Lament for a First Nation

Law and Society Series
W. Wesley Pue, General Editor

The Law and Society Series explores law as a socially embedded phenomenon. It is premised on the understanding that the conventional division of law from society creates false dichotomies in thinking, scholarship, educational practice, and social life. Books in the series treat law and society as mutually constitutive and seek to bridge scholarship emerging from interdisciplinary engagement of law with disciplines such as politics, social theory, history, political economy, and gender studies.

For a list of the titles in this series go to www.ubcpress.ca/books/series.

Peggy J. Blair

Lament for a First Nation
The Williams Treaties of Southern Ontario

UBC Press • Vancouver • Toronto

16 15 14 13 12 11 10 09 08 5 4 3 2 1

Printed in Canada on ancient-forest-free paper (100% post-consumer recycled) that is processed chlorine- and acid-free, with vegetable-based inks.

Library and Archives Canada Cataloguing in Publication

Blair, Peggy J. (Peggy Janice), 1955-
Lament for a First Nation : the Williams treaties of Southern Ontario / Peggy J. Blair.

Includes bibliographical references and index.
ISBN 978-0-7748-1512-3

1. Mississauga Indians – Treaties. 2. Ojibwa Indians – Ontario – Treaties. 3. Mississauga Indians – Land tenure. 4. Ojibwa Indians – Land tenure – Ontario. 5. Indians of North America – Canada – Government relations. 6. Mississauga Indians – Legal status, laws, etc. 7. Ojibwa Indians – Legal status, laws, etc. – Ontario. 8. Mississauga Indians – History. 9. Ojibwa Indians – Ontario – History. I. Title.

KE7709.B53 2008 342.7108'720899733 C2007-907480-4
KF8205.B53 2008

Canada

UBC Press gratefully acknowledges the financial support for our publishing program of the Government of Canada through the Book Publishing Industry Development Program (BPIDP), and of the Canada Council for the Arts, and the British Columbia Arts Council.

This book has been published with the help of a grant from the Canadian Federation for the Humanities and Social Sciences, through the Aid to Scholarly Publications Programme, using funds provided by the Social Sciences and Humanities Research Council of Canada.

Printed and bound in Canada by Friesens
Set in Stone by Robert Kroeger
Copy editor: Deborah Kerr

UBC Press
The University of British Columbia
2029 West Mall
Vancouver, BC V6T 1Z2
604-822-5959 / Fax: 604-822-6083
www.ubcpress.ca

Contents

Preface / ix

Introduction / xii

Part 1: Historical Background

1 History of the Williams Treaties First Nations / 1

2 Imperial Crown Policy / 14

3 A New Crown Policy / 38

4 Jurisdictional Disputes / 62

5 Bureaucratic Obstacles / 93

Part 2: The Williams Treaties

6 The Push for a New Treaty / 125

7 Differing Perceptions / 149

8 The *Howard* Case / 181

9 Analysis / 199

Conclusion / 235

Appendix: The Relevant Treaties / 240

Notes / 256

Bibliography / 302

Index / 310

An Indian's word, when it is formally pledged, is one of the strongest moral securities on earth; like the rainbow it beams unbroken, when all beneath is threatened with annihilation ... On our part, little or nothing documentary exists; the promises which were made, whatever they might have been, were almost invariably verbal – those who expressed them are now mouldering in their graves. However, the regular delivery of presents proves and corroborates the testimony of the wampums, and, by whatever sophistry we might deceive ourselves, we could never succeed in explaining to the Indians ... that their Great Father was justified in deserting them.

– Sir Francis Bond Head, *A Narrative*

Preface

In his 1965 book, *Lament for a Nation,* George Grant mourned the loss of Canadian identity due to assimilation by a dominant culture, the United States. My lament is not for Canada, however, but for the Hiawatha First Nation. It did not choose to go to court but was forced to defend the treaty rights of one of its members who had been charged with fishing without a licence. It lost the case, the result, I argue, of the same kind of assimilationist pressures and dominant cultural biases that Grant so eloquently described. Because of the ruling, six other First Nations are now trapped by the legalistic constraints of a decision which prevents them from hunting and fishing off-reserve, even though they were never charged, presented no evidence, and made no submissions. My lament, in that sense, is for all of them.

My interest in the subject matter of this book began late in the last century, when Bill Henderson invited me to watch him argue an appeal in the Supreme Court of Canada concerning the 1923 Williams Treaties. His client, George Howard, had been charged for fishing in the Otonabee River without a licence. The case – *Howard* – turned on the issue of whether the Williams Treaties had extinguished Howard's pre-existing treaty rights to fish there. As a lawyer practising Aboriginal law, I could sense at the time that Bill had lost his argument, although I wasn't familiar with the facts of the case and could not fully appreciate the arguments each party had made. When the Court's decision was released some months later, however, parts of it nagged at me. The Court's readiness to conclude that any First Nation would have surrendered its pre-existing treaty rights to hunt and fish was troubling, even if the surrender had occurred in 1923. I knew that my own First Nation clients would never have relinquished treaty rights to hunt or fish, as they considered these rights to be sacred. It seemed odd to me that a First Nation would have done so some seventy years earlier, at a time when one might assume it would be more, rather than less, dependent on the chase.

The paucity of evidence referred to in the Supreme Court decision also concerned me. It seemed to me that if such rights had been surrendered, there should have been all kinds of evidence supporting it. Ironically, what the Court considered to be strong evidence for surrender of rights was to me a virtual absence of evidence. Where were the discussions between the Treaty Commissioners and the First Nations about pre-existing treaty rights? Where was the debate? I would have expected not just discussion but some outraged dissent on the part of at least some band members before a decision with such profound consequences would have been reached by any Aboriginal community. Instead, the treaties had been completed with almost alarming haste. Why were treaty rights not mentioned anywhere?

The Court relied primarily on the recollections of an elderly former Chief, called by the Crown, who had been ten years old at the time of the surrender and knew some of the signatories. The Court seemed to think that his belief that he had no special rights was convincing, but I knew that Ontario, with whom I had sparred many times during similar litigation, had always claimed that Indians had no special rights in the province. I needed more than that to be convinced. I asked myself why a First Nation community would give up its protected rights to hunt and fish for the small sum of twenty-five dollars per person. If the Williams Treaties First Nations had traded their rights to hunt and fish in 1923, how did they make a living? What was going on at the time to compel such a surrender? And if they had surrendered their rights, why did George Howard continue to assert that he still had such rights? I knew that Howard had not funded an appeal to the Supreme Court of Canada. If his community was supporting his position, how could that be reconciled with the Court's decision that it had given up its treaty rights only seventy years before?

With these questions in mind, I began what I thought might someday be an article. Instead, it became a lengthy journey with many lateral turns and twists, before I could reconstruct what had happened during the Williams Treaties to my own satisfaction.

Since I am not a historian, historical geographer, or anthropologist, that journey could not have been completed without the assistance of those who have specialized knowledge in these areas. I owe a profound debt of gratitude to Dr. Janet Armstrong, who allowed me almost unlimited access to the many archival files that she had collected over the years in support of her own PhD thesis and research. Dr. José Brandão, Dr. Reg Good, Bill Henderson, Joan Holmes, Darlene Johnston, Dr. Victor Lytwyn, Jim Morrison, Dan Shaule, Tara Smock, and Dr. William Starna were equally generous in helping me to clarify certain references.

Thanks go also to Dr. Charles (Chuck) Cleland, an anthropologist and expert witness in the *Mille Lacs* trial, and Marc Slonim of the Seattle law firm of Ziontz, Chestnut, Varnell, Berley & Slonim, one of the lawyers involved in it, who provided me with a huge collection of materials filed in the case. The expert evidence from that trial, which includes reports from such well-known scholars as Thomas Lund, James McClurken, John Nichols, and Helen Tanner, as well as Chuck Cleland, has since been published as James M. McClurken, ed., *Fish in the Lakes, Wild Rice, and Game in Abundance: Testimony on Behalf of Mille Lacs Ojibwe Hunting and Fishing Rights* (East Lansing: Michigan State University Press, 2000) and was a very useful source.

I also acknowledge the contribution of the Department of Fisheries and Oceans, the Ontario Ministry of Natural Resources, and Indian and Northern Affairs Canada. These government offices released a great deal of information to me, and both the Ministry of Natural Resources and Indian Affairs made me aware of an exhaustive report on the Williams Treaties prepared by Tara Smock of Joan Holmes and Associates. The Holmes Report, as it is sometimes called, proved to be an invaluable resource.

This has been a long and sometimes difficult project, characterized by the usual conspiracy of late nights, computer glitches, broken printers, and looming deadlines. I would like to extend special thanks to Constance Backhouse for her consistent and unflagging encouragement and support. Similar thanks go to Randy Schmidt and Ann Macklem of UBC Press who were extremely patient with me on both a personal and professional level. I also acknowledge the very detailed and constructive feedback of Jamie Benidickson, Michael Coyle, Reg Good, Douglas Harris, Jean-Pierre Lacasse, and Michel Martin, who read and reviewed my efforts. The result is a much better work than would otherwise have been the case.

My final thanks go to my daughter, Jade, for her good-natured patience and acceptance of a time-consuming exercise that began when she was in elementary school and was still underway when she entered university. And of course to Bill Henderson, for inviting me to the Supreme Court of Canada in the first place, so many years ago.

As noted, I have had the help of some of the finest scholars in historical geography, Aboriginal law, anthropology, and history in developing this story. Any errors that remain are mine, and mine alone.

Introduction

With its 1994 decision in *R. v. Howard,* the Supreme Court of Canada effectively terminated the rights of seven Chippewa and Mississauga First Nations located in south-central Ontario to fish, hunt, and trap off-reserve. The Court declined to interfere with lower court judgments that had held that a "basket clause" in a 1923 treaty, one of the Williams Treaties, surrendering Indian title to certain lands within Ontario was unambiguous, and that the Aboriginal signatories understood that they had also surrendered their treaty rights to hunt, fish, and trap in all their traditional areas. In this regard, the seven Williams Treaties First Nations are unique among Aboriginal peoples in Canada. No other First Nations in Canada have ever been judicially held to have surrendered their subsistence rights to hunt and fish.

I argue that the circumstances in which the Williams Treaties First Nations find themselves are, in part, the result of a change in Crown policies that began in the mid-1800s. Before then, the Crown had affirmed and protected Aboriginal harvesting activities through treaties. As demonstrated by the recently discovered map of a 1701 treaty between the Imperial Crown and the Iroquois Five Nations, at that time the territorial extent of the Crown's treaty promises extended to waters and not merely lands. As settlement pressures developed, however, and as settler demands intensified, the Crown's policies changed to increasingly restrict Aboriginal hunting and fishing activities. Eventually, the Crown denied ever having made treaty promises protecting Aboriginal rights to hunt and fish. Restrictive legislation and aggressive enforcement actions throughout the nineteenth and twentieth centuries resulted in many Aboriginal people being charged and even jailed for exercising the rights promised by the Crown.

As will be seen, the Crown put forward differing justifications to explain its change in policies. At first, Crown officials argued that a reduced reliance on hunting and fishing was in the interest of Indians, as it would help to "civilize" them. Much later, Crown officials would suggest that restrictions were needed to protect and conserve game and fish, and accused First Nations peoples of abusing their hunting and fishing "privileges."

A review of the history leading up to the *Howard* decision, however, shows that Crown policies had little to do with protecting resources but instead provided a means by which large tracts of lands and resources could be opened up for the exclusive use of whites, while reducing competition in the increasingly lucrative fisheries. The steadily diminished ability of the Mississaugas and Chippewas to access their traditional lands and waters was then used to justify the Crown's argument that they no longer used their hunting grounds, and ought not to be compensated for them.

In 1923, as a series of stunning events unfolded on the international stage, the Crown reversed its decades-long position and agreed to negotiate a new treaty with the Mississaugas and Chippewas. The rushed surrenders that resulted – the Williams Treaties – were relied on by the Ontario government in *Howard* as evidence that the Mississaugas and Chippewas had not only relinquished all their rights to hunt and fish off-reserve, but that they had done so with the expectation that they would be treated in the same manner as the non-Aboriginal people who had settled around them.

The *Howard* decision raises troubling issues about the relationship between the Crown and First Nations in southern Ontario generally. At the end of the nineteenth century, the federal government allowed Ontario to assume both operational and jurisdictional authority over Indian fishing and hunting. This policy decision, as well as the federal Crown's refusal thereafter to become involved in issues around Aboriginal hunting and fishing, has left Ontario in sole control of interpreting whether or not Aboriginal and treaty rights exist. First Nations in general, and the Mississaugas and Chippewas in particular, have thus been left at the mercy of a government determined to advance "equal" rather than "special" rights for Aboriginal peoples.

The Ontario government has continually disavowed the Crown's original commitment to protect Aboriginal hunting and fishing rights, instead introducing policies that favour public interests over Aboriginal ones. These policies, however, are not sufficient to explain the outcome in *Howard*. In the United States, which developed game and fish laws similar to those of Ontario, a Chippewa community that in 1855 had signed a treaty almost identical to the Williams Treaties was found to have retained rather than surrendered its treaty harvesting rights. Because the principles of treaty interpretation applied in the American case were the same as those in *Howard,* but with such a different result, I suggest that the *Howard* decision and the extent to which Ojibway rights have been restricted have been determined as much by the Euro-centric and often erroneous cultural assumptions held by Canadian courts as by the continuing failure of the provincial and federal governments to live up to the "honour of the Crown."

The first step in understanding the implications of the *Howard* decision is to understand the significance of hunting and fishing to the Mississaugas and Chippewas. In the first part of this book, then, I examine the history of the Williams Treaties First Nations. I describe how the Crown at first recognized and protected Aboriginal rights but later allowed legalized encroachments into Aboriginal lands and waters. In Part 2, I discuss the backdrop against which the 1923 treaties were negotiated, and the provisions of the treaties themselves. A legal and historical analysis of the *Howard* case, based both on information that was put before the Supreme Court and on information of which it was unaware, suggests the *Howard* decision was wrong. Finally, I argue that the Canadian courts made a series of erroneous assumptions about the cultural needs of the Aboriginal people who had signed the treaties in question. I conclude that they did so in a manner that differed markedly from that of their American counterparts, and that their ignorance of Aboriginal culture and history caused a terrible injustice to those First Nations who had turned to the courts as their last resort.

Part 1
Historical Background

1
History of the Williams Treaties First Nations

The Mississaugas of South-Central Ontario

Like the majority of Aboriginal peoples in Ontario, the seven Ojibway First Nations that are the focus of this book belong to one linguistic family of Algonquian speakers – the Anishnabe, meaning "the people."[1] The Anishnabe also include the Algonquin (Algonkin), Nipissing, Ottawa (Odawa), and Cree peoples.[2] Archaeological evidence suggests that, for many thousands of years, the Anishnabe occupied large parts of what are now Ontario, Wisconsin, Michigan, and Minnesota. For example, in the United States, the Chippewa tribes are known to have lived in the Great Lakes–Upper Mississippi Valley from prehistoric times, and the Saugeen cultures of southern Ontario have been identified as one of the major cultures in the province between 1000 BC and AD 1000.[3]

Southern Ontario supported a greater population of Anishnabe than the north. There, local cultural groups interacted in a highly complex way.[4] Marriage partners had to be selected from outside the family clans, meaning that every family was connected to several clans and had multiple avenues to contribute to decision making. Anishnabe leaders were selected by their clan members in deliberations at seasonal councils.[5]

In general, the individual First Nations were distinguished by their dialect and their traditional hunting and fishing territories. The size of these family-based communities often varied, but seasonal hunting groups among the Anishnabe typically numbered between fifteen and twenty members. During the summer, small mobile groups came together around river mouths or favourite lakes and hunting grounds to socialize and contract marriages, and to participate in ceremonies and councils.[6]

Before European arrival, the Anishnabe were predominantly hunting and fishing tribes, and the importance of fish as a cultural and subsistence item among Ojibway peoples has been well established. Archaeological information indicates that, around 3000 BC, spears and harpoons were adapted to capture fish in the shallow Great Lakes and that hand-held seine nets came into use some time between 200 BC and AD 500. By about AD 800, the direct ancestors of the modern Ojibway people had modified the seine to produce the gill net, which enabled them to catch fish in deep water; their seasonal movements were adapted to the resource.[7]

The importance of fishing is also revealed by the location of Saugeen settlements. Most Saugeen villages and campsites have been discovered along rapids or at the mouths of rivers and creeks.[8] Some of these sites contain large quantities of fish bones from species that spawn from spring to early summer, suggesting that the Saugeen engaged in seasonal rounds of fishing, "when individual families gathered at a favourite fishing location ... and formed a larger community."[9]

The Anishnabe traded with their neighbours, the Ontario Iroquois and the St. Lawrence Iroquois. As Bruce G. Trigger points out, by about AD 1000 in northern Simcoe County an earlier intertribal trade in copper and beads among these groups had evolved into a trade extending across the southern margin of the Precambrian Shield. The Iroquois traded with the First Nations that lived on the shores of Georgian Bay, exchanging corn, fish nets, and tobacco for furs, dried fish, and meat.[10] According to James V. Wright, the Terminal Woodland period of post-European contact included three major cultural groups within Ontario. These were the Ontario Iroquois (who gave rise to the Huron, Petun, Neutral, and Erie Nations), the St. Lawrence Iroquois (who were first encountered by Jacques Cartier in 1534 but had disappeared when Samuel de Champlain visited the area in 1603), and the Ojibway, or Anishnabe.[11]

Early in the seventeenth century, as the fur trade with Europeans began, European visitors identified the inhabitants of southeastern and central Ontario as including Algonquin, Nipissing, and Ottawa tribes, the latter being a group closely related to the Ojibway.[12] At that time, the Ojibway lived somewhat to the west of the Ottawas, who were found south of Nottawasaga Bay and east of the Bruce, or Saugeen, Peninsula, in Lake Huron. Jesuit missionaries identified one "Outaouan" Band that claimed Manitoulin Island, as well as a number of other bands on the eastern and northern shores of Georgian Bay.[13] Ojibway peoples did not move into south-central Ontario until the latter part of the seventeenth century, however, following the Iroquois wars.[14] Those who did are commonly referred to as the Mississaugas.

The Mississaugas settled in the lush valleys of the Credit, the Thames (Ashkahnahseebee, or Horn River), the Otonabee (mouth-water), and the Moira (Saganashcocon) Rivers, which, together with the inland lakes between Lake Simcoe and the Bay of Quinte, formed their chief hunting and fishing grounds.[15] Some historians suggest that the Mississaugas came originally from the Mississagi River along the north shore of Lake Ontario, although there is little documentary evidence to support this claim. It is clear, however, that they were living farther north when they moved to Lake Ontario in the early eighteenth century.[16]

Presently, the seven Williams Treaties First Nations, named after Angus Seymour Williams, the Treaty Commissioner who negotiated with them, live on reserves at Scugog, Chemong, and Rice Lakes, as well as on islands in Lakes Simcoe and Huron. They are comprised of the Alderville (Alnwick), Curve Lake (Mud Lake or Chemong Lake), Hiawatha (Rice Lake), Scugog Island, Beausoleil (Christian Island), Georgina Island, and Mnjikaning (Rama) First Nations.

Today, the first four of these nations are known as Mississaugas; the remaining three are called Chippewas. As is so often the case with names applied to First Nations, these have a complex and sometimes confusing history. The word "Mississauga" means "persons who inhabit the country where there are many mouths of rivers." Fittingly, the first contact between European traders and the Mississaugas occurred at a river – the Credit River of Ontario (Mahzenahegaseebe, "the river where credit was given").[17] The name "Mississauga" was applied by French speakers to the group of Ojibway who came to live in the area around Lake Ontario. The French had taken the same approach with the Ojibway who lived near Sault Ste. Marie, designating them as Sauteurs or Saulteaux. "Chippewas" is simply an alternative spelling of "Ojibway" (Ojibwe), and the two words are often used interchangeably. In the US, their equivalents are "Chippewa" and "Ojibwa."

Because the Mississaugas are a branch of the Ojibway, European writers in the post-contact period often used the terms "Mississaugas" and "Chippewas" indiscriminately to describe tribes that belonged to the same linguistic group.[18] Adding to the confusion, in the post-contact era, as Anishnabe peoples began to settle in certain defined parts of Ontario, Europeans began to refer to the Ojibway of southwestern Ontario as "Chippewas" and the Ojibway of eastern Ontario as "Mississaugas," although this usage was not consistent.

At this time, as a result of this geographic separation, the terms "Chippewas" and "Mississaugas" refer to people who speak similar, although not identical, dialects. Whatever Europeans have called them, however, they prefer their own name, Anishnabe.

The Iroquois Wars

The desirability of south-central Ontario as a rich hunting and fishing ground is reflected in the oral traditions concerning the struggle between the Ojibway and the Iroquois for control of it. The wars between the Iroquois, or Five Nations Confederacy (formed of the Mohawk, Onondaga, Oneida, Seneca, and Cayuga Nations), and the Ojibway, supported by other First Nations allied to the French, are generally understood to have begun in the early to mid-1600s over the Iroquois desire to control the fur trade with Europeans. This was particularly so in the areas north of Lake Ontario, which constituted prime beaver-hunting grounds. By the early 1650s, Iroquois attacks had driven the Aboriginal peoples of southern Ontario to the north and west, and the Iroquois controlled the entire area north of Lake Ontario as a large hunting territory. Those Algonquian-speaking peoples who had not perished in the attacks or the preceding epidemics were mostly exiled to the furthest reaches of Ontario, where sporadic raids by Iroquois warriors continued.[19]

By 1689, with their enemies dispersed, Iroquois hunters obtained most of their furs from the lands north of Lake Ontario.[20] In the winter of 1690, "a considerable Party of the Five Nations" was observed hunting "Bever on the Neck of Land between Cataracckui Lake [Lake Ontario] and Lake Erie, with great security,"[21] as well as in the Ottawa Valley.[22]

Over two hundred years later, in 1923, the Williams Treaties Commissioners took much oral history from Chippewa and Mississauga witnesses concerning the Ojibway warfare with the Iroquois. One, seventy-eight-year-old Isaac Johnston of Scugog Island, testified that his grandmother had told him of the war with the Mohawks, which he said had occurred ten or fifteen generations before. "There was war with them, and they were mound-builders, those Mohawks," he explained. "They came from the States, I believe, and then along by the Mississauga River and she said that they fought right through on Couchiching Lake, and there were mounds built on the other side."[23] In his testimony during the commission hearings, Chief George Paudash of Rice Lake also referred to battles with the Mohawks, citing one that took place at Hatterick's Point near Rice Lake. Like Johnston, he too associated battles with burial mounds, commenting that, at another battle site, "there's a great Serpent Mound there, filled with Mohawks bones – and there are Turtle Mounds there beside it."[24]

Throughout Ontario, Aboriginal oral history maintains that the Iroquois dug mounds and tunnels as part of their warfare; the presence of pits and trenches associated with Iroquois warfare was noted as recently as 1906 near Mattawapik Falls, Temagami River.[25] According to James V. Wright, the sinuous excavations known as serpent mounds arose some two thousand years ago and were used as burial grounds, the most impressive of them being the "Serpent Mound" at Rice Lake.[26] His conclusion suggests that the serpent mounds predated the Iroquois wars. However, according to the 1896 *Peterborough Examiner*, David Boyle, the Curator of the Archaeological Museum of Toronto, accompanied by a "callow archaeological acolyte" identified as "Mr. A.F. Hunter of Barrie," examined a dozen mounds found on the north shore of Rice Lake that fall and discovered that they contained "historic" skulls, probably connected to these wars, as well as prehistoric ones, suggesting that the Iroquois had long used these grounds to bury their dead. "These historic or lower skeletons have been buried in a sitting position, and the 'intrusive' skeletons have been placed on the side with the knees drawn upward towards the chin. The Rice Lake mound system embraces, so far as explored scientifically, about a dozen examples of this aboriginal predilection for elevated burial places."[27]

In 1966, the oral tradition associating battles and mounds was recorded by George Cobb, a local historian commissioned by Trent University in 1962 to begin an experimental program in oral history. Over the next five years, he collected some seventy-eight audio reels of his interviews with elders, including those at Curve Lake. In 1966, a Curve Lake elder named Tom Taylor told Cobb that he knew the location of a mound but that he wouldn't tell a white man where it was "because they will dig it up."[28] Another Curve Lake elder explained that the Ojibway and Mohawks had "battles right out here on the big islands [on] Fox Island ... If you dig around you will find the skulls and everything there."[29]

The following three oral histories may point to this same battle. In 1905, the Ontario Historical Society was presented with an oral history prepared with the assistance of Chief Robert Paudash, which he claimed had come "from the mouth of Paudash, my father (son of *Cheneebeesh,* son of *Gemoaghpenasse*) who died aged 75 in the year 1893, the last hereditary chief of the tribe of Mississagas situated at Rice Lake and from the mouth of *Cheneebeesh,* my grandfather, who died in 1869 at the age of 104, the last Sachem or Head Chief of all the Mississagas, who in turn had learned, according to the Indian custom what *Gemoaghpenasse,* his father, had heard from his father and so on."[30] Chief Paudash described how the Mississaugas had battled with Mohawks all the way from Georgian Bay up the Severn River to Shunyung, or Lake Simcoe, where they had stopped at Machickning (fish fence) to get food, and then went east to Balsam Lake and down the valley of the Otonabee River, where the Mississaugas had villages.[31] Machickning is a reference to the Rama First Nation, which had (and still maintains) a fish fence at Atherley Narrows, near present-day Orillia.

In 1923, Johnson Paudash told the Williams Treaties Commissioners that an oral history passed on to him by his grandparents mentioned one of these battles. As a young boy, he had been told that fifteen hundred warriors of the Mississauga Nation, including O-ge-mah-be-nah-ke, his great-grandfather's grandfather, had fought with Mohawks at the mouth of the Severn River at a place called Skull Island, then down the Black River to the Narrows of Lake Simcoe, up the Talbot River, and over the heights of lands into Balsam Lake. At that point, the Mississauga war parties had separated into two groups. At Burlington Bay, a great battle then took place between the Mohawks and one Mississauga war party, while the other group of Mississauga warriors came toward Mud Lake, battled at Peterborough, and drove the Mohawks all the way to the mouth of the Otonabee River, at Hatterick's Point, where yet another fierce battle ensued.[32]

Almost seventy-five years earlier, George Copway, an Ojibway Chief and Methodist minister, published a history of the Ojibway in which he discussed the Iroquois battles in similar terms. He described the great war between the Iroquois and the Mississaugas as one of "the most bloody battles" and recounted how warriors had fought at Rama, Mud Lake, and Rice Lake until they reached the mouth of the Otonabee River, "where several hundred were slain. The bodies were in two heaps: one of which was the slain of the Iroquois; the other of the Ojibways."[33]

It has been suggested, on the one hand, that there was an Algonquian "diaspora" following the Iroquois wars, with the First Nations from southern Ontario dispersed or destroyed, and on the other, based on oral histories, that the Ojibway returned to drive the Iroquois out of southern Ontario.[34] The truth may be more complex. There is much evidence to suggest that far from being destroyed, Algonquian peoples maintained an involvement in the fur trade during and after the Iroquois wars, and that as skirmishes continued in disputed territories, negotiations were undertaken to bring an end to the conflict and to "overturn" the war kettles. The Mississaugas, in particular, entered into several peace agreements with the Iroquois that enabled them to occupy the lands in southern Ontario without further hostilities.

It is not possible in this particular work to provide a complete description of the diplomatic efforts leading to these intertribal treaties. A fascinating series of negotiations involving shuttle diplomacy between the Iroquois, the French and their Indian allies, and representatives of the English monarch, however, resulted in a series of multi-party agreements. These treaties form the basis from which both the Mississaugas and Iroquois claim treaty rights to hunt and fish in southern Ontario under the protection of the Crown, and are worthy of at least a cursory examination.

By the end of the seventeenth century, the Iroquois, like their enemies, had been weakened by disease and losses in battle. In the winter of 1672-73, Jesuit missionaries observed Iroquois and Mississauga warriors hunting together in the territory of Hudson's Bay, but elsewhere in Ontario, Iroquois warriors were being attacked by other French-allied Indians known as the "Far Indians."[35] In 1687, a Cayuga spokesman indicated that the current war with the "far nations" had rendered "our Bever hunting unfree and dangerous."[36]

In 1690, the Five Nations sent eight wampum belts to the First Nations who gathered for trade at Michilimackinac. The belts were made of shells or beads, and the symbolic images they depicted, like documents, were capable of being "read." According to French historian Bacqueville de la Potherie, one of the Iroquois wampum belts proposed a peace treaty by suggesting that the disputants should have "their own bowl, so that they might have but one dish from which to eat and drink," a metaphor for the shared use of the disputed hunting grounds.[37] The offer appears to have been rejected. In 1699, fifty-five Iroquois hunters were killed near Detroit while hunting beaver, apparently at the hands of Ottawa warriors.

Following the 1697 Treaty of Ryswick between England and France, King Louis XIV agreed to join with the English monarch in calling on their respective Indian allies to cease "all acts of hostility" in the lands north of Lake Ontario. Each King sent a dispatch to his Governor in North America directing each to work with the other and act to "unite their forces ... in obliging these Indians to remain at peace ... as His Majesty does not doubt but that will be productive of tranquility throughout the whole country."[38] The French King also noted that some of his First Nations allies hoped that a general peace would enable them to cross the otherwise hostile Iroquois homelands and thereby gain access to the lucrative fur markets at Albany, New York. He wrote of the "desire on the part of some of the French [Indian] allies" to have this access "and to share hunting grounds in order to enjoy free movement through Iroquois territory on the north shore rather than continue at war."[39]

In June 1700, five Chiefs of the Dowaganhaes (also referred to at times as the Waganhaes or Dowagenhaws), an unidentified group of the Algonquian-speaking "far nations" of the upper Great Lakes, sent a belt of wampum to Iroquois leaders at Onondaga confirming their desire for peace in the hunting grounds. They proposed their "hunting places to be one, and to boile in one kettle, eat out of one dish and with one spoon."[40] Later, in August, fifty Iroquois Chiefs reported these events to the English Governor Bellomont, stationed at Albany, who encouraged them to continue their peace-making efforts. He urged them to "try all possible means to fix a trade and correspondence with all those nations by which means you would reconcile them to yourselves ... and then you might at all times without any sort of hazard go a hunting into their country, which I understand is much the best for Beaver hunting."[41]

The Iroquois were able to make peace with four of these unidentified nations and reported that "we got some skins from the Waganhaes, which is a sign of peace."[42] That September, Iroquois Chiefs met at Montreal with Chiefs from nineteen of the French-allied Indian nations in the presence of the French Governor. There, the Iroquois again presented a wampum belt calling for the peaceful sharing of hunting grounds, "to make one joint kettle when we shall meet,"[43] and to eat from one bowl, with one spoon, again representing a desire to put an end to the fighting and share the disputed grounds. The Iroquois referred to their recent peace treaty with the Waganhaes by proclaiming that they had planted a "tree of Peace; now we give it roots to reach the Far Nations so that it may be strengthened."[44]

The following year, in July 1701, the Five Nations negotiated a treaty with Lieutenant-Governor John Nanfan, the acting English Governor at

New York. Nanfan promised the Iroquois that, in exchange for the cession of their beaver-hunting grounds to the King of England, they would be protected by the Crown when engaged in harvesting activities within the same territory.

The treaty refers to a "vast tract" of land described as eight hundred miles in length and four hundred miles in "bredth."[45] In the document, the Iroquois were promised that "wee [the Five Nations] are to have free hunting for us and the heires and descendants from us the Five nations forever and that free of all disturbances expecting to be protected therein by the Crown of England."[46] The territory of the treaty was referred to as the Beaver Hunting Ground and was described as "the country where the bevers, the deers, Elks and such beasts keep." It included all the lands lying between the "great Lake of Ottowawa [meaning the lake claimed by the Ottawas, namely, Lake Huron] and the lake called by the natives Sahiquage and by the Christians the lake of Swege [Lake Erie]."[47]

It is significant that the product of these prolonged cross-cultural discussions was a treaty reflecting negotiations among equals. Although written in English, it incorporated Iroquois words for places and for some of the First Nations with whom the Iroquois had battled. As well, it was written in terms of what the Iroquois ("wee") would acquire or retain rather than the rights to be acquired by the Crown.

Of equal significance is the fact that the treaty was accompanied by a map on which many of its key phrases appear, again written in both Iroquois and English. The map, long thought lost or destroyed, was recently found at the Public Records Office in England.[48] It provides a fascinating glimpse into the understanding brought by both parties to the lands at issue. It also reveals the fears of another time, referring, for example, to the Great Lake of the Ottawawa, or Ottawas, as reportedly inhabited by a monster.[49]

As important as the discovery of the map, however, is the revelation that the area in which Iroquois activities were to be protected by the Crown included waters. The lands depicted on the map by a "prick'd line" extend several miles into the waters of Lake Huron and include all of Lake Erie, thereby protecting rights in water, such as fishing, as well as hunting and trapping activities.

The Minutes of the 1701 conference between Lieutenant-Governor Nanfan and the Iroquois confirm that they had finally ended their lengthy hostilities with a number of First Nations. Importantly, the Iroquois informed Nanfan that they had made peace with "seaven nations," including the Assissagh, the Iroquois term for the Mississaugas.[50]

In September 1701, just after the treaty was concluded with Nanfan, a general peace agreement involving the Five Nations and all of the Indian nations allied to the French was reached at Montreal with the assistance of the French Governor, the Chevalier de Callieres.[51] As many as sixteen hundred Aboriginal delegates from the Great Lakes region attended this massive council as well as a large delegation from the Five Nations Confederacy. There, proposals put forward the year before by the Iroquois for a "tree of peace" and a "dish with one spoon" were ratified. The Aboriginal perspective of what was agreed to at that time, reflected in oral histories, has appeared in the historical record with remarkable consistency over the last three hundred years.[52]

For the Iroquois and the Ojibway, the "dish with one spoon" marked the end of violent conflict in the hunting grounds north of Lake Ontario. As Chief Jake Thomas explained to members of the Royal Commission on Aboriginal Peoples in 1993, the treaty signified that

> We shall only have one dish (or bowl) in which will be placed one beaver's tail, and we shall all have coequal right to it, and there shall be no knife in it, for if there be a knife in it, there would be danger that it might cut some one and blood would thereby be shed. This one dish or bowl signified that they will make their grounds one common tract and all have a coequal right to hunt in it. The knife being prohibited from being placed into the dish or bowl signifies that all danger would be removed.[53]

Chief Robert Paudash's oral history, referred to earlier, also described the arrangement as a treaty under which Mohawks and Mississaugas would intermarry and thus assure peace for the future. He explained that the Mississaugas, "seeing that the land conquered by them from the Mohawks, who had dispossessed the Hurons, was full of game and an excellent hunting ground, they came down from Lake Huron and settled permanently in the valley of the Otonabee, or Trent, and along the St. Lawrence as far as Brockville."[54] Victor Konrad disagrees, however, saying that the Mississauga villages located in the lands north of Lake Ontario were established "at the pleasure" of the Iroquois.[55]

Nonetheless, and whether they remained in the area as a result of war, consent, conquest, or diplomacy, the Ojibway remained virtually undisturbed in their possession of these lands until European settlement began. Indeed, by the late eighteenth century, the Mississauga and Chippewa occupation of southern Ontario was so well established that when the Crown needed lands in the area, it obtained land surrenders from them, and not from the Iroquois. These surrenders were obtained in general accordance with the provisions of the *Royal Proclamation of 1763* (discussed more fully below), and almost all were in exchange for promises that Aboriginal hunting and fishing activities would be protected by the Crown.

The Cultural Significance of Hunting and Fishing

As with other Aboriginal peoples in Ontario, hunting and fishing activities were important to the Mississaugas and Chippewas not just for subsistence but for cultural reasons as well. The earliest explorers to visit Ontario had noted the variety and ingenuity of Aboriginal harvesting techniques. In 1698, for example, Louis Hennepin described the intriguing methods by which the "Savages" fished:

> [They] catch all sorts of fish with Nets, Hooks and Harping-irons [harpoons or spears] as they do in Europe. I have seen them fish in a very pleasant manner. They take a fork of wood with two Grains or Points and fit a Gin to it, almost the same way that in France they catch partridges. After they put it in the water and when the Fish, which are in great plenty by far than with us go to pass through, and find they are entered in the gin, they snap together this sort of Nippers or Pinchers and catch the Fish by the Gills.[56]

Almost two centuries later, Johann Georg Kohl observed that the Ojibway language had a variety of specialized words to describe fishing that had no equivalents in English. The Ojibway, for example, had both a general word for fishing and specific words for each type of fishing they engaged in:

> "I fish" generically is *"Nin gigoike"* (literally the word signifies, "I make fish"); *"Nin pagidawa"* means: "I catch fish with nets"; *"Nin pagibad"*: "I catch fish with a line on which there are many hooks." *"Nin akwawa"* means: "I fish with a spear." We could certainly convey this idea in English with one word, "I spear," still it would not be so comprehensive as the Indian word, in which it is explained that *fish* are speared. They have also a separate term for spearing fish by torchlight; they call it *"wasswewin"* (fishing with a spear in the light). *"Nin wewebanabi"* signifies: "I fish with a hook"; it is the only term of the whole category which we can render in one English word, "I angle."[57]

Although the gill net was a major fishing technology in the development of the Aboriginal fishery, Anishnabe peoples invented many other diverse and creative devices for use in capturing fish. Kohl expressed his astonishment at the "many sorts of fish lances they [the Ojibway] have invented and how cleverly they use them ... They spear fish in winter and summer, by night and by day. They spear the huge sturgeon and the little herring often too, even smaller fish. In winter, spearing is almost the sole mode of catching fish." According to Kohl, fishing spears were called generically *anit,* but, again, there were special names for different sorts of spears, and all appeared to be "neatly made." Some had two prongs; others had three. "For catching larger fish, they also have a species of spear-head, which on striking, comes loose from the pole and is merely attached to it by a cord. The fish darts off, dragging the wooden bob after it, gradually becomes exhausted and is captured without difficulty."[58]

To lure fish, the Ojibway carved small *okeau* (decoy-fish) from wood or bone. Kohl saw several of these stained to look like real fish and attached to a long string, which was in turn connected to a piece of wood of about eighteen inches long. The string was "weighted with a piece of lead, so that it may sink perpendicularly in the water. The fisherman, lying over the hole ... lets his *okeau* play round the mouth of the fish he is decoying, draws it up in time and tantalises the poor wretch higher and higher until he can easily spear it."[59]

The Ojibway had a distinctive way of fishing in the winter, sometimes referred to as "peep-hole" fishing. They would cut a small hole in the ice and erect a tent above it, so that the fish could be seen swimming in the shade created by the tent and be more easily detected.[60] Thomas Need, who wrote *Six Years in the Bush* in 1838, described the Mississauga fishermen he saw engaging in such activities: "we observed some forty or fifty of them in their picturesque gypsy-like tents, watch for fish. They will stand many hours together over a hole in the ice, darkened by blankets, with a fish-spear in one hand, and a wooden decoy fish attached to a line in the other waiting for a muskelonge or pike which they strike with almost unerring certainty ... In this way, a skillful fisherman will catch 50 to 200 lbs. weight of fish in a day."[61]

Throughout the nineteenth century, Aboriginal fishermen used nets, spears, and stone weirs to catch fish. They sometimes used hooks, but, unlike Europeans, did not use lines with a single hook. As one Ojibway elder explained to an ethnologist, this was because they fished for subsistence: "With a hook you can catch only one fish at a time. With a net you can catch lots of fish at one time."[62]

The Mississaugas also created fishing weirs by placing stones in a creek so as to form a small channel where spawning fish could be pulled out by hand. At the peak of the spawning season, around a hundred fish a day could be caught. Fish were most commonly speared during ice fishing and at night by torchlight. The Indians did not ice fish at night for fear that the spirits would send a large man-eating snake to the ice-hole.[63]

Like those of other Ojibway communities, village sites were usually situated around areas where fish spearing could easily take place. As David Cusick wrote around 1840, the use of fish weirs and fish fences, such as that at Machickning, was well known:

> The use of the spear naturally caused villages and camps to be located at or near rifts and shallow parts of rivers. At such places, too, stone-weirs were made between the walls of which the fish were driven and one very large one still remains in the Seneca River. The Hurons made hurdles which brought the fish into their nets and the Oneidas had annual fishing feasts in the spring. When all were assembled a row of stakes was placed across the stream and woven with branches. Then the fish were driven down the creek and another row of stakes was placed behind them. When this was done the spearing commenced and the division of fish and the feast followed.[64]

Fishing, however, was not the only means of subsistence among the Ojibway. Hunters enjoyed great respect, with the community regarding "the active deer-slayer or brave beaver-trapper as a man to be respected, who can support a family, a brave who gains the women's hearts, and whose praises the songs repeat."[65] One early Mississauga name for Rice Lake, Pem-e-dash-cou tay-ang (Pamadusgodayong, Lake of the Burning Plains, Lake of Plains), reflects the use made of the hunting grounds on the south shore of the lake where vegetation was burned each spring to encourage the growth of a particular type of grass that attracted deer.[66]

Spiritually and culturally, there were many ceremonies and rituals associated with hunting. This was particularly the case at the time of *manido-gizisons* (the Manido moon) in early February and March, when it was believed that the supernatural man-eating Windigo would attack and destroy camps. In the harsh months of winter, stores of berries, sugar, and rice would quickly be depleted, leaving bands almost completely dependent on hunting and ice fishing. To ward off the Windigo, many precautionary steps were taken, such as making a feast with the first animal killed, but offering part of it in sacrifice. For some animals, specific hunting "medicines" were used to help in the hunt as well: "For hunting beaver, medicine would be smeared on the end of a stick, which is attached to the trap planted in the ground. The stick doused in medicine attracts the beaver without fail. For luck in deer hunting, a man usually chewed some kind of root, then rubbed it on the cheeks, eyes, hands or weapons. Other deer medicines were believed to 'poison' the animals' blood, which the hunter threw away as an offering to the *manidos,* spirits who helped him in his pursuit."[67]

Deadfalls were used for smaller animals such as porcupine and mink, and snares were set for rabbit and grouse. Larger species such as deer or moose were called with a trumpet and lured into a fenced enclosure. In 1888, A.F. Chamberlain visited the various Mississauga reserves to prepare a PhD thesis on the Scugog and other Mississauga dialects. He described the variety of means by which the Mississaugas hunted and fished: "The

Indians at Rice Lake used to shoot by night (in canoes with torches) the deer *(wawasque)* that came to feed on the rice-beds. They also hunted the deer with hounds obtained from the settler. The Indians of Chemong [Mud] Lake were accustomed to 'bark squirrels' *(atchitamon),* i.e. to make the bullet strike the tree under the animal, so that the splinters of bark killed it without injuring fur or flesh. The muskrat *(ozasque),* beaver *(amic)* and other animals they caught by setting traps."[68]

Each Mississauga hunting band was composed of an extended family sharing the same totem through male lineage, involving some twenty to thirty people, headed by a Chief, or *ogemah.* Fishing grounds, rice fields, and sugar bushes were communal property, available to any family member, but permission was required before these common grounds could be used by others.[69] Families had specific hunting territories. In 1838, Thomas Need remarked on the protocols that ensured that these hunting grounds were protected from encroachment by others: "I am now becoming acquainted with these Aboriginal peoples and mutual attentions and civilities pass on both sides: they are honest and civil ... On one point alone, that of hunting furs, they are said to be as tenacious as English landholders of their game ... Each family possesses a hereditary hunting ground, which is marked by bounds well known to the tribe and on which a trespass is highly resented."[70]

Given their reliance on hunting and fishing, then, it is not surprising that, in the treaty process, the Mississaugas and Chippewas took steps to protect their hunting grounds and fisheries from encroachments.

2
Imperial Crown Policy

Early Treaties and Surrenders

In 1755, the Imperial government placed the management of all Indian affairs within British North America in the office of the Superintendent General of Indian Affairs. Only a few years later, the Crown acknowledged the need to address the Aboriginal interest in land through negotiated agreements with First Nations. In 1761, King George III instructed Governor Robert Monckton to support and protect the "Indians in their just Rights and Possessions" and to "keep inviolable the treaties and compacts which have been entered into with them ... upon pain of our highest displeasure."[1]

With the 1763 Treaty of Paris, Aboriginal peoples in Canada fell under British jurisdiction, at least in terms of European law. Despite the Crown's assertion of sovereignty over "discovered" lands, however, the early practice of the British was to recognize the legal reality of Aboriginal title and rights through surrenders and treaties. In October 1763, King George issued a *Royal Proclamation* declaring that the Indian Territory, which included most of Ontario, was a hunting ground reserved for Aboriginal peoples until surrendered by them. As the Proclamation directed, "the several nations or Tribes of Indians with whom we are connected and who live under our protection should not be molested or disturbed in such part of our Dominions and territories as not having been ceded to us are reserved to them as their hunting grounds."[2]

The Proclamation was equal at law to an entrenched provision in the Constitution of the colonies of North America, and it set out the only protocols by which the Indian "hunting grounds" could be acquired by the Crown. Representatives of the Crown were required to meet in public and negotiate with those First Nations who had an interest in surrendering lands that the Crown desired. Lands could be purchased only by, for, and in the name of the Crown through its authorized representatives, and private individuals were forbidden from acquiring lands for themselves.[3] The Crown's interest at this time, however, was in obtaining title to the land, not the waters adjacent to it or the animals that roamed upon it. As a result, the Crown's policy was to acknowledge Aboriginal rights to hunt and fish, even in ceded lands, and even within waters.

In 1989, the Ontario Court of Appeal stated that the *Royal Proclamation* had been repealed by the *Quebec Act* of 1774,[4] although this conclusion is probably incorrect in light of higher court rulings that the Proclamation had the force of a statute equal to that of the *Magna Carta*.[5] However, the Ontario Court of Appeal has also said that "little turns on whether the surrender provisions of the *Royal Proclamation* had the force of law" since it set out an "established protocol between the Crown and First Nations peoples that Aboriginal title could be lost only by surrender to the Crown."[6]

The Proclamation was respected during the eighteenth century, as a comment from John Graves Simcoe, the first Lieutenant-Governor of the Province of Upper Canada, makes clear. Seven months after his 21 September 1791 appointment to office, he explained to the Lords of Trade that "The Indians can in no way be deprived of their rights to their Territory and Hunting Grounds, save and except as formerly stated, and any portion of Lands ceded by them held as a Reservation must and shall be fully protected, as well as rights reserved on certain Streams and Lakes for fishing and hunting privileges or purposes."[7]

Within a decade, the American Revolution had taken place. United Empire Loyalists, who had supported the British, together with members of what had become the Six Nations Iroquois (the Five Nations had been joined by the Tuscaroras in 1726), became exiles and began a vast migration into southern Ontario. To secure lands in which to settle its former allies, the Imperial government initiated a treaty process with the Ojibway.[8]

Despite the urgency, Lieutenant-Governor Simcoe confirmed England's early assurances that no First Nation territories would be claimed by the Crown unless first relinquished by the Indians. He told his Indian allies in 1793 that "no King of Great Britain has ever claimed absolute power or sovereignty over any of your lands or Territories that were not fairly sold or bestowed by your ancestors at Public Treaties."[9] Simcoe also reminded the Privy Council of the need to prevent encroachments on Aboriginal lands through colonial laws, noting that "no lands can be purchased of the Indians but by the consent of the Governor or Person administering the Government of the Province."[10]

The Imperial Crown also recognized that Aboriginal permission would be required before the King's subjects could safely travel navigable waters within southern Ontario, and it duly sought permission from the Mississaugas for this purpose. On 22 May 1784, the Mississaugas agreed that "the King should have a right to make roads thro' the Messissauge country, the navigation of the said rivers should be open and free for his vessels and those of his subjects."[11] No doubt in part due to their earlier agreement with the Iroquois, the Mississaugas also agreed to surrender lands for the use of the Six Nations, who had been driven from their homelands to the south. Nonetheless, the Mississaugas reminded the English that the Iroquois had a pre-existing right to use the area as a result of their earlier agreements. As Chief Pokquan stated during these negotiations, "We the Mississaugas are not the owners of all that Land laying between the three Lakes, but we have agreed and are willing to transfer our right of Soil & property to the King our Father, for the use of His people, and our Brethren the Six Nations ... we are Indians, and consider ourselves and the Six Nations to be one and the same people, and agreeable to a former, and mutual agreement, we are bound to help each other."[12]

The famous Iroquois spokesman Joseph Brant agreed with Chief Pokquan's sentiments. In 1793, as plans were discussed to set aside Mississauga lands for the Iroquois, he too reminded the English that "upwards of one hundred years ago a moon of Wampum was placed in this country with four Roads leading to the Centre for the convenience of Indians from Different Quarters to come and settle or hunt here a Dish with one Spoon was likewise put here with the moon of wampum, this shews that my Sentiments respecting the lands are not new."[13]

The Crown took steps to obtain other surrenders of the Mississauga territory in the late 1700s, although the policy of how to do so properly under the new Proclamation seems not to have been fully developed. An early surrender purportedly taken in 1784 for a tract of land along the north shore of Lake Ontario was never documented,[14] and an attempt to purchase Matchedash Bay produced only a "blank deed" with the marks of the Indians affixed to separate pages.[15] A 22 May 1784 treaty with Major John Butler for the "tract of country" located between Lakes Ontario and Erie was approved by the "Wabakanyne, Sachems, War Chiefs and Principal Women in band" but left its northern boundary undefined.

In 1785, Deputy Surveyor General John Collins investigated the route known as the "Toronto Carrying Place," from the Humber River to Lake Simcoe, as a means of communication with the interior. There is little information about the treaty he attempted to negotiate, and no copy of an actual surrender is known to exist. However, according to J.B. Rousseau, the French Canadian interpreter who accompanied him, and Collins' own journal of the transactions, the principal Chiefs of the Mississauga Nation unanimously agreed "that the King 'shall have a right to make roads through the Mississauga Country, that the Navigation of the Rivers and Lakes shall be open and free for his Vessels, and those of his subjects.'"[16]

In October 1783, William Redford Crawford of the Royal Regiment of New York negotiated an agreement with the Mississaugas for settlement lands at what are now Frontenac, Prince Edward, Lennox and Addington, Hastings, Glengarry, Stormont, Dundas, and Leeds Counties. Sir John Johnson of the

Department of Indian Affairs, however, indicated he had never received any deed of the Crawford purchase of lands "about Kingston and the Bay of Quinte," noting it had been left for Crawford to "fill up [mark in] the [water]Courses, since which I have never seen it." He reminded Crawford that the waterways had been incorrectly described in the original deed, stating, "If I recollect right, the Course running from the head of Lake Ontario to the River La Tranche is wrongly expressed in the Deed, as by Running a North west Course, it is thought it will not intersect any part of the River and the Intention was that it should."[17] No formal cession document exists for Crawford's purchase, the description of the tract is vague, and it seems the British made no payment to the Ojibway. Nonetheless, the First Nations kept their end of the bargain, and according to the late historian Robert J. Surtees, the Crown's claim to the area has never been questioned.[18]

The historical record is rife with errors in the written texts of these and many other treaties. For example, the so-called Gunshot treaty (Treaty No. 13) purported to affect certain lands north of Lake Ontario but omitted any description of the lands it was intended to cover.[19] From the English perspective, however, the Gunshot Treaty was probably intended to include adjacent waters since the use of a gunshot or cannon to determine the extent of the occupation and use of waters was a long-standing practice at the time. As pointed out by Lord Blackburn in 1859, "most of the writers on the subject refer to defensibility from the shore as the test of occupation; some suggesting therefore a width of one cannon shot from shore to shore, or three miles; some a cannon shot from each shore, or six miles; some an arbitrary distance of ten miles."[20] Obviously, these common-law concepts were not known to Aboriginal peoples, and as Johnson Paudash of the Hiawatha First Nation at Rice Lake would tell the Williams Treaties Commissioners in 1923, "Sure it was a mistake for them and it was a mistake for us that we don't know a cannon sounds further than a gun, too."[21]

The waters of Lake Ontario and the lands to its north, then, were clearly a focus of treaty negotiations. Indeed, in 1856, the government's Pennefather Report conceded that all of Rice Lake had been reserved by Lieutenant-Governor Simcoe for the sole and exclusive use of the Mississaugas. The report acknowledged that despite the informalities of the transaction, the Indians had carried out their share of the bargain and it was binding on the Crown.

As the Pennefather Report acknowledged, "at the time of the surrender of the country from the Head of the Bay of Quinte to the River Etobicoke in 1788, Rice Lake was expressly reserved and does not seem to have been expressly ceded. It is true that there were such informalities in the execution of this Treaty that Lt. Governor Simcoe declared it not to be binding except so far as the good faith of the Indians recognized it. They have carried out their share of the bargain, and we conceive that their claim to the Islands in Rice Lake should consequently be admitted."[22]

As errors in these and other surrenders came to light, Lord Dorchester, the Governor General, wrote to Simcoe informing him that the treaty purporting to cede Matchedash Bay was invalid, although he noted that no fraud had been intended. He warned that the omission "will set aside the whole transaction and throw us entirely on the good faith of the Indians for just so much Land as they are willing to allow and what may be further necessary must be purchased anew, but it will be best not to press that matter or shew any anxiety about it."[23] The error caused much consternation among Imperial authorities, who were afraid that if it were revealed, unrest might be caused among the settlers, along with increased demands from the First Nations.

However, in 1796, the possibility of resolving the issue passed from Simcoe's hands. After requesting a leave of absence, he left the office in July of that year and was replaced by Peter Russell, a member of the Executive Council of Upper Canada.[24] Simcoe himself, in recommending that Russell be his replacement, had described him as "the senior Executive Counsellor, (not a Roman Catholick) and ... in all respects the proper person."[25]

Russell was particularly concerned that the deficiencies in the surrenders of lands north of Lake Ontario could cause serious problems if they came to light. He feared that if either the Mississaugas or the settlers learned that the treaties were invalid, it might "shake the Tranquility of many respectable Persons, who have risked nearly their whole Property within its limits." He added that the Crown's claim to the lands, in the absence of a valid surrender, would then become very doubtful, "and our tenure of the intermediate space (involving a great many cultivated farms, as well as the Seat of Government) might consequently be at the mercy of the Messissagues, who, if they were apprized of the circumstance, might be induced to give trouble with a view of making their own advantage of it."[26]

On 22 May 1798, the Chippewas ceded "Penetangushene" Harbour, Georgian Bay, in Treaty No. 5. Russell recommended using this transaction to overcome the deficiencies of the earlier ones by surreptitiously rewording the preamble to confirm the earlier transactions.[27] However, James Green, the Secretary to the Executive Council of Upper Canada, warned against taking such a step.[28] Green, who felt the approach would have the "taint of ambiguity about it," cautioned that a new deed needed to be obtained with the informed consent of the appropriate Aboriginal parties. To do otherwise, he warned, "without the Sanction of the Indians previously had, might create alarms and produce consequences the most mischievous and dangerous to the King's interest with the Indians, if they should discover they were not openly and candidly dealt with."[29]

General Robert Prescott, who had replaced Lord Dorchester as Governor on 10 April 1796,[30] agreed with Green that a new deed of the faulty purchase was needed.[31] Despite the fears that the Mississaugas would make unreasonable demands, a confirmatory treaty and surrender was obtained from them in 1805. It described the land that was supposed to have been surrendered in 1787 as lying between the Etobicoke River and Lake Ontario.[32] However, even that treaty would prove to contain an inaccurate description of lands.

It is important to again note that under early Imperial policy in Ontario, no distinction was drawn between Aboriginal title in terms of lands and lands covered with water. This is reflected in the early treaties, which often included both, as well as in legislation. In fact, at the time of the *Royal Proclamation,* due to a general lack of familiarity with the Indian Territory, it was not known how much of it was covered with water and how much was dry land. As the Surveyor General observed in 1797,

> [It is] almost impossible to frame with any degree of accuracy a report on the ungranted Lands in this Province. Exclusive of this material uncertainty, the estimate must be founded upon old and incorrect maps, as but a very small proportion of the Province is sufficiently known so that a certain calculation may be had, of what may prove to be water and what may prove to be land, for although the interior parts of the Country have since the formation of this Government been made much better known than before, yet, even now, no calculation which can be with a certainty be depended upon, can be compiled until the course of the Grand or Ottawa River is known, and the shores of Lakes Huron and Superior, shall be ascertained.[33]

As a result, many treaties in Upper Canada made specific reference to waters. The 1798 "Penetangushene" Harbour surrender, for example, ceded "all that tract or space containing land and water or parcel of ground covered with water, be the same land or water, or both lying and being near or upon the Lake Huron and called Penetangushene ... together with the islands in the said Harbour of Penetangushene."[34] To give some further examples, in 1800, in Treaty No. 12, the Chiefs of the Ottawa, Chippewas, Potawatamie, and Wyandot Nations surrendered the land and water in a tract known as the Huron Church Reserve, whereas in Treaty No. 29, Chiefs of the Chippewa tribe surrendered lands that were completely described in navigational terms, and commenced "at the distance of fifty miles (on a course about north 84 degrees west) from the outlet of Burlington Bay on Lake Ontario, then on a course about north 84 degrees west so as to strike Lake Huron ten miles and three quarters of a mile north of the mouth of a large river emptying into the said lake."[35]

For the most part, however, regardless of whether they had surrendered lands or waters, the Aboriginal peoples who engaged in treaty discussions with the Crown were intent on continuing their hunting and fishing activities without interference. In 1790, for example, the Mississaugas warned that they would not allow white men to fish in the Credit River. John Butler, by then a colonel, reported that "the Chiefs of the Messesague Indians, [requested] me to make known their Intention in Writing respecting White people Fishing in their Creeks, I do therefore give this Warning to all concerned that they will not allow any Person of that description to fish in the Creek called the River of Credit which they reserve entirely to themselves, any other Creeks they have no objection to peoples fishing on."[36]

Earlier, in 1787, Simcoe had agreed to reserve the whole of Rice Lake for Mississauga use, and in 1796, he took steps to ensure that other waters were reserved exclusively for the Mississaugas as well. He wrote to Lord Dorchester recommending that the Crown take a cession "of the lands laying between the head of Lake Ontario or Burlington Bay and the Tobicoke [Etobicoke]" but purchase the lands "so as to leave the Mississaugas in full possession of their rivers and fishing grounds."[37] Accordingly, when the Crown obtained the 1805 surrender of lands north of Lake Ontario from the Mississaugas, it expressly reserved the "fishery in the said River Etobicoke" for the exclusive use of the Mississaugas.[38] A second treaty, Treaty No. 13a, was taken to confirm the Toronto purchase, and it too reserved the fishery for Mississauga use.

According to Council Minutes of the treaty meeting, the Aboriginal position concerning the fisheries had been very clear. The Mississaugas wanted to reserve "the sole right of the fisheries in Twelve Mile Creek, the Sixteen Mile Creek, the Etobicoke River, together with the flats or low grounds on said creeks and river which we have heretofore cultivated and where we have our camps. And also the sole right of the fishery in the River Credit with one mile on each side of the river."[39]

The reason the Mississaugas sought this protection was revealed at the treaty meeting by Chief Quinepono. Although described as a "head man" in the English records of these meetings, Quinepono (Quenepenon, or The Golden Eagle) was a principal Chief at a Mississauga village located at the Twelve Mile Creek near Lake Ontario. Said to be a "shrewd bargainer," the Chief complained that his people had been harassed by settlers.[40] He claimed that "Colonel Butler told us the Farmers would help us, but instead of doing so when we encamp on the shore they drive us off & shoot our Dogs and never give us any assistance as was promised to our old Chiefs. Father – The Farmers call us Dogs and threaten to shoot us in the same manner when we go on their land."[41]

Chief Quinepono indicated that he expected the Crown's protection for his people when they exercised their rights in surrendered lands, and made it clear that the Mississaugas would not relinquish control of the river in the new surrender:

> Father. We have considered again the subject of the Land we spoke about yesterday ... We therefore have altogether agreed to give all you ask, to do as our Father pleases with it, except this River which we must persist in keeping in the manner we represented yesterday ...
>
> We now rely on you Father to protect us when we want to encamp along the Lake and not suffer us to be driven off as we now are on the Lands we formerly sold our Father, altho we were promised to encamp and fish where we pleased. We also reserve all our fisheries both here [Credit River], at the Sixteen and Twelve Mile Creeks together with our Huts and cornfields and the flats or bottoms along these Creeks.[42]

A year later, in 1806, the Credit River Mississaugas executed yet another surrender that reserved for "the people of the Missisauga Nation of Indians and their posterity forever – the sole right of the fisheries in the Twelve Mile Creek, the Sixteen Mile Creek, the River Credit and the River Etobicoke together with the lands on each side of the said creeks and the River Credit ... the said right of fishery and reserves extending from the Lake Ontario up the said creeks and River Credit ... And the right of fishery in the River Etobicoke from the mouth of the said river to the allowance for road."[43]

Although the late eighteenth century had seen a flurry of surrenders involving the Mississaugas and Chippewas, in many ways the Crown's treaty process was just beginning. Following the War of 1812, the non-Aboriginal population of Ontario doubled in size; to accommodate the new arrivals, the government needed to conclude another series of treaties and surrenders. By this time, the British had discovered that the Rideau water system and the Trent River–Kawartha system offered passage from the Bay of Quinte to Georgian Bay, a route that would facilitate settlement. They once again approached the Mississaugas to surrender these valuable areas of land.

However, this round of treaty negotiations differed from those of the past in its allocation of payment to the First Nations. Prompted by its concern regarding the expense of the Indian purchases, Britain had decided to alter its approach to treaty making. In 1818, the Lords of the Treasury in England determined that the colonies themselves would be responsible for finding ways to pay for the acquisition of Indian lands.

Because of the limited funds available to the colony, Sir Peregrine Maitland, Lieutenant-Governor of Upper Canada between 1818 and 1828, devised a scheme under which the First Nations entering into treaties would be offered a small annual payment in perpetuity, rather than the considerably larger, one-time-only payments that had been negotiated previously.[44] To ensure that First Nations would agree to the new arrangements, the Crown made additional promises during treaty negotiations, often assuring them that they would be left undisturbed by white men in their own lands; in some cases, it went so far as to pledge that white men would be removed from traditional Aboriginal hunting and fishing grounds altogether. The series of treaties concluded in 1818 between the Crown and the Chippewas and Mississaugas for the Rideau and Trent River–Kawartha system would encompass a huge area. Just over a century later, in 1923, they would also play a key role in the Williams Treaties negotiations to surrender these valuable areas of land.

William Claus acted as the Crown representative during these negotiations. A prominent Loyalist during the American Revolution and a militia leader during the War of 1812, Claus would become a member of the legislative council of Upper Canada in 1818 while serving as the Deputy Superintendent General of Indian Affairs.[45]

Colonel Claus held a council with the Ojibway on 17 October 1818. He asked them to surrender an enormous tract of land, comprising over half a million hectares to the west and south of Lake Simcoe. He informed the Mississaugas and Chippewas of the Crown's new annuity plan but also promised them that following this surrender, there would be no further intrusions by white men, as it would be "many years after both of us and most of your people will have left the world before any settlement will come near your villages."[46]

Chief Joseph Yellowhead (Yellow Head), a Chippewa, led the Aboriginal delegation during these important negotiations. On 28 October 1818, the Chiefs and principal men of the Mississauga Tribe, under his leadership, surrendered the "Mississauga tract," some 648,000 acres, in exchange for the relatively small sum of £522 10s.[47] That November, another provisional agreement was entered into between Claus and the Chiefs and principal men of the Chippewa Nation.[48] Although it referred to the Chiefs of the Eagle, "Rein Deer," Crane, Pike, Snake, and White Oak Tribes, the Rein Deer Tribe was part of the Mississauga Nation, demonstrating again that the terms "Chippewa" and "Mississauga" were used interchangeably. Although the treaty referred to the Chippewas alone, annuities were later paid to the Mississaugas of Rice and Mud Lakes under its provisions.[49]

Treaty No. 20 does not record any hunting or fishing rights in its written text, but protection for these activities clearly formed a major concern of the Aboriginal signatories. A letter of complaint translated from Ojibway and signed by the principal men who had participated in the negotiations outlines the Crown promises that were made at the time. One of these men, Captain Paudaush (George Pahtaush), would later become the Chief of the Rice Lake reserve. He had fought in the War of 1812 together with Captain Nott and Captain Crowe (also referred to as John Crow), who also signed the letter. The letter sent to Lieutenant-Governor John Colborne referred to the treaty promises. It was signed, using their marks, by George Pahtaush, John Crow, Captain John (with the mark of a snake), Peter Watson, and Jacob Crane, and was witnessed by James Evany, a schoolteacher.[50]

In their letter, the men reported that the first council meeting with the Crown to surrender lands had been held at Port Hope. They described what their elders had told them had been discussed, and the promises the Crown had made:

> The Governor or Supt. General had come to make a treaty with my Grandfather. And the promise that he gave to my Grandfather was very sweet, of course, this was before my time ...
>
> When the Governor first asked our Indian people to surrender this land, he said my dear children, I want to ask you to surrender your land to me as you have already heard what I said or promised before. As long as you see the sun in the sky, as long as the Rivers flow and as long as grass grows, the Reserve shall be yours, whatever you will reserve, and my Grandfather did not wait long he got up and said Great father I do agree to surrender my land to you ...
>
> I will surrender on the mainland vis. we shall make a bee line from as far as you can hear a shot gun from the shore up this line shall leave me part of the main land, all the points, Islands and all the mouths of the Rivers, these shall be reserved for my hunting and fishing ground, and my children after me or the rising generation, as long as they live.[51]

Captain "Paudash" (Pahtoshe) had been present at a treaty negotiation at Port Hope in October, as well as at Treaty No. 20. He described in detail the exchange of Crown promises made then as well:

> another time while I was fishing it was very calm all at once I heard someone speaking to me when I looked I saw it was the Governor and he commanded me to rise and go to arrange to meet him at Port Hope. And I got up and went to Port Hope with a lot of other Chiefs and Warriors who wanted to hear what their great father the Governor was going to say. This is what he said. My dear children. I come to ask you again to surrender your land to me for my people that are coming from the East, they are on their way coming, they are very poor and hungry and some of them are starving.
>
> And again I agreed to surrender the land to him myself and this is one of the things I meant, that I reserved all the points along the shore ... and why I mention these things is because you did not give me any writing regarding the surrender and the promise but I am happy so is my people to know the surrender and the promise because its [sic] something we can never forget.

The last treaty involving Captain Paudash had taken place at Port Hope, and he asserted that this time, "I was the one who made the bargain thats why you often hear me say that I own all the Islands. And they were pretty well satisfied with the bargain. Colonel Claws [Claus] and Coll. Gibbins

[Givins] and this is what they said. Your great father will be very well satisfied with the bargain, and they mentioned the promise viz. the Rivers, grass and sun, so long as you see these you shall enjoy that blessing."[52]

William Claus' own journal of the treaty negotiations supports this account, confirming, for example, that the treaty was negotiated at Smith's Creek (Port Hope), as does the treaty itself. During the proceedings, Claus indicated that he had stressed the advantages of the government's new annual annuity plan, declaring it was the King's intention not "to do as formerly and pay you at once but as long as any of you remain on Earth to give you Cloathing in Payment every year."[53] In response, according to Minutes of Council, Chief Buckquaquet, a principal Chief, had responded that "From our lands we receive scarcely anything and if your words are true we will get more by parting with them than by keeping them – [since] our hunting is destroyed."

The Minutes of Council also reflect that Chief Buckquaquet asked Claus for specific assurances concerning his people's ability to continue hunting and fishing:

> Father. We hope that we shall not be prevented from the right of Fishing, the use of the Waters & hunting where we can find game. We hope that the Whites who are to come among us will not treat us ill ... The young men, I hope you will not think it hard at their requesting, that the Islands may be left for them that when we try to scratch the Earth, as our Brethren the Farmers do, & put any thing in it that it may come up to help our Women & Children.
>
> Father. We do not say that we must have the Islands but we hope our Father will think of us & allow us this small request – this is all we have to say.

To which Claus replied,

> Children. I have heard your answer & in the name of your Great Father thank you for the readiness with which you have complied with his desire. Your words shall be communicated to him. The request for the Islands, I shall also inform him of, & have no doubt but that he will accede to your wish. The Rivers are open to all & you have an equal right to fish & hunt on them.[54]

The November 1818 treaty resulted in the surrender of over 1,951,000 acres north of Lake Ontario in exchange for £740 annually in goods at the Montreal Price, fixed prices set by London for certain goods.[55] As in the earlier treaties, however, its description of lands would prove to be inaccurate. Indeed, in 1836, Captain Thomas Gummersall Anderson of the Indian Department learned that an 1818 Chippewa treaty involving lands on the east side of Lake Simcoe contained errors in its description, leaving some fifty thousand acres apparently still unsurrendered.[56]

Captain Anderson had been appointed as an officer of the Indian Department after the war. Stationed at Drummond Island, Penetanguishene, Coldwater, and Manitoulin Island, he succeeded Colonel Samuel Peters Jarvis as the Chief Superintendent of Indian Affairs in 1845.[57] He knew many of the treaty signatories personally, as they had fought together in the War of 1812. Nonetheless, he said nothing to them of the error and was commended by his superiors for having acted "prudently under the circumstances in not mentioning anything to the Indians about the 50,000 acres supposed still to remain unsurrendered by them to Government ... the matter had better rest as it is for the present uncommunicated to the Indians."

James Givins informed Anderson that he had found yet another error in the 1818 treaty and that the reference in it to an earlier surrender purportedly taken in 1805 was clearly a mistake, "as there is no trace and indeed there was no purchase from the Indians in 1805 that I can find."[58] However, this was not brought to the attention of the First Nations Chiefs who had signed the treaty either.

Promises of Protection

In the seventeenth and eighteenth centuries, the Anishnabe traded and bartered fish to Europeans, along with a huge variety of other resources, including canoes, meat, snowshoes, and maple sugar. Many First Nations, such as those at Parry Island, Georgian Bay, had learned to salt and store fish in barrels, enabling them to engage in relatively large-scale commercial activities.[59] By 1820, it was reported that the Chippewas of Rama had "advanced to a knowledge of the difference between barter and cash transactions – the main source of imposition by the trader and they are alive to the advantages of pursuing their fishing in the fall as a source of profit and not merely for their own food. To enable themselves to do this more extensively, they have built for themselves two batteaux, each capable of holding forty or fifty barrels of fish."[60]

During this era of relatively low harvesting, several species of fish grew to incredibly large sizes. A single lake trout, for example, could provide as much food as several caribou, and whitefish were called the *attikameg* or "caribou" of the water, because of their size and sheer abundance. William Dean points out that as late as 1922 at Batchewana, a sturgeon was caught weighing 140 kilograms; in 1960, a lake trout weighing thirty-one kilograms was caught in North Caribou Lake. As he puts it, "Considering that such large fish were the equivalent of from one to three caribou, their importance as a supply of food cannot be overlooked."[61]

Almost all domestic and commercial Aboriginal fishing activities took place on the "fishing islands" of the large freshwater lakes and rivers of inland Ontario. Because of their importance, Aboriginal peoples often reserved their fishing islands while surrendering other lands. In 1850, for example, Ojibway Chiefs reserved Batchewananaung Bay for their own use, together with a "small island at Sault Ste. Marie used by them as a fishing station." A later surrender, No. 91A of 29 July 1859, again retained the small fishing islands at Sault Ste. Marie specifically.[62]

The fishing islands provided a convenient spot to dry nets, to prepare fish for commercial trade by salting or drying, and to establish camps, enabling fishing activities to take place on a commercial scale.[63] As a result, Aboriginal peoples were determined to keep possession of them. In Ontario, all inquiries by non-Aboriginal persons concerning the use of unceded islands for fishing purposes were referred to the Indian Department, since as noted by the Chief Superintendent of Indian Affairs, Samuel Peters Jarvis, "islands within the tract of unceded lands have always been claimed by the Indians."[64] Jarvis referred to unceded "lands" but was clearly discussing fisheries in navigable waters. As late as 1845, a "W. Elliott," who had asked for the use of fisheries around "certain Islands in the occupation of the Indians on Lake Huron," was referred to the Indian Department.[65]

Although some non-Aboriginal commercial fishing interests in Upper Canada attempted to gain title to islands through private surrenders, the 1763 *Royal Proclamation,* as noted earlier, prevented such transactions with individuals. As a result, fishing companies and individuals sometimes entered into arrangements directly with First Nations to lease their fishing islands and adjacent waters. These leases were recognized and confirmed by the Imperial government as a means by which First Nations could protect their fisheries from unauthorized encroachments while receiving financial benefits from their lease.[66]

In the early 1830s, the Saugeen Ojibway Indians, who were Chippewas, began to lease their fishing islands and surrounding fisheries around the Saugeen Peninsula to third parties and to receive rents from the leases. In 1834, the Huron Fishing Company was granted the right by the Chiefs of the Saugeen Nation to occupy the Saugeen fishing islands of Lake Huron for a £25 fee over an unlimited term. The lease was confirmed by a formal licence of occupation issued by the Imperial government through Sir John Colborne, the Lieutenant-Governor, and conveyed exclusive rights to the leaseholders to the coast of Lake Huron between the Saugeen River and Cabots Head, as well as all the fishing islands along the coastline.[67] An examination of the lease makes it clear that it included a large block of waters adjacent to those islands, confirming that Aboriginal title to the islands included the waters around them.

The company was "to possess, occupy and enjoy" thirteen islands in Lake Huron, called the Gheghets Islands, which were north of the "River

Saugink [Saugeen], as numbered on a small plan prepared by Deputy Surveyor John McDonald." The licence commenced at a point within Lake Huron, running "west one mile and a quarter; then north five miles and three-eighths of a mile; then east two miles and a half, more or less, to the east shore of Lake Huron; then southerly along the water's edge of the Lake, following the several Points and Bays to the place of beginning." It included a map that showed a boundary extending into the water around the thirteen fishing islands.[68]

The Saugeen people, aware by that time of the threat to their fisheries posed by white fishermen, and particularly American interests, hoped that leases would restrict access to the fisheries and keep other white men out.[69] As the lease itself indicated, "we, the undersigned, will use our endeavours to protect the said Islands from Encroachment."[70]

The Imperial government approved of the Saugeen leases on the basis that the company employed many people, provided cheap food, trained "our hardy sailors," and would "create a nursery for the further encouragement in working the fisheries upon the splendid Lakes of Upper Canada and more especially, in the vast waters of Lake Huron."[71] Between 1834 and 1839, the Huron Fishing Company took 6,100 barrels of fish in Lake Huron; the Collector of Customs reminded the Governor General that the company had an obligation to pay the Indians an annual rent in return for this privilege,[72] indicating that the government recognized Aboriginal ownership of the fishing rights.

The Imperial government approved requests for licences only when the applicants could demonstrate that they had obtained the consent of the Aboriginal peoples involved. For example, in 1832, the Provincial Land Book record indicates that Alexander McGregor, an early Indian trader in the St. Lawrence and Georgian Bay areas, claimed he had a licence from the Indians to carry on an extensive fishery on a small island in Lake Huron. He complained that some time after he had taken occupation, Americans had dispossessed him of it, and he requested a lease or licence from Imperial authorities in order to dispossess them of it.[73] Because McGregor was apparently acting with the consent of the Indians, it was recommended that he should receive a licence of occupation during pleasure.[74]

The licences of occupation and leases held enormous economic value. One Alexander McDonald makes extensive comments concerning the potential of this industry in 1842, writing, "At the Saugeen and Manitoulin Islands, and at several of the points on the British Coast of Lake Huron, there is to be found an inexhaustible supply of fish, consisting principally of herring, trout and white fish, herring being in the greatest proportions and indeed of almost incredible abundance."[75] As the Huron Fishing Company reported, even a limited fishery involved almost inconceivable quantities and sizes of fish:

> I should recommend the Company to carry on the Fishery on a *limited* scale next season, by employing only eighty people; by such they can, with ease, put up: in herrings, 10,400 barrels; in white fish, 250 barrels; in salmon trout, 300 barrels – total of 10,950 barrels.
>
> ... As for Herring, I can safely state, that had we the means to cure them, not less than one thousand barrels could be taken during the height of the season; and, you will observe, that this is only at one station, – there are four as good. Indeed, the quantity that might be taken is so enormous, that, to make a calculation of it would appear quite incredible to those who have not had an opportunity of seeing this place, I therefore chose to leave the matter to your own imagination, rather than furnish a statement that could not be believed, save by eye-witnesses.
>
> With respect to Salmon Trout, it is so plentiful, that yesterday with only 105 lines with double hooks, 142 were brought to the curing house, some of which weighed from 25 to 40 pounds each.[76]

As the commercial fishing industry developed in earnest, white fishermen began to enter traditional Aboriginal fishing grounds without any formalized arrangements. First Nations peoples immediately protested that these encroachments violated their rights. Soon after the signing of the treaties at Credit River, for example, white settlers began to intrude on the Mississaugas' exclusive and reserved fishing areas, and in 1829, the Chief and Council of the Mississauga Band at Rice Lake petitioned the Lieutenant-Governor, Sir John Colborne, asking that these settlers be informed of the privileges "in law which the Indians are entitled to." James Adjitance, Peter Jones, Joseph Sawyer, and fifty-one other members of the Mississaugas of New Credit complained that the white men had taken all the Aboriginal fisheries except those at the Ten-mile creek and the Twelve mile creek. The Mississaugas reported that though "the two first are gone from us ... we are wishing to keep the Credit."

To support their right to the fisheries, and to convince the government to support them, the Mississaugas asserted that they had become "civilized" and "a new people; we have thrown away our sins; we live in houses where we worship the Great Spirit, and learn his word and keep his sabbath; our children and our young men learn to read." As well, they argued that they needed "the fish in our river that we may keep our children at home to go to school" rather than travel many miles to hunt for food. They also pointed out that the interference with their fisheries was preventing them from selling their fish commercially:

> We also catch salmon and sell them very cheap to industrious white men who bring us flour and other provisions and cattle, and they say it is much better than to fish themselves ... Others [white men] go to the mouth of

> the river and catch all the salmon: they put the offals of salmon in the mouth of the river to keep the fish from passing up, that they may take them with a seine near the mouth of the river in the lake and often in the dark they set gill nets in the river and stop all the fish.[77]

In response, the government passed *An Act the Better to protect the Mississaga tribes, living on the Indian Reserve of the River Credit*. This 1829 Act made it a specific offence for anyone to hunt or fish within the Mississauga reserves without the consent of three or more of their principal men or Chiefs.[78] In exchange for this legislation, the Mississaugas appear to have agreed to fish only five nights a week and to refrain from catching salmon for sale in the fall.[79]

At Rice and Mud Lakes, similar encroachments took place. Some of the Mississauga Chiefs who had signed the 1818 treaty, including George Pahtaush (Pahtoshe), Captain John Crow (identified by his *dodem* of a snake), Peter Watson, and Jacob Crane, complained bitterly to Lieutenant-Governor Colborne that the "only means of subsistence we and our children have is completely wrested from us by white people generally." They reminded Colborne that their hunting and fishing grounds were to have been retained for their exclusive use, and referred to the 1818 treaty as follows: "Your petitioners humbly shew that when we sold our land to our great Father, it was under a solemn promise that our hunting ground should not be encroached upon by the white people, but kept *solely* for the benefit of our people. Your petitioners now humbly beg your Excellency will interfere in their behalf and for the future assure your petitioners that justice which they hope and expect from their great Father."[80]

Although a marginal note from Colborne on the document asked if "there is no method of preventing these trespasses on the hunting grounds of the Indians?" no steps appear to have been taken by the Crown to prevent these incursions from continuing.

In September 1835, facing additional pressures as the "Indians from Lower Canada" also began to enter their hunting grounds, Chiefs George Pahtaush, John Copway, and John Crow of Rice Lake proposed that Colborne give them their annual presents of firearms early, enabling them to embark on that year's hunting "before their Game is destroyed." This time, their request for "three dozen Guns and Rifles and one hundred pounds of powder and three hundred pounds of shot" was approved by the Lieutenant-Governor.[81]

Pressure on the Mississaugas came from others as well. The Iroquois reminded them that they too had a right to hunt in the area as a result of the early treaties with the Ojibway, or the "dish with one spoon." In 1840, Peter Jones, a Mississauga leader, attended a meeting where Iroquois Chief John Buck "exhibited the wampum belts, the memorials of the old treaties and explained the talks contained in them. There were four belts, or strings of wampum. The first contained the first treaty made between the Six Nations and the Ojebways. This treaty was made many years before ... The belt was in the form of a dish or bowl in the centre which the chief said represented that the Ojebways and the Six Nations were all to eat out of the same dish; that is, to have all their game in common."[82]

During this period, interference with Aboriginal fishing grounds by white men holding Crown licences of occupation became a matter of considerable agitation. In 1839, a report on Indian affairs stated that "Indians should not be restricted in their fishing. The matter of licences and rights conferred [on others] should be reviewed."[83] J.W. Keating, the Assistant Superintendent of Indian Affairs, reported that those Indians who engaged in commercial fishing activities were regularly being taken advantage of by white traders, who "rob them of their stock, and leave them often without either clothing or provisions." He commented that these practices were reducing Indians to penury: "I have known Indians catching abundance of the finest trout, reduced to live even at the very time upon boiled acorns, not a fish returned to the lodge to feed either the hungering infant or the patient wife, whiskey was the sole reward or rather curse of their Tribes ... Were they civilized, the now wasted resources which providence has placed for their support could form a most fruitful source of prosperity, and even wealth."[84]

Aboriginal peoples throughout southern Ontario attempted to protect their lands but often with little success. As missionary Saltern Givens reported to Samuel Peters Jarvis, the Chief Superintendent of Indian Affairs, an attempt by Chief John Hill of Tyendinaga to remove the nets set by white men within the reserve's waters had resulted in his being sued in a civil action. Givens noted that Chief Hill had done no more than try to protect his community's fishing grounds: "You are aware that the lawsuit instituted against John W. Hill, a Mohawk Chief by certain whites for destroying their netts and driving them away from the Indian fishing ground has terminated unfavourable to him and the burden of costs and fines has fallen upon him ... The cause of action having arose in an attempt he made to protect the joint property of this nation from the acts of trespassers."[85]

In 1845, Sir Charles Bagot, the Governor General of British North America, issued a report to the Imperial government concerning the conduct of Indian Affairs.[86] Legislation had been passed that year making it illegal for anyone to fish for salmon "nearer the mouth of any of the rivers or creeks emptying into Lake Ontario or the Bay of Quinte than 200 yards or within two hundred yards up from the mouth of any such river or creek," precisely the areas that the Mississaugas had reserved for their own exclusive use.[87] The Bagot Report mentioned Aboriginal fisheries specifically, stating that all rangers, Chiefs, and officers should be informed of the new law and that any "insufficiency of the law" should be reported to the Governor

General "to prevent injustice and that if necessary, a legal enactment be introduced to supply additional power for its repression."[88] However, observing that Indians still relied on their traditional activities, the Bagot Report suggested that the "advance towards civilization" could be facilitated more easily if the Crown obtained surrenders of the remaining unceded fishing islands.[89]

As settlement efforts intensified, the Mississaugas resisted this supposed "advance towards civilization." Peter Jones, the noted Mississauga leader, began an intense lobbying effort to have First Nations provided with title deeds to their lands and waters that they could show to settlers and use to warn them off their lands:

> I wish also to say something about our Lands. My Indian Brethren feel much in their hearts on this subject, we see that the country is getting full of white people, and that the hunting will soon be destroyed. We wish our Great Father to save a sufficient quantity of lands for ourselves and our children to live upon & to cultivate. It is our desire that whatever lands may be marked out for us, to keep the right and title ourselves, and not be permitted to sell them, nor let any white man live on them unless he is recommended by our Council and gets a license from our Father the Governor; but we wish to feel that we stand on our own land that our fathers left us.
>
> I speak these words because I have since I have been in this Country heard that the lands on which the Rice Lake Indians are settled have been deeded to the New England Company to keep for them. I fear this will make them feel uneasy, I know that the Indians would feel better to keep the lands themselves, or that their Great Father should keep it for them, than to trust it with strangers that they know nothing about; every man always feels best when he is in his own house, and stands on his own ground.[90]

Captain Thomas G. Anderson of the Indian Department warned his superiors that the subject of title deeds was taking on growing importance to the First Nations "as they already talk of their Vast Forests and possessions beyond the limits of the Ceded Territory."[91] Colonel Bruce, the Superintendent General of Indian Affairs, confirmed that the Indians were anxious to obtain such deeds to their lands.[92] As well, he noted that applications had been made by white men for several of the "unconceded" Indian fishing islands, but that "negotiations cannot be opened on account of the uncertainty of the Indian tenure."[93]

Although the Indian Department had expressed its assurances that "the Government is most anxious to respect [Indian] rights and to afford them all proper protection,"[94] Anderson recommended that the Crown expropriate any remaining unceded Indian lands, since "it would relieve the Government, and this Department from much inconvenience and vexatious

Law Suits which must otherwise continue for years to come."[95] Anderson urged the government to extinguish all Aboriginal rights except those on reserves "and thus forever put an end to the question."[96] He argued that "if the Government [does] not take some speedy and effectual means of securing to the Natives some such portions of their lands, every inch of their Reserves will ere long be occupied by white settlers and the poor ignorant but confiding aborigines ... left without a spot on which to bring the expiring last of this once unrestrained and powerful race."[97]

Chief Superintendent Jarvis was opposed to providing title deeds to the First Nations, however, on the basis that "although there are some Indians at this moment fully competent to exercise these (political privileges), yet ... I cannot see in such a case how the advantages expected to be imparted to the less civilized, by keeping them from too great proximity with white men, can be secured for thus white men might enter upon these lands and no power whatever, in such case, would remove them."[98]

Jarvis' comments concerning the lack of power to remove squatters may have been based, in part, on events that had taken place at the Six Nations reserve at the Grand River. There, white squatters had moved onto reserved Aboriginal lands but refused to leave, and the Crown's efforts to remove them had resulted in their appealing to the courts and the Legislative Assembly for special protection. Ultimately, to remove the squatters from their own reserve, the Six Nations were ordered by the courts to pay the costs of the squatters' improvements, together with almost £8,000 (approximately $32,000) in eviction costs, an almost unimaginable sum of money at the time.[99]

Promises of Exclusivity

As the conflicts between settlers and Indians mounted, the Crown sought ways to ease Ojibway fears of being driven from their hunting and fishing grounds while getting the land cessions it so badly needed. During the ensuing treaty negotiations, Crown representatives promised the southern Ojibway that the Crown would create exclusive areas in which they would be wholly separated from whites and free to enjoy their treaty rights without interference. A series of treaties entered into at Manitoulin Island perhaps best evidence these commitments.

In 1826, as part of an early policy of "civilizing" Indians, Lieutenant-Governor John Colborne had established "model" Indian villages at Sarnia, Credit River, and Coldwater. Methodist missionaries were called on to assist in these developments, and the villages were placed under the superintendency of Thomas G. Anderson as the Superintendent of Indian Affairs. Three Chippewa First Nations, headed by Chiefs William Yellowhead, Joseph Snake, and John Aisance (Aissance, Assance), participated in the model-village experiment on the Coldwater-Narrows Reserve.

The Chiefs may have been chosen for this venture because they were perceived as loyal to the British. Chief William Yellowhead's father, also named William, had fought in the War of 1812 alongside Captain Anderson and had kept his men allied to the British during the fighting. When he was wounded in the defence of York in 1813, his son, Musquakie, or "William," took his place. Four years later, the younger William Yellowhead was appointed the principal Chief for the entire Deer Tribe, located on lands throughout Georgian Bay, Lake Simcoe, and Lake Muskoka.[100]

Chief Yellowhead and Chief Joseph Snake had settled their people primarily in the southern region of Lake Simcoe; Chief John Aisance and his people occupied the area of Kempenfelt Bay, stretching north to Georgian Bay. In 1830, Chiefs Yellowhead and Snake moved their communities to a model settlement at the Narrows of Lake Simcoe (at Orillia). There, along a road running west from the Narrows to Coldwater, houses and agricultural plots were constructed to accommodate their families, a Methodist minister, and a schoolmaster. Aisance and his people settled at Coldwater, at the western end of the Coldwater-Narrows Reserve.[101] William Hawkins, the Deputy Surveyor for the province, visited the reserve in 1833 and found that the Narrows village of some forty families comprised "sixteen houses, eleven old log shanties, a Methodist meeting room and school and some scattered wigwams. A fine frame house was constructed for William Yellowhead." At Coldwater, another thirteen houses, a sawmill, and six log shanties had been built, along with a meeting house and a house for Thomas G. Anderson.

In 1835, Anderson wrote to Lieutenant-Governor Colborne to passionately proclaim the successes of the Coldwater-Narrows Reserve in providing Indians with a "Knowledge of the Arts of civilized Life."[102] However, the government discontinued its support of the settlements in 1839. Subsequently, some of the Indians at the Narrows went north to Rama, and some of those at Coldwater went to Beausoleil Island in Lake Huron.[103] Chief Snake and his people returned to Snake Island in Lake Simcoe.[104]

During this period, as the Crown experimented with reserves, the American government had also begun to consider the formation of specific Indian colonies, or reserves, west of the Mississippi, where Indians could be kept together while they were "civilized." In 1830, it enacted the *Indian Removal Act* to facilitate this objective.[105] The *Act* authorized Indians residing in any of the states or territories to voluntarily exchange their lands for lands west of the Mississippi River. It provided support for those Indians who chose to emigrate to the new locations, as well as compensation for their abandoned improvements.

Many of the Ojibway and Pottawatomi who had supported Britain in its warfare against the Americans made their way into Upper Canada, where they asked the English Crown to provide them with a place to live.[106] In September 1835, Anderson advised Colborne that he felt the British had a moral debt to assist their former allies with their relocation. Perhaps influenced by the new American policies of concentrating Indians on reserves, he suggested creating a large reserve on Manitoulin Island, where Methodist missionaries had already extended their missions.[107] He felt that the island could provide a home to "our Indian allies emigrating from the United States and seeking our protection as well as the British Indian whose means of subsistence are exhausted," a reference to the reduction in available game and fish in the more populated southern areas.[108]

According to Anderson, creating a settlement at Manitoulin would not only satisfy the claims of the former allies upon England's "humanity" but would allow the government to "form one extensive establishment for the purpose of leading them to the arts of civilized life."[109] To do so, however, the Crown needed to obtain a surrender of Manitoulin Island from the Ottawas, who had long claimed title to the area.

Every year, a large council was held at Manitoulin Island where First Nations Chiefs and warriors received their annual presents of guns, ammunition, tobacco, blankets, and other items from the British government in recognition of their war-time alliance. In August 1836, Sir Francis Bond Head, the new Lieutenant-Governor of Upper Canada, took advantage of the council to obtain surrenders from those in attendance. Bond Head reported that "At the Great Manitoulin Island in Lake Huron ... I found about 1,500 Indians of various tribes assembled for their presents, the Chippewas and the Ottawas, at a great council held expressly for the purpose, [who] formally made over to me 23,000 islands."[110]

Those present during the negotiations would later claim that Bond Head induced them to enter into the treaty by promising them an exclusive right to fish in the many islands around Manitoulin.[111] Bond Head's own reports to his Home Office confirm that such promises were part of the treaty process.

According to Bond Head's dispatches, representatives of the Saugeen Indians had attended the council to receive their presents as well. Since they had already heard the proposal he had made to the Chippewas and Ottawas earlier that day relating to the surrender of the Manitoulin Reserve, Bond Head asked them to surrender the "Sauking [Saugeen] Territory which lies to the north of Owen Sound upon which proper houses shall be built for you and proper assistance given to enable you to become civilized and to cultivate land which your Great Father engages forever to protect for you from the encroachments of the whites."[112] Bond Head reported that the Saugeen Indians had then agreed to voluntarily surrender to him "a million and a half acres of the very richest land in Upper Canada."[113]

According to Chief Metigwob (Metigwab, Metiewabe, Medegwaub) of the Saugeen Nation,[114] however, the surrender was far from voluntary. Metigwob claimed that Bond Head had placed enormous pressure on him to agree to the proposal, telling the Chief that "if they did not listen to the words of the Great Father and comply with his wishes, he would cast them off and never do any of them [sic] for them in the way of giving presents." Although Chief Metigwob asked to consult with the Chiefs at St. Clair, River Credit, and Munceytown, Bond Head reportedly stated that "he had nothing to do with the Chiefs above-named, his treaty was with them and he must have an answer now."[115]

To induce them to surrender their lands, the Lieutenant-Governor asked the Chief if the Saugeen Indians would like to settle on the point from Owen Sound to Lake Huron. Metigwob finally agreed, but only after Bond Head promised that all whites who fished in the vicinity would be removed. Metigwob is reported to have done so on the basis that "there were many fish at that place."[116] With that promise alone, and despite receiving no financial compensation or annuities, Chief Metigwob and the other representatives of the Saugeen Nation signed Surrender 45½, relinquishing Aboriginal title to approximately one and a half million acres of land.[117]

As Robert J. Surtees writes, "No payment was made to the Indians for the lands they yielded to the government nor did any annuities flow to the signatory bands from these agreements. Instead, the Indians were simply promised that Manitoulin Island and the Bruce [Saugeen] Peninsula together with their fisheries would be protected from encroaching settlers and that the Indians there would be given assistance with agriculture."[118]

In an 1836 letter to Lord Glenelg, the Secretary of State for the Colonies, Bond Head explained his actions and his promises to the First Nations, observing that the Indians had long lived "in their Canoes" among the fishing islands, in part because the "surrounding Water abounds with Fish." He confirmed that he had made explicit promises to the Chiefs who attended the council, telling the assembled Indians that the Crown was doing what was best for them. He had warned them that if they did not agree, they could not expect the Crown to protect them, due to "an unavoidable increase of white population, as well as the progress of civilization, [which] have had the natural effect of impoverishing your hunting grounds ... In all parts of the world, farmers seek for uncultivated land as eagerly as you, my red children, hunt in your forest for game ... but uncultivated land is like wild animals and your Great Father, who has hitherto protected you, has now great difficulty in securing it for you from the whites, who are [hoping] to cultivate it."

Bond Head reported that he had told those present that since the islands of Manitoulin as well as those on the north shore of Lake Huron were surrounded by "innumerable fishing islands, they might be made a most desirable place of residence for the many Indians who wish to be civilized, as well as to be totally separated from the whites and I now tell you that your Great Father will withdraw his claim to these islands and allow them to be applied for that purpose."[119]

Francis Bond Head evidently believed that a policy that removed Aboriginal peoples from contact with white settlers would be far more successful than civilization efforts, which he personally considered a failure.[120] A few months after the treaties at Manitoulin, Bond Head sent Lord Glenelg a letter in which he confirmed these views, maintaining that the only practical course was "to remove and fortify [the Indians] as much as possible from communication with the Whites."[121] He then put forward his plan that Manitoulin Island and the islands surrounding it should become a reserve or locale for all the Indians in Upper Canada "to retire or fall back upon."[122]

On 4 August 1837, at a council of some seventy-five principal men and Chiefs, including Chiefs Aissance and Yellowhead, Samuel Peters Jarvis, who had replaced Colonel James Givins as the Chief Superintendent of Indian Affairs, carried out Bond Head's plan.[123] Using Ottawa interpreter Assikenack, he explained that those Indians who wished to continue receiving presents should "come and live under the protection of your Great Father," who is "willing that his red children should all become permanent Settlers on [Manitoulin] island." Reassuringly, he added that those who did so could support themselves by a moderate effort in agriculture and fishing: "If you cultivate the Soil with only moderate Industry, and exert yourselves to obtain Fish, you can never want; and your Great Father will continue to bestow annually on all those who permanently reside here [on Manitoulin Island], or in any Part of his Dominions, valuable Presents, and will from Time to Time visit you at This Place, to behold your Improvements."[124]

The 1839 annual report on Indian affairs in Upper Canada acknowledged that in 1836, Sir Francis Bond Head had promised the Saugeen peoples that His Majesty would "engage forever to protect them against the encroachments of the whites."[125] Despite these promises, within only a few years of the treaty, the Saugeen fishing grounds became "frequently the scene of violence with interlopers and trespassers."[126] It was reported that the abundance of fish at the mouth of the Saugeen River, where about 370 Chippewas and "Potawatomies" had settled, had "attracted the attention of white traders, thus annoying the Indians."[127]

Early in 1844, Jarvis informed J.M. Higginson, the Civil Secretary to the Governor General, that the Saugeen fishery was being interfered with by residents of Upper Canada as well as Americans, and that the "Indians are unable to prevent people from exploiting the fishery." A marginal note to the letter – "The Indians' interests must be protected"[128] – indicates that the Governor General was mindful of the Crown's earlier commitments. However, in response to a request from George Copaway (Copway), a Mississauga and Methodist minister, as to the legal rights of the Saugeen Indians to occupy the fishery, Jarvis suggested that the Imperial government should simply deny that islands in unceded waters and the fish around them belonged to Indians at all, stating, "[T]he fishing islands ... are part and parcel of the Wilderness of Canada West which has not yet been conceded to Her Majesty by the Indians but to assume that on that account they are the private property of a small band of Indians residing twenty miles from them and that the band have an exclusive right to the fish which resort to those Islands at certain Seasons or have the right to grant licences in any shape to others will not, I presume, be admitted by the Government."[129]

Despite this observation, Jarvis conceded that the practice of the British government had been to first extinguish Indian claims by surrender before other claimants could derive title.[130]

In March 1845, two Chiefs from Saugeen made their way to Toronto to present a petition to the Attorney General and to the Chief Superintendent of Indian Affairs, claiming that they had been defrauded by "wicked white men" who had taken possession of their fishing grounds.[131] It was reported again that year that the fishery had attracted white encroachment on what the Saugeen "consider their exclusive right and on which they rely much for provisions."[132]

In response, and apparently disregarding Jarvis' earlier advice, the Governor General issued a "declaration in favour of the Ojibway Indians respecting certain lands on Lake Huron" in the name of Queen Victoria, the only title deed of its type so far to be located. This extraordinary document, sometimes referred to as the 1847 *Imperial Proclamation,* was specific to the Saugeen Indians. Within the description of lands acknowledged as possessed and owned by the Saugeen Indians since time immemorial were included "any Islands in Lake Huron within 7 miles of the main land," together with the right to convey.[133] In light of Bond Head's earlier treaty promises during the 1836 surrender that white men would be removed from Saugeen waters, the Proclamation has been described as a "unique" document, clearly expressing the Crown's intent to protect Aboriginal fisheries.[134]

Despite this explicit endorsement of possession and protection, the Saugeen peoples, like other First Nations in southern Ontario, continued to face relentless and overwhelming intrusions into their territory by white fishermen, hunters, and settlers. Within months, the Crown concluded that it could no longer protect Aboriginal lands and fishing grounds from encroachment. Having determined that the Indian problem was best dealt with through "civilizing" Aboriginal peoples, the Crown decided to permit white men to hunt, fish, and even squat on Indian lands, with the expectation that this would aid in a new and aggressive policy of complete Indian assimilation.

3
A New Crown Policy

Legalized Encroachment

Very shortly after the *Imperial Proclamation* confirmed that the Saugeen people held Aboriginal title in the islands and waters around the Saugeen (Bruce) Peninsula, an 1847 government commission suggested a very different approach to dealing with the increasing "Indian problem." It recommended that the government should take steps to open up Indian lands to use by non-Indians, arguing that this would be beneficial for the Indians as it would aid in their more rapid assimilation.

The commission's "Report on the Affairs of the Indians in Canada" observed that the early policy of the government toward "this race was directed rather to securing their services in time of war than to reclaiming them from barbarism, and encouraging them in the habits and arts of civilization."[1] The Crown's concern for Aboriginal peoples, who were no longer needed as allies, had shifted to what was described as a "more enlightened policy" that would "endeavour, gradually, to raise the Tribes within the British Territory to the level of their white neighbours, to prepare them to undertake the offices and duties of citizens and by degrees, to abolish the necessity for its further interference in their affairs."[2]

This objective of the new Crown policy would be facilitated by discouraging Indians from pursuing their hunting and fishing activities. Separating Indians from their traditional activities to ensure their "civilization" would also allow their valuable hunting and fishing grounds to be opened up to white settlement, a point not missed by the report's authors:

> Experience has shown the Indians can no longer lead a wild and roving life, in the midst of a rapidly increasing white population. Their hunting grounds are broken up by settlement; the game is exhausted; their resources as hunters and trappers are cut off ... no choice is left but to remove beyond the pale of civilization or to settle and cultivate the land for a livelihood.

> But the settled and partially civilized Indians, when left to themselves, become exposed to a new class of evils. They hold large blocks of land, generally of the most valuable description which they can neither occupy nor protect against the encroachments of white squatters, with whom in the vain attempt to guard their lands, they are brought into a state of constant hostility and conflict.[3]

The report pointed out that it had once been necessary in Upper Canada, when Indians were more numerous and their alliances more important, to make treaties with them for the peaceful surrender of portions of their hunting grounds.[4] However, with the clock having turned, the government now had to recognize the "natural laws" of settlement and the inability of Indians or the Crown to protect even reserved areas due to the "incontrollable" forces of settlement before which even governments had to bend:

> the incapacity of the wild and untutored Indians to protect their lands and other property from the encroachment and frauds of the Whites first led the Crown to assume the office of Guardian in this respect and the Indians have become accustomed to depend entirely upon the protection and interference of the Government ... But the extent and isolation of Indian lands in Upper Canada, the impossibility of exercising a surveillance over those vast tracts, the incontrollable force of those natural laws of society to which even Government must bend have prevented the efficient protection of the Indian Reserves any more than the Crown lands under similar circumstances.[5]

During this period, the Imperial government had received reports of similar circumstances in other colonies as well.[6] Given what appeared to be a widespread problem in dealing with indigenous communities, the commission's report received serious consideration.

The commission recommended that a new policy should be introduced that recognized the "benefit" to the Indians of legalized encroachments. First, squatters who had "improved" Indian lands would be entitled to purchase them at an "upset price," a minimum bid fixed by the Crown. They would receive this consideration since "they not only enhanced the value of their own and surrounding land but their improvements offered a security for their ultimately making to the Indians full compensation."[7] Rather than protecting Indian lands, then, the new policy would encourage those who operated outside the law to benefit from their actions.

Second, no steps would be taken to prevent white men from overharvesting fish and game within the Indian territory or on reserve lands, since "its entire extinction or disappearance might be ultimately more beneficial to the Indians than its most rigid preservation for their use." Again, allowing white men to hunt and fish on Indian lands was considered to be good for Indians, as it would hasten their assimilation. The report outlined the inevitable outcome of this step toward civilization:

> The evidence which your Commissioners have received upon this point in every way confirms this view. As the Game is destroyed, the Indians take the cultivation of the land for sustenance. At first, when the hunting season comes round, they go further in search of it but year after year they are obliged to go further. Their journeys become lengthened, their absence from home prolonged, the fatigues and risk of the chase are increased, until gradually its followers fall off and remain at home to attend at their farms. After a while, hunting is only followed as a recreation for a few days in the spring and fall, and it is in evidence that in many of the old settlements, the practice may shortly be expected to cease altogether.[8]

To expedite the assimilation process, the commission recommended to the Executive Council that "the Indians be discouraged from looking to Game as a means of support and that all incentives to the chase be withheld from them."[9]

On the matter of Indian fisheries, the commission's recommendations were equally determined. The Commissioners argued that the same "natural laws" of settlement that had resulted in the encroachment of white men into Indian lands prevented the government from protecting Aboriginal fisheries in any meaningful way. They therefore suggested that "the same argument which the Chief Superintendent advances against any interference for the protection of Game on Indian Lands applies equally to the Fisheries; the severest penal statutes would scarcely prevent the white inhabitants from killing it." Further, the commission asserted that there should be no restrictions on white men fishing on Indian reservations, since "the law does not restrain the Indians from hunting and fishing on the property of whites [and], it would be unfair to make it penal to hunt and fish on reservations."[10]

The Imperial government also agreed that the solution was not separation of Indians from whites, as both Bond Head and Anderson had recommended, but a complete integration process. Adopting the commission's recommendations for a new "civilization policy," it directed that all of the southern Ojibway communities should be relocated to two areas where manual labour schools, one at the Bay of Quinte and another at Alnwick, would be established.

As Captain T.G. Anderson explained at a meeting of the Mississauga, Chippewa, and Iroquois Chiefs, the "great object" of raising Indians to the level of white men could be attained only if Indians were indoctrinated into white values and culture, and required to give up their own:

> Brethren. For many years past, the Government has used every means in its power to raise you upon a level with your white brethren ... but your unsettled state and wandering habits have rendered all their efforts insufficient for the full attainment of the great object in view ... It is as I have before told you the sentiment of the British Government to do even more for you now than ever it has done before. It wishes to raise you to the same rank in social life as your white brethren, and to make you an independent and happy people. But to accomplish this, you must assist in the great work by laying aside indolence, vie with each other in habits of industry and be obedient and kind to those who are appointed to instruct you.[11]

Anderson informed the Chiefs and principal men that the government wanted them to abandon hunting and fishing, and move to areas in which schooling would be provided for their children. He promised they would be given written documentation of whatever tracts of land they chose in these new locations, which would be secured "to you and your posterity forever."[12] Regardless of whether the adults chose to leave their traditional lands, however, he made it clear that their children would be required to be sent to residential schools "where they will forget their Indian habits and be instructed in all the necessary arts of civilized life and become one with your white brethren. In these Schools they will be well taken care of, be comfortably dressed, be kept clean and be given plenty to eat ... The management of the Manual Labour Schools will be entrusted to your Missionaries."[13]

The Chiefs of the River Credit, Alderville, Rice Lake, Mud Lake, Scugog Lake, and Snake Island Nations voted in favour of the school proposal, although just how much of the proposal was understood by those who attended is unclear. The proceedings were recorded by Henry Baldwin, a barrister from Peterborough and Secretary to the Chiefs in Council, who noted that the Mohawk speech was interpreted into English "or perhaps the substance of it, for the interpretation seemed rather brief" and that it was then interpreted from English into "Chippeway."[14]

Only Chief William Yellowhead of Rama and Chief John Aissance of Beausoleil Island refused to go along with the plans. Yellowhead protested that the government had moved his community once before, from the model community at Orillia, and that his young men had only just settled at Rama. He objected that he was "not willing to leave my village, the place where my Forefathers lived and where they made a great encampment; where they lived many generations; where they wished their children to live while the world should stand and which the white man pointed out to me and gave me for my settlement."[15] In fact, Chief Yellowhead did not move and spent the remainder of his life at Rama, where he died at around a hundred years of age.[16]

For his part, Chief Aissance complained that his community had been asked to relocate several times, most recently when requested to establish the model village at Coldwater and again when the Crown had abandoned the settlements. Referring to his band's seven-year residence at Coldwater, he stated that whenever he had complied with the wishes of

> our Great Father ... it has never continued so for any length of time. You see this road here, my Chiefs, the Portage Road; the land on half of that road was given to me and my Tribe to live upon. We remained there scarcely seven years when our white Father asked us to give it back ... What I have already stated are the causes that hinder me from favourably answering the question proposed. I do not wish to remove. I have already removed four times and I am too old to move again. You always credit me with too little in the account; when I ask for anything, you say "where shall I get it."[17]

Effects of the New Policy

The Crown's plans to facilitate access by white hunters and fishermen to unceded Indian lands, reserves, and traditional fishing grounds were supported by the Crown's Law Advisors. They offered legal opinions to the effect that Indians had no special rights to hunt and fish anyway.

Attorney General W.H. Draper simply ignored the treaties. Draper, who would go on to become Chief Justice, was an Englishman who had spent his early career as a seaman with the East India Company. (He was sometimes referred to as "Sweet William" for his oratorical skills.[18]) He informed J.M. Higginson, the Civil Secretary, that "the right to fish in public navigable waters in Her Majesty's dominions is a common public right – not a regal franchise – and I do not understand any claim the Indians can have to its exclusive enjoyment."[19]

Those who complained to the Superintendent of Indian Affairs regarding interference with Indian fishing activities were answered with a copy of Draper's opinion, which apparently received wide circulation. For example, although Thomas G. Anderson had written to one T.E. Campbell about a complaint from Indians concerning the intrusion of outsiders on their fishing islands, Campbell responded by quoting the opinion and the conclusion that the waters were "open to everyone."[20] Similarly, in a September 1848 letter, Campbell acknowledged receipt of a letter in which "the Indians complain of the interference of strangers with their fishing," and returned a copy of the opinion prepared by Attorney General W.H. Draper.[21]

The First Nations quickly noticed the effects of the new Crown policy. Shortly after the commission made its 1847 report, increasing numbers of white men entered the waters around Manitoulin Island. During an 1848 council, the Chiefs of the Manitoulin villages of Chitewainganing,

Shegwanaindand, and Wequameking (Wikwemikong) expressed their unease at these developments. George Ironside, a Superintendent of Indian Affairs stationed at a Manitoulin village, relayed their dissatisfaction to his superior:

> [T]wo of the principal men of this village [Manitowaning] were present as its representatives, [and] I was requested to state to you for the information of His Excellency the Governor General that they have long noticed, with feelings of distrust, the gradual encroachments of the whites upon their fishing grounds in the vicinity of their Island. That these places are yearly resorted to by persons under the pretence of mearly [sic] trading with the Indians while their real object is the catching and curing of fish, and, being always well prepared for carrying on the business, large quantities are annually secured and taken away by these intruders, to the great injury of the settlers here.[22]

The Chiefs at Manitoulin Island asked the Crown to protect them from these intrusions, but Ironside declined to do so. He defended his inaction on the basis that exposure to white fishermen would be good for the First Nations. However, as he explained a year later, it had had quite the opposite effect: "although I was aware last year of the feelings of the Indians, I did not interfere hoping that by their intercourse with the whites they would learn from them their mode of fishing and curing and be stimulated to further exertion, but it was carried on to such an extent as almost to produce a contrary effect and tended rather to depress than improve them."[23]

Ironside's position is rather difficult to comprehend. Born to a Shawnee mother and a father who worked in the Indian Department, he had been the head Chief at the Anderdon reserve in 1838 or 1839 and had been moved to Wikwemikong by the Indian Department because of a conflict that had developed over lands.[24] His lack of sympathy for the Aboriginal peoples on Manitoulin Island is thus somewhat surprising.

Nonetheless, as the intrusions into Indian lands intensified, instead of supporting their position, other Crown representatives also placed increasing pressure on First Nations to allow white men access to their traditional areas. For example, the Alnwick First Nation had a number of unceded islands located in the Bay of Quinte, South Bay, and Lake Ontario, and between Kingston and "Guananoque," a claim that the 1856 Pennefather Report had described as both "equitable" and "tenable."[25] These included reserves at Mississauga Point, about six miles below Belleville on the south side of the Bay of Quinte; at Grassy Point in Sophiasburgh; Cape Vesey near Point Pleasant; Bald Head at Weller's Bay at the southwest end of the Township of Ameliasburgh; and "all the islands eastward from Presqu'Isle to Guananoque"; as well as Green's Island, Timber Island, False Ducks, Duck, and other islands in South Bay.[26]

Even though they continued to use the fishing islands, members of the Alnwick First Nation were urged to surrender them as soon as possible, "it being clearly for their advantage that the matter should be speedily settled."[27] Colonel R. Bruce, the Superintendent General of Indian Affairs, recommended that the surrender should be made without "pecuniary cost to the Government," the only apparent "advantage" to the Mississaugas being an end to the controversy. However, Bruce himself admitted that the Crown had "on more than one occasion formally acknowledged the Indian title to Islands in the Bay of Quinte," including those not specially reserved to Alnwick.[28]

The Alnwick First Nation had asserted that a mistake had been made in respect of lands it had ceded in 1822 and that "the treaty as they intended it, and as it was explained to them, only yielded up a tract bounded in that direction by the height of land from which the waters flow into the Ottawa, a line corresponding nearly to the 45th parallel of north latitude." The First Nation complained that the treaty was being interpreted by the Crown "to extend 30 miles more to the southward to the headwaters of some of the principal streams flowing into Lake Ontario," and thus denied it access to its hunting grounds and fisheries.[29] The Indian Department concluded, however, that since the cession alluded to in the grant to the Mohawks of the Bay of Quinte was not on file, and the lands in question had been surveyed for white settlements, the claim would not be entertained. The fact that no treaty could be found, then, was used to deny a claim that no treaty had been entered into, a rather circuitous argument explained by the Department as justified since, "unless the first treaty of surrender is forthcoming, we do not feel justified in supporting the views of the Indians on this point."[30]

As white men rapidly depleted the fish and game in their ancient hunting and fishing grounds, many of the Mississauga and Chippewa First Nations were forced to leave their seasonal villages for locations further from populated areas. Despite the Crown's civilization policy, when establishing villages, the First Nations continued to select areas that gave them ready access to game and fish.

Ojibway Chief George Copway described how various bands of Mississaugas resettled themselves on reserves either adjacent to lakes or on islands, where they could fish. Copway, who had joined the Methodist ministry,[31] favoured these reserve settlements and wrote that the "Chippeways" at Rice Lake had been "reclaimed from their primitive wandering life." Rice Lake, as noted above, had earlier been reserved for the exclusive use of the Mississaugas, and the band had moved to the northern side of the lake, about twelve miles from Peterborough.[32] That the area had long been used for settlements is reflected in an old Mississauga name for it – Pamadusgodayong, or Lake of Plains, a reference to the lands cleared by

Iroquois for cornfields centuries earlier, then used as hunting grounds by the Mississaugas.[33]

The Chippewas of Alnwick (formerly the Mississaugas of the Bay of Quinte) had settled on Grape Island, in the Bay of Quinte. These were islands that the Mississaugas had specifically reserved when surrendering lands to the Crown to be set aside for the Mohawks of Tyendinaga in 1784.[34] Their desire to retain them is not surprising, since as late as 1891, the Bay of Quinte was described as an "exquisite Bay ... whose waters teem with all delights for the fisherman."[35]

Many of the Mississaugas settled in the Kawartha Lakes chain, north of Peterborough, an area described by Catharine Parr Traill as teeming with wildlife:

> The red, grey and black squirrels are abundant in our woods; the muskrat inhabits little houses that he builds in the rush parts of the lakes, these dwellings are formed of the roots of sedges, sticks and other materials of a similar nature and plastered with mud ... The Indians set traps to ensnare these creatures in their houses and sell their skins which are very thick and glossy towards winter. The beaver, the bear, the lynx and foxes are also killed and brought to the stores by the hunters, where the skins are exchanged for goods and money.[36]

One group of Mississaugas settled at Balsam Lake, on the Kawartha chain, but even in this more isolated region they were forced to leave their homes once the game became depleted by overhunting. Some of them moved to Lake Scugog (Scugog means "shallow waters"), while others moved to Snake Island and Mud Lake.[37] As Chief Jacob Crane described in 1855, the Balsam Lake Band had decided to leave for a variety of reasons, but primarily because "It is well known the game in the forest [is] becoming more scarce every year and we can no longer depend upon it for our food and clothing and the only way we can supply our want is to cultivate the land like the white man. For this purpose we are and have been for some time past, have been busy in clearing this land near our village in order to make big farms."[38]

The Crown's civilization policy would find the Mud Lake Band a greater challenge. The Mud Lake "Chippeways" had located on a peninsula jutting into the Mud, or Chemong (also referred to as "Curve") Lake, some sixteen miles northwest of Peterborough. Chemong is a variation of *oskigimong,* meaning "boat" or "canoe," which describes the shape of the lake.[39] Although pressure was brought to bear to induce the band to move from "their present unhealthy locations to Alnwick or to Rice Lake, the better to enable them to avail themselves of schools,"[40] the Methodist missionaries assigned to the task of civilizing the Indians at Mud Lake encountered great resistance to the enforcement of an agricultural, sedentary lifestyle.[41] Such attempts were unsuccessful primarily because the Mud Lake reserve "had the advantages of high quality fish all year round, abundant game and fowl, plenty of sugar maple, wild rice and cranberries as well as proximity to the growing centre of Peterborough."[42]

In 1850, the Indian Agent reported that "The only reason I believe why they [the Mud Lake Indians] continued here is because it affords them superior hunting grounds and while this is the case, it can scarcely be expected that they will turn their attention to agriculture and more especially since the greater part of the land belonging to the settlement is far from being adapted to that purpose."[43]

In 1856, the Pennefather Report observed that despite the various Crown attempts to divert them to agriculture, Ojibway peoples in southern Ontario persisted in relying on hunting, fishing, and other traditional activities. Even those who had converted to Christianity continued their traditional spiritual practices, such as vision quests in which a pubescent boy or girl fasted for ten days alone in a secluded spot while waiting "for a vision in which a spirit guide would appear and become the youth's guardian for life."[44]

The civilization efforts had proven uneven at best. The Pennefather Report noted that though the Saugeen, "Owens Sound," Colpoys Bay, Beausoleil, Rama, Snake Island, Alnwick, Rice Lake, Mud Lake, and Scugog Bands had settled in small villages, the Pottawatomies and Sandy Island Bands remained nomadic "heathens."[45] None of these First Nations had cultivated any farmlands but instead worked "occasionally for white people and gain a precarious existence by hunting, fishing, selling brooms and baskets."[46]

Another report described those Indians who persisted in their traditional activities as "savage" and "uncivilized." The Rama Indians, for example, were classed with the Mississaugas of the Bay of Quinte and Rice Lake but "in a more savage state."[47] The Snake Island Indians were also disparaged for continuing to "partake of the habits of their brethren at Rama. They spend the principal part of their time in fishing and hunting ... favoured by their location on the islands in Lake Simcoe."[48]

As for farming efforts, these had been a major disappointment. The Beausoleil Band had settled "on an Island near Penetanguishene, where from the bad quality of the soil, they cannot even raise potatoes and therefore plant patches of Corn &c on the adjacent Islands."[49] Captain Thomas G. Anderson complained that the Snake Island, Rama, and Beausoleil Bands had been unable to support themselves, "either from their bad location, from indolence or from want of some stimulous to exertion raise one half the food necessary to support their families. Their families are compelled by hunger to travel thro' the white settlements and make baskets and brooms which they exchange for food and whiskey."[50]

The Pennefather Report also discussed the level of education on the reserves, a topic that, many years later, would assume critical importance in *Howard*. It bemoaned the fact that these communities showed little interest in obtaining schooling for their children to help them make the transition to an agricultural life, commenting that the Snake Island Band school was "kept by Mr. Law, who sometimes counts 40 children under his tuition. The attendance is, however, variable, there being frequently but 8 or 10 pupils present, at other times none."[51] At Rama, "school is not taught more than half the time ... This Band are much given to hunting and basket making, consequently avoid tilling the soil, and are dragging through a life disgraceful to humanity."[52] Although Rice Lake had a school, "at present kept by a white woman," the Mud Lake Band had none. Scugog Lake had a school but "neither schoolmaster nor missionary resident among them."[53] Missionaries from Manitoulin Island reported that a Methodist manual labour school at Alnwick had "broken up, for reasons we are not in possession of" and recommended that an industrial school be established at Alnwick in its stead.[54]

Schools were often closed because of lack of teachers. At other times, children were kept home to assist with chores. The Reverend Peter Jacobs, situated at Rama, recommended that establishing schools with "strict orders that each child shall be at school one half day and work the other half and perhaps be rewarded would not be remiss."[55] One report complained that residential schools were required to address poor attendance, since "the Indians generally take their children from school for the most trifling reasons and perhaps keep them away for months, and when we succeed in inducing them to go again, they appear dissatisfied, hence the necessity of compelling their attendance."[56]

Most children simply did not attend school, being "prevented by the indifference of their parents, who in many cases keep them at home to assist in the labor of the fields, cutting up fire wood, &c."[57] As a result, in 1856, only ten of the forty school-aged children at Snake Island and Rice Lake attended school; similar numbers applied in other reserves.[58] Although Beausoleil Island, Rama, and Scugog had school-aged children, there was "no schoolmaster"; or records showed "Schoolmaster absent." The Sandy Island and Christian Island First Nations had no schools at all.[59] Even the manual labour school at Alnwick, which had been established in 1846 to train Indian children to farm, showed few signs of success for the government's agricultural policy. There, it was said that "The pupils receive a good plain education accompanied by religious instruction; the girls are also instructed in household affairs, and the boys are employed a portion of each day in working the farm."[60] Even so, the Alnwick Indians had only 250 acres of their 3,700 acres under "bad cultivation and they do not raise produce sufficient for their Support."[61]

Thomas G. Anderson admitted that he had made little progress in his efforts to civilize his charges. He urged his superiors to force the First Nations to give up their unceded lands, which he argued would finally enable them to become "civilized." Pointing out that white men had applied to purchase some of the islands in Lake Simcoe, Anderson complained that the Indians refused to sell although they had "no good reason for retaining them ... Under these circumstances, they have been repeatedly urged by the Government to remove to Owens Sound without any effect and for my own part, believing it to be to their advantage, I have taken the liberty to suggest the propriety of their being *compelled* by their guardian to use such means as are best adapted to serve their civilization and not allow their gross ignorance to exclude them from all advantages." He also complained that young Indian men had become disrespectful of government since they frequented taverns where "they meet the lowest grade of Society and with them join in what they term 'talk Politics' which to the ear and understanding of the unlettered Indian is generally disrespectful towards the Government and its officers – with his mind thus misled, he attends the next Council and right or wrong, opposes every measure which appears to emanate thro' the Chiefs from the Government."[62]

Although the Crown did not accept Anderson's recommendations, it was clearly frustrated with its failure to achieve its objectives. In 1857, the government passed legislation to encourage the "gradual civilization of Indians."[63] That same year, however, the Crown discovered a more effective way of advancing the civilization efforts. New fisheries legislation was enacted, and although it appeared neutral on its face, it was quickly used to restrict and prevent Aboriginal peoples from fishing in their traditional ways, and at the same time, to transfer their lucrative fisheries to white fishermen.[64]

The Fisheries Act

The first federal *Fisheries Act* was purportedly enacted to address what the Superintendent of Fisheries described as the "uncertainty of title" within the fisheries and the desirability of settling disputes.[65] However, the legislation also reflects the rather derogatory way in which Europeans perceived Aboriginal fishing practices as compared with their own. In the legislative debates, John Prince, a member of the Legislative Assembly of Canada, attacked Indian spear fishing and jack-lighting (night fishing with a light), arguing that these techniques were not "sportsmanlike" and therefore should be prohibited:

> There was no skill requisite to use the spear; it was a dastardly and mean thing to hold a torch at the surface of the water, waiting until the fish came up, and then to stick it with a fork. It was as bad to do this as to follow the practice of some individuals who go out into the woods with hounds, and hunt the poor deer into the lake, and then take a canoe, paddle over to the poor animal, and shoot it. No sportsman would follow such discreditable

> sport. He himself would rather take deer on the bound, or cast a fly at the fish he wished to capture.[66]

Described as an "an affluent English emigrant steeped in the literary lore of the rod and the chase," John Prince lobbied throughout his career to ban all Aboriginal hunting and fishing on the grounds that such activities were better left to sportsmen like himself. His comments are noteworthy, however, in that, during the 1860s, he would be appointed as a northern Ontario judge.[67]

Prince's belief that fishing was for recreation, not subsistence, characterized the approach taken by fisheries officials for many decades and showed a complete disregard for how Aboriginal people actually lived. His attitude toward them, however, was consistent with his views regarding non-whites generally. For example, in 1857, the year of the *Fisheries Act,* he referred to the "coloured" citizens of Toronto as the "greatest curse ever inflicted" on the two counties that he represented in the legislature.[68]

Scorn at the "unsportsmanlike" practice of spearing was shared by William Gibbard, the first Fishery Overseer appointed under the new fisheries legislation. Gibbard was determined to prevent the use of spears and nets by "Indians and half-breeds," as he believed this injured the regular net grounds of white fishermen.[69] He recommended that rules be developed to "abolish spearing (except on grounds reserved for the Indians)... the fish will not for many years perceptibly decrease; for owing to the storms, honey-combed and inaccessible shoals, there will be any number of places in all parts of Lakes Huron and Superior where fish of all kinds can spawn unmolested."[70]

Later, Gibbard urged that the *Fisheries Act* be amended to prohibit all forms of spearing, asserting that the practice was abused by Indians "too lazy" to fish "properly":

> Spearing should be prohibited altogether, unless in particular cases sanctioned by the Commissioner of Crown Lands. Indians under this clause give great annoyance to our lessees, as well as destroy fish in those places where they can spawn unmolested by nets, namely on honey-combed shoals and other places inaccessible to gill-nets or seines.
>
> The spearing is carried out at night, is difficult in consequence to detect, particularly where our lessees are in the neighborhood of the Indians; they get up in the morning and frequently find their nets torn by the spears of the Indians who too lazy to hunt for themselves, spear the fish in the lessees' nets.[71]

Under the new laws, the Governor-in-Council had the authority to issue special fishery leases and licences on lands belonging to the Crown for any term not exceeding nine years.[72] Although private property was exempted from the permission given to all "subjects of her Majesty" to fish for the purposes of trade and commerce in any of the harbours, roadsteads, bays, creeks, or rivers of the province,[73] reserve lands and waters were considered to be Crown lands rather than private property. As a result, the legislation enabled the Crown to issue licences and leases giving settlers increased, and in some cases exclusive, access to Indian waters, to the exclusion of the Aboriginal people who still retained Aboriginal title to them or held treaty rights to fish within them.[74]

Although depicted as "lazy," Aboriginal peoples expended considerable effort in fishing and were highly skilled at it. In fact, European settlers became concerned that Indians would provide unfair competition to the whites who were engaged in the commercial fishery. For one thing, Aboriginal people tended to sell their catches at lower prices than the white fishermen; for another, they had begun to engage in fairly large-scale commercial activities. For example, in 1842 Chief John Aissance and his band had moved to Beausoleil Island in Matchedash Bay, Georgian Bay, but because it was such a poor site for farming, they moved in 1856 to nearby Christian Island. Despite their surrender of their lands, in 1856, the Chippewas of Beausoleil Island in "Metchadash Bay" cured 150 barrels (3,000 pounds) of fish "caught at the fisheries near Beausoleil Island which abound in bass and pike."[75] Many barrels of fish were usually taken in a single haul and "cured and packed on the spot. The usual price of a barrel varies from five to six dollars."[76]

At Owen Sound and Cape Croker, where the Saugeen Ojibway villages were located, Aboriginal fishermen had taken 450 barrels (90,000 pounds) of an unidentified species of fish, 3,463 barrels (692,600 pounds) of herring, and 2,000 barrels (400,000 pounds) of salmon trout and whitefish at their fishing islands.[77] In 1856, a merchant and an unidentified buyer at Saugeen purchased 1,000 barrels of fish (200,000 pounds) from the Saugeen Indians. The unsurrendered fishing islands and the fisheries around them were reported to "constitute no inconsiderable part of the means of subsistence available for the [Saugeen] Band."[78] Concerned by what he perceived as unfair competition, however, William Gibbard observed that the "fish put up by Indians always sell at low rates."[79]

Despite Gibbard's views, some Indian Department officials thought that First Nations might be able to use their traditional fisheries as a source of revenue. All the inland lakes abounded "with fish of moderate sizes, such as trout, pike, white fish, perch, herring, loach and carp," and the fish in the Great Lakes were even larger. In 1857, a government report indicated that, "With reference to the fisheries about the [Manitoulin] Island, in the large bays in Lake Huron, we cannot but say that they are of great value, and that with proper management and protected from the encroachments of foreigners, they would suffice not only for the daily wants of the Indians, but contribute largely to their material welfare."[80]

Superintendent George Ironside also suggested that, if properly managed, the fisheries in Lake Huron could prove a source of considerable profit to the Manitoulin Indians as well as a food supply.[81] However, John McCuaig, the new Fisheries Superintendent, disagreed. He moved to reduce Aboriginal participation in the fishery by issuing Crown leases to white fishermen within Aboriginal fishing grounds. As one report indicated at the time, the value of the fisheries was no longer underestimated. McCuaig had no intention of allowing Aboriginal peoples to take economic benefits away from white men.[82]

McCuaig advised the government of the potential revenues it would acquire if it acted quickly to control access to the fisheries and, at the same time, took steps to deal with the increasing number of Americans who were inclined to hire "Indians and half-breeds." In 1858, in his first annual *Report of the Superintendent of Fisheries for Upper Canada,* McCuaig urged the government to move swiftly, warning that the wealth of the southern Ontario fisheries was, for the most part "lost to Canadian subjects. Like the prime fisheries skirting the north channel of Lake Huron, they are worked by Americans."[83] He recommended that Crown leases be granted to convey exclusive occupancy of fishing stations to the holders of the leases, granting the "entire fishing privileges in waters lying opposite or convenient to private lands, the same to vest the use of the beach and waters to mid-channel, inclusive."[84]

The most valuable fishing grounds were those that First Nations had traditionally occupied, but like Gibbard, McCuaig was convinced that white traders should not be undermined in their activities by Americans, supported by cheap Indian labour, who might undercut their prices:

> Fish is caught in rather large quantities during the spring and autumn, but all goes to the profit of the Traders who frequently supply the Indian with nets, and go with their schooners from one fishing ground to another and take the fish the moment it is hauled out of the water ... Fish, which at Collingwood, Saugeen, &c., was worth 9 and 10 dollars per quarter, was here bought from the Indians, and paid for in merchandize, for about 2 or 3 dollars. Flour was sold to the Indians for 12 dollars per barrel, which did not cost the traders more than 5 or 6 dollars, &c.[85]

Both McCuaig and Gibbard disapproved of the American practice of hiring "half-breeds," and complained that the "old established mercantile firms of the Sault Ste. Marie, (American side) who have been extensively engaged in the fisheries of these lakes for many years ... have invariably tendered higher than Canadians, and paid in advance; in the prosecution of their fisheries they will employ a Canadian half-breed just as soon as one from their side."[86]

Under the new system, First Nations were directed to notify the government regarding the specific fisheries they wanted to retain. Any fisheries they failed to reserve were to be reallocated to non-Aboriginal fishermen by leases and licences. The First Nations were promised that, in exchange for the loss of use of their lands and waters, the rents from the leases of unsurrendered waters would be paid to their credit.[87]

In 1858, William R. Bartlett, the Visiting Superintendent of Indian Affairs, asked the First Nations in Lake Huron to provide him with a list of the fishing stations they used and to let him know "if the Indians wished to reserve any of the Fisheries for their own use exclusively."[88] The Saugeen Chiefs were told that if their people wished to continue fishing, they would be required to pay rents. They were also told that "If therefore you have specified more fishing grounds than your people can actually make use of, you can let me know. The Supt. of Fisheries will arrange the details and boundaries of the grounds and of course his charge for rent will be in proportion to their extent. These are matters, however, with which we cannot interfere."[89]

Although the Saugeen Chiefs wanted to reserve their traditional fishing grounds, Gibbard informed Bartlett that he had already leased the Saugeen fishing islands and fisheries to white men. Obviously aware that his actions would not go unnoticed by the First Nations, he commented that the lessees were afraid they would be molested by the Indians. To stave off discontent, he asked Bartlett to let the Chiefs know he had also reserved some of the fisheries for the Cape Croker Band of Saugeen Indians.[90] However, of the ninety-seven leases he issued throughout Lake Huron and Lake Superior, only twelve went to First Nations.[91] Seventy-one went to what he instead described as "practical fishermen," and fourteen were issued to the Hudson's Bay Company. In the following four years, Aboriginal leases were reduced to virtually none.[92]

Aboriginal peoples learned to their anger that Crown leases to their own reserved and unceded fisheries, as well as to their fishing islands, had been issued to white men without their consent.[93] Despite their continuing protests, Gibbard issued a further six fishing leases to commercial fishing companies within the unceded waters of the Great Lakes. In 1861, these companies harvested about 2,500 barrels of fish (500,000 pounds) from Aboriginal waters in Lake Huron alone.[94]

In his first report, Gibbard described the magnitude of these fisheries, where "on one occasion ... 1,000 barrels and odd of herrings were landed in two hauls of the seine; 700 and then 300; at Cigar Island, 500 barrels were taken at one haul. At Smoke-House Island, one occasion, the seine was as full as it could be and for want of barrels and salt, thousands of herring were left in it."[95]

At Cape Croker, Gibbard ignored an offer from the band to pay whatever amount white men were paying to lease back its own unceded fishing islands. He also revealed his feelings toward Aboriginal activities generally, stating contemptuously, "I have allotted them three times as much as they will ever require and more than they will ever think of using. In my opinion, all the Indians would be better men and better off if they never saw a fish."[96]

Unhappy with the new legislation and their exclusion from their own traditional fishing grounds, First Nations throughout southern Ontario sent dozens of petitions and letters of protest to the federal government. The Chiefs and warriors of the Beausoleil and Christian Island Bands sent an angry letter to Bartlett objecting to being forced to pay rent for fishing in their own unceded fishing grounds. The letter was signed by Chief John Assance and Chief James Assance (Aissance) by their marks, and witnessed. It emphasized they had never agreed to surrender their game or their fish in their treaties:

> when the White Chief first came in America from the other side of the Big Salt Lake to make Treaty or Bargain to my forefathers he said I ask you to Surrender me some parcel of land to build my houses; I don't ask to surrender your hunting & fishing grounds – all the game is yours, and fisheries, now your law and regulation is laid down before us in prohibiting to kill our game for our living – our heart feel sick, we remember our forefathers Bargain, we still follow it, and we will still follow it as long as we are Indians, therefore we are at liberty to fish anywhere without lease rent to pay, the game and fish is ours, we never surrender to the Government yet and no remuneration for it.[97]

The Saugeen Ojibway Chiefs, joined by the Chippewas of Lake Huron and Lake Simcoe, sent a petition to the Imperial government in which they too reminded it that "when they surrendered their lands to the Government, they did not sign over all the game and fish."[98]

To deal with this discontent, the Indian Department and the Department of Crown Lands signed an agreement "for the Protection of the interest of Native Tribes," exempting Indians from paying fees for the fishery leases. However, the exemption applied only in circumstances "where the purport and object of title [was] to secure to the individuals and families of each tribe exclusive use of such fisheries for *bona fide* domestic consumption."[99] As the Ontario government itself would later admit,

> The Canada *Fisheries Act* was introduced in 1857 to control the impact of the rapidly-growing non-Aboriginal commercial fishing industry. Under the *Act* ... Aboriginal fishing activity became subject to (and conditional

upon) licensing and it became restricted to fishing for domestic purposes and subject to closed seasons. Some First Nations felt threatened by the imposition of licences, by exclusion from certain fishing grounds and by the prospect of non-Aboriginal commercial fishermen being allowed to fish in grounds that had traditionally been exclusively Aboriginal. Some refused to submit to the licensing regime only to find their access to the fishery was then denied.[100]

The provisions of the new food-fishing licences restricted First Nations to fishing within much smaller areas than they had traditionally used. In northern Ontario, where settlement had not yet taken place to any great degree, the leased areas were much larger than those leased to First Nations in the more populated areas to the south. At Garden River, for example, the First Nation's fishery lease included "all the waters within British boundaries along the Sault River, Little Lake George, Lake George to the West side of Camement D'ou Island including all the Lakes, Bays, mouths of rivers and creeks ... provided the rod and line fishery is open to those who fish for amusement only and not for gain or sale."[101] Nonetheless, complaints about the new leasing system were immediately received, even in these distant areas. Simon Dawson, who would later negotiate the 1873 North-west Angle Treaty on behalf of the federal government, objected that Indians would starve if the provisions were left unchanged:

> So far as I know, up to the summer of 1859, there has been no exclusive privilege granted for these fisheries, or if so, it had never been insisted on or maintained to the detriment of the Indians who had been in the habit, from time immemorial, of carrying on their fishing operations wherever they could do so to the greatest advantage, without any question being raised as to their right. Now, however, the case is altered. The fisheries have been leased, and those who hold them will not I am informed allow any of the Indians, except such as they choose, to fish at all and then only under the condition of giving the fish at a fixed price to them, the holders of the leases. Now the chief dependence of the Indians is on the fisheries, and if they are deprived of these they must starve. They have literally no way of laying in a winter's stock of provisions except from the fisheries.[102]

In the south, where settlement pressures were much greater, the largest of the leases extended only twelve miles into Lake Huron,[103] an area that Aboriginal peoples had previously fished without any restrictions. A lease to the Indians of Kettle Point extended only five miles into Lake Huron,[104] and despite the 1818 treaties promising them the use of fisheries throughout their ceded territory, the leases issued to the Chippewas and Mississaugas restricted them to the immediate waters around their island reserves. In the case of the Christian Island Indians, their lease included a right, within the lands encompassed by the lease, to cut timber for fishing purposes to a distance of eight rods inland.[105] Given that the Christian Island Band had not surrendered Christian Island and was supposed to have the exclusive right to use all its resources, the limited right to cut timber for "fishing purposes" under the lease could hardly be considered a privilege.

A lease was issued to the Rama Indians for a fishing station on Marion's Island in Lake Simcoe.[106] The Rama Band, which had never surrendered its rights to fish in the waters adjacent to its reserve, was engaged in commercial fishing activities at the time. Nonetheless, the fishing lease restricted Rama to a small fishery around the island for domestic purposes only.

In 1860, the British government formally transferred control over Indian affairs to the government of the Province of Canada. The Chief Commissioner of Crown Lands became the Superintendent General of Indian Affairs, with the power to dispose of Indian lands once these were surrendered.[107] Fisheries fell within the mandate of the Crown Lands Department as well, through a separate branch of that department, resulting in an obvious conflict of interest.[108] Although First Nations continued to send a flurry of petitions to the Governor General, these were generally treated with disinterest and forwarded to colonial officials to address. With its priorities directed to settlers and commercial interests rather than Aboriginal concerns, the new Fisheries Branch tended to ignore them altogether.

Enraged, Aboriginal fishermen damaged the nets set by the interlopers around their fishing islands. At Manitoulin Island, they lifted and removed a number of nets set "in trespass within their fishery."[109] A similar incident occurred when fishermen from the Christian Island Band removed nets set by non-Aboriginal fishermen within their fishing grounds adjacent to Christian Island and the surrounding islands in Georgian Bay.[110]

William R. Bartlett tried to placate the upset and angry Chiefs and warriors by suggesting that the rent from the islands, when added to annuity monies, would be "much better for you than these islands ... as they formerly have been subject to intrusion by everybody, besides being both unproductive and much trouble to both yourselves and the Department."[111] However, William Gibbard, displaying a complete disregard for Aboriginal concerns, complained that "The Indians still continue to give great annoyance to our lessees. They do not fish to any extent on their own grounds (of which the leasing system has given them more than a reasonable share) but seem jealous of everyone and are anxious to drive all others away from their neighborhood."[112]

The newly created Fisheries Branch now asserted that, rather than addressing the "uncertainty of title," as had been proclaimed at the time of its enactment, the *Fisheries Act* had been crafted to "preserve fish" from the harmful effects of out-of-season netting and spearing by Indians, so that these could become "productive fisheries" and "a source of revenue" for white settlers.[113] The real motivation behind the legislation, however, seems not to have been protecting fisheries, which were then thought inexhaustible, but obtaining revenues from their commercial exploitation. As John McCuaig reported in 1861, "The experience of the past three years has revealed, though imperfectly, the vast resources of the Upper Canada fisheries, and although we are not in possession of those data which would enable us to make an exact estimate of the annual value of the productions of our waters, yet there is abundance of evidence to show that my estimate of last year, viz. $2,000,000 is much below the actual amount annually realized."[114] McCuaig predicted that though annual rents in these early days had brought in only "$3,787, it was reasonable to assume an annual revenue from rents of $25,000 to $35,000 in a comparatively short time." In a period when the average labourer in England earned less than fourteen shillings a week, the value of the fisheries was enormous.[115]

With a newly informed appreciation of the full worth of the fisheries, the Fisheries Branch now asserted that fisheries had *never* been the subject of any special Aboriginal or treaty rights. It maintained that the leases of the past, entered into by the Chiefs with the approval of the Imperial Crown, did not evidence title to fisheries but rather only to fishing islands. It adopted this stance even though the leases themselves, as noted above, had invariably included water boundaries.

Nonetheless, and despite leases and licences that cited fisheries and waters in explicit terms, fisheries officials claimed that only Indian lands had been leased to third parties, and not the fisheries or waters around them. Indeed, the leases themselves were used to prove that the Indians had no monopoly over the waters, a circuitous argument at best:

> The Indians now assert that this *Act* trenches on their just rights, as they never surrendered the fisheries when they ceded their Land. I think that to establish this position, they should shew, that until the year 1857 they had enjoyed the monopoly of fishing in these waters. In reality this was not the case; the Lakes and rivers were considered open to all. Everyone aided in the destruction of fish, though in a very few instances, rent was paid to some of the Indian tribes, not for the fishery itself alone, but for use of *their Land* as a station for drying the nets, curing the fish, etc.[116]

Within a short time, white fishermen controlled virtually all of Georgian Bay and Lake Huron, as well as the Credit River, the Thames River, the Moira River, and Lake Simcoe. First Nations members responded by destroying the white fishing camps. In 1862, William Gibbard reported that fishing stations on all the fishing islands were being "regularly destroyed by Indians."[117] The next year, he complained that "The Indians ... still cause serious annoyance to fishery lessees and commit depredations upon *their* property. 'Tis very troublesome to arrange these difficulties in which the Indian tribes, and some half-breeds, are concerned."[118]

During the summer of 1863, in the waters around Manitoulin Island, Aboriginal unrest resulted in an armed confrontation between William Gibbard, supported by a vigilante posse, and several hundred warriors. Gibbard arrested an Aboriginal man but was ordered by the court at Sault Ste. Marie to release him. During his steamer trip home from Sault Ste. Marie, Gibbard drowned, apparently after being pushed overboard. The man he had arrested, who had travelled home on the same steamer, was alleged to be responsible, although charges were never laid.[119] As the *Manitoulin Expositor* wrote at the time,

> The Indian "revolt" was no more than a desperate stand by the natives of the islands who knew no more than that the Government inspector of fisheries in Lake Huron and Lake Superior, William Gibbard, J.P., had sold fishing rights to waters on the south side of Lonely Island. The natives for untold centuries had used the waters in the area for food.
>
> Mr. Gibbard leased the fishery to a Mr. Proulx for $4 per annum. According to a contemporary account "the consequences of keeping Mr. Proulx in the exclusive enjoyment of the fishery would have been to starve the whole of the Waquimakong [Wikwemikong] Indians who remained on the island." Mr. Gibbard paid dearly for his stubborn refusal to deal with the Indians in any but a highhanded manner.[120]

In retaliation for Gibbard's murder, William R. Bartlett was informed by his superiors that the Indians on Lake Huron would receive no further leases or licences and that, in addition, forthcoming amendments to the 1857 *Fisheries Act* would preclude any exclusive titles being "granted" in the fisheries.[121] He was also told that the lease he had requested for the Cape Croker Band had been issued to a white man rather than to "lawless [Aboriginal] fishermen."[122]

Legal Opinions

English common law had been received in the Province of Upper Canada in 1792. Although it has been suggested that the common law both recognized and protected Aboriginal title and Aboriginal rights to hunt and fish,[123] this rather generous interpretation of the law is not borne out by events that took place in Ontario.

When they surrendered their lands, First Nations granted certain rights to the Crown and reserved others to themselves. In unceded lands, they retained all their rights. As expressed in the provisions of the 1763 *Royal Proclamation,* the First Nations did not need the Crown to "grant" them an interest in their unceded waters and lands – they already had one. However, throughout the nineteenth century, Law Advisors to the Crown made the reverse argument, insisting that Indians had *only* the rights granted to them by the Crown. As Sidney L. Harring points out, Canadian legal doctrine was based on Victorian imperialist theories that denied Aboriginal peoples any rights not directly accorded them by the Crown.[124]

Law Advisors to the Crown insisted that Indians had no special rights, an approach that became entrenched in Canadian government policy and legal opinions although it wholly disregarded the *sui generis,* or legally unique, nature of treaties and Aboriginal title. The notion appears rooted in the *Magna Carta,* but since the *Royal Proclamation* had equal force of law to the *Magna Carta,* and postdated it by more than five hundred years, the claim that the *Magna Carta* could oust the provisions of the Proclamation makes no sense. In any event, the argument that the Crown could grant interests to anyone in lands that had not yet been surrendered is untenable.[125]

Taking their approach a step further, in the 1860s, the Crown's Law Advisors indicated that they gave little weight to the treaties anyway. They asserted that the Crown was required to keep only those promises it had recorded in writing in the treaties and not any oral promises that might have been made. This was an astonishing position to take, in light of the many errors in the written treaty texts, and the fact that the Indian leaders who had surrendered lands, usually unable to speak or read English, could rely only on the oral commitments provided to them by the Crown through interpreters.

In 1866, William R. Bartlett applied on behalf of the Cape Croker Band, part of the Saugeen Ojibway Nation, for leases of the fisheries around its reserves and islands. He pointed out that the band had been "deprived" of its fisheries, and urged that it needed to sell fish so that band members could "obtain comforts" and be removed from their "idle and vagabond lives."[126] The response he received from James Cockburn, the Acting Attorney General of Upper Canada, was that Indians had no special fishing rights at all.

Cockburn's reply was based on an 1863 legal opinion produced by Adam Watson, the Solicitor General. Watson, responding to a request as to whether navigable waters could be the subject of exclusive fishing rights, had advised that the public had a right of way over such waters as well as the right of fishing in them. Therefore, neither the Crown nor any private person could assert any special right or exclusive use within them.[127] Although Watson's opinion was prepared in relation to settler rights in surrendered lands, not to Aboriginal fishing in unceded or treaty waters, James Cockburn simply parroted it.

An elected politician who would soon become involved in the formation of Confederation as a delegate,[128] Cockburn was appointed Solicitor General of Upper Canada and a member of Cabinet.[129] Although he was educated at

Upper Canada College, it does not appear that he had any formal legal training.[130] Cockburn occupied the position of Attorney General of Upper Canada on an acting basis for only a few months while Watson, the Attorney General, was in Ireland, but his opinion would shape federal fisheries policies for at least the next hundred years.

As regards the *Royal Proclamation,* there was no reason to distinguish between its application to waters and to lands: indeed, the Proclamation itself made no such distinctions, and the early treaties had included both lands and waters. Cockburn's views, then, that the Proclamation applied only to Indian lands and not to Indian waters made no sense. Nonetheless, and without citing any cases to support his conclusion, Cockburn wrote that in the absence of an express *written* term in a treaty, and perhaps even with one, Indians were no different from other members of the public and had "no other or larger rights over the public waters of this province than those which belong at common law to Her Majesty's subjects in general."[131]

Cockburn went even further, arguing that the Crown had been given the authority to grant an exclusive right to fisheries only through the enactment of the *Fisheries Act.* A reference in that Act to the ability of the Commissioner of Crown Lands to grant licences for fishing in favour of private persons except "where the exclusive right of fishing does not already exist by law in favour of private persons" did not change his opinion. Instead, he concluded that "This exception was intended as I understand to exclude the application of the *Act* from certain Fishing rights which had been granted under the French law in Lower Canada before the Conquest; it certainly does not apply to the Indian tribes who have acquired no such rights by law unless it may be contended that in any of those treaties or instruments for the cession of Indian Territory there are clauses reserving the Exclusive right of fishing."[132]

Cockburn was equally dismissive of rights contained explicitly within treaties. He declared that parliamentary ratification was required before any such terms were enforceable: "I should say that without an Act of Parliament ratifying such a reservation no exclusive right could thereby be gained by the Indians as the Crown could not by treaty or act of its own (previous to the recent statute) grant an exclusive privilege in favour of individuals over public rights such as this, in respect of which the Crown only holds as trustee for the general public."[133]

Cockburn concluded his opinion, stating "The proviso in s.s. 8 of section 7 [of the *Fisheries Act*] is in accordance with this view, else why was it necessary to make any special stipulation for the Indian at all?"[134] A marginal note on the document, initialled by Cockburn, added that "Mr. Whitcher's proposal to set apart a portion of the reserve [funds] to be derived from the leases or licences of fisheries adjoining Indian Territory for the Indian fund" would be "in harmony with the generous and friendly policy which has been always maintained in our dealings with the Indian tribes," but that it would require further legislation. As a result, according to Cockburn, not even the rents the Crown had promised to First Nations for the use of their traditional waters by others could be paid to them without legislative change.

Despite Cockburn's strong statements, only seven years after his opinion that Indians could have no rights larger than those of the public, the Ojibway right to fish exclusively and free of the public common right in northern Ontario in exchange for a land surrender was expressly promised by the Crown. The North-west Angle Treaty was later agreed to by the Province of Ontario.[135] It would have been inconceivable that Ojibway peoples would have entered into the treaty without such commitments, given their reliance on fish. According to Cockburn's opinion, however, such promises could not be made by the Crown and thus were illegal.

Cockburn's opinion has been sharply criticized for ignoring the Crown's treaty promises, for favouring pre-existing rights in Lower Canada over Aboriginal rights, for not acknowledging Aboriginal title, for failing to cite relevant cases either in support of it or to the contrary, and for confusing the law of the sea with the common-law rules that applied to freshwater lakes and rivers.[136] Despite its many errors and omissions, however, the Crown would employ the Cockburn opinion to justify its future appropriation of Indian lands and fisheries in the name of the so-called public.

The Appropriation of Indian Fisheries

Following the receipt of Cockburn's opinion, the Acting Commissioner of Crown Lands directed the Fisheries Branch to sell off all Indian fisheries, including those around the unceded fishing islands, subject to a reserve of one chain (a measurement used at the time, representing 60 feet) for fishing purposes and those "fronting the mainland belonging to Indians." A "schedule of all Indian islands and riparian lands ceded and unconceded" was to be filed. In return for this unilateral appropriation of their reserved and unsurrendered fishing grounds, and following the advice outlined by Cockburn, the *Fisheries Act* was to be amended at the next sitting so that the government would then have the legislative authority to pay over "50 per cent of the rents derived from the fisheries occupied in connection with Indian lands ... for benefit of Indians."[137]

By this time, William F. Whitcher had taken charge of the Fisheries Branch, and, like Cockburn, he proved to be particularly unsympathetic to Aboriginal claims. The Nova Scotia–born Whitcher was an avid fly fisherman who had worked as a Fisheries Overseer on the Restigouche River and then on Lake Huron in the 1850s and 1860s. He blamed Aboriginal people for the majority of conservation problems and accepted Cockburn's opinion without any reservations.[138]

Under Whitcher's command, Indians would be free to fish for food in areas licensed to others for commercial use, but they were not to fish commercially or exclusively in any fishery. Whitcher advised one Fisheries Officer that "the substance of the legal opinion is that rights of fishery in all navigable waters are vested in the Crown for use and benefit of the public. Indians can have no exclusive right to the same either as original possessors of the soil or as present riparian owners and occupants."[139]

"Riparian" rights refer to a legal concept that permits the owners of land next to water to acquire title to those lands that are added by the deposit of soil carried by the water (accretion) while conversely losing title to those that are eroded. The concept also entails the right to a certain flow of, and access to, water. Such rights were always understood to accompany a patent of land. As early as 1904, the Supreme Court, applying the old law, held that a Crown patent of land awarded to Philomen Wright included the bed of waters as part of his riparian rights since "To read out of these letters patents the bed of this creek is to find therein a reservation thereof the Crown did not make and must be held not to have intended to make by the very fact that it did not make it."[140]

Whitcher's direction misapplied the concept of riparian rights as well, since at common law, Crown grants of land to settlers also *included* rights of fishing above the beds of adjacent waters. Whitcher's expanded interpretation of Cockburn's opinion gave settlers greater rights in surrendered Indian lands than the Indians themselves retained in lands they had not surrendered, a patently absurd result.

Like Cockburn, Whitcher insisted that the Crown would maintain a "friendly and generous policy" toward Indians. He proposed to dispose of the Indian fisheries by setting apart certain places as Indian fishing grounds for the common use of Indians generally. Other places would be leased to whites for commercial use, subject to Indians fishing there for their own domestic use but not for barter or trade. He promised that First Nations would be paid for these encroachments into their lands, writing that "As an equivalent for the use of so much Indian land as may be included in each lease, one half of the rent will be paid to the Indian Office as soon as sanction of Parliament is obtained." On the other hand, the fishing grounds to be reserved for the use of First Nations were to be "no more than [is] reasonably necessary."[141]

Despite Cockburn's opinion and Whitcher's commitments, the *Fisheries Act* was never amended, and rents were never paid for the flagrant use by non-Indians of unceded Aboriginal lands and waters.

4
Jurisdictional Disputes

Intra-Governmental Conflicts over Indian Fishing

In 1867, the newly formed Dominion had assumed responsibility for "Indians and lands reserved for the Indians," and the federal government then continued the procedures previously developed in Upper Canada and Canada West for managing Indian affairs. Through its Indian Branch, the Department of Secretary of State became responsible for First Nations.

In the early period after Confederation, some officials at the Indian Branch were acutely uncomfortable with the manner in which treaty promises had been disregarded. They maintained that First Nations were entitled to protection of their hunting and fishing activities as a result of their treaties and their unceded Aboriginal title. Others, however, had accepted Cockburn's opinion that unless treaties contained express written terms outlining hunting and fishing rights, Indians had no special rights.

Still others seemed unsure. William R. Bartlett, for example, acknowledged that the fishery authorities should take "immediate steps to protect the Indians in their rights to Fishery by putting a stop to the unlawful acts of white people."[1] On the other hand, he wrote of the Alnwick Band in 1867 that "Not only among this tribe of Indians (Alnwick) but all the other bands have a vague idea amongst them that a treaty was made by their forefathers with the British Govt by which the Indians are allowed to hunt & fish when ever and wherever they please. I try to dispel this idea whenever it is alluded to."[2]

The Indian Branch took full authority over Indians in 1876 with the passage of the first *Indian Act,* which placed responsibility for Indian lands in the hands of the Superintendent General of Indian Affairs.[3] Authority over fisheries, and therefore over Indian waters, was placed under the control of the Department of Marine and Fisheries. With W.F. Whitcher at its helm as the Deputy Commissioner of Marine and Fisheries, the Department began an aggressive and unprecedented campaign to restrict Aboriginal fishing activities.

A new close season banning fishing was introduced in April 1875 by Order-in-Council. It hit First Nations particularly hard throughout Ontario, where many of them had taken up farming but continued to depend on fishing for their winter stores of food.[4] As one Indian Agent reported, thirty-six band members were present at a joint council involving the Indians of Garden River and Batchewana, "a very large attendance considering it was haying season." The Joint Council discussed the imposition of the close season, and the Agent warned that

> should this Order be persisted in, I fear it will cause an immediate amount of misery to the two Bands as the close season is the only time during which great catches are taken, and it is chiefly on the fish they catch that they depend for the winter supply of pork and flour.
>
> Chief Nubinaugooching and several others present at the Robinson Treaty, states that Mr. Robinson assured them on making the surrender, that the Crown had no intention of interfering with their hunting or fishing, *but that the water would be free to them, the land was all that was required.* I therefore respectfully hope that all influence may be used to have this obnoxious Order repealed. I also understand that the white population are petitioning against it all through the district.[5]

First Nations at Manitoulin and Wikwemikong had a similar view of their treaties. As J.C. Phipps of the Manitowaning Indian Office confirmed,

> The Indians claim that the right to use the various Fishing Islands around the Manitoulin [Island] was one of the inducements offered to them to settle upon the island, under the Treaty with Sir Francis Bond Head; that the Fishery was leased to them for their exclusive use, that it has been annually renewed to them by the various Fishery overseers, that returns have been made annually of Fish sold ...
>
> I have thought it best to drop for a short time any distinct proposition for the curtailment of the fishery, to allow the excited feelings which at present exist to calm down; – the Indians are well aware of the futility of offering any opposition to the Government, and say that nothing shall ever induce them knowingly to break the law. I beg respectfully to remark that the question of the curtailment of the Fishery by leasing Fitzwilliam Island to whites was reported upon adversely in 1868 by the then Fishery Overseer, Mr. Plummer.[6]

William F. Whitcher made it clear that his goal was to prevent Aboriginal fishermen from being able to compete "unfairly" with white fishermen. He expected to achieve this by restricting Indians to capturing fish only within the area of their reserves, and then solely for their "immediate support."

This, he argued, would prevent Indians from competing unfairly with white men, who, unlike Indians, "pay rents and invest capital in faith of the permanent holding under leases or licences."[7]

If Indians who engaged in trading fish wished to continue doing so, Whitcher stated, they would be required to purchase a licence so that "whites would not complain about the competing traffic."[8] He added that if Indian licences interfered with the privileges exercised by white men, the Department would feel free "to restrain the Indians and to prescribe the extent and manner of their operations."[9] No such restraint was exercised, however, when white men interfered with Indians who fished for food or trade, or when they occupied the Indians' shore for fishing operations. As the numbers of such incidents increased, so too did conflict between non-Aboriginal and Aboriginal fishermen.[10]

Whitcher repeated James Cockburn's views that the fishery laws made no exception in favour of Indians, who were subject to the same restrictions as everyone else. If Indians wished to use any "fishing limits for domestic use or trade, they must have leases or licences, as do white men."[11] He later informed the Fishery Overseer at Collingwood that fisheries in Canadian public navigable waters belonged "*prima facie* to the public," and that Indians had no special rights in them, but that the "government acts towards [the Indians] with the same generous and paternal spirit with which the Indian tribes have ever been treated under British rule."[12]

Thus, if Indians wanted to fish for trade, they were required to pay a fee, and "since Indians are minors, leases and licences must be charged with Indian Affairs through the Department of the Interior." In terms of their domestic fishing reserves, however, Whitcher noted that "Indians do not have exclusive control of fishing in connection with Indian properties; thus they are not permitted to remove fishing gear of whites who have a lease or licence to these Indian fisheries."[13]

A Catholic Bishop contacted the Minister of the Interior to inform him that these developments had caused a great deal of uneasiness, particularly at Wikwemikong, on Manitoulin Island. In Treaty No. 45 of 1836, Sir Francis Bond Head had promised that the First Nations there would have exclusive access to the fisheries and fishing islands, but "[The Indians] say that they are threatened with being deprived of the right they have so far enjoyed of fishing round Squaw Island, Horse Island and Lonely Island. By the information which I have received, their rights of fishing on those Islands have been acknowledged by Sir Francis Bond Head, Governor General, by the Indian Superintendents Ironside and Plummer, by Mr. Whitcher himself, and last fall by Messrs J.C. Phipps of Manitowaning and Habrey [Abrey] of Little Current. I have also heard that the Hon. Mr. McDougall admitted their rights on these Islands in 1863."[14]

The Bishop's letter pointed out that the Manitoulin fisheries supported thousands of Indians, including the Saugeen Ojibway located at the Cape Croker and Saugeen villages:

> Now, Hon. Sir, you will please bear in mind there are some two thousand Indians fish every year near those Islands, alongside the reserve on the south side of Manitoulin Island. For, besides the Indians who actually live on the reserve, the Indians of Cape Croker and of Saugeen come regularly every year to fish in these waters. It is also a well known fact that fish is not always to be found in so great a quantity in the same place, so that if the reserve is again reduced to a smaller compass, many years they will be quite unable to catch many fish at all.
>
> If you add to this that certain parties circulate the report that the Indians require a permit to fish on which they want to sell, and that they receive no answer to the petitions which they have forwarded several times to the Indian Department, and in particular in February last, I think that there are good reasons for them to be uneasy. I expect, Hon. Sir, that in your anxiety to do whatever is possible to help the condition of the Indians you will favour me with such a reply that will quiet the minds of these poor people.[15]

Despite these concerns, the Marine and Fisheries Department remained firm that Indians were not entitled to special consideration. Aboriginal fishermen began to take matters into their own hands.

Whitcher reported an "incident" at Christian Island and Squaw Island in which the Indians had again lifted gear and nets belonging to white men. He blamed it on misinformation put about by local Fishery Overseers and Indian Agents who had "recognized the Indian pretension to control fishing privileges as belonging of right to themselves and after allowing them to select immense tracts of stations of sixteen miles or more ... as 'Indian Fisheries' and giving the Indians charts of the same, informing them that these bounds are to be defended from intrusion on the part of White men."[16] He also complained that Indian Agents supported the Indians in their beliefs that they had "greater rights" than other fishermen.[17] In particular, Whitcher accused William Plummer, the Visiting Superintendent of Indian Affairs, of fostering "illegal pretensions" and of putting forth "erroneous views."[18]

William Plummer had been an underground captain in the Wellington Mine in Bruce Mines before he joined the Indian Branch. In his first assignment with the Indian Branch in 1863, Plummer had been asked to investigate a situation on Manitoulin Island where an Indian Agent, Charles Dupont, had been accused of defrauding the Manitowaning Indians of lands. Following Plummer's investigation, Dupont was released from his duties, and although he was inexperienced, it was said that Plummer had "tackled" the problem "with sincerity and integrity."[19]

Between 1876 and 1881, Plummer became the Visiting Superintendent and Commissioner of Indian Affairs, based in Toronto. Charles Skene, another of Whitcher's antagonists, became the Visiting Superintendent of Indian Affairs based in Parry Sound, Lake Huron, then Indian Superintendent, a position he held until 1885.[20]

Early in 1876, Plummer wrote to the Department of Marine and Fisheries urging that fishing grounds be set aside for the Chippewas of Snake Island. He commented on the hardship of the thirty-dollar licensing fee imposed on them by the Department of Marine and Fisheries, pointing out that the First Nations had agreed to pay it only so that they could prevent white men from entering their licensed fisheries: "There should be set apart for these Indians, the water around the two small islands on which they reside, namely Georgina and Snake Islands in Lake Simcoe for home use only. The Fishery Overseer at Barrie has charged these Indians $30 a year for the privilege of fishing around Georgina Island which is considered by all to be a great hardship, but to which they have been compelled to submit in order to keep away a very undesirable class of white men who are in the habit of bringing whiskey and committing many worse abominations."[21]

Whitcher responded by dismissing Plummer's concerns as those of someone who was uninformed and a troublemaker:

> The Minister desires me to draw your attention to the erroneous view which Mr. Plummer entertains regarding the right of property in fishing grounds surrounding Indian islands. He pronounces their right to fishery privilege and fishery grounds the same as title to the soil. If, in the capacity of Indian Agent, Mr. Plummer teaches such *illegal* notions amongst Indian bands, although when formerly acting as a fishery overseer on Lake Huron he was always instructed directly to the contrary ... it is quite possible that the fishery officers may find some unnecessary trouble arising out of false advice given under the mistaken authority of Mr. Plummer.[22]

From that point on, Whitcher ignored all correspondence sent by Plummer. In June 1876, the Chiefs of the Rama, Georgina, Christian, and Snake Island Bands asked for Crown permission to use the fisheries in Sparrow Lake, Lake Couchiching, Lake St. John, and Lake Simcoe, including a number of fishing islands.[23] Chief Charles Big Canoe (sometimes referred to as Bigcanoe) of Georgina Island was told that his band would be entitled to a licence to fish for its own use, but not for barter; if it wished to fish for trade, it would be required to pay the same amount as non-Aboriginal fishermen.[24] Chief Big Canoe wrote to William Plummer, asking if his band had to pay for the licence "as we do not kill more fish than we require for our own needs."[25] Plummer's request to Whitcher asking that the First Nation be exempted, received no reply.[26]

At Rama, Chief J.B. Nagishking (Nagishkung, Nandgisking), like other members of his band, relied on hunting and fishing for a living.[27] He too wrote to William Plummer asking for the use of various fisheries for his band. Once again, Plummer's inquiry to Whitcher received no response.[28]

Whitcher wrote to Charles Skene, at Parry Island, explaining that because of white "settlement," Indian treaty fishing rights were subject to regulation and limitation, although he assured Skene that "Indians will secure by means of licences all the freedom of fishing that the most generous interpretation of these treaties could afford them and all the protection they can reasonably demand."[29] Despite his assurances, Whitcher sent a circular to fishery officers telling them that before Marine and Fisheries would issue *any* licences to Indians, it must be understood that the fishing privileges were subject to forfeiture if the holders failed to comply with fishery laws. As well, Indians were to be informed that white fishermen could occupy such portions of their reserves as were necessary.[30] Laws preventing trespass on Indian reserve lands had no application, in Whitcher's view, where fishing activities were concerned.

The policies Whitcher introduced during the 1870s resulted in numerous First Nations complaints that white men were trespassing on their reserve lands to fish, complaints that continued for many, many decades. As late as 1909, for example, J.D. McLean, the Secretary of Indian Affairs, noted that Chief Maracle and councillors of the Mohawks of the Bay of Quinte at Tyendinaga had "called at the Department today and state fishermen are camping all along the water front of the reserve stating they have a right to do so."[31]

The Cape Croker Indians of Georgian Bay tried a new approach, arguing in February 1876 that if they could hold their fishing grounds, it would prevent them from "roving amongst white settlement in search of employment and thus from being exposed to immorality and intoxicating drinks."[32] They told Plummer that their fishing grounds had become even more important to them as a source of food and for trade as their hunting grounds had become increasingly limited. They again offered to pay the same amount to rent their own unsurrendered islands as was paid by white men, pointing out that they had three large seines, two large scows, 150 barrels of salt, and 350 barrels left over from the previous season, thus attempting to present themselves as competent fishermen, worthy of a licence.[33]

Plummer forwarded the request, along with a similar one from the Christian Island Band, arguing that the current fishery was inadequate for the needs of the First Nations. He recommended that the request be granted.[34] Once again, Whitcher did not reply.

Eventually, Whitcher admitted that he had failed to answer Plummer's many letters requesting fishing limits for southern Ontario First Nations. He implied that he had not needed to respond because the entire matter was scheduled for review. In the winter of 1877, his Department and the Indian Branch had agreed to conduct an investigation and then refer the issue of Indian claims to fishing rights to the Department of Justice for an opinion that would place "the matter on a definite and permanent footing free from further doubt or disputes." However, he created a number of bureaucratic obstacles to ensure that white fishermen would not be interfered with in the interim.

First, the proposed reference of the claims of fishing rights advanced by Indians under existing treaties would have to be "accompanied by an official statement in regard to fisheries already reserved to Indians for their own use ... it would seem requisite to determine exactly what privileges and extent of fishing limits may be accorded ... to the various Indian Bands consistently with their *real* wants and needs." Second, the Department would refuse to recognize any rights that it considered incompatible with public rights or in conflict with public law. Given Cockburn's opinion, this meant that treaty rights and Aboriginal title would be disregarded by the Department of Marine and Fisheries as inconsistent with public rights.[35]

With these restrictions in place, two officers, one from the Indian Branch and the other from Marine and Fisheries, were assigned to conduct an investigation, after which a report would be made by the Justice Department and then the "whole matter" would be considered by the government "with a view to assigning the Indians such fishing stations as they in justice and equity should enjoy." For no particular reason, the preliminary investigation was not scheduled to start until the following summer, some nine months away.[36] In the meantime, "whites and Indians will be allowed to fish in common."[37] This course of action, Whitcher advised in another letter, had become "unavoidable, by the extravagant claims and extraordinary demands advanced on behalf of the Indians and [their] manifest unwillingness to accept any reasonable extent of fishing privileges."[38]

In July 1878, David Mills, Minister of the Interior and Superintendent General of Indian Affairs, notified Marine and Fisheries that he strongly disagreed with its policies, warning that the fishery regulations "seriously interfere with rights of Indians in Ontario ... in attaining, as they formerly did, the important part of their subsistence from waters in which from time immemorial they had been in the habit of fishing unrestricted by any regulations."[39]

Mills, in office during the Liberal government of Alexander Mackenzie, believed for a time that Indians in fact did hold some kind of "right or title" to their lands until it was extinguished. As Sidney L. Harring points out, Mills' position on Aboriginal title shifted, and Mills later described the Crown's recognition of Aboriginal title as a mere political expediency designed to protect good relations with the Indians.[40] Nonetheless, at this time, Mills complained that the regulations had obstructed the "exercise by the Indians of these unrestricted rights (in the enjoyment of which they were in many instances assured in Treaties made with them would never be disturbed)," thereby causing his Department "much embarrassment." He added, "The low price of furs and the rapid disappearance of game (which also formerly afforded an important means of a supply to the Indians) render the Indians all the more clamorous for a restoration to them of their ancient fishing privileges ... I submit that important modifications should be made in the present fishery regulations insofar as the Indians are affected thereby."[41]

In a September 1878 letter directed to Lawrence Vankoughnet, the Deputy Superintendent General of Indian Affairs, Whitcher responded to Mills' complaints. He retorted that protecting fish during their "breeding time" by preventing Indians from spearing them had benefited the whole country, particularly in areas where fish had been "netted and speared unrestrictedly and were almost exterminated." In his view, the rapid disappearance of game was "due almost entirely to unrestricted hunting, pursued also by Indians, and a similar condition of things would inevitably result to the inland fisheries were the habit of indiscriminate fishing restored, thus imposing still further deprivation on whites and Indians alike."

At the same time, Whitcher argued that the treaties did not guarantee Indians any right to unrestricted hunting or fishing, and that it was "well known that much of the laxity which prevailed in former times and the prevalence of destructive practices of fishing, particularly by Indians, were due to false sympathy with the pretended sufferings which it was alleged they must sustain if prevented from indulging their habitual preference for spearing fish on their spawning beds." In particular, Whitcher repeated his scathing criticisms of William Plummer and Charles Skene for convincing Indians that they were entitled to more than he believed was reasonable.[42]

Whitcher's true motivations were perhaps revealed in the final paragraph of his letter to Vankoughnet. Despite the fact that Indians had used the fishery resources for thousands of years before European arrival without any adverse consequences, Whitcher warned that the Indian claims should be ignored, since otherwise Indians would destroy a valuable "public" resource: "What claims are possible and sufficient in favouring Indians to injure and destroy a valuable public property that are paramount to the rights and interests of a great majority of the inhabitants to preserve and increase it for the benefit of the trade and industry of the whole country? Besides, it is well known that the Indians are themselves benefited from the operation of the present system."[43]

Skene and Plummer, provided with copies of Whitcher's letter, vociferously challenged his assertions. Skene pointedly commented that the reduction in fish was due to overharvesting not by Indians but by white men, and had nothing to do with Indian spear fishing or netting. He added that putting an end to the privilege of spearing "will come hard upon the Indians along the shores of the Lakes."[44] In Skene's view, environmental damage, along with pressure from the general society and American fishermen, in particular, were responsible for the precipitous decline in fish and game populations:

> I am at the same time of opinion that the scarcity of game and fish has been caused more by the pollution of the rivers & spawning Beds by throwing in Saw Dust and other Mill refuse and by the great quantities of fish and Game of all kinds killed by the white men for the purpose of sale than by the Indians spearing on the Shoals and Banks. As far as my experience goes all that the Indians killed by spearing or with the small nets or other limited means was not of much consequence – and certainly so long as only the Indians fished & hunted no one heard of the great scarcity of Game & fish that now prevails.[45]

As well, Skene argued that the Robinson-Huron Treaty had explicitly promised treaty rights to fish to the Aboriginal parties to it. He added, "I consider this clause very distinct and explicit and that unless it can be proved that the Indians did not at that time spear fish the right to do so cannot be taken from them without breaking faith with them."[46]

For his part, Plummer traced the problem to the fact that once exclusively Indian fisheries had been taken away from First Nations and given to white men without any justification except "public interest." He maintained that the public interest was in no way served by these decisions. Appealing for fairness in a December 1878 letter to David Mills, he noted that current policies prejudiced Aboriginal peoples:

> White men monopolize all the best fishing points, and further, it is a well known fact that the traders do not deal fairly with the Indians, and all the arguments that care to be used cannot overcome the prejudice of the Indians in these particulars.
>
> It cannot be for the public interest to lease the best fishing grounds to a few white men and to deprive several hundred Indians who reside in adjacent villages of the privileges which they have enjoyed from time immemorial, especially when it is well known that Indians can and do catch quite as many fish when left in undisturbed possession, as the whites do, and further, the surplus fish caught by the Indians are sold, and consumed by the people of the Dominion the same as those caught by white men, and the Indians as a rule are very law abiding and more strictly observant of the fishing regulations than the white fishermen.
>
> As to Indian treaties, it is well known that in the general surrenders, large tracts of land and adjacent islands were reserved and there are no

treaties in existence covering any surrender of these tracts and islands and the waters by which they are immediately surrounded.[47]

Plummer concluded his letter by reminding his superiors that they had agreed in the winter of 1877 that Whitcher and Vankoughnet would "investigate the cause of the complaints," which they had not done. Because of the agreement that an inquiry would take place, further violence had been prevented, as the First Nations had "kept quiet in expectation of this arrangement being carried out." However, Plummer noted, "the longer it is postponed, the greater will be the difficulty of making any change."[48]

Plummer's arguments had little effect on Whitcher. Instead, by 1879, he had successfully pushed through regulations banning Aboriginal spear fishing except with ministerial permission. J.C. Phipps of the Indian Office at Manitowaning protested to David Mills, the Minister of the Interior, that this restriction would cause further hardship to Aboriginal peoples because "spearing is a common mode of procuring fish for Domestic use by Indians, the prohibition of the practice as regards Trout, White fish, Sturgeon, Pike, Pickerel and Bass, except during the close seasons, would if strictly enforced, press very heavily upon them ... as without such permission these practices, which are common amongst the Indians appear to be illegal."[49] Mills did not respond to this letter, and it was probably forwarded to Whitcher, where it joined the pile of letters, protests, and petitions concerning Aboriginal rights that he had pointedly ignored.

As time passed, further changes to the fisheries legislation also made it illegal to sell fish without a licence, although many First Nations had historically depended on the sale of fish. Very few commercial fishing licences were issued to them in Ontario. Hayter Reed, the Deputy Superintendent of Indian Affairs, agreed with the Deputy Minister of Marine and Fisheries that the government should *not* issue commercial licences to Indians; doing so would not be "in the interest of the Indians" because the ensuing competition with white men would cause "agitation" and prompt whites to demand further restrictions of the "privileges" currently enjoyed by Indians.[50] As a result, when Indian Agents outlined First Nations requests for territories, these were generally rejected as unreasonable.[51]

Instead, Marine and Fisheries told the Deputy Superintendent General of Indian Affairs that granting all the Indian requests for licences would have exceeded the "real wants" of the Indians. In addition, "in complying with such evidently unfair demands, the Minister would have left himself open to the accusation of excluding whitemen from the untold wealth of Georgian Bay waters to the advantage of no-one in particular."[52]

Whitcher maintained that his Department had liberally provided for the "real wants" of the Indians. As proof, he noted that the Indians on the shores of Lake Huron were permitted to fish everywhere free for their own use and consumption. He used the fact that waters had been licensed in other locations, including at Christian Island, in support of his argument.[53] However, the Chippewas at Georgina and Snake Islands in Lake Simcoe, who had ice-fished for generations in the waters around their unceded islands, were each required to pay two dollars for the "privilege" of fishing for food through the ice in the winter.[54]

In 1896, only one Ontario First Nation, the Saugeen Ojibway village at Cape Croker, had received a licence enabling its members to fish commercially, and it too was required to pay twenty-five dollars annually for its licence.[55] The Saugeen village on the other side of the Bruce Peninsula, which held the same treaty rights, received no licence at all.

William Plummer's dogged efforts to ensure that the Aboriginal communities he worked with gained access to fisheries were undermined at every juncture. Even earlier arrangements that Plummer had made to benefit the Indians were cancelled by Whitcher. For example, Plummer, as Indian Superintendent, and the late Col. McKenzie, the Fishery Overseer at Barrie, had reached an agreement under which Plummer had secured a right for the First Nations to fish in the waters around their islands. In February 1888, the Secretary of Indian Affairs submitted the agreement to Marine and Fisheries, asking for a licence for the grounds and a refund of the fee based on the deal,[56] but was told that no licence would be issued. In refusing the request, J. Tilton, the Deputy Minister of Marine and Fisheries, took the extraordinary position that the arrangement between McKenzie and Plummer, both government officials, was a "private one," not binding on the Department of Marine and Fisheries. As far as he was concerned, Indian privileges were equal to those of white men and that was enough.[57]

Furthermore, even though by this time they were virtually excluded from the commercial fishery, Tilton depicted the Lake Simcoe Indians as having created a conservation problem:

> Since then, it was found necessary in view of the threatened destruction of fish in the above-named waters to prohibit all kinds of netting and to limit fishing operations to angling, trolling and spearing, during the winter months. Under this arrangement, which has proved most beneficial to the fish, the Indians of Lake Simcoe have enjoyed equal privileges with the whitemen; they can fish all over the lake should they please ... Under such circumstances, the Minister thinks that matters had better remain as they are, and not grant the Indians any special favour not enjoyed by the rest of the community at Lake Simcoe, and which would be sure to give rise to well-founded complaint.[58]

The Department of Marine and Fisheries continued to blame Indians for depleting the resource, although one Ontario First Nation, the Algonquins of Golden Lake, argued in its defence that the problem of overharvesting had been caused by white men. The Algonquins insisted that "if the Gov't would prohibit fishing by White people & appoint an Inspector, that the fish would soon multiply and give them enough."[59] Nonetheless, and, again, purportedly for conservation reasons, the Minister of Fisheries closed down the entire Aboriginal fishery in 1893, along with "the privilege hitherto granted to Indians on Lake Huron, Georgian Bay and Lake Superior of fishing during the close season."[60] Since the fishing was for domestic use, the decision deprived the First Nations in those areas of access to their food supply at a time when few alternatives were available.

Fisheries Officers were instructed to seize fish, destroy nets and boats, and prosecute Aboriginal violators for noncompliance.[61] Although the Deputy Superintendent General of Indian Affairs protested that a general prohibition would cause "great distress" to the Indians,[62] his views were completely ignored.

In August 1894, the Department of Marine and Fisheries again announced that it had "withdrawn" the privilege of fishing by Indians for domestic purposes during the close season throughout Ontario. Once more, Fishery Officers throughout the province were instructed to seize all fish caught and to destroy all nets used in contravention of the regulations.[63] Despite these highly arbitrary and unfair restrictions, First Nations in Ontario continued to challenge the fishing regulations and to fish for food, and for trade and barter, as they had for hundreds of years, although they did so under threat of charges. One elder from Curve (Mud) Lake, Mary Johnson, remembered that

> We used to fish through the ice, snow blowing, we just had little cedar boughs for shelter ... Sometimes I'd come home with 12 bass and that wasn't enough [I'd] go back again. We didn't salt those, we were allowed to sell fish at that time. But the government made a law that we weren't allowed to sell fish. I don't know why, whether the government wanted to starve us or not. And we couldn't eat only fish, so we'd go peddling, peddling fish. We'd get flour and potatoes and turnips, meat and we'd trade them for things to eat.[64]

Federal-Provincial Disputes over Lands

In the years leading up to Confederation, white settlement in the unceded lands of Ontario had taken place at an unprecedented rate, and in complete disregard of Aboriginal title and rights. In some instances, the government encouraged squatters to take over unsurrendered Indian lands. As reflected in Orders-in-Council throughout this period, the Crown's practice when learning of unceded Aboriginal title was not to remove the squatters, but to allow them to purchase the lands they had wrongly acquired.

In 1859, for example, squatters illegally occupied lands on the unceded island of Point au Pelee. The Crown obtained a judgment against them for illegal intrusion on Indian lands, but, seven years later, Parliament passed an Order-in-Council recommending that the land be patented to the squatters, thereby legitimizing their illegal occupation.[65]

The proceeds from the sale of lands to squatters were supposed to be paid to the trust accounts of the First Nations whose lands had been taken from them, at least theoretically, but in practice, the payments were made only after the First Nations had conclusively established the validity of their claims.[66] In fact, so little of this money made its way into Indian trust accounts that, in May 1895, the Dominion government filed a *Statement of Case* on behalf of the Chippewas and Mississaugas, alleging that Ontario had sold "and disposed of [the lands] as Crown lands, but no portion of the proceeds of the said sales was paid to the Indians or any compensation made to them."[67]

The Ontario government had refused to pay monies for what it considered to be a federal responsibility. As the federal claim alleged, "The claim of the Indians for compensation has, on many occasions, been brought by the Dominion to the notice of Ontario and although the Province of Ontario has acknowledged that no surrender or extinguishment of the Indian title to the said lands has ever taken place, yet Ontario has refused and declined to acknowledge the claim of the said Indians to be compensated, the allegation of the Province being that the Dominion and not Ontario must compensate the Indians for their right, title and interest in the said lands."[68]

At about this time, as will be discussed below, the Mississaugas and Chippewas began a long struggle to convince the government to address their claims regarding a large unceded territory lying north of the forty-fifth parallel and east of Lake Nipissing. Constantly frustrated in their efforts by government recalcitrance, the First Nations would be obliged to wait for some sixty years until their demands were finally addressed in the Williams Treaties of 1923.

As early as 1860, the Mississaugas had complained that their hunting grounds at "Cataraqua" [Cataraqui], or Kingston, had been "occupied" by "Indians and other Hunters from the United States and elsewhere who not only deprive us of our living by taking furrs [sic] but destroy the seed by killing animals when bearing their young." They asked the Governor General, Sir Edmund Walker Head, to protect them by "forbidding intruders to hunt or trespass on our rightful hunting ground."[69]

In 1866, a Rama Band member, one Paul de la Ronde, complained to William Spragge, Deputy Superintendent of Indian Affairs, that he too had been dispossessed of the unsurrendered hunting grounds belonging to his family.[70] Shortly afterward, in 1869, the Chiefs and councillors of Rice,

Mud, and Scugog Lakes wrote to Spragge, pointing out that some of their lands, lying north of the boundary set in an 1818 treaty, had never been surrendered by them, but that these too had been taken over by settlers, preventing them from hunting.[71]

A council meeting was convened. It included Joseph Whetung, who would be a prominent figure in the later 1923 treaty negotiations, as well as Paul de la Ronde, Thomas Jacobs, Isaac Jirons (Irons), John Tauney, Henry Crow, John Rice, and Henry Howard.[72] Under their direction, a lawyer, Alexander Gibb, wrote to William Spragge to protest the wrongful settlement of their unceded lands. However, he received a rather unsatisfactory response to the effect that no "precedent" existed for recognizing this kind of claim.[73]

Despite this reply, Joseph Howe, the Secretary of State, put the Commissioner of Crown Lands in Ontario on notice that the Mississaugas had advanced a claim to Aboriginal title to certain lands north of the lands they had surrendered in 1818. He admitted that the First Nations seemed to be the owner of the lands in question, and that he had located no records in the Indian Office to suggest that this "proprietorship," or title, had ever been conveyed to the Crown "by Deed of Cession or Surrender."[74]

By this time, however, the Crown had begun to argue that Indians had no actual proprietary interest in the soil, even in their own reserve lands.[75] Perhaps not surprisingly, in light of this position, the Crown took no steps to protect Aboriginal title in the unceded lands, although its awareness that the lands had never been surrendered is beyond question.

In May 1870, Spragge confirmed that the Aboriginal title of the Rice, Mud, and Scugog Lake Bands to their northern hunting grounds had never been extinguished.[76] Observing that their lands included "vast forests of merchantable timber of great quality," he suggested that perhaps they should be paid "some adequate annuity" in exchange for a surrender.[77] He wrote to the Lieutenant-Governor of Ontario, asking for "such proposals as may lead to a settlement of the Indian claims."[78]

Although the Crown considered the claim to the northern hunting grounds only in terms of monetary compensation, the claimants probably had a markedly different view. At this time, despite many decades of the purported "civilization efforts," the Chippewas and Mississaugas were still completely dependent on hunting and fishing for their livelihoods and subsistence, as is revealed in the 1871 Ontario census. This lists each adult male member of the Georgina Island Band of the District of Gwillimbury North as "Ojibway Indian, Hunter & Fisher."[79] At Rama, every adult male band member, even the very elderly, was described by the census as "Indian, Hunter and Fisher" or "Indian, Farmer & Hunter," including later signatories to the 1923 treaties Joseph Shilling Jr. and Gilbert Williams.[80] Others, whose occupation was recorded as "Hunter," included later witnesses and signatories to the 1923 treaties such as Edward Yellowhead, James Shilling, William Snake, William Bigwin, Benjamin Yellowhead, and Thomas Bigwind.[81] Only one, Frederick Copegog, was listed as an "Indian, Fisherman," without reference to hunting.[82] Obviously, members of these First Nations were very much affected when settlers and squatters interfered with access to their traditional hunting or fishing territories, and it is clear that they wanted their rights to hunt and fish protected, rather than money.

In 1872, Joseph de la Ronde, Paul de La Ronde's nephew, tried complaining directly to the Governor General of Canada. He wrote that his hereditary hunting grounds had been wrongly settled by whites, and that his family had suffered hardship as a result. Referring to his "need and distressed circumstances, and inasmuch as the Canadian government has taken possession of the said lands, he [the Petitioner] ventures to approach your Excellency in the hope that in accordance with the generous policy of the British government in their transactions with our unfortunate race, you may be pleased to afford some relief."[83] However, nothing was done. Ontario continued to ignore all federal government correspondence on the matter, while federal officials insisted that any compensation must be paid by Ontario before they would act. The idea that the Crown should recover the illegally occupied lands for the use of the Mississaugas was never once discussed.

William Plummer, however, pressed the Mississauga claim. In April 1878, he reminded the Minister of the Interior that, twelve years earlier, the Crown Lands Department had admitted the claim was valid but that nothing had been done.[84] The new Deputy Superintendent General of Indian Affairs, Lawrence Vankoughnet, assured him that the matter would be drawn to Ontario's attention.[85] Vankoughnet directed Plummer to tell the bands to leave the matter to the Department to resolve, expressing his confidence that Ontario would "pay a fair and reasonable price per acre for the Indian title to the lands."[86]

While Ontario and the federal government bickered over who was monetarily responsible for the problem, the Mississaugas and Chippewas watched with growing frustration as their northern hunting grounds were overtaken by farms and settlements. Because of their increasingly limited land base, Plummer felt sure they would want more than simple compensation for any surrender, and predicted that they would want additional reserve lands "away from the present settlements ... Some of these Bands do not have land enough, at present, on which it is possible to support themselves."[87]

On 6 June 1879, after several meetings with the bands, Plummer confirmed that they did indeed want more lands and access to more fish.[88] He noted that their desire was understandable, as they had few areas left where they could legally hunt and fish without interference. In particular, as one Chief complained, the fact that white men could fish commercially in the same waters where Indians fished for food had made fishing very difficult;

driving the point home, he added "as hunting is a failure we have to depend very much on fishing for a living."[89]

The Mississaugas and Chippewas had also found that white men were becoming increasingly hostile to their activities. When they attempted to access their northern hunting grounds, they were sometimes shot at; on other occasions, white farmers and trappers took their traps or the contents of the traps. Years later, in 1923, elders from the Williams Treaties First Nations described such incidents for the Treaty Commissioners. James Howard, a Hiawatha elder aged seventy-three, recalled that he had "quit" hunting in the northern grounds in the 1880s because

> [I]f I set a trap there would be some man come along behind me taking my traps up – white men – so it was no use of us going when our traps were taken up as fast as we set them.
>
> Q [Commissioners]. And that confined your hunting grounds just around here?
>
> A [Howard]. Yes, of course there is just muskrat and an odd mink but no big game and no beaver to hunt either. There was one old beaver down in the marsh for ten years and he is there yet. We never both [sic] him and he know we never bother him so he stays. Poor fellow, he's like us, he gets crowded out but we leave him [alone].

Johnson Paudash testified at the 1923 commission proceedings that his ancestors had always exercised the right to hunt or live in the northern grounds until they were interfered with by the white men, who bothered them and lifted their traps. Similarly, Chief George Paudash of Hiawatha testified that he had hunted only once in the northern hunting grounds because on that occasion his traps were lifted. He said that whenever members from his reserve went far from home, someone interfered with their traps. Sixty-three-year-old Madden Howard of Hiawatha gave similar evidence, remarking that he had hunted up north only once "because the white people lifted all our traps up, so I think once was enough."[90] In some places the traps themselves were taken; in others, the traps were left but "they take what is in them."[91] As far as he could recall, thirty years before, that is, in the 1890s, this had never happened.[92]

As the conflicts worsened, the Mississaugas and Chippewas pressed forward with their land claim, hoping it would gain them the additional lands they needed. William Plummer, planning to visit them in September 1880 and fully expecting them to inquire about the progress of their complaints, asked his superiors, "If nothing has yet been done, may I enquire as to when it is likely to be? I may state that the Indians interested in this matter have recently held councils on the subject ... They say this correspondence has been going on for many years and that a generation of their people have passed away without deriving any benefit from property to which they are entitled."[93]

Somewhat ironically, given that fifteen or so years had gone by without a response from Ontario, the Superintendent General of Indian Affairs recommended that Plummer call on the Ontario Crown Lands Department and urge the Province to "early" action.[94] Plummer immediately did so, only to learn from provincial officials that, though they admitted no treaty could be found surrendering the lands, they would not "admit their responsibility. They state that these lands were handed over to them at the time of Confederation and if anything has to be paid to quiet the Indian title, such payment must be made by the Dominion Government and not by the Crown Lands Department of the Province of Ontario. This, of course, is not official but I believe it to be the view generally entertained by the Crown Land's authorities."[95]

In turn, Lawrence Vankoughnet warned Sir John A. Macdonald, the Prime Minister and Minister responsible for Indian Affairs, that "The Indians who claim said tract are becoming yearly more impatient."[96]

In September 1881, the Chippewa Chiefs and councillors from Christian Island, Rama, and Georgina Island met with the Mississaugas of Rice, Scugog, and Mud Lakes at a General Council to discuss what to do next.[97] Joseph B. Nandgisking, the Chief of the Rama Band, and M.G. Pahtaush of Rice Lake were directed by the First Nations to meet with the Prime Minister in Ottawa as delegates of the six bands.[98]

When the federal government learned of the proposed visit, Plummer was told by his superiors to prevent it: the delegation "must not come ... the question at issue is a most intricate one, involving points of Constitutional law."[99] Nonetheless, in 1882 the Indian delegation made its way to Ottawa, where it was assured that the matter "will continue to engage the earnest attention of the Department until a solution of the question is arrived at."[100]

A year later, perhaps hoping to encourage official action on the claim, Chief "Nanigishking" sent a letter to Sir John A. Macdonald expressing his regret that the latter had been absent and unable to see them: "we would have been highly pleased to have met you, Sir, because of your knowledge of this territory, your willingness to do the tribes interested in this matter justice and especially as the Head or Great Chief of all the Indian Bands of the Dominion." The Chief's letter indicated that they had met with "Mr. Vankoughnet, your Deputy, who received us very kindly and promised this important matter would engage the attention of the Department."[101]

The provincial Treasurers of Ontario and Quebec were expected to meet with the federal government in 1884 to discuss and resolve outstanding Indian claims. Prior to the meeting, Vankoughnet was asked to submit any claims that the Department of Indian Affairs had pending, and he included those of the Mississaugas and Chippewas. He described their claim as involving a portion of lands included in another treaty, the Robinson-Huron Treaty, in error. Because the unceded lands were "nearest to the great centres of civilization and ... therefore ... the most valuable part of the territory covered by that treaty," Vankoughnet argued that the Mississaugas and Chippewas should receive as much "consideration for the relinquishment of their rights as the Ojibeways of Lake Huron received in compensation for their rights in a not more valuable tract."[102] Noting that the lands had been logged and settled, Vankoughnet proposed that the Mississaugas and Chippewas should be compensated for this loss, but he again asserted that the compensation should be paid by Ontario.[103]

The Treasurers' meeting of 1884 did not address this claim, however, and once again the Chippewas and Mississaugas were obliged to wait for the resolution of their land claims.

The Alnwick First Nation, which had a separate claim of its own, fared little better at official hands. Its claim related to unsurrendered territory lying north of lands ceded in 1822.

Although Vankoughnet referred to a claim concerning lands wrongly included in a different treaty, the Alnwick First Nation's claim actually related to lands that were much further south of the traditional northern hunting grounds claimed by the Mississaugas and Chippewas. On 4 February 1884, the Alnwick Band had passed a resolution signed by twenty-nine band members in which it expressed its willingness to surrender almost all of these non-reserve lands for the sum of $80,000.[104] Even so, their resolution made it clear that they wished to keep the fishing islands in the Bay of Quinte, the St. Lawrence, and Rice Lake, as well as "any other islands belonging to the said Band" for their own exclusive use.[105]

In December, the Indian Agent at Alnwick inquired as to what had become of their claim and was told that the matter was still under consideration.[106] A year later, with no news, the Alnwick Band passed another resolution asking its local Member of Parliament, George Guillet, to find out what was going on.[107] When Guillet asked for information on the progress of the claim,[108] he was advised that certain Commissioners had been appointed to settle claims against the old Province of Canada (Quebec and Ontario) and that when they met, the claim would considered.[109]

The claim was finally brought to the attention of the Commissioners, and to Ontario officially, in May 1889, but with no result.[110] Inquiring again a year later, Guillet was informed by the Justice Department that the federal government was supporting the position of the Mississaugas but that the "Governments of Canada, Ontario and Quebec are disputing about it and have been unable to come to any settlement."[111] Whether the response related to Alnwick's claim, or the broader claim of the Mississaugas and Chippewas, is unclear.

In 1893, almost thirty years after the Mississauga and Chippewa claim was first brought to light, Ontario finally provided its official response in a report written by J.P. MacDonnell. It rejected the claims on the basis that the First Nations had already been compensated for all their surrendered lands in the 1818 treaties.[112] MacDonnell used the success of the Crown assimilation policy as another ground to deny the claim, arguing that the Indians had been successfully "civilized" and had no need of hunting or fishing rights. According to him,

> They are ... settled upon reserves, and in every respect in a condition superior to their former state – the practical test of what the measure of their present rights should be ... Their rights of Occupancy of any territory to which they had proper title for the purposes of hunting and fishing have not been interfered with except by the natural process of settlement. Their residence upon the reserves and the pursuit of agriculture to a greater or less extent, have made them less dependent upon the chase & have consequently operated to render the hunting privileges of less consequence and value, if not wholly valueless, to them.[113]

However, despite MacDonnell's assertion that the Mississaugas and Chippewas were no longer dependent on the chase, those involved with them in the 1880s and 1890s thought otherwise. The Indian Agent at the Mud Lake Agency reported that though some of the men worked in lumber camps and others farmed, most "still followed the familiar lifestyle of hunting and fishing. The women were industrious making their baskets and fancy work ... nearly everyone owns a good board canoe in place of their heavy log dug-outs."[114] At Mud Lake, each family retained its own hereditary hunting ground, and trespass upon them continued to be highly resented.[115] Far from converting to an agricultural lifestyle, the Visiting Superintendent of Indian Affairs noted in 1890, "the Ojibways of Lake Huron are hunters and fishermen, agriculture being followed to only a very limited extent, hunting being by some bands considered the most honourable occupation."[116]

Although Ontario had pronounced what it considered the last word on the subject, the issue of Mississauga and Chippewa hunting and fishing rights was far from dead. Furthermore, the issue of just which government had jurisdiction over them had yet to be resolved.

The Fisheries Reference

Under the 1867 *British North America Act,* the federal government had jurisdiction over "Sea-Coasts and Inland fisheries," and the provinces had jurisdiction over "Property and Civil Rights."[117] Claiming that fish were property, Ontario passed its first fisheries legislation, the *Ontario Fisheries Act,* in 1885.[118] Like the 1857 federal *Fisheries Act,* the Ontario act permitted the granting of a lease or licence except where an exclusive right of fishing already existed by law.[119]

Although the new legislation did not mention Aboriginal peoples as having any particular or special rights, section 24 allowed the provincial Commissioner to "appropriate and licence or lease certain waters in which certain Indians shall be allowed to catch fish for their own use and at whatever manner and time and subject to whatever terms and conditions are specified in the licence or lease." This was in clear conflict with the federal fisheries legislation, which purported to do the same thing.[120]

In March 1886, John S. Thompson, the federal Minister of Justice, expressed concern to the Governor General that the Province's legislation encroached on Dominion authority. Nonetheless, he recommended against disallowance – Ottawa's power to revoke a provincial Act.[121] However, in 1892, the provincial legislature passed another piece of legislation, *An Act for the Protection of Provincial Fisheries*,[122] and this time the legislation was seen by the federal government as being more objectionable.

Many provisions of the new provincial Act were intended to curb the "illegal" trade in fish by Aboriginal peoples. For example, section 7 provided that no person "shall take or catch or kill in any provincial water or carry away the greater number than 50 speckled or brook trout on any one day."[123] Section 13 imposed a close season, preventing Indians from fishing even for food during the spawning period.[124] Section 9, which prohibited fishing for trout, pickerel, and maskinonge except "angling by hook and line,"[125] made it illegal for Aboriginal fishermen to use seine nets, gill nets, and spears, their traditional means of fishing. Instead, it required them to engage in fishing by hook and line only, even though "angling" was a foreign concept to Ojibway peoples, who generally did not engage in it and whose language had no word for it.[126]

Because of federal concerns over the constitutionality of this new legislation, Ottawa and Ontario decided to refer the issue to the Supreme Court of Canada for hearing and consideration.[127] They agreed, however, that Ottawa's jurisdiction over Indians and Indian lands would not be an issue in the hearing. As a result, the questions that the two governments agreed to put before the Court specifically excluded unsurrendered Indian lands and waters from the Court's consideration. For example, in its 1895 argument before the Court, Ontario contended that it had jurisdiction over the right of fishery "in the public waters as of common right within the territorial rights of the province," but conceded that unsurrendered Indian territories, including those covered with water, fell within exclusively federal jurisdiction.[128]

The Supreme Court's decision – the *Fisheries Reference* of 1895 – was not binding on either government, but it was highly persuasive. In its decision, the Court expressed the opinion that the beds of all lakes, rivers, public harbours, and other waters within the territorial limits of the provinces were vested in the provincial Crown under section 109 of the *British North America Act,* subject only to other constitutional provisions excepting pre-existing trusts and interests. These exceptions included the beds of public harbours and unsurrendered Indian lands covered with water, which the Court described as "vested" in the Dominion.[129] As a result, in unsurrendered Indian lands and waters, Parliament had exclusive jurisdiction.

In 1897, following the Supreme Court reference, Ontario passed a new piece of legislation, *An Act Respecting the Fisheries of Ontario.*[130] In recognition of the Supreme Court limits on provincial authority, the *Act* made it clear that Ontario could not authorize any interference with areas of purely federal jurisdiction, such as those affecting Indians.[131] Nonetheless, it contained many sections that again affected First Nations rights. For example, section 41 enabled the Lieutenant-Governor to issue "free licences" to frontier settlers "or to any Indians ... or any Band of Indians residing on any reserve to take fish in such waters ... by net or night or set line ... exclusively for the use and consumption of their own families." It restricted fishermen to no more than five set lines and excluded anyone receiving such a "free licence" from taking "sports fish" such as trout and bass. Again, the *Act* prohibited the sale of fish[132] and made it an offence to trespass or pass over any lands subject to a fishery lease.[133] Penalties for infringing this section were not less than ten dollars and not more than fifty dollars, but required *immediate* payment; those who did not pay were to be imprisoned for a period not exceeding one month.[134] As well, amendments to the legislation a year later required those engaged in commercial fishing to report the amount and weight of fish they caught, as well as the price they received per pound of fish, under oath to a fishery overseer, or be penalized.[135]

As early as 1875, the federal Fishery Overseer for the Lake Huron District had complained that "Most of the fishermen in this division are Indians, which accounts for the small amount of fees collected. It is also very difficult to procure reliable fishing statistics, fishermen pretending to believe it is in their best interest to under state their catch."[136] However, the understatement may not have been deliberate, as most Indians were unable to read, write, or even speak English. Now, under the new legislation, they were prosecuted for failing to report catches, as well as for fishing without a licence. Those unable to make "immediate" payment were to be jailed for a period not exceeding one month.[137]

Significantly, section 41(2) of the *Act* stated that Ontario had no jurisdiction to interfere with treaty rights or Aboriginal title. It also recognized that Indians *did* have special rights, maintaining that none of its provisions "shall prejudicially affect any rights specially reserved to or conferred upon Indians by any treaty or regulation in that behalf made by the Government of Canada nor shall anything herein as to which their claims have not been surrendered or extinguished apply to or prejudicially affect the rights of Indians, if any, in any portion of the Province."[138]

The catch was that neither government acknowledged there were any Aboriginal or treaty rights *to* prejudice. Instead, as noted by the Secretary of Indian Affairs in a memorandum prepared for the Minister of Marine and Fisheries, "the consistent course" of Marine and Fisheries had been not to recognize "the claims made by the Indians under Treaties entered into with them."[139] Although the Indians of Lakes Huron and Superior, Nipissing, Georgian Bay, and Rice Lake continued to "claim that under Treaties made with them, they have the right to fish in the waters mentioned without being subject to the Fishery Regulations, the Fisheries Dept ... contend(s) that treaties could not give larger rights than those enjoyed in common law, claims that are not compatible with public rights and which are in conflict with public law."[140]

By the late 1800s, Indian Affairs had adopted the Marine and Fisheries position that no enforceable treaty promises regarding hunting or fishing had been made to Indians generally, anywhere. The government's response to assertions that treaty promises had been made to the Mississaugas and Chippewas specifically was to deny that hunting or fishing had ever been mentioned in the treaties.

Aboriginal Rights Denied

In 1895, John Thackeray, the Indian Agent at Alnwick (Alderville), advised the Deputy Superintendent of Indian Affairs that the Indians at his reserve "are of the opinion that their forefathers when surrendering their lands etc. reserved the right to fish and hunt for meat at all times in the future ... Kindly let me know if such a Treaty was ever made and if so, whether it is in force now? I do not for a moment think that there is such a treaty, but to be sure I write to you herein. Two of the Alnwick Indians are at the present time cited before a game warden for violating the *Game Act of Ontario.*"[141]

Hayter Reed, the Deputy Superintendent of Indian Affairs, responded that the only treaty to "which these Indians were parties is that of 1822 and there is no mention of any right to fish or hunt being reserved to the Indians."[142] Reed again cited the Cockburn opinion to the effect that, in the absence of express *written* provisions within a treaty ratified by Parliament, no special rights existed:

> I find that when a similar question was raised in 1866, the Hon. Mr. Cockburn, then the Solicitor General, expressed the opinion that the Indians had no other or larger right over public waters than those which belonged at common law to Her Majesty's subjects in general ... the Indian had no special rights as to fishing other than such as might be conferred upon them by Parliament from time to time. I am therefore constrained to agree

> with you that the Indians have no special rights in this matter and no such plea can therefore be made by the two Alnwick Indians ... It would be well for you to advise the Indians of the position in which they stand, and point out to them that the laws for the preservation of fish and game are as much for their interest as that of the whites and they should be careful to observe them.[143]

Responding to the Crown's position and the increasingly restrictive laws, some Aboriginal peoples exercised their rights covertly, taking steps to avoid detection and enforcement action. The Ojibway had become highly skilled in this regard, continuing to "peep-hole" fish "practically under the noses of the game wardens,"[144] even though the technique had been outlawed by the provincial government. Federal regulations now totally banned spear fishing, due to the belief of the Minister of Marine and Fisheries that the spear was a "most wasteful, murderous and destructive instrument." When First Nations fishermen asked for permission to spear at Lake Simcoe, the Minister refused, writing, "Is it worthwhile to revive its use merely to meet a few exceptional cases ... My officers strongly oppose once more authorizing the use of the spear for some of the reasons already referred to in this letter but also because it maims and fatally injures five times more fish than it secures. It is used chiefly in the early spring, when the fish are full of spawn and about to breed and it is a mere pretext for slaughtering breeding maskinonge, bass &c."[145]

Nonetheless, the Mississaugas continued to spear salmon *(azaouamec)* as they had always done. As A.F. Chamberlain had described in 1888,

> in the use of the fish-spear, the Mississaugas were exceedingly skilful. Other kinds of fish were taken by spear, both by day and night. The mouth of the River Credit was a celebrated place for spearing salmon and on its banks, the Indians annually camped for that purpose. In the winter, the Indians of Rice and Mud (or Chemong) Lake obtained fish in the following manner: With his tomahawk, the Indian cut a hole in the ice, threw a blanket over him and stood or knelt for hours beside the hole. In one hand he held his fish-spear in the other a string, to which was attached a decoy-fish of wood serving to attract the prey. Their skill in this sort of fishing was remarkable, two hundred pounds of fish being frequently the result of a day's labour.[146]

An elderly man who had lived on Manitoulin Island recalled in 1952 that the Indians also fished at night, or "jack-lighted," a practice that had been banned by Ontario as well. He recalled that

> the Indians used to fish on the south shore, in Lake Huron. They would fish for sturgeon at night in Portage Bay, out in water 20 to 25 feet deep.

> For a light they burned fat pine knots, which they put in a wire basket in the bow of the boat. The fisherman with his spear would put a blanket on his head, so that he would be in the shade to look over the side of the boat. They would spear the sturgeon at a depth of 18 to 25 feet. The head or sharp end of the spear had a line on it, and would come free from the handle when the fish was speared. They would play the fish on the line until it was weakened and they could land it. They often would bring a sturgeon to our home. They would carry half a fish, with a piece of wood as big as a broom over their shoulders through the flesh behind the gills, and when they carried the fish, the tail would be trailing on the ground. I have seen half a fish that would weigh 50 pounds in some cases.[147]

Despite the ban on sales of fish, First Nations peoples depended on trade and barter, often selling their catches for small sums. Trout were the principal species taken through these methods, and those who caught them sold the larger ones in neighbouring communities for approximately a dollar a kilo.[148]

Elders at two of the Williams Treaties First Nations, Scugog and Curve (Mud) Lake, recalled participating as young children in large winter camps at which hunting and fishing took place. They described the sale and trade of fish as well as muskrats and other fur-bearing animals. Herb Irons, a Curve Lake elder interviewed in 1966 when he was eighty-one, said he sometimes sold fish for five cents a pound, as well as muskrat for twenty-five cents a pound. Remembering preparations for a deer hunt, Irons described precautions taken to avoid alarming the quarry: members of his First Nation would rake fallen leaves off the trail for some "seven or eight hundred yards I guess [so] you wouldn't make noise. You know, in the fall you could hear quite a ways, when you are stepping on the leaves."[149]

Short Tom Taylor remembered how he and his entire family would spend all winter hunting, fishing, and camping, "making baskets and fishing and hunting and every other thing. Anything to make a living." The family caught most of the food they ate, including "Deer and rats [muskrats] and the likes of that, fish, porcupine, ground hogs ... we lived on everything we could catch hold of."[150]

Tall Tom Taylor remembered a "great big" hunting camp "up around Pigeon Lake and Grassy Point, that is where we used to camp years ago. We used to camp there all winter, never had time to go to school in the winter time. Just a little while in the summer, and then we would go back again in the fall and camp again all winter there ... we made a wigwam out of cedar bark, tee-pee like, and we had a fire there in the middle, you put two logs on each side, and the smoke goes up to the roof of the camp." Taylor's family stayed in the wigwams, but they had "lots of visitors" from the Mud Lake reserve, who would come to fish.[151]

Along with limits on fishing, increasingly restrictive hunting laws had been introduced in Ontario over this same period. In 1892, for example, the Ontario government introduced *An Act for the Protection of Game and Fur-bearing Animals*. With the intent of protecting game, the legislation limited deer hunting to the first two weeks of November, although as Edward S. Rogers points out, Indians killed deer as necessity dictated, arguing they retained the right to do so under their treaties.[152]

The *Act* at least gave some consideration to the subsistence needs of settlers and Indians in the unorganized districts of the province, exempting both from its provisions when they killed game for their own immediate use. It made no provision for Aboriginal peoples who lived in southern Ontario. Importantly, however, the new provincial law acknowledged that Ottawa could enter into treaties or enact regulations to govern Aboriginal peoples hunting on their reserves or their hunting grounds, although "hunting grounds" were not defined. It also made it clear that treaties and federal regulations could not be affected by provincial laws, stating that "nothing contained herein shall be constructed to affect any rights specially reserved to or conferred upon Indians by any treaty or regulations in that behalf made by the Government of the Dominion of Canada with reference to their hunting on their reserves or hunting grounds, or in any territory specially set apart for the purpose, nor shall anything in the *Act* contained apply to Indians hunting in any portion of the Provincial territory as to which their claims have not been surrendered or extinguished."[153]

That aside, the legislation was primarily intended to legitimize sport hunting, and it did so by creating an enforcement system with wardens, bag limits (for deer), and bans (on moose, elk, and deer), and an even shorter hunting season for deer.[154] As William McKirdy, a trader at Lake Nipigon, complained in a letter to the Attorney General, the Indians in his region had "no means of living except from fishing and hunting and serious results would follow from applying Ontario fish and game laws."[155] On being informed by the Ontario Provincial Secretary, J.M. Gibson, that the laws enabled Indians to hunt and fish for food, McKirdy in turn pointed out that hunting was of little use unless the Indians could also sell the furs they caught.[156]

Amendments to the provincial legislation in 1893 further tightened hunting regulations. Limits were placed on the number of deer, elk, moose, and caribou that could be killed, restricting each hunter to only two of each during any one year.[157] The new restrictions extended to small game as well. Although the Mississaugas were highly dependent on the muskrat fur trade, section 8 of the *Act* prevented the shooting of muskrat during April. In addition, the *Act* forbid the destruction of "muskrat houses," whether by spears or through any other method, and it enabled "traps, snares, gins or other contrivances" to be destroyed by any person without incurring liability.[158]

Significantly, section 9 deemed the boundary of land that extended into waters or passed through marshes to be enclosed and considered private, if it was posted or placarded with signs that said that hunting or shooting were forbidden under Ontario game laws.[159] Other provisions of the *Act* imposed fines and immediate imprisonment in default of payment for violations of its terms. Despite these provisions, the Provincial Secretary advised the Department of Indian Affairs that "it has been the desire of this Government to interfere as little as possible ... in the northern portions of the Province" in the matter of Indian hunting.[160]

In 1896, Ontario amended its legislation to require that all hunters get licences to hunt deer, at a cost of two dollars per person, per season.[161] Only Indians and settlers resident in unorganized townships were excluded from these provisions.[162] New provisions of the *Act* enabled landowners to placard, or sign, their properties to prevent hunting or shooting on their lands generally, further restricting First Nations peoples from the rights they had previously exercised to hunt on privately owned lands.[163]

That these superficially neutral regulations targeted Indians is clear. For example, a province-wide prohibition against killing deer in the water was repealed in 1899, "excepting as to that portion of the County of Bruce known as the Indian Peninsula." Thus, the Saugeen Peninsula, where the Cape Croker and Saugeen Bands hunted within their own unceded lands, became the only place in Ontario where the practice remained illegal.[164]

Despite the laws, Mud Lake community members caught and sold a variety of animals, including beaver, otter, mink, and bullfrogs. As Tall Tom Taylor would later recount, they sold muskrat furs to Cliff Whetung's grandfather, who ran a small store in Peterborough, "for around ten cents, five cents, fifteen cents a pound"; beaver and otter got a "pretty good price." They also sold fish: Taylor recalled that his grandfather would come to the reserve with "a team to get the fish, in sleigh loads, and take the fish to Peterborough where he would sell them ... he used to come get fish over there ... he would bring the groceries and trade them for fish."[165]

The attempts by First Nations to sell or trade their fish without licences, however, were considered illegal by the Crown. As T.H. Elliott, the Fishery Overseer, reported in 1893, "the close season for pickerel is often violated by Indians who are encouraged in their illegal work by white traders supplying them with nets and buying their fish. Much illegal fishing could be prevented by prohibiting traders to buy fish from unlicensed fishermen or Indians under heavy penalties."[166] Noting that they were prevented by law from using seine nets, he complained that Indians were being supplied with seines by "unscrupulous" dealers:

> At Wikwemikong, between 25 and 30 tons of whitefish were caught by means of seines in four days and over 2/3 of this amount were spoiled as

> the men had to bring them 15 miles and no ice at this point in which to pack them. Seining for pickerel is also carried on the north shore of Georgian Bay during the close season and are packed in ice and secreted until the close-time is over. Many Indians have fished without licences a few days at a time with small nets. They are aware they are breaking the law.[167]

Perhaps they were breaking the law, but those few Aboriginal communities in southern Ontario that had been issued commercial fishing licences for "legal" fishing had been unable to use them, since the Crown continually issued commercial licences to white fishermen in the same areas. One such licence issued to the Mohawks of the Bay of Quinte, for example, was discontinued by band resolution "because in previous years, the Indians were of the opinion that when licences had been granted to them, they were of no use on account of the fact that the shore of the Bay of Quinte and far up Mud Creek was licensed to whites, and ... they monopolized the business."[168]

As Aboriginal peoples struggled to meet their subsistence needs and get by day-to-day, their plight was made significantly worse by the failure of the federal government to acknowledge that they held treaty rights. They, however, did not forget. In April 1895, when two members of the Scugog Band were charged for violating the provincial game laws by "cutting and destroying a number of muskrat houses," they claimed that "under a Robinson treaty or some other treaty privileges are accorded them that they have a right to kill Game and fish for their own use at any time."[169]

In the subsequent hearing, despite a clear conflict of interest, the band's Indian Agent, William Bateman, acted as the local Justice of the Peace. This was normal procedure, as Indian Agents had the same powers as police magistrates over any "infraction" under the *Indian Act*.[170] Bateman informed Hayter Reed that he had received a letter from Chief Charles Bigcanoe [Big Canoe] from Georgina Island, who was very upset by the charges. As Bateman observed, "This goes to show the impression the Indians are under in regard to rights reserved to them under some treaty regulations as to fishing and hunting. This prosecution is causing some excitement among the Indians as the facts have already reached the Bands at Rama and Georgina Island and they are waiting with considerable interest an answer from Ottawa expecting to be protected in the pursuit of game for their own use, particularly against these Ontario Deputy Game wardens."[171]

Bateman cautioned that unless the rights claimed could be established, he would be compelled to convict the two Indians.[172] Knowing full well that the Robinson-Huron Treaty had no application to the area in which the two Indians had violated the game laws, but that the 1818 treaty did, Reed informed him that the Department was unable to express an opinion as to whether the Robinson-Huron Treaty applied to the case before him.[173]

On 8 September 1895, Chief Bigcanoe, who would later sign the Williams

Treaty affecting Georgina Island, sent a follow-up letter to Bateman in which he protested that "you cannot arrest Indians or issue warrant to apply in your court ... I have some the old Treatys in my office that showed plain that the poor Indian never surrendered his game when he let his land go to the whiteman. To interfere the Indian for hunting his own game for he did not forget he reserved his rights and all the whild [sic] game and it showed in this Treaty that the white man consented to that part of the agreement."[174] His letter was ignored.

Indians continued to be charged under increasingly violent circumstances. John Simcoe of the Rama Band was arrested at gunpoint in 1895 for fishing in violation of the game laws. As J. Smith, the Deputy Minister of Marine and Fisheries, reported to Hayter Reed, "This Indian has for some years been very defiant and has openly stated that he would fish in spite of all laws, Overseers or Governments. It therefore became necessary to instruct Overseer Watson to enforce the law and make an example of him, and if he failed to pay the fine imposed to let the law take its course. These directions were necessary if the authority of this Department was to be maintained."[175]

Before taking further action, Smith asked Reed if he had any remarks. Reed – the Deputy Superintendent General of Indian Affairs – responded that he did not feel the Department of Indian Affairs had any reason to interfere.[176]

The federal government's policy regarding even those who "lawfully" engaged in domestic hunting and fishing was generally premised on an assumption that Indians would abuse any privileges they held. In early 1895, Indian Agent J.L. McPhee had requested free licences for the Georgina and Snake Islands First Nations for domestic use,[177] and also asked that the Indians be permitted to use nets.[178] The Acting Deputy Minister of Marine and Fisheries responded that the local Fishery Overseer opposed granting this "concession" because the Indians could "catch all the fish they require by means of trolling the same as the Rama Indians and although I do not mean to say that all the members of the Band abuse the privilege, yet I am sure that there are some of them who do so."[179] Marine and Fisheries refused permission to Aboriginal fishermen to seine in November as "destructive to breeding whitefish."[180] Later, when First Nations requested an extension of the fishing season due to poor harvests in Lake Huron, this too was denied.[181]

In November 1895, Hayter Reed prepared a memorandum for his Minister conceding that, throughout the Dominion, the Indians' perspective regarding their rights differed from that of the government. Indians everywhere claimed that when their respective treaties were made, "as explained to and understood by them ... the full and free privilege to fish was secured to them."[182] He acknowledged that, in some cases, such promises had been made "and this is universally asserted and tenaciously clung to all the more so because the Department's officials, like the undersigned, who attended some of the Treaties, have never had any doubt as to the intention and understanding of the stipulations and consequently have never tried to shake the Indians' convictions."[183]

In 1896, Daniel Whetung Sr. of Mud Lake, a later signatory to the 1923 Williams Treaty affecting his First Nation, told a lawyer, Henry Wickham, that "his father and grandfather before him used to trap, fish and hunt generally on Emily Creek and Emily Lake (leading off Sturgeon Lake)." Wickham wrote to Hayter Reed, saying "Mr. Daniel Whetung is under the impression that they possessed the *exclusive* right of hunting and fishing there and wishes to claim the same privilege. I have been under the impression that the right of hunting and fishing by members of such a Band were common in all adjacent waters but I may have been wrong in this and suppose that whatever these rights might be, they are governed by the original treaty made by these Indians."[184]

In response, Reed denied the existence of any treaty or other right that would exempt the Indians of Mud Lake from provincial fish and game laws. He added that the Department of Indian Affairs had been waiting for some time for Marine and Fisheries to respond to its proposal that a free licence be issued to the Mud Lake Indians to fish for domestic use. Until a response was received, he advised that "nothing more can be done in that direction."[185]

Reed had in fact recommended that Marine and Fisheries should issue free licences to Indians allowing them to fish for food, on the requisition of their respective Indian Agents, since otherwise the government would have to pay to feed them, an eventuality he declared would be "objectionable."[186] However, he opposed the issuance of commercial fishing licences to Indians, on the basis that preventing them from engaging in such activities was "in the interests of the Indians" themselves. He argued that

> the issue of licences to fish during the close season should be restricted to fishing for domestic consumption and confined to Indians who can support themselves by no other means ... and of course the Department will endeavour as fast as possible to bring such Indians to the point already reached by the great majority of them, at which they can manage to support themselves without fishing during the close season ... The alternative for the Government is to feed these Indians during the close season, and this is not only objectionable, as tending to pauperize them, but it would entail a very large expenditure to freight supplies to distant points, many of them most difficult of access.[187]

Why it would be in the Aboriginal interest to restrict a treaty right to fish for food only to those who could not support themselves, when no similar restrictions were placed on white men, was never fully explained. In response, however, Marine and Fisheries took the position that the Indians already had "many concessions and privileges not extended to white men," since they paid only one dollar for individual licences to fish, whereas white men paid five.[188] As well, citing the current appeal of the *Fisheries Reference* to the Privy Council, Marine and Fisheries advanced yet another reason for inaction, arguing that "the jurisdictional division of fisheries (federal/provincial) is before the Imperial Privy Council and it is not appropriate to enter into the discussion at this point."[189]

The hardline position of Marine and Fisheries rested not only on its longstanding views that Aboriginal peoples had no special rights but was also the result of pressure from the non-Aboriginal communities that opposed such rights. At Cape Croker, for example, the Indian Agent discouraged the band from applying for a commercial licence so that it would "not enter into competition with white fishermen." He pointed out that, should the band ignore his advice, white men would eventually pressure the government to cancel its existing limits.[190] The Agent warned the band of a "movement set on foot by whites to deprive the Indians of their Fishing Privileges" and added that there were "parties trying to take grounds now under licence to the Band which are amongst the most valuable in the Georgian Bay. White fishermen are anxious to have them."[191]

Marine and Fisheries was well aware of the public opposition to First Nations exercising their fishing rights. Its Deputy Minister, William Smith, indicated that he was reluctant to authorize free licences for Indians, even "for [reserve] waters where white men are not allowed to fish," since this caused dissatisfaction among white fishermen.[192]

Clifford Sifton, Superintendent General of Indian Affairs and Minister of the Interior, cautioned the Minister of Marine and Fisheries that there had been "considerable trouble for years as to the fishery rights of Indians in different parts of Canada."[193] Suggesting that the two departments reach a clear understanding as to what those rights were, he recommended that two representatives be appointed, one being J.D. McLean, the Secretary of Indian Affairs. In this capacity, McLean asked for a review of the privileges claimed by the Indians and a summary of what Marine and Fisheries had "conceded" in each case. Then, he prepared a rather unsympathetic memorandum in which he stated his belief that the "true cause" of Indian complaints was in "most cases the interference of the law with their reckless and prodigal destruction of fish."[194]

Soon after McLean wrote his memorandum, Reed prepared his own, in which he again argued that Indians had no exclusive fishing privileges. He added, "these Indians have refused in the past to consider the question of having their reserve subdivided ... for the purpose of inducing them to settle down to agriculture as a means of obtaining their livelihood. They persistently bring forward this question of their fisheries having been taken from them, and refuse to listen to the Department in matters which it urges for their general advancement."[195]

Since Marine and Fisheries had already decided that the Indian claims were "excessive," Indian Affairs concluded that a "meeting with the Department of Fisheries Officers would not be useful, given their attitudes."[196] From then on, Indian Affairs gave up any attempt to persuade Marine and Fisheries to take a more expansive view of Indian fishing, and declined all further requests to become involved in the issue. For example, when an Indian Agent asked the Department to persuade Marine and Fisheries to remove a close season on herring fishing because windy conditions had prevented Indian seine netting during the open season, his request was refused. The Department took this position even though the Agent had noted that "the Indians in asking for this asked for nothing but what is their right ... there is little use in giving them the right to fish and restrict them in a way that they receive little benefit from it."[197] With no protection from Indian Affairs, and in desperate need of food, Aboriginal fishermen hauled their seine nets in under cover of darkness to avoid being charged by the Province.[198]

Although Hayter Reed had told the Alnwick Indian Agent in 1895 that Indians had no special rights to fish, Reed himself was not completely sure of his position. In 1896, he wrote to the Deputy Minister of Justice, E.L. Newcombe, asking for an opinion as to whether Dominion regulations relating to fishing were applicable to Indians fishing in waters "entirely surrounded by and forming part of Indian reserves; 2nd, In waters so situated but connected by streams or rivers with other waters which do not form part of Indian Reserves; 3rd, In waters which are only bounded in part by Indian reserves."[199] Newcombe replied that he would defer an opinion until the Privy Council ruled in the *Fisheries Reference* appeal, which he expected would throw "considerable light" on Reed's questions.[200]

On the eve of the *Fisheries Reference* decision, J.D. McLean reached an understanding with Ontario that precluded the need for the commission that Sifton had suggested should inquire into Indian fishing rights. The fishery question, at least so far as it applied to Indians on Manitoulin Island and at Alnwick, would be resolved by prohibiting Indians from fishing in the close season. In return, Ontario agreed not to charge them fees for fishing during the open season. The agreement provided that in all other respects "The Indians are therefore subject to the Game Laws of Ontario, and are only exempted in the manner provided by those laws."[201]

By virtue of this informal and bureaucratic agreement, McLean effectively delegated all federal authority over Aboriginal hunting and fishing issues to the Province of Ontario. It would be a delegation with profound consequences for the First Nations living within the province.

5
Bureaucratic Obstacles

Delegation of Federal Authority

The Indian Affairs Secretary's informal delegation of federal fisheries authority to Ontario was formalized soon after the Judicial Committee of the Privy Council decision in the *Fisheries Reference* was released, although why this was done is unclear. For one thing, the second *Fisheries Reference* again confirmed that the federal government had exclusive jurisdiction in many of the waters of Ontario, including those flowing over, and adjacent to, Indian lands. For another, earlier that year, in a decision lauded as both "learned and elaborate,"[1] the Ontario High Court of Justice had ruled that unsurrendered waters adjacent to Indian reserve lands were subject to Indian title and therefore fell only within federal jurisdiction.[2]

When the *Fisheries Reference* reached the Judicial Committee of the Privy Council, the questions placed before the Court by the parties once again excluded any issue over who held jurisdiction in the beds of waters in unsurrendered and reserved Indian lands. These were agreed to be federal, and therefore not in dispute.[3]

Because of this, the Court did not have to deal with the issue of "public rights" in Indian lands. In dealing with *surrendered* lands, however, the Privy Council cautioned that even then, "public" rights were not absolute: the provinces did not get everything at Confederation, but only the proprietary, or ownership, rights they had possessed at the time of the new federation.[4] The Court stated that this excluded the "proprietary rights in relation to fisheries ... previously vested in private individuals."[5] Given that rights vested to third parties before Confederation had not passed to the provinces with Confederation, there is no reason to think that fishing rights within unsurrendered Indian lands or those preserved under treaties had somehow fallen within provincial jurisdiction. Nothing in the Court decision suggests anything to the contrary.

Indeed, in 1891, following consultations with the provinces,[6] Ottawa had introduced legislation making it clear that waters adjacent to Indian reserves were vested in the federal government and were therefore "the property of Canada and not of the Province."[7] During second reading, the House of Commons was informed that the bill had been arrived at following negotiations with the provinces, in light of the "uncertainty" over who owned the foreshores of Canada.[8] The intention of the legislation was to enable a transfer to be made to the provinces of the foreshore and bed of "every stream, river, lake, harbour, bay, open sea or other territorial waters of Canada ... to be dealt with as provincial public lands ... subject to the limitations contained in the Schedule."[9] Under the Schedule, however, if the federal government transferred title of any Dominion lands (such as public harbours) to the provinces, Indian lands and the waters adjacent to them extending to mid-channel were exempted from such transfers. The *Act* itself was even more specific: where such a transfer occurred, pre-existing fishing rights would not be affected.[10]

With the 1891 legislation filed as an exhibit before it, the Privy Council confirmed that the Province of Ontario had exceeded its jurisdiction when it purported to deal with federal lands covered with waters,[11] and also when it legislated provisions relating to the "manner of fishing."[12] Conversely, the Court ruled that the federal government had exceeded its own jurisdiction when it had issued licences for exclusive fishing in the non-Dominion waters of Ontario.[13]

When the decision was released, J.D. McLean, the Secretary of Indian Affairs, asked the Department of Justice for an opinion as to whether it affected Indian waters surrounding and adjacent to reserves.[14] The Acting Deputy Minister of Justice, A. Power, responded that it was not possible to answer McLean's questions, given their "generality."[15] However, he did point out that Parliament still had the authority to make regulations affecting inland fisheries and that such regulations could "extend to Indians fishing in such waters ... if they were expressed to do so."[16] He warned McLean that applying fishing regulations to restrict Indians generally, or "Indians entitled to the benefit of some treaty situation," might cause legal problems, and added "but as I have said, I have not considered it necessary to go into such question on this reference."[17]

McLean asked the Justice Department for another opinion as to whether the *Fisheries Reference* affected the water frontage of Indian reserves that the Indian Affairs Department had previously leased to third parties.[18] This time, without mentioning the *Fisheries Reference,* Reginald Rimmer, an Indian Affairs lawyer whose name would surface again in connection with the Williams Treaties, provided an opinion that differed greatly from Power's.

Rimmer, an English solicitor, emigrated to Canada in 1892 and was quickly called to the bars of Saskatchewan, Alberta, the Northwest Territories, and Manitoba, where he practised criminal law. Appointed solicitor to the Department of Indian Affairs in 1898, he was involved in the investigation of claims by the Dominion against Ontario arising out of the extinguishment of Indian title. Once he completed the special work for which he had been appointed, he resigned and returned to his criminal law practice in Regina, where three years later, he was appointed to the bench.[19] At the time of his opinion, however, he was still involved in the area of Indian land claims as the departmental law clerk.

Rimmer took a highly restrictive and legalistic view of the Crown's obligations. Adopting James Cockburn's position, he stated that "unless an *express grant* from the Crown can be shown, the Indians have no title in such lots as are covered by the water of a navigable lake." He also concluded that Indian Affairs had no reason to be involved in Indian fisheries, stating, "This question does not really affect this Department but is one for the consideration of the Department of Marine and Fisheries and the Ontario Government."[20] Yet again, the idea that the Crown needed to "grant" an interest to Indians before they could be said to have one had prevailed, though the question of how – or even if – the Crown had obtained a clear interest in unsurrendered Indian lands and waters had not been placed before the Court.

Immediately after the ruling, the Ontario government informed Ottawa that it would hire its own Fisheries Officers.[21] When the Attorney General of Ontario learned that the federal government had issued licences in parts of Georgian Bay, he objected strongly. He demanded to know if this had occurred after the decision of the Privy Council, since "Our understanding was that you were to issue no new licences ... If they are issued by your Department, I shall have to treat them as void and prosecute the offenders."[22]

In its defence, the federal government referred to a private agreement negotiated informally between the Minister of Marine and Fisheries and the Ontario Premier. Apparently, the two had agreed that Ottawa would continue issuing exclusive fishing licences in certain Ontario waters, but that the fees from these licences would be held in trust on behalf of the Province. In the meantime, the Dominion government would continue to appoint, and pay, for its own Fisheries Officers until Ontario was in a position to take over management of the fisheries itself.[23] As explained by Marine and Fisheries, the Minister and Premier had also agreed that the federal government would continue to administer the fisheries regulations, as "neither the Province of Ontario or Quebec were in a position to immediately assume control of the administration of the fisheries regulations."[24]

No direct documentary evidence exists of any more formal delegation of authority than this.[25] Indeed, shortly afterward, in October 1898, the Deputy Minister of Marine and Fisheries described the deal not as a legal or formal matter but as an agreement reached "purely" as a aspect of policy "which formed the subject of a personal discussion between the Minister of Marine and Fisheries and the Premier of Ontario."[26] Nonetheless, such a delegation of authority, effected in a backroom meeting of two elected politicians without the knowledge of the provincial Attorney General, can only be described as extraordinary.

Despite the agreement, Ottawa was highly reluctant to relinquish complete control over fisheries in Ontario. To ensure that Ontario complied with the proper enforcement of federal laws, three federal Fishery Inspectors were appointed to monitor provincial activities.[27] As well, Ottawa continued to maintain that the delegation had no effect on its overall authority to regulate the fisheries, asserting that it alone, and not Ontario, held "the sole and exclusive power to pass regulations with respect to the fisheries."[28]

That there were limits to the delegation seems quite clear. For example, in 1901 the Minister of Marine and Fisheries refused a request by Ontario to give full federal authority to provincial officers, informing Ontario rather prophetically that "your suggestion that the Provincial Overseers should be given Dominion authority involves some difficulties ... the question is, would the advantages counterbalance possible complications and confusion if full authority were given by the Dominion to officers over which they have no control, and whom we have no power to instruct."[29] In 1907, J.F. Boudreau, the Minister of Marine and Fisheries, described the parameters of the delegation as "restricted, permitting the province to issue licences, but otherwise leaving the federal government with all rights of regulation."[30]

The federal Justice Department anticipated further litigation concerning this issue. The Minister of Justice, R.A. Aylesworth, warned the Minister of Marine and Fisheries not to table any materials in Parliament that might become "embarrassing in the course of litigation or otherwise at some future time."[31] He recommended, though, that the Minister not object too strongly when the provinces claimed a right to grant exclusive fishing rights in provincial waters, but instead make it clear that this was a "privilege" and not a right.[32] Aylesworth recommended that the Minister stay clear of any other discussion of the *Fisheries Reference,* and in particular, that he avoid interpreting, explaining, or paraphrasing the decision, as "Anyone who wishes to know the law on the subject should study that decision for himself, or take legal advice about it. It is, I think, very objectionable that the Government should be asked to state categorically the interpretation which it puts upon the decision."[33]

Despite this cautionary advice, Aylesworth confirmed that, in his view, the federal government had the exclusive right to issue licences in certain waters. These included all navigable waterways in Ontario as well as those that Ottawa and Ontario had agreed were federal waters, such as those on and adjacent to Indian lands.[34]

It seems clear, then, that the federal government had the legal authority, by statute, case-law, and policy, not to mention the Constitution, to address Aboriginal interests in Indian waters, as well as in public harbours and navigable waters within Ontario. Nonetheless, J.D. McLean reported to his superiors that the *Fisheries Reference* decision had, at best, an "uncertain" effect on Indian fishing "privileges."[35] Throughout his tenure, the Department of Indian Affairs permitted Ontario to take over all the aspects of management and enforcement of Aboriginal fisheries, wherever they were situated, and claimed that Ontario had the right to do so as a result of the purported federal "delegation."

Ontario assumed the mantle of its new responsibilities by eagerly and aggressively enforcing federal and provincial laws against Aboriginal fishermen. In part, this was due to racism endemic in the province at the time. At Wiarton, the Reverend J. Cabot, a Roman Catholic missionary, complained in 1908 that "the Indians from Cape Croker" deeply resented being forced to eat at separate tables in local inns, where their tables were not cleaned and they were often not served.[36] In 1916, when two Aboriginal men escaped from a southern Ontario jail, their entire village was occupied by vigilantes who searched people's homes, abused those they found, and refused to allow the Aboriginal men there to leave for work. Even the Ontario Attorney General acknowledged that no white community would ever be treated in such a way.[37] Nonetheless, the federal government denied repeated First Nations pleas for aid, insisting that it no longer had any management authority over fisheries in Ontario.

As each level of government claimed that the other was responsible, the jurisdictional cracks that developed resulted in almost complete government inaction in the protection of Aboriginal rights. For example, even though the fishing islands in Chemong (Mud) Lake were administered by Indian Affairs as Indian property, complaints in 1914 that non-Aboriginal squatters were using them for fishing operations were referred to the provincial government. When J.H. Burnham, a Member of Parliament, complained about the unauthorized fishing activities on the islands, he was told by J.D. Haglan, a Marine and Fisheries official, that ever since the *Fisheries Reference* of 1898, the provincial Department of Fisheries at Toronto had administered all Ontario fisheries. Haglan told him to try there and added that, "if this matter is not one for the consideration of that Department, it probably can be dealt with by the Department of Indian Affairs as apparently the Islands referred to are under the jurisdiction of that Department."[38] Ontario did nothing to remove the squatters, and the Department of Indian Affairs finally, although reluctantly, intervened.[39]

In 1911, Johnson Paudash of the Hiawatha First Nation asked which level of government had jurisdiction over areas his band used for muskrat hunting. He was informed that the rice beds, marshes, and unsold islands in Rice Lake and other lakes connected with the Trent Canal system were under control of the Indian Affairs Department.[40] However, the many complaints made by the Hiawatha First Nation to the Indian Affairs Department that it was being interfered with by farmers when trapping in these areas were referred by that Department to the Province, which supported the farmers in their actions.

A few years later, the law firm of Evans and Evans was wrongly informed by Indian Affairs that the Indian islands in Scugog Lake were not under its control. This time, it was the *provincial* Deputy Minister of Lands and Forests who drew the attention of Indian Affairs to the fact that the islands in the entire chain of lakes in the Trent Valley were held in trust by the Department of Indian Affairs for the Mississauga Indians.[41] J.D. McLean reluctantly acknowledged that "It is considered *possible* that any island that may be in this lake would belong to the Indians under an arrangement come to with the Indians many years ago."[42]

As late as 1922, only a year before the Williams Treaties, W.C. Cain, the Deputy Minister of Lands and Forests Ontario, received a letter from a member of the public inquiring as to "what department of the federal or Provincial governments controls Rice Lake and connecting streams."[43] Ontario's response was that the matter fell within the jurisdiction of Indian Affairs, "and if you communicate with J.D. McLean, Secretary of that Department, no doubt he will be able to give you all the necessary information."[44]

Indeed, long after the Williams Treaties of 1923, and the supposed surrender of all previously unceded Mississauga lands under its provisions, the Secretary of the Department of the Interior advised an Oshawa lawyer that the Department of Indian Affairs, not Ontario, controlled certain islands in Lake Scugog.[45]

The First Nations Hire Lawyers

Despite being caught in a tangled net of bureaucratic finger pointing, the Mississauga and Chippewa First Nations were determined to pursue their land claims and protect their harvesting rights. William Plummer had retired, however, and without his advocacy, they had little support within the Department of Indian Affairs. Instead, the Department delayed responding to their claims, repeatedly denied their requests to retain legal counsel, and provided them with deliberately misleading information.

In 1895, John Thackeray, the Alnwick Indian Agent, inquired into the progress of the Alnwick claim, saying that "the Indians are continually asking me about the [progress] of their claim and they are [very] anxious to know."[46] He was informed that although two cases had gone to arbitration, the claim of "your Indians was not, however, one of those dealt with."[47] In 1896, Thackeray again requested information.[48] This time, he was told that the claim had not yet been presented but would be taken up in its turn.[49]

Clifford Sifton, the Minister of the Interior and Superintendent General of Indian Affairs, asked Reginald Rimmer and J.A.J. McKenna, another law clerk with Indian Affairs, to report confidentially to him on some of the outstanding disputes between the Department of Indian Affairs and Ontario, including the Mississauga land claim.[50] On 20 March 1899, Rimmer and McKenna recommended that the Department give up all "doubtful claims." A failure to do so, they asserted, would mean that "we shall have nothing to offer Ontario in return for the voluntary acquiescence in the Indian rights which we are endeavouring to assert and shall be put to litigation, expense and delay."[51]

Although it is not certain which rights Rimmer and McKenna were referring to, it is likely that these related to a dispute between Ontario and the federal government over whether the Province was liable to reimburse the Dominion government for the cost of extinguishing Aboriginal title in northern Ontario, as negotiations were then underway related to the North-west Angle Treaty.[52] In any event, Rimmer and McKenna considered the Mississauga claim to unsurrendered lands to be one of the "doubtful" ones that should be abandoned. In their report, published in 1901, they concluded that all the lands occupied and claimed by the Mississaugas and Chippewas south of the forty-fifth parallel had already been surrendered, and that "there was no evidence that either Tribe had ever used the lands north of there as hunting grounds, which had been used instead by Algonquins."[53]

Addressing the fact that there was no valid surrender dealing with the lands included in the Gunshot Treaty, they remarked that, in their view, this posed no threat to Crown title. They admitted that the surrender was invalid, but nonetheless concluded that "notwithstanding the invalidity in form of this purchase, the consideration having been paid, the Crown has been in possession of the land for one hundred and thirteen years without any regard to unextinguished Indian title."[54] Once again, the fact that the Crown had allowed settlers to take possession of the unceded lands in contravention of the *Royal Proclamation* was put forward as a basis to reject a valid claim for Aboriginal title.

Frustrated, but unaware of Rimmer and McKenna's conclusions, the Alnwick Band decided to hire a lawyer to help it secure its rights.[55] Their Indian Agent, John Thackeray, immediately asked the Indian Affairs Department if it would allow them to do so.[56] Rimmer advised against it, on the basis that he and McKenna had already reviewed the Alnwick land claim and "considered [that] it could not be successfully pressed. So far as I can learn, no fresh evidence has been presented. I cannot recommend any consent to the expenditure of Band funds for the purpose of retaining counsel."[57] The proper course, he recommended, was to protect the band's funds from the "wasteful expenditures" associated with hiring legal help.[58]

In January 1903, Thackeray wrote to Indian Affairs, warning his superiors that the band had already talked to John Kerr, a lawyer from Cobourg, and was determined to have the matter brought to a conclusion, as "they say this matter has been talked about [for] over 60 years."[59] With the news that legal action might be forthcoming, James J. Campbell, yet another Indian Affairs law clerk, was asked by the Deputy Superintendent General of Indian Affairs to review the Rimmer and McKenna report and provide a second opinion, given the "magnitude of the interests involved and of the responsibility of the Department in abandoning the interests of its wards specially intrusted to it at its own invitation."[60]

Campbell, to his credit, had an entirely different perspective on the issue. He criticized Rimmer and McKenna for taking information out of context, writing that "apparently reliance is placed in the cumulative force of certain minor findings to justify the main one ... [when] they are required to be considered individually." Campbell rebuked Rimmer and McKenna for requiring more proof than had ever been previously needed to establish a *prima facie* case for Aboriginal title. For him, the fact that the various tribes and bands understood the limits of the hunting grounds "without dispute on the part of other Indians," and that the "facts are still preserved by tradition" should have been sufficient.[61]

Campbell pointed out that the lands claimed by the Mississaugas were immediately adjacent to those they had surrendered in 1818 and "would naturally have formed their hunting grounds." Unless it could be shown that the grounds had been surrendered or claimed by others, he concluded that the evidence was *prima facie* in favour of the Indian claim.[62]

Despite this encouraging development, the claimants were never informed of Campbell's report. With no information as to the progress of their claim, the Chippewas of Rama, Georgina Island, and Christian Island decided that they, too, should hire a lawyer. They retained W.H. Hunter to represent them. John Yates, the Georgina Island Indian Agent, got wind of a meeting the lawyer planned to hold with his clients and tried to stop them from retaining Hunter by refusing to approve the funds needed:

> The Indians of Georgina and Snake Island, Rama, Christian Island and three other Bands, are geting reddy to press that Long talked of Claim against the Government. they have had a lawyer named Hunter among them for some time holding meetings. he tells them that he is sure to win and has got some money out of them, and he wants one thousand dollars now to enter the Case. I tryed my best to keep them from giving him any money ... the Indians thinks when they pas a Resolution, as they have in this case that I must obey it. the Indians dont seem to Excited over the Case but they think they will shurly get a large sum of money.[63]

Nonetheless, in the summer of 1903, the Mud Lake, Rice Lake, Scugog, Rama, Beausoleil, and Snake Island First Nations passed Band Council Resolutions appointing Hunter and G. Mills McClurg as their lawyers.[64] As their claim took shape, the lawyers asked Chief Big Canoe to look through the band's Minutes for any reference to the various petitions and deputations sent to Ottawa in the past. Alnwick's lawyer, John Kerr, also collected depositions in which Alnwick Band elders described their ancient hunting grounds[65] and forwarded them to Frank Pedley, the Deputy Superintendent General of Indian Affairs.[66]

In response to the mounting evidence, Clifford Sifton, Minister of the Interior, directed Indian Affairs to shut down the claim. Sifton instructed Pedley to let the lawyers know that "The Indian Bands cannot be permitted to employ counsel upon terms not approved by the Department and in cases in which the Department does not regard it as necessary that counsel should be employed."[67] Instead, the bands' lawyers were told to surrender all their evidence to Rimmer. If the information proved to justify the claim, they "might" be paid whatever amount the Department considered reasonable.[68] J.D. McLean suggested that the same position be taken with John Kerr, Alnwick's lawyer, and J. Hugh Hammond of Orillia, who acted for the Rama, Christian Island, and Georgina Island Bands.[69]

W.F. Hunter's outraged response to this directive was that his First Nation clients had as much right as anyone else in Canada to have a lawyer of their choice. He wrote, "It is perhaps unnecessary to call to your attention the fact that the courts of the land are open to the Indians equally with all other of His Majesty's Canadian subjects ... with all due respect, I cannot allow the matter to stand in this position for any length of time."[70]

Despite Hunter's threat of legal action, the Department stonewalled, refusing to allow the lawyers to see their clients' files. Frank Pedley warned his Minister that, in his view, giving outside lawyers access to government documents would be dangerous. He made the absurd suggestion that "if Mr. Hunter saw fit to place any of *his* papers in the custody of the Department, he would be at liberty at any time to see them and possibly withdraw them,"[71] an approach that Sifton enthusiastically approved.[72] In light of the federal position that Hunter might "possibly" get back his *own* documents but would not be permitted to see the Indian Affairs files, not surprisingly, Hunter informed his clients that the Department had denied the claim.

In 1905, Sifton unexpectedly resigned as Minister of the Interior in connection with an unrelated issue, and McClurg notified Chief Big Canoe that this would mean yet another delay, since "Nothing now can be done until after the appointment of a New Minister which in all probability will not occur until after the present Session ... We will now consider the advisability of putting the matter in Court and let the law dispose of it."[73]

In the meantime, the Mississaugas of Rice Lake had brought a third claim to the Department's attention. In May 1905, J.A. MacRae of Indian Affairs had met with Hiawatha First Nation Chief Robert Paudash of Rice Lake. Chief Paudash presented MacRae with clear evidence of an error in the 1818 treaty's description of its northern boundary. As a result, MacRae was convinced that this claim "should be taken seriously" since the treaty boundary, obviously incorrect, left a portion of lands north of it unceded.[74] In turn, J.D. McLean confirmed that "it looks very probable that an error was made in the description."[75]

However, Samuel Bray, the Indian Department's Land Surveyor, argued that the claim should be disregarded, asserting that the Indians had made little use of the lands and had waited too long to claim them. He criticized the band for not having brought the claim "to the attention of the Government until 20 yrs. after making the Robinson Huron Treaty and 48 years after making one of the Treaties affected and 52 years after making one of the other treaties affected."[76] Bray also maintained that since the Mississaugas had not used the lands, they should not be able to recover compensation for their loss: "There certainly appears to have been a tract of land in this locality which would not appear to be covered by any of the Treaties mentioned, and it has only been claimed by the Mississaugas. They, however, seem to have made very little use of it and as they also had been made in receipt of payments for all of the lands of which they had made practical use, their claim if admitted at all should also be for a small sum."[77]

McLean did not inform the Rice Lake Band that its claim had been validated; instead, he discouraged it from continuing further, writing to Paudash to tell him that his claim was "too indefinite" to proceed.[78] He sent a similarly disingenuous letter to W.H. Bennett, a Member of Parliament, informing him that the "evidence so far brought forward ... is not considered sufficient to lead to the conclusion that the claim for compensation is warranted."[79] In another letter to Manley Chew, a Member of Parliament and wealthy lumber merchant from the Midland area of east Georgian Bay, McLean was also deliberately misleading, stating that "on complete investigation ... we considered that the claim could not be successfully pressed. As nothing new has been added to the material already in the Department, it is not apparent in what manner the question could be re-opened."[80]

In 1911, Arthur Crozier, the lawyer for the Chippewa Bands, asked Indian Affairs to "let me Know Fully Just how this Claim of the Indians stands at this time. The Indians are of the opinion that very little has been accomplished considering the time which has elapsed."[81] McLean's response was almost identical to that sent to Chew.[82]

By this time, the unsurrendered Indian lands had been completely taken over by white settlers, who, under the provisions of the *Royal Proclamation,* were not entitled to obtain title to them. Even lands set aside as special reserves for Indians had been settled and encroached upon. In 1909, Chief Assance of Rama wrote to the Deputy Superintendent General complaining that lands near the Moon and Musquosh Rivers reserved by Lieutenant-Governor Simcoe as a hunting ground for the Chippewas had been taken away from them by white men:

> the said [area] was reserved by our forefarthers for their grandchildren in future settlement Location in time coming and has been Since repeatedly remind us, before their deaths that there is a Tract of Land lies, reserve for you & our children for your future settlement when time is Coming that, when the White Man will be crowd you to take away your land & hunting grounds.
>
> we Commence to see it now, on the Contarary, the Dept. dont recognize, we claim this reserve ... this Said reserve was never yet Ceded to the Crown to our best of Knowledge, but still White man is full through the country ... Now we strongly hold that Tract of Land our reserve will not be Ceded but Kept for future Location & Settlement and it Must be protected from trespassing. My granduncles whose Names I give, Manitowab, Negigance, Mahshkigance, claimed & reserve this Tract of Land, Mentioned this stands on the unceded hunting ground.[83]

In another letter, Chief Assance begged Manley Chew to communicate his "Statement Concerning this reserve" to the Deputy Superintendent General of Indian Affairs. He wrote that the "Indian Warriors for the British" claimed the entire unceded territory from "Sequine river To Colwater River and to Lake Simcoe there are Special reserves in Side the Mentioned Claim ... Some Members on this reserve will go and settle on Moon river reserve because Some are unable to farm to cultivate Soil and on that reserve there is much easier to support his family and raise stock easly for sale."[84]

A General Council of the Rama, Georgina, and Christian Island Bands held a meeting and decided to instruct lawyer J. Hugh Hammond to "act for us and in our name to protect and restore to us and our people the hunting, fishing and trapping rights that have been interfered with by the whites lately and [take] such steps as are necessary to gain this end as to him may seem proper."[85] Indian Agent Hagen's response upon learning of the meeting was that "some lawyer, I suppose is trying to make a little money out of the Indians." J.D. McLean agreed that "certain persons for their own ends are endeavouring to mislead the Indians in regard to this and other matters, but their interventions can lead to no good results."[86]

In the summer of 1911, the First Nations prepared to go to court with yet another lawyer, A.K. Goodman of the firm Goodman and Galbraith, as Hunter had retired. The *Indian Act* had been amended the previous year, however, to prohibit Indians from retaining lawyers without the written approval of the Superintendent General of Indian Affairs. This meant that Indian Affairs had the sole right to decide when and if lawyers could be hired by First Nations.[87] Goodman notified Indian Affairs that he was the bands' new solicitor,[88] and was informed by McLean that under the new rules, any agreement he might have with the Indians to represent them was invalid unless approved in writing by the Superintendent General.[89] Despite this warning, Goodman cautioned Sifton's replacement, Robert Rogers, that he intended to act for the bands and that the "Indians are becoming very restless at the long delay."[90]

Goodman prepared and sent another eight declarations from elders at Rama, Christian Island, and Georgina Island to the Minister directly, again pressing for more immediate action.[91] This time, McLean refused to take further steps unless the Indians provided originals.[92] However, because they had not been "fairly treated in regard to original documents deposited" in the past and had not had their documents returned to them, they declined.[93] In 1914, facing an array of lawyers determined to take the matter forward, McLean finally stopped stonewalling. He passed the contents of his departmental files to the Deputy Minister of Justice and asked that a "competent" lawyer be assigned to go thoroughly into the question.[94]

R.V. Sinclair, a Justice lawyer and former departmental solicitor for Indian Affairs, was assigned the task of reviewing the various materials compiled for the claim. In his report, completed in November 1916 and provided to E.L. Newcombe, the Deputy Minister of Justice, he concluded that "the Indian title to these lands has never been extinguished and I am of the opinion that some arrangement should be made for quieting the title by the payment to the claimants of some compensation in the same way that the Crown has dealt with other Indians whose title has been extinguished by Treaty ... The evidence so far as it goes seems to me to support the claim."[95] Like Campbell before him, Sinclair found that "The claim to the whole territory as hunting grounds is asserted by the declarations of 27 Indians in terms so positive and explicit as to render it extremely difficult to disregard the evidence." The lands were indeed "lands reserved for the Indians" within the meaning of the 1763 *Royal Proclamation* and were therefore subject to Aboriginal title.[96]

For sixty or more years, the Mississaugas and Chippewas had been told that they had no rights in their unceded hunting grounds. Now, in a clear statement, R.V. Sinclair had supported their claim to Aboriginal title. They were never told. Instead, their ongoing attempts to hunt and trap within the northern lands were not only left unprotected by the federal government but were obstructed by both Ontario and Ottawa. By 1916, Ontario had taken over the full enforcement of game and fish laws. It asserted, fully supported by Indian Affairs, that Indians had no special rights to hunt, fish, or trap in their traditional lands.

Provincial Enforcement Actions

For some decades after Confederation, as seen, the Department of Indian Affairs had argued in favour of Aboriginal rights and had opposed the restrictive measures taken by Marine and Fisheries. By the turn of the century, however, virtually all federal attempts to advocate or protect Aboriginal interests had been abandoned.

Shortly after the *Fisheries Reference,* Ontario passed new legislation to deal with both fish and game, despite the fact that under case-law at the time, the actions were unconstitutional.[97] The federal government made no public challenge to this step, though, internally, it knew the Province's actions were unconstitutional and considered disallowance.[98] In particular, the Dominion government objected to Ontario charging fees for provincial licences, since it considered that doing so itself might be both "*desirable,* and *necessary.*"[99] While the federal government pondered whether it should disallow the provincial legislation, Ontario agreed to make certain amendments to the law, conceding that its officials had "no right to define limits in the size, weight & number of fish to be taken and they surely have no right to define what shall be the minimum weight of fish that shall be trawled."[100]

F. Goudreau, the Acting Deputy Minister of Marine and Fisheries, wrote a strongly worded letter to the Deputy Minister of Justice, E.L. Newcombe, urging him to take legal action against the Province because the legislation professed to regulate fisheries and was therefore beyond provincial jurisdiction.[101] He insisted that "the federal government should not rest satisfied with a mere protest" but should instead let "it be clearly and firmly known what the position of the Dominion Government is on this point."[102] In response, Newcombe prepared a strong letter to the Attorney General warning that Ottawa was considering disallowance.[103] However, the Minister of Marine and Fisheries, Sir Louis H. Davies, disapproved of Goudreau's approach and chastised Newcombe for even considering it. Commenting that he did not like the "tone" of Newcombe's letter, he stated that he preferred to speak to the provincial officials personally.[104]

However, when Davies met with the Attorney General of Ontario and the Minister of Justice, he proved completely inept at preserving federal authority. Instead, he advised Ontario that Ottawa would not disallow the legislation even though the "Dominion has absolute jurisdiction and clauses in [the provincial] Acts trenching on fisheries jurisdiction were *ultra vires.*"[105] Davies, proud of the strong stance he had taken with Ontario, seems not to have realized that he had essentially surrendered all federal jurisdiction over fisheries to the Province, although he later commented somewhat wistfully that he had hoped to at least retain the authority to issue licences during the close season, "not because of any desire to merely retain any exclusive authority which may rest with the Dominion Government or for the sake of form, but because I apprehend difficulty and perhaps serious danger in the future, should Dominion permission be rendered superfluous in Ontario."[106]

Thus unchallenged, and with the passage of the new *Ontario Game and Fisheries Act* guaranteed, Ontario took over all aspects of Aboriginal fishing and hunting, advancing its position that Indians should be treated in the same manner as everyone else. In that regard, the Province received strong federal support.

For example, in 1899, J.M. Gibson, the Ontario Provincial Secretary and Commissioner of Crown Lands, asked Indian Affairs to join him in teaching Indian "law-breakers" a lesson. He explained,

> I have always endeavoured to avoid taking any course that could be considered antagonistic to the true interests of the Indians, but I fear there is a sort of feeling on the part of some of the Indians that our laws do not really affect them, and that in any case they will be protected against the Province by "big Government" at Ottawa ...
>
> What is wanted is cooperation between your Department and our Government in the matter of having the Indians taught that their true and permanent interests are to protect the deer and moose ... It is necessary that we should make an example of some of them who really know better than to openly violate the law.[107]

J. Smart of Indian Affairs responded that "the Department has never encouraged them to expect protection for violating the Provincial laws."[108]

Commissioner Gibson's own view was that treaty rights merely enabled Indians to have access to certain lands and exempted them from paying licensing fees. He believed that a treaty "could not bind Parliament as to prevent the making of laws with reference to hunting and fishing intended for the benefit of Indians as well as that of other persons."[109] This position, however, was inconsistent with the *Ontario Game Protection Act* itself, which contained clear provisions against prejudicing treaty rights and rights in unsurrendered lands.

Despite this, in 1900, an amendment to the *Ontario Game Protection Act* added a number of provisions that adversely affected Aboriginal peoples still dependent on the chase. Along with the requirement of a hunting licence, the concept of guiding licences was introduced. A five-year prohibition on the capture of beaver and otter was followed by an annual close season. As well, an annual eight-month close season on muskrat took effect immediately.[110] No exemption was provided for Aboriginal peoples, and almost immediately, the Mississaugas of Rice, Mud, and Scugog Lakes, represented by Chiefs Joseph Irons, Robert Paudash, George Goose, and Daniel Whetung Jr. as Secretary, vehemently protested the impact of these provisions on their ability to guide and trap. They sent a petition to the government that read in part, "Your Petitioners believe under the Gunshot Treaty and other treaties that they retained their right to hunt and fish generally, to capture and kill game and not only this but they also retained their right to at any time sell and dispose of any game caught as has formerly been their privilege on the continent. Your petitioners consider that it is their right to sell and dispose of such game at any time and they do not believe that they have at any time give over such rights."[111]

McLean responded that the Ontario game laws "are valid and binding even if they deprive Indians of rights assured to them by Treaty."[112] This position – that treaty rights could be infringed at the government's will – was defended as being in the "public interest."

Quite often, however, the "public interest" simply meant that non-Aboriginal people wanted greater access to hunting and fishing opportunities themselves. In 1902, for example, Ontario delayed issuing the Cape Croker Band a fishing licence because of protests it had received from the local non-Aboriginal community, which had complained about the "extensive territory" licensed to the band. It was reported that "whites are attempting to encroach on the Indian fishing reserve ... the Indians are uneasy."[113]

Responding to pressure from both sides, the Ontario Deputy Commissioner of Fisheries advised Indian Affairs that the Province would issue the licence to the First Nation, but that it would be limited to waters off the reserve and around Hay Island, a minuscule portion of the seven miles protected in the 1847 *Imperial Proclamation*.[114] Instead of defending their interests, J.D. McLean informed the Cape Croker Band through its Indian Agent that "Under the circumstances, the Department has allowed the Indians the largest limits it considers compatible with the due consideration of all interests involved."[115]

The Cape Croker Band protested the unilateral reduction of its limits, asserting that the new limits were "insufficient, unacceptable and unjustifiable." It called on the "Department of Indian Affairs, their rightfull protector and guardian," to protect its rights.[116] The response from Indian Affairs was that "The Department supports the province's action to make arrangements in the interests of all classes of the community concerned."[117]

Although the Assistant Secretary of Indian Affairs did point out to Ontario that the Cape Croker Band's new licence excluded it from fishing in part of its own reserve,[118] Ontario not only charged the First Nation the same fee that it had paid in the past for a larger area,[119] but licensed the territory covered by the band's licence to white men.[120] A letter from J. Campbell, Indian Affairs, to his Deputy Superintendent General indicated that it would be "bad policy to make any demands the reasonable nature of which cannot be demonstrated to provincial authorities," but pointed out that Barrier Island, the portion of the reserve denied to band members, was still an "Indian Island" and should be restored to the licence. Although the letter did suggest that the Province be asked why white men were licensed to fish there, the band's Indian Agent dismissed the band's further protests as emanating from "grumblers" and "fault finders" who "do not appreciate fairness but think they should own the whole earth."[121] In July 1902, Indian Affairs quietly informed Ontario that it had declined to intervene in the Cape Croker dispute to avoid "the risk of embarrassing your Department in its effort to afford equal justice to all interests concerned."[122]

With this, Ontario's jurisdiction over Indian hunting and fishing became an accepted fact. In 1906, when an Indian requested assistance after being fined for killing a moose, McLean remarked that "Indians who break the game or other laws do so at their own risk and the Department is powerless to protect them from the consequence even if it thought right to do so ... you must remember that there is no class or community who will ultimately benefit more from proper protection of game than Indians."[123]

As noted, amendments to Ontario's legislation required that Indians obtain, and pay for, a licence to act as guides.[124] However, a guiding licence could be obtained only if the applicant were certified by a local game warden as "fit and proper" to have one.[125] Chief Daniel Whetung Jr. of the Mud Lake Band, a later signatory to his nation's 1923 Williams Treaty, told his community members not to apply for a guide's licence no matter what, "as the Department has got no authority over them,"[126] and promised that his band would finance any legal fees if they were charged.[127]

In 1910, two Indians who were arrested for shooting a moose near Sturgeon Lake in northern Ontario argued that they had an express right under the Robinson-Superior Treaty to hunt. Once again, Ontario's position was that Indians were subject to the same fish and game laws as others.[128] Later that year, J.D. McLean wrote E.R. Tinsley, the Superintendent of Game and Fisheries in Toronto, pointing out that provincial authorities had instructed that charges be laid against Indians hunting and fishing even in the area of the Robinson-Huron treaties, where express promises to hunt and fish in ceded territories had been written into the treaties. He reminded the Province that, because the provincial legislation stated that treaty rights would not be infringed, its actions were inconsistent with its own game laws. Given this, he added, it was "little wonder, therefore, that the Indians should conclude that the Department also should hold the view that they were only exercising rights of which they could not be deprived."[129]

Tinsley, however, responded by arguing that Indians "have no more rights than other people. The most persistent and destructive poachers the Department [of Game and Fisheries] has had to deal with have been Indians, many of them boasting of their treaty rights empowering them to do whatever they felt inclined. It has long since been decided that all residents of the Province are amenable to the same laws, and they are not friends of the Indians who try to make them believe otherwise."[130] Tinsley claimed that he "had endeavoured to be lenient with the Indians of the province, but forbearance has ceased to be a virtue."[131]

Indian Affairs officials did not object to Ontario's restriction of Indian hunting rights to reserves. Internally, McLean conceded provincial jurisdiction, reporting that "Indian hunting ... is a claim that has frequently been advanced but so far as the Department is aware, never successfully in Ontario ... the Province has the sole and all the right governing game and the only exception in favour of Indians is such as may be provided by the Provincial Ordinances."[132]

In 1910, Kelly Evans, a Justice of the Ontario Court, was appointed Special Commissioner for a Game and Fisheries Commission in Toronto, tasked to inquire into the question of hunting and fishing in Ontario.[133] Judge Evans wrote to McLean, asking him a series of questions about federal policies on Aboriginal hunting and fishing issues. Since the provincial game legislation did recognize, at least in theory, that Aboriginal people had the right to hunt in hunting grounds and territories set apart for their use, Evans apprised McLean that Ottawa's views were particularly important, as "In the course of my investigations I have frequently been brought into contact with questions of Indian rights, in regard to territories other than their reservations especially."[134] Evans was particularly anxious not to clash in any way with general Indian Affairs policy in regard to Indian rights and privileges. He asked McLean whether Indian rights regarding hunting, fishing, and trapping off-reserve were greater than those of white men, and whether Indians had the right to trade in fish, fur, and game. He also asked "what extent of waters would be considered as included in their reservation, for fishing and shooting purposes."[135]

McLean replied that Ontario and "the Indians" (as opposed to the Department) held differing points of view. He explained that the position of the Ontario "Game Guardian," E.R. Tinsley, was that Indians had no special privileges except on-reserve, and that the only exemptions they had from the regulations were those contained within the provincial legislation itself. However, McLean informed Evans that Ontario's position was probably incorrect, since only the federal government could legislate in regard to Indians. He told Evans of a recent court decision that suggested that any provincial legislation attempting to limit Indian hunting rights was probably null and void, and that Indians could be restricted only by game laws applied to them under the *Indian Act*. He concluded that "it seems altogether probable that the courts will uphold the contention that they [Indians] are subject to Dominion but not to provincial legislation."[136]

In light of this, McLean's repeated advice to First Nations that only Ontario had jurisdiction over game laws seems particularly indefensible. However, McLean defended his actions on the basis that it was only "fit and proper" that Indians should conform to the same laws as white men. For this reason, he advised Evans that the Department of Indian Affairs discouraged the sale of game or fish by Aboriginal peoples, even if these had been taken on the reserve, "as that would undoubtedly open the way to like sale of fish or game taken elsewhere."[137]

In a second letter to Evans, McLean conceded that the "privileges" extended to Aboriginal peoples had been whittled away by the Province of Ontario's regulations and policies until no special privileges remained:

"Considerable latitude was given to them by the provincial authorities in regard to these matters until within recent years, but privileges formerly granted to them have one by one been withdrawn until at present they have no special privileges allowed to them by the Superintendent of Game and Fisheries of which the Department is aware. Recently, Indians have been heavily penalized for having hunted and trapped, relying apparently in good faith on the treaties made with them as well as upon the fact that they had trapped and hunted in these unoccupied territories for generations."[138]

The Evans report was released in 1911. In it, Evans expressed some definite opinions about Indians, stating that "one of the principal factors in the destruction of game is the Indian living in the wilder regions." As the founder of the Ontario Game Protection Association, a sportsmen's lobby, Evans was pointed in his description of Aboriginal people as "lazy" and not of the "better class" of men: "In the main also, it may be said that the Indian is not an energetic person, excepting when engaged in the pursuit of some wild creature, nor as a rule one possessed of great perspicacity in financial matters ... in general, they are loathe to undertake prolonged or steady work, and what money they make disappears with astonishing rapidity, so that during a great portion of the year, food is with them a question of no moment."[139]

The Evans report concluded that Indians were better suited to trapping than were white men, since trapping was a means by which the "shiftless and lazy" could gain a livelihood. Otherwise, as far as Evans was concerned, there was "but small advantage" to the community "from the existence of an Indian, other than through those functions which he can discharge in his native element, the woods, while the pursuit of trapping is not generally calculated to attract the better class of white men ... but on the contrary rather to serve as a means of gaining a competency for the shiftless and lazy." He suggested that since there was no advantage in encouraging white men to trap, an "advantage would exist in the case of the Indians, for not only would he thus be made to contribute materially to the public welfare but his energies would be applied in the direction most suited."[140]

Because he was a member of the bench, Evans' racist views about Indians are particularly troubling. However, his report was praised and adopted by Ontario, and changes to the provincial legislation incorporated its recommendations. From then on, for example, Ontario required that, even on their own reserves, Indians obtain licences to hunt and fish.[141]

A General Council of Indians from the Robinson-Huron and Manitoulin First Nations petitioned the federal government against these changes. They protested the fact that members of their communities were being jailed for exercising their rights, and that "many of our people have suffered the penalty thereof not only in fines but also in imprisonment."[142]

In a memorandum circulated to the Ontario Chiefs entitled "Re Hunting and Fishing rights reserved by the Indians in their different surrenders of territory to the Crown from the earliest period onward," G. Mills McClurg, a former Justice of the Peace and lawyer who had taken a leading role in the Mississauga and Chippewa land claim, advised the First Nations of the necessity of obtaining an Ontario licence to fish on their own reserves.[143] Despite conducting considerable research, McClurg could find nothing to assist them, reporting "I have ... consulted some of the best legal authorities both in Great Britain and in Canada and find the above to be the proper and only course to pursue."[144]

McClurg attempted to negotiate certain benefits for his clients but advised the Chief at Chemong (Mud) Lake that the provincial government had confirmed that, even on their own reserves, Indians could fish for food but not for sale.[145] He reported that he had managed to obtain some off-reserve concessions from Ontario concerning the Rama Band's ability to fish for food, and would try for others: "I have secured permission from Mr. Tinsley to allow the Indians at Rama to fish in Lakes Couchiching and Simcoe with night lines, using baited hooks, fish caught on these lines can be sold in the open market. I am trying for the same privileges in Muskoka Lakes."[146]

Given that the First Nations were being permitted to fish only in their reserve waters, these "concessions" did not amount to much. Even so, the First Nations had little choice but to comply. On 20 November 1911, Chief J.B. Stinson signed a Band Council Resolution asking Ontario for a licence to "fish with nets and night lines on our limited fishing grounds reserved by the Indian Department for us."[147] The resolution, sent to McClurg, was accompanied by a letter from Chief Stinson that said, "I hope you will succeed in getting this licence for us before the spring," when the fish would begin to spawn.[148]

The reaction from one band member at Rama, Sam Benson, to the news that his First Nation would be required to accept a licence from Ontario was poignant. He wrote that "as long as the rivers are flowing and the green grass grows and the Sun rises and sets the moon and Stars shining at nights ... for our race is our licence and will be forever flowing on certain limits of our reserves. The above will be cancelled if the Indians send in their applications to the province of Ontario. And then the Indians will pay licence to fish."[149]

Despite his knowledge of court decisions suggesting that provincial laws could not apply to Indian hunting, McLean advised First Nations peoples in a carefully worded letter that "I have to say it is held by the Provincial Government that the Indians are subject to the Game Laws to the same extent as white men. In this connection, the Province has been upheld by judicial decisions and you should be careful therefore to observe these laws as otherwise you leave yourself open to the penalties contained therein."[150] He made no mention of the fact that the federal government had a different view of the applicability of provincial laws.

By 1914, even in the sparsely populated and unsettled parts of the province, the legislative recognition of Indian treaty rights and rights in surrendered lands had been made a discretionary matter for provincial officials.[151] That discretion was clearly exercised to dissuade Indians from pursuing their traditional ways. For example, a 1914 request to the Indian Affairs Department by a member of the Algonquins of Golden Lake First Nation for a permit to fish at Clear Lake and trap muskrats was referred directly to Ontario. Victor Amicous, who was seventy-three, wrote sadly, "I am not able to go far away from home anymore. I am the only Indian on the Golden Lake Reserve who is trying to make his Living by Farming, but I have this year however, no Pork for the Winter. I am able to go to the above Lake [Clear Lake] and get some fish for myself and catch some Rats and Mink for a Week or Two."[152]

The Ontario Deputy Minister of Game and Fisheries responded that Ontario had decided to issue only a limited number of fishing licences to "settlers." If Amicous, whose status was now equated to that of a settler, wished to catch "herring" at Clear Lake, he would be required to pay a one-dollar fee for what amounted to a useless licence (because there were no herring in the lake) and to apply for the licence through his Indian Agent.[153]

Ontario continued its aggressive enforcement activities against Aboriginal peoples who exercised their treaty rights to hunt. In October 1914, Moses Commanda and his son, Barney, two Ojibway men from the Nipissing Band in northern Ontario, appeared before a High Court Justice in Sudbury facing charges of wounding a police officer with intent. The charges followed an incident in which provincial game wardens had entered the Commandas' reserve to charge them with illegally trapping beaver. Although the Commandas were exercising rights protected by the 1850 Robinson-Huron Treaty, the local magistrate sentenced them to a year in jail, just for possession of the furs, and then sent them on for criminal trial.[154] On appeal, and having heard the facts relating to the wounding charges, Justice Frank Latchford held that one of the game wardens had started the shooting, "and the only wounding that took place resulted from the fact that when one of the wardens had his revolver pointed at the younger Commanda, the father knocked it away with a stick, slightly injuring the game warden's hand."[155]

Although the Commandas were acquitted of the criminal charges, they were sent back to jail to finish their sentence for the illegal possession of furs. Justice Latchford appealed to both the Attorney General of Ontario and the Superintendent General of Indian Affairs to protest the "gross injustice" that had been done. Arguing that the Commandas' treaty rights should have been protected, he suggested that, on their behalf, Indian Affairs should claim compensation from the government for wrongful imprisonment:

> Under the Robinson-Huron Treaty which should be as sacred as any treaty, Shabokishick and his band to which the Commandas belonged – and other Indians inhabiting French River and Lake Nipissing – were accorded the full and free privilege to hunt over the territory which they ceded, in the same manner that they had heretofore been in the habit of doing. There seems to be no possible doubt as to the meaning of the Treaty in regard to the district in which the Commandas were hunting; and yet I find that the representatives of His Majesty, in violation of the Treaty made with His Majesty's predecessor, Queen Victoria, have interfered with the rights guaranteed by that Treaty and incarcerated the Indians for doing what they were given the right to do.[156]

The Commandas were eventually released by provincial Order-in-Council, but only after they had served well over two-thirds of their sentence.[157]

Meanwhile, the Province gained support from the federal government for its aggressive enforcement of both hunting and fishing laws. Perhaps not surprisingly, in light of its long-standing and narrow views of Aboriginal rights, Marine and Fisheries supported the provincial position that Aboriginal people had no special privileges except on their own reserves and only when domestic, not commercial, fishing was involved.

This position, put forward by the Deputy Minister of that Department, was again based on the old Whitcher correspondence and rooted in the erroneous legal opinions of James Cockburn and Adam Watson. As the Deputy Minister explained, "On looking over our files I found a letter from the Department of Marine and Fisheries at Ottawa to the Dep'ty Commissioner of Fisheries of Ontario which seems to define the position taken first of all by the Dept. of Marine and Fisheries and subsequently by this Dept. in which your Dept. appears to have acquiesced."[158] He added, "Indians have no exceptional privileges accorded them for commercial purposes and must comply with the fishery regulations in that respect as all other persons are bound to do. This would seem to respect the special rights of the Indians to take fish by any means and at any time for their own use strictly within their reserves, while placing them on the same footing as all other citizens of the Province while engaging in fishing as a business."[159]

In September 1916, after fishing in Lake Simcoe had been closed for the fall season, the Rama Band passed a resolution noting that "the Indians of Rama Reserve would like to know if they have the privilege to fish for their own use as this is a large part of their income for Rama Reserve."[160] The Rama Indian Agent forwarded the band's resolution to J.D. McLean, who in turn forwarded it to the Deputy Minister of Game and Fisheries in

Toronto.[161] McLean later informed the Indian Agent that the band's request had been refused by the Province.[162]

Provincial enforcement activities now precluded Aboriginal peoples from taking fish, even for food. Ralph Loucks, testifying many years later in the *Howard* case, recalled an incident that occurred in about 1919, when, at age six, he had gone fishing with his father. A game warden named Woodcock, who was stationed in Lakefield, "didn't charge anyone but he took half our fish. He took half our fish and left us the other half. That was prior to 1923."[163] The discriminatory nature of provincial policies is perhaps best evidenced by events at Georgina Island, where Ontario issued a licence to a white man, J. Garfunkle, to fish in the channel between the island and the mainland. Learning that Garfunkle had asked for permission to land his nets on its reserve, the Georgina Island Band objected.[164]

On asking for a copy of Garfunkle's licence,[165] Indian Affairs learned that the Province of Ontario had issued three seine licences to him. For its part, Ontario claimed to be unaware that the licences encroached on the reserve.[166] When J.D. McLean pointed out that these licences interfered with the rights of the Indians on the water frontage of their reserve,[167] the Acting Deputy Minister of Game and Fisheries asked him to submit a map showing the water frontage to which he thought the Indians were entitled.[168] However, when McLean duly sent the map, together with the Indian Agent's opinion that no licences should be issued to Garfunkle so as to "protect the fishing of both the Georgina and Snake Islands Indians,"[169] Ontario responded that "the Department cannot accept the water frontage which the Indians wish reserved ... Neither does the Department agree with your Indian Agent that no seine or net fishing should be granted to white men along the shore."[170]

When Ontario finally did change the location governed by Garfunkle's licences, it did so not because of the Indian Affairs claim, but because Garfunkle himself had determined that commercial fishing in the area was "unprofitable."[171]

However "unprofitable" the area was, Ontario refused to allow Aboriginal people to fish within it. When a member of the Georgina Island Band, Wellington Charles, sought permission to fish for carp – the same privilege given to Garfunkle – Ontario rejected his request. Asking Indian Affairs to intervene, Charles demonstrated that he had the support of the fish inspection advisor, who was willing to apply for the licence in his own name and assist him in selling the fish he caught.[172] McLean replied that the question of fishing privileges was entirely under the control of the provincial government.[173]

Overall, Ontario was able to prosecute Aboriginal people primarily because the Department of Indian Affairs was unwilling to defend them. Few Indians could pay fines, and most of those charged with hunting or fishing offences went to jail. According to Sidney L. Harring, one in four Indians from the Grand River reserve was jailed between 1873 and 1900. By 1906, the Kenora jail, in northern Ontario, was so full of Indians that it could no longer accommodate them.[174]

Frank Tough argues that, in claiming to know the "real interests" of the Indians while at the same time taking punitive action against them, Ontario hoped to shift Indian hunting skills toward guiding and to ensure the allocation of big game for sportsmen.[175] Others have suggested that the strong penalties were an attempt to force Indians to adopt white values.[176] Whatever the rationale may have been, the extent to which Ontario used its enforcement powers to prevent Aboriginal peoples from hunting and fishing is manifest throughout the record. Its ongoing efforts to shut Indians out of their traditional activities through legislation and increasingly punitive regulations were equally relentless.

Despite the recommendations of the Evans report only five years earlier that "shiftless" and "lazy" Indians be permitted to earn a livelihood through trapping, the *Ontario Game and Fisheries Act* was amended in 1914 to prevent muskrat trapping without a licence.[177] No such restrictions applied to white farmers and their sons who trapped in marshlands adjacent to their lands. The legislation had previously made no mention of Aboriginal peoples being excluded from marshes anywhere; now there were prohibitions against Indian trapping on private or leased lands.[178] The marshes, however, had been traditional Ojibway muskrat-trapping areas long before European farmers had arrived in North America, and the Ojibway protested bitterly at being denied access to areas they had always used.[179]

In 1916, the legislation was expanded to prevent *all* hunting and trapping of fur-bearing animals without a licence, but again exempted farmers and their sons who trapped or hunted in marshlands adjacent to their own property.[180] The Indian Agent for the Alnwick First Nation asked the Secretary of Indian Affairs to "intercede with the Dept. of Game and Fisheries Toronto to have them relax the law relating to trapping fur bearing animals." He pointed out that provincial game laws permitted farmers to put up signs, or "placard," the marshes adjoining their lands with "no trespassing" signs, and prevented Aboriginal hunters from entering lands they had traditionally used:

> As you are aware, Indians have to comply with the Regulations just the same as the white people, but ... no person can trap without a licence except farmers or their sons on their own land. Now in many cases, these Indians are unable to buy the Licence and those who do cannot trap, only in certain places, for the farmers placard their marshlands against trespassers who do, consequently the Indians are barred out as they have very little marsh land of their own. I may say further that I communicated with

the Department of Game and Fisheries Toronto last Fall but never had a reply ... A number of them are quite old people unable to do hard work and there is little to do at this time of year except a little wood cutting, which the younger men are employed at.[181]

The Hiawatha First Nation suffered from the placarding of marshlands by farmers at Rice Lake, a point it would raise during the 1923 Williams Treaties proceedings. R. McCamus, the band's Indian Agent, forwarded a Band Resolution to J.D. McLean in 1917, which complained that some farmers at the Otonabee, a river flowing into Rice Lake, had rented their marshland trapping rights to other white men, who then put up notices forbidding trespass. He explained, "The Indians have always had the privilege of trapping in those marshes and they are feeling very sore about being shut out."[182] McCamus asked that a man be sent down to investigate, or that a letter be written setting out very specifically what special rights the Rice Lake Indians had – "that is, if they have any other than what a white man has."[183]

Chief Alfred Crowe, who would later sign one of the Williams Treaties on behalf of the Hiawatha First Nation, wrote to Colonel Neil McNachten concerning the same issue. McNachten, the Secretary and Treasurer of the Canadian Patriotic Fund of the United Counties of Northumberland and Durham Branch, had a cottage at Rice Lake and had employed some First Nation members as guides. Chief Crowe told McNachten that he was thinking of consulting with "lawyer Hall" about his band's hunting rights, as he had been advised that the lawyer was "well acquainted with Indian Affairs and if he is, he would likely have the Treaty papers or papers regarding the hunting rights of our tribes." He added, "We are forbidden to hunt or trap on the Marsh lands of the Otonabee River and Rice Lake, which is all navigable water, also the main route of the Trent Valley, by notices prohibiting trespassing and hunting, by farmers who claim they own everything to clear water edge. Now on these marshes that we are prohibited from trespassing, the Indians of this Band have trapped for generations unmolested and which we have always understood was our legal hunting ground."[184]

In March 1917, McNachten wrote to J.D. McLean directly, asking him to send information about the treaties to Chief Crowe, with copies to him.[185] Ignoring the existence of the 1818 treaties, Indian Affairs replied that "the Department is not aware of any treaty entered into with the said Indians that contains a stipulation giving to them any special rights in the matter of hunting, trapping or fishing." By that time, Indian Affairs was in receipt of R.V. Sinclair's 1916 legal opinion upholding the Mississauga and Chippewa claim to Aboriginal title in the northern hunting grounds, but McLean told Chief Crowe in a carefully worded letter that Indians had no special hunting, trapping, or fishing rights under any *treaty*.[186] He made no mention of their rights to hunt and fish in lands still subject to their Aboriginal title.

Whereas Indian Affairs and the Department of Game and Fisheries consistently maintained that Aboriginal peoples needed a licence to trap in marshlands adjacent to their own reserves, McLean's letter nonetheless stated that in the view of the Department of Indian Affairs, white *farmers* had the right to trap exclusively in the marshlands adjacent to their lots without one, even though the legislation had conveyed no such right. In other words, Indian Affairs now took the position that water lots adjacent to private lands were owned by farmers, whether those waters had been expressly granted to them or not, and as a result, farmers could exclude Aboriginal peoples from trapping in them. At the same time, Indian Affairs asserted that Indians had no rights in the waters adjacent to their own unceded lands. Misrepresenting the outcome of the cases he had mentioned to Kelly Evans, McLean deliberately misled Chief Crowe, insisting that the courts supported his conclusions:

> Indians are held by the Department of Game and Fisheries to be subject to the Game Laws of the Province to the same extent as whitemen and this contention has been upheld by the courts in connection with prosecutions of Indians for offences against the provisions of these laws. As regards your claim to be allowed to enter upon the marsh lands of the Otonabee River and Rice Lake for the purpose of trapping or hunting, I have to say that as the property rights of the owners of lots on the mainland are understood to include the marsh attached to these lots, the owners thereof have the right to forbid trespassing thereon.[187]

Later that month, Ontario laid charges against Scugog Band members for trapping without a licence. Isaac Johnson, a Chief of the Scugog First Nation and a later signatory to the Williams Treaty on its behalf, wrote to the Superintendent General of Indian Affairs in May 1917 to complain that his 1818 treaty rights were not being respected: "The Game Warden of Scugog Island have summons one of the Indians to appear in court for trapping without a Licence there has been no explanation made to us on this subject from the Indian Department or the government. The Treaty that was made in 1818 was a provisional agreement since that time the Indians got their living from hunting and fishing as Chief of the Scugog Band I wish to know when did the government make a new Treaty this side of 1818. Hoping for an early reply."[188]

On 14 May 1917, Chief Joseph Whetung of Mud Lake told J.H. Burnham, his Member of Parliament, that he was "very anxious to obtain for my tribe the same privileges of fishing hunting trapping and selling furs without a licence that are granted to Indians north of Mattawa."[189] In response, Indian Affairs said, once again, that game laws were provincial and that it was therefore unable to grant any special privileges in connection with hunting, fishing, or trapping.[190] The Assistant Deputy Minister of Indian Affairs repeated that "these Indians have no rights in respect to hunting other than those granted to whites." He echoed the assimilationist policies of the Crown, saying, "I may add that it is considered that these Indians should occupy themselves with agricultural pursuits ... the Department is therefore not disposed to take up the matter of hunting privileges for them with the provincial government."[191]

Joseph Whetung sent another letter to his local Member of Parliament, J.H. Burnham, pointing out that he had written many times to Indian Affairs and had never received an answer. He asked Burnham to "see the proper persons and try and get the consent of the Department to the granting of our petition."[192] Burnham contacted Indian Affairs to find out what was going on. The Deputy Superintendent responded yet again that "the making and administering of the Game Laws come exclusively under the jurisdiction of the Provincial Governments." He added that the Department had endeavoured to secure "leniency" for the Indians to enable them to obtain a necessary food supply and that where its efforts had failed, this was due to the fact that "Indians in certain districts have not confined the killing of game to their requirements."[193]

According to the Deputy Superintendent, the Department recognized that the conditions brought about by the First World War would seriously affect Indians, and claimed it had brought the matter to provincial attention, obtaining a "relaxation of the game laws insofar as they related to Indians securing game for their own food supply." However, the Ontario Game and Fisheries Department had agreed only that Indians living in northern Ontario, north and west of the French and Mattawa Rivers and Lake Nipissing, could trap in those areas but only if they obtained a certificate from Indian Affairs. Indians living to the south and east of the Mattawa River were subject to the same game laws as white men. Despite knowing by this time that the Mississaugas had a genuine claim to Aboriginal title within these northern lands, Indian Affairs repeated, "The Department is unable to *grant* any special privileges to the Chemong [Mud] Lake Indians in the matter of hunting, trapping and fishing."[194]

Whetung persisted, writing to the Prime Minister in early 1919 to ask for the right to fish, hunt, trap, and sell furs without paying a licence fee. Howard Wallis, the Prime Minister's Secretary, replied that the matter would be placed in the hands of the Minister of Public Works for his attention.[195] Instead, the letter was passed on to Ontario.

Once again, the response came from the Deputy Minister of Game and Fisheries, who stated that Ontario's policy was not to demand a licence "from a Treaty Indian when trapping on his own reserve" but that "if you desire to trap without restrictions as to location you will be required to purchase a trapper's licence at a fee of $5.00."[196] One Mud Lake elder, Alex Knott, remembered that before this, there "was no such thing as a trapline. You could trap clear across Ontario."[197]

Having been told by Indian Affairs that his First Nation had no special rights, Chief Alfred Crowe signed another Band Resolution with Henry Cowie, another later signatory to the 1923 Williams Treaty for Hiawatha, asking "if they [Indian Affairs] will send us a man to Hiawatha who is acquainted with the hunting rights of the Indians as our trapping grounds along the Otonabee River where we trapped always unmolested and now notices have been put up all along the marshes prohibiting hunting & trapping and we want him to bring the Treaty book pertaining to hunting rights along with him and we wish him to come at once as the trapping season is open."[198] It does not appear that the two men received a response.

In 1913, Frank Pedley had been forced to resign from his position as Deputy Superintendent General of Indian Affairs because of improper speculation on the sale of Indian lands. He was replaced by Duncan Campbell Scott. Though best known as a poet, Scott was also a firm believer in the "great civilizing mission of the British Empire," namely, the transformation of Indians into a "civilized" state.[199] Because of this, Scott maintained that Ottawa should not interfere with provincial attempts to subject Indians to the same laws as non-Aboriginal residents of the province.

Scott prepared a lengthy memo to Arthur Meighen, the Minister of the Interior, observing that despite the express reservation of hunting and fishing rights in the Robinson-Huron and Robinson-Superior Treaties, Ontario had taken the position that the treaties were not binding. Scott referred to J.M. Gibson's 1899 view that this stance was in the "best interests" of Indians, as "the destruction of game would otherwise be unrestricted and would deprive the Indians of what to them is an important means of livelihood."[200] Indian Affairs, Scott noted, had responded to Ontario by pointing out that, though the federal government did not necessarily agree that the treaties were "subject to any legislation that Ontario might see fit to enact," it would not object to any reasonable legislation being applied to Indians.[201]

The question of whether treaties could be subject to provincial legislation had been referred to the Justice Department for an opinion. That Department had responded that the question was one of policy, not law. Despite his views that Indians were better off if they gave up their traditional activities, Scott suggested to Meighen that Ottawa could use its own constitutional authority over "Indians and Lands Reserved for the Indians" to regulate Aboriginal hunting and fishing, should Ontario refuse to pass laws respecting treaty rights. In fact, he noted that, should the federal government fail to do so, it might not be acting in accordance with its fiduciary obligations to Indians, and "In not insisting on the alleged rights of the Indians to hunt and fish as set forth in the Robinson Treaties, this government is of course open to a charge of breach of faith with the Indians ... the alternative appears to be to have Game Laws passed by the Dominion Government if the Provincial Government should be unwilling to pass such Game Laws as may be satisfactory to this Department."[202]

Meighen dismissed out of hand Scott's assertion that Aboriginal harvesting fell within federal, rather than provincial jurisdiction. Instead, he replied that "the view expressed by the Justice Department that there is nothing now ripe for the consideration of Judicial Tribunals, but only a subject of policy for the determination of this Department, is the right view. The constitutional power of the Province to regulate fishing and hunting, even as applicable to Indians, is undoubted. The question remaining is, as to how far this Department should, as representing the Indians, endeavour to modify the actual application of Provincial regulations in deference to the Robinson treaties as affecting such Indians."[203]

Meighen agreed, however, that the "territorial limits" in treaties should be protected and that any restrictions on Aboriginal hunting and fishing activities should be consistent with "the full and permanent enjoyment of these rights."[204] Nonetheless, in his view, the territorial protection afforded by treaties ended at the limits of Indian reserves. He insisted that "The Indian *outside* his reserve must comply with any Provincial restrictions with respect to hunting or the preservation of game – On the reserve itself, I am disposed to think the Indian is not so restricted and his Aboriginal rights to hunt in that reserve are quite free from any Provincial law. I do not want to give that case a final opinion but that is my opinion."[205] In connection with off-reserve hunting, Meighen concluded that "Game laws that are made for the reasonable protection of game are in the highest degree in harmony with these rights ... our agent should endeavour to make this point of view clear to the Indians and to urge them to comply with Provincial laws."[206]

For the First Nations in Ontario, the effects of the First World War had created additional hardship. Many First Nations men had enlisted, including all of the eligible men in the Cape Croker Band.[207] Francis Pagahmagabow of Parry Island, Johnson Paudash of Rice Lake, and Samson and Peter Comego of Alderville (Alnwick) would all become decorated soldiers and noted sharpshooters during the war, but many others did not return home.[208] Of the 292 members of the Six Nations at Brantford who enlisted, for example, 53 died, 55 were wounded, and 1 went missing.[209]

The 1918 *Report on Indian Affairs* referred to the "inspiring fact that these descendants of the Aboriginal inhabitants of a land so recently appropriated by our own ancestors should voluntarily sacrifice their lives on European battlefields, side by side with men of our own race, for the preservation of the ideals of our civilization."[210] Despite these fine sentiments, the Ontario government continued to charge and jail Indians for exercising their traditional rights. The 1915 case of Pierre Hunter, an Ojibway from Sioux Lookout, is just one example. Sentenced to jail time for hunting moose out of season, he was released from prison in the middle of winter with no money, and froze to death.[211] Asked to file a report about his death, George Fanning, the Ontario Game and Fish Officer who had arrested him, reported that he had no regrets, as "sending him to jail done him no harm ... but it did the Indians around here considerable good."[212]

Similar prosecutions took place in all regions of the province. The Grand General Indian Council met at Christian Island in 1918, pointing out that "more tribes of Indians are now included in the Game Laws of the Country which renders them helpless to secure their living."[213] Conditions were particularly desperate, since farmland on most southern Ontario reserves was poor, and Aboriginal peoples could not afford the machinery necessary to farm commercially. Under Indian Affairs policies, they were forced to sell their livestock to raise funds to purchase cars, but "once they had parted with their cattle, they could obtain no replacements."[214]

Despite these stark realities, Indian Affairs continued to promote agriculture. As Edward S. Rogers notes, some Aboriginal people migrated to urban centres, whereas others eked out an existence through seasonal employment in the lumber camps, on the railroads, as commercial fishermen, and as domestics, while continuing to procure much of their food from hunting, fishing, and gardening.[215] Obtaining subsistence from traditional activities became more difficult, however, as Ontario introduced additional restrictions, such as a new limit on the number of wild ducks that could be harvested, even for food.[216]

As the Royal Commission on Aboriginal Peoples comments, in asserting their trapping rights, Aboriginal peoples in northern Ontario did have one powerful supporter – the Hudson's Bay Company. In 1910, a Hudson's Bay manager at a northern post was convicted of the illegal possession of beaver furs that he had purchased from treaty Indians. The company defended him on the basis that provincial game legislation preventing treaty Indians from selling furs was unconstitutional. The company's lawyer, Leighton McCarthy, announced he was prepared to appeal the conviction all the way to the Privy Council, if necessary.[217]

The parties agreed in 1913 to put the legal issue directly to the Ontario Court of Appeal. Chief Justice William Meredith informed them a year later that he considered it best not to render a decision, and urged Ontario and the company to negotiate a deal instead.[218] McCarthy later claimed that Indian Affairs did not want the Court to find that treaty harvesting rights prevailed over Ontario's game laws.[219]

Eventually, regulations were negotiated by Ontario with the company. Through Orders-in-Council, Aboriginal peoples in northern parts of Ontario would be allowed to trap under individual quotas and by a special individual identification system allowing treaty Indians to trap without a licence. The new regime applied only to the north, however. Indians elsewhere in the province still required standard trapping licences.[220]

Although he resided south of the agreed-upon line, Daniel Whetung Jr., the Chief at Mud Lake, immediately wrote to the Indian Affairs Department asking for a certificate "to show that I am a treaty Indian etc."[221] In October 1921, J.D. McLean responded, "In reply, I have to state that you are an Indian of the Mud Lake Band and your number on the pay-list is 41."[222]

In March of the following year, Chief Whetung sent a letter to Indian Affairs indicating that "Indians here are having a pretty hard time of it"; the "winter has been long and no work – Can we catch fish (bass/grien) around near the reserve – for our use until the trapping starts we are starving for something to eat."[223] He received the standard response: the Department had no jurisdiction over the matter of Indian food fishing near the reserve. The Chief was told to write to the provincial Department of Game and Fisheries at Toronto.[224] However, the former Chief, Joseph Whetung, had already contacted Ontario, sending a petition signed by "many of the Indians" on the reserve to the Premier asking for hunting and trapping privileges. He had been told by the Province that he needed the consent of the Department of Indian Affairs at Ottawa "before the Toronto government will grant our request."[225]

As each government insisted that only the other had jurisdiction over the issues of Aboriginal harvesting, the Indians and their Indian Agents were shuffled back and forth between federal and provincial representatives. W.J. Kay, the Indian Agent at Sutton West, asked the provincial government for information as to what privileges the Indians had to fish in Lake Simcoe. He was told by the Game and Fisheries Department that they had none. Disbelieving, he wrote to Indian Affairs asking that his superiors "Kindly send me by return mail full particulars regarding Indians fishing in Lake Simcoe that is what privileges they have over a white man. I have asked the Game and Fisheries Dept. they only sent me a pamphlet of Laws etc. with no exemptions to Indians which I understood they have."[226] J.D. McLean repeated his often-stated position that "Indians as such have no special fishing privileges in the Province of Ontario."[227]

Part 2
The Williams Treaties

6
The Push for a New Treaty

The Canada-Ontario Agreement

For more than sixty years, the Mississaugas and Chippewas had been prevented from hunting and trapping within their unceded northern territories by white squatters, by provincial policies and laws, and by federal inaction. By the time of the 1916 Sinclair opinion upholding its Aboriginal title to those grounds, the Rama Band's northern hunting territories had been completely hunted out by white men. Chief Alder York, a signatory to the 1923 Williams Treaty on behalf of Rama, testified in 1923 that members of his band generally hunted "just around here ... They go to ancient hunting limit, but since the fur is killed out, the Indians don't go very far like they used to."[1] A clearer manifestation of the success of the Crown's assimilation policy could hardly be found.

In 1920, the Assistant Deputy Minister of Justice, W. Stuart Edwards, claiming that "pressures of work arising from the war" had prevented his Department from reviewing Sinclair's report, finally informed J.D. McLean that he had accepted Sinclair's conclusions.[2] Once an agreement with the Province was reached, he wrote, the federal government would be in a position to negotiate with the Indians, "unless, indeed, the Dominion is willing to assume some further responsibility upon its own behalf."[3] As for the unceded northern area, Edwards confirmed that there was no evidence of a surrender by any other band.[4]

The Mississauga and Chippewa First Nations were not informed for several more years that Ottawa had finally accepted their claim. In the meantime, they continued to press the government to address it. In September 1920, a member of the Christian Island Band wrote to the Deputy Superintendent General of Indian Affairs to say that he had "three times went to Rama Indian Reservation to see Yellowhead whose Grandfather had signed the surrender of lands to the Government and ask him to go with me and interview the Department of Indian Affairs regarding the old promises made to our Grand fathers by Government ... it is time the Government should compensate the Indians for their lands as there are many poor Indians who need the fulfillment of the promise the Government made to them."[5]

Yet another Chippewa delegation formed of members from the Christian Island, Rama, and Georgina Island Bands was sent to Ottawa to resubmit a "Hunting grounds" claim to Indian Affairs.[6] They had evidently heard of the Sinclair report, as the bands also passed a resolution trying to get a copy of a report concerning the "Hunting Ground – claims of the United Bands which it is understood to have been completed a few years ago."[7] McLean refused to comply and withheld other information they had requested in connection with their claim.[8]

On 15 November 1920, Johnson Paudash asked McLean for a map of the Indian surrenders affecting the Rice, Mud, and Scugog Lake Bands, as well as the Mississaugas of Alnwick, the Mississaugas of New Credit, and the "Chippays" of Lakes Huron and Simcoe.[9] In typically misleading fashion, McLean told him that there was no "published" map that could be sent to him, despite the fact that Sinclair had collected and reviewed a variety of materials, including many unpublished maps, in connection with his report.[10]

In 1921, McLean finally informed Chief Bigwin and Sampson George of Rama that the Chippewa claim had been referred to the Justice Department.[11] On 5 December of that year, Ottawa forwarded a copy of the Sinclair report, together with one of the supposedly non-existent maps showing the tract of unsurrendered land, to the Ontario Attorney General. In an accompanying letter, it asked Ontario to join it in establishing a treaty commission of inquiry to determine the extent and validity of the claim.[12] Less than three weeks later, the federal government received a positive response from Ontario. In light of the size of the territory, which was "a very large and important area of this Province," Ontario agreed to join the inquiry, "on the understanding that the question of provision for settlement of the claims should be left in abeyance until a claim has been fully established."[13]

Unaware of this development, the Rama, Georgina Island, and Christian Island Bands retained A.G. Chisholm, a lawyer from London, Ontario. Chisholm had represented the Six Nations the previous year as an intervenor in the appeal of *Sero v. Gault,* a case involving a Mohawk woman charged with the illegal possession of a fishing net in the waters of her reserve. In that case, Chisholm had unsuccessfully challenged the federal delegation of fisheries authority to the Province.[14] Although he lost the case, Chisholm, a prominent activist in Aboriginal legal matters, was a good choice.

Once again, McLean blocked First Nations access to counsel by trying to hold back their funds. In April 1922, he told Chief Frank Copegog at Christian Island that the band's trust monies could not be used for such a purpose and that Chisholm's retainer had not been approved by the Department.[15] Ignoring the Department's refusal to allow them to use their own funds to pay for their own lawyer, members of the Christian Island Band took up a collection to pay for their lawyer themselves.[16]

With Ontario's agreement in hand, the Department of Justice retained lawyer Oliver Mowat Biggar, more commonly referred to as O.M. Biggar, to negotiate the arrangements with the Province.[17] Colonel Biggar, an Edmonton lawyer, would later become the Judge-Advocate General in Ottawa. Appointed as Canada's first Chief Electoral Officer as well, he went on to become the Attorney General of Alberta.[18]

The Department notified Chisholm that his retainer was now unnecessary, since "a solicitor [Biggar] has been appointed to take up this claim on behalf of these Indians."[19] Prophetically, Chisholm warned the Superintendent General of Indian Affairs, Charles Stewart, that the Christian Island Band had a "natural right ... to choose their own counsel" and that, in the event of "an unfortunate determination of the claim," it would "inevitably blame your Department."[20]

In August, Chief Bigwin was told that the claim was "in the hands of a lawyer appointed by the Department of Justice who is investigating the matter with a view, if possible, of effecting a settlement with the Ontario Government. There is no necessity, therefore, of your coming to Ottawa again unless you are sent for by this Department."[21] Chief Henry Jackson of the Christian Island Band was also informed that the matter was in Biggar's hands.[22] Biggar, however, was not acting as counsel for the First Nations, but for the Government of Canada in its negotiations with Ontario. He never met with the First Nations and was never once present during the later treaty negotiations.

Ontario agreed that a formal agreement should be entered into outlining the terms for the appointment of a treaty commission.[23] W.C. Cain, the Deputy Minister of the provincial Lands and Forests Department, approved the terms of a draft agreement prepared by Biggar but with one additional demand.[24] The Province wanted a clause providing that if the Indians on any reserves set aside for them under the surrender became "extinct," the reserve lands were to revert back to the Province of Ontario.[25]

As these arrangements proceeded, the Mississaugas and Chippewas continued to push for a recognition of their existing rights to hunt and trap. At Mud Lake, during his testimony before the Treaty Commissioners in 1923, former Chief Joseph Whetung produced a letter of 9 May 1922 from J.D. McLean to himself.[26] Whetung had been part of a delegation sent to Ottawa to discuss hunting, fishing, and trapping rights. He had been accompanied by Henlon (Hanlon) Howard and Chief Robert Paudash of Hiawatha. The three were authorized by band resolution to go to Ottawa and "interview the proper authorities relative to hunting and fishing rights of the United Bands," and to take with them "any papers that ex-Chief Whetung may have in his possession and proving beneficial to the three united Bands."[27] Alfred McCue, a later signatory to the 1923 Williams Treaty, certified the resolution.[28]

According to a local minister who assisted the bands, a three-day meeting about trapping rights in Rice Lake, most likely the one referred to by the old Chief, resulted in a commitment from Duncan Campbell Scott that Indian Affairs "would protect the Indians by law enforcement and money" unless they were trespassing or breaching the close seasons.[29] Despite this promise of protection, as the muskrat season opened in the spring of 1923, there was escalating conflict between white farmers and Aboriginal trappers.[30] This time, shots were fired.

On 15 October 1923, I.E. Weldon, the lawyer for the Rice, Mud, and Scugog Lake Bands, wrote to Angus Seymour Williams, more commonly known as A.S. Williams, the newly appointed chairman of the treaty commission established to inquire into the claims. He advised Williams that "In the spring, at the opening of the muskrat trapping season, there was a row between a number of white men and the Indians. The white men lay in ambush and shot the Indians with shot guns, accusing the Indians of spearing muskrats in the muskrat houses. The Indians summonsed the white men before the criminal courts for shooting with intent and wounding, with the result that the white men were fined a very trifling amount. The Indians were then summonsed for illegally destroying muskrat houses and were all seven of them fined."[31]

Almost simultaneously, Ottawa and Ontario signed the Canada-Ontario Agreement to enter into new treaty negotiations with the Chippewas and Mississaugas.[32] In it, Ontario agreed to "concur in such Treaty as shall be negotiated by the said Commissioners."[33] The federal Cabinet was briefed about the agreement and the claim of the Chippewa and Mississauga Tribes that their rights to hunt and fish "in a certain area in the Province of Ontario, extending northwards and eastwards from Lake Simcoe and comprising some 10,719 square miles of territory [had] never been surrendered."[34] An Order-in-Council was passed on 23 June 1923 authorizing the Canada-Ontario Agreement to be signed by the Superintendent General of Indian Affairs.[35]

The Williams Treaties Commission

The Province of Ontario selected two of the three treaty commission members, and Canada chose the third. Ontario selected R.V. Sinclair, the Justice Department lawyer who had earlier upheld the validity of the claim, and Uriah McFadden, a lawyer in private practice at Sault Ste. Marie who had been a federal Post Office employee.[36] Canada chose A.S. Williams, the departmental solicitor for Indian Affairs, as the commission's chairman.[37]

The terms of the commission enabled it to investigate only some 10,719 square miles extending from the forty-fifth parallel to north of Lake Nipissing and from Georgian Bay east to the Ottawa River, the area claimed by the First Nations as the ancient hunting grounds of their ancestors. The territory was described as parts of the counties of Renfrew, Hastings, Haliburton, Muskoka, Parry Sound, and Nipissing, bounded by the lands included in the treaties of 1818, 1822, and 1850, a description that was clearly intended to prevent the Commissioners from considering the lands already surrendered under these early treaties. Under the *Inquiries Act,* the Treaty Commissioners had the power to summon any witnesses they wished and to require them to give evidence under oath and to produce documents. They were also authorized to engage the services of accountants, engineers, technical advisors, and other experts, as well as clerks, reporters, and assistants. They were to report their opinions, as well as the result of their treaty negotiations, to the Superintendent General of Indian Affairs.[38]

Under section 12 of the *Act,* the Commissioners also had the power to enable any party with an interest in the proceedings to be represented by a lawyer. Despite this authority, they denied virtually all attempts by the First Nations to have counsel represent them. For example, I.E. Weldon wrote to the Attorney General of Ontario on 20 September 1923 asking for permission to attend the inquiry to assist his clients, the Mississaugas of Rice, Mud, and Scugog Lakes, "in getting evidence, material etc. prepared ... Some of my clients are of the impression that this commission would not hear Counsel."[39] Although he had written to Ontario well before the inquiry began, Weldon was advised by Indian Affairs only after the Commissioners had finished hearing evidence that he would not be permitted to appear, as it was not the "normal policy" of Indian Affairs to allow legal counsel for Indians to be heard.[40]

In September 1923, a local newspaper reported that "an inquiry into the title of over 10,000 square miles of land in the Province of Ontario has been authorized by Order-in-Council. The inquiry is the result of a claim by the Indians of the Chippewa and Mississauga Tribes that all the Indian title to these lands has never been transferred to the Crown. The lands involved in the claim are situated in the northern portions of the counties of Renfrew Hastings, Haliburton and the Districts of Muskoka, Parry Sound and Nipissing, and the area is placed in the Order-in-Council at 10,719 square miles."[41]

MP Manley Chew congratulated J.D. McLean for reaching an agreement with Ontario. He suggested that before the "Committee" made a final settlement, it should perhaps meet with the Chiefs of the different bands and "hear their views on the case. I think this would be a very wise move, and no doubt the Indians would be grateful for the consideration. It would leave the impression that the Commission were anxious to do what is right in the matter."[42]

In August, shortly before the inquiry began, the provisions of the Canada-Ontario Agreement were brought to the attention of the First Nations. The

Indian Agents for the bands were directed to explain to them that the inquiry would relate to "a large tract of land ... which has been opened up for settlement but with respect to which no release of the Indian title of occupation has ever been taken by the Crown from the Indians."[43] Arthur S. Anderson, the Indian Agent at Rama, immediately called a Special Meeting of Council to inform his band of the developments,[44] as did Indian Agent W.J. Kay at Sutton West.[45]

On the first day of hearings at Georgina Island, the Commissioners explained the limits of their authority. A transcript of the proceedings, prepared by the commission's recording secretary, Indian Affairs stenographer Kathleen Moodie, states that the Commissioners said they were present "to take evidence concerning a claim for compensation for the *unsurrendered* Northern Hunting Grounds ... more fully described as the Hunting Grounds lying North of line 45 to the height of land near Lake Nipissing."[46]

A.S. Williams explained to the members of the Georgina Island First Nation that a claim had been asserted by the Mississauga and Chippewa Bands to "a large tract of territory ... which they allege comprised in earlier days the Hunting Grounds of the tribes mentioned and which apparently was never surrendered." Williams explained the agreement between Ottawa and Ontario, and added that "Under this Agreement, these Commissioners are authorized to investigate the claims of the Indians in regard to this territory and if the claims are established, to negotiate a Treaty of Surrender."[47]

To ensure that this was well understood, the Commissioners confirmed that, as the inquiry proceeded, "addresses were delivered by the Chair and members of the Commission at Georgina Island and at all reserves which were visited, designed to instruct the Indians as to the nature of the claim which in the event of its being surrendered, they would be asked to surrender."[48]

A careful review of the evidence and exchanges that took place during the proceedings reveals that the Commissioners clearly confined their focus to the former hunting grounds that had never been surrendered. Lands that had already been surrendered were not discussed, nor were currently used hunting grounds. Only the ancient ones were at issue. To emphasize this point, the Commissioners used a large map of Ontario that showed, within a boundary, the area said to correspond to the ancient hunting grounds, and they "plotted upon the map the various hunting limits which the evidence established had been occupied and used."[49] As witnesses testified, the old hunting grounds they described were marked off on the map with bold lines.

From the outset, Williams informed the Indians that the issue concerned not their treaty rights but their unceded lands. To establish their claim, he explained, "what you need to establish is that the territory in question was *formerly* the Hunting Ground of this tribe."[50] This point is apparent on the title page of the commission evidence transcript as well, which describes the "Evidence Taken by the Joint Commission appointed by The Dominion of Canada and the Province of Ontario in the Matter of Claim for compensation for *unsurrendered Northern Hunting Grounds* made by the Chippewas of Georgina Island, Christian Island and Rama and the Mississaugas of Scugog, Chemong, Rice Lake and Alnwick."[51]

The commission moved from community to community, beginning with the Chippewa First Nations at Georgina Island, Rama, and Christian Island, and ending with the Mississauga Nations at Scugog, Mud Lake, Hiawatha (Rice Lake), and Alnwick. Many of the witnesses who testified later signed the Williams Treaties. Of the five signatories from Georgina Island, for example, two had testified before the commission. One of these was the former Chief Charles Big Canoe, then some ninety years old. The 1871 census had listed him as a farmer, but Big Canoe told the Commissioners that though he had tried farming he was still engaged in trapping.[52] According to this elderly witness, his band had stopped using the northern area as a regular hunting ground when it moved to Georgina Island in 1859, although it still used it from time to time. Big Canoe said that his people "were very attentive of keeping their limits, like a farmer would be. They don't want anyone to hunt in their grounds."

John E. Big Canoe, the current Chief, testified that he too had moved from Snake Island to Georgina Island in 1859. Like Charles Big Canoe, he described his hunting territories in terms of proprietary rights, indicating that one branch of the Holland River, which flows into Lake Simcoe, belonged to his grandfather and the other to his great-uncle. The Commissioners informed him that the rivers south of Lake Simcoe were not within their mandate and were "not any part of the land we are talking about today." The current Chief remembered his father and grandfather going north to hunt. He himself still hunted deer in the northern area around Lake Joseph, where "there are no farmers ... [because] it is all rock." On his last trip to the "Old Hunting Ground," as he called it, he complained that Ontario had allowed his party to hunt deer only. He concluded by saying that "our people have been agitating the Government a good many years about this thing and the Department has promised from time to time that they would look after it as best they can and that the Indians would get fair treatment and be paid."[53]

James Ashquabe testified that he was "trying to farm a little" and that few band members now hunted on Georgina Island. The Commissioners found this "very strange," since Williams' own first memories were of "seeing the Indians around my home going off hunting." However, as Ashquabe explained, except for rabbits, no game was left on the island. These days, hunting took place off-reserve only.[54]

Benjamin Esquabe, a hunter and fisherman[55] who believed he was either seventy-four or seventy-five years old, told the inquiry that Lieutenant-Governor Simcoe had reserved a hunting area specifically for the Chippewas that ran from Moose Deer Point along the coast of Georgian Bay. He had met an elderly white man years earlier who had pointed out the rods and posts that Simcoe had used to set the limit. The white man had told Esquabe "that Governor Simcoe, he stand there on that spot and he done this (spreading his arms wide) and he say the line went in that direction and it shall belong on one side for the Chippewas Indians for their hunting grounds."

James Snake, frightened of the Commissioners, refused to take the oath for fear they might hang him after he gave evidence.[56] His father, who had been a hunter and fisherman,[57] had done his hunting of deer, mink, muskrat, "and fish hunting too, if you like ... around here." He himself had heard of the "big claim," and added "they would like to have it settled some time because it's been standing this many years and not paid for."[58]

After Snake completed his evidence, the Commissioners recalled Chief John Big Canoe, to ask him about the reserved hunting area south of Lake Simcoe that some witnesses had mentioned, and that had apparently not been surrendered. Big Canoe described the land as including West Gwillimbury "from the river that turns into Lake Simcoe ... Georgina Township and part of Scott Township and North Gwillimbury also."[59] This area, composed of seven townships, was described by many witnesses as hunting grounds reserved by Lieutenant-Governor Simcoe for their use under treaty.

The Commissioners then visited Rama. There would be six signatories to the treaty from Rama, and all six, including Chief Alder York, testified during the proceedings. Most witnesses at Rama told the commission that they relied on hunting and fishing. Former Chief J.B. Stinson, for example, said that he worked primarily as a guide but continued to hunt for his own purposes around Muskoka Lake and Lake Joseph. He described how his grandfather, Chief Joseph Benson (J.B.) Nanigishkung, had hunted up at the height of lands near Lake Nipissing every spring and fall. When Chief Stinson mentioned hunting along the Black River, the Commissioners prevented him from continuing: "That is in surrendered territory ... We want to find out the hunting limits in this territory that is *not* surrendered."[60]

Gilbert Williams, a fisherman, councillor, and also a signatory to the 1923 Williams Treaty involving Rama, testified that as a small boy, he used to carry a dozen traps back and forth for his father on the northern trips. They had camped at the mouth of the Muskoka River, often spending three to four weeks on each trip in the spring and fall. He said he still relied on trapping for a living and had a little house in Port Carling, where he hunted and kept his traps. Williams caught mostly "Small game. I did get beaver but they say I can't now. I get muskrat and mink, too ... Lots of [partridge] and ducks and geese, and fish, fine trout ... Bass, pike too. Good fishing country."[61]

Similarly, William Ingersoll told the Commissioners that he was still a trapper and that he hunted "not far from here."[62]

Joseph Yellowhead, now eighty years old, said he had always hunted. He told of going with his grandfather from Rama to Sparrow Lake and up to Muskoka. These hunting grounds, containing moose, beaver, otter, muskrat, marten, mink, and "all kinds of fur," were quite large: the Nanigishkung family's limit was at least fifty miles and the Shilling family's perhaps one hundred miles around. He himself had stopped going up to Lake Muskoka because "you see, white people are hunting all through our country and then we had to quit."[63] Later, the Rama Band would claim that, during the 1923 treaty negotiations, the Commissioners had promised these areas would be reserved.

Alex Ingersoll agreed that "now the white people come in my country and kill my game and I got to work in the land now like a farmer. I have not hunt for nine years. I guess I got enough of hunting. There's nothing in it anymore on account of them white people that come and take it all." However, he still hunted: "I hunt that west branch from Bracebridge away up and we get beaver, otter, muskrat, deer, bears and away back that way a little north we caught wolf and marten."[64]

Elijah Yellowhead's hunting limits were a little closer to Rama. He told the commission that "the Rama Indians belongs to that territory for hunting," but that "when the government have that land, tho', we never go there." Yellowhead produced three tickets to the House of Commons gallery to show that he had been to Ottawa personally to see the government about the claim.[65]

Former Chief John Bigwin, the next witness, explained that the Chippewas were made up of three tribes, namely, the Oak, Bear, and Reindeer Tribes, and that the Oak Tribe had limits up the Black River. Commissioner Williams again cautioned that the "Black River is out of the territory under discussion. That was surrendered in 1818." Asked if he knew how the Chippewas first got the land, Chief Bigwin responded, "Yes, and I got it yet. The white men did not get my hunting ground from me yet." Although the land may have been surrendered, the Chief clearly believed that he had retained treaty rights in his traditional hunting grounds.

Like an earlier witness, Bigwin pointed out that the hunting grounds had boundaries upon which Aboriginal people would not trespass: "We don't go over the lines like you people do, we keep our own hunting grounds. With our hunting grounds, we are like farmers with their fences, we would not think of going over our boundary any more than they would plow up another fellow's field." He explained that he sought other resources as well, such as the birch bark that he used to make canoes. Although he was seventy-eight years old, he still hunted, but he complained that white men interfered with his yearly hunting: "Yes, I hunt once in a while ... but the white man get him all. They use the steel traps and they go bang-snap like that and they get him all."[66] Well into his nineties, Chief Bigwin would insist that during the Williams Treaty negotiations with his band, the Commissioners had promised that his existing treaty rights to hunt and fish would not be affected by the new treaties.

Chief Bigwin's camping ground was on Bigwin Island, about sixty miles from the reserve, where he grew a little corn and potatoes. He described it as "the headquarters of the Bigwin family, my family, my island." He produced a map, given to him years before by J.D. McLean, which identified the hunting ground specifically. Long ago, the old Chief said, "before I understand the white people's talk, my grandfather told me, when you find Indians with hunting grounds, give him his reserve, keep off it. But I should have asked this old man before he died where these reserves are. This [Chief Alder] York, he is too young to know where."

Jonas George (Wa-sha-gee-siks), seventy-seven, whose evidence was interpreted for the Commissioners, had never seen any Aboriginal person from outside Rama hunt within the tribe's limits. Like many of the other Rama witnesses, he had dried and sold his furs at Minden, in the Kawartha Lakes chain.[67]

Another elder, Sampson Ingersoll, aged seventy-five, told the Commissioners that his father used to hunt down by Sparrow Lake and Koshee Lake, areas that Rama would also later say had been reserved to it in the 1923 surrender. As for lands included in the Robinson-Huron Treaty, Ingersoll testified that he "heard the Chippewa Nation should belong with them other Indians in the Robinson treaty ... We were licensed to that, it was ours."[68] Williams, demonstrating his lack of familiarity with the relevant treaties, asked him if the elders had ever told him that the "Hurons" had a right to the lands covered by this treaty. Not surprisingly, given that the Robinson-Huron Treaty referred to Lake Huron, not the Huron Nation, Ingersoll didn't think they did.

Sampson Yellowhead's family, which had hunted twenty-five miles back on both sides of the rivers, "hunt on the way as we go, too." He said the western end of the tribe's limits was near Coldwater and Penetang (Penetanguishene), "and it turns there and goes towards Nipissing ... toward the height of lands." Yellowhead raised the question of timber in the area of the claim, saying "You sell my timber without ask the Indian Chiefs, see? I would like to know which of you three fellows comes from the Government? ... Well, you fellows, you sell my timber and you not ask Chief Bigwin could you do so. When you sell my animals, my deers and my ducks and everything, you get for yourselves enemies, and I have to quit my hunting over there on my own grounds because I was pretty near shot when I was there last."[69]

Sam Snake (Snache), who interpreted for the Commissioners during these proceedings,[70] described the boundaries of the tribe as south to Balsam Lake (a Kawartha Lake), "not in the lake but on the mountain, and then westward along Talbot river until it strikes somewhere in Oro township, which I think is the line of what was surrendered in 1818 and along that line toward Penetang point and from there until it strikes Moose Deer Point again."[71]

Corroborating turn-of-the century reports that hunting territories were hereditary, David Simcoe testified that his father had left him his hunting ground when he died.

When Chief Alder York testified, he said that members of his band still hunted regularly, both around Rama and up north. A.S. Williams asked if any band members still went to the ancient limits. York replied, "Yes. But you know, since the fur is killed out, the Indians don't go very far. Not like they used to."[72] York's own family hunting grounds were at Balsam Lake. Like earlier witnesses, he was told by the Commissioners, "Well, that is not in the district we are talking of ... I suppose you know the area we are talking about. I will show it to you." Williams pointed out the boundaries on the Commissioners' map and asked Chief York if he was aware of the existence of the claim. "Oh my yes," York responded. "We have been crying about it for 70 years or more. I don't know if you are going to settle it now or not. Are you?"[73]

Other Rama witnesses mentioned Balsam Lake specifically, as part of their ancient grounds. Sampson George testified that he had camped on an island in Balsam Lake for about a year one time and had hunted all around "maybe 25 miles back and around, not only along the shore but back deer hunting." He and his group had portaged to Koshog where they had camped for two years and hunted. He remembered the areas because "I know them places. I hunt the poles for the wigwams, long ago, and I remember what I see. That was my job, to hunt the poles for the wigwams." He too described getting otter, beaver, deer, some bears, and "lots of muskrats in them days."[74]

At the conclusion of the Rama evidence, a "Mr. Tudhope, Barrister of Orillia, made a statement regarding the claims of the Indians, suggesting to them that they should make only reasonable demands. Mr. McFadden replied to this address."[75] At least one lawyer, then, was present to represent Rama at the hearings, although how he had obtained permission to attend is unknown. Still, the presence of Melvin B. Tudhope at the proceedings is important, since it means that at least one independent lawyer heard the Commissioners repeatedly insist that the commission had no interest in previously ceded lands.

On 17 September, the Commissioners took evidence from the Christian Island Band. Band member Walter Simon was sworn as an interpreter for the first witness, Thomas Kadegegwon (Spotted Feather). Kadegegwon, aged eighty-four, testified that he had moved from Beausoleil Island to Christian

Island about seventy years earlier. He described the Christian Island Band's hunting grounds as running from the east end of Lake Nipissing to the northern heights of land. However, Kadegegwon testified that members of the band had not hunted regularly in that territory for almost fifty years.

During his interpretation of Kadegegwon's evidence, Walter Simon himself answered one question put to the witness. Somewhat indignantly, he said that because of the settlement of Aboriginal lands and the recent game laws, his community was unable to exercise its rights: "ever since we can remember, we have always been in peaceable and unmolested possession of the said hunting grounds and our fathers before us ... until the time when the white people came into our country, who became very numerous and as the country became thickly populated, the Government took up our territory without negotiation ... and also enacted laws prohibiting the taking of game which molested the rights and deprived the claimants of the territory of their sustenance."[76]

Enoch Monague, who had been born on Beausoleil Island, remembered hunting with his father along the Ka-wa-gah-mong River, a river with no English name. Monague indicated that there was no hunting in the area any more, as it "is all full of farms." Again voicing his ignorance of the Robinson-Huron Treaty, Commissioner Williams asked Monague if the treaty included the lands he had spoken of, and if Monague's argument was that these "had been surrendered by the Hurons and the Hurons had no claim to it and that it should not have been in the treaty."[77] Again, since the Hurons had nothing to do with the Robinson-Huron Treaty, Monague had no idea what Williams meant.

Chief Henry Jackson, another 1923 signatory, testified that he had hunted at Nottawasaga, in southern Georgian Bay. However, as with earlier witnesses who had referred to already surrendered lands, A.S. Williams interrupted him, saying, "But we are not concerned with that district. Did you go anywhere else?" The Chief then described how he and his band members hunted at the Muskoka Lakes, near the Muskosh River, and at the mouth of the Moon River. These were all areas that Rama claimed as its current hunting grounds and that Rama would later allege were supposed to have been protected under the 1923 Williams Treaty for its exclusive use. Chief Jackson confirmed that his band claimed the County of York as well, but once again Williams expressed disinterest, saying, "That has all been surrendered."

The Chief raised the fact that a thousand square miles of Chippewa land had been wrongly included in the Robinson-Huron Treaty, and that the Crown had taken a surrender from Indians who did not own it. He described the land as having "some minerals in it, and the very best of timber and there is fine fishing and good hunting." He said he had made representations to Indian Affairs "and all we got was that it is all settled and nothing can be done but just the same, in our hearts we know that it is our property."

The Commissioners debated among themselves regarding whether to inquire further into this allegation. Although Williams pointed out that the Robinson-Huron Treaty area had not been referred to in the declarations, McFadden thought that it fell "within the scope of our duties," as a commission of inquiry.[78]

The commission took evidence at Scugog Island on 24 September 1923. The Scugog First Nation had moved from the Balsam Lake reserve to the Scugog Lake reserve in the mid-nineteenth century, and therefore a number of these witnesses, like earlier ones, mentioned that their fathers and grandfathers had hunted in the Balsam Lake area.[79] This land had already been surrendered, and the Commissioners again made it clear that they had no interest in it.

The first witness was Isaac Johnson, aged seventy-eight. A signatory to the 1923 Williams Treaty on behalf of Scugog, Johnson had described himself as an "Indian, hunter" in the 1871 census.[80] He had tried farming,[81] but, according to A.F. Chamberlain, a Mississauga linguist who had visited Scugog in the 1890s, none of the members of the Scugog First Nation were very good farmers. Even at Johnson's farm, considered one of the best, "The thistles, weeds and other evidences of inattention to proper methods of cultivation were but too visible ... That the Skugog Indians have not made the best of farmers, a glance at their fields and crops suffices to show."[82]

Mention of the seven townships that had been reserved as hunting grounds by Lieutenant-Governor Simcoe in the late eighteenth century surfaced again during this part of the inquiry. Isaac Johnson's wife told the Commissioners that "five or six" townships had never been surrendered – Scott, Brock, Georgina, North Gwillimbury, Uxbridge, and part of Reach – which she stated were "reserved as hunting grounds granted by Governor Simcoe." However, she explained that the Indians could not hunt there because "the white people is settled there."[83]

David Elliot, a Williams Treaty signatory and ex-Chief, explained that the band that had once lived at Balsam Lake had been a mixed group of Chippewas and Mississaugas, and so all the bands had hunting and fishing limits in the northern hunting grounds. His own limits were in Gull Lake, one of the Kawartha Lakes, which he visited every year, although he still hunted regularly at Minden and Haliburton, further north. He informed the Commissioners, however, that the unsurrendered lands claimed by Scugog were not to the north, where the Chippewas had their claim; instead, the Scugog claim referred to hunting grounds further west.

One of the few female witnesses was heard at Scugog. Rebecca Shilling, Joseph Shilling's daughter, was a Chippewa from Rama who had moved to Scugog. She remembered going with her father to the northern hunting grounds on the other side of Muskoka every fall and spring, and to the Rama hunting grounds with her mother "and some of them little wee ones too." They went up in October and stayed until Christmas. Although she herself had trapped mink, muskrat, and beaver, she had never hunted deer because "Father never allow me to take a gun." Enoch Shilling, her brother, said their father hunted every spring and fall for "rats, beaver, deer, mink and fish," but had stopped going hunting around 1872.[84]

Chief Thomas Marsden explained that his father's hunting grounds were at Balsam Lake, but, like earlier witnesses, he said that Scugog had its own claim to lands running from Lake Simcoe straight north to the heights of land. He explained that the Chippewa claim extended to Moose Deer Point, on Georgian Bay, and Lake Nipissing but that "[our claim] does not go that far." When asked how far it did go, Chief Marsden described it as following "along Burnt River and the boundary line of County of Ontario and Simcoe," but added that the Chippewas and Mississaugas disputed some of those grounds. Asked if he knew of a claim that lands south of Lake Simcoe were unsurrendered, Marsden responded, "No, only the islands in Simcoe. My grandfather – a man by the name of Simcoe – claims the islands. He lived at Rama."[85]

The commission heard from the last living band member who had resided at Balsam Lake, Sarah Marsden. She did not know how old she was, but testified that her husband, who had died forty-three years earlier, used to hunt at Burnt River and the Bushkong River.[86]

Then the commission moved on to Mud Lake. Like the other First Nations, most who testified in the Mud Lake proceedings were hunters, trappers, and farmers. Daniel Whetung Sr., listed as an "Indian, farmer," was twenty-six at the time of the 1871 census, making him seventy-eight at the time of the hearing.[87] As mentioned above, Chief Daniel Whetung Jr. and former Chief Joseph Whetung were themselves dependent on trapping for their livelihoods at the time of the inquiry.

Many of the exchanges at Mud Lake are extraordinary, as they demonstrate the extent to which the Treaty Commissioners erroneously insisted to band members that the earlier 1818 treaties had extinguished, rather than protected, their rights to hunt and fish, even though the 1818 treaty had protected the right to hunt and fish within the ceded territory as well as on islands, on portions of the mainland, and at the mouths of rivers. The following exchange between Daniel Whetung Sr. and A.S. Williams is instructive.

Whetung explained that he had asked a lawyer to help him get his rights in the Kawartha Lakes area, saying that, "when I was talking of where we go to hunt, I got a lawyer, Wickham, in Toronto. I got him to write to the government to give me what is my own because my grandfather and my father hunt on that creek between Bobcaygeon and Lindsay, and he wrote to the government and the answer he got was 'We would be glad to give it to Mr. Whetung but another party has come and said they own that creek too' and I never got it." Whetung was referring to a letter sent by Henry Wickham to Hayter Reed of Indian Affairs in 1896. At that time, Reed's response was not that the lands had been surrendered, but that Indian Affairs was not aware of any treaty or other right that would exempt the Mud Lake Indians from the operation of laws enacted for the protection of game and fish.

Williams retorted, however, that Whetung had no rights, as these had been surrendered: "But the answer to that is that it was surrendered in 1818 ... Under that surrender you were to get so much a year and I think you are getting it every season. The people who surrendered that land then were satisfied and that is the reason you could not get the concession there – because it now belongs to someone else. You can't have your apple and eat it at the same time, you know."[88]

Like their predecessors W.H. Draper, Adam Watson, and James Cockburn, the Commissioners obviously believed that unless a treaty contained express written terms reserving or "granting" rights, Indians had no rights, whatever oral promises might have been made at the time of the treaty. This is evident in another exchange between the Commissioners and Chief Daniel Whetung Jr., in which Williams seemed to understand that Aboriginal people might have had rights, but assumed they were surrendered at the time of the earlier treaties, except on reserve.

Whetung described how waters around the reserve, once used to trap muskrats, had been encroached upon through the placarding by farmers. Commissioner Williams responded, "of course, all this land has been surrendered but you can prevent me from trapping on this reserve, can't you? Well, is it not tit for tat?" Whetung replied, "it may be tit for tat, but just the same it has been handed down to us from our fathers and grandfathers that they did not surrender the game or the hunting rights." Williams dismissed his complaint, saying, "There is only one treaty where I know it was reserved and that was the Robinson-Huron treaty."

The following exchange reflects the commission's view that unless a treaty had specifically reserved hunting and fishing rights, these were effectively given up, regardless of the Aboriginal perspective. Williams asked, "But suppose you have given up that right, what do you want then?" Whetung responded,

> A. Well, at the time that Treaty was signed, the Indians were not advanced enough to read it. The Treaty would be written out, and they would believe what they were told and just put their mark.
>
> Q. [Williams] I know ... [But] while there would not be, and was nothing in these Treaties which said the Indians gave up the right of hunting

> or fishing, still, that was the effect of the Treaty, unless there was a special clause reserving the right, because in the absence of a clause reserving the right, the Indians would be subject to the general law governing the white man and the Indian. Now, what is the remedy you want – taking for granted that the Treaty of 1818 took away your right to hunt and fish except in the waters of your Reserve?
>
> A. We would like the privilege of following up our game, when we get it up, even to private property.

Despite the Commissioner's insistence that Whetung's First Nation had no treaty rights in its surrendered lands, Chief Whetung maintained that it *did* have rights to trap in the marshes, and he complained vehemently that lands it had used for generations had become the subject of interference and encroachments. A Commissioner commented, "I suppose you agree with the other witness that even today he can get all he wants right around here?" Whetung replied, "No at present all the marshes are leased where the Indians used to trap. We can go where it has not been leased but we find everything is taken up so that don't do no good."

During his testimony, Chief Whetung repeatedly expressed his concern that the game had been pushed back onto private property where the Mud Lake Band could not access it, and that all the marshes in which band members had formerly trapped were now leased to white men who prevented them from trapping there. He added that, due to flooding caused by construction of the Trent Canal, the reserve had been reduced by six hundred acres. As a result, there were only twelve hundred acres left.[89]

In fact, the reserve *had* been considerably reduced in size as a result of flooding from the Trent Canal system. When the reserve was first surveyed in 1899, it had 1,428 acres, plus considerable marsh and drowned lands.[90] In 1909, the Trent Canal system had flooded these lands, as well as portions of the Rice Lake Reserve.[91] At Mud Lake, the flooding destroyed three hundred acres of what would otherwise have been first-class farming land and turned them into swamp.[92] Portions of the mainland and many islands in Mud Lake that had been reserved in the 1818 treaty had been permanently submerged, and the line between what was water and what was land was not very clear. In 1914, five years after the flooding, a land surveyor had noted that many of the islands shown on an 1852 map "are no longer to be seen, but shoals, shallows and weed beds show now their former location."[93]

The band had claimed compensation for the flooding of six hundred acres, but its claim was rejected by the Assistant Deputy Minister of the Department of Railways and Canals on the basis of an opinion from none other than A.S. Williams himself.[94] Williams, then the Indian Affairs departmental solicitor, had advised Duncan Campbell Scott not to reimburse the band for the flooded lands, on the technical basis that they fell outside the jurisdiction of the Exchequer Court, meaning that the Indians had no "forcible claim." Samuel Bray, the Chief Surveyor, had noted his strong dissent in marginalia on the Williams opinion, writing, "This is an extraordinary decision."[95]

As Williams well knew, then, the effect of the flooding was to remove some of the most valuable land from the reserve and to reduce the area available for trapping and hunting. For Whetung, the result of this was that he worried most about "this hunting business. They are closing in on us and we can't get out of the Reserve to hunt. That is our worry. There are only about 1200 acres in our reserve and of that only four or five hundred acres that it would be possible to cultivate and if we can't hunt, what are we going to do?" He added that his band was particularly interested in the shorelines. "I'd like to mention that before these dams [a reference to the Trent Canal construction] were built, the game was further out on the lakes and creeks and we were free to hunt then altho' not right on what was then the shores but now the game is pushed back onto the private property and we can't get at it. What used to be marsh is deep water and that's all the place we can go."

When Commissioner Williams asked Chief Whetung if he would like to get "some other rights" concerning trapping, Whetung responded that he would, and added, "Well, if our fathers and fore-fathers did not give up the game, as they tell us always they did not, we want the privilege to hunt around these waters but it seems we can't do that no more." Williams asked, "You mean that regardless of leases, you should have the right to hunt and trap?" Whetung responded "yes."[96]

The Commissioners arrived at Rice Lake on 26 September 1923. Like the other First Nations, Rice Lake's Hiawatha Band relied on subsistence activities for its survival. In fact, in the latest Ontario census currently available, that taken in 1901, not a single member of Hiawatha was listed in any occupation other than hunting, fishing, or farming.[97] This is an important point, since the work history of this particular community would be relevant in the *Howard* case.

The first witness, Jeremiah Crowe, aged eighty-six, testified that his forefathers had "reserved" the northern hunting grounds.[98] Former Chief Robert Paudash, seventy-seven, who would sign the 1923 Williams Treaty on behalf of Hiawatha, had been a farmer, although he too had trapped in the northern territories and had sold his own furs at Keene and Peterborough.[99] Although uncomfortable with English, he described very clearly how earlier surrenders had distinguished between land and water. Apparently referring to the Gunshot Treaty, he attested,

> When they sold this in 1845 [sic] they make treaty that we should hunt on the creeks but the lands is not ours. The white man have the dry land, but

we have the wetland. Mr. Simcoe [Lieutenant-Governor Simcoe] say that. He did not take our land we live on, but now they want to take that away.

Williams. Tell me, do you know where we can find anything that would show that that was the understanding?

A. It must be somewhere.

Q. Have you seen any letter or correspondence or document that contains that statement? Have you ever seen it in writing? What surrender is it you refer to?

A. It is in 1788 and that is when the Dominion have its government in England and that writing is in England, I guess.

The Commissioners pressed Paudash further, asking him if his band had reserved its hunting rights. When he responded that it had, Williams asked,

Well, in your recollection, was this right of hunting reserved to you in the Treaty of 1788?

A. Yes, with Simcoe.

Q. And that if it is not here, it is in England?

A. Yes, I suppose it would be there. Maybe there was a mistake in the writing but it was a bargain. The white people say that and if they did not put it down it was mistake and would not have been mistake if we could have read that white writing. The Indian has a good head you know. And south of Simcoe, there was a reserve there for hunting – seven or eight townships not ever surrendered ...

Q. You say some land south of Simcoe was not surrendered?

A. Seven or eight townships, that is our hunting ground.

Q. Was it reserved to you for hunting?

A. It was reserved it [sic] Treaty with Simcoe.

Similar evidence was given by Madden Howard, another 1923 Williams Treaty signatory.

Johnson Paudash had informed himself fully as to the provisions of the 1818 treaty and other surrenders. He brought a number of maps and other exhibits that he had obtained from Indian Affairs on which unsurrendered lands were marked in red, and surrendered lands in blue. Paudash first attempted to describe the unsurrendered northern hunting grounds, but the Commissioners immediately directed his attention to the area south of Lake Simcoe that was marked on his map as "unsurrendered."

Paudash explained that this area had been reserved under a 1792 treaty with Simcoe as western hunting grounds for the Mississaugas. It included seven townships – Reach, what he referred to as "Brock Thora," North Gwillimbury, Georgina, Scott, Uxbridge, and a part of Scugog Township.[100] Paudash explained that the 1818 surrender was inaccurate. In 1905, on the basis of information provided to him by Robert Paudash, Johnson's father,[101] J.A. MacRae had pointed out to Indian Affairs that the treaty's northern boundary was supposed to run west along the forty-fifth parallel to a bay at the entrance of Lake Simcoe; instead, the line ran from Bracebridge to Moose Deer Point.[102]

The final Mississauga community interviewed by the Commissioners was Alnwick, or Alderville, whose members were also exclusively reliant on hunting, fishing, and trapping.[103] The Alnwick First Nation's claim differed somewhat from that of the other Mississauga communities. The band maintained that certain of its lands north of an 1822 treaty territory remained unsurrendered.[104] Alnwick, moreover, had a number of other reserves along the Bay of Quinte and the St. Lawrence River that it had offered to surrender to the government for $80,000 back in 1884, although it had expressed its intention then to reserve its fishing islands for its own hunting and fishing purposes.[105]

The Commissioners again made it clear that their inquiries related only to the northern hunting grounds. Williams asked the first witness, John Comego, if his father had a hunting limit in the northern part of Ontario, "which we are here to enquire about today." Comego, aged seventy-three, responded that his own hunting ground was "down this way more, towards the Bay of Quinte."

Comego had heard the old men of his band talk at council meetings about the treaty rights they had kept when they surrendered lands: "They said they had hunting grounds and I don't know whether they surrendered the land at that time or not, but they hold their hunting rights, the fur and the deer. That was all ours, that was our living, and the old men did not surrender that. That have made a surrender of land only, some time ago I believe, our forefathers did ... [b]ut they did not surrender the hunting."

However, Comego added that, unlike the Chippewas and other Mississaugas, his band generally hunted "back north *this* way. We hardly ever went up there [near Lake Nipissing] because there were Indians up there and we didn't want to bother going hunting up there."

Robert Gray, the next witness, had also hunted solely around Alnwick. He had heard the old people talk about hunting grounds "below here, but I never heard about up the other way." The only lakes Gray had heard mentioned were "away back North of the Bay of Quinte." Williams, still confused about the Alnwick claim, which was quite different from the others, asked, "But did you hear of them at Lake Nipissing or the Mississauga river near Saulte Ste. Marie?" The witness, not surprisingly, had not.

Calling Chief Robert Franklin to clarify matters, Williams asked him if he had ever heard his father refer to the limits the Commissioners "are speaking of today." Franklin responded that his father had spoken only of the hunting grounds and lands the band had never surrendered. He added,

"Our Band never claimed land in Nipissing District. I never heard of Nipissing or Muskoka at all, because we came from the east and our claims were that way." Williams persisted:

> Q. You of course know that the Mississaugas have been pressing a claim with the government in respect of unsurrendered hunting land. Now, have you any idea where these lands are said by the Mississaugas to be?
> A. Not any more than that I was hired to take the old men to Cobourg and I heard them give their affidavits to William Kerr, and I also heard them talking in Council here several times, and they claimed from Hastings County east and north to the Ottawa River and up that river – run north to the dividing line between Hastings and Northumberland. It ran east again and then North to Baptiste and over to Carleton County back to the St. Lawrence River but we never touched Lake Nipissing and I never heard the old hunters mention anything about Lake Nipissing.[106]

The Chief produced a letter in which the band's lawyer had put forward Alnwick's claim.[107] Williams, completely misconstruing the letter and its references to the Alnwick claim to the area north of the 1822 treaty, insisted,

> But you misunderstand the letter. This is a letter from Mr. Kerr ... at one time acting for you ... What he says is that this land which he describes is the furthest land north which the Mississaugas surrendered to the Crown. That is the land going up the west line of Hastings over to Carleton and back ... He says also that the Mississauga Indians claim this tract was the furthest north they surrendered but that all territory lying north of it remains their property insofar as the unextinguished title makes it their property. That is what we are here to enquire about. We know from the Treaty Book what has been surrendered but there is this bit north of that territory [which was] surrendered *and it is in respect of that* we are making this investigation.

Williams' insistence that, since at least 1884, the band had somehow been pursuing the wrong claim was more than a little paternalistic. Still, Williams demanded that the Chief provide information about "those old hunting grounds" around Nipissing, grounds in which the Alnwick Band had never hunted. All that Chief Franklin could tell him was that his father had once gone to Nipissing to hunt, some thirty-five years earlier, but that he knew no one else who had hunted there.

Chief Franklin again tried to explain the scope of Alnwick's claim, referring to the visit by William Plummer many years earlier to secure information about it:

> Well, a Commission something the same as yours came here and asked us what we would take for our share we had not surrendered and we set a price.
>
> Q. Was it you people set $80,000 as a price?
>
> A. Yes, but there was nothing more said, and we thought it was this land that you say we misunderstood about.

John Lake, the next witness, confirmed that the unsurrendered hunting grounds Alnwick wanted to discuss lay north of Belleville, on the Bay of Quinte, and that the band had never gone as far west as Nipissing.[108] Jack Smoke agreed that the band's regular hunting grounds were about fifty miles north of Kingston, where there was still "quite a bit of hunting, but the white people has got us beat out of it."[109]

Only one witness described lands falling outside of previously surrendered territory, a point the Commissioners commented on specifically. Norman Marsden testified that his grandfather had often talked of the hunting grounds and had gone north to hunt every spring and fall. He asked the Commissioners if his grandfather and father could keep an island at a place called Kosheewagama, where the grandfather had hunted and fished all his life. Williams commented, "Well, that at least is in the territory never surrendered."[110]

Like other members of his band, Moses Smoke had never hunted in the northern part of Ontario. Instead, he said, "We all hunt up – away up the river to Thompson's Lake. That would be the beaver creek ... catching deer and beaver and otter." He added a somewhat mistaken description of the Gunshot Treaty provisions, but made clear his position that the Alnwick First Nation had never surrendered its hunting and fishing rights and had no intention of doing so now: "You men had better settle up with us Indians what you owe us and that is nothing but right. And I tell you, the game is ours and we will kill it if we like because long ago the white man when he take our land say he does not take our game."[111]

The Commissioners, who had already heard reference to the Gunshot Treaty at Hiawatha, wanted more information about it. Asked if he had ever heard of it, David Crow said that the old men had spoken of it at a council. Back then, they had thought that entering into such a treaty was not a good idea because you "could hear a gun much further on one day than another day." Still, Williams asked if "there are such treaties" and Crow replied "yes." The final witness, John Chase, told the Commissioners that members of his band were good hunters and had never needed to go all that far to hunt.

The evidence ended with Sinclair explaining the position of the government regarding the claim. Although Moodie did not fully transcribe his comments, she did record that Sinclair asked "the Indians to think the matter over carefully and make only reasonable demands if the Commissioners returned with a view to making a treaty." Chief Franklin responded, "We don't want things that don't belong to us and they don't want what's ours, and the old people are all dead, but since the government is good enough to take what we have just heard from them and try to make some settlement with us, we should try to be kind of lenient and settle it up too."[112]

The Commissioners' Reports

In October 1923, following their visits to the reserves, the Commissioners prepared a lengthy memorandum for the Ontario Minister of Lands and Forests. Their report confirmed that their mandate had been to inquire only into the claim by the Chippewas and Mississaugas to a limited "area extending from the forty-fifth parallel of latitude north of Lake Nipissing and from the Georgian Bay east to the Ottawa River, alleged by the claimants to be the ancient hunting grounds of their ancestors."[113] They indicated that during the inquiry, the Chippewas had put forward an additional claim for a thousand square miles wrongly included in the Robinson-Huron Treaty of 1850, and that the Mississaugas had claimed that seven townships south of Lake Simcoe had never been surrendered. The Commissioners reported that these latter alone, constituting over 355,000 acres, were valued "moderately" at $30 million.

The Commissioners had also discovered that lands between the Bay of Quinte and the County of York "commonly supposed to be surrendered by what is known to be the Gunshot Treaty are not described in any Treaty." Therefore, they proposed an extension to their mandate so that they could obtain a new surrender of the lands originally intended to be covered by the Gunshot Treaty.[114] Ironically, the Commissioners described this as a "new" claim, when in fact, it was the same complaint that the Chippewas had pressed for many, many years.[115]

On the day they submitted their report to Ontario, the Commissioners wrote to Duncan Campbell Scott, Deputy Superintendent of Indian Affairs, informing him of their recommendations. They suggested that the First Nations be paid for the surrender of very specific tracts of land, namely, "the tract of land in question and some townships in the northerly part of the Counties of York and Lake Simcoe which apparently have never been surrendered."[116] In their report, the Commissioners did not mention any desire to obtain a surrender of any other rights within Ontario, or to extinguish rights held under other, earlier treaties. Nor had they informed the bands that they might seek to broaden their mandate to include these additional areas.

The following week, although the inquiry was over, I.E. Weldon was informed that his request to appear before the commission as counsel for his clients had been refused.[117] He wrote to the Commissioners, arguing that he had new evidence that might have been overlooked:

> One Indian, Johnson Paudash by name, was an educated, intelligent man, and with his assistance were unearthed many old treaties, documents, surrenders and other material which would go to show that these Indians had not been compensated for unsurrendered land ... I proposed appearing before your Commission when it should have its sittings but I found that the Department did not favour the intervention of solicitors in matters between the Indians and the Government, it having been found, or so I'm told, that frequently the lawyers showed greater anxiety on their own behalf than on behalf of their clients ... I might say that I would like very much indeed to have an opportunity to lay before the commission further evidence in corroboration of the evidence already given.[118]

In his letter, Weldon urged the Commissioners not to ask the First Nations to surrender their hunting and fishing rights, or to pay them cash amounts that might run into hundreds of thousands of dollars, as he felt they were not yet capable of managing their own financial affairs. Instead, he requested that his clients be provided with adequate hunting and fishing grounds for their use in perpetuity, pointing out that there were marsh and bog lands in the Kawartha Lakes where the Crown held title and where arrangements might be made for them to have the exclusive right to hunt and trap. He argued that "the general public is poaching on these lands for the purpose of taking muskrat and other fur animals and therefore there would be no loss if concessions were given to these Indians. However, the whole question is a large one and I would be exceedingly obliged if you would give me an opportunity of laying the whole matter before your Commission."[119]

Although the Commissioners would not allow Weldon to appear before them on the record, they did agree to meet with him privately in Toronto on 25 October.[120] What transpired at that meeting, if it ever took place, is not known.

On 18 October 1923, the Commissioners took a series of steps to prepare the necessary surrenders. Uriah McFadden wrote to W.C. Cain, asking him for information about Crown lands "within the territory over which those two Indian Nations claim compensation for hunting, trapping and fishing rights."[121] R.V. Sinclair wrote to Walter Simon at Christian Island, advising him that, with respect to the land said to be erroneously included in the Robinson-Huron Treaty, the commission wanted to take more evidence from Christian Island Band members living on Parry Island, Georgian Bay. He asked Simon to go with them to interpret.[122]

As well, the Commissioners sent letters to the Indian Agents at each reserve, notifying them that they intended to "visit the reserves again with a view of making a treaty with the various bands in respect of the said hunting grounds."[123]

The Surveys Branch of Indian Affairs was asked to prepare a statement of all the lands previously surrendered by the Mississaugas and Chippewas, as well as information about the size and location of their current reserves, presumably so that these areas could be excluded from the new surrender. The Commissioners also asked the Surveys Branch to prepare a careful description of the lands "forming the ancient hunting limits intended to be included in the Treaty," as well as the area claimed to have been wrongly included in the Robinson-Huron Treaty, "for the purpose of setting any question at rest as to title over these latter lands."[124]

The Commissioners later reported that they had also asked the Surveys Branch to describe the lands originally intended to be covered by the Gunshot Treaty. Once they obtained the information they needed, they wrote that they had "prepared two treaties, one to be signed by the three bands of Chippewas and the other to be signed by the four Bands of Mississaugas."[125]

7
Differing Perceptions

Although it had taken decades for the Chippewas and Mississauga claims to be investigated fully, the treaties prepared by the Commissioners were signed with breathtaking speed, in less than twenty-two days. Georgina Island signed on 31 October 1923, Christian Island on 3 November, and Rama the following day. Just over a week later, leaders from the Mississauga communities of Mud Lake (15 November), Rice Lake (16 November), Alderville (19 November), and Scugog (21 November) added their names. The speed with which the treaties were signed – less than two months after the commission proceedings began – is more than a little curious in light of the decades-long delay involved in getting the claims to the negotiation process. Interestingly, on 29 November, the Superintendent General of Indian Affairs, Charles Stewart, reported to Cabinet that the Commissioners had decided it was "advisable for the public good to press on the making of a Treaty without unnecessary delay so as to prevent as far as possible the bringing to bear upon the Indians the influence which the Commissioners became aware existed and which would be inimical to the signing of a treaty."[1]

What "inimical" influence Stewart had in mind is not specified. However, between August and December 1923, a series of extraordinary events had unfolded on the international stage. A Six Nations Iroquois Chief, Levi General, or Deskaheh, a member of the Cayuga Nation, had been sent by the Six Nations Iroquois to Geneva to urge the League of Nations to admit the Six Nations Confederacy as sovereign members of the league.[2] Before he left for Geneva, Deskaheh had been assisted by A.G. Chisholm, the lawyer hired by the Chippewas of Christian Island, Rama, and Georgina Island for their land claim only a year earlier. Ironically, Chisholm was a former associate of R.V. Sinclair, who had appeared with him on behalf of the Six Nations in a 1922 case involving a licence of occupation.[3] However, for his trip to Geneva, Deskaheh was accompanied not by Chisholm but by George Palmer Decker, a Rochester, New York, lawyer and former Deputy Attorney General who became his closest friend. When Decker died in

1936, his obituary referred to his "signal service" within his profession in the "defense of the American Indian" for whom he had laboured "without due compensation and [with] unremitting effort."[4]

Before approaching Geneva, Decker first took the Six Nations case to the Colonial Secretary in London. The documents he and Deskaheh assembled argued that Canada had mismanaged Indian affairs by misappropriating Indian trust funds, taking away valid land rights, and increasingly encroaching on matters of internal management and governance. They also alleged that Canada had prevented Aboriginal peoples from exercising rights on their reserved and unsurrendered lands, as well as those they had retained under their treaties. They pointed out also that monies had been withheld from the Six Nations, preventing them from hiring lawyers to put forward their legal claims and defence.[5]

On 7 August 1923, Deskaheh's petition for separate-nation status was presented to the League of Nations. The petition complained specifically about Canada's attempts to prevent the Six Nations from pursuing a land claim relating to unceded lands, and pamphlets were distributed in London detailing their allegations.[6] A furious Duncan Campbell Scott accused "Deskaheh and his faction" of misrepresenting the facts.[7]

By 28 August, Deskaheh had reached Geneva. There, he formally submitted the Six Nations application for League of Nations membership under the name *The Redman's Appeal for Justice*.[8] Alarmed by these developments, George P. Graham, Minister of Railways and Canals, immediately cabled home from Geneva for instructions. He also sent a personal letter to Charles Stewart, the Superintendent General of Indian Affairs, referring to the "trouble" Deskaheh had caused over the "Six Nations Indian question in Geneva ... Chief Darasek [sic] was not only there with his Yankee Solicitor, but they issued a Bill to every member of the League ... The Indian Chief seems to have made an impression among several of the Delegates."[9]

As Li Xiu Woo points out, support for the Six Nations came from various sources, including the Anti-Slavery and Aborigines Protection Society, and the Bureau pour la défense des indigènes. Equally disturbing to the Canadian government was the fact that Deskaheh received an extremely sympathetic response from the Netherlands and Ireland, as well as other countries. The press too paid considerable attention to Deskaheh's actions, intensifying what was rapidly becoming an international embarrassment for Canada, which was attempting to secure its own independence from Great Britain at the time. At the end of November 1923, as Deskaheh and his supporters lobbied the league's council to examine their claim, Prince Arfa-ed-Dowleh of Persia sent a telegram to the President of the league's council supporting their request. The session was to end in December, however, and since Canada was entitled to send a representative to the council when the matter was discussed, the Prince was asked to reconsider his position.[10]

Duncan Campbell Scott personally prepared Canada's reply to the Six Nations application. Ignoring the allegation that money had been withheld so that the Indians could not retain legal counsel, he insisted that their "ridiculous" and "frivolous" complaints were inventions; extraordinarily, he claimed that Canada had never entered into any treaties with the Six Nations. Overall, he defended Canada's actions as being in the interests of Indians, in keeping with its ultimate objective to "fit the Indians for full citizenship."[11]

Perhaps it is only coincidental that the Williams Treaties were rushed to signature during this period, just as it is only coincidental that Canada extended preferential trade tariffs to the Irish Free State on 21 September 1923 and to the Netherlands on 12 March 1924.[12] On the other hand, it is at least possible that Canada's swift action on the Williams Treaties was a means of avoiding further controversy over Aboriginal land claims while the international problems were sorted out. Certainly, by demonstrating that it had successfully concluded a major land claim and a new treaty at the same time that the Six Nations was accusing it on an international stage of failing to do either, Canada could only enhance its arguments against the Iroquois petition at the League of Nations.

The Williams Treaties Commissioners may also have feared that the Mississaugas, in particular, would be influenced by the actions taken by their long-time allies, the Six Nations. They were certainly aware that A.G. Chisholm had acted as counsel to the Chippewas of Rama, Christian Island, and Georgina Island, as well as the Six Nations, and it may be assumed that his clients followed the petition with much interest, given their close ties to the Six Nations. The Commissioners had also no doubt learned that I.E. Weldon, who had met with them only days before the treaties were signed, was opposed to the surrender of Mississauga hunting and fishing rights.

Although all of this is speculative, and there is no documentary link associating the Williams Treaties with Deskaheh's application to the league, the fact remains that the treaties were negotiated, signed, and executed in an extraordinarily short period of time. It is also a fact that the Commissioners did not permit Weldon to be present during the hearings and that mere days after the treaties were signed, Britain informed the Canadian government that it completely supported opposing the Iroquois petition.[13]

In fact, so quickly were the treaties signed that they were completed even before Ontario had authorized the amount of funds that could be tabled in the negotiations. A cheque drawn in favour of the Department of Indian Affairs was sent by Ontario to Charles Stewart, the Superintendent General of Indian Affairs, on 6 November 1923, several days after the first three treaties had been signed at Georgina Island, Christian Island, and Rama. The cheque was accompanied by a letter indicating it was conditional "on the specific understanding that the final settlement on the Treaty ... must not involve a sum in excess of approximately half a million dollars"; otherwise, the cheque was to be returned.[14]

What might have happened if, during the treaty negotiations, the Indians had insisted on more money than the Commissioners were authorized to pay is not known. This does suggest, however, that the treaties were understood to be conditional, even by the Commissioners themselves, an argument supported by the fact that at the time the treaties were signed, the amount of compensation was left blank.

As A.S. Williams explained to the Premier of Ontario on 4 December 1923, more than a month after the first of the treaties had been signed, he had yet to determine what amount was to be inserted. He said it had been agreed that the commission would pay the sum of $500,000 to be divided equally between the Chippewas and the Mississaugas and that "out of this sum the cash payment of $25.00 per head is to be made." However, until that had been done, "the exact balance which will remain in the hands of the Dominion Government to be administered for the Indians cannot be inserted in the Treaty." Once it was calculated, he indicated that a completed copy of the treaties would be sent to Ontario.[15]

As it turned out, the amount of compensation paid out was not what had been agreed upon. Instead, it was calculated according to the population of the various First Nations. Rice Lake, for example, with a population of 104, received a mere $36,615.59 in exchange for the extinguishment of its rights to the northern grounds.[16] Georgina Island, with a population of 120, received only $42,045.03.[17]

To place the twenty-five-dollar one-time per capita payment to the Mississaugas and Chippewas in its proper financial context, one need only note that, by the early 1900s, a "typical, rising professional" earned approximately $2,000 a year.[18] For their services, Williams and the other Commissioners themselves received a payment of "at least One Hundred Dollars ($100.) *per diem* in addition to travelling and other necessary expenses."[19] In other words, for each day they were involved in the treaty-making process, each Commissioner received four times as much money as individual community members were paid for the all-out surrender of their rights.

Reports of the Negotiations

On 1 December 1923, the Commissioners reported to both the Superintendent General of Indian Affairs and the Minister of Lands and Forests for Ontario on the completion of the successful negotiations. The Commissioners made little mention of the actual representations made during the negotiations, and for some reason, these were not transcribed, although Kathleen Moodie had accompanied the Commissioners throughout the negotiations.[20]

Those present from the First Nations would later claim that their own attempts to record the proceedings were discouraged. According to Chief

John Bigwin, one of the signatories to the treaties, not only had the Commissioners not provided copies of the treaties to the bands, they would not permit the band to transcribe the proceedings either, although some boys "learning shorthand" took notes of what was said. The Chief was interviewed by the *Orillia Packet and Times* in 1938. As the paper reported, he maintained that "at the time the treaty was made the Indians were given to understand it did not interfere with their right to hunt and fish." In a written statement he had brought with him, the Chief informed the reporter that

> In September 1923 a Treaty was made between the Ontario Government and the Mississaugas and Chippewa Indians by which the Indians gave up all rights to certain lands in the northern part of Ontario.
>
> When the Commissioners approached the Indians in a friendly manner, hunted up all the evidence and put it together, they finally came to a satisfactory settlement. Before signing the treaty, each commissioner got up and said these very words, – that the Indians would still be able to hunt, fish and trap. Restrictions on fishing wasn't to be included in the treaty ... Fishing and hunting were not included in the sale of land. Its the resource for our living. These words were caught by school boys learning shorthand ... We should have had an interpreter or a stenographer so as to take both sides of the question. The commissioners didn't let us [take down] anything.[21]

Despite the lack of a transcript for the negotiations, there are some hints in other documents as to what was said. In their December 1923 report, the Commissioners indicated that they had discussed the amount of compensation during the negotiations at Rama and "made a very special effort ... to convince the Indians that the amount which the Commission was prepared to offer would be a full and ample compensation for such rights as they were being asked to surrender." At the same time, the Commissioners observed that most of the Rama reserve consisted of rough rocky and swampy land; they added that its small farms, "owing to the character of the ground, are not cultivable."[22] Significantly, in their December report, they suggested that the departmental policy of inducing Indians to turn to agriculture would be more easily achieved if Indian Affairs acquired land that could be cultivated by the Indians – in other words, if it added to the reserves.

The Commissioners made similar comments about Mud Lake. Of the 1,664 acres on that reserve, only 500 were said to be cultivable, and the work of clearing the land was said to be "so great that it is impossible to induce the Indians to do so and consequently only a very limited number of them are engaged in farming. If better land in the vicinity could be obtained, the Commission is of the opinion that many more members of the Band could be induced to turn their attention to agriculture." Similarly, at Scugog, the Commissioners noted that Wilson Garrow, the Indian

Agent, had informed them that he had been unable to persuade the Indians to take up farming.[23]

The Commissioners commented that the trapping issue raised by Chief Daniel Whetung Jr. at the Mud Lake hearings had been raised at Hiawatha as well. They reported that Hiawatha witnesses had complained that "owing to the leasing to whites of muskrat trapping privileges upon the borders of the lakes, they had been deprived of the right formerly enjoyed by them of trapping muskrat, upon the avails of which trapping, many of the Indians are largely dependent for support. This question will be further referred to in another report to be made by the Commission."[24]

If the Commissioners planned to investigate the protection of these rights in a further report, it is unlikely that they intended the band's hunting, fishing, and trapping rights to be extinguished at the moment the band signed the treaty. The Commissioners, and especially R.V. Sinclair, had some sympathy for the Aboriginal people they dealt with: this much seems clear. It also seems clear that Parliament had little knowledge of the agreement, and little interest in it. *Hansard* records only a July 1924 exchange involving the treaty, one that shows a complete ignorance of even its most basic aspects. In July, the House of Commons was asked to approve the Governor General's warrants for the previous year, so as to "provide for the expenses of investigating claim and negotiating treaty for cession of Indian title to 10,719 square miles in the Province of Ontario." Arthur Meighen, the leader of the Opposition, asked if the request was related to "Colonel Thompson's investigation," to which the Minister of Justice replied "I think so." Meighen commented, "A pretty barren investigation."[25]

Despite this, Ontario would later argue in *Howard* that the terms of the treaties expressly and intentionally extinguished the rights of all the bands to hunt, fish, or trap anywhere in Ontario except on their reserves, and that this was clearly understood by the Aboriginal parties, Canada, and Ontario.

The Terms of the Treaties

The "Articles" of the Mississauga treaty signed by Mud Lake, Hiawatha, Alnwick, and Scugog were identical to those of the Chippewa treaty signed by Georgina Island, Christian Island, and Rama. Its terms begin as follows:

> Whereas the Mississauga Tribe above described having claimed to be entitled to certain interests in the lands in the Province of Ontario hereinafter described such interests being the Indian Title of the said Tribe to fishing, hunting and trapping rights over the said lands, of which said rights, His Majesty through his said Commissioners is desirous of obtaining a surrender ... [the tribe] by their Chiefs and Headmen duly authorized thereunto as aforesaid do hereby cede, release, surrender and yield up to the Government of the Dominion of Canada for his Majesty the King and his Successors

> forever all their right, title, interest, claim, demand and privileges whatsoever in, to, upon or in respect of the lands and premises described.[26]

In the Chippewa treaty, the word "Mississaugas" was replaced with "Chippewas," but in all other respects the treaties were the same. Both treaties focused on two geographical areas: the first was the ancient northern hunting grounds described by the witnesses; the second lay further to the south. For both areas, the legal description prepared by the Surveys Branch was highly technical, but essentially used various outside reference points that demarcated and excluded the boundaries of lands affected by the earlier treaties.[27] For example, in the treaty's first clause, the boundary of the northern parcel is described as running to that "point on Matchedash Bay where the land included in the surrender of the Eighteenth day of November 1815 of record in Book of Surrenders Volume One is reached" and continuing to the "Western Northwest corner of the parcel surrendered on the Twenty-eighth day of November, 1822." In describing the southern area, the treaty's second clause cited the Gunshot Treaty lands "said to have been ceded in 1787, which was confirmed on the First of August, 1805, of record as Number Thirteen in Volume One of the Book of Surrenders."

As well, the treaty described all the islands in Georgian Bay but excluded Rice Lake. This was consistent with the mandate of the Commissioners and with the many instructions to witnesses that they discuss only those lands that had not previously been surrendered, or those in which present rights might exist.

The legal description of lands in the second clause, with its reference to the Gunshot Treaty, included the seven townships that had often been mentioned during the commission of inquiry. The townships were not identified by name in the treaty, although this was how many of the witnesses had referred to them. In the absence of any explanation that these lands were to be affected, it is not at all clear that the First Nations would have known that the treaty purported to surrender lands that they stated were reserved for them by Lieutenant-Governor Simcoe, particularly since the next clause in the treaty expressly said it would not affect any lands previously reserved.

In its third clause, the so-called basket clause, the treaty broadened its scope to include "all the right, title, interest, claim, demand and privileges whatsoever of the said Indians *in, to, upon or in respect of all other lands situate in the Province of Ontario* to which they have ever had, now have, or now claim to have any right, title, interest, claim, demand or privileges, except such reserves as have heretofore been set apart for them by His Majesty the King." Ontario would later argue that this clause had extinguished all of the Mississauga and Chippewa treaty rights throughout the province, enabling them to hunt and fish only on their reserves.

As worded, the clause itself would seem not to refer to the areas covered by the earlier treaties, since, in its own preamble, the treaty stated that it applied only to "the Indian Title of the said Tribe." Indian title no longer existed within the territory covered by earlier treaties – the Aboriginal title in them had been extinguished when the lands were surrendered, although certain treaty rights had been agreed to within these ceded lands.

The treaty also stated that it was subject to the agreement reached in April 1923 between the Dominion of Canada and the Province of Ontario, "a copy of which is hereto attached." No copy, however, was appended to the copies of the treaty that were filed, perhaps as a result of the speed with which the treaties had been signed.[28]

A final and important provision of the Williams Treaties was that the Chiefs and headmen,

> on their own behalf and on behalf of all the Indians whom they represent do hereby solemnly covenant, promise and agree to strictly observe this Treaty in all respects and that they will not, nor will any of them, nor will any of the Indians whom they represent, molest, or interfere with the person or property of anyone who now inhabits or shall hereafter inhabit any portion of the lands covered by this Treaty ... and that they will assist the officers of His Majesty in bringing to justice and punishment any Indian party to this Treaty who may hereafter offend against the stipulations hereof or infringe the laws in force in the lands covered hereby.[29]

As will be seen, those who signed the treaties continued to hunt and fish in violation of the game laws, and insisted that they had retained a treaty right to do so.

Duncan Campbell Scott received his copy of the treaties on 13 December 1923. The cover letter that accompanied it read, "We beg to hand you herewith our report in connection with the Treaty recently made between the Mississaugas of Rice, Mud [Curve] and Scugog Lakes and of Alderville, and the Chippewas of Lakes Huron and Simcoe and the Crown for the surrender by these Indians of their Aboriginal hunting rights over a large portion of Northern Ontario."[30] There was no suggestion in the Commissioners' correspondence that any other lands in Ontario were affected by the treaties.

With the execution of the treaties, the Commissioners commented with apparent relief that "the Indian title which formerly covered all the lands in the old Province of Ontario has finally been released."[31] However, in all the Commissioners' reports, letters, memoranda, and requests, there is not a single mention of the so-called basket clause. Moreover, there is not a single reference in any of these records to suggest any intention on the part of the Treaty Commissioners to effect the extinguishment of any pre-existing treaty rights, or indeed, to include within the surrender any lands already ceded. Nor does it appear that Ontario viewed the surrender as doing so at the time.

The Deputy Minister of Lands and Forests, W.C. Cain, prepared a memorandum on 22 February 1924, briefing his Minister on the treaties. He summarized events, describing how the Indian tribes had made claim for compensation for their unsurrendered lands comprising some eleven or twelve thousand square miles within Renfrew, Hastings, Haliburton and Muskoka, Parry Sound, and Nipissing, and pointed out that further claims had been put forward during the hearings

> showing that an additional 1,000 square miles had by mistake been included in the Robinson Huron Treaty in 1850, this area extending North along the shore of Georgian Bay from Moose Deer Point to the French River. Furthermore, it was discovered that seven townships lying immediately south of Lake Simcoe, belonging to the Mississaugas, had never been surrendered ... [and] that an area supposed to have been surrendered by what was known as the "Gun-Shot Treaty" lying between the Bay of Quinte and the County of York had never been included in the Treaty and it was therefore deemed advisable that all these claims should under the Commission vested be absolutely cleaned up so that there be no remaining area in the whole Province unsurrendered to the Crown.[32]

It seems clear from Cain's summary that only unsurrendered lands were addressed by the new treaties. Ontario's argument that the Williams Treaties First Nations had relinquished all their rights, including those previously protected under their early treaties, would be developed much, much later on.

The executed copies of the treaties and the Minutes of a Special General Meeting of each First Nation authorizing the surrender were filed with the Deputy Registrar General of Canada on 24 June 1924.[33] These Minutes indicate that "Special General Meetings" were held at each reserve so that the bands could consider "a proposal from His Majesty the King, though his Commissioners, for a surrender of all right, title and interest of the said Band in certain lands in the Province of Ontario, particularly described in the draft Treaty submitted to this Council meeting."[34] Both the specific reference to the fact that only "certain" lands were to be discussed and the use of the term "draft" treaty suggest that further changes in the Williams Treaties could be negotiated.

Indeed, according to these Minutes, those empowered to sign the treaties were authorized to act as negotiators "appointed and authorized on behalf of the said Band to conduct the negotiations with the said Commissioners for a surrender of all the right, title and interest of the said Band in the said lands."[35] Given this, it seems obvious that the Minutes authorized negotiations for additional terms beyond those contained in the Commissioners' draft proposals; otherwise, the appointment of band negotiators would have been unnecessary. As will be seen, negotiations did take place, although the requests made by the various First Nations and the undertakings provided by the Commissioners in response were not reflected in the written terms of the treaties.

The Aboriginal Perspective

According to the limited record of the negotiations, it seems the Aboriginal negotiators had no idea that the Williams Treaties would affect their pre-existing treaty rights. In 1966, for example, a Mud Lake elder, aged eighty-one, recalled that "they had a meeting at Clifford's [Clifford Whetung's] barn, not this new one, but a store house, that is years ago, and he [Whetung] told the fellows, the old fellows never to sell the hunting, and he says: 'Oh that will never happen.'"[36]

There is one Minute of the representations made by the Commissioners at Rama in November 1923 that was confirmed as accurate by the Indian Agent at Rama who attended the negotiations himself.[37] According to this record, the Commissioners gave a simplified account of their demands, encouraging the First Nation to give up title to lands that they described "as not much value" to the communities any more: "Crown asks Indians to give up their rights to hunt, fish and trap on these lands as the rights which their ancestors exercised. These lands are not much value to the Indians now. They would not give up what civilization has brought to them. *Some limits will be reserved for hunting, fishing and trapping.* The Ontario Government wants to deal fairly and equitably with the Indians and has considered all evidence."[38]

Since hunting, fishing, and trapping were already protected on reserves, the only possible interpretation of "some limits" being reserved is that it related to additional areas in which hunting and fishing rights would be protected off-reserve, and possibly, given the Commissioners' reports, to the provision of additional lands as well. Indeed, under the Canada-Ontario Agreement, Ontario had already agreed to set aside such reserves as were negotiated, provided these reverted back to it should any of the First Nations become "extinct."[39] Again, since the First Nations already had reserves, this can only mean the setting aside of additional reserve lands.

A few weeks after the treaties were signed, the Commissioners confirmed that during the negotiations, the Rama Indians had requested additional areas as reserves, as well as the right to hunt and fish for food throughout the year without licences:

> The Rama Indians also requested the Commission to include in the Treaty some provision which would enable the Indians signing the Treaty to hunt

> and fish for domestic purposes at any time during the year. The Commission stated it had no power to include such a provision in the Treaty but that it would bring the request of the Indians to the Department. The Rama Indians also desired the Commission to grant them a piece of land hitherto and now used by them as camping grounds, situate between Moon and Muskosh Rivers near Moose Deer Point. The Indians stated that the land in question is rocky and quite unsuitable for farming purposes. The Commission promised to bring this matter to the attention of the Department.[40]

The Commissioners' report to Duncan Campbell Scott described the particular areas that the Rama First Nation wanted reserved. These were composed primarily of the fishing islands, although a hunting ground at Port Carling, where Councillor Gilbert Williams had his "little house," was also included in their demands.[41] As the Commissioners' report noted, "These Indians also stated that they had been in the habit for many years of using the following islands and points as grounds, namely: Chief Island in Lake Couchiching; Green Island and Eight Mile Point in Lake Simcoe; Snake Island in Sparrow Lake, one island in the Mud [Curve] Lake, a small portion of land in Port Carling and one island in Lake Koshee and said they would like the Commission to include a provision in the Treaty securing to them the above-mentioned islands."

Once again, the Commissioners stated that they had told the Aboriginal negotiators that they themselves had no power to make these reservations, "but would draw the attention of the Department thereto."[42]

Far from surrendering these hunting grounds and fishing islands in the new treaty, then, Rama wanted additional protection from the Crown. Nonetheless, the treaty, as signed, was silent on the assurances of the Commissioners that certain areas could be set apart for hunting and fishing. Nor does it reflect the fact that Rama's surrender of lands was conditional on these stipulations being met.

That this was the Aboriginal perspective, however, is fairly clear when one considers the cultural values of the Ojibway. Working primarily from his observations of Cree, Ojibway, and Iroquoian peoples in Ontario, Clare Brant, the noted Mohawk psychiatrist, identified common behaviours among First Nations. He described how these tribes promoted positive inter-personal relations through complex but unspoken rules.[43] His findings were corroborated by Roger Spielmann, an anthropologist who has studied Ojibway culture extensively.

Spielmann noted that the Ojibway place great value on maintaining harmony in relationships in this manner. Cooperation is assumed, rather than negotiated.[44] Therefore, in Ojibway culture, a request is not easily made and should not be refused. As he has written, maintaining harmony in relationships by not refusing requests is one of the primary values in Ojibway culture. He comments, "Most non-Native people [do not] understand the extreme importance of maintaining harmony in the moment rather than allowing any kind of tension to develop by having to refuse a request. These Native values are completely contrary to the non-Native way of obtaining commitments and promises for future events."[45]

Therefore, the Ojibway would not have refused the Commissioners' request that the treaties be signed in blank, even though their own requests had not yet been met. At the same time, they would have fully expected their own requests to be fulfilled. From the Aboriginal perspective, the Commissioners' agreement to take the matter back for consideration was a promise to honour the requests made of them, as will be demonstrated below. Nor would the Commissioners' representations that they would take these matters back for discussion have altered the Aboriginal perception of the commitments made, since in Ojibway culture, to reject a request would entail a loss of face, an outcome to be avoided.[46]

Certainly, the First Nations behaved as if their requests had been met. For one thing, in the early 1930s, the Mississaugas of New Credit appointed Johnson Paudash to negotiate with the Department of Indian Affairs in regard to their own unsurrendered lands in the County of York, something they would probably not have done had they considered the 1923 treaty at all controversial.[47] And as evidenced by their post-treaty conduct, the Rama First Nation signatories believed they had received the promises they had requested. This is confirmed by the comments of hereditary Chief John Bigwin, made only a few short years after he had signed the Rama treaty.

In 1928, when three members of the Rama Band were charged with violating the game laws, Chief Bigwin insisted they had a treaty right to hunt and fish. As the *Toronto Star* reported,

> Chief John Bigwin of the Ojibway Nation has a grievance. Three of his tribe are in jail for hunting and trapping. And Chief Bigwin, who has a long memory, recalls that in the reign of George III, a treaty was made with Governor Simcoe by which the Indians surrendered their land on the promise that so long as grass grew and water ran they were to be permitted to hunt and fish without bar or bound. The big chief's protest was written in his own hand and forwarded to Attorney-General Price: "Would you kindly tell me if these treaties made by Queen Victoria and King Edward still stand good and a treaty by King George III said just the same?" It said in part, "I want to stay by Confederation, so will you kindly see about these Indians and let them go free or I will have to see King George."[48]

Covering the same story in a 9 May 1928 article, the *Montreal Gazette* observed that Bigwin had written to W.H. Price, the Ontario Attorney General, to complain that members of his band had been imprisoned for violating hunting and trapping laws. The *Gazette* commented that "Mr. Price considers the case one for the Indian Department at Ottawa and he will take the matter up with them ... D. McDonald, deputy Minister of Fish and Game stated today that a few years ago they paid the Indians $500,000 for all rights in the Simcoe-Peterboro-Haliburton area and he expressed the opinion that an identical agreement had been made with the Washago (Rama) Indians."[49]

The *Globe* ran a similar story, indicating that Attorney General Price had promised an "investigation of the complaint made by Chief John Bigwin that three of his Indians have been put in jail for hunting and fishing." It reproduced Bigwin's letter to Colonel Price, which read, in part,

> Dear Sir: I am writing to let you know that three Indians had been put in jail for hunting and traping [sic] and I would like to see if you can do anything about it as I would like to get these men free as the treaty said that we would have free hunting and fishing as long as the grass grows and water runs ... as I am the chief of the nation now I would like peace with the white people as well as the Indians and I don't want any Indians put in jail for hunting on their own ground nor do I want any white people put in jail. I want to stay by confederation so will you kindly see about these Indians and let them go free or I will have to go see king George hopping [sic] this is not asking to much I am as ever yours. (signed) Chief John Bigwin.

The article concluded with,

> This naive appeal of the Indian will strike a responsive chord in public sentiment. Most people have a profound sympathy with the Indians whose rights it has often been recognized have not always been protected by Governments as well as they might have been. Chief Bigwin retains the Indian's unspoiled confidence that the King can set his grievance right and that the way to the foot of the Throne is open to him. His statement that he will appeal to King George if his men are not released may be ingenuous but it illustrates again that sublime confidence that native peoples in all parts of the British Empire have that justice and fair dealing are the foundations of the British Throne and that any treaty Britain has set her signature to is no mere "scrap of paper," but a document to be honoured and its provisions carried out. If the Indian was given the right to hunt and fish on his own property "while grass grows and water runs," that right should be maintained today. The complaint should be investigated and if a wrong has been done, it should be set right.[50]

Certainly, at that time, there was nothing to indicate that any of the parties to the Williams Treaties understood them to extinguish earlier treaty rights, and Chief Bigwin's complaint had received a sympathetic response.

In 1930, Arthur S. Anderson, the Indian Agent for Rama, informed the Indian Affairs Secretary that he had learned that Councillor Gilbert Williams was prepared to go to jail to protect his rights to fish. Anderson said that the Rama Band, who fished in Muskoka waters during the summer, had often complained to him that "they cannot sell any fish they catch in that District. In one particular case of Gilbert Williams, this Indian for a number of years has visited Muskoka and from the sale of fish made his living, but now this year, he states he has been notified that he cannot sell any. This I consider a hardship on this old Indian for he depends on the sale of his fish to make his living."[51] Williams told Anderson, "I am going to fish and if caught I will go to jail before I pay a fine."[52] Importantly, while the Rama Band member was being told he could not sell his fish, no one seems to have suggested that he could not freely fish for food.

In 1931, Rama treaty signatory Chief Alder York visited Ottawa and left behind a Memorial. It stated that "the Indians were promised by the Three Commissioners who took the Chippewa Treaty in 1923 that they would have the privilege of hunting and fishing within the bounds of the territory ceded without a licence and also were promised a certain area of the said ceded territory in the vicinity of the Moose Deer Point for their own special hunting grounds."[53] That same year, the Rama Band Council passed a resolution asking Indian Affairs for its assistance in protecting the same fishing islands that it had referred to during the treaty negotiations:

> We, the members of the Rama Band of Indians do humbly ask to intercede for us to the officials of the Game and Fish Department to give us a special privilege to fish and sell the fish this summer as there is no work in the country. And we don't see any other way could make our living this summer ... We catch fish by trolling and as a rule we dont catch very many and *the name of the lakes where our people fish as follows,* – Lake Simcoe, Couchiching, Sparrow Lake, Muskoka Lake, Rousseau Lake, Lake Joseph and Skeleton Lake.[54]

Thus, long after the 1923 treaties, Rama members had continued to hunt and fish for food in the lands that Ontario would later claim they had willingly agreed to surrender.

As noted earlier, Sparrow Lake, a few miles north of Lake Simcoe, had been mentioned during the treaty commission hearings as an area where band members continued to hunt and fish. The Rama Band Council passed another resolution on 6 June 1931, that "agent Anderson be requested to notify the Department of Indian Affairs that members of Rama are determined to fish notwithstanding results and will oppose any actions resulting from prosecution for fishing."[55] The resolution was signed by Chief York, former Chief J.B. Stinson, Sam Williams, and William Martell, all signatories to the 1923 treaty.

In October, Rama passed a similar band resolution with respect to the trapping and hunting of fur-bearing animals, including deer, "without paying a licence fee, during open season, notwithstanding any results," and added that it would "oppose with legal assistance any prosecution taken against any member of the Rama Band."[56] Indian Agent Anderson forwarded the resolution to Indian Affairs, noting that he had told the Rama Band Council that if "they carried out their threat, it would lead them into very expensive litigation." He also remarked that "They still maintain that under the old Treaties, they should not have to pay a licence."[57]

That November, Chief York sent Indian Agent Anderson a letter instructing him to explain to the Indian Affairs Department on the band's behalf that under the *Royal Proclamation,* "the Indians were to enjoy the full enjoyment of their rights in hunting and fishing and lands, and to live without molestation or hindrance."[58] The letter closed with, "Now Mr. Anderson, you've heard what the commissioner said in 1923, before the presence of the people that the Indians could hunt and fish on the lands now ceded without being molested."[59] It also attached a resolution in which the Rama Band Council demanded to know under what authority its right to hunt and trap without licences had been taken away.[60] Anderson forwarded the resolution to A.F. Mackenzie, Secretary of Indian Affairs, adding that the Rama Council had not been satisfied with Mackenzie's explanation and commenting that "you will notice they go a long way back in dealing with the question."[61]

In November 1933, Sam Snache (Snake), who had interpreted for the Commissioners at the Rama hearings, prepared another Memorial of Stipulation and Memorial of "Greivience" in which he outlined what he understood was promised at the time of the treaty proceedings. The areas to which it refers are exactly those mentioned in the Commissioners' 3 December 1923 letter to Duncan Campbell Scott reporting on the negotiations at Rama. There, the Commissioners had simply noted that the band had requested the areas, but Snake wrote that the band had received promises of protection:

> Lands been promised at the time of the signing of the Surrender Nineteen Hundred and Twenty-Three. Viz:- Moose Deer Point lying between Mosquosh and Moon Rivers as for our perpetual Reserve and near by hunting ground a rocky country not settled. Viz: Matchadash township and also small parcels of Land; Viz- Chief Island in the proximity of the reserve and Eight mile point for our fishing ground and one Island on Lake Dalyrymple and One Island in Sparrow Lake known as the Indian Island and Port Carling

> for our summer camp grounds and also another Island in Xoshee Lake. These lands were faithfully promised by the Dominion and the Provincial Government Commissioners A.W. [sic] Williams, McFadden Sinclair and Miss Moody Sec. and they also promised a privelege to hunt and trap and fish within the bounds of territory ceded to the Crown without a licence. Under nearly three hundred witnesses. And now we hope that the Indians of Rama Indian Reservation that these promises be carried out.[62]

Anderson advised A.F. Mackenzie that "This question comes up annually when they are required to [get] their licences."[63]

In May 1938, four members of the Rama Band, Jacob St. Germain, Sanford Stinson, Stanley Shilling, and Russell Fawn, were charged with spearing pickerel. Covering the case, the *Toronto Star* ran the following headline: "May Fish While Grass Grows and Water Runs, Chief of 98 Pleads – Need Food Is Plea." The *Star* continued:

> "Your worship, these Indians will starve if they are deprived of rights to fish," declared Boulton S. Marshall in Police Court. Counsel for Rama Reserve, he appeared before magistrate Bick to plead in charges of spearing pickerel on Lake St. John.
>
> ... "We were supposed to have free fishing rights as long as the grass grows and the waters run" testified John Bigwind [sic], 98 year old hereditary Chief of the reserve. "The great white queen signed an agreement to give us these rights. I have a copy of the treaty and I don't think my boys should be punished."[64]

On 10 May, another newspaper reported that Chief Bigwin, the "92 year old patriarch who claims the hereditary chieftainship of the Ojibway Indian Tribe of the Rama reserve came out of retirement yesterday to plead for his children, four Rama reserve Indians who appeared in police court on charges of spearing fish in [the] close season." The paper added that Chief Bigwin, clad in the full regalia of his tribe, and by then almost blind, had been led into the courtroom by one of his younger followers for what was described as a "test case." "The Indians claim the territory on which they were fishing was part of the reserve where they have special privileges and provincial game laws do not apply. 'Queen Victoria told my grandfather, my father and myself that so long as the grass grows and the water runs I and my children may hunt and fish forever and ever,' Chief Bigwin told Magistrate C.F. Bick. He brandished a time yellowed document which the chief claimed was the original Treaty Queen Victoria made with the red men."[65]

Two days later, another newspaper article stated that "Officials of the Indian Affairs Branch believe Indians have the right to fish in Lake St.

John, on the Rama Reserve near Orillia under the terms of old treaties ... The understanding here is that the lake is entirely surrounded by reserve land. If this is found to be so, the Indians may spear fish under the old treaties giving them the right to take game and fish on their land 'so long as the grass grows and the water runs.'"[66]

According to the lawyer representing the accused, Indian Affairs had assured the Indians "that they could not possibly be prosecuted under the circumstances and in view of this, they contested these cases."[67] These were not the assurances one would have expected, had treaty rights to hunt and fish been extinguished voluntarily only fifteen years earlier.

When he was almost one hundred years old, Chief John Bigwin gave an interview to the *Orillia Packet and Times* in which he again asserted that the Commissioners, at the time of the signing, had said that Indians would be able to hunt, fish, and trap, and that fishing and hunting were not included in the surrender. The *Packet and Times* commented that

> Chief John Bigwind [sic], the patriarch of the Rama Reserve, visited Orillia on Saturday afternoon to obtain publicity for his protest against the claim that the Indians had given up their alleged right to fish and hunt outside the reserve in the treaty made in 1923.
>
> Chief Bigwind, who will be one hundred years old on the 20th of August, was one of those who negotiated the Treaty. Indeed, he was said to be chiefly instrumental in bringing it about as the result of a chance interview he had on the Train with the Hon. G. Howard Ferguson. Under these treaties the Indians were allowed a half million dollars for their claims to the lands north of Orillia, which had never been formally surrendered ... Chief Bigwind, whose mind is remarkably clear and his memory good ... declares that at the time the treaty was made, the Indians were given to understand that it did not interfere with their right to hunt and fish ...
>
> Before signing the treaty, each commissioner got up and said these very words, – that the Indians would still be able to hunt, fish and trap. Restrictions on fishing wasn't to be included in the treaty ... "We don't want the fish or game," they said ... Fishing and hunting were not included in the sale of land. Its the resource for our living ... Even in May and June it is really hard for us in the reservation and we have to do something to live. We ask the Indian Department for relief. What do they say? Go and fish and hunt. Then the inspectors or wardens stop us. We must have some way to live.[68]

From the Aboriginal perspective, then, the Williams Treaty signed at Rama was conditional on the First Nation receiving the concessions it requested when the treaty was signed, namely, the right to hunt and fish without a licence. However, the Commissioners claimed to have "no recollection" of making any such promises.[69] A.F. Mackenzie informed Chief

Alder York on 12 May 1931 that the most the Commissioners had promised was to "take up with the Provincial authorities" the question of setting apart a special area in the vicinity of Moose Deer Point as hunting grounds, but that "the Province was unwilling to make such a concession after having paid the Indians generously in the making of the treaty."[70]

Whether the misunderstanding as to what was promised in 1923 resulted from cultural differences, interpretation difficulties, or perhaps unintentionally misleading statements by the Commissioners is not clear. However, as the Royal Commission on Aboriginal Peoples commented many years later, treaty negotiations are complex and often the subject of cultural misunderstandings. The Royal Commission observed, "These contradictions were often not evident, or remained unspoken, in the negotiation and conclusion of solemn treaty agreements. Over time, treaties became more complex and difficult to negotiate. In many cases, it is questionable whether the Indian parties understood the legal and political implications of the land conveyance documents they were asked to sign."[71]

The Royal Commission also noted that tremendous barriers are created when two cultures with very different world views and experiences attempt to understand and come to terms with one another. These obstacles often result in oversimplified explanations, with common understanding thus reached only at the broadest levels, and often require the parties to rely on mutual trustworthiness and good faith.[72] That good faith and good intentions did exist with the Williams Treaties is evident in the fact that the treaties were not even complete when they were signed. However, within a decade, this good faith was replaced by the technical reliance of Ontario bureaucrats on the restrictive legal effect of the basket clause, as will soon be seen.

Regardless of Ontario's later views of the treaty, there is little doubt that the Aboriginal signatories, at least at Rama, believed they had been promised additional protection for their rights. Their actions, unlike those of the government officials who advised them, remained consistent over time. Whatever internal matters the Commissioners might have needed to address with Ontario, the post-treaty conduct of Rama Band members evidences their understanding that they had retained their treaty rights. Indeed, they could hardly have known otherwise, since the Crown did not provide them with written copies of the treaties for almost nine years after they were signed.

A.S. Williams completed the treaties with the missing information and filed them with the Registrar in June 1924. When no copies were forthcoming, Rama's lawyer, Melvin B. Tudhope, who, as noted, had attended the commission hearings, tried to get them. In October 1924, he wrote, "I would like to get copies of the Treaties made in November, 1923, with the Indians of the Rama Reserve and with the Peterborough Indians. These treaties have a definite bearing on the enforcement of game laws here and I would like to have copies of the treaties on file so that the Indians may have information from time to time."[73] Indian Affairs replied that the treaties had not been printed and were therefore not available for distribution. However, J.D. McLean advised him that "these treaties have no bearing whatsoever on the game laws of the Province."[74]

In April 1931, Johnson Paudash wrote to the Secretary of Indian Affairs also asking for a copy of the 1923 treaty,[75] but he received no response. Later that year, when Arthur Whetung of the Mud Lake Band was charged with trapping on private lands, he too requested a copy of the treaty from Indian Affairs.[76] He received the astonishing answer that "the department has no copies of the treaty entered into between the Dominion Government and the Province of Ontario in 1923."[77] Whetung then wrote to the Indian Lands and Timber Branch clarifying that the treaty he wanted was the one entered into between the Mud Lake Band of Indians and the Dominion of Canada "and concurred in by the Government of the Province of Ontario ... please send me a copy of the Treaty."[78] A.F. Mackenzie replied, giving the same incredible response – that the Department of Indian Affairs "has no copies of the Treaty entered into between the Government of the Dominion of Canada and the Mississaugas of the Mud Lake Band of Indians."[79]

Joseph Mangan, the Oshawa lawyer defending Arthur Whetung against the charges, tried to get a copy of the treaty as well. He wrote to the Secretary of Indian Affairs asking for a copy of the "Agreement or Treaty dated the 15th of November 1923 made between the Mud Lake band of Indians and the Crown and which we believe also affects the Counties of Victoria and Peterborough or perhaps the lands adjacent thereto on the East. We would accordingly ask you to be good enough to let us have a copy of the latter Treaty also."[80] It does not appear that he received a response.

It seems beyond question that the Department's insistence that it had no copies of the treaty was deliberately misleading. J.E. Anderson, the Lindsay lawyer prosecuting Arthur Whetung, wrote directly to A.S. Williams, by then the Assistant Deputy Minister and Departmental Solicitor for Indian Affairs, asking for a copy of the treaty to use in his case.[81] A.F. Mackenzie, the Secretary of Indian Affairs, clarified that the Department had no "copies" of the treaty, but only the originals, adding that "If, however, there is any particular subject concerning the Treaty in which you are interested, I shall be pleased to forward you an extract. I may add for your information that there is nothing in the treaty with respect to Indian hunting or fishing rights, and I am not aware of any manner in which the treaty could be invoked with any hunting or fishing case."[82]

How J.E. Anderson was supposed to identify what might interest him in the text of a treaty he had never seen perhaps requires no further comment. Nonetheless, at least Canada had acknowledged that it possessed the treaty and had offered to provide him with extracts for his prosecution. The First Nations actually involved in the treaty received no such information. In fact, it was not until 1932, after a frustrated Arthur Whetung complained directly to the Privy Council, that the First Nations finally received copies of the completed treaties.[83] Six copies were forwarded to the Rice Lake Indian Agent,[84] and Arthur Whetung was informed by the Secretary of Indian Affairs that a copy of the treaty had been sent to the Agent at Hiawatha.[85] At that time, perhaps not coincidentally, the King's Printer finally published the treaties.[86]

Soon after the treaties were circulated, some nine years after they were signed, A.S. Williams contacted the presiding magistrate in Whetung's case to ask for leniency in the charges. He wrote that Arthur Whetung was "well and favourably known to the Department."[87] He also noted that

> [this] type of case is one that is frequently brought to our attention. The [Mud Lake] Indians cling persistently to the belief that they are entitled to hunt and fish over all lands which were formerly used by their ancestors, and the Department has experienced great difficulty in making them realize that they are subject to the laws of the Province, except when on their own reserve, where it is held that the laws of the Province do not apply. It is particularly difficult to convince them with respect to lands covered with water.
>
> ... To revert to the present case, I may say after having interviewed Mr. Arthur Whetung at some length, I am fully satisfied that he was convinced in his own mind that he was within his rights in hunting on the lands in question and that if he had understood the position of the matter as it has now been explained to him, he would not have committed the offence.[88]

Williams made no mention of the 1923 surrender as having had any effect on Mud Lake's pre-existing treaty rights but instead pointed out that provincial laws applied to all Indians whenever they hunted or fished off-reserve. Perhaps more important is his observation that Whetung was "convinced in his own mind that he was within his rights." In light of the fact that both men participated in the same treaty process, it would be harder to find a clearer statement of the Aboriginal perspective.

The Intention of the Crown

The intention of the Aboriginal parties appears to have been clear: to obtain redress for lands they could no longer use as hunting grounds, to secure the Crown's protection for the areas they continued to use, and, in the case of Rama, to gain additional protected territories. The Crown's intention, however, is also important to consider.

As already observed, the Commissioners had repeatedly stated throughout the hearings that their mandate was to deal only with lands that had not previously been surrendered. What, then, can one make of the basket clause, which purported to extinguish all rights except those on-reserve?

Answering this question requires a close examination of the language used in other agreements. A basket clause of the type used in 1923 re-appeared shortly afterward, in the 1929 adhesions to Treaty No. 9, but to a very different effect. This time, the actual treaty negotiations were carefully recorded by the Treaty Commissioners, one of whom, W.C. Cain, had been involved in the approvals of the Williams Treaties as Deputy Minister of Lands and Forests for Ontario. Significantly, in his capacity as Commissioner in the Treaty No. 9 adhesions, he promised the First Nations with whom he negotiated that their fishing, hunting, and trapping rights would be protected, and that some areas in the lands they surrendered would even be made exclusive for their use.

The process that culminated in the 1929 negotiations may have resulted from a 1923 article that appeared in the *Ottawa Citizen*. In it, the Premier of Ontario, G.H. Ferguson, erroneously remarked that the Williams Treaties had dealt with the last remaining Aboriginal title claims anywhere in the province, and that "every tribe that could possibly have a claim on the white man's government had been taken care of."[89] The *Ottawa Citizen* happily proclaimed that Ontario's payment for "the loss of the Chippewa and Mississauga hunting and fishing grounds" would be the last one the Province would ever have to make on that account and that, "As the matter of settlement of Indian claims for compensation for lost territory has exercised governments for a century or more, the premier is naturally glad to have seen the last of the problem. Since Toronto was a village, municipalities, corporations and governments have periodically been confronted with compensation demands from the Indians, who felt themselves entitled to reparations for lands claimed by civilization."[90]

However, Ferguson soon learned that his announcement had been premature. Duncan Campbell Scott reminded the Premier that a large portion of Ontario north of the Albany River had not yet been ceded: "I noted yesterday's despatch from Toronto ... in which you are reported as having stated that the last claim of the Indians of the Province of Ontario had been dealt with. I wish to draw your attention to the fact that the Indian title to a large portion of the Province north of the Albany River has not yet been ceded ... Certain Indians in this district who trade at posts on the Albany River are already annuitants under Treaty 9, but the remaining population of approximately 1500 have not relinquished their Aboriginal rights to this territory."[91]

Premier Ferguson thanked Scott for his letter and explained that he had "understood from the Commission that we cleaned up the whole question of Indian claims against the Province ... I am communicating with the

Commission today upon the subject."[92] The result of these communications was that Ontario and Canada agreed to enter into yet another treaty, this time involving the northern First Nations.

Although the Crown had repeatedly insisted that Aboriginal peoples had no special rights or Aboriginal title in waters, the surrender document prepared in the Treaty No. 9 adhesion negotiations clearly indicated that they did. Indeed, the Treaty No. 9 adhesions specify "land covered by water" in the surrender, whereas the 1923 treaties do not. This is important, as the description of the northern surrender was prepared by Scott himself and included "All that tract of land *and land covered by water* in the Province of Ontario, comprising part of the District of Patricia, containing one hundred and twenty-eight thousand three hundred and twenty square miles, more or less ... and including all islands, islets and rocks, waters and lands covered by water within the said limits."[93]

In preparing for the treaty adhesions, F.E. Titus, the solicitor for Ontario's Lands and Forests Department, was asked for an explanation of the general background to Treaty No. 9. He prepared a memorandum for Cain in which he summarized the Williams Treaties. These he referred to as effecting only the surrender of "portions" of land, or about 10,719 square miles; nowhere did he mention that the Indians had surrendered their interests in any other lands in Ontario. Indeed, in the same report, Titus informed Cain that

> [a]ccording to a letter dated May 1, 1926 received by the Premier of Ontario from the Department of Indian Affairs ... it appears that Indians claiming title to lands in an alleged unceded portion of Ontario which roughly speaking is all that portion of Ontario lying north of the Albany River, west of James Bay and East of the Manitoba Border have applied for a treaty ... The Premier of our Province agrees it will be quite proper to have this Indian situation cleared up as rapidly as possible and states that the Government would be glad to co-operate with the Indian Department in the working out of a treaty to take care of the Indians in question.[94]

Titus explained how two other groups entering into similarly worded treaties had sought and received assurances that a basket clause would not confine them to hunting and fishing on their reserves. In both Treaty No. 5 with the Saulteaux and Swampy Cree Tribes and Treaty No. 9 with the Ojibway, Cree, and other Indians, Titus noted that although the "subscribing Indians surrendered their rights, not only to the areas therein specifically described, but also to other lands wheresoever situated in Canada," the Indians were insistent that their fishing and hunting rights should not be interfered with. Also, Titus added, they "feared that if they signed the treaty they would be compelled to reside upon the Reserve to be granted to them and would be deprived of their fishing and hunting privileges which they now enjoy. On being informed that their fears in regard to both these matters were groundless, as their present manner of making a livelihood would in no way be interfered with, the Treaty was signed."[95]

In 1929, W.C. Cain and Herbert Awrey, a senior accounting clerk with the Department of Indian Affairs, were appointed as Treaty Commissioners for the northern negotiations. This time, unlike their 1923 Williams Treaty counterparts, the Commissioners had an express mandate: first, they were to obtain a surrender of lands *and* waters; second, they were to secure a treaty that would operate as a full release of rights – "to release and surrender also all Indian rights and privileges whatsoever of the said Indians to all or any other lands wherever situated in Ontario, Quebec, Manitoba or the District of Keewatin, or in any other portion of the Dominion of Canada."[96] This mandate was confirmed in the Order-in-Council that appointed them.[97]

As the negotiations for the Treaty No. 9 adhesions progressed, several drafts were prepared for the surrender. All contained a basket clause involving a surrender of all rights, titles, and privileges "to the said territory ... and also all the said Indian rights, titles and privileges whatsoever to all other lands and lands covered by water wheresoever situated in the Dominion of Canada."[98] Each First Nation, on signing the treaty, was to receive a flag and a copy of the treaty. Reserves would be set aside of not more than 640 acres for each family of five, and the Aboriginal signatories would "in turn cede any rights they may have and promise to abide by the law and ... maintain peace between each other and with other tribes of Indians, halfbreeds and whites."[99]

Duncan Campbell Scott wrote to Cain indicating that, during the negotiations, the First Nations in the area were likely to ask that the government make some provision for their continued hunting. As was the case in the Williams Treaties, he indicated that the Commissioners should assure the Indians that they would get sympathetic treatment from the Province, adding, "I am hopeful that after giving the matter every consideration you may be disposed to suggest to your Government the justice of setting apart various tracts within which the Indians shall have the sole right to take game, or that the game laws may be so modified, or such other provisions made, as will preserve to the Indians a continuance of living."[100]

Scott told Herbert Awrey that he had impressed upon Cain the "justice of ensuring to the Indians a continuance of their right to take game for a living. I shall be glad if you keep this matter before you in taking the adhesion to Treaty No. 9 and support the views expressed in this letter."[101]

Cain's report on the subsequent treaty negotiations indicates that he and Awrey heard many Indian grievances regarding hunting and fishing, and that, in response, the Commissioners had explained the application of provincial game laws to Indians. Nonetheless, the Commissioners recommended that a large part of northern Ontario be set aside as an exclusive hunting and trapping area for the Indians, so that they "may be assured of a continuous source of natural supply for their sustenance."[102]

Reporting on the progress of the negotiations, a newspaper article noted that the adhesions had been signed at Trout Lake and "The last great treaty negotiations are over ... The Indians have gone back to their fishing and their potato growing."[103] A *Toronto Star* article described the negotiations, quoting Awrey as saying that the Commissioners had assured the bands that, along with annuities, "they would still have the privilege to hunt and fish as usual in return for the lands they ceded."[104] Despite the clear mandate of the Commissioners to extinguish all rights, then, the basket clause seems to have been regarded as mere boilerplate and of less significance than the other clauses of the treaty.

Oral histories concerning the Treaty No. 9 adhesions suggest that the Aboriginal signatories did not intend to surrender their rights in the land either. Chief Frank Beardy, describing the understanding of his grandfathers when they signed the 1929 adhesion, said, "They didn't say anything about the land being taken. They agreed to share the land. How Native people look at the land is that no one person owns that land. The Creator owns that land. How can our forefathers, our grandfathers, give away something that they didn't own in the first place?"[105]

The Post-1923 Period

In the years immediately following the Williams Treaties and the northern adhesions, First Nations throughout Ontario continued to insist that they had special rights to hunt and fish, and Ontario continued to lay charges against them under provincial and federal legislation. In other words, very little changed.

As the Royal Commission on Aboriginal Peoples has noted, internal squabbling between federal government departments as to the existence and scope of Aboriginal and treaty rights added to the problems faced by First Nations peoples trying to exercise their rights. For example, employees of the federal Department of Mines explicitly rejected statements from Indian Affairs that treaty Indians had any specific harvesting rights on public lands.[106] As well, even though the official Indian Affairs position was that Indians were subject to provincial fishing laws, the Department sometimes supplied seine nets to First Nations even though the use of these was illegal under both provincial *and* federal fisheries laws.[107]

Ottawa's official position, however, was that Indians had no special rights in Ontario. For example, despite Sir Francis Bond Head's promise in 1836 to remove white men from the waters around the Saugeen Peninsula, the Chief Surveyor for Indian Affairs advised the Acting Secretary of Indian

Affairs in 1928 that he could find no evidence "that the Saugeen Indians have any fishing rights in the waters adjoining their reserves other than those to which claim could be made as a riparian owner."[108] In 1929, a request by L. Ritchie of the Saugeen Band that the Fishery Department provide him with a copy of the "old treaty" and a chart showing the reserved waters[109] produced the response that "there is no need to send maps or documents to this Indian."[110] Ritchie's Indian Agent was directed to tell him that Indians had no special privileges or rights.[111] Sixty-five years later, the courts would disagree, finding that, under the Bond Head treaty, the Saugeen Ojibway Nation had Aboriginal and treaty rights to fish commercially in priority to other users, a right extending seven miles into Georgian Bay and Lake Huron.[112]

Despite governmental nonrecognition of their rights, Aboriginal peoples continued to rely on hunting and fishing as their primary means of support. The Indian Affairs annual report for 1929, released only six years after the Williams Treaties were signed, noted that "hunting and fishing are Aboriginal vocations of the primitive Indians." It observed that white men were depleting fish and game in Indian hunting territories, and that there had been a "commercialization of fishing waters in the vicinity of Indian reserves without consideration of the needs of the Indian population." The report commented that, in some cases, the Crown had granted exclusive licences to white fishing interests covering waters fronting reserves "upon which the Indians had originally located themselves expressly on account of the fishing advantages. To be cut off in this arbitrary manner from their natural food supply is a serious and unmerited misfortune for the Indians concerned. These conditions, needless to say, are not within the control of this Department, which, however, loses no opportunity to obtain redress and protection for its wards."[113]

In reality, Indian Affairs continued to do little to protect the interests of Aboriginal peoples against provincial enforcement actions. At the Tyendinaga Mohawk territory on the Bay of Quinte, a seine net owned by Elizabeth Sero, a widow, and used by several band members for food and commercial purposes had been seized by provincial authorities two years before the Williams Treaties, in 1921. When Sero sued for the value of the net, she lost in an extraordinary judgment issued by Justice Riddell, who stated that "to talk of treaties with the Mohawk Indians, residing in the heart of one of the most populous districts of Upper Canada, upon lands purchased for them and given to them by the British government, is much the same in my humble opinion, as to talk of making a treaty of alliance with the Jews of Duke Street." It should be noted that Riddell, a fellow member of the Royal Society along with Duncan Campbell Scott, informed Scott that he had personally searched the archives for material to counter the Tyendinaga claim before rendering his decision.[114]

The Indian Affairs Department reported that the Mohawks of the Bay of Quinte at Tyendinaga, however, took the stand that they were "not amenable to the fisheries regulations ... The Indians were still stubborn, and notwithstanding the judgment against them, adhered to the view that they did not require any licence."[115] When the Band Council called on Indian Affairs to intervene, the Department did ask the Department of Game and Fisheries in Toronto to permit a band member to use a seine net, but it failed to pursue the matter when Ontario refused to give authorization.[116]

When the Mohawks continued to fish in the Bay of Quinte using seine nets, the Department of Indian Affairs characterized their practice as "illegal." An internal report indicated that "the Indians have continued to fish with nets in the bay and sell their fish illegally to buyers from adjacent towns. The provincial authorities are well aware of this condition and there is a constant game of hide and seek between them and the Indians. This Department could not very well interfere in the matter of low prices paid to the Indians for illegal taking of fish."[117]

In 1930, as the dispute between the Mohawks of the Bay of Quinte and the provincial Fishery Overseer regarding their use of seine nets heightened, the overseer directed a company dredging material from a Bay of Quinte channel to dump stone along the shore of the reserve, destroying the Aboriginal fishery altogether.[118] The Department of Public Works confirmed that the step had been taken with the consent of the Deputy Minister of Game and Fisheries.[119]

Although section 12 of the *Ontario Game Protection Act* had provided that game laws would not apply to Indians or to settlers in the unorganized districts of Ontario when it came to domestic hunting and fishing,[120] this clause had been dropped by the 1920s. Recreational hunting and angling now trumped Aboriginal rights. Fish and game were seen as a public resource, one in which Aboriginal people should not hold special entitlements. As David Taylor, Ontario Deputy Minister of Game and Fisheries, explained to Indian Affairs in 1936, his government believed that the fish and game resources of the province were far too important to be left to Aboriginal people to "slaughter."[121]

The Province soon decided that Aboriginal peoples were not to be permitted to fish even in the waters adjacent to their reserves, a position it took without any challenge from the Indian Affairs Department at Ottawa. In 1931, James Farrington, the Assistant to the Deputy Minister of Game and Fisheries, Ontario, asked A.F. Mackenzie, the Secretary of Indian Affairs, to inform him whether the waters adjoining the islands in Buckhorn, Little Mud, and Chemong Lake were part of the Indian reservations and just what privileges the Indians had in those waters. Farrington's letter was forwarded to the Chief Surveyor at Indian Affairs, D. Robertson, for his reply. Without mentioning the 1923 treaty, Robertson simply asserted yet again that Indians had no better rights than any other riparian landowners, writing to T.R.L. MacInnes that "you are probably in a better position to reply to this letter than I am. I do not see how the waters adjoining these islands can be considered within the reservations and as far as I am aware, the Indians have no special privileges in these waters other than those to which the general public or riparian owners would be entitled."[122]

Since the Mud Lake First Nation had no waters on its reserve, even a narrow interpretation of the 1923 Williams Treaty promises that it could continue to fish would necessitate its doing so in the waters adjacent to its reserve. Nonetheless, the Secretary of Indian Affairs informed Ontario that "so far as this department is aware the waters adjoining these islands do not constitute part of the reserves, nor is the department aware of any special privileges enjoyed by the Indians in those waters other than those to which the general public or riparian owners would be entitled."[123] The Ontario Game and Fisheries Department confirmed to Chief Daniel Whetung of Mud Lake that "no special privileges are enjoyed by Indians in these waters other than those to which the general public or riparian owners are entitled."[124]

In 1933, members of the Mud Lake Band petitioned Indian Affairs "intimating they are in hard case and in need of relief, and stating they cannot understand why they are not permitted to sell fish." The Deputy Minister of Indian Affairs advised the band's Indian Agent that, "With regard to fishing, this is subject to the laws and regulations of the Province. If the Indians desire to have a group or Band licence which would entitle them to fish commercially, and will submit applications through you, the Department will be glad to take the question up with the provincial authorities."[125]

The Province refused to issue such licences to Indians, and in 1934, a member of the Mud Lake Band was convicted of having forty pounds of muskellunge in his possession for commercial sale.[126] He was sentenced to a week in jail for violating the federal *Fisheries Act,* and since he was unable to pay a ten-dollar fine, he spent an extra ten days in jail for the "illegal" possession of fish under the *Game and Fisheries Act* of Ontario.[127]

In 1936, Pauline Jewett, then a candidate for election in Northumberland, contacted the Indian Affairs Department to inquire why the Rice Lake Band's "privilege" to ice-fish for food had been removed simply because the tourist, outfitter, and other associations were opposed to Indians fishing in winter for their domestic needs.[128] Again, Indian Affairs responded that the control and management of fishery resources in Ontario was a provincial matter. The Department suggested that "A solution to the problem of obtaining fish during the winter for domestic needs might be best secured by a submission to the Minister of Lands and Forests requesting relaxation of the ban on winter fishing." Extraordinarily, Indian Affairs did not bother to check its own files, writing instead that "There does not appear to be any record of the Band requesting assistance from this Branch in obtaining authority to fish during the winter."[129] There was little point in the Rice Lake Band making another attempt to secure permission from Ontario, when a request from Alnwick to ice-fish in the same waters had already been denied.[130]

J. Ashquabe, a signatory to the 1923 treaty and councillor at the Georgina Island First Nation, wrote to the Department of Indian Affairs in 1936, indicating his understanding that, under the terms of the treaty, he was supposed to be able to fish without a licence. He wrote that his gill net had been seized, contrary to his understanding of the promises exchanged: "Sirs, am I in error to think we Indians could fish for our own use anytime and in any way? My gill net was confiscated by Game Warden Frank Lyons of Virginia, Ontario. I had it set in an ice crevasse approximately ½ mile from the shoreline on our reserve in about forty feet of water he also confiscated 1 trout 16 whitefish which were caught. Please instruct me on what steps I may take."[131] A.F. Mackenzie, the Secretary of Indian Affairs, directed the Indian Agent at the reserve to advise Ashquabe that "Indians ... are subject to the Provincial regulations in the same manner as other people."[132]

In 1937, William Taylor, Hirum Taylor, and David Jacobs, members of the Mud Lake Band, were charged with ice-fishing 150 and 200 yards offshore from their reserve. As their lawyer reported to Indian Affairs, "the Indians believed that they were within their reserve and that they had a perfect right to fish for food off their own reserve."[133] The Indian Affairs Secretary responded with his stock answer that "in so far as I am aware these Indians have no special privileges in respect to fishing but are in the same position in regard thereto as other citizens."[134]

Indeed, regardless of their specific treaties, Indians throughout Ontario were consistently told that they had no special rights and would be prosecuted like other members of the public. "This department," J.D. McLean stated, "has recognized the exclusive right of the provinces to legislate with respect to hunting and fishing and has advised the Indians that they must obey the laws of the provinces with respect thereto."[135]

T. Murray Mulligan, a Sudbury lawyer, asked Indian Affairs if the Indians of the band at Naughton, Ontario, required a licence to net fish. He indicated that "It would appear from what the Chief tells me that licences were not heretofore required, but the Game Warden has issued a warning."[136] A.F. Mackenzie replied that "I have to advise you that the Indians are subject to the same laws and regulations of the province with regard to fishing licences in the same manner as other people."[137]

Even in northern Ontario, where Aboriginal peoples depended completely on fish and game, provincial officials saw these as "public" resources, not subsistence items to which Indians had any special claim. For example, in

1939, Kenora Indian Agent Frank Edwards asked David Taylor, the Ontario Game and Fisheries Deputy Minister, "how the Indians were going to make a living if they could not hunt or fish." Taylor replied that "it was nothing to do with him ... It was our department's baby, not his, and the Indians were not going to live on the province's moose, deer, fish, etc. and some other way of their making a living should be devised by us."[138]

Ontario courts supported this position, finding that the Province had the authority to unilaterally extinguish treaty rights and even rights on-reserve if it chose to do so. For example, in 1939, a judge of the Ontario High Court of Justice held that "it does not matter whether the Indians have any rights flowing from the reservation in the Robinson treaty or not. Such rights may be taken away by the Ontario Legislature without any compensation ... So even if the Indian had any rights within the reservation in section 109, the destruction of the same by the Ontario Game and Fisheries *Act* is *intra vires* the Provincial Legislature."[139]

With such rulings behind it, Ontario permitted non-Aboriginal fishermen unfettered access to fisheries, even within reserve waters. Lawrence James of the Chief Point Indian Reserve protested to Indian Affairs that white fishermen had been given licences to fish within three miles of his reserve, thereby "breaking Indian laws as I understand them."[140] H.R. Conn, Indian Affairs fur supervisor and a later advisor to the National Indian Brotherhood, responded that this was "not a question of law but a matter of Ontario Department policy."[141]

East of Ontario's Algonquin Park, not a single member of the Algonquins of Golden Lake First Nation who applied for registration of his existing traplines following his return from Second World War military service was successful. Conn complained to the head of Ontario's Fish and Wildlife Branch in 1947 that "Military service is apparently not taken into consideration as we find approved applications of men without military service in preference to Indians with four years' overseas service."[142] Conn pointed out that, when Algonquin Park was created in the 1890s, and hunting and trapping were banned within its boundaries, the Algonquins had lost most of their traditional trapping territories "without compensation."[143]

The Algonquins of Golden Lake claimed Aboriginal title to the area, a land claim considered sufficiently valid to be under negotiation with Ottawa and Ontario as a comprehensive claim currently.[144] Nonetheless, in 1954, when the Algonquins sought permission to fish and kill deer for their own use at any time during the year, they were refused. The Band Council passed a further resolution asking Indian Affairs to supply each family with a gill net and a rifle, but the Director of Indian Affairs responded that "The Golden Lake Band ... cannot claim any special right with regard to game except when on their reserves ... This Department does not have any jurisdiction over provincial crown lands ... Fishery regulations, being federal legislation, apply to all."[145] The last resolution of the band was described as both "unpractical and unrealistic."[146]

Despite its public denial of virtually all treaty rights in Ontario, Indian Affairs seems to have been aware that certain First Nations might indeed have special rights, but made a conscious policy decision to mislead them. In 1954, as the Superintendent of Welfare for Indian Affairs advised one of his officers with respect to an individual who had been charged with a hunting offence, "it is not the desire of the Branch to inform Indians fully concerning their Treaty rights because conservation and management could be defeated by so doing."[147]

Ontario's aggressive prosecutions against treaty Indians for hunting on unoccupied Crown lands continued well into the 1970s. For the first time, however, the Province began to lose in the courts, as judges examined more closely the extent to which it could regulate Indian harvesting rights. In 1970, for example, citing the *Game and Fish Act,* Ontario prosecuted a member of the Henvey Inlet Band for hunting moose illegally. Ontario argued that since the 1923 Williams Treaty territory overlapped part of the Robinson-Huron Treaty, the 1923 treaties had extinguished treaty rights there as well.[148] Moses, the accused, was originally convicted but was acquitted on appeal. This time, with a much more liberal tone than in prior decisions, and with the retired H.R. Conn testifying on behalf of the band, the Court concluded that Ontario could not apply its legislation to restrict treaty rights under the Robinson treaties:

> The sole right to legislate on behalf of Indians, and lands reserved for Indians is conferred on the Parliament of Canada by s. 91(24) of the *B.N.A. Act, 1867.* The Robinson Treaty was between the Province of Canada (Ontario and Quebec) and counsel for the Crown on this appeal raised the question, but without pressing it, as to whether in this case "property and civil rights" rather than "Indians and lands reserved for Indians" were involved ... I must reject this contention as I am satisfied from the authorities that it is only the Parliament of Canada which has power to abrogate the privilege to hunt which the Indians retained under the Robinson Treaty.[149]

Soon after this victory, the Mississaugas living at Mud Lake won their first court battle for recognition of their rights. On 7 February 1975, one hundred members of the Mud Lake Band ice-fished "illegally" in Buckhorn Lake to protest provincial legislation making it illegal for them to fish for food. Three were charged but all were acquitted on the basis of a band bylaw that enabled members to fish off-season in waters between Fox Island and the mainland.[150]

The Province persisted in its attempts to prove that the Williams Treaties

First Nations had no existing treaty rights. In 1977, Doug Williams and Wayne Taylor, both members of Mud Lake (which by then had become known as Curve Lake) were charged under the *Game and Fish Act* for taking bullfrogs out of season. They claimed an exemption from the provincial legislation on the basis of an "oral tradition which states that the Indian people never gave up their hunting and fishing rights in the provisional Agreement of 1818."[151] They were convicted when the Minutes of the negotiations that recorded the Crown's oral promises during the treaty were ruled inadmissible by the presiding judge.[152] However, Williams and Taylor appealed, and in 1981 the Ontario Court of Appeal overturned their convictions. Thus, in *R. v. Taylor and Williams,* a Canadian court held for the first time that oral promises made to Aboriginal peoples in a treaty proceeding formed part of the treaty itself.

The Court noted that "although the written articles of the [1818] treaty with the Chippewas contain no guarantee of fishing and hunting rights, an examination of minutes taken at a council meeting between the Deputy Superintendent of Indian Affairs, William Claus, and the chiefs of the six tribes who were parties to the treaty reveals that those rights were discussed at the time the treaty was signed."[153] It found that the promises made to the Mississaugas and Chippewas – that they could continue to hunt and fish – were binding, and that members of the First Nations were entitled to rely upon them. As the Court of Appeal observed in its decision, "If the Indians were to remain in the area one wonders how they were to survive if their ancient right to hunt and fish for food was not continued."

As a result of this ruling, the 1818 treaty was found to have preserved the historic right of the Mississaugas to hunt and fish on the lands they had surrendered in that year. After more than a hundred years in which the provincial government had denied them the exercise of their rights, and some 163 years after the Mississaugas had entered into the treaty, the Court concluded that provincial game laws did not, in fact, apply to the exercise of their treaty rights.[154]

During its arguments before the appellate court in *Taylor and Williams,* the Ontario government abandoned its call for a new trial on the charges. Although the record does not give a reason as to why Ontario changed its position, between 1979 and 1981, the Ontario Ministry of Natural Resources, the Indian Commission of Ontario, and the Union of Ontario Indians had joined together to interview the elders of the Williams Treaties. Given the probable nature of their evidence, which has not been located, the Court's acceptance of oral history in *Taylor and Williams* may have influenced Ontario's decision. The fact that the *Taylor and Williams* defence counsel, Paul Williams, had participated in the interviews as the representative of the Union of Ontario Indians may also have prompted the Province's decision. Had a new trial proceeded on the issue of the 1923 treaties, it may be assumed that he would have presented the elders and their oral history in support of his clients' defence.

One year after the decision in *Taylor and Williams,* the Canadian Constitution was amended to recognize and affirm pre-existing Aboriginal and treaty rights. Sections 35 and 52(1) of *Constitution Act, 1982* state that

> The existing Aboriginal and treaty rights of the Aboriginal peoples of Canada are hereby recognized and affirmed.
>
> The Constitution of Canada is the supreme law of Canada, and any law that is inconsistent with the provisions of the Constitution is, to the extent of the inconsistency, of no force or effect.

Despite this constitutional protection, the Ontario Ministry of Natural Resources decided to challenge the hunting and fishing rights of the Williams Treaties First Nations yet again. A detailed historical report on the Williams Treaties was prepared by a researcher in the Office of Indian Resource Policy, a branch of the Ministry of Natural Resources. Two weeks later, in December 1984, the Ministry laid new charges against four members of the Williams Treaties First Nations who had fished for food in waters near their reserve. Of these, only one proceeded to trial. The result was *R. v. Howard.*

8
The *Howard* Case

The Trial

George Henry Howard, a member of the Hiawatha First Nation at Rice Lake, was charged for fishing without a licence. The primary issue was whether he had an "existing" treaty right to fish protected by section 35 of the Constitution or whether his rights in the Otonabee River, where he had been fishing, had been extinguished by the 1923 Williams Treaties.

The trial was very brief. It proceeded by an Agreed Statement of Facts and only two witnesses, and was completed in less than a day. In part, this was due to the nature of such trials at the time. In 1986, when the *Howard* case went to trial, the Supreme Court of Canada had not yet set out guidelines for how a case involving Aboriginal rights should proceed, and with section 35 of the Constitution and the *Charter of Rights* in their infancy, rules of procedure involving evidentiary burdens and even the extent of Crown disclosure had yet to be established. Five years later, the Supreme Court of Canada would rule in *Stinchcombe* that the defence is entitled to full disclosure of all relevant information in the possession of the Crown, including statements obtained from persons the Crown does not propose to call as witnesses, but at the time of *Howard* there was no such requirement.[1]

The Crown and defence entered an Agreed Statement of Facts that established that George Howard was "a status Indian pursuant to the *Indian Act* of Canada and he is a member of the Hiawatha Band of Indians whose reserve is located on the shore of Rice Lake in the County of Peterborough; that the Hiawatha Band was and continues to be parties [sic] to treaties concluded with the Crown and that on January 18th, George Henry Howard took a few pickerel from the Otonabee River near to, but not on the Hiawatha reserve property ... at a time when the fishing season was closed."[2] Immediately after this Agreed Statement of Facts was read into court, the defence called its evidence.

Usually, in *quasi*-criminal cases such as *Howard,* the burden of proving its case beyond a reasonable doubt rests with the Crown. In cases invoking Aboriginal rights, the burden of proving extinguishment of an Aboriginal or treaty right also falls on the Crown, which must meet the test of "strict proof" akin to proof beyond a reasonable doubt. As the Supreme Court would state in another later ruling, *R. v. Sparrow,* this burden is due to the "serious and far-reaching consequences of a finding that a treaty right has been extinguished."[3]

Given that onus, the Crown should probably have been required to present its evidence of extinguishment first. Instead, for no reasons apparent on the record, Ian Johnson, a defence expert, was called as the first witness in the trial. Johnson, a claims co-ordinator with the Union of Ontario Indians, held a Master's degree in history. Unfortunately, although Johnson indicated that he had completed a historical narrative of the 1923 Williams Treaties over a six-month period prior to the trial, neither his research papers nor his *curriculum vitae* appear to have been filed with the Court.[4]

Johnson described the evolution of the Mississauga land claim, explaining that after decades of inaction, the federal government had finally agreed "at the instance of Ontario" that the best way to deal with the unsurrendered territory was to enter into a new treaty. He mentioned that although the First Nations had asked for legal representation during these treaty proceedings, "they were actually specifically forbidden to have independent legal counsel ... They were told that there was no need for independent legal counsel because the treaty commissioners themselves were lawyers and that based on the trust relationship that the Indians had with the federal government, the treaty commissioners would represent their best interests."[5]

Johnson noted that the Williams Treaties Commissioners had taken evidence from band members at the various Mississauga communities regarding their traditional family hunting territories in the north. He explained to the trial judge, R.B. Batten, that the Treaty Commissioners had told witnesses throughout the inquiry that they were not interested in any hunting and fishing grounds outside the area of their mandate, but on learning of additional unsurrendered areas, had nonetheless decided to include them in the 1923 treaty affecting the Mississaugas.[6]

Johnson testified that the inclusion of the additional lands was never the subject of any discussion with the First Nations, and that the federal and provincial governments had very limited knowledge that these additional clauses had been inserted into the treaty text either.[7]

In response to a question from the Court as to how the 1923 surrender affected the provisions of the earlier 1818 treaty, Johnson himself flagged the issue of the basket clause. Having already described the first two clauses of the Williams Treaty, he pointed out that "it is in fact the third paragraph, I would guess, that purports to deal with the 1818 treaty area ... So I would guess that that catch-all phrase is purporting to include any lands that the Mississaugas had ever had interest in or any privileges deriving out of that land tenure."[8]

Johnson expressed the opinion that the First Nations could not have intended to surrender their treaty rights, since the Commissioners had said during the treaty negotiations that they would approach the Department of Indian Affairs on the subject of protecting Hiawatha's hunting and fishing rights within Rice Lake and the southern 1818 treaty area. Therefore, Johnson's opinion was that the Hiawatha signatories did not realize that they "were signing anything other than a surrender of their hunting and fishing rights with respect to the 10,000 square miles in the northern part of old Ontario."[9] In support of his opinion, he raised an issue that was to play a determining role in the case, that of language. Although the Commissioners had retained interpreters who spoke both English and Ojibway, he had seen no indication that interpreters had been present during the proceedings. Instead, Johnson testified, there was a great deal of evidence to the effect that "most of the Chiefs, and headmen, being elder members of the Hiawatha Band, for example, did ... either not speak English or had limited grasp of the English language."[10]

Johnson also pointed out that the Hiawatha Band believed it had retained rights to hunt and fish under its 1818 treaty and had immediately begun protesting once it became aware that the 1923 treaty had taken these away.[11] The expert concluded his evidence with the opinion that the Mississauga Indians had not intended to surrender any hunting or fishing rights that they might have had in the 1818 treaty. "The evidence," he said, "would suggest quite the contrary, that they understood they had those rights and would have them protected from encroachment by the Province of Ontario."[12]

In reply, the Crown called only one witness, a former Chief from Hiawatha named Ralph Loucks. The fact that Loucks was not called as the Crown's first witness but as a reply witness allowed the Crown to avoid making disclosure of his evidence. It also permitted the Crown to put forward his evidence with little defence opportunity for preparation or rebuttal. Had Loucks testified as the trial's first witness, the defence might have had an opportunity to address some of the points he raised, or adjourn to locate other reply witnesses such as elders from Hiawatha. However, this was not possible, as Johnson had already completed his evidence when Ralph Loucks was called. In essence, the defence was left not knowing the case it was supposed to meet until its evidence had been completed, an unfairness that can only have affected the outcome of the trial. However, perhaps because the litigation was perceived as an Aboriginal case, rather than a criminal one, no objections to this procedure were raised by either the Crown or the defence.

Born in 1913 at Hiawatha, Ralph Loucks had been only ten years old when the Williams Treaties were signed. In response to Johnson's opinion that the Aboriginal signatories did not speak English and did not understand the implications of the treaty, Loucks testified that he had attended school at Hiawatha, and that English was the only language taught at that time, although most people spoke both languages. Regarding the treaty, given his age, Loucks testified that "I don't remember that much but what I do remember, I didn't know that I had any special rights."[13] After 1923, Loucks did not feel that he had any more rights to hunt or fish than anyone else, and "never was aware ever in my life that [game and fish laws] did not apply to me ... I have always lived by them and done what I had ... I had gone fishing, sure, as much as anybody, but as I said, if I got caught, I paid the fine. I wasn't aware that there was any difference. I'm not saying there wasn't, but I was not aware of it."

Loucks had been the Chief at Hiawatha for approximately twenty-five years and had first heard of the 1923 treaty after 1950, when he had become Chief. He testified that he personally knew the treaty signatories, George Paudash, Hanlon Howard, Johnson Paudash, Henry Cowie, William Anderson, Alfred Crowe, and Madden Howard, and testified that three or four of the seven had been Chiefs at Hiawatha.[14] Loucks disagreed with the defence contention that the seven would not have understood what was on a treaty written in English, saying all could read English, and that three or four of them were "businessmen":

> Madden Howard, for example, had cottages and boats to rent and he was a businessman. He knew right from wrong. Henry Cowie – Hank Cowie – he built the camp that I now own. He built it in 1922 and 3 and he started to read and write and certainly could read and write and understand [English] ... and two men amongst those seven, Hanlon Howard and Johnson Paudash, they were almost as smart as any lawyer regarding Indian treaties or legal papers ... almost quicker than some of them ... Well, because they made several trips for the Band to Ottawa ... They made several trips to Ottawa regarding legal papers of some kind and they were quite knowledgeable in that area.

On cross-examination, Loucks said he had no knowledge of delegations being sent from the reserve to deal with hunting and fishing issues.[15]

With the evidence completed, argument began. The Ontario Court of Appeal had ruled in *Taylor and Williams* that the 1818 treaty had *protected* rights to hunt and fish in the lands ceded by the Mississaugas.[16] Nonetheless, the Crown argued that the 1818 treaty had instead "extinguished the Indian title ... where this alleged offence occurred and consequently the laws as to hunting and fishing applied thereafter to all persons including those who lived on the reservation." The Crown argued, in the alternative, that the 1923 treaty "basket clause" covered the balance of lands in the

Province of Ontario and would therefore have extinguished the Mississaugas' 1818 treaty rights in any event.[17]

In reaching his decision, Judge Batten outlined the various arguments both counsel had raised, but, citing an Ontario Court of Appeal decision, *R. v. Hare and Debassige,*[18] concluded he was bound to find that whatever treaty rights the defendant might have to fish had been extinguished by the tight restrictions imposed under federal fisheries legislation, rather than as a result of either treaty.[19] Given this finding, the judge's further rulings were *obiter,* or essentially unnecessary to his conclusion. However, having disposed of the central issue because of this technicality, the judge proceeded to consider the 1923 treaty, simply because "a great deal of evidence was adduced" concerning it. As he put it, despite efforts of the government commission to "restrict" the evidence to the northern lands within its mandate, "Time and time again ... there was evidence given as to the use of the other lands, which were heretofore thought to be covered by pre-existing treaties. In particular, one Johnson Paudash, a First World War veteran, and a civil servant with the federal government, pointed out with the assistance of maps and other documents that the description of land in an earlier treaty was inaccurate."[20] The trial judge dismissed Mr. Johnson's evidence that members of Hiawatha were unaware of the effect of the treaty, or that they did not understand English well, on the basis that "this witness had not ever in fact attended at the Hiawatha Reservation."[21]

Since the treaty had been signed sixty years earlier, it is not known why the trial judge considered Johnson's failure to visit the reserve to have had any effect on his expert opinion about the language spoken at the time. Nonetheless, the judge concluded that he preferred Ralph Loucks' evidence, since Loucks "was well acquainted personally with the signatories to the 1923 treaty and referred to several of them as intelligent, capable businessmen, all of whom spoke English and some of whom represented the Band by going to Ottawa on specific matters of interest. His recollection was that the game laws were recognized by members of the Band when not on reserve property ... With respect to the issue of the capabilities of the signatories ... the evidence of Mr. Loucks is to be preferred."

Finally, the judge seems to have concluded that there was no need for the band to retain its treaty rights, since "there was no reference to the hardships as claimed in 1818 before the reserve was created, when there were complaints of want and privation by the Indians." As a result, he held that the lands where the offence took place had been ceded in either 1818 or 1923, and that any "special" rights to fish had been included in the cession.[22]

Howard was appealed to the District Court, where the appeal court judge observed that he was constrained to consider only whether the trial judge erred in law or if his findings of fact were clearly unsupported by the evidence.[23] Unlike the trial judge, Justice J.A. Jenkins was persuaded that he should consider the circumstances surrounding the execution of the 1923 treaty on the same basis as the Ontario Court of Appeal had considered the 1818 treaty in *Taylor and Williams*. Having read the transcripts of the commission filed with the Court, however, he found no evidence that "the Indians were misled nor can I conclude that there exists an 'appearance of sharp dealings' on the part of the Commission."[24] Without evidence of misconduct, he reluctantly concluded that section 35 could not create new rights or reconstitute rights that had been contracted away by agreement.[25]

Judge Jenkins dismissed the appeal, adding that "I might say I have sympathy with the Aboriginal people of Canada and I wish them the best of good fortune in their dealings with the various governments [but] I am bound by two decisions in this case. First of all, the trier of fact, and also by the court of appeal."[26]

A further appeal was launched, and the Ontario Court of Appeal rendered its decision on 13 March 1992. By then, the Supreme Court of Canada's decision in *R. v. Sparrow* had been released, and the Court had ruled that even the detailed regulation of Aboriginal fishing rights under legislation did not extinguish them.[27] Therefore, the original ruling by Judge Batten to the effect that Howard's treaty rights had been extinguished as a result of federal fisheries legislation was wrong and could no longer stand.[28]

Despite this, rather than ordering a new trial, the Court of Appeal proceeded to consider the issue of whether Howard had ever held any section 35 rights or whether these had been extinguished in some other way. New evidence, in the form of materials not previously before the trial judge, was introduced by both the defence and the Crown. In many ways, this significantly changed the nature of the case, and though it is understandable that both sides wanted to present a fuller record, much of the contextual information around the additional materials was not provided, since no further witnesses could be called.

In his argument, Bill Henderson, Howard's lawyer, urged the Court to find that the Crown had not met the onus of establishing that the Aboriginal signatories to the 1923 treaty had sufficient knowledge and understanding of its terms to bind them to it. The Court of Appeal easily rejected this argument. Although they were not introduced at trial, Minutes of the Special Meeting of the surrender had been filed by the Crown on the appeal. Reviewing these, the Court of Appeal, referring to evidence that Johnson Paudash was "recognized by the Band as an expert in the matter of Indian treaties," pointed out that Paudash had attended the meeting of the Band in Council, had moved the adoption of the resolution to enter into the treaty, and was one of the band's signatories to it. The Court noted as well that Hanlon Howard, another signatory mentioned in Loucks' evidence as able to speak and read English, "was the secretary to the Band in Council. It was he who read the Treaty to Council and certified the Minutes of the meeting. He too was one of the Band's signatories to the Treaty."

Supported by this new evidence, the Court suggested that there was only one piece of evidence "which could suggest some misunderstanding of the Treaty on the part of some members of the Band. It is the reference in a report made by the Commissioners to a complaint about the issuing by the Ontario Government of muskrat leases along the shore of Rice Lake. In our opinion, that evidence is very ambiguous and is not sufficient to cast doubt upon the evidence of Mr. Loucks." It dismissed the appeal on the grounds that the evidence "amply" justified that findings of fact and that the Crown had satisfied its onus of establishing that the representatives of the band knew and understood the treaty and its terms.[29]

With only one remaining avenue of appeal, Howard took his case to the Supreme Court of Canada. There, Henderson again argued that the 1923 treaty had resulted in a surrender of the Indian title to specified areas only, and was not intended to include the 1818 treaty territory.[30] Extrinsic evidence, he urged, suggested that the Indians would not have understood the meaning of the basket clause for a variety of reasons, including its ambiguity and the fact that they were "deprived of legal advice ... There is no indication that the clause was explained to the Indians at Hiawatha as having the effect now argued for by the Crown ... There is indeed, evidence to the contrary."[31]

Henderson argued that the Crown could not provide the strict proof of extinguishment required because the Commissioners had a fiduciary duty to provide full disclosure, to make a full record of the negotiations, to ensure that the Indian parties had independent legal advice, and to refrain from any dealings that would have brought the honour of the Crown into disrepute – none of which had been done.

Perhaps Howard's strongest argument was the fact that the record of the proceedings disclosed no evidence of interest on the part of the Commissioners in any hunting or fishing rights other than those in the northern hunting grounds. Furthermore, during the proceedings, Hiawatha had specifically raised the issue of its muskrat harvest; Henderson asserted that if the Commissioners had intended the treaty to extinguish these harvesting rights, they had misled the band in promising to make representations to Indian Affairs to protect these same rights.[32] Finally, he maintained that the federal Crown had breached its fiduciary duties by failing to intervene in the current court proceedings to provide its own understanding of the meaning of the 1923 treaty.[33]

The Ontario Attorney General's reply to these arguments is of interest. As we shall see in Chapter 9, Ontario's arguments were almost identical to those put forward by the State of Minnesota in a similar case involving the Mille Lacs tribe of Chippewa. The Chippewa in the American case had won, however; the State's appeal had worked its way to the United States Supreme Court almost simultaneously with the *Howard* case.

Ontario responded that the Mississauga First Nations had expressly ceded all their rights in all lands in Ontario, and did so knowingly, because the treaty had been read aloud and was considered by the Hiawatha Band Council before it was signed.[34] Although Ontario conceded that Howard's band had an Aboriginal right to fish preserved by the treaty of 1818, it argued that the right was expressly given up under the terms of the 1923 treaty, which was "clear and unambiguous on that point. The cession, including the cession of the fishing right, was for valuable consideration. And the members of the appellant's Band, parties to the Treaty, fully understood and appreciated the terms and effect of the Treaty and freely entered into it."[35]

Ontario relied heavily on Loucks' evidence, asserting that he had proven that "All members of the appellant's Band in 1923 spoke, wrote and read English. The Chief and the six other representatives of the Band who signed the Treaty spoke, wrote and read English. Three or four of them were businessmen. And two especially 'were almost as smart as any lawyer regarding Indian treaties or legal papers.'"[36] As well, after the draft treaty had been read, interpreted, and explained to them, it was voted into force by "a unanimous vote of all 15 male members of the Band of the full age of 21 years present at the meeting."[37]

Because the Mississaugas had ceded title to the government without an "express" retention of rights, Ontario argued that the right to hunt and fish on those lands was gone.[38] It pointed to Ralph Loucks' evidence that he had been unaware of ever having special rights, and the fact that even though he fished regularly, he expected the game and fish laws to apply to him. Ontario urged the Court to consider the fact that the Indian parties had the same right to fish in the same way as other members of the public, and that "it was clearly contemplated by all parties that the Indian parties would thereafter continue to take game and fish subject to the law in force in the province." The only evidence suggesting that the treaty should not be given effect, Ontario noted, had come from Ian Johnson, whose evidence had been rejected.[39]

Ontario urged the Court not to "ignore" the actual terms of the treaty and the understanding of the parties by substituting a different treaty.[40] Asserting that the courts should be reluctant to "re-negotiate" agreements between Indian parties and the Crown, it accused Howard of seeking not a "just, broad and liberal construction of the treaty" but rather its recission.[41]

For the first time, Canada intervened in the litigation, appearing before the Supreme Court,[42] but only to challenge the appellant's position that it had a duty to intervene earlier in the proceedings. Counsel for Canada argued that the federal government was not obliged to support the position taken by an Indian litigant, and that intervention was discretionary.[43]

On 22 February 1994, the Supreme Court of Canada released its decision, written by Justice Charles Gonthier. He agreed with the trial judge that Ian

Johnson had "no personal knowledge of the events or persons involved," and that, by contrast, Ralph Loucks had testified to knowing the seven Hiawatha signatories personally.[44]

In a relatively short decision, Justice Gonthier reviewed the findings of the lower courts and agreed with them that there was no ambiguity in what had transpired. He concluded, "The historical context summarized above does not provide any basis for concluding that the terms of the 1923 Treaty are ambiguous or that they would not have been understood by the Hiawatha signatories. The basket clause was a conveyance in the broadest terms."[45]

Importantly, the Supreme Court decided that a treaty entered into in the 1920s did not raise the same concerns as those signed in the more distant past, where one could "legitimately" question the understanding of the Indian parties. Instead, the Court concluded that the 1923 treaty concerned lands "in close proximity to the urbanized Ontario of the day. The Hiawatha signatories were businessmen, a civil servant and all were literate. In short, they were active participants of the economy and society of their province. The terms of the Treaty and specifically the basket clause are entirely clear and would have been understood by the seven signatories. By the clear terms of the 1923 Treaty, the Hiawatha Band surrendered any remaining special rights to hunt and fish in the Otonabee River area."[46]

The immediate effect of the *Howard* decision was devastating. Members of the Williams Treaties First Nations, whose treaty rights to hunt and fish off-reserve had been affirmed in *Taylor and Williams* only thirteen years earlier, became the first Aboriginal peoples in Canada ever found to have surrendered their subsistence rights to hunt and fish off-reserve.

Aftermath of the Decision

Although it will be argued below that the *Howard* decision was misinformed, it should be noted that after the *Howard* ruling, under certain provisions of the 1923 treaties, the Williams Treaties communities did retain a right to fish in the waters adjacent to their reserves.

In 1991, in a case called *Howard # 2,* Justice Murphy of the Ontario General Division held that, under this exception, the Hiawatha First Nation had an existing section 35 right to hunt and fish in waters adjacent to its reserve. However, Justice Murphy declined to determine how far the right extended, holding it was sufficient to find that the right included the location in which Mr. Howard had been fishing.[47] Shortly after, however, in *R. v. Jackson,* Judge Eddy acquitted members of the Kettle Point First Nation of charges arising from fishing three and a half nautical miles offshore from their Lake Huron reserve, specifically following Judge Murphy's ruling in *Howard # 2.*[48] In his ruling, Judge Eddy was harshly critical of the actions taken by the Ontario Ministry of Natural Resources in attempting to arbitrarily restrict the members of the Kettle Point First Nation to a smaller area. He wrote that there was no evidence of formal acknowledgment or consent by the Kettle Point First Nation to this limit, but instead,

> There is evidence before me that members of the Ministry of Natural Resources charged with enforcing the *Ontario Fishery Regulations* and pursuant to the *Fisheries Act,* R.S.C. intended to conduct their subsequent enforcement activities based upon this arbitrary boundary offered to the Band. There is no evidence before me that the boundary has any relationship to natural fish populations or topography as to fishing ground or allocation or identification of existing resources or priorities respecting the same. Further there is no evidence before me that such boundaries were established pursuant to any consideration of the *Fisheries Act* or federal legislation.[49]

Despite the judge's very pointed criticisms of Ontario's arbitrary actions in similar circumstances, only days after the Supreme Court's ruling in *Howard,* the Ontario government moved to restrict the fishing activities of the Williams Treaties First Nations to no more than one hundred yards offshore from their reserves.

Members of the Williams Treaties First Nations were notified that, in light of the Supreme Court of Canada's decision, their off-reserve harvesting activities would result in charges. In May 1994, the Deputy Minister of the Ministry of Natural Resources informed the Williams Treaties Chiefs that "Ontario now has no alternative but to resume normal compliance activities consistent with Ontario and Federal law regarding hunting and fishing carried out by members from your community ... officers will have no option but to investigate any alleged violations and take the normal enforcement action required under the law. However, hunting and fishing *on* reserve have not been affected by the Supreme Court of Canada ruling."[50] Ontario would begin its enforcement in just one month, on 15 June.

Ron Irwin, the federal Minister of Indian Affairs, wrote to the Ontario Minister of Natural Resources, Howard Hampton, expressing his reservations about the 15 June deadline. He encouraged Hampton to "reconsider your approach to enforcement and to try to negotiate a resolution with the First Nations concerned."[51]

Hampton responded to both Minister Irwin and the federal Fisheries Minister, Brian Tobin, arguing that it was up to Ottawa to deal with the problems arising from *Howard.* He took the position that because "Indians" and "fisheries" fell within federal jurisdiction, only the federal government could amend the law or the treaty to provide any privilege to the Williams Treaties First Nations respecting the harvesting of game and fish.[52] In response, Irwin denied that the matter was federal, stating that the issue was "not limited to fishing but also includes hunting activity that is within your direct responsibility."[53]

To enable the Williams Treaties Nations to meet their subsistence needs while these issues were addressed, Hampton and the Williams Treaties Chiefs agreed that the bands would accept communal licences. First, however, new federal regulations were required under the *Fisheries Act* to allow Ontario to issue such licences. As part of this agreement, Hampton made a commitment that Ontario would work with the Chiefs and Canada to reach a resolution of the issue through a harvesting agreement and, later, through an amendment to the treaty itself.[54]

A meeting was held that June involving representatives of the Department of Fisheries and Oceans, the Ministry of Natural Resources, the Ontario Office of Native Affairs, and the Department of Indian and Northern Affairs. Meanwhile, however, vociferous opposition to any negotiated agreements restoring hunting and fishing rights had been expressed by a sports lobbying group, the Ontario Federation of Anglers and Hunters.

As the Royal Commission on Aboriginal Peoples commented in its final report, opposition from this group was unsurprising: "A century of effective prohibition of activities that treaty beneficiaries believed had been guaranteed to them by treaty has had a major impact on government and on society generally. Part of the corporate memory of provincial resource management agencies is that Aboriginal and treaty rights do not exist. It is no accident that groups such as the Ontario Federation of Anglers and Hunters continue to maintain that 'Treaty Indians do not possess any exclusive claims to Crown land or resources within the geographic boundaries of Ontario, with the exception of their reserves.'"[55]

The Ontario Federation of Anglers and Hunters mounted a well-funded and vigorous advertising campaign opposing any new arrangements. Both Ottawa and Ontario became concerned as to which of them would bear the brunt of the federation's anger as well as the expected opposition from other Ontario hunting and fishing organizations should new legislation be introduced. Each government attempted to shift responsibility for the problem to the other, with Ontario putting the onus on the federal government to resolve the harvesting situation, while the Department of Fisheries and Oceans insisted the issue was solely provincial.

As in the past, despite having constitutional jurisdiction over "Indians and Lands Reserved for the Indians" as well as over "Sea-Coasts and inland Fisheries," Ottawa maintained that the controversy fell within purely provincial authority. It insisted that in non-tidal waters, the underlying *solum,* or bed of the waters, whether provincial or privately owned, fell within provincial jurisdiction over property and civil rights.[56] As well, Ottawa noted that any remaining federal authority over fisheries had been delegated to Ontario long before. It claimed that as a result of arrangements and agreements "which started nearly a hundred years ago," as implemented under the federal *Ontario Fishery Regulations,* it had delegated all of its administrative management responsibility for fisheries within Ontario to the Province and that "in its own right ... Ontario has the right to decide who may harvest fish and this is not a delegated authority."[57]

The ability to issue a communal licence was not a new development. Back on 16 June 1993, the federal government had enacted certain *Aboriginal Communal Fishing Licences Regulations* (ACFLR) under the *Fisheries Act*. However, it had excluded Ontario from their provisions, probably as a result of its views that the regulation of Aboriginal fishing issues involving non-tidal or coastal waters fell within provincial, and not federal, jurisdiction anyway.

The effect of the new regulations was to remove fishing and any other related activities agreed to under a communal Aboriginal Fishing Agreement from the application of other *Fisheries Act* regulations. This meant that where an agreement existed, band members fishing under the terms of a communal licence could not be prosecuted for what would otherwise be considered violations.

The notion of communal licences was rooted in the Supreme Court of Canada's 1990 *Sparrow* decision, which had recognized Aboriginal rights as collective, not individual. As the Regulatory Impact Analysis Statement that accompanied the legislation noted, "Individual food fishing licences were found to be inconsistent with the concept of communal Aboriginal fishing opportunities as identified [in] the Supreme Court of Canada's *Sparrow* decision."[58]

When the ACFLR were first introduced, the then Minister of Fisheries and Oceans, John Crosbie, canvassed Ontario as to whether it wished to be part of the amendments. Opposition from the Ontario Federation of Anglers and Hunters almost instantaneously appeared in full-page ads in major newspapers throughout Ontario. Under the catchphrase of "A Deal is a Deal" – a reference to the Williams Treaties – the federation ads harshly criticized what they described as secret meetings entrenching special, rather than "equal," rights for Indians. The federation demanded that the Williams Treaties should be "honoured for everyone's benefit."[59] Another of its campaigns called on federal Minister John Crosbie to "Just say no!" to any secret deals.[60]

In January 1994, just four months before the release of the Supreme Court of Canada decision in *Howard,* Brian Tobin, the new federal Minister of Fisheries, again asked Minister Hampton if Ontario wanted to exercise the authority conveyed by the new *Aboriginal Communal Fishing Licences Regulations* to issue communal licences.[61] In May, after the Supreme Court of Canada's ruling, Hampton quickly accepted.

Hampton urged Ottawa to move rapidly on the changes but continued to express surprise at its insistence that Ontario could act unilaterally to deal with Aboriginal fishing issues, writing "the only circumstance which would allow discretion regarding enforcement ... is a confirmation from you that you intend to proceed with the application of [ACFL] regulation in Ontario."[62]

The federal government apparently felt it had provided that confirmation. On 17 June, Brian Tobin indicated that he had instructed his officials to commence processing the regulatory amendment to the ACFLRs on a priority basis and expressed his hope that the provincial Ministry would "maintain the *status quo* regarding management of fishing by the Williams Treaty First Nations who are fishing for food purposes."[63] Astonishingly, Hampton responded that Canada had not made a firm commitment to regulatory change, leaving Ontario "no alternative but to resume normal compliance activities."[64]

Later that day, the Deputy Minister of the Ministry of Natural Resources notified the Chiefs of the Williams Treaties First Nations that Ministry staff would begin enforcement activities against band members the very next morning; he claimed Ontario had no other option.[65] An Enforcement Appendix attached to his letter stated that Ontario was unable to enter into full discussions around Community Harvesting Conservation Agreements "due to a lack of federal regulatory authority regarding fishing."[66]

It seems likely that the provincial threats of enforcement against members of the Williams Treaties First Nations were intended to pressure Ottawa to push through the new legislation, while publicly reinforcing the idea that Ontario had no independent authority to address the *Howard* decision. By then, the lobbying campaign of sports organizations who opposed Williams Treaties First Nations hunting and fishing off-reserve had gathered considerable momentum. Casting blame on the federal government allowed Ontario to avoid the criticisms of those opposed to the Williams Treaties First Nations being permitted to hunt and fish without licences, while also permitting it to breach the commitments it had made to the Chiefs by claiming it lacked federal authority to act. However, Ontario's continued attempts to blame Ottawa for its own decision to take enforcement action even after the requested federal commitments were provided infuriated Minister Tobin. He wrote an angry letter to Ontario Premier Bob Rae that referred to Hampton's 17 June letter to the Chiefs as containing "untrue" statements. According to Tobin, the federal government had made the necessary commitments on more than one occasion, first writing to Minister Hampton to ask if Ontario wished to be part of the ACFLRs, then confirming on 14 June 1994 "that I was willing to move forward with a revision to the ACFLRs expeditiously, as soon as Ontario forwarded the wording it required; and on June 17, 1994, I informed Mr. Hampton that I had instructed officials of the Department of Fisheries and Oceans to commence processing the regulatory amendment requested by Ontario on a priority basis."[67]

Although sports groups had demanded that the Williams Treaties members' harvesting activities be restricted, or shut down altogether, the communities had retained treaty rights to fish in waters adjacent to their reserves, as noted above. Some provincial officials accepted this fact only reluctantly. Since the Supreme Court of Canada's ruling in *R. v. Howard* mentioned fishing "near to" the reserve, the Ministry of Natural Resources (MNR) decided that "this adjacency principle should be very narrowly construed," and concluded, unilaterally, that one hundred yards offshore was more than sufficient. It informed the First Nations that "Within these defined waters, MNR enforcement officers will not interfere with Williams Treaty community members who are fishing in manners consistent with their right to fish on reserve lands. When fishing in these defined waters, community members do not have to comply with closed seasons, creel limits etc. nor possess an Outdoors Card fishing licence."[68] Outside the hundred-yard limit, however, any members fishing for food would be charged.

The federal government responded quickly to the provincial enforcement threats. On 27 June, Ron Irwin, the Minister of Indian Affairs, informed the Chiefs of Ontario, the provincial wing of the Assembly of First Nations, that amendments to the *Aboriginal Communal Fishing Licences Regulations* delegating authority to Ontario to issue communal licences to the Williams Treaties First Nations would be adopted. However, this would occur only because Ontario had indicated it would use the regulations "exclusively to provide the Williams Treaties First Nations with increased post-*Howard* access to fish and wildlife."[69] The federal Cabinet approved the requested amendments on 2 August 1994, again with the understanding that "the provincial government is expected to use its authority to issue communal fishing licences to Williams Treaty First Nations," although strong criticism from the Ontario Federation of Anglers and Hunters was expected.[70]

On 3 August, the *Aboriginal Communal Fishing Licences Regulations* were amended, but only temporarily. They defined "Minister" responsible for the non-tidal waters of Ontario as the "Minister of Natural Resources for Ontario," thus delegating federal authority to the provincial Minister to issue ACFLs within Ontario.[71] However, even though the legislation was federal, Ottawa decided that Ontario would conduct the consultations required under *Sparrow* with Aboriginal groups.

This was surprising, given that Minister Tobin had expressed concerns to the Ontario Premier to the effect that Ontario was not living up to its fiduciary obligations in this regard. In the heated letter mentioned above, Tobin warned the Premier that "I had, and continue to have, concerns about the consultation process conducted by the Province of Ontario ... the requirement to consult with Aboriginal people when government actions touch on their interests is not frivolous; it was emphasized by the Supreme Court of Canada in 1990 in the *Sparrow* decision. Only the government of Ontario can explain to the Native people resident in the Province how it intends to use the authority it will receive pursuant to these regulations." Tobin noted that Minister Hampton had proposed to conduct consultations only after revisions to the regulations had passed. He pointed out that consultations were supposed to enable "the parties being informed to have a real opportunity to influence the proposed regulatory change and not merely to inform them after the fact." He ended his letter by expressing the hope that "the government of Ontario recognizes and acts upon its responsibilities regarding consultation while DFO [Department of Fisheries and Oceans] moves forward with the processing of the amendments."[72]

The urgency of the situation is reflected in the unusual speed with which Ottawa had acted. For example, as Tobin explained, pre-publication of the amendments had been waived by the federal government "because of the extraordinary circumstances of this case and to assist the government of Ontario in managing urgent Aboriginal fisheries issues in the province as quickly as possible."[73]

The Ministry of Natural Resources issued a news release on 1 September indicating that the fishing portion of the proposed communal licensing agreements had been authorized by the federal government under the new regulations. The release mentioned that such agreements would help "establish a consistent relationship" as well as an "orderly and conservation-minded approach to harvesting" in the region.[74] However, despite Ontario's many representations that, once the regulations were changed, it would refrain from enforcement actions against Williams Treaties First Nations engaged in hunting and fishing, the Deputy Minister of Natural Resources again informed the Chiefs that the Province would continue to enforce federal and provincial regulations off-reserve until they actually signed Community Harvesting Conservation Agreements.[75]

A permanent delegation of federal authority to Ontario awaited proof of the adequacy of Ontario's consultations with those affected by the changes. On 21 October, the Director of Aboriginal Policy for the Ministry of Natural Resources, David deLaunay, wrote to Marion Lefebvre, Director-General of Native Affairs at the Department of Fisheries and Oceans, to advise her that Ontario had completed its consultations and to ask that the final amendments be put through at the earliest possible date. He informed her that those Aboriginal organizations and First Nations consulted about the regulations had been assured that the new regulations would be used only to benefit the Williams Treaties First Nations and would never be imposed on any other Aboriginal communities in the absence of an agreement:

> At a lengthy meeting held in September, 1994 between the Ontario Minister of Natural Resources and the Ontario Regional Chief of the Chiefs of Ontario, the Minister explained that it was Ontario's intention to apply the

> ACFLR to First Nations who were signatories to the Williams Treaties of 1923 and not to other Aboriginal peoples in Ontario. Accordingly, Ontario advised the Ontario Regional Chief that the Regulations would have no adverse impact upon other Aboriginal peoples in Ontario.
>
> ... The Government of Ontario has advised the Williams Treaty First Nations through their negotiator that it wishes the Government of Canada to enact the necessary amendment to make the ACFLR applicable in Ontario only for the benefit of the Williams Treaty First Nations.[76]

The Department of Fisheries and Oceans, meanwhile, continued to view the *Aboriginal Communal Fishing Licences Regulations* as a provincial matter.[77] One official confirmed that "DFO has long held the position that Ontario could, by way of its own jurisdiction as manager of the resource, allocate increased access to fish to the [Williams Treaties] First Nations without the involvement of the federal government."[78] However, if this were so, there is no explanation for why Ottawa had made legislative changes to the federal regulations, or on such an accelerated schedule. Early that November, Minister Howard Hampton urged Minister Brian Tobin to process the permanent regulations as quickly as possible, stating it was of "primary importance" to Ontario that "these regulations be amended as expeditiously as possible so that we can address the fishing activities of the Williams Treaty First Nations."[79]

In response to concerns by Ontario First Nations that the regulations might be used to impose licences on other First Nations with existing treaty rights, the provincial Minister personally confirmed to them that this would never happen. That December, Hampton wrote to Chief Gord Peters of the Chiefs of Ontario Office, assuring him that "my greatest priority in relation to this matter is ensuring that a remedy is provided as soon as possible to the situation of those First Nations that are signatory to the Williams Treaty First Nations ... I believe I have been quite clear about my intention to apply the Regulation only to First Nations that do agree to its application."[80] Two days later, Hampton wrote again to Chief Gord Peters, repeating his assurances that "the Regulations will have no impact upon Ontario First Nations that are not affected by the Supreme Court of Canada decision in R. v. Howard. Licences will not be issued to any First Nations in Ontario unless the First Nation's agreement has first been obtained."[81]

The amendments Ontario had requested were pre-published in the *Canada Gazette* on 17 December 1994, and became permanent in February 1995.[82] The Regulatory Impact Analysis Statement confirmed that "Ontario has indicated that a situation where it intends to use the regulation to issue licences is to meet the personal and community needs of the Williams Treaty First Nations where fishing rights are confined to reserve lands as a result of the recent decision of the Supreme Court of Canada in *R. v. Howard*."[83]

Later that month, harvesting agreements were signed between the Williams Treaties First Nations and Ontario. Each agreement contained a clause allowing cancellation on thirty days' notice, but also included commitments by Ontario that, to the fullest extent of its jurisdiction, it would continue negotiating with a view to resolving outstanding issues. However, during the lead-up to the Ontario provincial election of 1995, rumours circulated that if the Harris Conservatives were elected, the new government would cancel the Williams Treaties First Nations Conservation and Harvesting Agreements. On 30 August 1995, the newly elected Conservative Minister of Natural Resources, Chris Hodgson, did exactly that. He claimed that "The Government wishes to act in a manner consistent with the Supreme Court of Canada decision in *R. v. Howard,* which confirmed that rights to harvest fish and game off-reserve were extinguished by the Williams Treaty, 1923, for those communities which were signatories to the treaty."[84] Members of the Williams Treaties First Nations were informed that they would be required to have individual licences to hunt and fish off-reserve.

A Ministry press release quoted the provincial Minister as saying that "The termination of the agreements help fulfil a commitment by the current government to restore balance to hunting and fishing agreements ... This will ensure fair hunting and fishing opportunities for everyone."[85] Chief Gord Peters of the Chiefs of Ontario Office responded that he was sad but not surprised "that the fears of First Nations have come to pass. Without a shred of pre-consultation, the new Ontario Government announced today its intention to cancel effective September 30 the Williams Treaty communal licences authorized under the ACFLR."[86]

In September 1995, the Ministry of Natural Resources issued a field direction instructing conservation officers and field managers effective midnight to resume normal "compliance" activities involving the Williams Treaties First Nations. The document indicated that "Fishing adjacent to the shoreline of Reserve lands (up to a maximum of 100 yards out from shore) will be treated in the same manner as fishing on reserve lands, at present."[87] Chief Gord Peters asked Minister Tobin for his assistance, but Tobin replied that the responsibility for managing the fishery rested solely with Ontario and that he did not think a meeting with the Chiefs would be appropriate.[88]

Despite the assurances by Ontario during its consultations that it would use the ACFLR only to benefit the Williams Treaties First Nations and in no instances without Aboriginal consent, it then proceeded to unilaterally impose licences on the two Saugeen Ojibway Nations that had rights to fish commercially arising from the 1836 Bond Head treaty. Among other things, the new licences precluded the Chippewas of Nawash at Cape Croker and the Chippewas of Saugeen from fishing in areas used by sports fishermen in the unsurrendered waters around their fishing islands. In 1993, the Chippewas of Nawash had won a court decision that had upheld the Saugeen

Ojibway Aboriginal and treaty rights to fish commercially in many of the same areas.

An application by the Williams Treaties First Nations for an injunction to stop the government from cancelling the harvesting agreements was dismissed by the Ontario courts. A General Division judge held that "The provincial government, in what appears to have been the legitimate exercise of its contractual right, gave the 30 days' notice and said that the reason was that it had decided that all members of the Ontario community should be treated equally and in the same way in regard to non-reservation fishing rights, in a situation in which it had finally been determined by our highest court that the Aboriginal community had no right to be treated specially."[89]

9
Analysis

Legal Perspectives

When one considers how the various courts approached the evidence in *Howard,* it is important to acknowledge that the courts are limited in what they may and may not do, particularly on appeals. An appeal court is restricted in its ability to receive new information and is limited to the record before it. The concept of "judicial notice," that is, of accepting certain notorious facts without further proof, is, and should be, sparingly used.

That said, in cases involving Aboriginal issues, the courts have also noted that "primary findings based on credibility of witnesses [should] be displaced ... where in a complex pattern of events, incontrovertible evidence can only be fitted into the pattern if a different view of the credibility of a witness is taken by the [appellate] court."[1] This was acknowledged by the Supreme Court of Canada most recently in *Delgamuukw* when Justice Lamer commented that "appellate intervention is warranted" in cases of Aboriginal rights "by the failure of a trial court to appreciate the evidentiary difficulties inherent in adjudicating Aboriginal claims when, first, applying the rules of evidence and, second, interpreting the evidence before it."[2]

Where factual issues are involved, the rule is that an appellate court should not reverse the trial judge in the absence of palpable and overriding error in assessing facts.[3] This rule, of course, is grounded on the assumption that the facts found by the lower courts are accurate, have been placed in their proper context, and are not subject to any subconscious or overt biases that might affect their judicial interpretation. A misapprehension of facts warranting appellate intervention is much harder to determine when the same misapprehension of "facts" arising at trial governs the appellate court's review.

In *Van der Peet,* the Supreme Court of Canada stated that the challenge of defining Aboriginal rights stems from the "meeting of two vastly dissimilar legal cultures," adding that "a morally and politically defensible conception of Aboriginal rights will incorporate *both* legal perspectives."[4] In *Delgamuukw,* the Court again highlighted the need to take Aboriginal perspectives into account, given that Aboriginal rights "cannot be completely explained by reference either to the common law rules of real property or to the rules of property found in Aboriginal legal systems [but] must be understood by reference to *both* common law and Aboriginal perspectives."[5]

The reality, however, is that although the common law is somehow supposed to intersect with traditional Aboriginal laws and customs, Canadian courts all too often apply a European or Euro-Canadian legalistic approach, rather than fully understanding the Aboriginal perspective. This is not in itself surprising. There were no Aboriginal judges on the Ontario Court of Appeal or Supreme Court of Canada to offer a perhaps different interpretation of the facts in *Howard.* Instead, the judges viewed the evidence through a prism of the values, knowledge, and experience they had acquired as non-Aboriginal people and as lawyers trained in a culture of English common law. This is so in most cases: as one scholar writes, the application of English common law to resolve outstanding cross-cultural issues is "almost never expressly justified, beyond the justification implicit in its mere existence."[6]

Because of their own implicit cultural beliefs, the courts in this case often displayed a remarkably mistaken filter of assumptions about Aboriginal people when making findings of fact about their way of life in the time period under examination. For example, Ontario had employed Ralph Loucks' statement that he was unaware of having any special rights either before or after the treaty as persuasive evidence that he had none. For their part, the courts accepted this as evidence that his rights had been extinguished; why Loucks had reached this conclusion was not questioned.

That Ralph Loucks might have been dissuaded from believing he had special rights as part of an assimilation policy never crossed the judges' minds. Yet Loucks' statements are understandable in light of the persistent efforts of the federal and provincial governments to deny that Aboriginal people had special rights to hunt or fish.

Despite this omission in *Howard,* the Court has shown an awareness of the Crown's assimilation policy toward Aboriginal peoples in other cases: in *Corbiere,* for example, the Court referred to discrimination against off-reserve members as "a consequence, in part, of historic policies toward Aboriginal peoples."[7] In that case, the Court observed that assimilation policies were designed to "encourage Aboriginal people to renounce their heritage and identity, and to force them to do so if they wished to take a full part in Canadian society."[8] As a result, the Court held that excluding off-reserve members from voting in Band Council elections was discriminatory, and therefore wrong, because they were excluded on the assumption that they had no interest in preserving their cultural identity.[9]

While questioning the lawyers during oral argument in *Corbiere,* Justice

McLachlin suggested that stereotyping had occurred, saying "maybe the stereotype is that they're ... like assimilated people, that they're like non-Indian people and wouldn't have the interest" in voting.[10] Justice L'Heureux-Dubé agreed that it was wrong to assume that "they are less Aboriginal because they just don't care about Aboriginal culture, stereotypically."[11] In its judgment, the Court referred with approval to statements made by the Royal Commission on Aboriginal Peoples to the effect that "Aboriginal identity lies at the heart of Aboriginal peoples' existence," that this cultural identity "is also tied to a land base or ancestral territory," and that "For many, the two concepts are inseparable."[12]

It is not clear why the Supreme Court of Canada would so easily understand the cultural significance of a land base to contemporary First Nations members, yet fail to appreciate its significance to those who had preceded them. Perhaps it is because *Corbiere* involved voting, something the members of the Court were more likely to have experience with than the need to hunt and fish in order to survive.

Applying only one cultural perspective to the facts put before the court in treaty cases can raise other problems. For example, the Supreme Court of Canada held in *Howard* that it found "no ambiguity in the Treaty which would justify interpreting the Treaty against the Crown."[13] When one looks at the facts in *Howard* from the perspective of those who hunted and fished to survive, however, there is considerable ambiguity in the treaty.

In examining the information that was filed in the Supreme Court during *Howard,* one notes considerable ambiguity as to just what the Aboriginal witnesses before the 1923 commission understood would happen as a result of the treaty. Exactly where they would be free to hunt and fish on lands already reserved to them, and therefore protected under the exception to the 1923 treaty, is certainly not clear. Many of the Aboriginal witnesses in the 1923 inquiry had referred to the seven townships -- described in the surrender document solely in geographic terms – as lands "reserved" to them by Lieutenant-Governor Simcoe long before. Others had asked the Commissioners to "reserve" certain areas for their exclusive use. The Alnwick Band had always excluded its fishing islands and waters from discussion, as already "reserved" to it. Other witnesses referred specifically to what they believed were already "reserved" hunting grounds. Many of these reserved lands had also become submerged as a result of the Trent Canal flooding. In such circumstances, the understanding of the First Nations as to what they had surrendered, and what rights they had reserved, is not at all clear.

Another obvious example is reflected in the muskrat-trapping issue raised by Hiawatha during the proceedings. The Commissioners had agreed to examine the issue through a further report, but failed to do so. This was mentioned by the Ontario Court of Appeal in *Howard* as "very ambiguous" but not sufficient to raise any doubt as to the evidence put forward that

Hiawatha intended to surrender its rights throughout the province.[14] However, in light of the importance of the issue to Hiawatha, it is not plausible that the band would have signed a treaty giving up its rights to trap at the Otonabee River while simultaneously – in fact, on the same day – seeking assurances from the Commissioners that its rights to trap both there and in Rice Lake would be protected by the Crown.

Another level of ambiguity arises from the Commissioners' own quite erroneous belief that the pre-existing treaty rights held by the Mississauga and Chippewa Nations had already been extinguished. Their perspective was clearly not shared by the Aboriginal parties who testified before them, as the transcripts of those hearings reveal. But there were many ambiguities and areas of misunderstanding reflected in the treaties, as the following analysis will show.

At the time of the 1923 treaties, the Commissioners clearly believed that there were no pre-existing treaty rights to protect. If they thought about it at all, they probably believed that band members engaged in harvesting activities simply as a matter of provincial largesse. As the Commissioners pointed out themselves during the hearings, they had little knowledge of the hunting and fishing activities undertaken by the First Nations. Their mandate was to get a surrender of unsurrendered lands, not to address issues that had already been covered in previous treaties. Also, as they warned one witness, "we must ask you to realize that ... if you ask us questions about timber, or game regulations or things of that sort we cannot answer simply because we do not have the necessary knowledge to do so."[15]

Although the Supreme Court concluded in *Howard* that the "basket clause" had content and meaning to the parties, E.L. Newcombe, the Deputy Minister of Justice, told the Supreme Court of Canada in 1909 that many standard clauses appeared in treaties simply because they appeared in other treaties. Citing a clause in Treaty No. 3, in which Aboriginal peoples promised to abide by laws in place from time to time, Newcombe stated that it was a meaningless clause and had been inserted only because it appeared in many other treaties of the day. He criticized opposing counsel for suggesting otherwise:

> Now, my learned friend wants to make the tail wag the dog, because he reads this last covenant here; the undersigned chiefs solemnly promise to be good and loyal subjects, to obey the treaty and observe the law and all that sort of thing. That is what he says is the principal consideration, but what is the fact; that form is the usual form; if they had printed forms of treaties that would be printed in every one of them. It is a common form of covenant which they put in, because it is a good enough thing, no doubt, to impress upon these Indians that they ought to obey the law, but does any one suppose if they had had no title to surrender that we would have gone

up there and paid a lot of money to them to take a covenant from them to keep the peace?

During his submissions, Newcombe introduced several treaties to support his point that treaties often contained clauses that had no meaning. In that litigation, the Court agreed that it would draw "no inference" from a clause that "appears to have been common to many, if not all, treaties with the Indians made by Canada."[16]

In the end, it is not known why, or when, the "basket clause" was inserted in the 1923 treaties, or at whose request. An exhaustive review of archival files does not disclose its author; nor is it mentioned a single time in the dozens of Commissioners' reports and memoranda concerning the treaties. Had the Commissioners intended it to extinguish the bands' rights to hunt and fish for subsistence, however, one would have expected them to raise it with the bands rather than offer to relay First Nation concerns about hunting and fishing to their superiors.

As lawyers with the Department of Indian Affairs and the Department of Justice, Commissioners R.V. Sinclair and A.S. Williams would also have known of a recent common-law ruling that applied in their situation. Only two years before the Williams Treaties were signed, in *Amodu Tijani v. Secretary, Southern Nigeria,* the Privy Council had determined that pre-existing Aboriginal rights were to be fully respected by the Crown in any dealings concerning Aboriginal title.[17]

The Commissioners' conviction that the 1818 treaties contained no hunting and fishing rights made inserting a basket clause to extinguish those rights unnecessary. That a similar – indeed, broader – basket clause was inserted in a treaty only three years later during the negotiations around the Treaty No. 9 adhesions and was understood not to affect harvesting rights adds considerable force to this argument.

Historical evidence suggests that it was not unusual for the Crown to prepare its treaties before embarking on the negotiations themselves. Although the treaties often contained standard clauses and covenants that were completely inappropriate in the circumstances, these were frequently left unrevised despite the promises exchanged in the negotiations. The northern numbered treaties negotiated with the Cree of the Northwest Territories in 1899, as one example, were drafted long before negotiations took place. They contained many inappropriate terms, including a commitment to provide livestock and farming equipment in an area in which agriculture was laughably impossible.[18]

On the other hand, verbal promises made by the Crown were frequently left out of treaty texts. As the Royal Commission on Aboriginal Peoples observed, the Cree and Dene Nations involved in Treaty No. 8 negotiations had refused to sign any treaty unless they received promises that their manner of making a living as hunters and trappers would not be restricted in any way. In response, the Treaty Commissioners promised that "they would be guaranteed full freedom to hunt, trap, and fish in the Northwest Territories if they would sign the Treaty." These oral promises were repeated and confirmed by a Catholic Bishop who was aware that the written treaty did not include them but gave the Indians his own "word of honour" that the promises would be kept.[19] Like the Williams Treaties, however, Treaty No. 8 included the usual "cede, surrender and yield up" clause, although this was never discussed by the parties at any time during their negotiations.[20] The Royal Commission on Aboriginal Peoples suggests that the Commissioners' failure to explain the concept of land surrender to the Aboriginal signatories probably arose from their haste to conclude the treaties. As they note, however, with remarkable understatement, these omissions are "disturbing."[21]

At other times, the written texts of treaties placed limits on the rights to be exercised, without the knowledge of the Aboriginal parties. For example, hunting and fishing rights might be limited to Crown lands despite oral promises not to interfere, in any way, with Aboriginal use of fish and game.[22]

It is most likely that the Commissioners put the basket clause in the treaty to prevent claims for unsurrendered lands from arising in the future. Having just resolved a long-standing Aboriginal title claim, they undoubtedly wished to ensure that no further land claims were put forward. This is far from wanting to make sure that all previous treaty rights were also extinguished, however.

It is hard to imagine that the Aboriginal fishermen and hunters who signed the Williams Treaties would have understood the technical language of the basket clause. Indeed, it seems abundantly clear that they were unaware of either its existence or its effect. In its submissions before the Supreme Court of Canada in *Howard,* Ontario argued that the continuous exercise of a right and subsequent conduct of the parties after a treaty were factors that might be useful in interpreting the treaty, although it asserted that "these might lead to a conclusion other than that proposed by the Indian party."[23] In this case, there is evidence of continuous subsequent conduct to the effect that the treaty signatories believed they had retained their rights to hunt and fish, and in the instance of Rama, that they had received additional protection as well.

The Aboriginal understanding of the 1818 treaty and evidence of subsequent conduct were advanced in the 1981 case of *R. v. Taylor and Williams,* regarding the two Curve (Mud) Lake Band members who had taken bullfrogs out of season. There, the Ontario Court of Appeal held that "it is part of the oral tradition of the tribes that this right [to hunt and fish in the area covered by the 1818 treaty] was not only recognized at the time of the treaty, but that they continued to exercise the right without interruption up until the present. The respondents' evidence ... was not disputed by the Crown."[24]

Given the finding that, despite the terms of the 1923 treaty, Curve (Mud) Lake Band members had hunted and fished continuously up to the time of *Taylor and Williams,* it is surprising that not a single judge in *Howard* commented on the fact that this particular Williams Treaties First Nation had successfully established its continual exercise of the same treaty rights that the Crown argued were extinguished in 1923. The courts in *Howard,* if they turned their minds to the question at all, must have assumed that the band had either exercised its rights illegally after the 1923 treaty, despite pledging to obey all laws in force, or that it had intended to violate the treaty from the moment it was signed.

Perhaps the courts assumed that treaty promises were not important to the Aboriginal signatories, although there is certainly no evidence to support such an inference. And if they were not deliberate liars and perjurers in 1981, one must wonder at what point the First Nation members at Hiawatha who had continuously exercised their rights "forgot" that they had actually surrendered them in 1923.

Instead, their conduct strongly suggests that the Williams Treaties First Nations believed that they had retained the rights their ancestors had protected under earlier treaties in the hunting grounds that they continued to use, and that the 1923 surrender affected only the ancient hunting grounds that they could no longer safely access. In this regard, their views were supported by the many instances in which the Williams Treaties Commissioners told them to refrain from mentioning lands that had already been surrendered.

Finally, and perhaps most compelling, is the fact that the basket clause, if taken literally, would have confined the seven First Nations to fishing only on the limits of their reserves. Six of the seven First Nations, including Hiawatha, have no waters on their reserves. Since the 1923 treaty reserved a right to hunt and fish on-reserve, where could George Howard have exercised his remaining treaty rights, if not on the Otonabee River?

In fairness, the courts did not wholly dismiss the Aboriginal perspective. In considering it, however, they relied exclusively on the testimony of Ralph Loucks, dismissing Ian Johnson's expert evidence of how other band members had acted and reacted in 1923. No member of any level of court reviewing *Howard* noted that, because Loucks was only ten at the time of the treaty, his understanding of it was hardly immediate. By his own admission, Loucks had been unaware of the treaty for some three decades after it was signed, and therefore could only have formed his opinions of the treaties many years later. What his parents might have thought at the time the treaties were negotiated is an entirely different matter.

Loucks' evidence that some of the treaty signatories were "businessmen" raises particular concerns as to how much understanding he had of how adults earned their livelihoods during his own childhood so long before.

Although he testified that some of the treaty signatories ran camps and were guides and businessmen, his understanding of when exactly they had engaged in these activities was not clear in the evidence. The Supreme Court and the lower courts seem to have assumed that they were businessmen in 1923. Loucks may perhaps have been referring to the less distant past, after 1951 *Indian Act* amendments removed some of the restrictions affecting Aboriginal peoples, or he may simply have been mistaken.

The Court's finding that the Hiawatha signatories were "active participants in the economy and society of their province" in 1923, however, is particularly hard to support. Although the Williams Treaties Commissioners did report conditions on the reserve, they noted only the poor quality of its agriculture; not a single report referred to any "businesses" on the reserves. Some witnesses had testified before the commission that they were continuing to trap and fish, whereas others were wage labourers or guides.

The most recent census information available, that from 1901, refers to virtually all of the treaty signatories at Hiawatha as "farmers" or "farm labourers." Not a single one is listed as a "merchant" or "gentleman," the terms used to describe those with either education or businesses.[25] The same may be said of the signatories in the other Williams Treaties communities. There were, as Loucks testified, some members engaged in guiding at his community. However, according to one elder, guiding involved paddling in canoes, as "No one owned a motor boat."[26]

Accepting Loucks' evidence that some of the signatories were businessmen, none of the judges in *Howard* thought to inquire as to how other First Nations members made a living in 1923. Instead, their assumption was that hunting and fishing were no longer important to them, an assumption that was demonstrably wrong.

Although the census information was not before the courts, the treaty commission's transcripts were. They indicate that the Williams Treaties First Nations, like other southern Ojibway communities, were composed of hunters, trappers, fishermen, and farmers desperately trying to make a living in the harsh times of the 1920s. As their exchanges with the Commissioners over muskrat trapping reflect, hunting and especially trapping were extremely important to them, and they were particularly concerned about the Province's restrictive laws and regulations. For instance, the transcripts note that Chief Daniel Whetung Jr. of Curve Lake was distressed about the encroachments into, and placarding of, his community's muskrat-trapping areas. He expressed his concerns to the Commissioners, as well as his despair at what would happen to his community if it lost its rights to hunt and trap. Just a year before, in 1922, he had described his community as "having a pretty hard time of it," since the "winter has been long and no work ... we are starving for something to eat."[27]

Conditions at the other reserves were equally desperate. The flooding of the Trent-Severn waterway in the 1920s had drowned the wild rice beds around Georgina Island, destroying a major staple in the band's diet. With farming virtually impossible due to the high cost of equipment, and logging limited by the island's small land base, the impact on the community was devastating.[28]

According to the inquiry transcripts, many of the witnesses and signatories told the Commissioners that they were trying "a little farming."[29] Perhaps the courts assumed that farming was somehow more profitable in the 1920s than it is today. However, farming was a difficult business for anyone in the 1920s and 1930s, particularly for Aboriginal peoples, who did not receive the same assistance offered to non-Aboriginal peoples. Just as they had faced opposition to their fishing activities due to the fear that they might provide "unfair competition," Aboriginal farmers encountered equal opposition to their agricultural efforts. As the Royal Commission on Aboriginal Peoples has noted, the fact was that "Indian people were not eligible for the information and assistance that settlers themselves received from federal and provincial departments of agriculture."[30] As a result, few band members farmed successfully in 1923, and despite Ralph Loucks' evidence, there were even fewer businessmen.

In fact, at the time of the treaties, Aboriginal people were considered minors and were legally incapable of entering into contracts. As a result, they were unable to gain licences to conduct businesses. At Tyendinaga, for example, an Aboriginal man who attempted to operate a horse ferry had been forced to shut down his business because of that reality. He complained to the Indian Affairs Department that "I was told they could make no legal contract with me being an Indian. This is the point where I ask advice can I make a legal contract?"[31] The response he received was that "Your only course is to associate a white man with yourself and try to run a ferry with a licence in his name."[32] It was for this reason that Wellington Charles, a band member at Georgina Island, had requested in 1920 that a fishing licence be issued in the name of a local fisheries inspector so that he himself could fish and sell carp.[33]

The reality is that in the 1920s, Aboriginal people were still wards of the government. As such, they were unable to vote in general elections, and were therefore unrepresented in the legislatures, even though the franchise had by then been extended to women.[34] The 1906 *Indian Act* went so far as to define a "person" as an individual *other* than an Indian,[35] a definition that precluded Indians from contracting, voting, standing for office, or owning real property.

In 1920, Indians were still being referred to as "children in the broadest sense."[36] In a Senate speech made that June, Sir James Lougheed, the Minister of Soldiers' Civil Re-establishment, said that "the Indian has not those characteristics which it make proper to leave to his discretion whether he shall assume responsibility or not." Referring to Indians as "nomadic," he added that "My experience in the West was that in most cases when you educated an Indian, you spoiled a good Indian and made a poor citizen."[37]

Even I.E. Weldon, the counsel for the Rice, Mud, and Scugog Lake Bands, had informed the Williams Treaties Commissioners that his clients would be unable to properly look after their own affairs for at least another generation:

> My clients may not thank me now but I think that their children will. Until such time as the Indians are able to look after their own affairs better than they have done to the present time, I must respectfully submit that no large sums of money be paid to them. I have found the average Indian is not to be put into the same class as the average Negro, and I submit that with adequate training and education for a generation or two that these particular Indians, in any event, would be able to take their places as citizens of Canada with the average white person.[38]

The Aboriginal leaders who appeared before the Commissioners were intelligent, charming, persistent, and well informed, but unlike the Commissioners, they were not lawyers, and they were definitely not the well-educated businessmen the Court decisions would suggest. The Treaty Commissioners' verbatim transcripts do not reflect a balanced or respectful exchange of negotiations among equals, but are rife with examples in which they behaved in a patronizing way, such as A.S. Williams' reference to the elderly Sampson Fawn as a "little deer." Even as late as 1928, a University of Toronto thesis prepared for a PhD in education investigated the "mental capacity of southern Ontario Indians."[39]

These unconsciously superior attitudes were shared by those to whom the Commissioners reported. In 1947, for example, Duncan Campbell Scott provided his view of the "sophistication" of Indians in legal matters, writing of negotiations he had been involved in personally during Treaty No. 9, and pointing out the need he had found to be "simple" in his discussions with them:

> They were to make certain promises and we were to make certain promises but our purpose and our reasons were alike unknowable. What could they grasp of the pronouncement on the Indian tenure which had been delivered by the law lords of the Crown, what of the elaborate negotiations between a dominion and a province which had made the treaty possible, what of the sense of traditional policy which brooded over the whole? *Nothing*. So there was no basis for argument. The *simpler facts* had to be stated, and the parental idea developed that the King is the great father of the Indians, watchful over their interests and ever compassionate.[40]

Scott himself was convinced that Aboriginal peoples were a waning race of "tragic savages" doomed to extinction.[41] However objectionable this view is now, it was also held by the Province of Ontario in the 1920s, as is revealed by its insistence that the Canada-Ontario Agreement, which led up to the Williams Treaties, provide for the return of lands to Ontario should any of the bands involved become extinct.[42]

At the time of the 1923 treaties, because of these widespread beliefs, Aboriginal people were not allowed to retain lawyers, spend their own money, sell land, enter into wills, or manage their own funds without the approval of Indian Affairs. It is inconceivable that the Commissioners themselves would ever have referred to those appearing before them in 1923 as urbanized, sophisticated businessmen. It is difficult to accept the Supreme Court of Canada's conclusion, some seventy years later, that they were.

Cultural Misunderstandings

The Supreme Court rested its findings that the treaty signatories were well educated and able to read and speak English on the evidence of Ralph Loucks, who had testified that there had been a school on the reserve when he was a child of ten. The Court thus concluded that those signing the treaty must have been educated themselves. This points to a startling misapprehension of conditions on most reserves.

Many of the treaty signatories had never attended school, and even those who had would have received only the barest of educations. The mere fact that a school existed on a reserve in 1923 did not mean that any education had been available to the signatories when they themselves had been of school age. For example, Charles Big Canoe of Georgina Island was born almost ninety years earlier, in 1834, at a time when no schools were established for any Indians anywhere in Ontario.[43] Isaac Johnson, Joseph Whetung, and former Chief Robert Paudash were in their mid- to late seventies at the time of the treaty. They would have attended school, if at all, in the 1850s and 1860s, but few schools were available at that time, and even fewer Indian students attended them.

As the Pennefather Report had described, no schools were available in 1856. By 1869, when an even larger number of signatories and First Nation members involved in the Williams Treaties would have been school aged, there were only some thirty schools in all of Ontario providing education to Aboriginal students.[44] The newly established industrial school at Alnwick was one.

The quality of the education for Aboriginal children, however, was not very high. The extent to which girls from the various reserves were instructed in household affairs is perhaps evidenced by an incident that occurred when A.F. Chamberlain, the Mississauga linguist, visited the Scugog

Island reserve. At John Bolen's house, he found himself teaching a delighted "Mrs. Bolin [Bolen] how to operate a sewing machine which she had received from the Dominion Government." Chamberlain observed that Mrs. Bolen was illiterate, and although she could speak English, she could not read or write it. Visiting the house of Isaac Johnson, a 1923 signatory, Chamberlain commented that "not much information was obtained as [Mrs. Johnson] spoke nothing but Indian, as did also the young squaws."[45]

By 1884, the churches had established some schools for Indian children, but attendance still fell well below expectations. More than ten years later, Court records involving four Ojibway men accused of horse stealing in 1899 showed that none were able to read; obviously, even the most basic formal education had not reached their particular reserve.[46]

That conditions did not improve after the turn of the century was revealed by Muriel Whetung in a 1976 interview. Not long before the 1923 treaties, in 1916, she had married Chief Daniel Whetung Jr. and moved to Mud Lake. She had tried to get good teachers there, "so my three kids could get an education, because I didn't have any education to speak of – a little public school." Her efforts had been unsuccessful. Mrs. Whetung also explained that the qualifications for teaching were very low, and that belonging to the church was considered sufficient.[47] Mastery of Book 4 (Grade 8) was viewed as adequate education, but "few were encouraged to go that far, as most girls were needed to do chores at home and most boys were encouraged to find a job to help to support the family."[48] In fact, according to the Williams Treaties Commissioners' reports, the Mud Lake negotiators were still asking in 1923 that a schoolteacher be provided for their reserve.[49]

Short Tom Taylor, a Curve (Mud) Lake elder who was in his forties at the time of the Williams Treaties, recalled that

> There were no schools here in my time; never bothered with schools. All hunting and camping out in them days. There was a little wee one [school]. And the school teachers in them days would take you in the school and then they would go to sleep and you could do what you wanted. That's how they teached in my time. The school was way down near the lake. By gosh, he'd ring his little bell and we'd go in and we'd sit down and he'd lie over on his chair and he'd sleep there until about a quarter to twelve and tell us to go home and have our dinner.[50]

It was not until 1920, when Ralph Loucks was around seven, that the Department of Indian Affairs finally made education compulsory for all Indian children between the ages of seven and fifteen. Ralph Loucks had certainly attended school, but he was among the first of the Aboriginal students to be required, or able, to do so. Thus, the suggestion that adults on the reserve were educated at the time of the treaties is simply not supportable.

Indeed, the signatories' lack of education was evident in the Commissioners' transcripts. During the negotiations, for example, Chief Daniel Whetung told the Commissioners he had spent only three or four years in school, which meant he had completed, at best, Grade 4.[51] Johnson Paudash, the main spokesman and member of many hunting and fishing delegations prior to the commission inquiry, told the Commissioners that he had not passed his entrance exams to high school and had only an elementary school education.[52] Nonetheless, the band's own lawyer, I.E. Weldon, had described him to the Commissioners as "an educated man," a comment that ought to have highlighted to the Court the extent to which other members of his band lacked formal education.[53]

The Court's assumptions that the Mississaugas who signed the treaty were fluent in English and would therefore have understood the treaty terms clearly shaped its thinking. Basing its argument on Loucks' evidence, Ontario had held that the Chief and the six other representatives of the band who signed the treaty spoke, wrote, and read English and would have easily understood legal papers.[54] This assertion was apparently persuasive, as was Ontario's submission that "the evidence shows beyond any doubt that the members of the band were entirely aware of the terms of the written treaty when they signed it."[55] However, what transpired after 1923, as well as contextual information not considered by the Court, suggests that these submissions, and the Court's acceptance of them, greatly oversimplified the context of the times.

The Minutes of Surrender that were filed as exhibits with the Supreme Court of Canada suggest that the signatories' actual facility with English was not as strong as the Court believed. The claim that all band members were fully literate in English is far from accurate: in fact, there were wide variances within each community as to the level of literacy among the band members authorizing the negotiations for the surrender. A more careful examination of the Minutes of Special Meeting, also filed as exhibits with the Supreme Court of Canada, might have flagged some of these issues. For example, of the sixty-six band members who voted to approve Mud Lake's Minutes, thirteen were unable to sign their own names and signed with an "X" as "his mark." Although the Minutes required that only men over the age of twenty-one vote, "Mrs. Wellington Irons," "Mrs. Herbert Irons," and "Mrs. Amos Johnson" signed along with their husbands. This suggests that the explanation of the resolution requirements – that it was to be signed only by the male members of the band – may not have been perfectly understood.[56]

At Rice Lake, one individual of the fifteen approving the resolution was illiterate and signed with an "X" as "his mark."[57] At Alderville, the names of those present and approving the resolution were very obviously written by one person. However, all are marked with an "X," leaving it unknown whether any or all of the forty-two band members of the fifty-eight eligible to vote were able to read or write.[58] However, as Charles E. Cleland points out, in the convention of the Ojibway treaty process, those who were non-literate generally signified assent by means of an "X" placed beside their written names.[59] As well, former Chief Alfred McCue's name appears on both the Minutes of Surrender and the treaty itself, though he could have read neither, since he was completely blind by the 1920s.[60]

The fact that Aboriginal peoples were *required* to use English in the treaty proceedings does not necessarily mean they were completely comfortable with it. The Supreme Court of Canada claimed it found no evidence to rebut the inference of knowledge and understanding that it drew from a reading of the Minutes of the Hiawatha Band in Council when the treaty was signed.[61] A review of the commission proceedings, however, discloses that the ability of many witnesses and signatories to speak English was limited. At Rama, for example, when a Mrs. Jacobs testified before the Commissioners and was asked if she could answer their questions in English, she replied, "A little. I used to speak English but I cannot to do it very well now. I never been to school."[62]

Chief Robert Paudash, a signatory from Hiawatha, had only limited comfort with English himself. Asked a question during his testimony, he responded, "I can't say it. That [English] is not my language and you must excuse me."[63]

Because of this, interpreters were present during the Williams Treaties proceedings. The text of each treaty notes that it was "signed and sealed ... after first having been interpreted and explained."[64] The inquiry transcripts indicate that the Commissioners relied on Walter Simon, Sam Snake, and Daniel Whetung as interpreters, but they were asked to interpret only when the Commissioners wanted to understand the evidence of an Ojibway-speaking witness.[65] These transcripts reveal that no arrangements were made to ensure that evidence presented in English was interpreted for the benefit of those participating in the proceedings whose first language was Ojibway: they would have had little understanding of what the evidence, or even the questions posed by the Commissioners, entailed.

Nonetheless, interpreters were necessary, as is indicated by the Commissioners' own account that when they went to Parry Sound to interview members of the Christian Island Band, they asked Walter Simon to accompany them to interpret.[66] Equally obvious is the fact that if all the members of the Hiawatha Band spoke, wrote, and read English, as was argued in *Howard* and accepted by the Court, interpretation of the treaties would not have been required.

The suggestion, then, that all members of the various First Nations could read, write, and fully understand English is contradicted by the Commissioners' own actions and the explicit wording of the treaties themselves. These are points that a Court perhaps more attentive to cultural differences might have noted.

It is possible to forgive the courts for not understanding that, even with interpretation, the translation of Aboriginal concepts into English and back is not an easy task. The Algonquian language spoken by Ojibway peoples is not capable of exact translation at the best of times.[67] What is problematic, however, is that the courts in *Howard* did not make note of the linguistic difficulties present in the information they did have when they concluded there were none. Instead, the Supreme Court of Canada determined that if the signatories spoke and read English, they must have necessarily understood the meaning and import of the basket clause. Since the meaning of the basket clause was clear to *them,* the judges concluded it must also have been clear to the Aboriginal signatories. However, even now, some eighty years after the 1923 treaty negotiations, translators are required in many court proceedings involving Aboriginal witnesses who speak some English. In *Delgamuukw,* for example, a trial dating from the 1990s, sixty-one witnesses gave evidence, many using translators from their native Gitksan or Wet'suwet'en language.[68]

Aboriginal peoples continue to assert that English legal language and legal processes, originating in a foreign system, are unfamiliar to them and require interpretation. Aboriginal lawyers continue to complain that the assumption that Aboriginal people are fluent in English, when they are not, is still all too common: "If an Indian can speak some English, the tendency is for the Judge to say that he understands English well enough."[69]

Perhaps the most important reasons militating against the courts' conclusion that Aboriginal peoples willingly surrendered their right to hunt and fish, however, are not the economic, but the cultural ones. Many dominant cultures are based on the assumption of individual and "equal" rights. Aboriginal collectivist cultures have a very different set of expectations. The divergence of these two cultural perspectives can, during negotiations, cause a good deal of miscommunication, and as seen in *Howard,* can lead to later attributions of bad faith.[70] Indeed, as Jeffrey Z. Rubin and Frank E.A. Sander point out, some of the most important effects of culture are felt even before the negotiations begin, with each culture operating as the "profoundly powerful organizing prism" through which information is integrated and understood.[71]

When people from two cultures approach negotiations, their cultural differences can cause considerable confusion. In some collectivist cultures, such as that of China, for example, negotiators will often consider that a memorandum of agreement merely formalizes a relationship and "signals the start of negotiations," whereas Americans will interpret the same agreement as a binding contract, concluding the negotiations.[72] Similarly, it would appear that the Williams Treaties First Nations, and Rama in particular, believed that the documents they signed were "provisional," forming only part of the negotiations. From their perspective, based on their cultural assumptions, the Commissioners had given certain promises, which according to Ojibway culture, should not have been refused. From the Euro-Canadian perspective of the Commissioners, on the other hand, they had made no commitments but had instead agreed only to take certain matters back to their superiors for further consideration.

In light of these differing cultural perspectives, I suggest that a fair assessment of what transpired in the Williams Treaties requires giving greater weight to the Aboriginal parties' intentions than to the Crown's, since it was they who were giving up rights, not the Crown. Given the reality of their daily lives, the Aboriginal parties to the treaty were unlikely to have ever contemplated surrendering their long-term means of subsistence. As the Royal Commission on Aboriginal Peoples commented, "First Nations would not consider making a treaty unless their way of life was protected and preserved."[73]

What *Howard* reflects, however, is the rather troubling judicial assumption that hunting and fishing rights were no longer important to Aboriginal peoples by the 1920s because they were no longer reliant on them, or in other words, that the assimilation policies of previous decades had been successful.

The courts in *Howard* were evidently unaware of the extent to which First Nations throughout Ontario continued to depend on hunting, trapping, and fishing for their physical and cultural subsistence, even in the 1920s. Significantly, it did not occur to them that hunting, fishing, and trapping might be lifestyles that were vital to the First Nations. Yet the Aboriginal perspective on the importance of both the land and their relationships to it through hunting and fishing were then and are now fundamental to Aboriginal cultural identities.

Aboriginal peoples do not perceive land as "owned" by them, but as something "made by the Creator. We can use it as long as we live."[74] As one witness told the Royal Commission on Aboriginal Peoples, "The hunting, all the game and fishing around the area there, we looked at that just like our money. It was our money, because that is our food."[75]

As the Royal Commission on Aboriginal Peoples observes, the economic relations "embedded" in this cultural perspective are very different from those of the West. Aboriginal cultures emphasize the conservation of renewable resources, limit harvesting activities to meet actual needs, and distribute resources equitably within the community, normally through family networks.[76] If hardship strikes because of bad weather or the supply of food fluctuates, everyone suffers equally.[77] At the same time, everyone has equal access to the necessities of life.[78] As the Federal Court noted during a 2000 trial involving the Saugeen Ojibway people, these values remain strong today. "The fishery was stated to be 'a vital source of our cultural heritage, and of the values and attitudes that inform our spiritual beliefs.'"[79]

The Chiefs of Ontario, the Ontario wing of the Assembly of First Nations, considers cultural rights such as hunting and fishing to be completely inalienable. In June 1994, at an "All Ontario Chiefs" meeting held at the Bay of Quinte, Chief Keith Knott of Curve (Mud) Lake, supported by Chief Vernon Syrette of the Batchewana First Nation, called for the Ontario Regional Chiefs to work with the Williams Treaties First Nations to "ensure recognition of the inherent Aboriginal rights of these First Nations." Their resolution set out that the Williams Treaties First Nations had entered into the treaties "with the intent to share some of the resources within their traditional territory" but "absolutely did not intend to alienate their basic and fundamental rights to resources which essentially includes the livelihoods and way of life of the citizens of these First Nations." It noted the support of the Chiefs of Ontario to the "inalienable Aboriginal rights of all First Nations citizens to their traditional pursuits of hunting and fishing." The resolution passed with full support.[80]

Despite the fact that the courts have often acknowledged the very strong spiritual and cultural ties Aboriginal peoples have to hunting and fishing, no judge in *Howard* questioned the apparent willingness of First Nations to surrender these cultural and spiritual relationships in exchange for a small amount of money. On the other hand, no Canadian court would assume that a group of non-Aboriginal people would willingly exchange their own religious and cultural beliefs for a mere twenty-five dollars.

Nor was any comment forthcoming from the Supreme Court of Canada in response to Ontario's argument that it was "advantageous" for the First Nation in *Howard* to surrender rights since these had never been protected by the Crown, or to even question *why* protection for its sacred treaty promises had not been offered by the Crown. This failure to raise obvious questions has been said to result from "cultural blindness." A 1991 task force examining the impact of the criminal justice system on Aboriginal peoples described such blindness as a form of "judicial bias," an unconscious imposition of Eurocentric values by courts that do not understand the cultural importance to Aboriginal peoples of hunting, fishing, and trapping, and that "consider urban middle-class life-style and wage economy to be the only viable way of life."[81] As Joan Ryan and Bernard Ominayak have said, "in so doing [the courts] fail to comprehend the magnitude of their decisions."[82]

It seems, then, that the Canadian courts have accepted, however unconsciously, that Aboriginal people have indeed been assimilated, and that this forms one of their starting assumptions.

However, at the time of the Williams Treaties, although Aboriginal peoples may have appeared to be integrated, urbanized, and assimilated, they were not. When one reviews who the treaty signatories actually were, it seems even more improbable that they would ever have agreed to give up their pre-existing treaty rights to hunt, trap, and fish. The treaty signatories included such people as Chief Daniel Whetung Jr., described by his own Mud Lake community as an "early activist in Indian rights."[83] Whetung was the secretary of the Mississauga Council of Rice, Scugog, and Mud Lakes Land Claims Committee, and a leader in the fight for recognition of his community's treaty rights.[84] His contemporaries, Chiefs Joseph Whetung, Robert Paudash, Charles Big Canoe, John Bigwin, and Alder York, had sent petitions and delegations to Ottawa for years before the treaties were concluded, attempting to gain government recognition of their hunting, fishing, and trapping rights. On occasion, Johnson Paudash and Hanlon Howard, treaty signatories mentioned specifically by the courts in *Howard,* formed part of these delegations.

Indeed, Chief Henry Jackson, a Chippewa signatory from Christian Island, would go on to become one of the founders of the North American Indian Brotherhood, now known as the Assembly of First Nations, created during the 1940s in response to new legislation requiring that all traplines be registered. Jackson and his co-chair, Chief Andrew Paull of British Columbia, urged Aboriginal trappers not to take out licences or registrations on the grounds that they violated treaty and Aboriginal rights, statements for which they were soundly denounced by Indian Affairs.[85] Signatories such as Councillor Gilbert Williams, and Sam Snake, as well as many others, depended on the commercial sale of fish, furs, and game for a living even at the time of the negotiations. There is no rational reason why they would have given up their livelihood for a one-time payment of twenty-five dollars.

Perhaps because it lacked understanding of the conditions affecting Aboriginal peoples in the early part of the twentieth century, the Supreme Court in *Howard* decided that a treaty entered into in the 1920s in an urban area did not raise the same concerns as those signed in the more distant past. However, regardless of whether the Hiawatha reserve was located close to an urban centre, the conditions of poverty and discrimination affecting Aboriginal people were still very much in place early in the twentieth century. One Curve (Mud) Lake elder, Alex Knott, remembered that in the 1920s, despite serving in the war, he had been unable to find work because he was an Indian: "I volunteered to go into the army. I was overseas for three years ... You got paid $1.41 a day ... When I got back home from the war, I went to Buckhorn Lake about a job and he asked if I was from Curve Lake so I didn't get the job. I worked on farms before I went overseas and also a tannery, in the 30s."[86]

In other cases, such as *R. v. Williams* and *R. v. Gladue,* the Supreme Court of Canada has recognized that conditions attributed to racism in more recent times have resulted in marginalization and discrimination for Aboriginal peoples throughout Ontario. In its 1998 *Williams* decision, the Court stated that "Racism against Aboriginal peoples includes stereotypes that relate to credibility, worthiness and criminal propensity ... It reflects a view of native people as uncivilized and without a coherent social or moral order. The stereotype prevents us from seeing native people as equals."[87]

The following year, in *Gladue,* the Supreme Court repeated its observations of widespread bias against Aboriginal people within Canada. Importantly, the Court concluded that "The unbalanced ratio of imprisonment for Aboriginal offenders flows from a number of sources, including poverty, substance abuse, lack of education, and the lack of employment opportunities for Aboriginal people."[88] Why the Court would have concluded that conditions were somehow better in 1923 at a time when there were fewer schools, greater poverty, and no social safety net than there are now remains something of a mystery.

The American Approach in Mille Lacs

The kinds of legal and cultural assumptions made by the Canadian courts throughout the *Howard* case are markedly different from those that have been applied by American courts when addressing similar issues. The notion that rights were "granted" by the sovereign to Aboriginal peoples, for example, rather than from Aboriginal peoples to the sovereign through treaties, has been expressly rejected in the United States. Applying an approach that differed subtly from that of its Canadian counterpart, the United States Supreme Court has found that an Indian treaty is not a "grant of rights to the Indians, but a grant of rights *from* them."[89] As a result, the courts presume that any rights not expressly extinguished by a treaty or granted away by tribes continue to exist.

Since the purpose of treaties of cession was to take away rights, the United States Supreme Court has observed that treaties rarely list those rights that are to be reserved.[90] Therefore, silence in a treaty is not assumed to mean an absence of protection for rights but quite the opposite; rights not expressly mentioned in the treaty are not affected by it. This distinction is of paramount importance in a case such as *Howard,* where the Williams Treaties made no mention of previously protected treaty rights. Under the American approach, silence in a later treaty is more likely to mean that it ignored previous rights, than to have included, and thus extinguished, them.

One must ask, why the difference? The principles of treaty construction in the United States – that treaty ambiguities must be resolved in favour of Indians,[91] that treaties must be interpreted as they would have been understood by Indians,[92] and that treaties must be construed liberally in favour of Indians[93] – are identical to those applied in Canada. The answer seems to be that unlike their Canadian counterparts, the American courts have superimposed Aboriginal cultural assumptions over Eurocentric legal ones. Where Aboriginal fishing is concerned, for example, the United States Supreme Court has started with the assumption that if fishing was not discussed, no rights were adversely affected, since fishing was the Indians' primary means of securing a livelihood. The Court's rationale has been that, in the absence of discussion, the Indians would have assumed their fishing rights remained intact, and that these assumptions are entitled to protection.[94]

The American courts have been similarly disinclined to find extinguishment. Instead, their operative assumptions have worked the other way. In almost all instances, the American courts have assumed that the right to fish exists whether it is mentioned in a treaty or not.[95] A treaty creating a reservation has therefore been presumed to include water, so as to enable residents to fish, and a reservation created on an island has been presumed to include fishing rights where the primary food source is fish.[96] Conversely, if a treaty was intended to convert a tribe from nomadic ways into agrarian ones, the courts have assumed it would include sufficient grazing rights to achieve its purpose.[97] Even the termination of a reservation itself has been held not to have affected hunting and fishing rights, on the basis that "every tribe retains its original rights unless these have been extinguished in clear terms by Congress."[98]

Even where rights have been described as being in "common" with those held by settlers, the American courts have considered these as conferring special, not equal, protection for Indian tribes.[99] In 1987, pronouncing on the nature and scope of Chippewa rights under early treaties that promised "equal" rights with settlers,[100] the courts found that this entitled a tribe to 100 percent of the available fisheries resources where less would not afford a modest subsistence to them, even though it appeared the band was not physically capable of harvesting, processing, and gathering all of them.[101]

As a result, American government bureaucracies have been forced to modify their policies accordingly. Recognizing that Native American governments are "governmental sovereigns," the United States Wildlife Service acknowledges that tribal governments have responsibilities for fish and wildlife resource management, both within their reservations and even over certain non-reservation lands. It also recognizes that tribal governments may have shared responsibilities with state governments to co-manage fish and wildlife resources. Importantly, the Wildlife Service "supports the rights of Native Americans to be self-governing, and further supports the authority of Native American governments to manage, co-manage or cooperatively manage fish and wildlife resources."[102]

The American judicial presumption that, in the absence of explicit discussion, tribes would not willingly surrender rights that were necessary to their livelihoods makes sense, and is congruent with Aboriginal cultural realities. More importantly, when American courts applied it to litigation regarding a treaty containing a basket clause similar to that of the Williams Treaties, their decisions differed markedly from those reached in *Howard*.

A Minnesota case, involving the Mille Lacs Band of Chippewa and facts greatly resembling those in *Howard,* wound its way through the American courts at the same time that *Howard* was being heard in Canada. In fact, the *Mille Lacs* case was heard by the United States Supreme Court in the same year that the Canadian Supreme Court heard *Howard*. Nonetheless, the conclusion ultimately reached by the US courts was in every respect diametrically opposed to that reached by the Supreme Court of Canada.

Like the Hiawatha First Nation, the Mille Lacs Band of Chippewa in Minnesota had signed two treaties, the 1837 Treaty of St. Peters and the 1855 Treaty of Washington. The latter contained the basket clause, which, if read literally, purported to extinguish Chippewa "rights, title and interest" throughout Minnesota and elsewhere. Accordingly, the opponents of the Chippewa argued in court that the 1855 treaty had extinguished the rights enshrined in that of 1837. The US Supreme Court, however, concluded that the earlier protected treaty rights had not been surrendered in the ceded lands. As a result, the American Chippewa not only exercise treaty rights in the ceded territories, but are engaged in the full management of their members wherever harvesting issues are concerned, to the exclusion of state regulation.[103] The tribes can even block state regulation if they themselves are effectively protecting legitimate state conservation, health, and safety interests through their own laws.

The depth and scope of evidence presented in the *Mille Lacs* case may itself explain why its outcome differed from that of *Howard*. However, although the American and Canadian courts applied almost identical principles of treaty interpretation to the facts presented to them, as will be seen, they differed markedly in terms of the cultural assumptions and the legal presumptions they applied.

Prior to white settlement, numerous bands of Chippewa inhabited the woodlands of what is now Wisconsin, Michigan, and Minnesota. Like their Canadian counterparts, the Chippewa historically followed a pattern of seasonal movements depending on the availability of resources at different times of the year.[104] In 1860, Johann Georg Kohl noted that "The migrations of the fish, their regular arrival and departure, the periods of their spawning, being out of season and being in condition again, hence [had] a material influence on the movements of the population." In particular, the "people of the interior" travelled long distances to profit from the Chippewa fisheries.[105]

The families of these Chippewa bands came together during the summers, forming villages of up to several hundred people on the shores of lakes where they hunted and fished, gathered wild rice, and planted small gardens of corn, beans, and squash.[106] Late fall fishing was particularly important to the American Chippewa. This was a time when fish that spawn in the fall, primarily lake trout and whitefish, could be captured using gill nets and frozen for winter.[107] After fall, families departed for their hunting grounds, returning in the late spring to capture sturgeon and suckers, which spawn in the spring.[108]

That notable cultural similarities exist between the American and Canadian Chippewa tribes is revealed in the work of Frances Densmore, an ethnologist with the Smithsonian Institute. Between 1907 and 1925, she visited the American Chippewa to study their traditional culture, and included the Mille Lacs Band in her study. She collected a detailed oral history from a Mille Lacs resident, a seventy-four-year-old woman named Nodinens. Nodinens described activities closely paralleling the cultural life of the Mississaugas and Chippewas on the other side of the border, and that dated back to her own childhood:

> My home was on Mille Lac and when the ice froze we started for the game field ... There were six families in our party, and when we found a nice place in the deep woods, we made our winter camp. The men shoveled away the snow in a big space and the six wigwams were put in a circle and banked with evergreen boughs and snow ...
>
> Towards the last of winter ... [o]ur sugar camp was always near Mille Lac and the men cut holes in the ice, put something over their heads and fished through the ice. There were plenty of big fish in those days and the men speared them.[109]

From the very beginning of their contact with Europeans, the American Chippewa supplied deer, moose, whitefish, lake trout, passenger pigeon, and other natural resources to their new neighbours.[110] After contact, as animal populations diminished, the Chippewa became increasingly dependent on fish for subsistence and trade.[111] They participated in the fur trade with both English and French traders, and later actively traded food and natural resources with the miners and lumbermen who began working the lands they ceded to the United States.[112]

However, as to the north, there were many conflicts between Indians and whites. Indians had not assimilated into white culture, and "many whites blamed the lack of progress on the Indians themselves [claiming] that the 'savage mind was incapable of adopting civilized pursuits.'"[113] The continuing white hostility to Aboriginal peoples who engaged in their traditional practices derives from the very different cultural attitudes each group held toward property. In European culture, fences and trespass laws were the means by which one asserted proprietary rights. By contrast, although the Chippewa had hereditary hunting areas, and would defend territories occupied or entered without their consent, there seems to have been no similar concept of, and indeed, there is no Ojibway word for, "personal ownership" of property.[114] As Charles E. Cleland explains, "No person owned land, animals or any of nature's abundance. Certainly one might acquire a vital interest in such things by virtue of habitual use or the investment of labour, but not ownership ... Properly, it could be said that the Chippewa recognized territorial boundaries over which they claimed stewardship of resources. These use prerogatives were on occasion vigorously defended but were also shared by simple permission. The Chippewas did not think of themselves as owners in the American sense of the word."[115]

Conflicting views regarding animals formed another major source of strife between Americans and Chippewa. The Chippewa practice was to take what they needed from others as they needed it. Since settlers let their livestock forage at liberty in the woods, the Chippewa felt free to "borrow" what they required. At other times, Chippewa killed farm animals to emphasize their anger at the expropriation of their own resources without their consent.[116] In some instances, the destruction of property was deliberate. When loggers entered the Chippewa and St. Croix Valleys to take lumber without Chippewa permission, the Chippewa chased the white men out of their traditional lands and destroyed their improvements, actions similar to those of their Canadian counterparts in addressing the invasion of their fishing islands by unauthorized whites.[117]

The American Constitution authorized the President to enter into treaties on behalf of the United States,[118] to address the pre-existing Indian title in lands.[119] A number of treaties were entered into with the Chippewa during the early part of the nineteenth century, and most included provisions enabling them to hunt and fish on their ceded lands.[120]

By the mid-nineteenth century, however, American leaders believed that "civilization" efforts were needed to assimilate Indians. They attempted to persuade the Indians to give up their traditional beliefs and lifestyles in favour of farming. Like William Gibbard, the federal Fishery Overseer who associated Indian fishing techniques with laziness, Americans tended to view those Chippewa who continued their traditional harvesting patterns as "lazy" and "uncivilized" because they thought of hunting and fishing as recreations, rather than work.[121] However, the expectation that Indians could easily adapt to agriculture, or even that they wanted to, was equally inaccurate:

> American subsistence expectations for the Chippewa proved a good example of the difficult trap in which the Chippewa found themselves. Because the climate and soils of most of the Chippewa country was not sufficient for agricultural production, the Chippewa traditionally planted small gardens ... but did not rely on these crops to feed themselves in the winter. Their main foods came from hunting, fishing and collecting wild plant food which required constant movement from one activity to another. Americans who associated hunting and fishing with leisure rather than as labour, considered these activities a sign of laziness.[122]

Despite the pressure on Aboriginal peoples to take up farming, trade in wild rice, fish, and meat became particularly important to them as the fur trade waned. The production of salted fish in Lake Superior for trade, for example, became a very large-scale operation,[123] and by the late 1830s, fur companies had developed sophisticated systems for Great Lakes fish production and sale to eastern markets.[124]

In both the US and Canada, it was largely Aboriginal people who worked in the industry, making the nets, cleaning and packing fish in salt barrels, and otherwise engaging in wage labour.[125] As noted in an 1836 report by the Acting Superintendent of Michigan for Indian Affairs to the Commissioner of Indian Affairs, "The Chippewa cultivate corn and potatoes to a limited extent but devote most of their time in quest of food in the chase or in fishing."[126] The extent of their dependence on fishing is revealed in the terms of an 1836 treaty with the Chippewas and Ottawas in the State of Michigan that provided for the delivery of ten thousand fish barrels and two thousand barrels (400,000 lbs.) of salt to the Indians over a twenty-year period to be used in the commercial fishing business.[127]

As in Canada, the abundance of fish in the large inland lakes and the American Great Lakes resulted in competition between the Chippewa and Europeans over access to the fisheries.[128] The Chippewa sought to safeguard their rights by securing government protection through treaties, and initially, the American government offered them that protection. For example, in 1834, following complaints from the Chippewa that white men were encroaching on their unceded lands, Henry Schoolcraft issued a circular requiring white men entering Chippewa territories to obtain a permit at Mackinac and to pay the Chippewa compensation for entering their lands. All trespasses by non-Indians were prohibited, as were hunting, fishing, or trapping on Indian lands, again paralleling developments in Upper Canada.[129]

When its early efforts to civilize Indians proved unsuccessful, the US government changed its tactics, passing the 1830 *Indian Removal Act* as a means of achieving its objectives. Under the terms of the *Act,* Indian's living in any state or territory could voluntarily exchange their lands for lands west of the Mississippi. The *Act* provided support for Indians who relocated, as well as compensation for their abandoned improvements. President Andrew Jackson, a strong supporter of the policy, advocated that the Indian tribes be removed "as fast as their consent can be obtained."[130] In 1837, Congress appropriated the funds necessary for the negotiation of treaties with the Indians so that the government could obtain land cessions and move the Indians west of the Mississippi. Twelve such treaties were concluded under the *Northwest Ordinance* of 1787, which, along the lines of the *Royal Proclamation,* required that "the utmost good faith shall always be observed towards the Indians; their lands and property shall never be taken from them without their consent; and in their property, rights and liberty, they never shall be invaded or disturbed."[131]

One of these, the 1837 Treaty of St. Peters, involved the Chippewa in what is now Michigan, Wisconsin, and Minnesota, including the Mille Lacs Band. The treaty was based on discussions very similar to those around the 1818 treaty negotiations involving the Mississaugas of south-central Ontario.

For example, Chief Maghegabo indicated a desire on the part of his people to retain rights in their rivers and streams, saying that, "Of all the country we grant you, we wish to hold onto a tree where we get our living and to reserve the streams where we drink the waters that give us life."[132] Commission Secretary Ver Planck Van Antwerp later remarked that he understood this as a "metaphorical reference" to the desire of the Indians to continue hunting, fishing, and making maple sugar from the trees on the ceded lands.[133] For his part, Chief Flat Mouth stated the same position more directly: "My father, your children are willing to let you have their lands, but they wish to reserve the privilege of making sugar from the trees and getting a living from the lakes and rivers as they have done heretofore ... It is hard to give up the lands. They will remain and cannot be destroyed – but you may cut down the trees and others will grow up. You know we cannot live deprived of our lakes and rivers."[134]

During the negotiations, Governor Dodge indicated that he would "make known to your Great Father your request to be permitted to take sugar on the lands and you will be allowed, during his pleasure, to hunt and fish on them."[135] In fact, Article 5 of the treaty preserved "the privilege of hunting and fishing and gathering wild rice upon the lands, the rivers and the lakes included in the territory ceded ... during the pleasure of the President of the United States."

Witnesses to the treaty negotiations observed that the government interpreters were not very capable, and that translation from English to Chippewa was extremely difficult. Throughout the process, however, three things were clear: the Chippewa had emphasized that they needed to continue hunting, fishing, and gathering on the ceded lands; they had been assured that they could do so; and they had been told that it "will probably be many years before your Great Father will want all these lands for the use of his white children."[136]

By the 1840s, it had become obvious that the voluntary Indian removal policy was a failure. Officials met to discuss and plan the eventual removal of Chippewa west of the Mississippi by other means. A 6 February 1850 executive order by President Taylor unilaterally cancelled all usufructuary rights – the rights to hunt and fish – granted in the early treaties and ordered the Chippewa to vacate their ceded territories. The order stated that those privileges granted "temporarily" to the Chippewa under the July 1837 treaty were revoked, and required them to move to their unceded lands.[137] The order was intended to drive the Chippewa from their lands, since hunting, fishing, and gathering were such an integral part of the Chippewa occupation of their lands. The policy, however, did not work since "As a practical matter, there was no way the Chippewa would simply stop feeding themselves."[138]

Government officials tried to implement the order by moving the Chippewa Indian Agency, where the Indians collected their annuity payments, to unceded lands in the Minnesota Territory, timing the payments in such a way as to make it difficult for them to return home, but this too was unsuccessful.[139] On 25 August 1851, the Acting Secretary of the Interior suspended the order, and the removal effort effectively ended. In 1853, President Franklin Pierce reversed the federal policy of removal: now, reservations would be created on Chippewa lands, where it was believed that a "progressive" civilization policy toward Indians could be more easily achieved.[140]

In 1854, the United States negotiated a treaty that ceded all remaining lands east of the Mississippi occupied by the Lake Superior Chippewa. The 1854 treaty established reservations within the lands ceded under earlier treaties and provided for certain annuities including guns, traps, and ammunition. Although the Wisconsin bands were signatories, some bands were not. A year later, the Treaty of Washington acquired the remaining unceded Chippewa lands. Over a hundred years later, this treaty would result in litigation strikingly similar to *Howard*.[141]

A key figure in the Treaty of Washington was George Manypenny, the Commissioner of Indian Affairs, who entered into some fifty-two treaties during his tenure. All of Commissioner Manypenny's treaties were virtually identical in wording. But for a few clauses, they were drafted long before he met to negotiate with the tribes. The Williams Treaties Commissioners had concluded seven identical treaties in little more than ten days; Manypenny raced through three Michigan treaties and negotiated another seven in less than a month in 1854.[142] As a result of this speed, and the fairly consistent language in the treaties, there is some question as to how much actual negotiation took place, or to what extent the Indian signatories understood the legalities of the documents they signed.[143]

The negotiations leading to the 1855 Treaty of Washington were particularly rushed. Indian Agent Henry Gilbert had been instructed to begin the treaty negotiations with the Chippewa and was specifically mandated to "acquire all the country" the Chippewa owned or claimed in Minnesota and Wisconsin.[144] With passage of a treaty authorization bill in December 1854, Manypenny summoned representatives of the Mississippi, Pillager, and Lake Winnibigoshish Bands of Chippewa to Washington in February 1855, where he told them they needed to act quickly while Congress was still in session. As none of the Chiefs spoke English, the treaty negotiations were again conducted through interpreters. According to those involved, there were many difficulties in translation.[145] Like most of Manypenny's treaties, the 1855 treaty was essentially drafted and written up before the negotiations took place.[146]

In submitting the treaty for ratification, Manypenny noted that additional, or even overlapping, claims might one day be advanced by other Chippewa groups. To prevent such claims from developing, he inserted a clause into the treaty similar to that considered in *Howard.* Article 1 of the 22 February 1855 treaty expressly extinguished the Chippewa title to certain specific lands occupied, owned, and claimed by the bands in the Territory of Minnesota. To deal with the other classes of land that might be claimed by Chippewa outside the described boundaries, Manypenny inserted his own version of the basket clause, a catch-all provision noting that "the said Indians do further fully and entirely relinquish and convey to the United States any and all right, title and interest of whatsoever nature the same may be which they may now have in and to any other lands in the Territory of Minnesota or elsewhere."[147]

Like the Williams Treaties, the 1855 treaty made no mention of pre-existing treaty rights to hunt and fish, although it did provide for the creation of various reservations, including one for the Mille Lacs Band. Accordingly, the Chiefs of the band carefully selected a reservation at Mille Lacs, in their traditional Minnesota territory, which would allow them access to the resources on which they depended, such as fishing sites, maple groves, and cranberry bogs.[148]

A number of nineteenth-century observers had commented on the rich resources of Mille Lacs. Fish and rice were particularly plentiful, and the Mille Lacs Chippewa harvested and traded fish as well as cranberries, waterfowl, and venison.[149] In fact, unlike other Chippewa bands whose subsistence needs required them to move to their hunting grounds seasonally, the Mille Lacs Band was able to establish a large sedentary village at the lake because of the quantity of fish and rice there.[150] In 1852, at least one hundred families fished in the lake and hunted in the area. There were nearly "a hundred wigwams. Indian children frolic on the ice. The hunters return loaded with game. White blankets are planted every few hundred yards on the ice, denoting fishing grounds. The frozen fish sparkle in the moonlight."[151]

After the treaty, however, when the Chippewa attempted to exercise their traditional harvesting activities, settlers objected. The conflicts that developed between Aboriginal hunters and fishermen and white farmers closely paralleled those that took place in Ontario. By 1871, American settlers had begun to complain that the Indians were violating the newly enacted game laws by hunting out of season; they urged the government to confine Indian hunting, fishing, and gathering to reserve lands.[152]

When the Chippewa asserted that they had treaty rights to hunt and fish, they were opposed by the State of Minnesota, which supported a policy of "equal" rights, rather than "special" ones. This policy was echoed by United States Commissioner Henry Rice, who visited Mille Lacs in 1889. When the Chippewa asked him about off-reservation deer hunting, he replied, "that is a matter for the legislature of the State to determine. You can hunt deer in any event, wherever you find them during the season set apart for hunting, and wherever the white man may hunt, your young men will have the same right to do so."[153]

Historian James McClurken argues that, in practical terms, the government's failure to acknowledge the Mille Lacs Band treaty rights did not pose much of a problem initially, since there were no restrictions on the number of deer a hunter could take, and there was little enforcement of game laws.[154] By the late 1800s, however, as game decreased, the Chippewa faced increasing state restrictions and enforcement but continued to rely on off-reservation hunting and fishing for their subsistence and commercial needs. In 1883, Agent John Wright reported that the Mille Lacs Band, particularly poor at farming, "live in teepees, though there are a few old log houses in tolerably fair condition. They have no oxen and but a few ponies or plows, consequently their garden patches are small and poorly cultivated."[155]

A similar report prepared a year earlier indicated that the Indians at Mille Lacs held no interest in agriculture, and that "To plant seed and prepare for coming want is a consideration he [the Indian] cares nothing about ... No attention is given to agriculture. There is not a yoke of oxen nor a team of any kind."[156] The report added that "Women plant corn and potatoes with weeds as high as the crop."[157]

Prevented from selling fish and game legally, like their Canadian counterparts, the American Chippewa became door-to-door peddlers, selling fish and resource-based items such cranberries, wild rice, maple sugar, and venison, as well as baskets and other containers.[158]

In the opening decades of the twentieth century, hundreds of Chippewa hunters were arrested and charged with violating state game and fish laws. Like the Mississaugas and Chippewas in Ontario, they argued that these laws were superceded by the provisions of their treaties, but their rights were equally ignored. As the regulations became increasingly restrictive, the State insisted that it alone held the right to enforce these laws, even on reservations.[159]

When whites objected to the Mille Lacs practice of netting pike in the lake, the band was prohibited from doing so, although it had fished in that manner for generations.[160] In 1919, a local resident suggested that the State of Minnesota should issue licences to the Mille Lacs Band so it could legally catch and sell fish as this "was a livelihood to their liking and one which they are capable and willing to follow."[161] However, the band was told that it could not fish, even though "[fishing] gives a useful occupation to Indians about the Lake ... they make a little money to properly provide for their families. They have spent money to get ready for the present season and are now informed that they cant [sic] fish at an industry that they do know how to do."[162]

In 1924, shortly after Congress passed an *Indian Citizenship Act,* the states claimed that all Indians were subject to state fish and game laws, although the *Act* itself indicated it would not "impair or otherwise affect any right of any Indian or tribe."[163] By 1930, the Commissioner of Indian Affairs took the position that the 1855 Treaty of Washington had extinguished all of the Chippewa's earlier treaty rights, a position commonly repeated by government officials thereafter.[164]

Despite the nonrecognition of their treaty rights, the American Chippewa continued their activities, protesting their fines, arrests, and imprisonment to the Bureau of Indian Affairs. Increasingly, they too hired their own attorneys to defend themselves,[165] and in 1994, the matter of the Mille Lacs Band's pre-existing treaty rights finally made its way to court.

Unlike *Howard,* the *Mille Lacs* case took the form of a civil action, with a higher burden of proof on the plaintiff band. The Mille Lacs Chippewa filed suit in the Federal District Court against the State of Minnesota, asking for a declaratory judgment to the effect that they retained their usufructuary (harvesting) rights under the original 1837 treaty. In *Howard,* Canada did not intervene; in *Mille Lacs,* by contrast, the United States intervened to support the Mille Lacs Band. Nine counties and six private landowners intervened as defendants to support the state position.[166] In August 1994, a United States trial court was asked to determine whether the Mille Lacs Band of Chippewa had surrendered its previous treaty rights when it signed the 1855 treaty, as a result of the basket clause.

The arguments at trial, and on appeal, were very similar to those presented at *Howard.* At trial, like their Canadian counterparts, the Chippewa plaintiffs argued that the language in the 1855 treaty was not clear, and that neither the Chippewa nor the United States had intended that the Chippewa would relinquish the usufructuary privileges guaranteed by the 1837 treaty. Instead, they contended "that the Chippewa continued to hunt, fish and gather on the 1837 ceded territory after the 1855 treaty, indicating that they believed their usufructuary privilege still existed."[167] In reply, the respondents claimed that the Chippewa had understood they were losing their sovereignty on off-reservation lands and had agreed to give up their usufructuary privileges under the treaty. As in *Howard,* they argued that the treaty was intended to subject the Chippewa to state regulation when they were off-reserve.[168]

However, during the *Mille Lacs* trial, and unlike in *Howard,* many experts from many different disciplines were called to give testimony. Along with an anthropologist, two historians, a legal historian, and an Ojibway linguist, Dr. Charles E. Cleland was qualified as an expert ethnohistorian for the defence. A professor of anthropology and curator of Great Lakes archaeology and ethnology at Michigan State University, Cleland has authored many articles on Great Lakes Native American pre- and post-contact archaeology, history, and ethnohistory, and has also testified in a wide variety of treaty rights cases on behalf of the Chippewa, Ottawa, and Menominee people of Minnesota, Wisconsin, Michigan, and Ontario.[169]

In his evidence regarding the effect of the basket clause, Dr. Cleland pointed out that it was inserted because Commissioner Manypenny wanted to prevent further claims from being filed, rather than to extinguish pre-existing treaty rights, so that the government would not be put in the position of paying for the same land twice.[170] As well, in cementing the treaty of 1842, the Commissioner had assured the Indians that its clause providing for their removal from their own territories "was only inserted as a matter of form," and that "compliance with it would never be urged or insisted on by the government."[171]

It seems clear that the understanding of the Mille Lacs Chiefs during the 1855 treaty negotiations was that they had secured the resources of the reservation and the surrounding areas for themselves. As another expert, Dr. James M. McClurken, an ethnohistorian and anthropologist, would testify, "it is inconceivable that a people who had so long relied upon the resources located in and around their future reservation would have ceded rights to them."[172] All the band's experts agreed that the Mille Lacs Chippewa would have necessarily understood they had secured additional rights to hunt and fish under the 1855 treaty, since their previous treaty had already guaranteed them the right to hunt and fish within the territories ceded at that time. As well, all agreed that if Manypenny had even suggested the surrender of such pre-existing treaty rights, the Chippewa would most certainly have protested.[173] Indeed, it was pointed out that, given the band's poor agricultural development in 1855, it would have starved to death had it attempted to rely solely on farming for a living, something "so obvious to those concerned that the entire record of the negotiations does not even mention the subject."[174]

John D. Nichols, an expert in Ojibway languages who testified at trial, prepared a report as to the translation of key phrases in the 1837 and 1855 treaties. He indicated to the Court that other concerns arose from cultural misunderstandings around language. As he pointed out, English and Ojibway are "about as different as two languages can be ... They package information in very different ways. English tends to have one or two ideas per word; Ojibway tends to wrap up many ideas into a word."[175] Nichols explained that most Ojibway words have no direct equivalents in English. As a result, accurate translation between the two is extremely difficult, and information must either be left out or added, to make sense.[176]

Noting that Ojibway communities had no legal systems similar to those of Europeans, Nichols explained that they possessed no words for English legal concepts regarding the ownership of land. As he observed, interpretive problems continue even today: "The Ojibway vocabulary for English legal institutions and processes is still extremely limited and inexact even after over a century of contact with them. An interpreter today, as in the nineteenth century, has little in the way of matching vocabulary to work with, especially when translating documents and negotiations of a legal nature between English and Ojibway."[177]

Nichols explained, much as Johann Georg Kohl had in 1860, that no single word existed to connote something as simple in English as the concept of "fishing." Instead, with the exception of one noun, *giigoonh,* meaning "a fish," all related Ojibway words are equivalents for specific fishing techniques, rather than descriptions of the concept of fishing itself.[178] Having gathered Ojibway words from various sources during twenty-five years of research, Nichols had been unable to locate any Ojibway equivalents for the English concepts of "right, title, and interest." As a result, he believed that efforts to translate these European legal concepts into Ojibway were meaningless.[179] He added that the problem still persisted and not just in the United States but also in Ontario and Manitoba, where attempts by interpreters to find new words to explain English legal terms did not necessarily mean that these were understood.[180] As a result, Nichols maintained that even if the 1855 interpreters had used what they felt to be accurate Chippewa equivalents for the concepts outlined in the basket clause, it is unlikely that these would have been understood, given that the words in the treaty cannot be accurately interpreted even today.

Another expert, legal historian Thomas Lund, explained to the Court that the Commissioners themselves would not have considered the provisions of the 1855 treaty to have any effect on the 1837 treaty rights, because none of these rights constituted a "right, title or interest" in land as defined under nineteenth-century law, and therefore would not have been seen as such by the drafters of the treaty.[181] As he explained, a "privilege" such as a treaty right to take fish and game was not considered a legal right at any point in the nineteenth century, as such a right would have entitled the Indians to enter private lands without committing a trespass, an eventuality to which the government would never have agreed.[182] Recognizing that Indians held any right, title, or interest in game or fish would also have meant acknowledging that they had the right to exclude others from access to them, a common-law monopoly that Lund argued the government would have been reluctant to acknowledge in any formal document, particularly a surrender.[183]

According to Lund, under nineteenth-century law, any person could enter all "wild" or uncultivated lands that were not enclosed or farmed. Unless these were "posted," or placarded against trespassing, anyone was free to enter and take the fish and game found on another's property. Therefore, a surrender of right, title, and interest in lands had no effect on the hunting and fishing activities that anyone could conduct on private, unposted lands anyway.

Lund pointed out that American common law had adopted the English common-law view that the landowner had no general property right to the fish and game found on his land, as these were owned "in common" with other members of the public.[184] Under common law, only when the landowner captured or killed a wild animal did he acquire property rights in it.[185]

This point is important in connection with the Williams Treaties. During the 1923 commission proceedings, R.V. Sinclair, clearly subscribing to this common-law view, told Daniel Whetung Jr. that Indians had no right or proprietary interest in wild animals until they were caught, and therefore had no treaty rights to hunt or fish in the first place, saying, "animals were wild and could not be the subject of property until they were caught ... You see it's difficult to say to whom a beaver belongs at any particular time or a fox because he is here today and he may be somewhere else tomorrow and 100 miles away the next day. No one has any property right in game or fish until he has killed or caught them – they are wild."[186]

Ultimately, Lund's legal-historical opinion of the Treaty of Washington basket clause was that it had nothing to do with pre-existing treaty rights to take fish and game. This opinion was accepted, as was all the other expert evidence put forward by the Mille Lacs Band's witnesses.

The trial judge held that the treaty language conveying all right, title, and interest in unceded lands was not a clear reference to a surrender of the usufructuary rights in lands, and that the intent and understanding of the Chippewa as to what they had surrendered must therefore be considered.[187] In reaching his conclusions, the trial judge observed that huge cultural differences existed between Chippewa peoples and settlers, and that these had added to the misunderstandings between them: "To be sure the record shows instances of cultural differences where Chippewa and settlers had varying perceptions which led to misunderstandings. Perhaps the most striking single piece of trial evidence to illustrate this was about glass windows. Settlers regarded them as something to look out of, and the Indians regarded them as something to look into, oblivious of the settlers' concept of privacy. Other examples include Indians' cultural expectation that food be shared with hungry travellers, or that animals in the fields constituted game."[188]

The Court accepted Nichols' evidence that the Ojibway and English language structures differed so radically as to make the accurate translation of the treaty's complex legal terms extremely difficult, especially under the time pressures involved in immediate translation.[189] It concluded that "Even the best translators would have had difficulty translating some treaty terms because the Chippewa did not have analogous words for many of the concepts developed in the highly complex and refined English vocabulary."[190] The trial judge, as well, was persuaded that even the combination of the terms "hunting, fishing and gathering" would have been unusual in the Chippewa language.[191]

Trial testimony from band members in *Mille Lacs* indicated that hunting, fishing, and gathering remained an important part of their culture, lifestyle, and economy, even at the time of trial. Unlike the Canadian courts in *Howard,* the Court found the fact that they had continued to hunt and fish to be important evidence, concluding that if the Chippewa had understood that they had given up their rights, they would not have continued to hunt and fish on the ceded territory.[192]

Although the Supreme Court of Canada placed weight on Ralph Loucks' testimony that his First Nation had complied with the game laws, equating this compliance with knowledge that its rights had been extinguished, the American judge decided that this kind of evidence held very little weight. He said that such evidence was not proof of extinguishment, and that "it would be unreasonable to expect Band members to incur criminal penalties to show that they still believed that their usufructuary privilege exists."[193]

Perhaps more importantly, the American Court relied on the fact that the Chippewa had repeatedly complained to federal officials that state enforcement of game regulations violated their treaty rights as evidence that they had no intention to surrender them.[194]

Other arguments raised in *Howard* and accepted by the Canadian courts were dismissed by the American Court with equal ease. In *Howard,* Ontario asserted that the 1818 treaty rights to hunt and fish were simply the "residue of the Indian title" and therefore were captured in the Williams Treaties' extinguishment of Indian title. When this argument was raised in the *Mille Lacs* case, it was rejected out of hand. The American judge affirmed that treaty rights were not simply an interest left over after a surrender, but special reserved rights that were entitled to protection.

The Court noted that the Treaty Commissioner's authorization was to extinguish Indian title, not treaty rights. His mandate, it concluded, could not apply to land that had been the subject of the 1837 treaty, because that land was no longer owned and claimed by the Chippewa: "Moreover, the usufructuary privilege guaranteed by the 1837 treaty is not just an incident of Indian title; it is a treaty-recognized right of use."[195]

In *Howard,* the Crown called no evidence to show that the terms used in the Williams Treaties basket clause had ever been explained to the Chippewas and Mississaugas, in either English or Ojibway. As noted, nothing in the historical record shows that any such explanation was given. In the *Mille Lacs* case, the Court found the lack of discussion regarding the 1855 basket clause to be of great consequence.

Significantly, the judge concluded that the Chippewa could not have intended to surrender their pre-existing treaty rights in the absence of any dialogue on this point. He noted that "The lack of discussion by the Chippewa about a privilege so important to them shows that they did not understand the treaty to have what the defendants urge is a 'plain meaning.'"[196]

The State of Minnesota appealed the *Mille Lacs* trial decision to the United States Court of Appeals for the Eighth Circuit, where, once again, its arguments closely paralleled those advanced by Ontario during *Howard*.[197] For example, the State argued that "the Court should not look beyond the plain language of the Treaty; modifying it would change the interpretation that naturally flows from the text as written ... Despite the doctrine of treaty interpretation that heavily favours the Indians, there are limits beyond which a court cannot stretch, no matter how morally compelling the Indians' case may appear in historical hindsight."[198]

The State maintained that the District Court erred when it ruled that the Treaty of Washington had not, as a matter of law, extinguished the Mille Lacs Band's usufructuary rights under the 1837 treaty. For one thing, Minnesota argued that the exchange included a promise by the Mille Lacs Band to "settle down in the peaceful pursuits of life, commence the cultivation of the soil, and appropriate their means to the erection of houses, opening farms, the education of their children and such other objects of improvement and convenience as are incident to well-regulated society."[199] The "other side" of the exchange was the so-called basket clause, which the State argued was an express relinquishment of all right, title, and interest and therefore extinguished any off-reservation hunting and fishing rights.[200]

The State, like Ontario, complained that any other conclusion would have the effect of reading the basket clause right out of the treaty, and argued that by including it, Congress had clearly intended to subject the Chippewa's off-reservation activities to state regulation.[201] Finally, using language eerily similar to that of Ontario, the State argued that the Court ought not to grant relief "founded upon any merely moral obligation ... because of supposed injustice to the Indians."[202]

As mentioned above, although Canada did not intervene in *Howard,* the American federal government intervened in *Mille Lacs* to support the Chippewa in defending their treaty rights. It argued, among other things, that, in the absence of very clear intent, early treaty rights were not affected by later treaties, and that the 1855 record of negotiations did not refer to the earlier treaty rights purportedly affected by the later surrender. Federal lawyers argued that "the absence of any discussion in the record of the negotiations clearly indicated that they [the Chippewa] did not understand that they would be relinquishing rights essential to their subsistence way of life ... their subsequent behaviour implied that they continued to feel free to exercise the rights allegedly revoked by the treaty."[203] Overall, the federal lawyers argued that both parties to the Treaty of Washington understood it to be a land cession agreement only, and that neither had intended it to revoke the 1837 treaty rights to hunt and fish.[204] "In these circumstances," they asserted, "silence ... cannot reasonably be construed to extinguish those rights."[205]

On the subject of state regulation, the federal government also sided with the Chippewa. Instead of insisting that regulation fell under state jurisdiction, it argued that Congress had the authority to preserve Indian fishing and hunting rights from the power of a State. It also pointed out that the US Supreme Court had determined in a wide variety of cases that off-reservation hunting regulations were an appropriate subject for federal, rather than state, regulation.[206]

The Court of Appeals for the Eighth Circuit agreed. It upheld the trial judge's ruling.[207] In particular, it concluded that previously protected hunting and fishing rights had not been discussed during the treaty negotiations and therefore were not revoked.[208]

Once again, the State appealed the decision, and in 1999, the Supreme Court of the United States agreed to hear the appeal.[209] As before, the State of Minnesota urged the Court to find that the Mille Lacs Band of Chippewa had "unambiguously" relinquished its rights, given the explicit terms of the "basket clause."[210] The United States Supreme Court, however, disagreed.

The Court decided it was necessary to look beyond the written words of the document to the larger context of the history of the treaty, the negotiations, and the practical construction adopted by the parties, since the historical record would provide insight into how the parties understood the terms of the agreement: "This insight is particularly helpful to the extent that it sheds light on how the Chippewa signatories to the Treaty understood the agreement because we interpret Indian treaties to give effect to the terms as the Indians themselves would have understood them."[211]

When reviewing this evidence, the Court noted that other Aboriginal tribes had reserved treaty rights to hunt and fish in the ceded territory, and that the State had proposed no explanation "compelling or otherwise – for why the United States would have wanted to abrogate the Mille Lacs Band's hunting and fishing rights while leaving intact the other Bands' rights to hunt and fish on the same territory."[212] This line of reasoning is particularly compelling when one recalls that the Robinson-Huron Bands had expressly reserved rights to hunt and fish under the 1850 Robinson-Huron Treaty in parts of the territory ceded in 1923. There too, there is no explanation as to why the Canadian or Ontario governments of 1923 would have felt the pressing need to extinguish the Aboriginal rights of the Chippewas or Mississaugas in an area in which other Aboriginal people could continue to hunt and fish.

Basing its decision on all the evidence, the United States Supreme Court concluded that the pre-existing treaty rights of the Mille Lacs Chippewa were not extinguished merely because their Indian title to the land had been surrendered. Much more than that was required. A contextual analysis of the history, purpose, and negotiation of the treaty supported the Court's ultimate ruling that the Mille Lacs Band had not intended to relinquish its treaty rights through the later treaty.[213] Any *other* conclusion, the Court warned, would reflect a fundamental misunderstanding of the basic principles of treaty construction.[214] The same may be said of *Howard.*

Conclusion

The 1763 *Royal Proclamation* recognized that Aboriginal peoples held a form of ownership, or Aboriginal title, to their traditional territories, which was not to be disturbed unless willingly surrendered by them. According to the Supreme Court of Canada, because treaty rights are negotiated agreements, they can be extinguished, or cancelled, only by the consent of the parties.[1] Because of the treaties, a special relationship has developed between the Crown and Aboriginal peoples, which has been described by the Court as engaging the "honour of the Crown."[2] Thus, relationships between the Crown and Aboriginal peoples are supposed to be "trust-like rather than adversarial," and the special trust relationship (the responsibility that the government holds toward Aboriginal peoples) is supposed to be the first consideration in determining whether legislation or action restricting their activities can be justified.[3]

The "honour of the Crown" seems to have been forgotten throughout most of the nineteenth century, at least in Ontario. The Royal Commission on Aboriginal Peoples has suggested that problems concerning the nonfulfillment of treaty promises arose shortly after Confederation, when almost all of the British Crown's rights and powers were transferred to Ottawa and the provinces. The Royal Commission describes how after 1867, a government preoccupied with building the new Dominion of Canada largely forgot the treaties, as "immigration and settlement took precedence in the corridors of power, nor did the government's corporate memory with respect to the historical treaties survive within the Indian Affairs administration."[4]

The commission concludes that the government failed to live up to treaty promises because no effective government office was given responsibility for fulfilling Crown treaty commitments in the post-Confederation era. As well, it points out that treaty implementation was left to a small group of civil servants who lacked the knowledge, power, and authority to act for the Crown in meeting treaty obligations or to hold off other government departments and the private sector if they had conflicting agendas.[5]

As a result, the commission concludes that governments unwittingly – and in some important instances, consciously – violated treaty and Aboriginal rights.[6] Its report implies that it is not difficult to see why provincial officials historically thought Aboriginal peoples should be treated no differently than the non-Aboriginal population when it came to hunting and fishing regulations, since the provinces were not accountable for Aboriginal peoples, who instead were wards of the federal government.

With respect, this interpretation of events seems far too charitable to the Imperial, colonial, and federal governments. The historical record reveals that the change in government policy toward Aboriginal peoples came long before Confederation, when the Imperial government, although aware of the special rights of Aboriginal people, decided as a matter of policy to ignore them. Once it had determined that the "Indian problem" was best solved by "civilizing the Indians," and that the goal of civilization was best achieved if Indians were separated from their traditional activities, a recognition of treaty promises would have conflicted with its stated objectives.

In practical terms, once it decided to assimilate Indians, the government could hardly acknowledge that they had special rights to hunt and fish. Recognizing special rights would mean that Indians would continue their traditional ways. Worse, they would have the right to call on government protection of activities that the government had already decided should be ended "for their own good."

That denying special rights would have the incidental effect of freeing up valuable lands for the use of non-Aboriginal peoples is hardly a coincidence. The overt recognition of squatters' rights where these conflicted with Aboriginal land rights was not inadvertent but deliberate.[7] That it took place at a time when Aboriginal peoples were precluded from asserting their rights except through the Crown can only be described as deeply troubling.

The Royal Commission's explanation for the nonfulfillment of treaty obligations after Confederation unfortunately fails to ask the questions of *why* treaty rights were left in the hands of a few federal officials, *why* the issues of settlement and immigration took precedence over Aboriginal rights, and *why* the provinces were allowed to deal with treaty rights at all. It seems clear that under the newly crafted *British North America Act,* the transfer of obligations and rights involving treaties was not supposed to disturb the special fiduciary relationship between Aboriginal peoples and the Crown.[8] Nonetheless, the history of the Williams Treaties shows that in the post-Confederation period, the federal government did little to protect Aboriginal rights but instead used rather dubious jurisdictional issues to disavow its own responsibilities.

Despite its official position, internal records show that by the end of the nineteenth century, the Department of Indian Affairs had come to believe that the provincial government had no constitutional authority to deal with

Indian harvesting issues. Nonetheless, Ottawa permitted Ontario to take over all aspects of management of Indian hunting and fishing, even allowing the uncontested passage of legislation it believed was unconstitutional.

This was not simple distraction or mere forgetfulness, as suggested by the Royal Commission. Instead, the federal government's policies demonstrate a markedly consistent effort to deny treaty rights and a decidedly continuous pattern of both withholding information and misleading First Nations as to the extent of the rights they had. The determined efforts of officials such as William Plummer and Charles Skene to have treaty promises upheld were constantly undermined by their superiors. As for corporate forgetfulness, it is perhaps obvious to note that what are now archival records of the promises made during treaty negotiations were contained in the same governmental files that detail their denial, files that were just as available to Indian Affairs then as they are to scholars today. Far from absent, then, corporate memory appears to have been dangerously deceptive.

Perhaps the clearest example of Ottawa's deliberate attempts to escape its responsibilities is its purported delegation of fisheries authority to Ontario, a delegation that has since allowed it to claim it has no remaining responsibilities. The most charitable interpretation of its actions is that the federal government may have delegated limited authority over inland fisheries to Ontario in the belief that the Privy Council's ruling in the *Fisheries Reference* case made delegation necessary. The evidence suggests otherwise. As well, it is unlikely that the Privy Council ever intended its decision to be interpreted as authorizing a wholesale delegation of fisheries authority to the Province, since at the time of the *Reference,* the overwhelming weight of judicial authority was that any such delegation would be unconstitutional.[9]

Since that delegation, Ottawa has used constitutional arguments and finger pointing to assert that Ontario alone holds jurisdiction in dealing with Aboriginal harvesting issues. Still, as described by Justice Idington of the Supreme Court of Canada long ago, the federal government was assigned section 91(24) constitutional powers over "Indians and Lands Reserved for the Indians" for a reason, so the "high, honourable and onerous duties" owed to Indians could be "discharged as [the] occasion called for."[10] As the Court then remarked, such "high duties of national importance" were discharged all the better if they were not confined to the "narrow views [of] the provincial range of vision."[11]

Using somewhat similar wording ninety years later, the Supreme Court of Canada concluded in *Delgamuukw* that jurisdiction over "Indians and Lands Reserved for the Indians" had been entrusted to the federal government so that the "core of Indianness" could be protected from provincial intrusion.[12] In this way, federal jurisdiction over Indians would not be separated from federal jurisdiction over their lands. Otherwise, the Court warned, there could be a "most unfortunate result ... if the government vested with primary constitutional responsibility for securing the welfare of Canada's Aboriginal peoples [found] itself unable to safeguard one of the most central of native interests – their interest in their lands."[13]

From the Aboriginal perspective, the fragmentation of the Crown into "federal" and "provincial" governments has never shaken the belief that the Crown – writ large – is responsible for keeping its word. As Chief Justice Brian Dickson of the Supreme Court of Canada once commented, the Aboriginal relationship with the Crown does not depend on the particular representatives of the Crown involved, since from the Aboriginal point of view, any divisions that the Crown has imposed on itself, such as the federal and provincial Crown, are internal to itself.[14] Nonetheless, in *Howard,* the appellant's argument that Canada should have intervened in the proceedings, or at least put forward its own interpretation of the 1923 treaties, was dismissed without comment by the Supreme Court.

For some unexplained reason, during that appeal, the federal government was not called on to explain its views of a treaty document to which it was a party, even though federal lawyers appeared to make submissions on other points. It is hard to imagine a situation in which a signatory to a disputed contract of any type might participate in proceedings concerning its interpretation but be permitted to sit silent while the other parties disputed what was intended. In light of the long-standing adversarial relationship between the Province of Ontario and First Nations, it is equally difficult to imagine how the federal government could have permitted Ontario to advance evidence concerning the "Crown's" position on the nature and scope of George Henry Howard's rights without making any comment.

Despite Ontario's position in court that all pre-existing treaty rights had been extinguished, Canada settled a claim shortly after the *Howard* case arising from a 1785 treaty that had allowed the Crown a right of passage through Mississauga territory. Clearly, Canada must have taken the position that that particular pre-existing treaty right was not affected by the 1923 treaties. What is of concern, however, is the fact that the planning conferences that discussed the settlement of this claim began on 5 April 1994, only a few months after the federal Crown had presented its arguments to the Supreme Court of Canada in *Howard.*[15]

If a legislative objective must be attained in a way that upholds the honour of the Crown, little supports the manner in which the federal government has permitted Ontario to encroach on Aboriginal hunting and fishing rights in favour of "public rights" and "equal rights" for all. *Howard* is simply one of the more recent examples of how the federal government, vested with primary constitutional responsibility for securing the welfare of Canada's Aboriginal peoples, has proven itself not unable, but unwilling, to safeguard the most central of Aboriginal interests.

As a result, First Nations in Ontario have been exposed to the arbitrary actions of an aggressive provincial government determined to treat them in the same fashion as it treats non-Aboriginal peoples, except with fewer privileges. In such circumstances, Aboriginal peoples have turned for justice to their last resort, the courts. Unfortunately, a close analysis of *Howard* leaves one with the uncomfortable feeling that the courts have not been sufficiently attentive or sensitive to the information placed before them to provide the justice sought.

In light of past history, it is perhaps not surprising that Ontario argued in *Howard* that because treaty fishing rights enjoyed no special protection, it was "advantageous" to the Aboriginal parties to surrender them. However, the Crown's failure to protect its own treaty promises should never be allowed to minimize the extent of the treaty obligations it has chosen to ignore. That the federal government permitted Ontario to make such an argument without objection reveals the extent to which it has separated itself from its constitutional responsibilities to Indians generally. That the Supreme Court of Canada accepted Ontario's arguments raises equally serious concerns about the judicial protection Aboriginal peoples may expect when the Crown is indifferent to their rights.

The Supreme Court of Canada has previously said that the failure of colonial governments to legally recognize rights cannot be equated with a "clear and plain" intention to extinguish them, since to find otherwise would perpetuate the historical injustice suffered by Aboriginal peoples at the hands of colonizers who failed to respect the distinctive cultures of pre-existing Aboriginal societies.[16] In *Howard,* the insistence of the Crown that Aboriginal peoples in Ontario had no "special rights," the erroneous belief of the Williams Treaties Commissioners that the First Nations had no pre-existing treaty rights, and the evidence of an elderly man who had been told he had no "special rights" became the basis of an evidentiary finding that can only be described as unjust. That the little evidence put forward was then interpreted in the context of mistaken cultural assumptions about how Aboriginal people behave can only add to that injustice.

As the Iroquois spokesman Deskaheh, impoverished and in failing health, asked the public in his last speech, made over the radio only a few months before his death in 1925, "We have only a little territory left – just enough to live and die on. Don't you think your governments ought to be ashamed to take that away from us by pretending it is part of theirs?"[17]

Appendix: The Relevant Treaties

Table 1

The Williams Treaties

Date	First Nations, as named in the Treaties	Treaty	Signatories	Witnesses	Source
23 September 1787	Surrender by [blank] and the "Honble Sir John Johnson" of [blank] tract of land, indenture made at the Carrying Place, head of the Bay of Quinté.	Treaty 13 ("Gunshot Treaty")	Wabukanyne, Neace, Pakquan (by their totems)	John Collins, Louis Protle, Nathnl Lines, *Interpr.*	*Indian Treaties and Surrenders*, vol. 1 (Ottawa: Queen's Printer, 1891) at 32-34.
7 December 1792	**Messissaque Indian Nation.** Surrender of a tract of land between Lakes Ontario and Erie, ratifying a unanimous agreement reached at a "conference held by John Collins and William R. Crawford, with the principal Chiefs of the Messissague Nation, Mr. John Russeau [sic], Interpreter, it was unanimously agreed that the Kin should have a right to make roads thro' the Messissague Country, that the navigation of the said rivers and lakes should be oen and free for His vessels..."	Treaty 3 (confirming the 1785 Collins/ Crawford agreement)	Wabakanyne, Wabanip, Kautabus, Wabaninship, Mattotow (by their totems) J. Graves Simcoe	John Butter [sic], R. Hamilton, R. Kerr, Peter Russell, John McGill, David William Smith	*Ibid.*, at 5-7.
1 April 1793	**Six Nations.** Grant by Lieutenant Governor Simcoe of lands at Tyendinaga Township to Six Nations in recompense of the losses sustained in the war and in recognition for the "Attachment and Fidelity of the Chief Warriors and People of the Six Nations to us and Our Government ... made	Treaty 3½	J.G.S. Wm. Jarvis, *Secy*.		*Ibid.*, at 7-8.

▶

Date	First Nations, as named in the Treaties	Treaty	Signatories	Witnesses	Source
	manifest on divers occasions by their spirited and zealous exertions and by the bravery of their conduct." Grant to enable the Six Nations to use, hold and enjoy the land "in the most free and ample manner and according to the several Customs and usages by them."				
21 August 1797	**Mississagua Nation of Indians.** Surrender of three thousand four hundred and fifty acres between those purchased from the Mississagues and the lands intended to be purchased from the Missassagues for Capt. Joseph Brant (Six Nations) beginning on the north bank of Burlington Bay, in exchange for blankets, blue strouds, black strouds, linen, calico, butchers knives and brass kettles valued at seven five pounds two shillings and six pence.	Treaty 8	W. Claus, *Supt. I.A. on behalf of the Crown.* Wabanip, Quanibbenon, Potaquan, Okemabenasse, Wabanosh, Tabandon (by their totems)	Robt. Nelles, George Chisholm, *Commissioners on behalf of the Province of Upper Canada*; Howard Douglas, *Lt. R.A.*, John Bronhead, *Lieut. 24th Regt.*, J.B. Rousseaux, *D.R.*	*Ibid.* at 22.
24 October 1797	**Messissague Nation.** Surrender of three thousand four hundred and fifty acres between Burlington Bay and Lake Ontario in exchange for "one hundred pounds of good and lawful money."	Treaty 3¾	Wabakanyne, Wabanip, Wanapenant, Tabandan, Okamapenes, Patopkquan (by their totems)	John Buller [sic], *Adjutant.* R.H. Sheaffe, *Captain 5th Regt.* J.M. Masor, *Lieut. 5th Foot.* Wm Gainfort, *Ens. 15th Regt.*, W. Johnson Chew, *Indian Dept.*, A.Jones, *D.P.S.*	*Ibid.* at 8.

22 May 1798	**Chippeway tribe or Nation of Indians.** Surrender of tract of land lying near Lake Huron "called the Harbour of Penetagushene" together with the islands in the harbour.	Treaty 5	W. Claus, *Superintendent Indian Affairs on behalf of the Crown.* Chabondashea, Aasance, Wabenenguan, Ningawson, Omassanahsqutawah (by their totems)	Will. Willcocks, Alex. Burns, *Commissioners on behalf of the Province;* Sam. Smith, *Major, J.S. Rangers,* Arthr. Holden Brooking, *Lt. 2nd Regt.* John McGill, *Adjt. 2nd Regt.,* J. Givins, *Agent of Indians,* W. Johnson Chew, *Indian Department,* Geo. Cown, *L.D.*	*Ibid.*, at 15.
1 August 1805	**Mississaugue Nation.** Confirmatory Surrender, confirming the Gunshot Treaty, Treaty 13 (23 September 1787) but excepting out the fishery in the "River Etibicoke which only they the said Chiefs, Warriors and people expressly reserve for for the sole use of themselves and the Missaugue Nation."	Treaty 13	William Claus, *Depy. Sup. Genl, on behalf of the Crown.* Chechalk, Quenepenon, Wabukanyne, Okemapenesse, Wabenose, Kebonecence, Osenego, Acheton (by their totems)	J.W. Williams, *Capt. 49th Regt.,* Jno. Blackenbury, *Ens. 49th Regt.,* P. Selby, *Asst. Sec'y, I.A.,* J.B. Rousseaux	*Ibid.*, at 34.
2 August 1805	**Mississaugue Nation.** Provisional surrender, signed at the River Credit. Part of Toronto Townships, Peel County and parts of Trafalgar Nelson Townships, Halton County, "reserving the sole right of fisheries in the Twelve Mile	Treaty 13a	W. Claus, *Deputy Superintendent General, on behalf of the Crown* Chechalk,	J.W. Williams, *Capt. 49th Regt.,* Jno. Brackenbury, *Ens. 49th Regt.,* P. Selby, *Assistant Secretary, I.A.,*	*Ibid.*, at 35.

▶

Date	First Nations, as named in the Treaties	Treaty	Signatories	Witnesses	Source
	Creek, the Sixteen Mile Creek, the Etobicoke River, together with the flats or low grounds on said creeks and river, which we have heretofore cultivated and where we have our camps. And also the sole right of the fishery in the River Credit with one mile on each side of the river."		Quennippenon, Wabukanyne, Okemapenesse (by their totems)	J.B. Rousseaux	
5 September 1806	**Missisague Nation.** Surrender of 85,000 acres of woods and waters thereon, in exchange for five shillings and the yearly rent of one peppercorn, payable on demand to Chechalk, Quenepenon, Wakanye, Okemapenesse, Wabenose, Kebonecence, Osenego, Acheton, Patequan and Wabakegego.	Treaty 14	Wm. Claus, *DSG on behalf of the Crown* Chechalk, Quenepenon, Wakanye, Okemapenesse, Wabenose, Kebonecence, Osenego, Acheton, Patequan, Wabakegego (by their totems)	D. Cameron, Donald McLean, *Com's. on behalf of the Prov.*, Geo. R. Ferguson, *Capt. Canadian Regt.*, Wm. L. Crowther, *Lieut. 41st Regt.*, James Davidson, *Hospital Staff*; H.M. Smith, P. Selby, *Asst. Secy. I.A.*, J.B. Rousseaux, David Price, *Interpreter*	*Ibid.*, at 36-37.
6 September 1806	**Mississague (also Missisague) Nation.** Confirmatory surrender of Treaty 13a, reserving the sole right of Fisheries in the Twelve Mile Creek, the Sixteen Mile Creek, the River Credit and the River Etobicoke, together with lands on each side of the said creeks and the River Credit, "the said right of fishery and reserves extending from the	Not numbered	W. Claus, *D.S.G. on behalf of the Crown.* Chechalk, Quenepenon, Wabukanyne, Okemapenesse,	D. Cameron, Donald MacLean, *Commissioners on behalf of the Province*; H.M. Smith, Geo. R. Ferguson, *Capt. Canadian Regiment*, Peter Selby, *Asst. Secy*,	*Ibid.*, at 37-39.

	Lake Ontario up the said creeks and River Credit ... and the right of fishery in the River Etobicoke from the mouth of the said river ...”		Wabanose, Kebonecence, Osenego, Acheton, Patequan, Wabakagego (by their totems)	*I.A.*, J.B. Rousseaux, Wm. M. Crowther, *Lieut. 41st Regt.*, James Davidson, *Hospital Staff*, David Price, *Interpreter*	
17 November 1815	**Chippawawa Nation.** Provisional sale of parcel of 250,000 acres of land between Kempenfelt Bay upon Lake Simcoe and Lake Huron to the bottom of “Nottawaysague” Bay, following the shore of Sturgeon Bay and the shore of Matchedas Bay easterly ... “along the western boundary of a purchase said to have been made in 1785 ... in exchange for rent of one Pepper Corn ... payable on demand.”	Treaty 16	J. Givins, *S.I.A on behalf of the Crown* Kinaybicoinini, Aisance, Misquuckkey (by their totems)	Elisha Beman, Henry Procter, *Commissioners on behalf of the Province*, W.M. Cochrane, *Capt. Com. Lt. Infty*, Alex. Ferguson, *Lieut. Ind. Dept.*, William Gruet, *Interpreter*	*Ibid.*, at 42-43.
18 November 1815	**Chippawa Nation.** Confirmatory surrender of lands outlined in Treaty 16 in exchange for four pounds.	Also recorded as Treaty 16	J. Givins, *S.I.A. on behalf of the Crown.* Kinaybicoinini, Aisance, Misquuckkey (by their totems)	Elisha Beman, Henry Procter, *Commissioners on behalf the Province*; W.M. Cochrane, *Capt. Com. Lt. Infty*, Alex. Ferguson, Lieut. *Ind. Dept.*, William Gruet, *Interpreter*	
17 October 1818	**Chippewa Nation.** Provisional Surrender by Chiefs and principal men of the Rein Deer, Cat Fish, Otter and Pike Tribes for “the area bounded by the District of London on the west, by Lake Huron on the north, by the Penetangueshine	Treaty 18	W. Claus, *Dep. Supt. Gen., on behalf of the Crown* Musquakie or Yellow Head (Chief of the	J. Givins, *Supt. Indian Affairs*, Alex McDonell, *Asst. Sec'y Indian Affairs*, John Claus	*Ibid.*, at 47.

▶

◄ *Table 1*

Date	First Nations, as named in the Treaties	Treaty	Signatories	Witnesses	Source
	purchase (made in 1815) on the east, by the south shore of Kempenfelt Bay, the western shore of Lake Simcoe and Cooks' Bay and the Holland River to the north-west angle of the Township of King containing by computation one million five hundred and nine-two thousand acres" in exchange for twelve hundred pounds currency in goods at the Montreal price, yearly and for every year forever.		Rein Deer Tribe), Kaqueticum, or Snake (Chief of the Cat Fish Tribe), Muskigonce, or Swamp (Otter Tribe), Manitonobe, or Male Devil (Pike Tribe), Manitobinince, or Devil's Bird (by their totems)		
28 October 1818	**Mississagua Nation.** Provisional surrender by Chief of the Eagle Tribe and principal men of the "Mississagua Nation of Indians inhabiting the River Credit, Twelve and Sixteen Mile Creeks, on the north shore of Lake Ontario" of a tract of land "called the Mississagua tract, bounded southerly by the purchase made in 1806; on the east by the Townships of Etobicoke, Vaughan and King; on on the southwest by the Indian purchase, extending from the outlet at Burlington Bay ..."	Treaty 19	W. Claus, *D.S.G. on behalf of the Crown* Adjutant (Chief of the Eagle Tribe), Weggishigomin (Eagle Tribe), Kawwahkitahqubi (Otter Tribe), Cabibonike (Otter Tribe), Pagitaniquatoibe (Otter Tribe) (by their totems)	J. Givins, *Supt. Indian Affairs* Wm. Hands, Jr., *Clerk Indian Dept.* Wm. Gruet, *Intr. Indian Dept.*	*Ibid.*, at 47-48.
5 November 1818	**Chippewa Nation.** Provisional surrender by Chiefs and principal men of the Eagle, Rein Deer, Crane, Pike, Snake, and White Oak Tribes of one one million nine hundred and fifty-one thousand acres from the western boundary of the Home	Treaty 20	W. Claus, *Depy. Supt. Gen. I.A, on behalf of the Crown* Buckquaquet (Chief	J. Givins, *S.I.A.*, Wm. Hands, *Sen., Clerk Ind. Dept.*, Wm. Gruet, *Interpreter, Ind. Dept.*	*Ibid.*, at 48-49.

	District northerly to a bay at the northern entrance of Lake Simcoe, in exchange for annual payment of seven hundred and forty pounds in goods at the Montreal Price.		of the Eagle Tribe), Pishikinse (Chief of the Rein Deer Tribe), Pahtoshe (Chief of the Crane Tribe), Cahgahkishinse (Chief of the Pike Tribe), Cahgagewin (Snake Tribe), Pininse (White Oak Tribe) (by their totems)		
31 May 1819	**Mississaguas of Bay de Quinté.** Provisional agreement for surrender of tract of land containing "two millions seven hundred and forty-eight thousand acres" in exchange for six hundred and forty-two pounds, ten shillings, Province currency in goods at the Montreal price.	Treaty 27	John Ferguson *on behalf of the Crown* Papiwom, Wobekenense, Nongonseway, Kechegom, Komonjeveweny, Shebeshe, Nakawagan, Wabosek, Nawacamigo, Antenewayay, Itawabonen, Kabiatsiwaybegebe, Wobukeek, Shiwitagon, Katouche, Nawakeshecom, Shawondaise, Kiwaishe, Nitinowinin, Kakekijick (by their hands and seals)	D. Washburn, Henry Murney, Benjamin Fairfield, Jr.	*Ibid.* at 62-63.

▶

◀ *Table 1*

Date	First Nations, as named in the Treaties	Treaty	Signatories	Witnesses	Source
28 February 1820	**Mississauga Indians.** Surrender of lands in the eastern part of the Mississaqua Indian Reserve, Township of Toronto "together with all the woods and waters therein lying and being and all and singular the rights, privileges and appurtenances thereto belonging and especially all sole and exclusive rights of fisheries on the said Twelve and Sixteen mile creeks and the said River Credit heretofore reserved to or possessed by the said Nation of Mississauga Indians.	Treaty 22	W. Claus, *Dy. S.G. of I.A. on behalf of the Crown* Acheton, Nevoiquequah, Weiguesquome, Paushetaunonquitohe, Wabakagigo (by their totems)	J. Givins, *Supt. Indian Affairs,* D. Cameron, N. Coffin, J.P. Catty, *Lt. Royal Engineers Commanding,* D.J. Skene, *Lt. 68th Light Regiment,* J.L. Tighe, *H. Assist. Surg. to the Forces,* Alex. McDonnell, *Asst. Secy, I.A.,* Wm. Gruet, *Interpreter*	*Ibid.*, at 51-53.
28 November 1822	**Mississauga Indians.** Confirmatory Surrender of Treaty 27 (31 May 1819).	Treaty 27¼	Nawacamigo, Antenewayway, Kabratsiwaybiyebe, Wabakeek, Shewitigan, Nawaquarkecom, Shawandais, Pejehejeck, Papewan, Wabeckeneme, Naganasaway, Shebeshee, Naiquakan, Wabanzik (by their totems)	J.P. Hawkins, *Major 68th Regt. and Lt.-Col.,* Wm. Smyth, *Lieut. 68th Regt.,* John Ferguson, *I.I.D.*	*Ibid.*, at 63-65.

15 December 1835	**"Mississgua" Tribe of Indians of the Bay of Quinté.** Surrender of lots 28, 29, 30, and 31 on the Bay of Quinte.	Treaty 40½	John Sunday, Jacob Pathegezhick, Jacob Sunday, James Sahgahnahquothoabe, Jacob Pahbewun, James Nahwahquashkum, (each by marking an "X" and by seal)	J.B. Clench, *Supt. Indian Affairs,* Silvester Hurlburt, Charles W. Warren	*Ibid.*, at 99.
9 August 1836	**Ottawas and Chippewas.** Surrender, in form of a proposal by Sir Francis Bond Head, asking that the Ottawas and Chippewas relinquish their claims Manitoulin Island and the north shore of Lake Lake Huron so that these may form a reserve "under your Great Father's control) of all Indians whom he shall allow to reside on them; if so, affix your marks to this my proposal."	Treaty 45	F.B. Head J.B. Assekinack (signed?); Mokommunish, Tawackkuck, Kimewen, Kitchemokomon, Pesciatawick, Paimausegai, Nainawmutteebe, Mosuneko, Kewuckance, Shawenauseway, Espaniole, Snake, Pautunseway, Paimauqumestcam, Wagemauquin, (by their totems)	Not witnessed	*Ibid.*, at 112-13.

▶

◀ *Table 1*

Date	First Nations, as named in the Treaties	Treaty	Signatories	Witnesses	Source
9 August 1836	**Saukings (Saugeen) Indians.** Surrender of the Sauking Territory.	Treaty 45½	F.B. Head, Metiewabe, Alexander Kaquta Bunevairear, Kowgisawis, Mettawansh (by their totems)	T.G. Anderson, *S.I.A.*, Joseph Stinson, *Genl. Supt. of Weslayan Missions*, Adam Elliott, James Evans, F.L. Ingall, *Lieut. 15th Regt. Commandg. Detacht.*, Talfourd W. Field, *Dist. Agent*	*Ibid.*, at 113.
26 November 1836	**Chippewa Tribe of Indians of Lakes Huron and Simcoe, now occupying the the tract of land on the public high road leading from Colewater to the Narrows of Lake Simcoe.** Proposal to surrender tract, described in index as the high road from Coldwater to Narrows of Lake Simcoe in Medonte and North and South Orillia Townships, Simcoe County.	Treaty 48	Yellow Head, John Aisance, Thomas Naineshunk, Wahbone Young, Shawgashe (by their totems) James Bigwing, Joseph Shilling, Benjamin Joseph, Henry Jones, Henry Stanour, John Pawgawaznine, Shawwenwabung (each by marking an "X")	J. Givins, *C.S.I.A.*, W.B. Robinson, *M.P.P.* William Hepburn	*Ibid.*, at 117.
15 June 1838	**Mississagua Tribe of Indians of Kingston and the Bay of Quinté now settled in the Township of Alnwick.** Surrender of Wahboose. Island in Midland.	Treaty 49	John Sunday, Jacob Sunday, Jacob Pazhegezhick, James Sahgahnaquottwabe,	Charles Anderson, Silvester Hurlburt	*Ibid.* at 119.

			Jacob Pahbewun, James Hah-wah-quash-kum (by their totems)		
7 September 1850	**Ojibway Indians inhabiting the north shore of Lake Superior.** Surrender of lands from Batchewananaung Bay to Pigeon River to the height of lands covered by the charter of the Hudson's Bay Company, "reserving the full and free privilege to hunt over the territory now ceded by them and to fish in the waters thereof as they have heretofore been in the habit of doing ..."	Treaty 60 (Robinson-Superior Treaty)	W.B. Robinson Joseph Peau de Chat, John Ininwayu, Mishe-muckqua, Totomenai, Jacob Wasseba, Ahmutchiwagabow, Michel Shebageshick, Manitonshanise, Chigenaus (each by marking an "X")	George Ironside, *S.I. Affairs*, Arthur P. Cooper, *Capt. Comg. Rifle Bde.*, H.N. Balfour, *2nd Lieut. Rifle Brigade*	*Ibid.*, at 147-49.
9 September 1850	**Ojibway Indians inhabiting and claiming the eastern and northern shores of Lake Huron, from Penetanguishene to Saulte Ste. Marie and thence to Batchewanaung Bay, together with the islands in the said lakes opposite to the shores thereof.** Surrender of those lands "as well as all unconceded lands within the limits of Canada West to which they have any just claim" reserving "the full and free privilege to hunt over the territory now ceded by them, and to fish in the waters thereof, as they have heretofore been in the habit of doing ..."	Treaty 61 (Robinson-Huron Treaty)	Shinguakouce, Nebenaigoching, Keokonse, Mishequonga, Tagawinini, Shabokeshuk, Dokis, Ponekeosh, Windawtegowinini, Shawenakeshick, Namassin, Muckata Mishaquet, Mekis, Maisquaso, Naoquagabo, Wabokekik, Kitchipossegun by Papasainse, Wagemake, Pamequonaishcung, John Bell	Astley P. Cooper, *Capt. R. Bde.*, George Ironside, *S.I. Affairs*, T.M. Balfour, 2nd *Lt. Rifle Bde.*, Allan MacDonell, Geo. Johnston, *Interpreter*, Louis Cadot, J.B. Assikinock, T.W. Keating, Jos. Wilson, Witness to the signatures of Muckata Mishaquet, Mekis, Mishoquette, Asa Waswanay and Pawiss, T.G.	*Ibid.* at 149.

▶

◀ *Table 1*

Date	First Nations, as named in the Treaties	Treaty	Signatories	Witnesses	Source
			Paqwatchinini, Mashekyash, Idowe-kesis, Waquacomiek, Mishoquetto Asa Waswanay, Pawiss (each by marking an X)	Anderson, *S.I.A.*, W.B. Hamilton, W. Simpson, Alfred A. Thompson	
			W.B. Robinson		
			Ocheek, Metigomin, Watachewana, Mimewawapenasse, Shenaoqum, Oningegun, Panaissy, Papasainse, Ashewasega, Kagishewawetung by Baboneung, Baboneung, Shawonebin (each by marking an X)		
17 June 1852	**Chippewas of Lakes Huron and Simcoe.** Sale of the northern division of the Township of Orillia, including the estate and interest of William Yellowhead, Thomas Naningeshkung, James Bigwind, George Young, Joseph Snake, John Aissance, James Aissance, Peter Gadahgegwun, and John Jones.	Treaty 66	Chief William Yellowhead, Chief Thomas Naningeshkung, Chief James Bigwind, Chief George Young, Chief Joseph Snake, Chief John Aissance,	Read, explained in Council, signed, sealed and delivered in the presence of Adam Paterson, *Comm'r. Queen's Bench*, John Simpson, Joseph Naningeshkung,	*Ibid.* at 159-60.

			Chief James Aissance, Chief John Jones, Peter Gadahgegwun (by their totems)	*Interpreter* W.B. Hamilton, witness to signature of of James Aissance John Simpson, witness to signature of John Jones, Charles Keeshick, *interpreter* John Simpson, Frederick C.M. Fraser, witness to signature of Peter Gadahgegwun John Simpson (marking an "X")	
	Duplicate of Treaty 66 but with interpreter recorded as Joseph Nanegeshkung, and with variations in names of signatories.		Chief William Yellow-head, Chief Thomas Naningishkung, Chief James Bigwind, Chief George Young, Chief Joseph Snake, Chief John Aissance, Chief James Aissance, Chief John Jones, Peter Gadahgegwun (by their totems)		
5 June 1856	**The Tribe of the Chippewa Indians residing on the shores of Lakes Couchiching, Simcoe, and Huron.** Four islands in Lake Simcoe, Pumpkin Island in Lake Coucheching, and all those islands lying and being in Georgian Bay except the Christian Islands "which three islands hereby excepted and reserved to our own use."	Treaty 76	Thomas Nanegeshking by his son Joseph Nanegeshkung; (signature?); James Bigwind; George Young, Joseph Snake, John Aisence, Peter Gade-que-gun	"Signed, sealed and delivered in the presence of (having been read over explained and interpreted, which they appeared to perfectly understand)."	*Ibid.* at 203-4.

▶

◀ *Table 1*

Date	First Nations, as named in the Treaties	Treaty	Signatories	Witnesses	Source
			(by their totems)	David Laing Sanson, Adam Paterson, John Beattie, Thomas Shilling, Joseph Nanegeshkung, *Interpreter*	
19 June 1856	**"Mississaga Tribe of Indians formerly living on 'Grape Island' in Lake Ontario" but now settled at Alnwick.** Surrender of islands in Bay of Quinte and Weller's Bay, Lake Ontario and in St. Lawrence River.	Treaty 77	John Sunday, John Simpson, Jacob Sunday, John Pigeon, Joseph Skunk, Thomas Frasure, James Indian, John Storm (by their totems) Thomas Marsden, John Rice, *Interpreter*	Thomas Marsden, John Rice, *Interpreter* T.G. Anderson, *S.I.A.*	*Ibid.*, at 205.
24 June 1856	**A part of the Mississaga Tribe settled and inhabiting the borders of Rice Lake, Mud Lake, and Scugog Lake.** All islands in Rice Lake previously unceded.	Treaty 78	George Paudash, John Crow, Robert Soper, Peter Nogee, John Bigman, Jacob Crane, James McCue, Peter Patchey, Isaac Irons, Joseph Muskrat (by their totems) Jno. Short, Luke T. Skye, M.G. Paudauh, *Interpreter*, John Fawn, James Schofield, William Marsden, Jacob Crane, Jr.	T.G. Anderson "In witness whereof we have set out hands, seals and totems ..."	*Ibid.*, at 206-7.

Notes

Chapter 1: History of the Williams Treaties First Nations

1 E.S. Rogers, "Southeastern Ojibwa" in Bruce G. Trigger, ed., *Handbook of North American Indians: Northeast,* vol. 15 (Washington, DC: Smithsonian Institute, 1978) 760 at 760. See also Edward S. Rogers and Donald B. Smith, "Introduction" in Edward S. Rogers and Donald B. Smith, eds., *Aboriginal Ontario: Historical Perspectives on the First Nations* (Toronto: Dundurn Press, 1994) xix at xxi.

2 Rogers and Smith, *supra* note 1 at xxi.

3 Charles E. Cleland, "Preliminary Report of the Ethnohistorical Basis of the Hunting, Fishing and Gathering Rights of the Mille Lacs Chippewa" in James M. McClurken, ed., *Fish in the Lakes, Wild Rice, and Game in Abundance: Testimony on Behalf of Mille Lacs Ojibwe Hunting and Fishing Rights* (East Lansing: Michigan State University Press, 2000) 1 at 8.

4 James V. Wright, "Before European Contact" in Rogers and Smith, *supra* note 1, 21 at 22.

5 Canada, *Report of the Royal Commission on Aboriginal Peoples: Looking Forward, Looking Back,* vol. 1 (Ottawa: Royal Commission on Aboriginal Peoples, 1996) at 660.

6 *Ibid.* at 661.

7 See, for example, Charles E. Cleland, "The Historical Development of the Great Lakes Aboriginal Fishery" (Paper presented at CBA-Ontario/Canadian Aquatic Resources Section, American Fisheries Society Conference, "Aboriginal Fishing: Traditional Values and Evolving Resource Stewardship," Wahta Mohawk Territory, Bala, Ontario, 29 September 1996).

8 Wright, *supra* note 4 at 31.

9 *Ibid.* at 32. What happened to the Saugeen culture is not known. It is believed that, between AD 500 and AD 1000, it may have developed into the Princess Point culture at the western end of Lake Ontario.

10 Bruce G. Trigger, "The Original Iroquoians" in Rogers and Smith, *supra* note 1, 41 at 44.

11 Wright, *supra* note 4 at 35.

12 Robert J. Surtees, "Land Cessions, 1763-1830" in Rogers and Smith, *supra* note 1, 92 at 95.

13 Bruce G. Trigger and Gordon M. Day, "Southern Algonquin Middlemen: Algonquin, Nipissing and Ottawa, 1550-1780" in Rogers and Smith, *supra* note 1, 64 at 64.

14 Cleland, *supra* note 3 at 8.

15 A.F. Chamberlain, "Notes on the History, Customs and Beliefs of the Mississauga Indians" (1888) 1 *Journal of American Folklore* 150 at 150, 154.

16 My thanks to Victor Lytwyn for this information.

17 Chamberlain, *supra* note 15 at 154.

18 Rogers, *supra* note 1 at 760.

19 Trigger and Day, *supra* note 13 at 72. For oral histories of Iroquois warfare and raiding extending far into parts of northern Ontario such as York Factory, Ghost River, and James Bay, see Victor Lytwyn, *The Hudson's Bay Lowland Cree in the Fur Trade to 1821: A Study in Historical Geography* (PhD Thesis, University of Manitoba, 1993) at 62; C. Douglas Ellis, ed.,

Atalohkana Nest Tipacimowina: Cree Legends and Narratives from the West Coast of James Bay (Winnipeg: University of Manitoba Press, 1995) at 177; and James Wesley, *Stories from the James Bay Coast,* ed. by Norman Wesley and Andy Faries (Cobalt, ON: Highway Book Shop, n.d.) at 1-8.

20 See "Memoir on the Advantage of the Establishment of a Fort at Niagara, from 1686-1689" in E.B. O'Callaghan, ed., *Documents Relative to the Colonial History of the State of New York,* vol. 9 (Albany: Weed and Parsons, 1853-87) at 399.

21 Cadwallader Colden, *The History of the Five Indian Nations of Canada* (London: T. Osborne; Toronto: Coles Publishing, 1972) at 132.

22 "Narrative of the Most Remarkable Occurrences in Canada, 1694, 1695" in O'Callaghan, *supra* note 20, vol. 9 at 594-632.

23 *Evidence Taken by the Joint Commission appointed by The Dominion of Canada and the Province of Ontario in the Matter of Claim for compensation for unsurrendered Northern Hunting Grounds made by the Chippewas of Georgina Island, Christian Island and Rama and the Mississaugas of Scugog, Chemong, Rice Lake and Alnwick,* Library and Archives Canada [LAC] (formerly the National Archives of Canada), Ottawa, Record Group [RG] 10, vol. 2331, file 67,071 A at 161-62.

24 *Ibid.* at 252. See "Another Rice Lake Serpent Mound; Asphodel (Township) Furnishes the Second Great Find" *Peterborough Examiner* (5 September 1896).

25 See Ellis, *supra* note 19 at 177; and Samuel Stewart, Diary of James Bay Treaty (no. 9), summer of 1906, LAC, RG 10, vol. 11, file 2, 399 (microfilm reel T-6924).

26 Wright, *supra* note 4 at 30.

27 "Another Rice Lake Serpent Mound," *supra* note 24. A.F. Hunter was a well-known historian who co-edited the Simcoe Papers of the Ontario Historical Society with E.A. Cruikshank in 1924.

28 George Cobb, taped interview with Tall Tom Taylor, aged eighty-one, 12 June 1966, Trent University Archives, Peterborough, Ontario, tape 49, box 4, 82-006. Some transcripts of these tapes are available at Trent: see Professor Kenneth Kidd fonds, tape 41, box 1, 93-011. Others were copied onto audio cassettes in February 2002 and are now available to researchers. My thanks to Janet Armstrong for directing me to this source and for providing me with her own transcriptions of some of the relevant tapes.

29 George Cobb, taped interview with Short Tom Taylor, aged eighty-seven, 29 May 1966, Trent University Archives, tape 47, box 2, 82-006.

30 J. Hampden Burnham, "The Coming of the Mississaugas" (1905) 6 *Ontario Historical Society Papers and Records* 7 at 7.

31 *Ibid.* at 8.

32 *Evidence Taken, supra* note 23 at 253.

33 George Copway, *The Traditional History and Characteristic Sketches of the Ojibway Nation* (London: Charles Gilpin, 1850) at 88-92.

34 Darlene Johnston argues quite convincingly that Richard White's description of the Algonquian "diaspora" in his book *The Middle Ground: Indians, Empires and Republics in the Great Lakes Region, 1650-1815* (New York and Cambridge: Cambridge University Press, 1991) ignores significant evidence of involvement by Algonquian peoples in the fur trade during the same time period. See Darlene Johnston, *Litigating Identity: The Challenge of Aboriginality* (LLM Thesis, University of Toronto, 2003).

35 Reuben Golden Thwaites, ed., *The Jesuit Relations and Allied Documents,* vol. 57 (Cleveland: Burrows Brothers, 1897) at 21-23.

36 "Propositions Made by the Cayuga to the Magistrates at Albany" in Lawrence H. Leder, ed., *The Livingston Indian Records, 1666-1723* (Stanford, NY: E.M. Coleman, 1979) at 120-22.

37 Quoted in Anthony Wallace, "Origins of Iroquois Neutrality: The Grand Settlement of 1701" (1978) 24 *Pennsylvania History* 223 at 228.

38 *New York Colonial Manuscripts 1638-1800,* Paris Documents, New York State Archives, Albany, New York, A1894, vol. 5 at 698-99.

39 *Ibid.*

40 O'Callaghan, *supra* note 20, vol. 4 at 694.

41 *Ibid.* at 735-36, dated 29 August 1700. See also "Private conference between the Earl of

Bellomont and two of the principal Sachems of each of the Five Nations at Albany," in Charles H. McIlwain, ed., *An Abridgement of the Indian Affairs Contained in Four Folio Volumes, Transacted in the Colony of New York from the Year 1678 to the Year 1751 by Peter Wraxall* (Cambridge: Harvard University Press, 1968) at 34-37.

42 O'Callaghan, *supra* note 20, vol. 3 at 442-43, dated 23 June 1701.

43 "Treaty Between Governor de Callières and the Chiefs of the Five Iroquois Nations," *ibid.*, vol. 9, 715 at 717, dated 3 September 1700.

44 *Ibid.*

45 John Nanfan to the London Council of Trade, in O'Callaghan, *supra* note 20, vol. 9 at 907.

46 "Deed of the Beaver Hunting Ground" in O'Callaghan, *supra* note 20, vol. 9 at 908-10.

47 *Ibid.* For further clarification, the lands to be protected were to include an area previously occupied by seven nations called Aaragaritkas, a group with which, according to the treaty, the Iroquois had warred, then "subdued and driven out." Unfortunately, linguists have been unable to identify just who the Aaragaritkas were because the term has fallen out of use by Iroquois speakers and does not appear elsewhere in contemporary documents.

48 In 1996, with the kind assistance of John Woods of the Readers Room, I located the map (reference C0700-15) at the Public Records Office, Kew, England. A copy was loaned to Dr. Victor Lytwyn for his examination and was later provided to Dr. José Brandão, who announced the map's discovery in a presentation entitled "The Newly Rediscovered Map of Iroquoia and of Iroquois Hunting Territory," at the Annual Conference on Iroquois Research, Rensselaerville, New York, in October 2000. Since then, two publications have included copies of the 1701 map. These are Brian Leigh Dunnigan, *A Frontier Metropolis: Picturing Early Detroit, 1701-1838* (Detroit: Wayne State University Press, 2001); and Sara Stidstone Gronim, "Geography and Persuasion: Maps in British Colonial North America" (2001) 57 *William and Mary Quarterly* 373. I have recently learned that Erminie Wheeler-Voegelin was aware of the map in the early 1970s and included a schematic drawing of it in her *Ethnohistory of Indian Use and Occupancy in Ohio and Indiana Prior to 1795,* vol. 1 (New York and London: Garland, 1974). Thanks to Dr. Reg Good for bringing this to my attention.

49 In August 1701, shortly after its execution, Nanfan sent a copy of the "deed" to the Council of Trade in London, stating, "I now enclose ... the conference [minutes] with our Five Nations with an instrument I have procured from them whereby they convey to the Crown of England a tract of land 800 miles long by 400 broad including all their beaver hunting, with a draught [map] the most accurate I have been able to procure, of the situation of our Five Nations as well as the land conveyed to H.M. which your Lordships may please to observe begins at Jarondigat and is within the prick'd line." Nanfan, *supra* note 45, vol. 9 at 907.

50 Ives Goddard, "Synonymy of Southeastern Ojibwa" in Trigger, *supra* note 1, 768 at 769. The reference to peace with the "Assissagh" appears in "Meeting Between Lieutenant-Governor John Nanfan and the Five Nations at Albany," McIlwain, *supra* note 41 at 39, dated 14 July 1701.

51 For a complete description of this conference, see Gilles Havard, *Le Grand Paix de Montreal de 1701: Les voies de la diplomatice francoamérindienne* (Montreal: Recherches Amerindiennes au Québec, 1992).

52 See, for example, Hugh Hastings ed., *The Papers of Sir William Johnston,* vol. 2 (Albany: University of New York, 1922) at 705 and vol. 13 at 431.

53 Canada, *supra* note 5, vol. 1, *Looking Forward, Looking Back,* at 656. According to footnote 46 of the Royal Commission report, Thomas was quoting from a 1907 work compiled by a committee of Chiefs at Grand River.

54 Burnham, *supra* note 30 at 10. Chief Robert Paudash of Hiawatha's oral history, taken in the form of a statutory declaration, was relayed by J. Hampden Burnham, a local politician and lawyer to the Mississaugas.

55 Victor Konrad, "An Iroquois Frontier: The North Shore of Lake Ontario during the Late Seventeenth Century" (1981) 7 *Journal of Historical Geography* 129 at 142.

56 Louis Hennepin, *A New Discovery of a Vast Country in America,* ed. by Reuben G. Thwaites (Chicago: A.C. McClurg, 1903; repr., Toronto: Coles Publishing, 1974) at 522-23.

57 Johann Georg Kohl, *Kitchi-gami: Wanderings around Lake Superior* (London: Chapman and Hall, 1860) at 328.

58 *Ibid.* at 328, 330-31.
59 *Ibid.* at 330-31.
60 Edward S. Rogers, "The Algonquian Farmers of Southern Ontario, 1830-1945" in Rogers and Smith, *supra* note 1, 122 at 132.
61 Thomas Need, quoted in Mae Whetung-Derrick, *History of the Ojibwa of the Curve Lake Reserve and Surrounding Area,* vol. 1 (Curve Lake: Curve Lake Indian Band, 1976) at 27.
62 Roger Spielmann, *You're So Fat! Exploring Ojibwe Discourse* (Toronto: University of Toronto Press, 1998) at 89.
63 Whetung-Derrick, *supra* note 61, vol. 2 at 27.
64 William M. Beauchamp and David Cusick, *The Iroquois Trail, or Footprints of the Six Nations: In Customs, Traditions and History* (Fayettesville, NY: published by W.M. Beauchamp, 1892) at 92-93.
65 Kohl, *supra* note 57 at 327.
66 Donna S. McGillis, "A History of Rice Lake," http://www.ricelakeinfo.com/hstrybuf.htm.
67 Whetung-Derrick, *supra* note 61, vol. 2 at 63.
68 Chamberlain, *supra* note 15 at 154.
69 Whetung-Derrick, *supra* note 61, vol. 1 at 27.
70 Thomas Need, quoted in Whetung-Derrick, *supra* note 61, vol. 2 at 1.

Chapter 2: Imperial Crown Policy

1 Instructions from King George to Governor Robert Monckton, 9 December 1761, Public Records Office, London, England, CO/1130: 31d-80.
2 *Royal Proclamation* issued by King George, 7 October 1763, in Adam Shortt and Arthur G. Doughty, eds., *Documents Relative to the Constitutional History of Canada, 1759-1791,* pt. 1 (Ottawa: Historical Documents Publication Board, 1918) at 163-68; in *Sessional Papers,* No. 18 (1907) at 121-23; and at R.S.C. 1985, App. II, No. 1.
3 For a good summary of the requirements of the Proclamation, and an example of a surrender found not to meet them, see Indian Specific Claims Commission, *Report on Boblo Island* (Ottawa: Indian Claims Commission, 2000).
4 *Ontario v. Bear Island Foundation et al.* (1989), 68 O.R. (2d) 394 (C.A.), affirmed but without comment on this point, [1991] 2 S.C.R. 570.
5 See comments of Justice Hall in *Calder v. A.G.B.C.,* [1973] S.C.R. 313, and Lord Denning in *R. v. Secretary of State,* [1981] 4 C.N.L.R. 86 at 91 (Eng. C.A.).
6 *Chippewas of Sarnia v. Canada (Attorney General)* (2000), 51 O.R. (3d) 641 (Ont. C.A.).
7 J.G. Simcoe, Quebec, to the Lords of Trade, London, 28 April 1792, A.E. Williams/United Indian Bands of Chippewas and Mississaugas Papers, Public Records Office extracts, Archives of Ontario, Toronto, F 4337-2-0-11 (microfilm reel MS 2605) [hereafter A.E. Williams/United Indian Bands Papers].
8 Edward S. Rogers and Donald B. Smith, "Introduction" in Edward S. Rogers and Donald B. Smith, eds., *Aboriginal Ontario: Historical Perspectives on the First Nations* (Toronto: Dundurn Press, 1994) xix at xxvi.
9 Speech of Colonel Simcoe to the Western Indians, Navy Hall, 22 June 1793, in the Simcoe Papers, quoted in Donald B. Smith, *Sacred Feathers: The Reverend Peter Jones (Kahkewaquonaby) and the Mississauga Indians* (Toronto: University of Toronto Press, 1987) at 163.
10 John Graves Simcoe to the Committee of the Privy Council for Trade and Plantations, n.d., in E.A. Cruikshank, ed., *The Correspondence of Lieut. Governor John Graves Simcoe,* vol. 3 (Toronto: Ontario Historical Society, 1931) at 56, 61-62.
11 *Indian Treaties and Surrenders: From 1680 to 1890,* vol. 1 (Ottawa: Brown Chamberlin, 1891) at 6.
12 "Notes on a Meeting held at Niagara with the Mississauga Indians, accompanied by the Chiefs and Warriors of the Six Nations, Delewares, etc." in Charles M. Johnston, ed., *The Valley of the Six Nations: A Collection of Documents on the Indian Lands of the Grand River* (Toronto: Champlain Society and University of Toronto Press, 1964) at 46-48.
13 Joseph Brant to Alexander McKee, 4 August 1793, in Cruikshank, *supra* note 10, vol. 3 at 66-67.

14 The Crawford purchase is referred to in a letter dated 25 March 1791 from John Johnson to John Collins, in Alexander Fraser, *Third Report of the Bureau of Archives for the Province of Ontario 1905* (Toronto: L.K. Cameron, 1906) at 455.
15 Lord Dorchester, Governor General, to Lieut. Governor Simcoe, in Cruikshank, *supra* note 10, vol. 1 at 137-38.
16 Memorandum by John Collins, dated at Lake le Clie, 9 August 1785, regarding a council with the Mississaugas, Simcoe Papers, Archives of Ontario (microfilm reel MS 1797); F.B. Murray, ed., *Muskoka and Haliburton, 1615-1875* (Toronto: Champlain Society, 1963) at 97.
17 Johnston to Collins, in *supra* note 14 at 455, dated at Montreal, 25 March 1791.
18 Robert J. Surtees, "Land Cessions, 1763-1830" in Edward S. Rogers and Donald B. Smith, eds., *Aboriginal Ontario: Historical Perspectives on the First Nations* (Toronto: Dundurn Press, 1994) 92 at 106.
19 Treaty No. 13, dated 23 September 1787, in *Indian Treaties, supra* note 11, vol. 1 at 32.
20 *R. v. Cunningham* (1859), Bell C.C. 72 at 419.
21 *Evidence Taken by the Joint Commission appointed by The Dominion of Canada and the Province of Ontario in the Matter of Claim for compensation for unsurrendered Northern Hunting Grounds made by the Chippewas of Georgina Island, Christian Island and Rama and the Mississaugas of Scugog, Chemong, Rice Lake and Alnwick,* Library and Archives Canada [LAC], Ottawa, Record Group [RG] 10, vol. 2331, file 67,071 A at 38.
22 *Report of the Special Commissioners appointed on the 8th day of September 1856, to Investigate Indian Affairs in Canada* (Toronto: Stewart Derbyshire and George Desbarats, 1858), Appendix 21 at A21-87 to A21-88 [hereafter Pennefather Report]. This was acknowledged by the Ontario government in 1930, when confirmed by J.L. Morrice, the Ontario Land Surveyor, in a note to F.E. Titus, Solicitor for the Department of Lands and Forests, 31 July 1930, attached to a memorandum sent by Titus to W.R. Cain, Deputy Minister of Lands and Forests, "pursuant to his instructions dated 16th May last," Ministry of Natural Resources archives, Peterborough, Ontario, file 19,380.
23 Lord Dorchester, Governor General, to Lieut. Governor Simcoe, 27 January 1794, in Cruikshank, *supra* note 10, vol. 1 at 142.
24 D.B. Read, *The Lieutenant Governors of Upper Canada and Ontario 1792-1899* (Toronto: W. Briggs, 1900) at 25, 36.
25 *Dictionary of Canadian Biography Online,* http://www.biographi.ca/, *s.v.* "Peter Russell." See also Charles R. Tuttle, *Tuttle's popular history of the Dominion of Canada: With art illustrations from the earliest settlement of the British-American colonies to the present time, together with portrait engravings and biographical sketches of the most distinguished men of the nation* (Montreal/Boston: D. Downie and Co./Tuttle and Downie, 1877).
26 Peter Russell to Robert Prescott, 9 April 1798, in E.A. Cruikshank and A.F. Hunter, eds., *The Correspondence of the Honourable Peter Russell with Allied Documents relating to his administration of the Government of Upper Canada during the Official Term of Lieut.-Governor J.G. Simcoe, While on Leave of Absence,* vol. 2, 1798 (Toronto: Ontario Historical Society, 1935) at 137-39, no. 34.
27 Treaty No. 5 in *Indian Treaties, supra* note 11, vol. 1 at 15-17.
28 See Minutes in Edith Firth, ed., *The Town of York, 1793-1815: A Collection of Documents of Early Toronto* (Toronto: Champlain Society, 1962) at 123.
29 James Green to Sir John Johnson, 12 March 1798, in Cruikshank and Hunter, *supra* note 26, vol. 2 at 117-18.
30 Henry J. Morgan, *Sketches of Celebrated Canadians and persons connected with Canada; from the earliest period in the history of the province down to the present time* (Montreal: R. Worthington, 1865) at 130.
31 Robert Prescott to Peter Russell, 9 April 1798, in Cruikshank and Hunter, *supra* note 26, vol. 2 at 137-39.
32 Indenture listed with Treaty No. 13, 1 August 1805, in *Indian Treaties, supra* note 11, vol. 1 at 34.
33 Copy of a letter from D.W. Smith, Surveyor General, to Peter Russell, 16 April 1797, A.E. Williams/United Indian Bands Papers, F 4337-2-0-1 (microfilm reel MS 2605).

34 Treaty No. 5, *supra* note 27 at 15.
35 Treaty No. 29 in *Indian Treaties, supra* note 11, vol. 1 at 72.
36 J. Butler to unknown, dated at the Head of Lake Ontario, 16 October 1790, Simcoe Papers, Archives of Ontario (microfilm reel MS 1797).
37 J.G. Simcoe to Lord Dorchester, York, 9 April 1796, in Cruikshank, *supra* note 10, vol. 4 at 239, with thanks to Dr. José Brandão for providing this reference.
38 Treaty No. 13, and Indenture, Mississauga Nation of Credit River and William Claus, Deputy Superintendent General, Indian Affairs, 1 August 1805, in *Indian Treaties, supra* note 11, vol. 1 at 34-35.
39 Treaty No. 13a, 2 August 1805, in *Indian Treaties, supra* note 11, vol. 1 at 35-36.
40 Greg Curnoe, *Directory of First Nations Individuals in Southwestern Ontario, 1750-1850,* Occasional Publication of the London Chapter, ed. by Frank Davey and Neal Ferris (London: Ontario Archaeological Society, 1996), web version edited by Nick Adams, http://www.adamsheritage.com/deedsnations/edit.htm.
41 Minutes of a Council Meeting with the Mississaugues at the River Credit, 1 August 1805, recorded by P. Selby, LAC, RG 10, vol. 1.
42 *Ibid.* 2 August 1805.
43 Treaty No. 14, 6 September 1806, in *Indian Treaties, supra* note 11, vol. 1 at 76.
44 Surtees, *supra* note 18 at 112-13.
45 "William Claus," Events, Places, People and Times in Canadian History, http://www.edunetconnect.com/cat/candict/c.html.
46 Surtees, *supra* note 18 at 116.
47 Treaty No. 19, 28 October 1818, in *Indian Treaties, supra* note 11, vol. 1 at 47-48.
48 Treaty No. 20, 5 November 1818, in *Indian Treaties, supra* note 11, vol. 1 at 48-49.
49 Sir Charles Bagot, "Report on the Affairs of the Indians in Canada, Laid before the Legislative Assembly on 20 March 1845," *Journals of the Legislative Assembly of the Province of Canada,* 1844-45 (Montreal: Rolo Campbell, 1847) Appendix No. 67 [hereafter Bagot Report].
50 Undated letter, LAC, RG 10, vol. 118 at 169,439-782. My thanks to Dr. Reg Good for providing this reference.
51 Documents contained in file named "Gunshot Treaty," A.E. Williams Papers, Archives of Ontario, F 4337-11-0-8 (microfilm reel MS 2607). See also David T. McNab, "The Promise That He Gave to My Grandfather Was Very Sweet: The Gun Shot Treaty of 1792 at the Bay of Quinte" (1996) 2 *Canadian Journal of Native Studies* 293.
52 "Gunshot Treaty," A.E. Williams Papers, Archives of Ontario, F 4337-11-0-8 (microfilm reel MS 2607).
53 Surtees, *supra* note 18 at 115.
54 Quoted in *R. v. Taylor and Williams,* [1981] 3 C.N.L.R. 114 at 119 (Ont. C.A.). Note that no primary source is given for this evidence.
55 Treaty No. 20 in *Indian Treaties, supra* note 11, vol. 1 at 48, and "Gunshot Treaty," A.E. Williams Papers, Archives of Ontario, F 4337-11-0-8 (microfilm reel MS 2607).
56 James Givins to Thomas G. Anderson, 13 April 1836, LAC, RG 10, vol. 2330, file 67,071-3, pt. 2.
57 Anderson's diaries, which may be found at the Trent University Archives, fonds 77-1014, are also referred to in S. Rowe, "Anderson Record from 1699 to 1896" (1905) 6 *Ontario Historical Society Papers and Records* at 109-35.
58 James Givins to Thomas G. Anderson, 3 May 1836, LAC, RG 10, vol. 2330, file 67071-3, pt. 2.
59 Edward S. Rogers, "The Algonquian Farmers of Southern Ontario, 1830-1945," in Edward S. Rogers and Donald B. Smith, eds., *Aboriginal Ontario: Historical Perspectives on the First Nations* (Toronto: Dundurn Press, 1994) 122 at 132.
60 T.G. Anderson, Indian Superintendent at Manitoulin Island, 1828, quoted in Bagot Report, *supra* note 49, Appendix EEE, ch. 11. See also Pennefather Report, *supra* note 22 at 82.
61 William G. Dean, "The Ontario Landscape, circa A.D. 1600" in Edward S. Rogers and Donald B. Smith, eds., *Aboriginal Ontario: Historical Perspectives on the First Nations* (Toronto: Dundurn Press, 1994) 3 at 17.
62 *Indian Treaties, supra* note 11, vol. 1 at 151, 227.

63 There are many references to these areas as "camping grounds" in the evidence placed before the Commissioners in 1923: see, for example, *Evidence Taken, supra* note 21 at 108.
64 S.P. Jarvis to J.M. Higginson, 10 April 1844, LAC, RG 10, vol. 508 at 194.
65 State Book, Upper Canada, 3 September 1845, State Books, LAC, RG 1, vol. Y (microfilm reel C-124).
66 For a full discussion of these leases, see Peggy J. Blair, *The Supreme Court of Canada's "Historic" Decisions in Nikal and Lewis: Why Crown Fishing Policy Makes Bad Law* (LLM Thesis, Faculty of Law, University of Ottawa, 1998) at 22-27, published in two parts as "Settling the Fisheries: Pre-Confederation Crown Policy in Upper Canada and the Supreme Court's Decisions in *R. v. Nikal* and *Lewis*" (2001) 31 *R.G.D.* 87, and "No Middle Ground: *Ad Medium Filum Aquae,* Aboriginal Fishing Rights and the Supreme Court of Canada's Decisions in *Nikal* and *Lewis*" (2001) 31 *R.G.D.* 515.
67 Lease to the Huron Fishing Company from Saugeen Chiefs issued by Sir John Colborne, 2 September 1834, LAC, RG 10, vol. 56 (microfilm reel C-11,018); Executive Council Minutes, 21 May 1834, Upper Canada Land Books, LAC, RG 1, L1, vol. Q at 414 (microfilm reel C-105).
68 Licence of Occupation from Sir John Colborne to the Huron Fishing Company, signed by William Rowan, 3 July 1834, copy printed in *Report of the Huron Fishing Company,* Colonial Office Papers, Public Record Office, London, England.
69 Trial transcript, *R. v. Jones and Nadjiwon* (15 June 1992), Orangeville, Ontario (Testimony, Dr. Victor Lytwyn at 68-69) (Ont. Prov. Ct. Crim. Div.).
70 Lease of Fishing Islands to the Huron Fishing Company, signed by Jacob Metegoob (var. Metigwab, Metigwob), John Assance, and Alexander Matwayash, 2 September 1834, in *Report of the Huron Fishing Company, supra* note 68. My thanks to Darlene Johnston for supplying this reference.
71 E.C. Taylor, Secretary of Huron Fishing Company, to Sir John Colborne, 18 April 1835, LAC, RG 5, A1, vol. 152.
72 John Galt, Collector of Customs, to T.M.C. Murdoch, Chief Secretary to Governor General, 14 March 1842, LAC, RG 10, vol. 130 at 73,609 and 73,611 (microfilm reel C-11,484).
73 Petition from Alexander McGregor to Lieutenant-Governor Sir John Colborne, dated at York, 4 September 1832, LAC, RG 1, L10.
74 Executive Council Minutes, 15 December 1832, Upper Canada Land Books, LAC, RG 1, L1, vol. P at 394 (microfilm reel C-105). Lytwyn, *supra* note 69, suggests that McGregor, who was fishing from unceded lands, did not in fact have Aboriginal consent to do so. Nonetheless, McGregor did receive a licence of occupation from the Crown.
75 Alexander McDonald, Goderich, to T.M.C. Murdoch, Chief Secretary to the Governor General, 14 March 1842, LAC, RG 10, vol. 130 at 73,591-7.
76 Report of E.C. Taylor, Secretary, to the Directors of the Huron Fishing Company, n.d., in *Report of the Huron Fishing Company, supra* note 68 [emphasis added].
77 Petition of the Mississauga Indians of Rice Lake in the Newcastle District to Sir John Colborne, Lieut. Governor, 27 January 1829, LAC, RG 10, vol. 5 at 2038.
78 *An Act the Better to protect the Mississaga tribes, living on the Indian Reserve of the River Credit,* 1829 (10 Geo. IV), c. 3 (Upp. Can.).
79 Smith, *supra* note 9 at 79.
80 Undated Petition, LAC, RG 10, vol. 118 at 169,565-67 [emphasis added]. My thanks to Dr. Reg Good for supplying this reference.
81 George Pautaush, John Copeway, and John Crowe to Lieutenant-Governor John Colborne, and requisition marked "W.H.," LAC, RG 10, vol. 59 at 60, 105-7. My thanks to Dr. Reg Good for supplying this reference.
82 Peter Jones, *History of the Ojebway Indians with Especial Reference to Their Conversion to Christianity* (London: A.W. Bennett, 1861; repr., Freeport, NY: Books for Library Press, 1970) at 119.
83 J.B. Macaulay, "Report on Indian Affairs," NAC, RG 10, vol. 117 at 168748.
84 J.W. Keating, Assistant Superintendent of Indian Affairs, answer to the queries of the Commissioners of 1840, in Bagot Report, *supra* note 49, Appendix T.

85 Saltern Givens, Missionary, to S.P. Jarvis, 21 December 1840, LAC, RG 1, E3, vol. 36.
86 Bagot Report, *supra* note 49, Appendix EEE, ch. 11.
87 *An Act to repeal and reduce into one Act the several laws now in force for the Preservation of Salmon in that part of this Province formerly Upper Canada, and for other purposes therein mentioned,* 1856 (8 Vict.), c. 47.
88 Bagot Report, *supra* note 49.
89 *Ibid.* Appendix EEE, ch. 11, "Chippewas of Rama."
90 Kahkewaquonaby, alias Peter Jones, Indian Chief and Missionary, to Lord Goderich, Colonial Secretary, 25 July 1831, Council Minutes, 1835-48, Paudash Papers, LAC, RG 10, vol. 1011.
91 T.G. Anderson to Bruce, 27 January 1852, LAC, RG 10, vol. 538 at 51 (microfilm reel C-13,355).
92 Col. Bruce, Superintendent General of Indian Affairs, to J.H. Price, Commissioner of Crown Lands, 6 March 1851, LAC, RG 10, vol. 268 at 164,214 (microfilm reel C-126,533).
93 *Ibid.*
94 Col. Bruce, Superintendent General of Indian Affairs, to T.G. Anderson, 1 April 1851, LAC, RG 10, vol. 514 at 180 (microfilm reels C-13,345 and C-13,346).
95 Report by T.G. Anderson, Superintendent of Indian Affairs, 10 June 1848, LAC, RG 10, vol. 268 at 163,887 (microfilm reel C-12,653).
96 T.G. Anderson to Col. Bruce, 27 January 1852, LAC, RG 10, vol. 538 at 51 (microfilm reel C-13,355).
97 T.G. Anderson to L. Oliphant, Superintendent General of Indian Affairs, 29 August 1854, LAC, RG 10, vol. 541 at 121-29.
98 "Report on the Affairs of the Indians," *supra* note 84 at 365.
99 Sally M. Weaver, "The Iroquois: Consolidation of the Grand River Reserve, 1847-1875" in Edward S. Rogers and Donald B. Smith, eds., *Aboriginal Ontario: Historical Perspectives on the First Nations* (Toronto: Dundurn Press, 1994) 182 at 184.
100 "Orillia Hall of Fame," Scenic Orillia, http://www.scenicorillia.com/orilliahalloffame/halloffame20.html.
101 Bagot Report, *supra* note 49, Appendix EEE at 27-29.
102 "The Reserves and the Changing Circumstances of Native Peoples in Canada," ch. 15 in *The Native Peoples of Simcoe County,* 1999, Innisfil Public Library, http://innisfil.library.on.ca/natives/natives/chp15.htm.
103 Rowe, *supra* note 57 at 130.
104 See http://aboriginalcollections.ic.gc.ca/simcoe/ community/georgina.
105 Charles E. Cleland, "Preliminary Report of the Ethnohistorical Basis of the Hunting, Fishing and Gathering Rights of the Mille Lacs Chippewa" in James M. McClurken, ed., *Fish in the Lakes, Wild Rice, and Game in Abundance: Testimony on Behalf of Mille Lacs Ojibwe Hunting and Fishing Rights* (East Lansing: Michigan State University Press, 2000) 1 at 79.
106 Rogers, *supra* note 59 at 123. In 1837, for example, nearly thirty-seven hundred Ottawa, Ojibway, Pottawatomi (var. Potawatomie, Pottawatomie), Winnibago, and Menominee came from the United States.
107 *Ibid.* at 126.
108 Quoted in James A. Clifton, *A Place of Refuge for All Time: Migration of the American Potawatomi into Upper Canada, 1830 to 1850,* Canadian Ethnology Service Paper No. 26 (Ottawa: National Museums of Canada, 1975) at 90.
109 *Ibid.*
110 Francis Bond Head, Toronto, "Memorandum on the Aborigines of North America," to Lord Glenelg, 20 November 1836, in Sir Francis Bond Head, *A Narrative* (London: John Murray, 1839) Appendix A at 1a-15a. See also Olive P. Dickason, *Canada's First Nations* (Toronto: MacClelland and Stewart, 1992) at 237-38.
111 See, for example, J.C. Phipps, Manitowaning Indian Office, to the Minister of the Interior, Indian Branch, 10 February 1876, LAC, RG 10, vol. 1972, file 5530.
112 Treaty No. 45½ in *Indian Treaties, supra* note 11, vol. 1 at 113.
113 Bond Head, *supra* note 110, Appendix A at 1a-15a.

114 Treaty No. 45½ refers to him as "Metiewabe." See *supra* note 112, vol. 1 at 113.
115 Statement of Metigwab on the surrender of the Saugeen Territory, 13 September 1836, Six Nations Land Research Office, Six Nations, Brantford, Ontario, Cat. No. 836-9-13-1.
116 *Ibid.*
117 *Indian Treaties, supra* note 11, vol. 1 at 113.
118 Robert J. Surtees, *Indian Land Surrenders in Ontario, 1763-1867* (Ottawa: Department of Indian Affairs and Northern Development, 1984) at 91-92.
119 Sir F. Bond Head, Lieutenant-Governor of Upper Canada, to Lord Glenelg, Secretary of State, 20 August 1836, *Imperial Blue Books,* 1839, No. 93, 1212-23.
120 Rogers, *supra* note 59 at 127.
121 Bond Head, *supra* note 110, Appendix A at 1a-15a.
122 *Ibid.*
123 James Givins was Chief Superintendent of Indian Affairs from 1830 to 1837, Samuel Peters Jarvis from 1837 to 1845. Douglas Leighton, "The Compact Tory as Bureaucrat: Samuel Peters Jarvis and the Indian Department, 1837-1845" (1981) 73 *Ontario History* 40 at 40-41.
124 "Address of the Chief Superintendent of Indian Affairs to the Indians Assembled in General Council at the Great Manitoulin, 4th August 1837" in *Parliament, House of Commons, Volume 12, 1839* (Great Britain: Cambridge, 1839) at 383-84.
125 J.B. Macaulay, "Report describing Various Aspects of Indian Affairs in Upper Canada," April 1839, LAC, RG 10, vol. 719 at 123-24 (microfilm reel 13,411).
126 *Ibid.*
127 Extract from the *Annual Report on Indian Affairs,* taken from correspondence of S.P. Jarvis, Chief Superintendent of Indian Affairs, 20 July 1838, LAC, RG 10, vol. 124 (microfilm reels C-11,481 and C-11,482).
128 S.P. Jarvis to J.M. Higginson, 4 April 1844, LAC, RG 10, vol. 130 at 73,582 and 73,584.
129 S.P. Jarvis to J.M. Higginson, 25 October 1844, LAC, RG 10, vol. 509.
130 *Ibid.*
131 J.M. Higginson to S.P. Jarvis, 2 May 1845, LAC, RG 10, vol. 510 at 296-97.
132 Bagot, *supra* note 49, Appendix EEE.
133 *Imperial Proclamation* of 1847, 29 June 1847, Liber. A.G. Special Grants, 1841-54, LAC, RG 68 (microfilm reel C-4158).
134 See *R. v. Jones and Nadjiwon* (1993), 14 O.R. (3d) 421 at 438 (Ont. Prov. Div. Crim. Ct.).

Chapter 3: A New Crown Policy

1 Sir Charles Bagot, *Report on the Affairs of the Indians in Canada laid before the Legislative Assembly,* 20 March 1845, in *Journals of the Legislative Assembly of the Province of Canada,* 1844-45 (Montreal: Rolo Campbell, 1847) Appendix T at 349 [hereafter Bagot Report].
2 *Ibid.*
3 *Ibid.*
4 *Ibid.* at 363.
5 *Ibid.* at 369.
6 See, for example, Sir Paul Hasluck, *Black Australians,* 2d ed. (Melbourne: Melbourne University Press, 1970) at 63.
7 *Report on the Indian Affairs, supra* note 1, Appendix T at 370.
8 *Ibid.*
9 *Ibid.* at 371.
10 *Ibid.*
11 *Minutes of the General Council of Indian Chiefs and Principal Men: Held at Orillia, Lake Simcoe Narrows, on Thursday the 30th, and Friday the 31st day of July, 1846 on the proposed removal of the smaller gommunities* [sic] *and the establishment of manual labour schools* (Montreal?: s.n., 1846) at 6.
12 *Ibid.*
13 *Ibid.*
14 *Ibid.* at 13.
15 *Ibid.* at 20.

16 "Orillia Hall of Fame – Chief William Yellowhead – Musquakie, (1769-1864)," Scenic Orillia, http://www.scenicorillia.com/orilliahalloffame/halloffame20.html.
17 *Minutes of the General Council, supra* note 11 at 21.
18 Constance Backhouse, *Petticoats and Prejudice: Women and Law in Nineteenth Century Canada* (Toronto: Women's Press, 1991) at 56-57.
19 Attorney General W.H. Draper to J.M. Higginson, Civil Secretary, 16 April 1848, Library and Archives Canada [LAC], Ottawa, Record Group [RG] 10, vol. 612 at 215.
20 T.E. Campbell to T.G. Anderson, Superintendent, Indian Affairs, 25 September 1848, LAC, RG 10, vol. 513 at 93.
21 Campbell to Ironside, 25 September 1848, LAC, RG 10, vol. 612 at 214.
22 George Ironside, Superintendent of Indian Affairs, Manitowaning, to Major Campbell, Superintendent General of Indian Affairs, Montreal, 17 February 1848, LAC, RG 10, vol. 169, no. 3029 at 98,090-93.
23 *Ibid.*
24 Greg Curnoe, *Directory of First Nations Individuals in Southwestern Ontario, 1750-1850,* Occasional Publication of the London Chapter, ed. by Frank Davey and Neal Ferris (London: Ontario Archaeological Society, 1996), web version edited by Nick Adams, http://www.adamsheritage.com/deedsnations/edit.htm.
25 *Report of the Special Commissioners appointed on the 8th day of September 1856, to Investigate Indian Affairs in Canada* (Toronto: Stewart Derbyshire and George Desbarats, 1858) at 90-91 [hereafter Pennefather Report].
26 *Ibid.* at 91.
27 R. Bruce to T.G. Anderson, 19 March 1852, LAC, RG 10, vol. 515 at 31.
28 R. Bruce to Commissioner of Crown Lands, 29 August 1854, LAC, RG 10, vol. 541 at 121-29.
29 Pennefather Report, *supra* note 25 at 92.
30 R. Bruce to T.G. Anderson, 19 March 1852, LAC, RG 10, vol. 515 at 31.
31 See G.S. French, *Parsons & Politics: The Role of the Wesleyan Methodists in Upper Canada and the Maritimes from 1780 to 1855* (Toronto: s.n., 1962) ch. 6.
32 George Copway, *The Traditional History and Characteristic Sketches of the Ojibway Nation* (London: Charles Gilpin, 1850) at 186.
33 J. Hampden Burnham, "The Coming of the Mississaugas" (1905) 6 *Ontario Historical Society Papers and Records* at 10.
34 Chief John Sunday, Minutes of Council held at the Post of York on 30 January 1828, LAC, RG 10, vol. 791 at 102, reporting the information received from elders at the time of the Simcoe Deed of 1794. See Donald B. Smith, *Sacred Feathers: The Reverend Peter Jones (Kahkewaquonaby) and the Mississauga Indians* (Toronto: University of Toronto Press, 1987) at 99.
35 Charles G.D. Roberts, *The Canadian guide-book: The tourist's and sportsman's guide to eastern Canada and Newfoundland: Including full descriptions of routes, cities, points of interest, summer resorts, fishing places etc. in eastern Ontario, the Muskoka district, the St. Lawrence region; the Lake St. John country, the Maritime provinces, Prince Edward Island, and Newfoundland: With an appendix giving fish and game laws and official lists of trout and salmon rivers and their lessees* (New York: D. Appleton, 1891) at 39.
36 Catharine Parr Traill, *The Backwoods of Canada: Being letters from the wife of an emigrant officer, illustrative of the domestic economy of British America* (London: C. Knight, 1836) at 208.
37 Copway, *supra* note 32 at 186-93.
38 Chief Jacob Crane to T.G. Anderson, *ca.* 1855, Ministry of Natural Resources archives, Peterborough, Ontario, file 184,361.
39 Burnham, *supra* note 33 at 10.
40 Report by T.G. Anderson, Superintendent of Indian Affairs, 10 June 1848, LAC, RG 10, vol. 268 at 163,887 (microfilm reel C-12,653).
41 Mae Whetung-Derrick, *History of the Ojibwa of the Curve Lake Reserve and Surrounding Area,* vol. 1 (Curve Lake: Curve Lake Indian Band, 1976) at 54.
42 *Ibid.* at 67.
43 Quoted in *ibid.* at 68.
44 Edward S. Rogers, "The Algonquian Farmers of Southern Ontario, 1830-1945" in Edward S.

Rogers and Donald B. Smith, eds., *Aboriginal Ontario: Historical Perspectives on the First Nations* (Toronto: Dundurn Press, 1994) 122 at 141.

45 Pennefather Report, *supra* note 25 at 80-93, and Appendices 29, 31, and 32 at 248-59.

46 *Ibid.*

47 Bagot Report, *supra* note 1, Appendix EEE, ch. 11, "Chippewas of Rama."

48 Pennefather Report, *supra* note 25 at 80-93.

49 T.G. Anderson to L. Oliphant, Superintendent General of Indian Affairs, 29 August 1854, LAC, RG 10, vol. 541 at 121-29.

50 *Ibid.*

51 Pennefather Report, *supra* note 25 at 86-88.

52 *Ibid.*

53 *Ibid.*

54 Evidence of Captain Ironside, Rev. D. Omeara [O'Meara], Rev. [T.] M. Hannipeaux, and M. Férard [Ferrard] (regarding Manitoulin Island Indians) in *ibid.* Appendices 23, 24, and 25. Hannipeaux and Férard were Roman Catholic missionaries residing on Manitoulin Island. Dr. O'Meara was the Anglican missionary residing at Manitowaning.

55 See Pennefather Report, *supra* note 25, Appendix 31.

56 *Ibid.* at 257.

57 *Ibid.* Appendix 29 at 251.

58 *Ibid.* Saugeen, with thirty school-aged children, had an average attendance of ten; Owens [sic] Sound, with fifty, had twenty-two.

59 *Ibid.*

60 *Ibid.* The Alnwick school and that at the Bay of Quinte were established as part of the Crown's assimilation policy in which small Ojibway communities were to relocate to areas near the schools. *Minutes of the General Council, supra* note 11 at 6.

61 *Ibid.*

62 T.G. Anderson to L. Oliphant, Superintendent General of Indian Affairs, 29 August 1854, LAC, RG 10, vol. 541 at 121-29 [emphasis added].

63 *An Act to Encourage the Gradual Civilization of the Indian Tribes in this Province and to Amend the Laws Respecting Indians,* 1857 (20 Vict.), c. 26.

64 Peggy J. Blair, *The Supreme Court of Canada's "Historic" Decisions in Nikal and Lewis: Why Crown Fishing Policy Makes Bad Law* (LLM Thesis, Faculty of Law, University of Ottawa, 1998) at 61-84; and J. Michael Thoms, *Ojibwa Fishing Grounds: A History of Ontario Fisheries Law, Science, and the Sportsmen's Challenge to Aboriginal Treaty Rights, 1650-1900* (PhD Thesis, University of British Columbia, 2004). For a contrary opinion, see Roland Wright, "The Public Right of Fishing, Government Fishing Policy and Indian Fishing Rights in Upper Canada" (1994) 86 *Ontario History* 337, which argues that the *Fisheries Act* of 1857 was intended to *protect* Aboriginal fishing.

65 "Annual Report of the Superintendent of Fisheries for Upper Canada, by John McCuaig, Superintendent of Fisheries" (1859) *Journals of the Legislative Assembly,* Appendix 1, dated 31 December 1858.

66 R. Alan Douglas, ed., *John Prince, 1796-1870: A Collection of Documents* (Toronto: Champlain Society, 1980) at 155, 158.

67 See Canada, *Report of the Royal Commission on Aboriginal Peoples: Restructuring the Relationship,* vol. 2, part 2 (Ottawa: Royal Commission on Aboriginal Peoples, 1996) at 499 [hereafter *Restructuring*].

68 Quoted in Robin W. Winks, *The Blacks in Canada: A History,* 2d ed. (Montreal and Kingston: McGill-Queen's University Press, 1997), quoted in "Racism in Canada," http://www.aclc.net/antiba_endnotes.html.

69 "Report of William Gibbard, Fishery Overseer for the Division of Lakes Huron and Superior for 1859" in "Annual Report of the Superintendent of Fisheries for Upper Canada, for the Year 1859" in *Sessional Papers,* No. 12 (1860) 23 Vict., Appendix No. 31 at 84.

70 *Ibid.* at 91.

71 "Reasons given by the undersigned, William Gibbard, for suggesting the accompanying amendments to the Fishery Act," 28 April 1863, in "Report of the Select committee on the Working of the Fishery Act &c., &c., &c." *Sessional Papers No. 5,* 26 Vict. 1863.

72 *Fisheries Act* (1857) 22 Vict., c. 62, s. 2.
73 *Ibid.* s. 3.
74 *Ibid.* In 1865, *An Act to amend Chapter 62 of the Consolidated Statutes of Canada and to provide for the better regulation of fishing and protection of Fisheries* was passed with identical provisions.
75 Pennefather Report, *supra* note 25 at 83.
76 Samuel Strickland, *Twenty-Seven Years in Canada West; or, the Experience of an Early Settler,* vol. 1 (London: Richard Bentley, 1856) at 76-77.
77 John Hamilton McCuaig, "First Report of the Superintendent of Fisheries for Upper Canada" (1858) *Journals of the Legislative Assembly* Appendix 15.
78 Pennefather Report, *supra* note 25, Appendix No. 21.
79 *Ibid.*
80 T. Hannipeaux and M. Férard, *Report upon the Present State of the Great Manitoulin Island, and upon that of the Nomadic Bands or Tribes on the Northern Shore of Lake Huron* (n.p., August 1857) at 233-34.
81 Evidence of Captain Ironside, Rev. D. O'Meara, Rev. "M." Hannipeaux, and M. Ferard (regarding Manitoulin Island Indians) in Pennefather Report, *supra* note 25, Appendices 24, 25, and 26.
82 Strickland, *supra* note 76, vol. 1 at 76-77.
83 McCuaig, *supra* note 77.
84 *Ibid.*
85 "Annual Report of the Superintendent of Fisheries for Upper Canada for the year 1861" in *Sessional Papers,* No. 11 (1862) at 241.
86 "Report of William Gibbard," *supra* note 69 at 91.
87 W.R. Bartlett to Saugeen Chiefs, 23 June 1859, LAC, RG 10, vol. 544 at 228.
88 "Annual Report of the Superintendent of Fisheries for Upper Canada" (1859) *Journals of the Legislative Assembly* Appendix 1.
89 W.R. Bartlett, Visiting Superintendent of Indian Affairs, to the Saugeen Chiefs, 23 June 1859, LAC, RG 10, vol. 544 at 228.
90 William Gibbard, Department of Crown Lands, to W.R. Bartlett, 9 August 1859, LAC, RG 10, vol. 418 at 573-74.
91 "Report of William Gibbard," *supra* note 69 at 84, 87.
92 *Restructuring, supra* note 67 at 499.
93 Blair, *supra* note 64 at 102-14.
94 Victor Lytwyn, "Waterworld, the Aquatic Territory of the Great Lakes First Nations" in Dale Standen and David McNab, eds., *Gin Das Winan Documenting Aboriginal History in Ontario* (Toronto: Champlain Society, 1996) 14 at 24.
95 "Report of William Gibbard," *supra* note 69 at 91.
96 William Gibbard, Report, 9 August 1859, LAC, RG 10, vol. 418.
97 Chiefs John Assance and James Assance to W.R. Bartlett, Deputy Superintendent General of Indian Affairs, witnessed, 21 June 1859, LAC, RG 10, vol. 415. My thanks to Darlene Johnston for this particular reference.
98 Petition signed by the "Chippewa Indians of the Saugeen and Lakes Huron and Simcoe," 4 May 1860, Archives of Ontario, Toronto, RG 1, vol. A-1-7, n.p.
99 Lise Hansen, "Treaty Fishing Rights and the Development of Fisheries Legislation in Ontario: A Primer" (1991) 7 *Native Studies Review* 1 at 6.
100 "Aboriginal Fisheries on Lake Huron," in *Annual Report of Lake Huron Management Unit* (Toronto: Ministry of Natural Resources, 1994) at 7.
101 Fishery Lease, Garden River, Goulais Bay, 4 October 1859, LAC, RG 10, vol. 252, pt. 2 at 150,617. My thanks to Darlene Johnston for supplying this reference.
102 Memorandum from Simon J. Dawson, Three Rivers, to Pennefather, 24 July 1860, Dawson Family Papers, Archives of Ontario, MU 831, file 42 n.p.
103 Fishery Lease in the name of Wm. R. Bartlett for Station Frenchman's Bay to Chiefs Point, LAC, RG 10, vol. 252, pt. 2 at 150,617.
104 Special Fishery Licence and Licence of Occupation to Froome Talfourd, Indian Superintendent, on behalf of the Kettle Point Indian Band, signed by William Gibbard, Collingwood, Wawanosh Family Papers, D.B. Weldon Library, University of Western Ontario, London, box 4381, file I-1-1.

105 Fishery Lease, Christian Island, 22 October 1859, LAC, RG 10, vol. 252, pt. 2 at 150,625.
106 Fishery Lease in the name of Wm. R. Bartlett for Station Marion's Island in Lake Simcoe, LAC, RG 10, vol. 252, pt. 2, no. 150,653.
107 Later, in 1868, responsibility for Indian matters was transferred to the Department of Secretary of State; the *Department of Secretary of State Act* appointed the Secretary of State the Superintendent General of Indian Affairs. "History of the Indian Act, Part One" (1978) 8 *Saskatchewan Indian* 1 at 4.
108 My thanks to Jim Morrison for helping me to clarify these lines of authority and their chronology.
109 Report of William Gibbard, 9 August 1859, LAC, RG 10, vol. 418.
110 *Ibid.*
111 W.R. Bartlett to Indian Chiefs and Warriors at Cape Croker, 19 August 1859, LAC, RG 10, vol. 544.
112 "Report of William Gibbard on the Fisheries of Lakes Huron and Superior" in *Sessional Papers,* No. 11 (1862). Gibbard's report is dated 31 December 1861.
113 Richard Pennefather to Duke of Newcastle, Secretary of State for the Colonies, 1 November 1860, LAC, RG 10, vol. 11,026, file 7; see also Public Record Office, CO42, vol. 624, folios 266-306 (LAC microfilm reel B-446). My thanks to Dr. Reg Good for bringing these references to my attention.
114 "Annual Report of the Superintendent," *supra* note 85.
115 *Ibid.* Wages for the mid- to late 1860s obtained from James Skipper and George P. Landow, "Wages and Cost of Living in the Victorian Era," The Victorian Web: Literature, History and Culture in the age of Victoria, http://www.victorianweb.org/economics/wages2.html.
116 Richard Pennefather to the Duke of Newcastle, Secretary of State for the Colonies, 1 November 1860, PRO, CO42. vol. 624, folios 266-306 (microfilm reel B-446) [emphasis in original]. See also LAC, RG 10, vol. 11026, file 7. Thanks to Dr. Reg Good for this information.
117 Quoted in Lytwyn, *supra* note 94 at 24.
118 William Gibbard, "Report on Fisheries of Lakes Huron and Superior" in *Sessional Papers,* No. 5 (1863) Appendix No. 42(b) [emphasis added].
119 The Manitoulin incident is described in Victor Lytwyn, "Ojibwa and Ottawa Fisheries around Manitoulin Island: Historical and Geographical Perspectives on Aboriginal and Treaty Rights" (1990) 6 *Native Studies Review* 21 at 21-22. See also D. Leighton, "The Manitoulin Incident of 1863: An Indian-White Confrontation in the Province of Canada" (1977) 69 *Ontario History* 113 at 121-24.
120 "Fishing Rights Stirred Revolt on Manitoulin Island" *Manitoulin Expositor,* repr. in *London Free Press* (15 June 1950).
121 W.R. Bartlett to Indian Chiefs and Warriors, Cape Croker, 19 January 1864, LAC, RG 10, vol. 547 at 72.
122 A. MacNabb to W.R. Bartlett, 26 August 1864, LAC, RG 10, vol. 421, pt. 10.
123 *State of Western Australia v. Ward* (2000), 170 A.L.R. 159 at para. 107, [2000] F.C.A. 191.
124 Sidney L. Harring, "The Liberal Treatment of Indians: Native People in Nineteenth Century Ontario Law" (1992) 56 *Saskatchewan Law Review* 297 at 299.
125 See remarks of Lord Denning in *R. v. Secretary of State,* [1981] 4 C.N.L.R. 86 at 91 (Eng. C.A.).
126 William Bartlett to William Spragge, Deputy Superintendent of Indian Affairs, 9 January 1866, LAC, RG 10, vol. 549 at 187-90.
127 *Ibid.*
128 Charles R. Tuttle, *Tuttle's popular history of the Dominion of Canada: With art illustrations from the earliest settlement of the British-American colonies to the present time, together with portrait engravings and biographical sketches of the most distinguished men of the nation* (Montreal/Boston: D. Downie and Co./Tuttle and Downie, 1877) at 460.
129 Henry J. Morgan, *The Canadian Parliamentary Companion* (Montreal: s.n., 1869) at 81.
130 *Ibid.*
131 *Ibid.*
132 A. Russell, Assistant Commissioner of Crown Lands, to Indian Branch, attaching copy of opinion of James Cockburn, Solicitor General, 8 March 1866, LAC, RG 10, vol. 323 at 216,137-38 (microfilm reel C-9577).

133 *Ibid.*
134 Opinion of James Cockburn, Solicitor General, *ca.* 1866, with typed version containing addendum, LAC, RG 10, vol. 323.
135 Blair, *supra* note 64 at 114-20.
136 See Peggy J. Blair, "Solemn Promises and *Solum* Rights: The Saugeen Ojibway Fishing Grounds and *R. v. Jones and Nadjiwon*" (1996-97) 28 *Ottawa Law Review* 125 at 139; Blair, *supra* note 64 at 61-71; and Mark D. Walters, "Aboriginal Rights, Magna Carta and Exclusive Rights to Fisheries in the Waters of Upper Canada" (1998) 23 *Queen's Law Journal* 301.
137 Commissioner A. Russell, Commissioner of Crown Lands, to unknown, 3 April 1866, LAC, RG 10, vol. 323.
138 *Restructuring, supra* note 67 at 500. It appears that Whitcher was quite wealthy. His custom-built mid-Victorian residence, *ca.* 1869, has been described as "a fine example of the Tudor style" and one of the largest and best instances of this type of architecture existing in the Ottawa area. It is now the Turkish embassy. Information provided by Edward J. Cuhaci and Associates, Ottawa.
139 W.F. Whitcher, Crown Lands Department of Fisheries, to C.J. Dupont, Esq., Manitowaning, 12 May 1866, LAC, RG 10, vol. 323.
140 *Quebec (A.G.) v. Scott* (1904), 34 S.C.R. 603 at 610 (S.C.C.).
141 W.F. Whitcher, Crown Lands Department of Fisheries, to C.J. Dupont, Esq., Manitowaning, 12 May 1866, LAC, RG 10, vol. 323.

Chapter 4: Jurisdictional Disputes

1 W.R. Bartlett to W.F. Lamorandiere, Interpreter, Cape Croker Indians, 14 September 1867, Library and Archives Canada [LAC], Ottawa, Record Group [RG] 10, vol. 550, and to Geo. Miller, Superintendent of Fisheries, Owen Sound District, 12 November 1867, LAC, RG 10, vol. 551.
2 W.R. Bartlett to William Spragge, Deputy Superintendent General of Indian Affairs, 25 March 1867, LAC, RG 10, vol. 550 at 208-9.
3 "History of the Indian Act, Part One" (1978) 8 *Saskatchewan Indian* 1 at 4.
4 Referred to in report of William Van Abbott, Indian Lands Agent, Sault Ste. Marie, to the Minister of the Interior, Ottawa, 7 August 1875, LAC, RG 10, Red series, vol. 1967, file 5184 (microfilm reel C-11,123).
5 *Ibid.* [emphasis added].
6 J.C. Phipps, Manitowaning Indian Office, to the Minister of the Interior, Indian Branch, 10 February 1876, LAC, RG 10, vol. 1972, file 5530.
7 W.F. Whitcher to E.A. Meredith, Deputy Minister of the Interior, 9 May 1876, LAC, RG 10, vol. 1972, file 5530.
8 W.F. Whitcher to E.A. Meredith, 10 June 1876, LAC, RG 10, vol. 1972, file 5530, (microfilm reel C-11,124).
9 W.F. Whitcher to E.A. Meredith, Deputy Minister of the Interior, 9 May 1876, LAC, RG 10, vol. 1972, file 5530.
10 See Peggy J. Blair, *The Supreme Court of Canada's "Historic" Decisions in Nikal and Lewis: Why Crown Fishing Policy Makes Bad Law* (LLM Thesis, Faculty of Law, University of Ottawa, 1998) at 110-11 for examples of interference with Aboriginal fishing, such as instances in which white men set their nets at river mouths to prevent the upstream passage of fish.
11 W.F. Whitcher to E.A. Meredith, 10 December 1875, LAC, RG 10, vol. 1972, file 5530.
12 W.F. Whitcher to James Patton, Fishery Overseer, Collingwood, 17 December 1875, LAC, RG 10, vol. 1972, file 5530.
13 *Ibid.*
14 John Francis Jamet, Bishop, Sault Ste. Marie, to D. Laird, Minister of the Interior, 6 September 1876, LAC, RG 10, vol. 1972, file 5530.
15 *Ibid.*
16 W.F. Whitcher to E.A. Meredith, 29 December 1875, LAC, RG 10, vol. 1972, file 5530.
17 W.F. Whitcher to E.A. Meredith, 10 December 1875, LAC, RG 10, vol. 1972, file 5530.
18 See Peggy J. Blair, "Solemn Promises and *Solum* Rights: The Saugeen Ojibway Fishing Grounds and *R. v. Jones and Nadjiwon*" (1996-97) 28 *Ottawa Law Review* 125 at 137-39.

19 Shelley J. Pearen, "Sheguiandah after the Treaty of 1862," Manitoulin Island, http://www.manitoulin.on.ca/Expositor/treaty_series_part_1.htm.
20 *The Canadian Almanac and Miscellaneous Dictionary,* vol. 1 (Toronto: Copp Clark, 1895).
21 W. Plummer, Report Extract, 9 March 1876, quoted in Joan Holmes and Associates, "Williams Treaty Claim, Draft Historical Report," vol. 1 (Report prepared for Specific Claims, Indian and Northern Affairs Canada, Ottawa, May-August 1990) para. 43, doc. 42.
22 W.F. Whitcher to L. Vankoughnet, LAC, RG 10, vol. 6960, file 475/20-2, pt. 1 [emphasis added].
23 J.B. Nagishkung (var. Nagishking), Rama, to W. Plummer, 15 June 1876, cited in Joan Holmes and Associates, *supra* note 21, vol. 1 at para. 44, doc. 45.
24 Alex McKenzie to Chief Charles Big Canoe, 14 October 1876, LAC, RG 10, vol. 6960, file 475/20-2, pt. 1.
25 Chief Big Canoe, Georgina Island, to William Plummer, 18 October 1876, LAC, RG 10, vol. 6960, file 475/20-2, pt. 1.
26 William Plummer to E.A. Meredith, Minister of the Interior, 25 October 1876, LAC, RG 10, vol. 6960, file 475/20-2, pt. 1.
27 The Chief is listed in the 1871 Ontario census as James B. Nanaghskung, Rama, Indian, "Hunter & Fisherman." *Federal Census of 1871 (Ontario Index),* LAC, RG 31, entry 109 (microfilm reel C-9977). All 1871 entries for adult Rama males record them as hunters and/or fishermen. Note the 1871 census is accessible online at http://www.collectionscanada.ca/02/020108_e.html.
28 J.B. Nagishkung, Rama, to W. Plummer, 15 June 1876, cited in Joan Holmes and Associates, *supra* note 21, vol. 1, at para. 44, doc. 45.
29 W.F. Whitcher to Charles Skene, 19 January 1876, LAC, RG 10, vol. 1972, file 5530.
30 Whitcher on behalf of the Minister of Marine and Fisheries, Circular, 20 January 1876, LAC, RG 10, vol. 1972, file 5530.
31 J.D. McLean, Secretary, Memo to Law Clerk, 12 August 1909, LAC, RG 10, restricted file 40-34.
32 F. Lamorandiere, Interpreter, to William Plummer, Superintendent and Commissioner of Indian Affairs, 10 February 1876, LAC, RG 10, vol. 1972, file 5530.
33 Chiefs of Saugeen Band to William Plummer, 15 February 1876, LAC, RG 10, vol. 1972, file 5530.
34 William Plummer to Minister of the Interior, 9 March 1876, LAC, RG 10, vol. 1972, file 5530.
35 W.F. Whitcher to E.A. Meredith, 10 June 1876, LAC, RG 10, vol. 1972, file 5530 [emphasis added].
36 *Ibid.*
37 W.F. Whitcher to J.C. Phipps, Indian Agent, 6 September 1876, LAC, RG 10, vol. 1972, file 5530.
38 W.F. Whitcher to E.A. Meredith, 10 June 1876, LAC, RG 10, vol. 1972, file 5530 (microfilm reel C-11,125).
39 David Mills to Albert Smith, Minister of Marine and Fisheries, 18 July 1878, LAC, RG 10, vol. 2064, file 10,099½.
40 Sidney L. Harring, "The Liberal Treatment of Indians: Native People in Nineteenth Century Ontario Law" (1992) 56 *Saskatchewan Law Review* 297 at 333.
41 Quoted in *ibid.*
42 W.F. Whitcher to L. Vankoughnet, Deputy Superintendent of Indian Affairs, 15 September 1878, LAC, RG 10, vol. 2064, file 10,099½.
43 *Ibid.*
44 Charles Skene, Parry Sound Superintendency, to William Buckingham, Deputy Minister of the Interior, 22 October 1878, LAC, RG 10, vol. 2064, file 10,099½.
45 Charles Skene to Lawrence Vankoughnet, 24 October 1878, LAC, RG 10, vol. 2064, file 10,009½, quoted in Canada, *Report of the Royal Commission on Aboriginal Peoples: Restructuring the Relationship,* vol. 2 (Ottawa: Royal Commission on Aboriginal Peoples, 1996) pt. 2 at 504.
46 *Ibid.*

47 William Plummer to David Mills, Minister of the Interior, 3 December 1878, LAC, RG 10, vol. 563.
48 *Ibid.*
49 J.C. Phipps, Manitowaning Superintendency, to the Minister of the Interior, 10 February 1879, LAC, RG 10, vol. 2064, file 10,099½.
50 Hayter Reed, Deputy Superintendent of Indian Affairs, to William Smith, Deputy Minister of Marine and Fisheries, 22 April 1896, LAC, RG 10, vol. 2439 (microfilm reel C-11,221).
51 Blair, *supra* note 10 at 109-10.
52 S.P. Bennett, Marine and Fisheries, to L. Vankoughnet, Deputy Superintendent General of Indian Affairs, 4 July 1884, LAC, RG 10, vol. 6964, file 488/20-2.
53 Quoted in Lise Hansen, "Treaty Fishing Rights and the Development of Fisheries Legislation in Ontario: A Primer" (1991) 7 *Native Studies Review* 1 at 13.
54 Secretary of Indian Affairs to J. Tilton, Deputy Minister of Marine and Fisheries, Ottawa, 16 February 1888, LAC, RG 10, vol. 6960, file 475/20-2, pt. 1.
55 A.N. McNeill, Department of Indian Affairs, to Deputy Minister of Indian Affairs, 11 November 1896, LAC, RG 10, vol. 2439, file 91,338.
56 Secretary of Indian Affairs to J. Tilton, Deputy Minister of Marine and Fisheries, Ottawa, 16 February 1888, LAC, RG 10, vol. 6960, file 475/20-2, pt. 1.
57 J. Tilton, Deputy Minister of Marine and Fisheries, to L. Vankoughnet, Deputy Superintendent of Indian Affairs, 7 May 1888, LAC, RG 10, vol. 6960, file 475/20-2, pt. 1.
58 *Ibid.*
59 E. Burnett, Indian Agent, South Algoma, to Secretary of Indian Affairs, 25 January 1898, LAC, RG 10, vol. 3909, file 107,297 at 191,819.
60 L. Vankoughnet, Deputy Superintendent General of Indian Affairs, Memorandum, to T.M. Daly, Superintendent General of Indian Affairs, 5 January 1893, LAC, RG 10, vol. 2439, file 91,338 (microfilm reel C-11,221).
61 William Smith, Deputy Minister of Marine and Fisheries, Canada, to L. Vankoughnet, Deputy Superintendent General of Indian Affairs, 30 December 1892, LAC, RG 10, vol. 2439, file 91,338 (microfilm reel C-11,221).
62 L. Vankoughnet, Deputy Superintendent General of Indian Affairs, Memorandum, to T.M. Daly, Superintendent General of Indian Affairs, 5 January 1893, LAC, RG 10, vol. 2439, file 91,338 (microfilm reel C-11,221).
63 J. Hardie, Acting Deputy Minister, Marine and Fisheries, to H. Reed, Deputy Superintendent General of Indian Affairs, 8 August 1894, LAC, RG 10, vol. 2439, file 91,338 (microfilm reel C-11,221).
64 Mary Johnson, elder, quoted in Mae Whetung-Derrick, *History of the Ojibwa of the Curve Lake Reserve and Surrounding Area,* vol. 2 (Curve Lake: Curve Lake Indian Band, 1976) at 34. Mary Johnson was also interviewed by George Cobb in 1966; see George Cobb, taped interview with Mary Johnson, aged ninety-six, undated, Trent University Archives, Peterborough, tape 42, box 4, 82-006, copy on tape 85, box 5.
65 Harring, *supra* note 40 at 311.
66 F.E. Titus, Memorandum, to W.R. Cain, Deputy Minister of Lands and Forests, 31 July 1930, Ministry of Natural Resources archives, Peterborough, Ontario, file 19,380 at 4.
67 *Statement of Case of the Dominion on behalf of the Chippewa Indians of Lake Huron and Simcoe and the Mississauga Indians of Mud Lake, Rice Lake, Alnwick and Scugog,* 6 May 1895, filed by W.D. Hogg, Counsel for the Dominion, LAC, RG 10, vol. 2329, file 67,071, pt. 1B, paras. 5, 6, and 7.
68 *Ibid.*
69 Peter Crow, Joseph [illegible], Robert Mitchell, John Mitchell, and Lewis Antoine by their marks to the Governor General, Sir Edmund Walker Head, 11 May 1860, LAC, RG 10, vol. 255, pt. 1, file 201-300 at 153,123. My thanks to Dr. Reg Good for supplying this reference.
70 Paul de la Ronde, Hester Wakaonah, and Anne Wakaonah to William Spragge, Deputy Superintendent of Indian Affairs, 24 September 1866, LAC, RG 10, vol. 2329, file 67,071, pt. 1B (microfilm reel C-11,202).
71 Chiefs and Councillors of Rice, Mud, and Scugog Lakes to Spragge, 22 December 1869, LAC, RG 10, vol. 2329, file 67,071, pt. 1B.

72 *Ibid.* Note that Whetung is spelled Wetongue in the letter.
73 Gibb to Spragge, 26 January 1870, with marginal note, initialled W.S. dated 28 January 1870, Irving Papers, Archives of Ontario, Toronto, MU 1464 26/30/9.
74 Joseph Howe, Secretary of State, to Commissioner of Crown Lands, 9 February 1870, Irving Papers, Archives of Ontario, MU 1464 26/30/4(I).
75 A comment from an 1869 Upper Canada Queen's Bench case illustrates this view: J. Martin, representing the Crown in the prosecution of one Fegan for trespassing on the Grand River reserve, stated, "Indians on reserve lands have no interest in the soil. They have the right of occupation and cultivation and of clearing the land ... they have not the right of cutting and selling the timber." *Fegan v. McLean* (1869), 29 U.C.Q.B. 202, quoted in Harring, *supra* note 40 at 312.
76 Wm. Spragge, Deputy Superintendent General of Indian Affairs, Report, 19 May 1870, LAC, RG 10, vol. 2328, file 67,071, pt. 1 (microfilm reel C-11,202).
77 *Ibid.*
78 William Spragge to the Lieutenant-Governor, 23 May 1870, LAC, RG 10, vol. 2328, file 67,071, pt. 1.
79 *Federal Census of 1871 (Ontario Index),* LAC, RG 31, District of York North, Subdistrict of Gwillimbury North, Division 1-2 at 58-60 (microfilm reel C-9977).
80 *Ibid.* at 30-32.
81 *Ibid.* at 11 (microfilm reel C-9963).
82 Frederick Copegog, aged twenty-seven, *ibid.* District of Simcoe North at 2 (microfilm reel C-9963).
83 Joseph de la Ronde to Baron Lisgar, 27 May 1872, LAC, RG 10, vol. 2328, file 67,071, pt. 1.
84 William Plummer to Minister of Interior, 15 April 1878, LAC, RG 10, vol. 2328, file 67,071, pt. 1 (microfilm reel C-11,202).
85 Superintendent General of Indian Affairs to William Plummer, 9 May 1878, LAC, RG 10, vol. 2329, file 67,071, pt. 1B (microfilm reel C-11,202).
86 L. Vankoughnet, Deputy Superintendent General of Indian Affairs, to William Plummer, 1 August 1878, LAC, RG 10, vol. 2329, file 67,071, pt. 1B.
87 Plummer to Minister of the Interior, 27 August 1878, LAC, RG 10, vol. 2329, file 67,071, pt. 1B.
88 Plummer to Minister of the Interior, 6 June 1879, LAC, RG 10, vol. 2328, file 67,071, pt. 1.
89 Chief Anawagose [his mark], Grumbling Point, to J.C. Phipps, Visiting Superintendent of Indian Affairs, dated at Killarney, 19 March 1879, LAC, RG 10, vol. 6964, file 488/20-2.
90 *Evidence Taken by the Joint Commission appointed by The Dominion of Canada and the Province of Ontario in the Matter of Claim for compensation for unsurrendered Northern Hunting Grounds made by the Chippewas of Georgina Island, Christian Island and Rama and the Mississaugas of Scugog, Chemong, Rice Lake and Alnwick,* LAC, RG 10, vol. 2331, file 67,071 A at 243.
91 *Ibid.* at 247.
92 *Ibid.*
93 Plummer to Deputy Superintendent General of Indian Affairs, 22 September 1880, LAC, RG 10, vol. 2329, file 67,071, pt. 1B.
94 Unidentified Indian Affairs official to Plummer, 26 February 1881, LAC, RG 10, vol. 2329, file 67,071, pt. 1B.
95 Plummer to Superintendent General of Indian Affairs, 1 March 1881, LAC, RG 10, vol. 2329, file 67,071, pt. 1B.
96 Lawrence Vankoughnet to Sir John A. Macdonald, 11 March 1881, LAC, RG 10, vol. 2328, file 67,071, pt. 1.
97 Petition of Chiefs and Councillors of Christian Island, Rama, Georgina Island, Rice Lake, Scugog, and Mud Lake, 23 September 1881, LAC, RG 10, vol. 2329, file 67,071, pt. 1.
98 *Ibid.*
99 Unidentified, Indian Affairs, to William Plummer, 12 December 1881, LAC, RG 10, vol. 2329, file 67,071, pt. 1B.
100 Unidentified, Indian Affairs, to J.B. Nanningishking (var. Nankishung, Nanishking) and M.G. Pahdash, 8 August 1882, LAC, RG 10, vol. 2329, file 67,071, pt. 1B.

101 Chief J.B. Nanigishking to Sir John A. Macdonald, 20 August 1883, LAC, RG 10, vol. 2329, file 67,071, pt. 1B.
102 L. Vankoughnet to Sir John A. Macdonald, 2 October 1884, LAC, RG 10, vol. 2329, file 67,071, pt. 1B.
103 *Ibid.* He recommended that they be paid $4,908 plus arrears of annuities estimated at $166,872.
104 Alnwick Band Resolution, 4 February 1884, LAC, RG 10, vol. 2329, file 67,071, pt. 1B.
105 *Ibid.*
106 Unidentified, Indian Affairs, to D.J. McPhee, 31 December 1884, LAC, RG 10, vol. 2329, file 67,071, pt. 1B.
107 Band Council Resolution, Alnwick, 29 December 1885, LAC, RG 10, vol. 2329, file 67,071, pt. 1B.
108 George Guillet to the Superintendent General of Indian Affairs, 20 April 1887, LAC, RG 10, vol. 2329, file 67,071, pt. 1B.
109 Indian Affairs to George Guillet, 28 April 1887, LAC, RG 10, vol. 2329, file 67,071, pt. 1B.
110 Unknown to R. Sedgewick, Deputy Minister of Justice, 22 May 1889, LAC, RG 10, vol. 2399, file 83,002.
111 *Ibid.*
112 J.P. MacDonnell, Memorandum, The Mississaugas of the Rice Mud and Scugog Lakes, the Mississaugas of Alnwick and the Chippewas of Lakes Huron and Simcoe, 9 February 1893, Irving Papers, Archives of Ontario, MU 1464 26/30/87.
113 *Ibid.* Supplement "C."
114 Quoted in Whetung-Derrick, *supra* note 64, vol. 1 at 69.
115 A.F. Chamberlain, "Notes on the History, Customs and Beliefs of the Mississauga Indians" (1888) 1 *Journal of American Folklore* 150 at 155.
116 "Report of J.C. Phipps, Visiting Superintendent of Indian Affairs, Northern Superintendency, Division No. 1, Manitowaning" in "Annual Report of the Department of Indian Affairs" in *Sessional Papers,* No. 18 (1891) at 4. Phipps' report dates from 30 August 1890.
117 *British North America Act, 1867,* s. 92(13).
118 *An Act to Regulate the Fisheries of this Province,* 1885 (48 Vict.), c. 9.
119 *Ibid.* s. 2.
120 *Ibid.* s. 24.
121 "Report of the Honourable the Minister of Justice approved by his Excellency the Governor General in Council on March 6, 1886" in W.E. Hodgins, ed., *Correspondence, Reports of the Ministers of Justice and Orders in Council upon the Subject of the Dominion and Provincial Legislation, 1867-1895, compiled under the direction of the Honourable the Minister of Justice* (Ottawa: Government Printing Bureau, 1896) at 198.
122 *An Act for the Protection of Provincial Fisheries,* 1892 (55 Vict.), c. 10.
123 *Ibid.*
124 *Ibid.*
125 *Ibid.*
126 Roger Spielmann, *You're So Fat! Exploring Ojibwe Discourse* (Toronto: University of Toronto Press, 1998) at 89.
127 Hansen, *supra* note 53 at 15.
128 *In the Matter of Jurisdiction over Provincial Fisheries* (1895), 26 S.C.R. 444 (S.C.C.) at 448 (Question 11), 487-88.
129 *Ibid.* at 514, Chief Justice Strong, King concurring.
130 *An Act Respecting the Fisheries of Ontario,* 1897 (60 Vict.), c. 9 [hereafter *Fisheries of Ontario Act*].
131 *Ibid.* s. 2.
132 *Ibid.* s. 41.
133 *Ibid.* s. 8. Note that s. 3(1) of the *Act* defined "Crown lands" as meaning and "including such ungranted lands of the Crown or public lands or Crown domain as are within and belong to the Province of Ontario and whether or not any waters flow over and cover the same."
134 *Ibid.* s. 48.

135 *Ontario Fisheries Act,* 1898-99 (62 Vict.), c. 34, s. 13.
136 "Report of G.B. Abrey, Fishery Overseer, Lake Huron Division" in "Annual Report of the Department of Marine and Fisheries" in *Sessional Papers,* No. 5 (1875) at 157.
137 *Fisheries of Ontario Act, supra* note 130, s. 48.
138 *Ibid.* s. 41(2).
139 Memorandum to the Minister of Marine and Fisheries from the Secretary, Indian Affairs, 7 June 1898, LAC, RG 10, vol. 3909, file 107-297-3.
140 S. Stewart, Indian Affairs, "Fishing Privileges Claimed by Indians – Ontario," *ca.* 1897, LAC, RG 10, vol. 3908, file 107,297-1.
141 Indian Agent, J. Thackeray, Alnwick, to Deputy Superintendent of Indian Affairs, 18 July 1895, LAC, RG 10, vol. 6960, file 475/20-2, pt. 1.
142 Hayter Reed to John Thackeray, Alnwick, 23 July 1895, LAC, RG 10, vol. 6960, file 475/20-2, pt. 1.
143 *Ibid.*
144 *Ibid.* at 134.
145 L.H. Davies, Minister of Marine and Fisheries, to F. Latchford, Toronto, 6 March 1901, LAC, RG 23, vol. 123, file 164, pt. 1.
146 Chamberlain, *supra* note 115 at 154-55.
147 Joe Noland, interviewed by Frank Meyers, in "Manitoulin Pioneers and Obidgewong Indians" *Gore Bay Recorder* (20 November 1952) 7-8. Noland was born on Manitoulin Island in 1881.
148 *Ibid.* at 13-14.
149 George Cobb, taped interview with Herb Irons, age not provided, 2 July 1966, Trent University Archives, tape 43, box 4, 82-006.
150 George Cobb, taped interview with Short Tom Taylor, aged eighty-seven, 29 May 1966, Trent University Archives, tape 47, box 2, 82-006.
151 George Cobb, taped interview with Tall Tom Taylor, aged eighty-one, 12 June 1966, Trent University Archives, tape 47, box 4, 82-006.
152 Edward S. Rogers, "The Algonquian Farmers of Southern Ontario, 1830-1945" in Edward S. Rogers and Donald B. Smith, eds., *Aboriginal Ontario: Historical Perspectives on the First Nations* (Toronto: Dundurn Press, 1994) 122 at 133.
153 *An Act for the Protection of Game and Fur-bearing Animals,* 1892 (55 Vict.), c. 58, s. 12. It should be noted that under s. 15, half of any fine collected was to be paid to the prosecutor.
154 Frank Tough, "Ontario's Appropriation of Indian Hunting: Provincial Conservation Policies vs. Aboriginal and Treaty Rights, CA 1892-1930" (Paper prepared for the Ontario Native Affairs Secretariat, Toronto, Ontario, January 1991) at 2.
155 William McKirdy to Attorney General, 1892, Archives of Ontario, RG 8 Series, 1-I-D, no. 3257, quoted in Harring, *supra* note 40 at 326.
156 J.M. Gibson to William McKirdy, 4 July 1892, and response, Archives of Ontario, RG 2 Series, 1-I-D, no. 3257, cited in Harring, *supra* note 40 at 326.
157 *An Act to Amend and Consolidate the Laws for the Protection of Game and Fur-bearing Animals,* 1893 (56 Vict.), c. 49, s. 2(3).
158 *Ibid.* s. 8.
159 *Ibid.* s. 9.
160 See Tough, *supra* note 154 at 3.
161 *Act to Make Further Provision for the Protection of Game,* S.O. 1896 (59 Vict.), c. 68, s. 2(1).
162 *Ibid.* s. 2(8).
163 *Ibid.*
164 *Amendment to the Ontario Game Act,* 1898-99 (62 Vict.), c. 33, s. 3.
165 Cobb, *supra* note 151.
166 "Report of T.H. Elliott, Fishery Overseer" in "Annual Report of the Department of Marine and Fisheries" in *Sessional Papers,* No. 10A (1893) at 167.
167 "Report of T.H. Elliott, Fishery Overseer" in "Annual Report of the Department of Marine and Fisheries" in *Sessional Papers,* No. 11 (1894) at 293.
168 Copy of Extract, note to file, Tyendinaga fishing file, H.R. Conn, Fur Supervisor, undated, LAC, RG 10, restricted file 40-34.

169 William Bateman, Indian Agent, Port Perry, to Deputy Superintendent General of Indian Affairs, 5 April 1895, LAC, RG 10, vol. 6960, file 475/20-2, pt. 1.
170 *Ibid.*
171 William Bateman to Deputy Superintendent General of Indian Affairs, 6 April 1895, LAC, RG 10, vol. 6960, file 475/20-2, pt. 1.
172 *Ibid.*
173 Hayter Reed, Deputy Superintendent General of Indian Affairs, to William Bateman, 10 April 1895, LAC, RG 10, vol. 6960, file 475/20-2.
174 Chief Bigcanoe to William Bateman, 8 September 1895, LAC, RG 10, vol. 6960, file 475/20-2, pt. 1.
175 J. Smith, Deputy Minister of Marine and Fisheries, to Hayter Reed, Deputy Superintendent of Indian Affairs, 9 October 1895, LAC, RG 10, vol. 6960, file 475/20-2, pt. 1.
176 Hayter Reed to Smith, 14 October 1895, LAC, RG 10, vol. 6960, file 475/20-2, pt. 1.
177 D.C. Scott to J.L. McPhee, referring to application, 3 February 1895, LAC, RG 10, vol. 6960, file 475/20-2, pt. 1.
178 John Hardie, Acting Deputy Minister, to Hayter Reed, referring to an application to use nets in waters around Georgina and Snake Islands, 21 February 1895, LAC, RG 10, vol. 6960, file 475/20-2, pt. 1.
179 *Ibid.*
180 Deputy Minister of Marine and Fisheries to Deputy Superintendent General of Indian Affairs, 26 May 1897, LAC, RG 23, vol. 181, file 727, pt. 1.
181 F. Goudreau, Deputy Minister of Marine and Fisheries, to J.D. McLean, Secretary of Indian Affairs, 4 November 1897, LAC, RG 23, vol. 181, file 727, pt. 1.
182 Memorandum for the information of the Minister in re Fishing privileges claimed by the Indians prepared by Hayter Reed, Department of Indian Affairs, 18 November 1895, LAC, RG 10, vol. 107,297-1.
183 *Ibid.*
184 H. Wickham to Hayter Reed, 10 December 1896, LAC, RG 10, vol. 2405, file 84,041, pt. 1 [emphasis added].
185 Hayter Reed to H. Wickham, 12 December 1896, LAC, RG 10, vol. 2405, file 84,041, pt. 1.
186 *Ibid.*
187 *Ibid.*
188 F. Goudreau, Deputy Minister of Marine and Fisheries, to J.D. McLean, Secretary, Department of Indian Affairs, 12 November 1897, LAC, RG 10, vol. 3908, file 107,297-1.
189 F. Goudreau to J.D. McLean, 12 November 1897, LAC, RG 10, vol. 3908, file 107,297-1.
190 J. Jermyn, Indian Agent at Cape Croker, to Hayter Reed, 16 April 1896, LAC, RG 10, vol. 2439, file 92,338.
191 J. Jermyn to Hayter Reed, 6 November 1896, LAC, RG 10, vol. 2439, file 92,338, attaching Band Council Resolution, 31 October 1896, Archives of Ontario, Toronto, MS 108 (microfilm reel 1).
192 William Smith, Deputy Minister of Marine and Fisheries, to Hayter Reed, 2 April 1896, LAC, RG 10, vol. 2349, file 91,338.
193 Clifford Sifton to Louis Davies, Minister of Marine and Fisheries, 20 December 1897, LAC, RG 10, vol. 3909, file 107,297-3.
194 J.D. McLean to J.D. Stewart, Indian Affairs, 28 December 1897, LAC, RG 10, vol. 3909, file 107,297-3.
195 Hayter Reed, Memorandum, 26 November 1897, LAC, RG 10, vol. 3909, file 107,297-3.
196 J.D. McLean, Memorandum, 7 June 1898, LAC, RG 10, vol. 3908, file 107,297-1.
197 John Scoffield, Agent, to Department of Indian Affairs, 21 April 1897, LAC, RG 23, vol. 181, file 727, pt. 1.
198 "Report of T.H. Elliott, Fishery Overseer, Manitoulin Island Division" in "Annual Report of the Department of Marine and Fisheries" in *Sessional Papers,* No. 11A (1897) at 186.
199 Hayter Reed to E.L. Newcombe, 23 May 1896, LAC, RG 13, vol. 2422, file 480/1931.
200 E.L. Newcombe to Hayter Reed, 1 June 1896, LAC, RG 13, vol. 2422, file 480/1931.
201 J.D. McLean, Memorandum, 26 November 1897, LAC, RG 10, vol. 3908, file 107,297-1.

Chapter 5: Bureaucratic Obstacles

1 See W.D. McPherson and J.M. Clark's treatise, *The Law of Mines in Canada* (Toronto: Carswell, 1898) at 15-16.

2 *Caldwell v. Fraser,* Copy of Judgment of Rose J. delivered 31 January 1898 at Barrie, Ontario, Irving Papers, Archives of Ontario, Toronto, MV 1469 31/37/17. For a complete discussion of this case, see Peggy J. Blair, *The Supreme Court of Canada's "Historic" Decisions in Nikal and Lewis: Why Crown Fishing Policy Makes Bad Law* (LLM Thesis, Faculty of Law, University of Ottawa, 1998) at 34-36.

3 *A.G. Canada v. A.G. Ontario et al.,* [1898] A.C. 700 at 703, question number 11 (P.C.).

4 *Ibid.*

5 *Ibid.* at 712. The Court declined to comment on the right of riparian owners, however, as they were not parties to the litigation.

6 Bill 111, *An Act to Authorize the Transfer of Certain Public Property to the Provincial Governments,* was introduced by Sir John Thompson on 22 June 1891; it was, as he put it, the bill "relating to the foreshores." *Hansard* (22 June 1891) at 1101.

7 *An Act to Authorize the Transfer of Certain Public Property to the Provincial Governments,* 1891 (54-55 Vict.), c. 7.

8 *Hansard* (17 August 1891) at 3986.

9 *Ibid.* at 3988.

10 *An Act to Authorize the Transfer, supra* note 7; see also extract on file, Library and Archives Canada [LAC], Ottawa, Record Group [RG] 10, vol. 2449, file 94,121, pt. 1.

11 *A.G. Canada v. A.G. Ontario et al.,* [1898] A.C. 700 at 714.

12 *Ibid.* at 714, 716.

13 *Ibid.*

14 J.D. McLean to E.L. Newcombe, Deputy Minister of Justice, 28 June 1898, LAC, RG 10, vol. 2422, file 480/1931.

15 A. Power, Acting Deputy Minister of Justice, to J.D. McLean, Secretary of Indian Affairs, 8 July 1898, LAC, RG 10, vol. 2422, file 480/1931.

16 *Ibid.*

17 *Ibid.*

18 J.D. McLean to E.L. Newcombe, 29 June 1898, LAC, RG 10, vol. 2271, file 54,380.

19 "The Hon. Reginald Rimmer" in John Hawkes, *Saskatchewan and Its People,* vol. 3, Saskatchewan Genealogical Project, http://www.rootsweb.com/~cansk/SaskatchewanAndIts People/VolumeIII/RimmerReginald.html.

20 Reginald Rimmer, Law Clerk, to Superintendent General of Indian Affairs, 7 November 1901, LAC, RG 10, vol. 2397, file 82,200 [emphasis added].

21 S. Bastedo, Office of the Attorney General of Ontario, to F. Goudreau, Deputy Minister of Marine and Fisheries, 26 July 1898, LAC, RG 23, vol. 123, file 164, pt. 1.

22 *Ibid.*

23 Deputy Minister, Marine and Fisheries, to John R. Cartwright, Deputy Attorney General of Ontario, 17 October 1898, LAC, RG 23, vol. 123, file 164, pt. 1.

24 Department of Marine and Fisheries to Arthur S. Hardy, Attorney General of Ontario, 17 October 1898, LAC, RG 23, vol. 123, file 164, pt. 1.

25 The informal agreement between the Governments of Canada and Ontario in 1898 is referred to in a federal Order-in-Council, P.C. 714, 8 May 1926. The Department of Fisheries and Oceans Canada has confirmed that no documentary evidence exists for the agreement. See, however, para. 6 in *Chippewas of Nawash v. Canada* (9 November 2000), T-730-99 (F.C.T.D.), in which Justice Dawson of the Federal Court, Trial Division, referring to a handwritten memorandum, stated that, "on or about February 27, 1899, a memorandum submitted by the federal Minister of Marine and Fisheries for the approval of the Governor General of Canada called for dispensing with the services of certain federal fisheries officers in Ontario, and leaving the administration of certain fisheries matters in Ontario to provincial authorities." Later in the decision, the judge erroneously dated the memorandum to 3 March 1899 and remarked that it was directed to the Auditor General.

26 Deputy Minister of Marine and Fisheries to J.L. McDougall, 24 October 1898, LAC, RG 23, vol. 123, file 164, pt. 1.

27 A memorandum to the Governor General *ca.* 1899 reads, "The Minister further recommends that with a view to ensuring that the regulations made with respect to the Fisheries are being properly observed and enforced by the Provincial officials, the Province of Ontario be divided into three Inspectional divisions, and that Inspectors be appointed for each such division. The boundary of each division to be defined as follows." See Transcript of Evidence, *Chippewas of Nawash v. Canada, supra* note 25 at 164, Cross-Examination of Michel Leclerc. The document cited by Leclerc is probably the 27 February 1899 Marine and Fisheries memorandum for the approval of the Governor General.

28 David Mills, Minister of Justice, to unknown, 23 June 1899, LAC, RG 23, vol. 123, file 164, pt. 1.

29 L.H. Davies, Minister of Marine and Fisheries, to F. Latchford, Toronto, 6 March 1901, LAC, RG 23, vol. 123, file 164, pt. 1.

30 J.F. Boudreau, Minister of Marine and Fisheries, to R. Aylesworth, Minister of Justice, 28 February 1907, LAC, RG 13, vol. 2399, file 565/1906.

31 R. Aylesworth to J.F. Boudreau, 25 March 1907, LAC, RG 13, vol. 2399, file 565/1906.

32 *Ibid.*

33 *Ibid.*

34 *Ibid.* See also Indian Affairs to John Kent, Bewdley, 14 November 1922, LAC, RG 10, vol. 7753, file 2,702,502, which repeats Canada's position that the navigable waterways in Ontario were within exclusively federal jurisdiction.

35 J.D. McLean, Memorandum, 7 June 1898, LAC, RG 10, vol. 3908, file 107,297-1.

36 J. Cabot to Attorney General of Ontario, 9 January 1908, Archives of Ontario, RG 4, file 109.

37 Attorney General to Superintendent of Ontario Police, cited in *ibid.* file 109 at 358.

38 J.D. Haglan to J.H. Burnham, 22 April 1914, LAC, RG 10, vol. 2400, file 83,002, pt. 2.

39 Indian Agent R. McCamus to Secretary, Indian Affairs, 28 May 1914, LAC, RG 10, vol. 2400, file 83,002, pt. 2.

40 Indian Affairs to Johnson Paudash, Scugog, 20 February 1911, LAC, RG 10, vol. 6613, file 6025-4.

41 Aubrey White, Lands and Forests, to J.D. McLean, 27 November 1914, LAC, RG 10, vo. 2400, file 83,002, pt. 2, referring to the advice given to Evans and Evans by Indian Affairs.

42 J.D. McLean to Evans and Evans, 9 December 1914, LAC, RG 10, vol. 2400, file 83,002, pt. 2 [emphasis added].

43 John Kent, Bewdley, Ontario, to W.C. Cain, Deputy Minister of Lands and Forests Ontario, 30 October 1922, LAC, RG 10, vol. 7753, file 27,025-2.

44 W.C. Cain to John Kent, 30 October 1922, LAC, RG 10, vol. 7753, file 27,025-2.

45 Secretary, Department of the Interior, to J.A. McGibbon, Barrister, Oshawa, 23 November 1925, LAC, RG 10, vol. 2400, file 83,002, pt. 2.

46 John Thackeray to Deputy Superintendent General of Indian Affairs, 23 February 1895, LAC, RG 10, vol. 2329, file 67,071, pt. 1B.

47 Deputy Superintendent General of Indian Affairs to John Thackeray, 29 November 1895, LAC, RG 10, vol. 2329, file 67,071, pt. 1B.

48 John Thackeray to Deputy Superintendent General of Indian Affairs, 28 September 1896, LAC, RG 10, vol. 2329, file 67,071, pt. 1B.

49 Deputy Superintendent General of Indian Affairs to John Thackeray, 1 October 1896, LAC, RG 10, vol. 2329, file 67,071, pt. 1B.

50 Referred to in a letter from J.D. McLean to Clifford Sifton, 5 December 1903, LAC, RG 10, vol. 2329, file 67,071, pt. 1B, recommending against the meeting with W.H. Hunter.

51 "Report," J.A. McKenna and R. Rimmer, 20 March 1899, LAC, RG 10, vol. 2545, file 111834. See also *Matters in Dispute between the Dominion and Ontario, Joint Report to the Superintendent General of Indian Affairs by Messrs. McKenna and Rimmer* (Ottawa: Government Printing Bureau, 1901).

52 See *Ontario v. Canada,* [1905-1907] 10 Ex. C.R. 445 (Exch. Ct.); *Ontario v. Canada,* [1910] 42 S.C.R. 1 (S.C.C.); and *Canada v. Ontario,* [1910] A.C. 637 (P.C.).

53 *Matters in Dispute, supra* note 51, paras. 2, 4, and 5.

54 *Ibid.* Case No. 5.

55 Band Council Resolution, Alnwick, 1 December 1902, LAC, RG 10, vol. 2329, file 67,071, pt. 1B.

56 Thackeray to Superintendent General of Indian Affairs, 25 December 1902, LAC, RG 10, vol. 2329, file 67,071, pt. 1B.
57 R. Rimmer, Law Clerk, to Deputy Superintendent General, Indian Affairs, 7 January 1903, LAC, RG 10, vol. 2329, file 67,071-2.
58 *Ibid.*
59 Thackeray to Deputy Superintendent General, Indian Affairs, 15 January 1903, LAC, RG 10, vol. 2329, file 67,071, pt. 1B.
60 James Campbell to Deputy Superintendent General of Indian Affairs, 8 April 1903, LAC, RG 10, vol. 2328, file 67,071, pt. 1A.
61 *Ibid.*
62 *Ibid.*
63 John Yates to Deputy Superintendent General, Indian Affairs, 4 August 1903, LAC, RG 10, vol. 2329, file 67,071, pt. 1B.
64 Resolution and Powers of Attorney, 10-29 August 1903, LAC, RG 10, vol. 2329, file 67,071, pt. 1B.
65 George Blaker, Declaration, 15 May 1903, LAC, RG 10, vol. 2328, file 67,071, pt. 1; Thomas Marsden, Declaration, 15 May 1903, LAC, RG 10, vol. 2328, file 67,071, pt. 1; Peter Crowe, Declaration, 15 May 1903, LAC, RG 10, vol. 2328, file 67,071, pt. 1.
66 Kerr to Pedley, 19 May 1903, LAC, RG 10, vol. 2328, file 67,071, pt. 1.
67 Clifford Sifton, Minister of the Interior, to Frank Pedley, 27 November 1903, LAC, RG 10, vol. 2329, file 67,071, pt. 1B.
68 *Ibid.*
69 J.D. McLean to Clifford Sifton, 27 November 1903, LAC, RG 10, vol. 2329, file 67,071, pt. 1B.
70 Hunter to Sifton, 15 December 1903, LAC, RG 10, vol. 2329, file 67,071, pt. 1B.
71 Pedley to Sifton, 16 January 1904, LAC, RG 10, vol. 2329, file 67,071-2 [emphasis added].
72 *Ibid.*, marginalia initialled "C.S."
73 G. Mills McClurg to Chief Big Canoe, 6 March 1905, quoted in Joan Holmes and Associates, "Williams Treaty Claim, Draft Historical Report," vol. 2 (Prepared for Specific Claims, Indian and Northern Affairs Canada, Ottawa, May-August 1990) para. 181, doc. 180.
74 Summary of Claims of Rice Lake Indians, J.A. MacRae, 9 May 1905, LAC, RG 10, vol. 2329, file 67,071-2.
75 McLean to Deputy Superintendent General of Indian Affairs, 19 January 1906, LAC, RG 10, vol. 2329, file 67,071-2.
76 Bray to Deputy Minister, Indian Affairs, 26 April 1909, LAC, RG 10, vol. 2329, file 67,071-2.
77 *Ibid.*
78 J.D. Maclean to Johnson Paudash, 30 January 1906, LAC, RG 10, vol. 2328, file 67,071-2.
79 J.D. McLean to W.H. Bennett, 5 May 1908, LAC, RG 10, vol. 2329, file 67,071.
80 J.D. McLean to Manley Chew, 11 May 1909, LAC, RG 10, vol. 2329, file 67,071-2.
81 A. Crozier to J.D. McLean, 18 February 1911, LAC, RG 10, vol. 2329, file 67,071-2.
82 J.D. McLean to Crozier, 23 February 1911, LAC, RG 10, vol. 2329, file 67,071-2.
83 Chief Assance to Deputy Superintendent General of Indian Affairs, 19 February 1909, LAC, RG 10, vol. 2329, file 67,071-2.
84 Chief Assance to Manley Chew, 19 March 1909, LAC, RG 10, vol. 2329, file 67,071-2.
85 Resolution, 14 September 1909, LAC, RG 10, vol. 6743, file 420-8, pt. 1.
86 Quoted in Frank Tough, "Ontario's Appropriation of Indian Hunting: Provincial Conservation Policies vs. Aboriginal and Treaty Rights,' CA 1892-1930" (Paper prepared for the Ontario Native Affairs Secretariat, Toronto, Ontario, January 1991) at 6.
87 *An Act to Amend the Indian Act,* 1910 (9-10 Ed. VII), c. 28, s. 2. See also s. 37(a), which allowed claims to be brought "at the suit" of the Crown alone.
88 A.K. Goodman to J.D. McLean, 25 September 1911, LAC, RG 10, vol. 2329, file 67,071-2.
89 McLean to Goodman, 10 October 1911, LAC, RG 10, vol. 2329, file 67,071-2.
90 Goodman to the Hon. Robert Rogers, Minister of the Interior, 7 February 1912, LAC, RG 10, vol. 2329, file 67,071-2.
91 Goodman to Robert Rogers, 7 May 1912, LAC, RG 10, vol. 2329, file 67,071-2.
92 J.D. McLean to Goodman, 25 June 1912, LAC, RG 10, vol. 2329, file 67,071-2.

93 Goodman to McLean, 17 October 1912, LAC, RG 10, vol. 2329, file 67,071-2.
94 J.D. McLean to Deputy Minister of Justice, 15 January 1914, LAC, RG 10, vol. 2329, file 67,071-2.
95 R.V. Sinclair to E.L. Newcombe, 23 November 1916, LAC, RG 13, vol. 2510, file C498.
96 *Ibid.*
97 In *In Re Gray* (1918), 57 S.C.R. 150 at 176, Justice Anglin of the Supreme Court stated that "A complete abdication by Parliament of its legislative functions is something so inconceivable that the constitutionality of an attempt to do anything of the kind need not be considered." See also *R. v. Brodsky et al.*, [1936] 1 D.L.R. 578 (Man. C.A.) and *Nova Scotia (Attorney General) v. Canada (Attorney General),* [1951] S.C.R. 31 at 34.
98 E. Newcombe to Sir Louis Davies, Minister of Marine and Fisheries, 29 April 1901, LAC, RG 23, vol. 123, file 164, pt. 2.
99 E.E. Prince, Memo re. Disallowing Certain Clauses of the Ontario Provincial Legislation, 1900, 26 April 1901, LAC, RG 23, vol. 123, file 164, pt. 2 [emphasis in original].
100 *Ibid.*
101 F. Goudreau, Acting Deputy Minister of Marine and Fisheries, to E.L. Newcombe, 7 December 1900, LAC, RG 23, vol. 123, file 164, pt. 1.
102 F. Goudreau, Acting Deputy Minister of Marine and Fisheries, to E.L. Newcombe, 28 December 1900, LAC, RG 23, vol. 123, file 164, pt. 1.
103 Draft, E.L. Newcombe to Ontario Legislature, marginal note signed L.H. Davies, 7 December 1900, LAC, RG 23, vol. 123, file 164, pt. 1.
104 *Ibid.*
105 Note to file, signed "E.E.P" for E.E. Prince, undated, LAC, RG 23, vol. 123, file 164, pt. 2.
106 L.H. Davies to F. Latchford, Ottawa, 6 March 1901, LAC, RG 23, vol. 123, file 164.
107 J.M. Gibson to J. Smart, Indian Affairs, 27 April 1899, LAC, RG 10, vol. 2405, file 84,041, pt. 1.
108 J. Smart to J.M. Gibson, 27 April 1899, cited in
109 J.M. Gibson to J. Smart, Indian Affairs, 27 April 1899, LAC, RG 10, vol. 2405, file 84,041, pt. 1. See also Tough, *supra* note 86 at 3-4.
110 *Ontario Game Protection Act,* 1900 (63 Vict.), c. 49, ss. 5(1), 24, 28.
111 Petition, 1 January 1901, LAC, RG 10, vol. 2405, file 84,041, pt. 1.
112 J.D. McLean to Chiefs, undated, LAC, RG 10, vol. 2405, file 84,041, pt. 1.
113 J. McIver, Indian Agent, to J.D. McLean, 5 April 1902, LAC, RG 10, vol. 2439, file 91,338.
114 S.T. Bastedo, Deputy Commissioner of Fisheries, to J.D. McLean, Secretary, Indian Affairs, 23 April 1902, LAC, RG 10, vol. 2439, file 91,338.
115 J.D. McLean to J. McIver, 18 July 1902, LAC, RG 10, vol. 2439, file 91,338.
116 Cape Croker Band Council Resolution, 13 August 1902, LAC, RG 10, vol. 2439, file 91,338.
117 J.D. McLean, Acting Deputy Minister of Indian Affairs, to J. McIver, Indian Agent, Cape Croker, 25 August 1902, LAC, RG 10, vol. 2439, file 91,338.
118 Barrier Island, which formed part of the reserve, was excluded. S. Stewart to S.T. Bastedo, Deputy Commissioner of Fisheries Ontario, 15 October 1902, LAC, RG 10, vol. 2439, file 91,338.
119 S.T. Bastedo to S. Stewart, 28 October 1902, LAC, RG 10, vol. 2439, file 91,338.
120 J. Campbell, Indian Affairs, to the Deputy Superintendent General of Indian Affairs, 4 June 1904, LAC, RG 10, vol. 2439, file 91,338.
121 J. McIver, Indian Agent, Cape Croker, to J.D. McLean, 9 December 1902, LAC, RG 10, vol. 2439, file 91,338.
122 J.D. McLean to Superintendent of Game and Fisheries Ontario, 27 July 1902, LAC, RG 10, vol. 2439, file 91,338.
123 J.D. McLean to unknown, 23 July 1906, LAC, RG 10, vol. 6743, file 420-8, pt. 1.
124 The 1914 *Ontario Game and Fisheries Amendment Act* made it clear that "restrictions requiring a licence when fishing applied to Indians as well as to all other guides." R.S.O. vol. 11, c. 262, s. 27(2). This clarified an earlier amendment that had stated only that guides required a licence or permit "for hunting, shooting or fishing in any part of Ontario." *An Act Respecting the Game, Furbearing Animals and Fisheries of Ontario,* 1913 (3-4 Geo. V), c. 69, s. 52.

125 *An Act Respecting the Game, ibid.*
126 Unknown to Minister of Fisheries, *ca.* 1916, LAC, RG 10, vol. 2406, file 84,041, pt. 2.
127 Mae Whetung-Derrick, *History of the Ojibwa of the Curve Lake Reserve and Surrounding Area,* vol. 2 (Curve Lake: Curve Lake Indian Band, 1976) at 11.
128 Sidney L. Harring, "The Liberal Treatment of Indians: Native People in Nineteenth Century Ontario Law" (1992) 56 *Saskatchewan Law Review* 297 at 327.
129 J.D. McLean to E. Tinsley, 15 December 1910, LAC, RG 10, vol. 6743, file 420-8-1 (microfilm reel C-8101).
130 E. Tinsley to J.D. McLean, 12 April 1912, LAC, RG 10, vol. 6743, file 420-8-1 (microfilm reel C-8101).
131 Quoted in Tough, *supra* note 86 at 7.
132 J.D. McLean to unknown, 15 February 1910, LAC, RG 10, vol. 6743, file 420-8, pt. 1, quoted in *ibid.* at 5.
133 Larry Turner and John de Visser, *Rideau* (Erin: Boston Mills, 1995) at 63.
134 Kelly Evans, Special Commissioner, Game and Fisheries Commission, Toronto, to J.D. McLean, Assistant Deputy and Secretary, Department of Indian Affairs, Ottawa, 14 December 1910, LAC, RG 10, vol. 6743, file 420-8-1 (microfilm reel C-8101).
135 *Ibid.*
136 J.D. McLean to Kelly Evans, Special Commissioner, 26 December 1910, LAC, RG 10, vol. 6743, file 420-8-1 (microfilm reel C-8101).
137 *Ibid.*
138 J.D. McLean to Kelly Evans, 10 January 1911, LAC, RG 10, vol. 6743, file 420-8-1 (microfilm reel C-8101).
139 *Final Report of the Ontario Game and Fisheries Commission, 1909-1911* (Toronto: L.K. Cameron, 1911) at 199, 201.
140 *Ibid.* at 210-11.
141 G. Mills McClurg to the Chiefs, 5 September 1911, A.E. Williams/United Indian Bands of Chippewas and Mississaugas Papers, Archives of Ontario, F 4337-1-0-13 (microfilm reel MS 2604) [hereafter A.E. Williams/United Indian Bands Papers].
142 Petition, 22 March 1911, LAC, RG 10, vol. 6743, file 420-8, pt. 1, quoted in Tough, *supra* note 86 at 6.
143 Along with A.E. Williams, a researcher of Aboriginal history, McClurg collected a vast amount of materials on behalf of the United Indian Bands of the Chippewas and Mississaugas, a grassroots movement that asserted rights to hunt, fish, and vote between 1903 and about 1920. McClurg, Secretary and Treasurer of the organization, as well as its counsel, gathered legal documents, band census lists, speeches, and research materials. This document collection is held by the Archives of Ontario, Toronto, as the A.E. Williams/United Indian Bands of Chippewas and Mississaugas Papers, F 4337.
144 Memorandum, G. Mills McClurg, "Re Hunting and Fishing rights reserved by the Indians in their different surrenders of territory to the Crown from the earliest period onward," 5 September 1911, A.E. Williams/United Indian Bands Papers, F 4337-1-0-13 (microfilm reel MS 2604).
145 G. McClurg to Chief Joseph Irons, Chemong, 23 April 1904, A.E. Williams/United Indian Bands Papers, F 4337-1-0-4 (microfilm reel MS 2604).
146 G. Mills McClurg, Toronto, to Walter Simon, General Secretary, Christian Island, 17 October 1911, A.E. Williams/United Indian Bands Papers, F 4337-1-0-48 (microfilm reel MS 2605).
147 Band Council Resolution, Rama Reserve, signed by Chief J.B. Stinson, 20 November 1911, A.E. Williams/United Indian Bands Papers, F 4337-1-0-27 (microfilm reel MS 2604).
148 Chief J.B. Stinson to G. Mills McClurg, 28 November 1911, A.E. Williams/United Indian Bands Papers, F 4337-1-0-27 (microfilm reel MS 2604).
149 Sam Benson, Rama, to G. Mills McClurg, 12 September 1911, A.E. Williams/United Indian Bands Papers, F 4337-1-0-13 (microfilm reel MS 2604).
150 McLean to unidentified, 6 February 1913, LAC, RG 10, vol. 6743, pt. 2, quoted in Tough, *supra* note 86 at 8.

151 *Ontario Game and Fisheries Act,* R.S.O. 1914, vol. 2, c. 262, s. 8(i).
152 Vincent Amicous, Golden Lake, to Department of Indian Affairs, 3 October 1914, archives not identified, file 194,819, document no. 455,523. Thanks to Brant Bardy for supplying this and the two documents cited in the next note.
153 A. Sherriff, Esq., Deputy Minister Game and Fisheries Ontario, to the Secretary of the Department of Indian Affairs, file 194,819, document no. 456,336. See also J.D. McLean to Vincent Amicous, 17 October 1914.
154 Canada, *Report of the Royal Commission on Aboriginal Peoples: Restructuring the Relationship,* vol. 2 (Ottawa: Royal Commission on Aboriginal Peoples, 1996) pt. 2 at 496 [hereafter *Restructuring*].
155 *Ibid.*
156 Quoted in *ibid.* at 497.
157 *Ibid.*
158 Deputy Minister of Marine and Fisheries to Indian Affairs, *ca.* July 1916, LAC, RG 10, restricted file 40-34.
159 *Ibid.*
160 Band Council Resolution moved by Alfred Williams, seconded James York, 23 September 1916, LAC, RG 10, vol. 6960, file 475/20-2, pt. 1.
161 Chas. Myers to J.D. McLean, 26 September 1916, LAC, RG 10, vol. 6960, file 475/20-2, pt. 1; J.D. McLean to A. Sherriff, 29 September 1916, LAC, RG 10, vol. 6960, file 475/20-2, pt. 1.
162 J.D. McLean to Chas. Myers, 19 December 1916, LAC, RG 10, vol. 6960, file 475/20-2, pt. 1.
163 Transcript of Trial, *R. v. George Henry Howard* (1 October 1985), at 90 (Ont. Prov. Ct. Crim. Div.) (copy in author's file).
164 J. Bourchier, Indian Agent, to Secretary, Indian Affairs, 8 June 1917, LAC, RG 10, vol. 6960, file 475/20-2, pt. 1.
165 J.D. McLean to E. Tinsley, Superintendent of Game and Fisheries, 12 June 1917, LAC, RG 10, vol. 6960, file 475/20-2, pt. 1.
166 D. McDonald, Acting Deputy Minister of Game and Fisheries, to J.D. McLean, 19 June 1917, LAC, RG 10, vol. 6960, file 475/20-2, pt. 1.
167 J.D. McLean to D. McDonald, 26 June 1917, LAC, RG 10, vol. 6960, file 475/20-2, pt. 1.
168 D. McDonald to J.D. McLean, 30 June 1917, LAC, RG 10, vol. 6960, file 475/20-2, pt. 1.
169 J.D. McLean to D. McDonald, 20 July 1917, LAC, RG 10, vol. 6960, file 475/20-2, pt. 1.
170 Acting Deputy Minister of Game and Fisheries Ontario to J.D. McLean, 8 August 1917, LAC, RG 10, vol. 6960, file 475/20-2, pt. 1.
171 *Ibid.*
172 Wellington Charles to Department of Indian Affairs, 9 June 1920, LAC, RG 10, vol. 6960, file 475/20-2, pt. 1.
173 J.D. McLean to Wellington Charles, 5 July 1920, LAC, RG 10, vol. 6960, file 475/20-2, pt. 1.
174 Harring, *supra* note 128 at 352, 357.
175 Tough, *supra* note 86 at 5.
176 Harring, *supra* note 128 at 349.
177 *Ontario Game and Fisheries Act,* R.S.O. 1914, vol. 22, c. 262, s. 11.
178 *Ibid.* s. 11(2).
179 Since the Trent Canal system, which linked the Bay of Quinte with Georgian Bay via the Kawartha Lakes and Lake Simcoe, fell under purely federal jurisdiction, it is not at all clear that the provincial legislation should have affected waters or marshes used by the Mississaugas; however, it was used to prevent them from trapping.
180 *Ontario Game and Fisheries Amendment Act,* 1916 (6 Geo. V), c. 60, s. 5(2).
181 W.R. Coyle, Indian Agent, Alnwick, to J.D. McLean, Indian Affairs, 5 March 1917, LAC, RG 10, vol. 2406, file 84,041, pt. 2.
182 R. McCamus, Indian Agent, Rice Lake, to J.D. McLean, 15 March 1917, LAC, RG 10, vol. 2406, file 84,041, pt. 2.
183 *Ibid.*
184 Chief Alfred Crowe, Hiawatha, to Col. McNachten, Cobourg, Ontario, 15 March 1917, LAC, RG 10, vol. 2406, file 84,041, pt. 2.

185 Neil McNachten to J.D. McLean, 21 March 1917, LAC, RG 10, vol. 2406, file 84,041, pt. 2.
186 J.D. McLean to Chief Alfred Crowe, 24 March 1917, LAC, RG 10, vol. 2406, file 84,041, pt. 2.
187 *Ibid.*
188 Chief Isaac Johnson to Superintendent General of Indian Affairs, 17 May 1917, LAC, RG 10, vol. 2406, file 840,041, pt. 2.
189 Joseph Whetung, Chief of the Reindeer Tribe, Curve Lake, to J.H. Burnham, M.P. House of Commons, 14 May 1917, LAC, RG 10, vol. 2406, file 84,041, pt. 2.
190 Deputy Superintendent General of Indian Affairs to J.H. Burnham, 19 May 1917, LAC, RG 10, vol. 2406, file 84,041, pt. 2.
191 Assistant Deputy Minister, Indian Affairs, to J.H. Burnham, 3 April 1917, LAC, RG 10, vol. 2406, file 84,041, pt. 2.
192 Chief Joseph Whetung to J.H. Burnham, 14 May 1917, LAC, RG 10, vol. 2406, file 84,041, pt. 2. As mentioned above, using information provided by Chief Robert Paudash and his son, Johnson, concerning the Mississaugas, Burnham had prepared a lengthy oral history for the Ontario Historical Society and was apparently sympathetic to their problems.
193 Deputy Superintendent of Indian Affairs to J.H. Burnham, 19 May 1917, LAC, RG 10, vol. 2406, file 84,041, pt. 2.
194 *Ibid.* [emphasis added].
195 Howard Wallis to Joseph Whetung, Chief of the Reindeer Tribe, Mississauga Indians, Curve Lake, 12 March 1919, LAC, RG 10, vol. 6745, file 420-8, pt. 3.
196 D. McDonald, Deputy Minister, Game and Fisheries Ontario, to Joseph Whetung Sr., 18 March 1919, LAC, RG 10, vol. 6745, file 420-8, pt. 3.
197 Quoted in Whetung-Derrick, *supra* note 127, vol. 2 at 39.
198 R. McCamus to J.D. McLean, 12 March 1919, LAC, RG 10, vol. 2406, file 84,041, pt. 2, forwarding Crowe and Cowie's resolution.
199 Li Xiu Woo (Grace Emma Slykhuis), *Canada v. The Haudenosaunee (Iroquois Confederacy) at the League of Nations: Two Quests for Independence* (LLM Thesis, University of Quebec at Montreal, 1999) at 112-13.
200 Duncan Scott, Memorandum, to the Hon. Arthur Meighen, Minister of the Interior, 6 March 1918, LAC, RG 10, vol. 6731, file 420-1 (microfilm reel C-8093).
201 *Ibid.*
202 *Ibid.*
203 Memorandum from A.M., Office of the Minister of the Interior, to Duncan C. Scott, [undated, but received on 31 October 1918], LAC, RG 10, vol. 6731, file 420-1 (microfilm reel C-8093).
204 Meighen to Scott, 31 October 1918, LAC, RG 10, vol. 6731, file 420-1 (microfilm reel C-8093).
205 Unsigned memorandum entitled Opinions – Department of Justice, undated, in file named "Application of Game Laws to the Indians in Manitoba, Saskatchewan and Alberta, 1915-1939," LAC, RG 10, vol. 6731, file 420-1 (microfilm reel C-8093), 8 June 1920, attaching page 3379 of *Hansard* (8 June 1920) [emphasis added].
206 Meighen to Scott, 31 October 1918, LAC, RG 10, vol. 6731, file 420-1 (microfilm reel C-8093).
207 "Report on Indian Affairs" in *Sessional Papers,* No. 27 (1918).
208 Edward S. Rogers, "The Algonquian Farmers of Southern Ontario, 1830-1945" in Edward S. Rogers and Donald B. Smith, eds., *Aboriginal Ontario: Historical Perspectives on the First Nations* (Toronto: Dundurn Press, 1994) 122 at 153.
209 Woo, *supra* note 199 at 104.
210 "Report on Indian Affairs," *Sessional Papers of Parliament,* Vol. 27, 1918 (8 Geo. V).
211 Harring, *supra* note 128 at 327.
212 Quoted in *ibid.,* citing report as LAC, RG 4, file 1572.
213 Grand Indian Council to Duncan Scott, *ca.* September 1918, LAC, RG 10, vol. 2406, file 84,041, pt. 2.
214 Rogers, *supra* note 208 at 156.
215 *Ibid.* at 157.

216 *An Act to Amend the Ontario Game and Fisheries Act,* 1922 (12-13 Geo. V), c. 97, ss. 6, 5, 4 respectively. Prohibitions against nets and snares also applied to deer, moose, and caribou.
217 *Restructuring, supra* note 154 at 508.
218 *Ibid.* at 510.
219 *Ibid.*
220 For a detailed description of this arrangement, see Tough, *supra* note 86 at 8-9.
221 Daniel Whetung, Curve Lake, to Department of Indian Affairs, 20 October 1921, LAC, RG 10, vol. 6745, file 420-8, pt. 3.
222 J.D. McLean, Secretary, Indian Affairs, to Daniel Whetung, 24 October 1921, LAC, RG 10, vol. 6745, file 420-8, pt. 3.
223 Chief D.E. Whetung Jr. to Duncan Scott, Indian Affairs, 28 March 1922, LAC, RG 10, vol. 6961, file 481-20-2, pt. 3.
224 J.D. McLean to D.E. Whetung, 5 April 1922, LAC, RG 10, vol. 6961, file 481-20-2, pt. 3.
225 Chief Whetung to J.H. Burnham, M.P. House of Commons, 14 May 1917, LAC, RG 10, vol. 2406, file 84,041, pt. 2.
226 W.J. Kay, Indian Agent, to Indian Affairs, 7 October 1922, LAC, RG 10, vol. 6960, file 475/20-2, pt. 1.
227 J.D. McLean, Assistant Deputy and Secretary, Indian Affairs, to W.J. Kay, 11 October 1922, LAC, RG 10, vol. 6960, file 475/20-2, pt. 1.

Chapter 6: The Push for a New Treaty

1 *Evidence Taken by the Joint Commission appointed by The Dominion of Canada and the Province of Ontario in the Matter of Claim for compensation for unsurrendered Northern Hunting Grounds made by the Chippewas of Georgina Island, Christian Island and Rama and the Mississaugas of Scugog, Chemong, Rice Lake and Alnwick,* Library and Archives Canada [LAC], Ottawa, Record Group [RG] 10, vol. 2331, file 67,071 A at 69.
2 W. Stuart Edwards, Assistant Deputy Minister of Justice, to J.D. McLean, 8 January 1920, LAC, RG 10, vol. 2330, file 67,071-3, pt. 1.
3 *Ibid.*
4 Edwards to unknown, 4 February 1920, LAC, RG 10, vol. 2510, file C498.
5 Cain Aissance to Duncan Scott, 9 September 1920, LAC, RG 10, vol. 2330, file 67,071-3, pt. 2.
6 Christian Island Band Council Resolution, 21 January 1921, LAC, RG 10, vol. 2330, file 67,071-3, pt. 2.
7 Wm. Assance, President, United Bands, Rama, Georgina Island, and Christian Island, to Indian Affairs, 27 October 1920, LAC, RG 10, vol. 2330, file 67,071-3, pt. 2.
8 J.D. McLean to Johnson Paudash, 7 February 1921, LAC, RG 10, vol. 2330, file 67,071-3, pt. 2.
9 Johnson Paudash to J.D. McLean, 15 November 1920, LAC, RG 10, vol. 2330, file 67,071-3, pt. 2.
10 McLean to Paudash, 24 November 1920, LAC, RG 10, vol. 2330, file 67,071-3, pt. 2.
11 J.D. McLean to Chief Bigwind [sic] and Sampson George, 16 June 1921, LAC, RG 10, vol. 2330, file 67,071-3, pt. 2.
12 Duncan Scott to W.E. Raney, Attorney General for Ontario, 5 December 1921, LAC, RG 10, vol. 2330, file 67,071-3, pt. 2.
13 E. Bayly, Deputy Attorney General, Ontario, to D.C. Scott, 22 December 1921, LAC, RG 10, vol. 2330, file 67,071-3, pt. 2.
14 Resolution, Christian Island Band, 12 April 1922, LAC, RG 10, vol. 2330, file 67,071-3, pt. 2. In the appeal of *Sero v. Gault,* a case involving the seizure of an Aboriginal seine net on the Tyendinaga reserve, one of the arguments advanced by the plaintiff was that "The exclusive right to legislate in regard to Indians and their lands or affairs cannot be delegated by Parliament so as to divest the Dominion of such right in favour of a Provincial or other legislative body, and in no other case has any such delegation in regard to Indians ever been attempted." Notice of Appeal, *Eliza Sero v. Thomas Gault and John Fleming,* Supreme Court of Ontario, 13 July 1921, prepared by Porter, Butler and Payne, Solicitors for the Plaintiff, A.G. Chisholm, Solicitor for the Six Nations, intervenor, copy found in LAC, RG 10, restricted file 40-34, original in LAC, RG 10, vol. 6960, file 481/20-2, pt. 1. Unfortunately,

how the Court responded to this argument is not known, as the benchbooks of Mr. Justice William Nassau Ferguson, who heard the appeal on 13 July 1921, have gone missing, and, as with many other cases involving Aboriginal rights, the decision was never reported. The benchbooks were turned over to the Law Society of Upper Canada, which has the benchbook for the months before and after the appeal but not for the month of the appeal itself.

15 J.D. McLean to Chief Frank Copegog, 29 April 1922, LAC, RG 10, vol. 2330, file 67,071-3, pt. 2.

16 Christian Island Band Council Resolution, 3 May 1922, LAC, RG 10, vol. 2330, file 67,071-3, pt. 2.

17 E.L. Newcombe, Deputy Minister of Justice, to D.C. Scott, 18 May 1922, LAC, RG 10, vol. 2330, file 67,071-3, pt. 2.

18 Earlier in his career, however, Biggar had acted as counsel to an Edmonton liquor merchant who, contrary to the provisions of the *Indian Act,* had sold alcohol to Indians. In defending his client, Biggar had brought a number of "half-breeds" into court, intending to demonstrate the difficulty of distinguishing between them and Indians. He lost the case when the judge concluded that Ward, one of the purchasers, "looked a good deal like an Indian," and that "the Parliament of Canada, knowing, as it is a matter of general knowledge, that Indians are so constituted as to be unable to withstand the appetite for liquor." *R. v. Pickard* (1908), 14 C.C.C. 33 (Alberta D.C.).

19 Letter marked for Minister's signature to A.G. Chisholm, 31 May 1922, LAC, RG 10, vol. 2330, file 67,071-3, pt. 2.

20 A.G. Chisholm to C. Stewart, 14 June 1922, quoted in Joan Holmes and Associates, "Williams Treaty Claim, Draft Historical Report," vol. 2 (Prepared for Specific Claims, Indian and Northern Affairs Canada, Ottawa, May-August 1990) para. 274, doc. 275.

21 J.D. McLean to Chief Big Wind [sic], 9 August 1922, LAC, RG 10, vol. 2330, file 67,071-3, pt. 2.

22 J.D. McLean to Henry Jackson, 14 September 1922, LAC, RG 10, vol. 2330, file 67,071-3, pt. 2.

23 O.M. Biggar to Edward Bayly, Deputy Attorney General, 9 June 1922, LAC, RG 10, vol. 2330, file 67,071-3, pt. 2.

24 O.M. Biggar to J.D. McLean, 31 January 1923, LAC, RG 10, vol. 2330, file 67,071-3, pt. 2.

25 O.M. Biggar to Duncan Scott, 9 March 1923, LAC, RG 10, vol. 2330, file 67,071-3, pt. 2.

26 *Evidence Taken, supra* note 1 at 201. The transcript simply notes that a copy of the letter was "on file in Department."

27 *Ibid.*

28 Mae Whetung-Derrick, *History of the Ojibwa of the Curve Lake Reserve and Surrounding Area,* vol. 2 (Curve Lake: Curve Lake Indian Band, 1976) at 11.

29 Andrew McLachlin, Keene Methodist Church, to Indian Affairs, 15 June 1924, LAC, RG 10, vol. 7753, file 27,025-2.

30 According to an oral account from Dow Taylor, an elder, muskrats can be caught for approximately one week only, just after the ice melts, when they leave their homes to breed. Cited in Whetung-Derrick, *supra* note 28, vol. 2 at 31. For George Cobb's interview with Dow Taylor, 16 July 1966, see Trent University Archives, Peterborough, tapes 42 and 46, box 4, 82-006.

31 Weldon to A.S. Williams, 11 October 1923, LAC, RG 10, vol. 2330, file 67,071-3.

32 Memorandum of Agreement between the Dominion and the Province of Ontario, dated April 1923, LAC, RG 10, vol. 2330, file 67,071-3, pt. 2.

33 Order-in-Council, Ontario, 22 May 1923, LAC, RG 10, vol. 2330, file 67,071-3, pt. 2.

34 Chas. Stewart to Governor-General-in-Council, 11 June 1923, LAC, RG 10, vol. 2330, file 67,071-3, pt. 2.

35 Certified Report of the Privy Council, approved by His Excellency the Governor General on the 23rd June, 1923, 23 June 1923, LAC, RG 13, vol. 2510, file C498.

36 W.C. Cain to D.C. Scott, 16 August 1923, LAC, RG 10, vol. 2330, file 67,071-3, pt. 2.

37 Charles Stewart to Governor-General-in-Council, 22 August 1923, LAC, RG 10, vol. 2330, file 67,071-3, pt. 2.

38 Commission appointing A.S. Williams *et al.* to investigate into the validity of claims made by certain Indians to Lands in the Province of Ontario, 31 August 1923, LAC, RG 10, vol. 2330, file 67,071-3, pt. 2.
39 I.E. Weldon to W.P. Nicholls, 20 September 1923, LAC, RG 10, vol. 2330, file 67,071-3.
40 Indian Affairs to I.E. Weldon, 11 October 1923, LAC, RG 10, vol. 2330, file 67,071-3, pt. 1.
41 Clipping from unidentified newspaper (5 September 1923), Ministry of Natural Resources archives, Peterborough, Ontario, file 19,388.
42 Manley Chew to J.D. McLean, 7 September 1923, LAC, RG 10, vol. 2330, file 67,071-3.
43 J.D. McLean to Indian Agents, 27 August 1923, LAC, RG 10, vol. 2330, file 67-071-3, pt. 2.
44 Arthur S. Anderson to J.D. McLean, 30 August 1923, LAC, RG 10, vol. 2330, file 67,071-3, pt. 2.
45 W.J. Kay to J.D. McLean, 4 September 1923, LAC, RG 10, vol. 2330, file 67,071-3.
46 *Evidence Taken, supra* note 1 at 1 [emphasis added].
47 *Ibid.* at 2.
48 Commissioners' Report to Superintendent General of Indian Affairs and the Minister of Lands and Forests, 1 December 1923, LAC, RG 10, vol. 2330, file 67,071, pt. 1 at 3.
49 *Ibid.*
50 *Evidence Taken, supra* note 1 at 2 [emphasis added].
51 *Ibid.* title page [emphasis added].
52 *Ibid.* at 11.
53 *Ibid.* at 4-5, 11, 16-19.
54 *Ibid.* at 14-15.
55 *Federal Census of 1871 (Ontario Index),* LAC, RG 31 at 59 (microfilm reel C-9966).
56 *Evidence Taken, supra* note 1 at 26, 28-29.
57 *Federal Census of 1871, supra* note 55 at 59.
58 *Evidence Taken, supra* note 1 at 29.
59 *Ibid.* at 31-32.
60 *Ibid.* at 99 [emphasis added].
61 *Ibid.* at 145-47.
62 *Ibid.* at 126.
63 *Ibid.* at 75, 77.
64 *Ibid.* at 106-7.
65 *Ibid.* at 85-86. At the following day's proceedings, he produced his grandfather's 1896 will, in which Sampson Yellowhead had bequeathed to him "my hunting ground, situate on Trading Lake and extending from said Lake to Trout Lake and better known as the Hunting Ground belonging to the Chief of the Yellowhead family." Page 119 of the transcript noted that the will had been witnessed by J.H. Hammond, Solicitor, Orillia (deceased by 1923).
66 *Ibid.* at 88-89.
67 *Ibid.* at 92, 94, 101.
68 *Ibid.* at 105.
69 *Ibid.* at 110, 111.
70 See *ibid.* at 135. The use of an interpreter is an important point, as the Supreme Court in *Howard* would later conclude that all the treaty signatories understood and spoke English.
71 *Ibid.* at 113.
72 *Ibid.* at 68.
73 *Ibid.* at 70, 78.
74 *Ibid.* at 120-21.
75 *Ibid.* at 79.
76 *Ibid.* at 34-42.
77 *Ibid.* at 50-54.
78 *Ibid.* at 62-63, 65-66.
79 *Ibid.* at 171.
80 *Federal Census of 1871, supra* note 55 at 68 (microfilm reel C-9986-C-9987).
81 *Evidence Taken, supra* note 1 at 160.
82 Chamberlain wrote that three band members, "McCew," Marsden Jr., and Elliott, "claim to

be the oldest settlers on the island [and at] the other end of the village lives Isaac Johnston (whose farm is considered to be the best)." A.F. Chamberlain, *The Language of the Mississaga Indians of Skugog: A Contribution to the Linguistics of the Algonkian Tribes of Canada* (Philadelphia: MacCalla, 1892) at 9.

83 *Evidence Taken, supra* note 1 at 170.

84 *Ibid.* at 179-80.

85 *Ibid.* at 182-87. It should be noted that Johnson Paudash from Hiawatha, a signatory to the 1923 treaty to whom the Supreme Court referred in *Howard,* was present at the Scugog hearings. *Ibid.* at 189.

86 *Ibid.* at 176.

87 *Federal Census of 1871, supra* note 55 at 61 (microfilm reel C-9986-C-9987). Others from the Mud Lake and Rice Lake Reserves, where the census was apparently done at one time, who were recorded as "Indian, hunter" include Isaac Johnson, Miles Johnson, Thomas Johnson, Joseph Iron, Solomon Fawn, Peter Nogeh, James Bigman, George Taylor, William McCue, Thomas Taylor, Isaac Irons, Joseph Muskrat, John Fawn, John Reigo, John Ricelake, James Taylor, James Saniard, and William Coppewy.

88 *Evidence Taken, supra* note 1 at 208.

89 *Ibid.* at 211-15.

90 A.J. Cameron, Ontario Land Surveyor, to Superintendent General of Indian Affairs, *ca.* 1899, LAC, RG 10, vol. 7753, file 27,025-1.

91 J.D. McLean, Secretary, Indian Affairs, to L.K. Jones, Secretary, Railways and Canals, 10 April 1909, LAC, RG 43, series B, vol. 1579, file 8059, pt. 1.

92 R.H. Abraham, Indian Affairs, to S. Bray, 2 October 1916, LAC, RG 10, vol. 6613, file 6025-3.

93 Report of F.W. Wilkins, Land Surveyor, 16 June 1914, LAC, RG 43, vol. 1554, file 7435, pt. 1.

94 Band Council Resolution and letter from Chief Jas. Whitung [Whetung] and Secretary L.D. Taylor to the Superintendent General of Indian Affairs, LAC, RG 10, vol. 6613, file 6025-3.

95 Memorandum from A.S. Williams to Duncan Scott, 16 February 1917, LAC, RG 10, vol. 6613, file 6025-3.

96 *Evidence Taken, supra* note 1 at 214, 215.

97 With thanks to Dr. Janet Armstrong for providing this information from her July 2000 examination of the original handwritten (and hard to read) census books held at Library and Archives Canada.

98 *Evidence Taken, supra* note 1 at 3.

99 He is listed as Robert Potash in *Federal Census of 1871, supra* note 55 at 68 (microfilm reel C-9987).

100 *Evidence Taken, supra* note 1 at 230-48.

101 J.A. MacRae, Summary of Claims of Rice Lake Indians, 9 May 1905, LAC, RG 10, vol. 2329, file 67,071-2.

102 *Evidence Taken, supra* note 1 at 238.

103 The 1871 Ontario census category of "Indian, hunter" included John Eshevince, Moses Black, John Peters, John Snowstorm, John Bever, James Shipegew, John P. Chase, Robert Wilkins, William Comigo, John S. Shilling, George Comingo, Isaac Bever, William Jack, and William Crow. *Federal Census of 1871, supra* note 55 n.p. Thomas Marsden is listed as an "Indian, farmer" in *ibid.* at 2 (microfilm reel C-9984). George "Comingo" (Comego) is listed as an "Indian, Hunter Fisher" in *ibid.* at 22.

104 J.W. Kerr, Barrister, to Frank Pedley, 2 February 1903, LAC, RG 10, vol. 2329, file 67,071, pt. 1B.

105 Alnwick Band Resolution, 4 February 1884, LAC, RG 10, vol. 2329, file 67,071, pt. 1B.

106 *Evidence Taken, supra* note 1 at 259-64.

107 The letter was from J.W. Kerr, Barrister, to Frank Pedley, 2 February 1903, LAC, RG 10, vol. 2329, file 67,071, pt. 1B.

108 *Evidence Taken, supra* note 1 at 265-67, 269.

109 *Ibid.* at 269, 271.

110 *Ibid.* at 275.

111 *Ibid.* at 277.

112 *Ibid.* at 281-83.
113 Williams, Sinclair, and McFadden to Hon. James Lyons, Minister of Lands and Forests, 10 October 1923, LAC, RG 10, vol. 2331, file 67,071-4A at 3.
114 *Ibid.* at 4.
115 See, for example, L. Vankoughnet to Sir John A. Macdonald, 2 October 1884, LAC, RG 10, vol. 2329, file 67,071, pt. 1B.
116 A.S. Williams to Duncan Scott, 10 October 1923, Department of Indian Affairs and Northern Development, Ottawa, Ontario, file 1/1-11-15, vol. 1.
117 Commission to I.E. Weldon, 11 October 1923, LAC, RG 10, vol. 2330, file 67,071-3.
118 Weldon to A.S. Williams, 15 October 1923, LAC, RG 10, vol. 2330, file 67,071-3, pt. 1.
119 *Ibid.*
120 Williams to Weldon, 18 October 1923, LAC, RG 10, vol. 2330, file 67,071-3, pt. 1.
121 Uriah McFadden to W.C. Cain, 18 October 1923, Ministry of Natural Resources archives, Peterborough, Ontario, file 19,388.
122 R.V. Sinclair to Walter Simon, Christian Island, 18 October 1923, LAC, RG 10, vol. 2330, file 67,071-3, pt. 1.
123 Commission to Indian Agents Gerow, Kay, Picotte, Coyle, McCamus, and Anderson, 19 October 1923, LAC, RG 10, vol. 2330, file 67,071-3, pt. 1.
124 Commission to Surveys Branch, Indian Affairs, 18 October 1923, LAC, RG 10, vol. 2330, file 67,071-3, pt. 1. The commission also asked for figures regarding how much compensation the government held for the Mississaugas and Chippewas in respect of the already surrendered lands, the monies from the sale of reserves or timber, and the amounts of per capita annuities. Commission to Accounts Branch, Indian Affairs, 18 October 1923, LAC, RG 10, vol. 2330, file 67,071-3, pt. 1.
125 *Ibid.* at 4-5.

Chapter 7: Differing Perceptions

1 Charles Stewart to Governor General of Canada, 29 November 1923, Library and Archives Canada [LAC], Ottawa, Record Group [RG] 10, vol. 2330, file 67,071-3, pt. 1.
2 For a full discussion of these events, see Li Xiu Woo (Grace Emma Slykhuis), *Canada v. The Haudenosaunee (Iroquois Confederacy) at the League of Nations: Two Quests for Independence* (LLM Thesis, University of Quebec at Montreal, 1999).
3 *R. v. New England Company* (1922), 63 D.L.R. 537 (Ex. Ct.).
4 "Eulogy, George Palmer Decker, 1861-1936" in George Palmer Decker collection, Decker Papers, Lavery Library, St. John Fisher College, Rochester, New York, http://library.sjfc.edu/docs/Decker%20Eulogy.doc.
5 Woo, *supra* note 2 at 19, 221.
6 *Ibid.* at 111, 199-200.
7 *Ibid.* at 205.
8 *The Redman's Appeal for Justice,* the 6 August 1923 petition submitted by Deskaheh to James Eric Drummond, Secretary General of the League of Nations, should not be confused with a book entitled *The Redman's Appeal for Justice: The Position of the Six Nations That They Constitute an Independent State,* published by the Six Nations in March 1924. My thanks to Dr. Reg Good for providing this information.
9 Graham to Stewart, 6 October 1923, LAC, RG 10, vol. 2285, file 57,169-1B, pt. 3. My thanks to Dr. Reg Good for providing me with this source.
10 Woo, *supra* note 2 at 208-11.
11 *Ibid.* at 188, 225.
12 *Ibid.* at 230.
13 *Ibid.*
14 Minister, Department of Lands and Forests, to Charles Stewart, 6 November 1923, LAC, RG 10, vol. 2330, file 67,071-3, pt. 1.
15 A.S. Williams to Premier Howard Ferguson, 7 December 1923, LAC, RG 10, vol. 2330, file 67,071-3, pt. 1.
16 Memo from the accountant at Indian Affairs to D.C. Scott, 25 July 1924, cited in Joan

Holmes and Associates, "Williams Treaty Claim, Draft Historical Report," vol. 2 (Prepared for Specific Claims, Indian and Northern Affairs Canada, Ottawa, May-August 1990) at para. 345.

17 *Ibid.*

18 Amount obtained from James Skipper and George P. Landow, "Wages and Cost of Living in the Victorian Era," The Victorian Web: Literature, History and Culture in the Age of Victoria, http://www.victorianweb.org/economics/wages2.html. See also John Burnett, *A History of the Cost of Living* (Harmondsworth: Penguin, 1969) for other references.

19 Minister of Lands and Forests to D.C. Scott, 16 August 1923, cited as document 303 in Joan Holmes and Associates, *supra* note 16, vol. 2 at paras. 299-300. The amount was approved on 20 August 1923 by Charles Stewart, Superintendent General of Indian Affairs.

20 Report to the Superintendent General of Indian Affairs and the Minister of Lands and Forests, 1 December 1923, LAC, RG 10, vol. 2330, file 67,071-3, pt. 1.

21 "Indians Claim Right to Fish and Hunt Not Given Up" *Orillia Packet and Times* (13 June 1938), LAC, RG 10, vol. 6960, file 475/20-2, pt. 1.

22 Report to the Superintendent General of Indian Affairs and the Minister of Lands and Forests, 1 December 1923, LAC, RG 10, vol. 2330, file 67,071-3, pt. 1 at 10-11.

23 *Ibid.* at 16.

24 *Ibid.* at 13

25 House of Commons, *Official Report of Debates (Hansard)* (July 1924) at 4857.

26 *Indian Treaty and Articles of a Treaty, together with Minutes of Special General Meeting,* filed with Deputy Registrar General of Canada, Lib. 297, fol. 40, Reference No. 77929 [hereafter *Articles of Treaty*]; see also *Copy of the Treaty made between His Majesty the King and the Chippewa Indians of Christian Island, Georgina Island and Rama* (Ottawa: Queen's Printer, 1967). The Mississauga version of the treaty is at Indian and Northern Affairs Canada, http://www.ainc-inac.gc.ca/pr/trts/trmis_e.html, and the Chippewa version is at http://www.ainc-inac.gc.ca/pr/trts/trchip_e.html.

27 *Ibid.*

28 *Ibid.* at 8 [emphasis added].

29 *Ibid.* at 7.

30 A.S. Williams and R.V. Sinclair to D.C. Scott, 13 December 1923, LAC, RG 10, vol. 2330, file 67,071-3.

31 Report to the Superintendent General of Indian Affairs and the Minister of Lands and Forests, 1 December 1923, LAC, RG 10, vol. 2330, file 67,071-3, pt. 1.

32 W.C. Cain to Minister of Lands and Forests, 22 February 1924, Ministry of Natural Resources, Ontario Indian Resource Policy, file 19,388, vol. 1.

33 *Articles of Treaty, supra* note 26; see also *Copy of the Treaty, supra* note 26.

34 See, for example, Minutes of a General Meeting of the Alnwick Band in Council dated 19th day of November 1923, filed as part of the *Articles of Treaty, supra* note 26.

35 *Ibid.* at 2.

36 George Cobb, taped interview with Herb Irons, age not provided, 2 July 1966, Trent University Archives, Peterborough, tape 43, box 4, 82-006.

37 Arthur S. Anderson, Indian Agent, Rama, to Secretary of Indian Affairs, 9 November 1933, Department of Indian Affairs and Northern Development [DIAND], Ottawa, Ontario, file 1/1-11-15, vol. 1.

38 Indian Claim, Rama, marked "RHW," November (date torn), DIAND, file V1-11-15, vol. 1, "Williams Treaties" [emphasis added].

39 Memorandum of Agreement between the Dominion and the Province of Ontario, April 1923, LAC, RG 10, vol. 2330, file 67,071-3, pt. 2.

40 Commissioners to Duncan Scott, 3 December 1923, LAC, RG 10, vol. 2330, file 67,071, pt. 1.

41 *Evidence Taken by the Joint Commission appointed by The Dominion of Canada and the Province of Ontario in the Matter of Claim for compensation for unsurrendered Northern Hunting Grounds made by the Chippewas of Georgina Island, Christian Island and Rama and the Mississaugas of Scugog, Chemong, Rice Lake and Alnwick,* LAC, RG 10, vol. 2331, file 67,071 A at 146.

42 Commissioners to Duncan Scott, 3 December 1923, LAC, RG 10, vol. 2330, file 67,071, pt. 1.

43 Canada, *Report of the Royal Commission on Aboriginal Peoples: Looking Forward, Looking Back,*

vol. 1 (Ottawa: Royal Commission on Aboriginal Peoples, 1996) ch. 15, s. 9 "Culture and Social Relations," n. 43 [hereafter *Looking Forward*].

44 Roger Spielmann, *You're So Fat! Exploring Ojibwe Discourse* (Toronto: University of Toronto Press, 1998) at 28.

45 *Ibid.* at 32-33.

46 *Ibid.* at 79, 84-85.

47 Mississaugas of New Credit Band Resolution, 28 May 1931, DIAND, file 1/1-11-15, vol. 1.

48 *Toronto Star* (8 May 1928).

49 *Montreal Gazette* (9 May 1928).

50 *Globe* (9 May 1928).

51 Anderson to Secretary, Indian Affairs, 10 June 1930, LAC, RG 10, vol. 6960, file 475/20-2, pt. 1.

52 Anderson to Secretary, Indian Affairs, 13 June 1931, LAC, RG 10, vol. 6960, file 475/20-2, pt. 1.

53 A.F. Mackenzie, Secretary of Indian Affairs, to Chief Alder York, referring to Memorial, 12 May 1931, DIAND, file 1/1-11-15, vol. 1.

54 A.F. Mackenzie to D. McDonald, 6 May 1931, LAC, RG 10, vol. 6960, file 474/20-2, pt. 1 [emphasis added].

55 Resolution, Rama Reserve, signed Agent Anderson, Alder York, Chief, and J.B. Stinson, Secretary, 6 June 1931, LAC, RG 10, vol. 6960, file 475/20-2, pt. 1.

56 Resolution, Rama Reserve, *ca.* October 1931, LAC, RG 10, vol. 6746, file 420-8C.

57 Anderson to A.F. Mackenzie, Secretary of Indian Affairs, 24 October 1931, LAC, RG 10, vol. 6746, file 420-8C.

58 Chief York to Indian Agent Anderson, *ca.* November 1931, LAC, RG 10, vol. 6746, file 420-8D.

59 *Ibid.*

60 Resolution, Rama Reserve, 16 November 1931, LAC, RG 10, vol. 6746, file 420-8C.

61 Anderson to Secretary of Indian Affairs, 21 November 1931, LAC, RG 10, vol. 6746, file 420-8C.

62 Arthur S. Anderson, Indian Agent, Rama, to Secretary of Indian Affairs, 9 November 1933, attaching Memorial of Greiviance [sic] signed Samuel Snache, DIAND, file 1/1-11-15, vol. 1.

63 Arthur S. Anderson, Indian Agent, Rama, to Secretary of Indian Affairs, 9 November 1933, DIAND, file 1/1-11-15, vol. 1.

64 "Great White Queen's Pact Quoted by Indian in Court" *Toronto Star* (12 May 1938), LAC, RG 10, vol. 6960, file 475/20-2, pt. 1.

65 "Indian Chief Claims Rights for Fishing" article from unidentified newspaper (10 May 1938), LAC, RG 10, vol. 6960, file 475/20-2, pt. 1.

66 Clipping from unidentified newspaper (12 May 1938), LAC, RG 10, vol. 6960, file 475/20-2, pt. 1.

67 *Ibid.*

68 "Indians Claim Right to Fish and Hunt Not Given Up" *Orillia Packet and Times* (13 June 1938), LAC, RG 10, vol. 6960, file 475/20-2, pt. 1.

69 A.F. Mackenzie, Secretary of Indian Affairs, to Chief Alder York, referring to Memorial, 12 May 1931, DIAND, file 1/1-11-15, vol. 1.

70 *Ibid.*

71 *Looking Forward, supra* note 43 at 173.

72 *Ibid.* Ch. 5, "Differing Assumptions and Understandings."

73 M.B. Tudhope to J.D. McLean, 27 October 1924, DIAND, file 1/1-11-15, vol. 1.

74 J.D. McLean to Tudhope, 13 November 1924, DIAND, file 1/1-11-15, vol. 1.

75 Johnson Paudash to Secretary, Indian Affairs, 10 April 1931, DIAND, file 1/1-11-15, vol. 1.

76 Arthur Whetung to Department of Indian Affairs, 15 October 1931, DIAND, file 1/1-11-15, vol. 1.

77 T.M.L. MacInnes, Acting Secretary, Indian Affairs, to Arthur Whetung, 22 October 1931, DIAND, file 1/1-11-15, vol. 1.

78 Whetung to Mr. J.C. Caldwell, Director of Indian Lands and Timber Branch, 24 October 1931, DIAND, file 1/1-11-15, vol. 1.

79 A.F. Mackenzie, Secretary of Indian Affairs, to Arthur Whetung, 29 October 1931, DIAND, file 1/1-11/15, vol. 1.

80 Joseph P. Mangan to Secretary, Indian Affairs, 2 April 1932, LAC, RG 10, vol. 7753, file 27,025-1.
81 J.E. Anderson, Barrister, to A.S. Williams, 4 May 1932, DIAND, file 1/1-11-15, vol. 1.
82 A.F. Mackenzie to J.E. Anderson, 6 May 1932, DIAND, file 1/1-11/15, vol. 1.
83 Arthur Whetung to the Honourable the Clerk of the Privy Council, 23 May 1932, DIAND, file 1/1-11/15, vol. 1. The request was forwarded by E.J. Lemaire, the Clerk of the Privy Council, to the Acting Superintendent General of Indian Affairs, 25 May 1932, DIAND, file 1/1-11/15.
84 A.F. Mackenzie, Secretary, to Agent M. Eastwood, 25 June 1932, DIAND, file 1/1-11/15, vol. 1.
85 *Ibid.*
86 See *Copy of the Treaty Made November 15, 1923 between His Majesty the King and the Mississauga Indians, reprinted from the edition of 1932,* prepared by Edmond Cloutier, Queen's Printer and Controller of Stationery (Ottawa: Queen's Printer, 1957).
87 A.S. Williams to Police Magistrate E.A. Jordan, County of Victoria, Provisional County, Haliburton, Lindsay, 6 May 1932, LAC, RG 10, vol. 6746, file 420-8D.
88 *Ibid.*
89 "Indian Claims Are Now Taken Care Of" *Ottawa Citizen* (26 November 1923), LAC, RG 10, vol. 3033, file 235,225, pt. 1A.
90 *Ibid.*
91 Duncan Scott to G.H. Ferguson, 27 November 1923, LAC, RG 10, vol. 3033, file 235,225.
92 Ferguson to Scott, 29 November 1923, LAC, RG 10, vol. 3033, file 235,225.
93 Duncan C. Scott, "Description of Lands," 1 June 1926, LAC, RG 10, vol. 6819, file 490-2-17 [emphasis added].
94 F.E. Titus to W.C. Cain, 20 June 1928, Ministry of Natural Resources archives, Peterborough, Ontario, Land file 11,479, vol. 1.
95 *Ibid.*
96 Charles Stewart, Superintendent General of Indian Affairs, to Governor-General-in-Council, 11 May 1929, LAC, RG 10, vol. 6819, file 490-2-17.
97 Order-in-Council, 30 May 1929, LAC, RG 10, vol. 6819, file 490-2-17.
98 See, for example, draft Adhesion, 1 March 1929, LAC, RG 10, vol. 6819, file 490-2-17.
99 W.C. Cain to unknown, 26 March 1926, Ministry of Natural Resources archives, Land file 11,479, vol. 1.
100 D.C. Scott to W.C. Cain, 27 May 1929, LAC, RG 10, vol. 6819, file 490-2-17.
101 D.C. Scott to H.N. Awrey, 28 May 1929, LAC, RG 10, vol. 6819.
102 W.C. Cain and H.N. Awrey, Treaty Nine Commisssioners, "Report to Superintendent General of Indian Affairs," 30 August 1929, LAC, RG 10, vol. 6819, file 490-2-17.
103 "Indian Chief Marries Son so Squaw Will Get Treaty Money" clipping from unidentified newspaper (30 July 1929), LAC, RG 10, vol. 6819.
104 "Trout Lake Indians Marvelled at Planes" *Toronto Star* (3 August 1929), LAC, RG 10, vol. 6819, file 490-2-17.
105 Chief Frank Beardy, Muskrat Dam First Nation, Big Trout Lake, Ontario, 4 December 1992, quoted in *Looking Forward, supra* note 43 at 655.
106 Canada, *Report of the Royal Commission on Aboriginal Peoples: Restructuring the Relationship,* vol. 2, part 2 (Ottawa: Royal Commission on Aboriginal Peoples, 1996) at 506 [hereafter *Restructuring*].
107 A.F. Mackenzie, Secretary of Indian Affairs, to T. Murray Mulligan, Barrister, Sudbury, 13 April 1933, LAC, file 40-25.
108 Robertson, Chief Surveyor, to T.M.L. MacInnes, Acting Secretary, 27 July 1928, LAC, RG 10, vol. 10283, file 478/20-2.
109 L. Ritchie, Saugeen Band, to Dept. of Ind. Affairs, 29 July 1929, LAC, RG 10, vol. 10283, file 478/20-2.
110 A.F. Mackenzie, Acting Assistant Deputy Minister, Indian Affairs, to D. Robertson, Indian Agent, Port Elgin, 15 August 1929, LAC, RG 10, vol. 10283, file 478/20-2.
111 *Ibid.*
112 *R. v. Jones and Nadjiwon* (1993), 14 O.R. (3d) 421 (Ont. Crim. Div.).

113 "Annual Report of the Indian Affairs Department" in *Sessional Papers* (1929).
114 Judgment in *Sero v. Gault and Fleming,* 2 March 1921, LAC, RG 10, vol. 6960, file 481/20-2, pt. 1. For further analysis of *Sero v. Gault* in the general context of First Nations rights, see ch. 4 in Constance Backhouse, *Colour Coded: A Legal History of Racism in Canada, 1900-1950* (Toronto: University of Toronto Press, 1999).
115 Copy of extract of earlier document, note to file, Tyendinaga Fishing file, H.R. Conn, Fur Supervisor, *ca.* 1952, LAC, RG 10, restricted file 40-34.
116 *Ibid.*
117 *Ibid.*
118 G.M. Campbell, Indian Agent, to T.M.L. MacInnes, Secretary, Indian Affairs, 19 December 1930, LAC, RG 10, vol. 6960, file 481/20-2, pt. 1.
119 N. Desjardins, Secretary of Public Works, to Secretary of Indian Affairs, 9 January 1931, LAC, RG 10, vol. 6960, file 481/20-2, pt. 1.
120 *Restructuring, supra* note 106 at 505.
121 *Ibid.*
122 D. Robertson, Chief Surveyor, to T.M.L. MacInnes, 14 July 1931, LAC, RG 10, vol. 7753, file 27,025-1.
123 A.F. Mackenzie to Jas. Farrington, 21 July 1931, LAC, RG 10, vol. 7753, file 27,025-1.
124 D. McDonald to Chief Daniel Whetung, 4 August 1931, LAC, RG 10, vol. 7753, file 27,025-1.
125 A.F. Mackenzie to V.M. Eastwood, 4 January 1933, LAC, RG 10, vol. 6961, file 481/20-2, pt. 3.
126 Clipping from unidentified newspaper (27 June 1934), LAC, RG 10, vol. 6746, file 420-8E.
127 H. Darling, Acting Superintendent, R.C.M.P., to Deputy Superintendent General, Indian Affairs, 31 May 1934, LAC, RG 10, vol. 6746, file 420-8E.
128 Note to file re. phone call, unsigned, Department of Indian Affairs, *ca.* 1936, LAC, RG 10, vol. 6961, file 481/20-2, pt. 3.
129 J.H. Gordon, Acting Director, Indian Affairs, to Pauline Jewett, 20 February 1936, LAC, RG 10, vol. 6961, file 481/20-2, pt. 3.
130 D. McDonald, Deputy Minister of Game and Fisheries, to D.C. Scott, 26 January 1931, LAC, RG 10, vol. 6961, file 481-20-2, pt. 3.
131 J.R. Ashquabe to the Department of Indian Affairs, 14 January 1936, LAC, RG 10, vol. 6960, file 475/20-2, pt. 1.
132 A.F. Mackenzie to O.J. Silver, 30 January 1936, LAC, RG 10, vol. 6960, file 465/20-2.
133 W.J. Arthur Fair to Superintendent General of Indian Affairs, 6 February 1937, LAC, RG 10, vol. 8863, file 1/18-11-8, pt. 2.
134 T.M.L. MacInnes, Secretary, to W.J. Arthur Fair, 8 February 1937, LAC, RG 10, vol. 8863, file 1/18-11-8, pt. 2.
135 Quoted in *Restructuring, supra* note 106 at n. 174.
136 T. Murray Mulligan, Barrister, to Department of Indian Affairs, 11 April 1933, LAC, RG 10, file 40-25.
137 A.F. Mackenzie, Secretary of Indian Affairs, to T. Murray Mulligan, Barrister etc., Sudbury, 13 April 1933, LAC, RG 10, file 40-25.
138 Quoted in *Restructuring, supra* note 106 at 513.
139 *R. v. Commanda,* [1939] O.J. No. 287 at paras. 20, 22 (Ont. H.C.J.).
140 Lawrence James, Chief Point Indian Reserve, to Department of Indian Affairs, Ottawa, 8 January 1954, DIAND, file 8/20-2.
141 H.R. Conn, Fur Supervisor, Ottawa, to F.R. Butchart, Superintendent, Cape Croker Indian Agency, 19 February 1954, DIAND, file 8/20-2.
142 Quoted in *Restructuring, supra* note 106 at 512.
143 *Ibid.*
144 According to the Indian Affairs website, Ontario initiated these negotiations in June 1991, and Canada joined the process on 7 December 1992. The negotiations are part of a comprehensive claim filed by the Algonquins of Golden Lake asserting unextinguished Aboriginal title to thirty-four thousand square kilometres in the Ottawa Valley. Indian and Northern Affairs Canada, http://www.inac.gc.ca/pr/info/info52_e.html.
145 H.M. Jones, Director, to Francis Benoit, Golden Lake, 22 December 1954, PA 11/20-2. This

memorandum contains both the Band Council Resolution and the response. My thanks to Brant Bardy for supplying this document.
146 *Ibid.*
147 Quoted in *Restructuring, supra* note 106 at 506.
148 *R. v. Moses,* [1970] 3 O.R. 314 (Dist. Ct.).
149 *Ibid.*
150 Mae Whetung-Derrick, *History of the Ojibwa of the Curve Lake Reserve and Surrounding Area,* vol. 2 (Curve Lake: Curve Lake Indian Band, 1976) at 83.
151 Quoted in Brian Bedwell, "Hunting and Fishing Rights of the Mississauga Indian People, Curve Lake Reserve No. 35" (Report prepared for Office of Indian Resource Policy, Ministry of Natural Resources, Toronto, Ontario, 6 September 1979) n.p.
152 *Ibid.*
153 *R. v. Taylor and Williams,* [1981] 3 C.N.L.R. 114 at 118 (Ont. C.A.).
154 *Ibid.* at 123.

Chapter 8: The Howard Case

1 *R. v. Stinchcombe,* [1991] 3 S.C.R. 326.
2 Transcript of Trial, *R. v. George Henry Howard* (1 October 1985), at 1 (Ont. Prov. Ct. Crim. Div.).
3 *R. v. Sparrow,* [1990] 3 C.N.L.R. 161 at 174, 175 (S.C.C.).
4 Transcript of Trial, *R. v. George Henry Howard, supra* note 2 at 12-14.
5 *Ibid.* at 30.
6 *Ibid.* at 25.
7 *Ibid.* at 74.
8 *Ibid.*
9 *Ibid.* at 54. Note that, in the treaties themselves, the northern area is given as 17,600 square miles and the southern area as 2,500 square miles "more or less."
10 *Ibid.* at 72.
11 *Ibid.* at 70, 75.
12 *Ibid.* at 82.
13 *Ibid.* at 86, 87, 90.
14 *Ibid.* at 90, 93, and cross-examination at 102.
15 *Ibid.* at 94-96.
16 *R. v. Taylor and Williams,* [1981] 3 C.N.L.R. 114 at 114 (Ont. C.A.).
17 Oral Judgment, *R. v. Howard,* R.B. Batten, Provincial Court, Peterborough, dated 10 January 1986, unreported, cited from *Case on Appeal,* Supreme Court of Canada at 491-92 [hereafter Oral Judgment, Batten].
18 *R. v. Hare and Debassige,* [1985] 20 C.C.C. (3d) 1 (Ont. C.A.).
19 Oral Judgment, Batten, *supra* note 17 at 495. This finding would later be completely undermined by the Supreme Court of Canada in *R. v. Sparrow, supra* note 3 at 174 (discussed more fully below).
20 Oral Judgment, Batten, *supra* note 17 at 497.
21 *Ibid.*
22 *Ibid.* at 498.
23 *R. v. Howard,* Oral Judgment of Jenkins J. on Appeal to District Court, Peterborough, dated 9 March 1987, unreported, cited in *Case on Appeal,* Supreme Court of Canada at 501.
24 *Ibid.* at 502.
25 *Ibid.*
26 *Ibid.* at 503.
27 *R. v. Sparrow, supra* note 3 at 174. Note that this conclusion has also been reached in Australia: in *Mason v. Tritton* (1994), 34 N.S.W.L.R. 572 at para. 86 (N.S.W.C.A.), the Court of Appeal upheld a trial decision to the effect that fisheries legislation had not extinguished Native title.
28 *R. v. Sparrow, supra* note 3 at 174.
29 *R. v. Howard* (1992), 8 O.R. (3d) 225 at 229-30 (Ont. C.A.).

30 *R. v. Howard,* [1994] 2 S.C.R. 299 (Factum of the Appellant George Henry Howard at paras. 4, 5) (S.C.C.) [hereafter Appellant's Factum].
31 *Ibid.* at paras. 49, 50.
32 *Ibid.* at paras. 74-77.
33 *Ibid.* at para. 89.
34 *R. v. Howard, supra* note 30 (Factum of the Respondent Ontario at paras. 1, 10).
35 *Ibid.* at paras. 16, 17.
36 *Ibid.* at 19.
37 *Ibid.* at 12.
38 *Ibid.* at para. 23.
39 *Ibid.*
40 *Ibid.* at para. 25.
41 *Ibid.* at 15, para. 29.
42 *R. v. Howard, supra* note 30 (Factum of Intervenor Attorney General of Canada at para. 10).
43 *Ibid.* at paras. 34, 37.
44 *R. v. Howard, supra* note 30 at 303.
45 *Ibid.* at 304.
46 *Ibid.* at 307.
47 *R. v. Howard (Howard # 2),* [1991] O.J. No. 548 (Ont. Gen. Div.), decision released 3 January 1991.
48 *R. v. Jackson,* [1992] 4 C.N.L.R. 121 at 132 (Ont. Prov. Ct. Crim. Div.).
49 *Ibid.*
50 Robert Mitton, Deputy Minister, Ministry of Natural Resources Ontario, to Chief Gord Peters, 13 May 1994, document provided under Access to Information Request, copy on author's file. Note that the majority of the documents cited below were acquired as a result of requests made under provincial and federal access to information legislation.
51 Draft, Ron Irwin to Howard Hampton, undated, but would appear to have been sent in mid-May 1994, since it refers to a meeting of 17 May 1994.
52 Howard Hampton, Minister of Natural Resources, to Ron Irwin, Minister of Indian and Northern Affairs, and Brian Tobin, Minister of Fisheries and Oceans, 12 May 1994.
53 Draft, Ron Irwin to Howard Hampton, undated, *ca.* 17 May 1994.
54 Howard Hampton, Minister of Natural Resources, to Brian Tobin, Minister of Fisheries, 24 May 1994.
55 Canada, *Report of the Royal Commission on Aboriginal Peoples: Restructuring the Relationship,* vol. 2 (Ottawa: Royal Commission on Aboriginal Peoples, 1996) at 507.
56 Marion Lefebvre, Director-General, Native Affairs, Department of Fisheries and Oceans, to Peggy J. Blair, undated, *ca.* June 1993.
57 *Ibid.*
58 *Aboriginal Communal Fishing Licences Regulations,* S.O.R./1993-332 and Regulatory Impact Analysis Statement at 2903; *Aboriginal Communal Fishing Licences Regulations,* S.O.R./1994-390 and Regulatory Impact Analysis Statement at 2270.
59 "A Deal is a Deal?" Ontario Federation of Anglers and Hunters, newspaper advertisement, undated, *ca.* 1993, *Access to Information and Privacy Act* application [ATIP] no. 000265.
60 "Strange Bedfellows," Ontario Federation of Anglers and Hunters, newspaper advertisement, undated, *ca.* 1993, ATIP no. 000264.
61 Brian Tobin to Howard Hampton, 18 January 1994.
62 Howard Hampton, Minister of Natural Resources, to Brian Tobin, 15 June 1994.
63 Brian Tobin to Howard Hampton, 17 June 1994.
64 Howard Hampton to Brian Tobin, 17 June 1994.
65 Deputy Minister of Natural Resources to Chiefs, with attachment, 17 June 1994.
66 *Ibid.*
67 Brian Tobin to Premier Bob Rae, 28 June 1994.
68 Deputy Minister of Natural Resources, *supra* note 65.
69 Ron Irwin to Chief Gord Peters, 27 June 1994.

70 Memorandum to the Deputy Minister, Department of Fisheries and Oceans, from Director-General, Communications, 26 August 1994.
71 *Aboriginal Communal Fishing Licences Regulations,* Amendment S.O.R./1994-531, dated 3 August 1994.
72 Fisheries Minister Brian Tobin to Premier Bob Rae, 28 June 1994.
73 Brian Tobin to Howard Hampton, 9 August 1994.
74 Ministry of Natural Resources, News Release (1 September 1994).
75 Robert Mitton to Vice-Chief, Union of Ontario Indians, 11 October 1994.
76 David deLaunay to Marion Lefebvre, 21 October 1994.
77 Memorandum, "Williams Treaties: Ontario's Third Party Consultations," 24 October 1994.
78 Audrey Stewart, Director of Treaty Policy and Review, Department of Indian and Northern Affairs, to George Da Pont, Director General of Government Relations Branch, 2 November 1994.
79 Howard Hampton to Brian Tobin, 7 November 1994.
80 Howard Hampton to Chief Gord Peters, 13 December 1994.
81 Howard Hampton to Chief Gord Peters, 15 December 1994.
82 Regulatory Impact Analysis Statement, 17 December 1994 at 4744.
83 *Aboriginal Communal Fishing Licences Regulations* Amendment, S.O.R./1995-106, 21 February 1995, Regulatory Impact Analysis Statement at 523.
84 Chris Hodgson to Chief Gord Peters, 30 August 1995.
85 Ministry of Natural Resources, News Release (30 August 1995).
86 Chief Gord Peters to Brian Tobin, date obscured but fax-stamped 7 September 1995.
87 Memo from Cam Clark, Assistant Deputy Minister, Operations, to Regional Directors, District Managers, Lake Managers, Compliance Specialists, and Conservation Officers, 30 September 1995.
88 Brian Tobin, Minister of Fisheries and Oceans, to Chief Gord Peters, 20 September 1995.
89 *Knott v. A.G. Ontario* (28 September 1995), 95-CU-91257 (Ont. Gen. Div.) (Endorsement, Coo J.).

Chapter 9: Analysis

1 *Agbaba v. Winter* (1977), 51 A.L.J.R. 503 at 508.
2 *Delgamuukw v. British Columbia,* [1997] 3 S.C.R. 1010 at para. 80 (S.C.C.).
3 *Ontario (A.G.) v. Bear Island Foundation et al.,* [1991] 2 S.C.R. 570.
4 *R. v. Van der Peet,* [1996] 2 S.C.R. 507 at paras. 42, 49, and 232.
5 *Delgamuukw v. British Columbia, supra* note 2 at para. 112 [emphasis added].
6 Sidney L. Harring, "The Liberal Treatment of Indians: Native People in Nineteenth Century Ontario Law" (1992) 56 *Saskatchewan Law Review* 297 at 361.
7 Canada, *Report of the Royal Commission on Aboriginal Peoples: Looking Forward, Looking Back,* vol. 1 (Ottawa: Royal Commission on Aboriginal Peoples, 1996) at 137-91 [hereafter *Looking Forward*], quoted in *Corbiere v. Canada (Minister of Indian and Northern Affairs),* [1999] 2 S.C.R. 2 at para. 83 (S.C.C.).
8 *Corbiere v. Canada, ibid.* at para. 88.
9 *Ibid.* at para. 18.
10 Transcript of oral argument before the Supreme Court of Canada in *ibid.* at 77 (copy in author's file).
11 *Ibid.* at 78.
12 Canada, *Report of the Royal Commission on Aboriginal Peoples: Perspectives and Realities,* vol. 4 (Ottawa: Royal Commission on Aboriginal Peoples, 1996) at 521 and 535, quoted in *Corbiere v. Canada, supra* note 7 at para. 17.
13 *R. v. Howard* (1992), 8 O.R. (3d) 225 at 228 (Ont. C.A.).
14 *Ibid.* at 229-30.
15 *Evidence Taken by the Joint Commission appointed by The Dominion of Canada and the Province of Ontario in the Matter of Claim for compensation for unsurrendered Northern Hunting Grounds made by the Chippewas of Georgina Island, Christian Island and Rama and the Mississaugas of Scugog, Chemong, Rice Lake and Alnwick,* Library and Archives Canada [LAC], Ottawa, Record Group [RG] 10, vol. 2331, file 67,071 A at 124.

16 *Ontario v. Canada,* [1910] 42 S.C.R. 1 at 60-61 (S.C.C.).
17 *Amodu Tijani v. Secretary, Southern Nigeria* (1921), 2 A.C. 399 at 407 (P.C.); *In re Southern Rhodesia* (1919), A.C. 211 at 233.
18 *Looking Forward, supra* note 7 at n. 81.
19 *Ibid.* at n. 82
20 *Ibid.*
21 *Ibid.* ch. 1.5, "Differing Assumptions and Understandings."
22 *Ibid.*
23 *R. v. Howard,* [1994] 2 S.C.R. 299 (Factum of the Respondent Ontario at 18) (S.C.C.) [hereafter Respondent's Factum].
24 *R. v. Taylor and Williams,* [1981] 3 C.N.L.R. 114 at 120.
25 1901 census, LAC. My thanks to Dr. Janet Armstrong for supplying this information.
26 Elder Ester Taylor, quoted in Mae Whetung-Derrick, *History of the Ojibwa of the Curve Lake Reserve and Surrounding Area,* vol. 2 (Curve Lake: Curve Lake Indian Band, 1976) at 11.
27 Chief D.E. Whetung Jr. to Duncan Scott, Indian Affairs, 28 March 1922, LAC, RG 10, vol. 6961, file 481-20-2, pt. 3.
28 Georgina Island information from Department of Indian Affairs website, Aboriginal Collections, http://aboriginalcollections.ic.gc.ca/simcoe/community/georgina/index2.htm.
29 See the following examples in *Evidence Taken, supra* note 15: Chief Charles Big Canoe at 11, Isaac Johnson at 160, James Ashquabe at 14, and Alex Ingersoll at 107.
30 *Looking Forward, supra* note 7, ch. 4, s. 4.3, "Failure of Alternative Economic Options." *Looking Forward* notes that, "In the Cowichan area of British Columbia, for example, the only assistance available to Indian farmers was a single inspector whose job was to make sure that their orchards were sprayed with pesticides – not to improve their crop, but to prevent pests from spreading to adjacent non-Aboriginal orchards." *Ibid.* at n. 118.
31 William Powless to Vankoughnet, 30 August 1887, LAC, RG 10, vol. 2337, file 68,122, pt. 1.
32 Secretary, Indian Affairs, to Powless, 24 October 1887, LAC, RG 10, vol. 2337, file 68,122, pt. 1.
33 Wellington Charles to Department of Indian Affairs, 9 June 1920, LAC, RG 10, vol. 6960, file 475/20-2, pt. 1.
34 Li Xiu Woo (Grace Emma Slykhuis), *Canada v. The Haudenosaunee (Iroquois Confederacy) at the League of Nations: Two Quests for Independence* (LLM Thesis, University of Quebec at Montreal, 1999) at 153, 158.
35 *Ibid.* at 231.
36 Comments in *House of Commons Debates* (25 June 1920) at 4175, quoted in Woo, *supra* note 34 at 123.
37 *Ibid.* at 124, 125.
38 I.E. Weldon to A.S. Williams, 15 October 1923, LAC, RG 10, vol. 2330, file 67,071, pt. 3.
39 E. Jameson Paed, *The Mental Capacity of Southern Ontario Indians* (PhD Thesis, University of Toronto, 1928).
40 Duncan Campbell Scott, *The Circle of Affection* (Toronto: McClelland and Stewart, 1947), extracts in Department of Indian Affairs and Northern Development, Ottawa, Ontario, file 1/1-11-12, vol. 1 [emphasis added].
41 See, for example, Duncan Campbell Scott, *Labour and the Angel* (Boston: Copeland and Day, 1898) at 15.
42 O.M. Biggar to Duncan Scott, 9 March 1923, LAC, RG 10, vol. 2330, file 67,071-3, pt. 2.
43 Chief Big Canoe's birthdate is extrapolated from the 1871 census, which lists his age as thirty-seven in that year. *Federal Census of 1871 (Ontario Index),* LAC, RG 31 at 56 (microfilm reel C-9966).
44 Henry Hind, *The Dominion of Canada: Containing a historical sketch of the preliminaries and organization of confederation: Also the vast improvements made in agriculture, commerce and trade, modes of travel and transportation, mining and educational interests etc etc etc for the past eighty years under the provincial names with a large amount of statistical information from the best and latest authorities* (Toronto: L. Stebbins, 1869) at 429, table at 479.
45 A.F. Chamberlain, *The Language of the Mississaga Indians of Skugog: A Contribution to the Linguistics of the Algonkian Tribes of Canada* (Philadelphia: MacCalla, 1892) at 10-11.

46 Harring, *supra* note 6 at 350.
47 Muriel Whetung, elder, quoted in Whetung-Derrick, *supra* note 26, vol. 2 at 105.
48 *Ibid.* at 106-7.
49 Report to the Superintendent General of Indian Affairs and the Minister of Lands and Forests, 1 December 1923, LAC, RG 10, vol. 2330, file 67,071-3, pt. 1.
50 George Cobb, taped interview with Short Tom Taylor, aged eighty-seven, 29 May 1966, Trent University Archives, Peterborough, tape 47, box 2, 82-006.
51 *Evidence Taken, supra* note 15 at 234.
52 *Ibid.* at 235.
53 Weldon to A.S. Williams, 15 October 1923, LAC, RG 10, vol. 2330, file 67,071-3, pt. 1.
54 Respondent's Factum, *supra* note 23 at 12.
55 *Ibid.* at 14, para. 24.
56 Minutes of Council, 15 November 1923, Mud Lake.
57 Minutes of Council, 1 November 1923, Rice Lake.
58 Minutes of Council, 19 November 1923, Alderville.
59 Charles E. Cleland, *Rites of Conquest: The History and Culture of Michigan's Native Americans* (Ann Arbor: University of Michigan Press, 1992) at 207.
60 Whetung-Derrick, *supra* note 26, vol. 2 at 11.
61 *R. v. Howard, supra* note 23 at 305, 141.
62 *Evidence Taken, supra* note 15 at 142.
63 *Ibid.* at 229.
64 *Indian Treaty and Articles of a Treaty, together with Minutes of Special General Meeting,* filed with Deputy Registrar General of Canada, Lib. 297, fol. 40, Reference No. 77929 at 12.
65 *Evidence Taken, supra* note 15 at 195.
66 R.V. Sinclair to Walter Simon, Christian Island, 18 October 1923, LAC, RG 10, vol. 2330, file 67,071-3, pt. 1.
67 Chamberlain, *supra* note 45 at 13.
68 *Delgamuukw v. British Columbia, supra* note 2 at para. 89, citing from the trial judge's reasons at 116-17.
69 Leonard Mandamin, "Submission to the Task Force on the Criminal Justice System and Its Impact on the Indian and Metis People of Alberta" (Report prepared for the Indigenous Bar Association, Calgary, 1990) at 8-9.
70 M. LeBaron Duryea, "Mediation Conflict Resolution and Multicultural Reality" in E. Kruk, ed., *Mediation and Conflict Resolution in Social Work and the Human Sciences* (Chicago: Nelson-Hall, 1997) 315 at 321-23.
71 Jeffrey Z. Rubin and Frank E.A. Sander, "Culture, Negotiation and the Eye of the Beholder" (1991) 7 *Negotiation Journal* 249-54.
72 R.J. Lewicki, J.A. Litterer, J.W. Minton, and D.M. Saunders, *Negotiation,* 2d ed. (Chicago and Toronto: Irwin, 1994) at 421.
73 *Looking Forward, supra* note 7 at 174.
74 *Ibid.*, ch. 15.1 at 53.
75 Chief William George, Sekani Nation, Stoney Creek, British Columbia, 18 June 1992, quoted in *ibid.* at 54.
76 *Ibid.* at 55.
77 *Ibid.*
78 *Ibid.* at 59.
79 *Chippewas of Nawash v. Canada* (9 November 2000), T-730-99 at para. 12 (F.C.T.D.).
80 Resolution No. 94/31, All Ontario Chiefs Conference, Mohawks of the Bay of Quinte, 7-10 June 1994 (copy in author's file).
81 Alberta, *Report of the Task Force on the Criminal Justice System and Its Impact on the Indian and Metis People of Alberta* (Edmonton: Queen's Printer, 1991) at 5-6.
82 Joan Ryan and Bernard Ominayak, "The Cultural Effects of Judicial Bias" in Sheilah L. Martin and Kathleen E. Mahoney, eds., *Equality and Judicial Neutrality* (Toronto: Carswell, 1987) 345 at 352-53.
83 Whetung-Derrick, *supra* note 26, vol. 2 at 11.

84 Whetung was Chief between 1913 and 1943.
85 Canada, *Report of the Royal Commission on Aboriginal Peoples: Restructuring the Relationship*, vol. 2 (Ottawa: Royal Commission on Aboriginal Peoples, 1996) at n. 199.
86 Alex Knott, elder, quoted in Whetung-Derrick, *supra* note 26, vol. 2 at 39.
87 *R. v. Williams,* [1998] 1 S.C.R. 1128 at para. 58 (S.C.C.).
88 *R. v. Gladue,* [1999] 1 S.C.R. 688 at para. 65.
89 *U.S. v. Winans,* 198 U.S. 371 (1905).
90 Stephen Pevar, *The Rights of Indians and Tribes* (Carbondale: Southern Illinois University Press, 1992) at 38.
91 *Decoteau v. District Court,* 420 U.S. 425 at 447 (1975); *Bryan v. Itasca County,* 426 U.S. 373 at 392 (1976).
92 *Jones v. Meehan,* 175 U.S. 1 at 10 (1899).
93 *Tulee v. Washington,* 315 U.S. 681 at 684 (1942).
94 *Ibid.* at 690.
95 Pevar, *supra* note 90 at 190.
96 *Alaska Pacific Fisheries v. U.S.,* 248 U.S. 78 (1918).
97 Pevar, *supra* note 90 at 42.
98 *Menominee Tribe v. United States,* 391 U.S. 404 (1968).
99 In 1979, the US Supreme Court defined a Pacific Northwest tribe's treaty, which contained a clause enabling it to fish "in common" with all citizens of the territory, as guaranteeing the tribe an equal percentage of the catch. As a result, the Indians were entitled to take 50 percent of the available fish, unless a lesser amount would provide them with a "moderate living" described as "so much as is necessary to provide the Indians with a livelihood." *Washington v. Washington State Commercial Passenger Fishing Vessel Assoc.,* 443 U.S. 658 at 664 (1979).
100 *Lac Courte Oreilles v. Wisconsin (LCO III),* 653 F.Supp. 1420 (W.D. Wis. 1987). The judgment was delivered by Judge James Doyle, who, upon his death, was replaced by Judge Barbara Crabb.
101 *Lac Courte Oreilles Band of Lake Superior Chippewas Indians v. Wisconsin,* 686 F.Supp. 226 (W.D. Wis. 1988).
102 *The Native American Policy of the U.S. Fish and Wildlife Service* (Washington, DC: U.S. Department of the Interior, Fish and Wildlife Service, 1984) at 3-4.
103 See *Lac Courte Oreilles v. Wisconsin (LCO IV),* 668 F.Supp. 1233 (W.D. Wis. 1987), as well as *Settler v. Lameer,* 507 F.2d 231 at 237-238 (9th Cir. 1974). In *U.S. v. Washington,* it was held that tribal members can hunt and fish only to the extent allowed by the tribe and that this is not a matter for state intervention with the exception of two limitations, namely, that the tribe may not take so much wildlife as to endanger propagation of the species and may not take any wildlife that Congress has expressly prohibited it from taking. *U.S. v. Washington,* 384 F.Supp. 312 (W.D. Washington 1974), aff'd 520 F.2d 676 (9th Cir. 1975), cert. denied 423 U.S. 1086 (1976). As well, the US Supreme Court has recognized that Indian tribes have the power to manage fish and wildlife use by both tribal members and non-members. *Pyullap Tribe Inc. v. Department of Game,* 433 U.S. 165 (1977); *U.S. v. Williams,* 898 F.2d 727 (9th Cir. 1990). Perhaps as a result of the American decisions, in 1975 the United States Congress passed a ruling enabling tribal governments to contract for and administer federal funds for services previously provided through the bureaucracy, under provisions of the *1975 Indian Self-Determination Act.*
104 The term "Chippewa" will be applied to the American tribal grouping, in keeping with the convention used by American scholars.
105 Johann Georg Kohl, *Kitchi-gami Wanderings around Lake Superior* (London: Chapman and Hall, 1860) at 32.
106 Charles E. Cleland, "Preliminary Report of the Ethnohistorical Basis of the Hunting, Fishing and Gathering Rights of the Mille Lacs Chippewa" in James M. McClurken, ed., *Fish in the Lakes, Wild Rice, and Game in Abundance: Testimony on Behalf of Mille Lacs Ojibwe Hunting and Fishing Rights* (East Lansing: Michigan State University Press, 2000) 1 at 9 [hereafter "Preliminary Report"].

107 *Ibid.*
108 *Ibid.*
109 Quoted in *ibid.* at 13.
110 "Preliminary Report," *supra* note 106 at 15.
111 Robert H. Keller, "An Economic History of Indian Treaties in the Great Lakes Region" (1978) 4 *American Indian Journal* 2 at 20.
112 Brief for the federal Appellee, *Mille Lacs Band of Chippewa Indians and U.S. v. State of Minnesota et al.,* U.S. Court of Appeals, 8th Circuit, Nos. 97-1757, 97-1764, 97-1768, 97-1770, 97-1771, 97-1772, 97-1774, 97-1737, and 97-1938 (May 1997) [hereafter Brief of the Appellants] at 10.
113 "Preliminary Report," *supra* note 106 at 80.
114 Roger Spielmann, *You're So Fat! Exploring Ojibwe Discourse* (Toronto: University of Toronto Press, 1998) at 31.
115 "Preliminary Report," *supra* note 106 at 45-46.
116 *Ibid.* at 48.
117 *Ibid.*
118 U.S. Const. art. II, s. 2, cl. 2.
119 *Worcester v. State of Georgia,* 31 U.S. 515 at 548 (1832).
120 For example, in the *Treaty of Detroit,* 17 November 1807, 7 Stat. 105, 2 Kapp 92, art. 5 provided that "Indian nations shall enjoy the privilege of hunting and fishing on the lands ceded as aforesaid, as long as they remain the property of the United States." Similar provisions are contained in the *Treaty of Greenville,* 3 August 1795, 7 Stat. 49, 2 Kapp 39, art. 7; *Treaty of Fort Industry,* 4 July 1805, 7 Stat. 87, 2 Kapp 77, art. 6; *Treaty of Brownstown,* 25 November 1808, 7 Stat. 112, 2 Kapp 991, art. 4; *Treaty of Miami Rapids,* 29 September 1817, 7 Stat. 160, 2 Kapp 145, art. 11; *Treaty of Saginaw,* 24 September 1819, 7 Stat. 203, 2 Kapp 185, art. 5; *Treaty of Chicago,* 29 August 1821, 7 Stat. 218, 2 Kapp 198, art. 5.
121 "Preliminary Report," *supra* note 106 at 46.
122 *Ibid.*
123 *Ibid.* at 15.
124 See, for example, Grace Nute, "The American Fur Company's Fishing Enterprise on Lake Superior" (1926) 12 *Mississippi Valley Historical Review* 12.
125 Charles E. Cleland, "The Historical Development of the Great Lakes Aboriginal Fishery" (Paper presented at "Aboriginal Fishing: Traditional Values and Evolving Resource Stewardship," CBA-Ontario, Canadian Aquatic Resources Section, American Fisheries Society conference, Wahta Mohawk Territory, Bala, Ontario, 27-29 September 1996) at 4.
126 Referred to in *State of Michigan v. Leblanc,* 248 N.W. 2d 199 (1976).
127 Article 4 of the 1836 Treaty between U.S. and Chippewa and Ottawa Tribes, 7 Stat. 491 (1836), cited in *ibid.* By contrast, as Europeans in Upper Canada became increasingly interested in the fisheries, certain steps were taken to curtail Aboriginal participation in the commercial fishery. For example, an *Act for the preservation of salmon in Lake Ontario,* 1823 (47 Geo. III) was amended to prohibit any person "from employing Indians or buying or receiving under any pretence whatever from any Indian or Indians any salmon taken or caught ... during the closed season."
128 "Preliminary Report," *supra* note 106 at 15.
129 *Ibid.* at 26.
130 Quoted in Brief of the Appellants, *supra* note 112 at 6.
131 *Northwest Ordinance,* 1787, 1 Stat. 51, art. 3, quoted in *ibid.*
132 Quoted in "Preliminary Report," *supra* note 106 at 29.
133 Quoted in *ibid.*
134 Quoted in *ibid.* at 31.
135 Quoted in *ibid.*
136 Quoted in *ibid.* at 8.
137 *Ibid.* at 10.
138 *Ibid.* at 64.
139 Brief of the Appellants, *supra* note 112 at 10.

140 *Ibid.*
141 *Ibid.* at 11.
142 "Preliminary Report," *supra* note 106 at 81.
143 *Ibid.* at 82.
144 Justice Sandra Day O'Connor, Opinion of the Court, quoted in James M. McClurken, ed., *Fish in the Lakes, Wild Rice, and Game in Abundance: Testimony on Behalf of Mille Lacs Ojibwe Hunting and Fishing Rights* (East Lansing: Michigan State University Press, 2000) at 532.
145 "Preliminary Report," *supra* note 106 at 89.
146 *Ibid.* at 92.
147 Article 1 of 1855 treaty, quoted in *Mille Lacs Band of Chippewa v. U.S.,* Civ. No. 4-90-605, U.S. Dist. Ct., D. Minn., 4th Div., at 104. See also 861 F.Supp. 784 (1994) and Civ. No. 3-94-1226 (D. Minn., 29 March 1996) for other rulings concerning this treaty during the various actions.
148 James M. McClurken, "The 1837 Treaty of St. Peters Preserving the Rights of the Mille Lacs Ojibwa to Hunt, Fish and Gather: The Effect of Treaties and Agreements since 1855" in James M. McClurken, ed., *Fish in the Lakes, Wild Rice, and Game in Abundance: Testimony on Behalf of Mille Lacs Ojibwe Hunting and Fishing Rights* (East Lansing: Michigan State University Press, 2000) 329 at 334-35 [hereafter "St. Peters"].
149 *Ibid.*
150 *Ibid.*
151 *Ibid.* at 335.
152 Charles E. Cleland, "Off-Reservation Hunting, Fishing, and Gathering in the Post-Treaty Era" in James M. McClurken, ed., *Fish in the Lakes, Wild Rice, and Game in Abundance: Testimony on Behalf of Mille Lacs Ojibwe Hunting and Fishing Rights* (East Lansing: Michigan State University Press, 2000) 103 at 105 [hereafter Off-Reservation Hunting].
153 *Annual Report of the Commissioner of Indian Affairs of the United States,* 1889, quoted in "St. Peters," *supra* note 148 at 404.
154 "St. Peters," *supra* note 148.
155 Quoted in *ibid.* at 343.
156 Quoted in *ibid.* at 381.
157 *Ibid.*
158 "Preliminary Report," *supra* note 106 at 16.
159 "St. Peters," *supra* note 148 at 440.
160 *Ibid.* at 441.
161 Quoted in *ibid.*
162 Swanson to Carlos Avery, 10 May 1920, quoted in "Preliminary Report," *supra* note 152 at 106.
163 *Indian Citizenship Act* (1924), quoted in "Off-Reservation Hunting," *supra* note 152 at 106.
164 *Ibid.* at 107.
165 *Ibid.*
166 Referred to by Justice Sandra Day O'Connor, Opinion of the Court, *supra* note 144 at 533.
167 *Mille Lacs Band of Chippewa v. U.S., supra* note 147 at 106.
168 *Ibid.* at 104. It should be noted that, following its initial ruling upholding the existence of hunting and fishing rights, the District Court permitted several other Wisconsin bands to intervene as plaintiffs. At the same time, the Fond du Lac Band of Chippewa Indians filed suit against Minnesota for a similar declaration. In March 1996, the District Court held that the Fond du Lac Band had retained its hunting and fishing rights. *Fond du Lac Band of Chippewa v. Carlson et al.,* Civ. No. 5-92-159 (D. Minn., 18 March 1996) App. to Pet. for Cert. 419. The Fond du Lac litigation was consolidated with the Mille Lacs litigation for Phase II of the trial, which involved issues of management and regulation.
169 The experts for the defence also included Dr. James M. McClurken, an anthropologist and ethnohistorian; Dr. Helen Tanner and Dr. Bruce White, both historians; John D. Nichols, an expert on the Ojibway dialect spoken at Mille Lacs; and Thomas Lund, a legal historian. See McClurken, *supra* note 11 at viii for an outline of the experts called by the defence during the trial. Cleland, *supra* note 59 is particularly worthy of study.

170 "Preliminary Report," *supra* note 106 at 93.
171 *Ibid.* at 40.
172 "St. Peters" *supra* note 148 at 337.
173 McClurken, for example, describes such an agreement as "inconceivable," *ibid.*
174 "Preliminary Report," *supra* note 106 at 96.
175 John D. Nichols, "The Translation of Key Phrases in the Treaties of 1837 and 1855" in James M. McClurken, ed., *Fish in the Lakes, Wild Rice, and Game in Abundance: Testimony on Behalf of Mille Lacs Ojibwe Hunting and Fishing Rights* (East Lansing: Michigan State University Press, 2000) at 514.
176 *Ibid.* at 515.
177 *Ibid.* at 516.
178 *Ibid.* at 518.
179 *Ibid.* at 520.
180 *Ibid.* at 521.
181 Thomas Lund, "The 1837 and 1855 Chippewa Treaties in the Context of Early American Wildlife Law" in James M. McClurken, ed., *Fish in the Lakes, Wild Rice, and Game in Abundance: Testimony on Behalf of Mille Lacs Ojibwe Hunting and Fishing Rights* (East Lansing: Michigan State University Press, 2000) 486 at 489.
182 *Ibid.*
183 *Ibid.* at 495.
184 *Ibid.* at 489.
185 *State v. Rodman,* 58 Minn. 393 (1894).
186 *Evidence Taken, supra* note 15 at 215.
187 *Mille Lacs Band of Chippewa v. U.S., supra* note 147 at 106-7.
188 *Ibid.* at 98.
189 *Ibid.* at 18.
190 *Ibid.*
191 *Ibid.* at 22.
192 *Ibid.* at 108.
193 *Ibid.* at 109.
194 *Ibid.*
195 *Ibid.* at 110-11.
196 *Ibid.* at 107.
197 As noted above, the *Mille Lacs* action was consolidated with another, *Fond du Lac,* and the state appeal proceeded with respect to these two cases: *Mille Lacs Band of Chippewa Indians v. Minnesota,* Civ. No. 4-90-605, decision of the Hon. Diana E. Murphy, U.S. Dist. Ct., D. Minn., 3d Div., 13 May 1994, unreported, and decision of 24 August 1994, reported at 861 F.Supp. 784, and the decisions of the Hon. Michael J. Davis, U.S. Dist. Ct., D. Minn., 3d Div., 29 March 1996, unreported, and 29 January 1997, unreported. As well, the case of *Fond du Lac Band of Chippewa Indians v. Carlson et al.,* Civ. No. 5-92-159, U.S. Dist. Ct., D. Minn., 5th Div., decision of the Hon. Richard H. Kyle dated 18 March 1996 and of the Hon. Michael J. Davis, released concurrently with the decision in *Mille Lacs,* was also appealed.
198 Factum of the Appellant at 16, 18, *Minnesota v. Mille Lacs Band of Chippewa Indians,* 124 F.3d 904 (1997), affirmed 119 S.Ct. 1187 (1999).
199 10 Stat. 1165, quoted in *ibid.* at 24, Part II.
200 *Ibid.* at 24.
201 *Ibid.,* citing 1858 Minn. Laws, chs. XIX, XLIV, SAA 416-21.
202 *Ibid.* at 34, citing *U.S. v. Mille Lacs Band,* 229 U.S. 498 at 500-1, 33 S.Ct. 811 at 812-13 (1913).
203 *Ibid.* at 29.
204 *Ibid.* at 30.
205 *Ibid.* at 32, 33.
206 *Ibid.* at 39.
207 *Minnesota v. Mille Lacs Band of Chippewa Indians,* 124 F.3d 904 (1997), affirmed 119 S.Ct. 1187 (1999).

208 *Ibid.* at 920.
209 *Minnesota v. Mille Lacs Band of Chippewa Indians,* 524 U.S. 172 (1999).
210 Justice Sandra Day O'Connor, Opinion of the Court, *supra* note 144 at 537.
211 *Ibid.* at 1201.
212 *Ibid.* at 1202.
213 *Ibid.* at 1203.
214 *Ibid.*

Conclusion

1 *R. v. Sioui,* [1990] 1 S.C.R. 1025 at 1077 (S.C.C.).
2 *R. v. Sparrow,* [1990] 3 C.N.L.R. 161 at 180 (S.C.C.).
3 *Ibid.* at 180, 187; see also *R. v. Marshall (Marshall # 1),* [1999] 3 S.C.R. 456 at para. 92.
4 Canada, *Report of the Royal Commission on Aboriginal Peoples: Looking Forward, Looking Back,* vol. 1 (Ottawa: Royal Commission on Aboriginal Peoples, 1996), ch. 6, "Non-fulfilment of Treaties."
5 *Ibid.*
6 Canada, *Report of the Royal Commission on Aboriginal Peoples: Restructuring the Relationship,* vol. 2 (Ottawa: Royal Commission on Aboriginal Peoples, 1996) pt. 2 at 486.
7 *Reference re Secession of Quebec,* [1998] 2 S.C.R. 217 (S.C.C.).
8 *Bear Island Foundation et al. v. Ontario* (15 November 1999) dockets C22677, C22678, C22682, C23434, and C23435, at 7 (Ont. C.A.).
9 See *Citizen's and The Queen Ins. Cos. v. Parsons* (1881), 4 S.C.R. 215 at 314; also *St. Catherine's Milling Co. v. The Queen* (1887), 13 S.C.R. 577 at 637; *C.P.R. v. Corporation of the Parish of Notre Dame de Bonsecours,* [1899] A.C. 367 (P.C.); *The Mayor, Aldermen, and Commonalty of the City of Fredericton et al. v. Barker* (1880), 3 S.C.R. 505 (S.C.C.).
10 *Ontario v. Canada,* [1910] 42 S.C.R. 1 (S.C.C.).
11 *Ibid.*
12 *Delgamuukw v. British Columbia,* [1997] 3 S.C.R. 1010 at para. 177 (S.C.C.).
13 *Ibid.*
14 *Mitchell v. Peguis Indian Band,* [1990] 2 S.C.R. 85 at para. 105 (S.C.C.).
15 "Chippewa Tri-Council Report" (1998) 10 *Indian Claims Commission Proceedings* 33 at 57.
16 *R. v. Côté,* [1996] 2 S.C.R. 139 at paras. 52, 53.
17 "The Last Speech of Deskaheh," delivered on 10 March 1925, quoted in Li Xiu Woo (Grace Emma Slykhuis), *Canada v. The Haudenosaunee (Iroquois Confederacy) at the League of Nations: Two Quests for Independence* (LLM Thesis, University of Quebec at Montreal, 1999) at 251.

Bibliography

Historical Articles, Journals, and Texts

Beauchamp, William M., and David Cusick. *The Iroquois Trail, or Footprints of the Six Nations: In Customs, Traditions and History* (Fayettesville, NY: published by W.M. Beauchamp, 1892).

Burnham, J. Hampden. "The Coming of the Mississaugas." (1905) 6 *Ontario Historical Society Papers and Records* 10.

Chamberlain, A.F. *The Language of the Mississaga Indians of Skugog: A Contribution to the Linguistics of the Algonkian Tribes of Canada* (Philadelphia: MacCalla, 1892).

–. "Notes on the History, Customs and Beliefs of the Mississauga Indians" (1888) 1 *Journal of American Folklore* 150.

Colden, Cadwallader. *The History of the Five Indian Nations of Canada* (London: T. Osborne; Toronto: Coles Publishing, 1972).

Copway, George. *The Traditional History and Characteristic Sketches of the Ojibway Nation* (London: Charles Gilpin, 1850).

Cruikshank, E.A., ed. *The Correspondence of Lieut. Governor John Graves Simcoe* (Toronto: Ontario Historical Society, 1931).

Hannipeaux, T., and M. Ferard. *Report upon the Present State of the Great Manitoulin Island, and upon that of the Nomadic Bands or Tribes on the Northern Shore of Lake Huron* (N.p., 1857).

Head, Sir Francis Bond. *A Narrative* (London: John Murray, 1839).

Hennepin, Louis. *A New Discovery of a Vast Country in America*. Ed. by Reuben G. Thwaites (Chicago: A.C. McClurg, 1903; repr., Toronto: Coles Publishing, 1974).

Hind, Henry. *The Dominion of Canada: Containing a historical sketch of the preliminaries and organization of confederation: Also the vast improvements made in agriculture, commerce and trade, modes of travel and transportation, mining and educational interests etc etc etc for the past eighty years under the provincial names with a large amount of statistical information from the best and latest authorities* (Toronto: L. Stebbins, 1869).

Johnston, Charles M., ed. *The Valley of the Six Nations: A Collection of Documents on the Indian Lands of the Grand River* (Toronto: Champlain Society and the University of Toronto Press, 1964).

Jones, Peter. *History of the Ojebway Indians with Especial Reference to Their Conversion to Christianity* (London: A.W. Bennett, 1861; repr., Freeport, NY: Books for Library Press, 1970).

Kohl, Johann Georg. *Kitchi-gami Wanderings around Lake Superior* (London: Chapman and Hall, 1860).

Leder, Lawrence H., ed. *The Livingston Indian Records, 1666-1723* (Stanford, NY: E.M. Coleman, 1979).

Morgan, Henry J. *The Canadian Parliamentary Companion* (Montreal: s.n., 1869).

–. *Sketches of Celebrated Canadians and persons connected with Canada; from the earliest period in the history of the province down to the present time* (Montreal: R. Worthington, 1865).

O'Callaghan, E.B., ed. *Documents Relative to the Colonial History of the State of New York* (Albany: Weed and Parsons, 1853-87).

Ontario Historical Society Papers and Records, vol. 6 (Toronto: Ontario Historical Society, 1905).

Roberts, Charles G.D. *The Canadian guide-book: The tourist's and sportsman's guide to eastern Canada and Newfoundland: Including full descriptions of routes, cities, points of interest, summer resorts, fishing places etc. in eastern Ontario, the Muskoka district, the St. Lawrence region; the Lake St. John country, the Maritime provinces, Prince Edward Island, and Newfoundland: With an appendix giving fish and game laws and official lists of trout and salmon rivers and their lessees* (New York: D. Appleton, 1891).

Rowe, S. "Anderson Record from 1699 to 1896" (1905) 6 *Ontario Historical Society Papers and Records* 109.

Scott, Duncan Campbell. *Labour and the Angel* (Boston: Copeland and Day, 1898).

Shortt, Adam, and Arthur G. Doughty, eds. *Documents Relative to the Constitutional History of Canada, 1759-1791* (Ottawa: Historical Documents Publication Board, 1918).

Strickland, Samuel. *Twenty-Seven Years in Canada West; or, the Experience of an Early Settler,* vol. 1 (London: Richard Bentley, 1856).

Traill, Catharine Parr. *The Backwoods of Canada: Being letters from the wife of an emigrant officer, illustrative of the domestic economy of British America* (London: C. Knight, 1836).

Tuttle, Charles R. *Tuttle's popular history of the Dominion of Canada: With art illustrations from the earliest settlement of the British-American colonies to the present time, together with portrait engravings and biographical sketches of the most distinguished men of the nation* (Montreal/Boston: D. Downie and Co./Tuttle and Downie, 1877).

Primary Sources: Government Reports (Historical)

Bagot, Sir Charles. "Report on the Affairs of the Indians in Canada, Laid before the Legislative Assembly on 20 March 1845." *Journals of the Legislative Assembly, 1844-45* (Montreal: Rolo Campbell, 1847).

Copy of the Treaty made between His Majesty the King and the Chippewa Indians of Christian Island, Georgina Island and Rama (Ottawa: Queen's Printer, 1967).

Copy of the Treaty Made November 15, 1923 between His Majesty the King and the Mississauga Indians, reprinted from the edition of 1932, prepared by Edmond Cloutier, Queen's Printer and Controller of Stationery (Ottawa: Queen's Printer, 1957).

Evidence Taken by the Joint Commission appointed by The Dominion of Canada and the Province of Ontario in the Matter of Claim for compensation for unsurrendered Northern Hunting Grounds made by the Chippewas of Georgina Island, Christian Island and Rama and the Mississaugas of Scugog, Chemong, Rice Lake and Alnwick, Library and Archives Canada, Ottawa, Record Group 10, vol. 2331, file 67,071 A.

Federal Census of 1871 (Ontario Index), Library and Archives Canada, Ottawa, Record Group 31. http://www.collectionscanada.ca/02/020108_e.html.

Final Report of the Ontario Game and Fisheries Commission, 1909-1911 (Toronto: L.K. Cameron, 1911).

Fraser, Alexander, ed. *Third Report of the Bureau of Archives for the Province of Ontario, 1905* (Toronto: L.K. Cameron, 1906).

House of Commons. *Official Report of Debates,* Third Session, Fourteenth Parliament, 14-15 Geo. V (1924).

Indian Treaties and Surrenders: From 1680 to 1890, 3 vols. (Ottawa: Brown Chamberlin, 1891).

Journal of the Legislative Assembly of Canada, 1839.

Journals of the Legislative Assembly of Canada, 1844-45.

Journals of the Legislative Assembly of Canada, 1859, Appendix 1.

Matters in Dispute between the Dominion and Ontario, Joint Report to the Superintendent General of Indian Affairs by Messrs. McKenna and Rimmer (Ottawa: Government Printing Bureau, 1901).

Minutes of the General Council of Indian Chiefs and Principal Men: Held at Orillia, Lake Simcoe Narrows, on Thursday the 30th, and Friday the 31st day of July, 1846 on the proposed removal of the smaller gommunities [sic] *and the establishment of manual labour schools* (Montreal?: s.n., 1846).

Province of Canada. *Journals of the Legislative Assembly of Canada,* 1844-45, Appendix EEE, "Report on the Affairs of the Indians in Canada, Laid before the Legislative Assembly on 20 March 1845."

Report of the Special Commissioners appointed on the 8th day of September 1856, to Investigate Indian Affairs in Canada (Toronto: Stewart Derbyshire and George Desbarats, 1858).

"Report on the Affairs of the Indians in Canada Submitted to the Legislative Assembly" (1847) 6:1 *Journals of the Legislative Assembly of the Province of Canada* Appendices No. 67 and Appendix T.

Sessional Papers, No. 12 (1860) Appendix No. 31.

Sessional Papers, No. 11 (1862).

Sessional Papers, No. 5 (1875).

Sessional Papers, No. 18 (1891).

Sessional Papers, No. 10A (1893).

Sessional Papers, No. 11 (1894).

Sessional Papers, No. 27 (1918).

Statement of Case of the Dominion on behalf of the Chippewa Indians of Lake Huron and Simcoe and the Mississauga Indians of Mud Lake, Rice Lake, Alnwick and Scugog, 6 May 1895, filed by W.D. Hogg, Counsel for the Dominion, Library and Archives Canada, Record Group 10, vol. 2329, file 67,071, pt. 1B.

Government Reports and Commissions (Contemporary)

Annual Report of Lake Huron Management Unit (Toronto: Ministry of Natural Resources, 1994).

Canada. *Report of the Royal Commission on Aboriginal Peoples,* 7 vols. (Ottawa: Royal Commission on Aboriginal Peoples, 1996).

"Chippewa Tri-Council Report" (1998) 10 *Indian Claims Commission Proceedings* 33.

Indian Specific Claims Commission. *Report on Boblo Island* (Ottawa: Indian Claims Commission, 2000).

The Native American Policy of the U.S. Fish and Wildlife Service (Washington, DC: U.S. Department of the Interior, Fish and Wildlife Service, 1984).

Legislation

Aboriginal Communal Fishing Licences Regulations, Amendment S.O.R./1994-531, 3 August 1994.

Aboriginal Communal Fishing Licences Regulations, Amendment S.O.R./1995-106, 21 February 1995.

Aboriginal Communal Fishing Licences Regulations, S.O.R./1993-332.

An Act for the Protection of Game and Fur-bearing Animals, 1892 (55 Vict.), c. 58.

An Act for the Protection of Provincial Fisheries, 1892 (55 Vict.), c. 10.

An Act Respecting the Game, Furbearing Animals and Fisheries of Ontario, 1913 (3-4 Geo. V), c. 69.

An Act the Better to protect the Mississaga tribes, living on the Indian Reserve of the River Credit, 1829 (10 Geo. IV), c. 3 (Upp. Can.).

An Act to Amend and Consolidate the Laws for the Protection of Game and Fur-bearing Animals, 1893 (56 Vict.), c. 49.

An Act to Amend the Indian Act, 1910 (9-10 Ed. VII), c. 28.

An Act to Authorize the Transfer of Certain Public Property to the Provincial Governments, 1891 (54-55 Vict.), c. 7.

An Act to Encourage the Gradual Civilization of the Indian Tribes in this Province and to Amend the Laws Respecting Indians, 1857 (20 Vict.), c. 26.

Act to Make Further Provision for the Protection of Game, S.O. 1896 (59 Vict.), c. 68.

An Act to Regulate the Fisheries of this Province, 1885 (48 Vict.), c. 9.

An Act to repeal and reduce into one Act the several laws now in force for the Preservation of Salmon in that part of this Province formerly Upper Canada, and for other purposes therein mentioned, 1856 (8 Vict.), c. 47.

Amendment to the Ontario Game Act, 1898-99 (62 Vict.), c. 33.
Ontario Fisheries Act, 1898-99 (62 Vict.), c. 34.
Ontario Game and Fisheries Act, R.S.O. 1914, vol. 2, c. 262.
Ontario Game Protection Act, 1900 (63 Vict.), c. 49.

Jurisprudence

A.G. Canada v. A.G. Ontario et al., [1898] A.C. 700 (P.C.).
Agbaba v. Winter (1977), 51 A.L.J.R. 503.
Amodu Tijani v. Secretary, Southern Nigeria (1921), 2 A.C. 399 (P.C.).
Calder v. A.G.B.C., [1973] S.C.R. 313 (S.C.C.).
Caldwell v. Fraser, Copy of Judgment of Rose J. delivered 31 January 1898 at Barrie, Ontario, Irving Papers, Archives of Ontario, Toronto, MV 1469 31/37/17.
Chippewas of Nawash v. Canada (9 November 2000), unreported, T-730-99 (F.C.T.D.).
Chippewas of Sarnia v. A.G. Canada et al. (21 December 2000), unreported, C32170, C32188, C32202 (Ont. C.A.).
Citizen's and The Queen Ins. Cos. v. Parsons (1881), 4 S.C.R. 215 (S.C.C.).
Corbiere v. Canada (Minister of Indian and Northern Affairs), [1999] 2 S.C.R. 2 (S.C.C.).
C.P.R. v. Corporation of the Parish of Notre Dame de Bonsecours, [1899] A.C. 367 (P.C.).
Delgamuukw v. British Columbia, [1997] 3 S.C.R. 1010 (S.C.C.).
Fond du Lac Band of Chippewa v. Carlson et al., Civ. No. 5-92-159 (D. Minn., 18 March 1996).
Howard v. The Queen, [1994] 2 S.C.R. 299 (S.C.C.).
In Re Gray (1918), 57 S.C.R. 150 (S.C.C.).
In the Matter of Jurisdiction over Provincial Fisheries (1895), 26 S.C.R. 444 (S.C.C.).
Jones v. Meehan, 175 U.S. 1 (1899).
Knott v. A.G. Ontario (28 September 1995), unreported, 95-CU-91257 (Ont. Gen. Div.).
Lac Courte Oreilles Band of Lake Superior Chippewas Indians v. Wisconsin, 686 F.Supp. 226 (W.D. Wis. 1988).
Lac Courte Oreilles v. Wisconsin (LCO III), 653 F.Supp. 1420 (W.D. Wis. 1987).
Lac Courte Oreilles v. Wisconsin (LCO IV), 668 F.Supp. 1233 (W.D. Wis. 1987).
Mason v. Tritton (1994), 34 N.S.W.L.R. 572 (N.S.W.C.A.).
The Mayor, Aldermen, and Commonalty of the City of Fredericton et al. v. Barker (1880), 3 S.C.R. 505 (S.C.C.).
Mille Lacs Band of Chippewa v. U.S., Civ. No. 4-90-605, U.S. Dist. Ct., D. Minn. 4th Div., 861 F.Supp. 784 (1994); Civ. No. 3-94-1226 (D. Minn., 29 March 1996).
Minnesota v. Mille Lacs Band of Chippewa Indians, 124 F. 3d 904 (1997), affirmed 119 S.Ct. 1187 (1999).
Mitchell v. Peguis Indian Band, [1990] 2 S.C.R. 85 (S.C.C.).
Nova Scotia (Attorney General) v. Canada (Attorney General), [1951] S.C.R. 31 (S.C.C.).
Ontario (A.G.) v. Bear Island Foundation et al. (1989), 68 O.R. (2d) 394 (C.A.), affirmed [1991] 2 S.C.R. 570 (S.C.C.).
Ontario v. Canada, [1910] 42 S.C.R. 1 (S.C.C.).
Pyullap Tribe Inc. v. Department of Game, 433 U.S. 165 (1977).
Quebec (A.G.) v. Scott (1904), 34 S.C.R. 603 (S.C.C.).
R. v. Brodsky et al., [1936] 1 D.L.R. 578 (Man. C.A.).
R. v. Commanda, [1939] O.J. No. 287 (Ont. H.C.J.).
R. v. Côté, [1996] 3 S.C.R. 139 (S.C.C.).
R. v. George Henry Howard (1 October 1985), unreported (Ont. Prov. Ct. Crim. Div.).
R. v. Gladue, [1999] 1 S.C.R. 688 (S.C.C.).
R. v. Howard (1992), 8 O.R. (3d) 225 (Ont. C.A.).
R. v. Howard, [1994] 2 S.C.R. 299 (S.C.C.).
R. v. Howard (Howard # 2), [1991] O.J. No. 548 (Ont. Gen. Div.).
R. v. Jackson, [1992] 4 C.N.L.R. 121 (Ont. Prov. Ct. Crim. Div.).
R. v. Jones and Nadjiwon (1993), 14 O.R. (3d) 421 (Ont. Prov. Ct. Crim. Div.).
R. v. Marshall (Marshall # 1), [1999] 3 S.C.R. 456.
R. v. Moses, [1970] 3 O.R. 314 (Dist. Ct.).
R. v. Nikal, [1989] 4 C.N.L.R. 143 (B.C. Prov. Ct.).

R. v. Secretary of State, [1981] 4 C.N.L.R. 86 (Eng. C.A.).
R. v. Sioui, [1990] 1 S.C.R. 1025 (S.C.C.).
R. v. Sparrow, [1990] 3 C.N.L.R. 161 (S.C.C.).
R. v. Taylor and Williams, [1981] 3 C.N.L.R. 114 (Ont. C.A.).
R. v. Van der Peet, [1996] 2 S.C.R. 507.
R. v. Williams, [1998] 1 S.C.R. 1128 (S.C.C.).
Reference re Secession of Quebec, [1998] 2 S.C.R. 217 (S.C.C.).
Settler v. Lameer, 507 F.2d 231 (9th Cir. 1974).
St. Catherine's Milling and Lumber Co. v. The Queen (1887) 13 S.C.R. 577 (S.C.C.).
St. Catherine's Milling and Lumber Co. v. The Queen (1888), 14 A.C. 46 (P.C.).
State of Michigan v. Leblanc, 248 N.W. 2d 199 (1976).
State of Western Australia v. Ward, [2000] F.C.A. 191; (2000), 170 A.L.R. 159.
State v. Rodman, 58 Minn. 393 (1894).
Tulee v. Washington, 315 U.S. 681 (1942).
U.S. v. Washington, 384 F.Supp. 312 (W.D. Washington 1974), aff'd 520 F.2d 676 (9th Cir. 1975), cert. denied 423 U.S. 1086 (1976).
U.S. v. Williams, 898 F.2d 727 (9th Cir. 1990).
U.S. v. Winans, 198 U.S. 371 (1905).
Washington v. Washington State Commercial Passenger Fishing Vessel Assoc., 443 U.S. 658 (1979).
Worcester v. State of Georgia, 31 U.S. 515 (1832).

Secondary Sources: Articles, Books, and Reports

Blair, Peggy J. "No Middle Ground: *Ad Medium Filum Aquae,* Aboriginal Fishing Rights and the Supreme Court of Canada's Decisions in *Nikal* and *Lewis*" (2001) 31 *R.G.D.* 515.
–. "Settling the Fisheries: Pre-Confederation Crown Policy in Upper Canada and the Supreme Court's Decisions in *R. v. Nikal* and *Lewis*" (2001) 31 *R.G.D.* 87.
–. "Solemn Promises and *Solum* Rights: The Saugeen Ojibway Fishing Grounds and *R. v. Jones and Nadjiwon*" (1996-97) 28 *Ottawa Law Review* 125.
–. *The Supreme Court of Canada's "Historic" Decisions in Nikal and Lewis: Why Crown Fishing Policy Makes Bad Law* (LLM Thesis, Faculty of Law, University of Ottawa, 1998).
–. "Taken for 'Granted': Aboriginal Title and Public Fishing Rights in Upper Canada" (2000) 17 *Ontario History* 31.
Brandão, J.A., and William Starna. "The Treaties of 1701: A Triumph of Iroquois Diplomacy" (1996) 43 *Ethnohistory* 2.
Burnett, John. *A History of the Cost of Living* (Harmondsworth: Penguin, 1969).
Cleland, Charles E. "The Historical Development of the Great Lakes Aboriginal Fishery" (Paper presented at "Aboriginal Fishing: Traditional Values and Evolving Resource Stewardship," CBA-Ontario, Canadian Aquatic Resources Section, American Fisheries Society Conference, Wahta Mohawk Territory, Bala, Ontario, 27-29 September 1996).
–. "The Inland Shore Fishery of the Northern Great Lakes: Its Development and Importance in Prehistory" (1982) 7 *American Antiquity* 761.
–. "Preliminary Report of the Ethnohistorical Basis of the Hunting, Fishing and Gathering Rights of the Mille Lacs Chippewa" in James M. McClurken, ed. *Fish in the Lakes, Wild Rice, and Game in Abundance: Testimony on Behalf of Mille Lacs Ojibwe Hunting and Fishing Rights* (East Lansing: Michigan State University Press, 2000) 1.
–. *Rites of Conquest: The History and Culture of Michigan's Native Americans* (Ann Arbor: University of Michigan Press, 1992).
Clifton, James A. *A Place of Refuge for All Time: Migration of the American Potawatomi into Upper Canada, 1830 to 1850.* Canadian Ethnology Service Paper No. 26 (Ottawa: National Museums of Canada, 1975).
Dean, William G. "The Ontario Landscape, circa A.D. 1600" in Edward S. Rogers and Donald B. Smith, eds. *Aboriginal Ontario: Historical Perspectives on the First Nations* (Toronto: Dundurn Press, 1994) 3.
Dunnigan, Brian Leigh. *A Frontier Metropolis: Picturing Early Detroit, 1701-1838* (Detroit: Wayne State University Press, 2001).
Duryea, M. LeBaron. "Mediation Conflict Resolution and Multicultural Reality" in E. Kruk,

ed. *Mediation and Conflict Resolution in Social Work and the Human Sciences* (Chicago: Nelson-Hall, 1997) 315.

Ellis, C. Douglas, ed. *Atalohkana Nest Tipacimowina: Cree Legends and Narratives from the West Coast of James Bay* (Winnipeg: University of Manitoba Press, 1995).

French, G.S. *Parsons & Politics: The Role of the Wesleyan Methodists in Upper Canada and the Maritimes from 1780 to 1855* (Toronto: s.n., 1962).

Goddard, Ives. "Synonymy of Southeastern Ojibwa" in Bruce G. Trigger, ed. *Handbook of North American Indians: Northeast,* vol. 15 (Washington, DC: Smithsonian Institute, 1978) 768.

Gronim, Sara Stidstone. "Geography and Persuasion: Maps in British Colonial North America" (2001) 57 *William and Mary Quarterly* 373.

Hansen, Lise. "Treaty Fishing Rights and the Development of Fisheries Legislation in Ontario: A Primer" (1991) 7 *Native Studies Review* 1.

Harring, Sidney L. "The Liberal Treatment of Indians: Native People in Nineteenth Century Ontario Law" (1992) 56 *Saskatchewan Law Review* 297.

Harris, Douglas C. *Fish, Law, and Colonialism: The Legal Capture of Salmon in British Columbia* (Toronto: University of Toronto Press, 2002).

Hasluck, Sir Paul. *Black Australians,* 2d ed. (Melbourne: Melbourne University Press, 1970).

Joan Holmes and Associates. "Williams Treaty Claim, Draft Historical Report," 2 vols. (Report prepared for Specific Claims, Indian and Northern Affairs Canada, Ottawa, May-August 1990).

Keller, Robert H. "An Economic History of Indian Treaties in the Great Lakes Region" (1978) 4 *American Indian Journal* 2.

Konrad, Victor. "An Iroquois Frontier: The North Shore of Lake Ontario during the Late Seventeenth Century" (1981) 7 *Journal of Historical Geography* 129.

Leighton, D. "The Manitoulin Incident of 1863: An Indian-White Confrontation in the Province of Canada" (1977) 69 *Ontario History* 113.

Leighton, Douglas. "The Compact Tory as Bureaucrat: Samuel Peters Jarvis and the Indian Department, 1837-1845" (1981) 73 *Ontario History* 40.

Lund, Thomas. "The 1837 and 1855 Chippewa Treaties in the Context of Early American Wildlife Law" in James M. McClurken, ed. *Fish in the Lakes, Wild Rice, and Game in Abundance: Testimony on Behalf of Mille Lacs Ojibwe Hunting and Fishing Rights* (East Lansing: Michigan State University Press, 2000) 486.

Lytwyn, Victor. *The Hudson's Bay Lowland Cree in the Fur Trade to 1821: A Study in Historical Geography* (PhD Thesis, University of Manitoba, 1993).

–. "Ojibwa and Ottawa Fisheries around Manitoulin Island: Historical and Geographical Perspectives on Aboriginal and Treaty Rights" (1990) 6 *Native Studies Review* 21.

–. "Waterworld, the Aquatic Territory of the Great Lakes First Nations" in Dale Standen and David McNab, eds. *Gin Das Winan Documenting Aboriginal History in Ontario* (Toronto: Champlain Society, 1996) 14.

McClurken, James M. "The 1837 Treaty of St. Peters Preserving the Rights of the Mille Lacs Ojibwa to Hunt, Fish and Gather: The Effect of Treaties and Agreements since 1855" in James M. McClurken, ed. *Fish in the Lakes, Wild Rice, and Game in Abundance: Testimony on Behalf of Mille Lacs Ojibwe Hunting and Fishing Rights* (East Lansing: Michigan State University Press, 2000) 329.

McNab, David T. "The Promise That He Gave to My Grandfather Was Very Sweet: The Gun Shot Treaty of 1792 at the Bay of Quinte" (1996) 2 *Canadian Journal of Native Studies* 293.

McPherson, W.D., and J.M. Clark. *The Law of Mines in Canada* (Toronto: Carswell, 1898).

Murray, F.B., ed. *Muskoka and Haliburton, 1615-1875* (Toronto: Champlain Society, 1963).

Nichols, John D. "The Translation of Key Phrases in the Treaties of 1837 and 1855" in James M. McClurken, ed. *Fish in the Lakes, Wild Rice, and Game in Abundance: Testimony on Behalf of Mille Lacs Ojibwe Hunting and Fishing Rights* (East Lansing: Michigan State University Press, 2000) 514.

Nute, Grace. "The American Fur Company's Fishing Enterprise on Lake Superior" (1926) 12 *Mississippi Valley Historical Review* 12.

Pevar, Stephen. *The Rights of Indians and Tribes* (Carbondale: Southern Illinois University Press, 1992).

Read, D.B. *The Lieutenant Governors of Upper Canada and Ontario 1792-1899* (Toronto: W. Briggs, 1900).
Rogers, E.S. "Southeastern Ojibwa" in Bruce G. Trigger, ed. *Handbook of North American Indians: Northeast,* vol. 15 (Washington, DC: Smithsonian Institute, 1978) 760.
Rogers, Edward S. "The Algonquian Farmers of Southern Ontario, 1830-1945" in Edward S. Rogers and Donald B. Smith, eds. *Aboriginal Ontario: Historical Perspectives on the First Nations* (Toronto: Dundurn Press, 1994) 122.
–, and Donald B. Smith, eds. *Aboriginal Ontario: Historical Perspectives on the First Nations* (Toronto: Dundurn Press, 1994).
Rubin, Jeffrey Z., and Frank E.A. Sander. "Culture, Negotiation and the Eye of the Beholder" (1991) 7 *Negotiation Journal* 249.
Ryan, Joan, and Bernard Ominayak. "The Cultural Effects of Judicial Bias" in Sheilah L. Martin and Kathleen E. Mahoney, eds. *Equality and Judicial Neutrality* (Toronto: Carswell, 1987) 345.
Schmalz, Peter. *The History of the Saugeen Indians.* Research Publication No. 5 (Ottawa: Ontario Historical Society, 1977).
Skipper, James, and George P. Landow. "Wages and Cost of Living in the Victorian Era." The Victorian Web: Literature, History and Culture in the Age of Victoria. http://www.victorianweb.org/economics/wages2.html.
Smith, Donald B. *Sacred Feathers: The Reverend Peter Jones (Kahkewaquonaby) and the Mississauga Indians* (Toronto: University of Toronto Press, 1987).
Spielmann, Roger. *You're So Fat! Exploring Ojibwe Discourse* (Toronto: University of Toronto Press, 1998).
Surtees, Robert J. "Land Cessions, 1763-1830" in Edward S. Rogers and Donald B. Smith, eds. *Aboriginal Ontario: Historical Perspectives on the First Nations* (Toronto: Dundurn Press, 1994) 92.
Tanner, Helen. "The Mille Lacs Band and the Treaty of 1855" in James M. McClurken, ed. *Fish in the Lakes, Wild Rice, and Game in Abundance: Testimony on Behalf of Mille Lacs Ojibwe Hunting and Fishing Rights* (East Lansing: Michigan State University Press, 2000) 463.
Thoms, J. Michael. *Ojibwa Fishing Grounds: A History of Ontario Fisheries Law, Science, and the Sportsmen's Challenge to Aboriginal Treaty Rights, 1650-1900* (PhD Thesis, University of British Columbia, 2004).
Tough, Frank. "Ontario's Appropriation of Indian Hunting: Provincial Conservation Policies vs. Aboriginal and Treaty Rights, CA 1892-1930" (Paper prepared for the Ontario Native Affairs Secretariat, Toronto, Ontario, January 1991).
Trelease, Allan W. *Indian Affairs in Colonial New York: The Seventeenth Century* (New York: Cornell University Press, 1960).
Trigger, Bruce G. "The Original Iroquoians: Huron, Petun and Neutral" in Edward S. Rogers and Donald B. Smith, eds. *Aboriginal Ontario: Historical Perspectives on the First Nations* (Toronto: Dundurn Press, 1994) 41.
–, and Gordon M. Day. "Southern Algonquin Middlemen: Algonquin, Nipissing and Ottawa, 1550-1780" in Edward S. Rogers and Donald B. Smith, eds. *Aboriginal Ontario: Historical Perspectives on the First Nations* (Toronto: Dundurn Press, 1994) 64.
Wallace, Anthony. "Origins of Iroquois Neutrality: The Grand Settlement of 1701" (1978) 24 *Pennsylvania History* 223.
Weaver, Sally M. "The Iroquois: Consolidation of the Grand River Reserve, 1847-1875" in Edward S. Rogers and Donald B. Smith, eds. *Aboriginal Ontario: Historical Perspectives on the First Nations* (Toronto: Dundurn Press, 1994) 182.
Whetung-Derrick, Mae. *History of the Ojibwa of the Curve Lake Reserve and Surrounding Area,* 2 vols. (Curve Lake: Curve Lake Indian Band, 1976).
White, Richard. *The Middle Ground: Indians, Empires and Republics in the Great Lakes Region, 1650-1815* (New York and Cambridge: Cambridge University Press, 1991).
Woo, Li Xiu (Grace Emma Slykhuis). *Canada v. The Haudenosaunee (Iroquois Confederacy) at the League of Nations: Two Quests for Independence* (LLM Thesis, University of Quebec at Montreal, 1999).

Wright, James V. "Before European Contact" in Edward S. Rogers and Donald B. Smith, eds. *Aboriginal Ontario: Historical Perspectives on the First Nations* (Toronto: Dundurn Press, 1994) 21.

Wright, Roland. "The Public Right of Fishing, Government Fishing Policy and Indian Fishing Rights in Upper Canada" (1994) 86 *Ontario History* 337.

Index

Note: Page numbers followed by "(a)" refer to pages in the Appendix.

Aaragaritkas, 258n47
Aasance. *See* Aisance, Chief John
Aboriginal Communal Fishing Licences Regulations, 192-94, 196, 293n58
Aboriginal title: affecting land and water, 19; in American law, 231; and basket clause in Williams Treaties, claim by Mississaugas to, 75, 78, 100, 104; and claim by Algonquins of Golden Lake, 177, 291n144; confirmed by fishery leases, 26; disregarded by Crown officials, 58, 60, 68, 73, 75, 99; early Crown policy recognizing, 14; and English common-law, 57; exclusion of Aboriginal peoples from fisheries despite, 68; as grant of privileges, 118; Imperial Proclamation confirming, 37-38, 50, 57-58, 235; legal opinion of R.V. Sinclair concerning Mississauga claim to, 104, 116, 125; and legislation, 292n27; lost by surrender, 15; and Ontario, 82; and pre-existing Aboriginal rights, 203; and *Royal Proclamation* (1763), 235; and Samuel Jarvis, 37; surrendered by Saugeen people, 35, 99, 169; and Williams Treaties, 156, 203, 204
Acheton (Mississauga): signatory to Treaty 13, 243(a); signatory to Treaty 14, 244(a); signatory to Treaty 22, 248(a)
Act for Preservation of Salmon in Lake Ontario (1823), 298n127
Act for the Protection of Game and Furbearing Animals (1892), 86, 274n153
Act for the Protection of Provincial Fisheries (1892), 81
Act Respecting the Fisheries of Ontario (1897), 82
Adjitance, James, 44
Adjutant, Chief (Mississauga, Eagle Tribe): signatory to Treaty 19, 246(a)
Ahmutchiwagabow (Ojibway): signatory to Robinson-Superior Treaty, 251(a)
Aisance, Chief John (Chippewa), 32-33; hunting grounds of, 102-3; and model villages at Coldwater, 32-33; move to Beausoleil Island, 50; presence at Manitoulin treaties, 36; protests by, 53; response to industrial school policy, 41-42; sale of estate and interest in Orillia (Treaty 66), 252(a), 253(a); surrender of Coldwater Tract (Treaty 48), 250(a); surrender of fishing islands (Treaty 76), 253(a); and Treaty 5, 243(a); and Treaty 16, 245(a)
Aisence, Chief John. *See* Aisance, Chief John
Aissance, Chief James (Chippewa), 53; sale of estate and interest in Orillia (Treaty 66), 252(a), 253(a)
Aissance, Chief John. *See* Aisance, Chief John
Albany, 7
Albany River, 169
Alderville First Nation. *See* Alnwick First Nation
Algonkin. *See* Algonquin
Algonquian-speaking peoples, 1; diaspora, 6; in fur trade, 6, 213, 257n34. *See also* Chippewas; Dowaganhaes; Far Indians; Mississaugas; Nipissing; Ojibway; Ottawas
Algonquin, 1. *See also* Anishnabe
Algonquins of Golden Lake, 72-73, 112, 177, 291n144
Alnwick: fishing islands, 44, 79, 143; Indians of, 92; request to ice-fish, 176;

school at, 266n60; surrender of fishing islands, 254(a). *See also* Alnwick First Nation
Alnwick, Township of: settlement of by Mississaugas, 250(a)
Alnwick First Nation, 3, 41, 201, 211; claim to unsurrendered lands by, 44, 46, 79, 143, 145; and 1822 treaty, 44, 79; Indian Agent for, 83, 98, 115; land claim of, 99; surrenders by, 44, 79, 250(a); and unsurrendered fishing islands, 43-44; Williams Treaties Commission hearings at, 143-46. *See also* Mississaugas of the Bay of Quinte
Ameliasburgh, 43
Americans: cultural differences in interpretation of contracts, 113; fishing in Great Lakes, 51; hiring half-breeds, 52; Native, self-governing, 218; settlers, and Chippewa, 221
Amicous, Victor, 112
Anderson, Arthur S., 130, 162-64
Anderson, Captain Thomas Gummersall: Chief Superintendent of Indian Affairs, 25; Coldwater settlement, 32-33; Crown civilization policy, 40-41, 47-48; diaries of, 261n5; errors in 1818 treaty, 24-25; extinguishment of Aboriginal title, 32; Manitoulin Island reserve, 34; response to encroachments on Indian fishing islands, 42; signatory to Treaty 77, 254(a); witness to Treaty 78, 254(a); and title deeds, 31-32; witness to Robinson-Huron Treaty, 254(a); witness to Treaty 45½, 250(a)
Anderson, Charles: witness to Treaty 49, 250(a)
Anderson, J.E., 167
Anderson, T.G. *See* Anderson, Captain Thomas Gummersall
Anderson, William: signatory to Williams Treaty, 184
angling: and Ojibway language, 10
Anishnabe, 2-3, 25; and Algonquin, 1; and Cree, 1; defined, 1; fishing technologies of, 10, and Nipissing, 1; and Ottawa, 1; trade and barter by, 2, 25
Antenewayay (Mississauga of the Bay of Quinte): signatory to Treaty 27, 247(a); signatory to Treaty 27¼, 248(a)
Antenewayway. *See* Antenewayay
Anti-Slavery and Aborigines Protection Society, 150
Arfa-ed-Dowleh, Prince, 150
Armstrong, Janet, x
Ashewasega (Ojibway): signatory to Robinson-Huron Treaty, 252(a)
Ashkahnahseebee (Horn) River, 2
Ashquabe, James, 131, 176; signatory to Williams Treaty, 176
Assance, Chief James. *See* Aissance, Chief James
Assance, Chief John. *See* Aisance, Chief John
Assembly of First Nations, 214
Assikenack. *See* Assekinack, J.B.
Assekinack, J.B. (Ottawa): interpreter at Bond Head treaties, 36; signatory to Treaty 45, 249(a); witness to Robinson-Huron Treaty, 251(a)
Assikinock, J.B. *See* Assekinack, J.B.
Assissagh, 8. *See also* Mississaugas
Atherley Narrows, 5. *See also* fish fence
attikameg. *See* whitefish
Awrey, Herbert, 171
Aylesworth, R.A., 96

Baboneung (Ojibway): signatory to Robinson-Huron Treaty, 252(a)
Backhouse, Constance, xi
Bagot, Sir Charles: Governor General of British North America, 30; and report on Indian Affairs, 30-31
Baldwin, Henry, 41
Balfour, Second Lieutenant H.N.: witness to Robinson-Superior Treaty, 251(a)
Balfour, T.M.: witness to Robinson-Huron Treaty, 251(a)
Balsam Lake: Mississauga settlement at, 45; move from, 45; referred to in Williams Treaties Commission hearings, 135; and Scugog Band, 137-38; warfare at, 5
Balsam Lake Band: move to Lake Scugog, 45
Barrier Island, 279n118
Bartlett, William R., 52-53, 55, 58, 62
basket clause: in adhesions to Treaty 9, 169; ambiguity of, 205; as boilerplate, 172; extinguishment of hunting and fishing rights in *Howard* due to, xiii; evidence of in *Howard,* 182; in *Mille Lacs* case, 218-19, 225, 227-32; not explained to Mississaugas, 231; reliance on by Ontario, 166, 184; and Supreme Court of Canada, xii, 187, 189, 202, 213; in Treaty 5, 170; in Treaty 9, 170-72; and US Supreme Court, 232; in Williams Treaties, 155-57, 169, 203-4
Batchewana: size of fish caught at, 25
Batchewana Band, 62
Batchewananaung Bay: referred to in Robinson-Superior Treaty, 251(a); reservation of, 26

Bateman, William, 88-89
Batten, R.B., 182, 185
Bay of Quinte, 2, 21, 40, 43, 45, 79, 215; chiefs meeting at, 215; and Crawford Purchase, 17; industrial school at, 40, 266n60; linked to Georgian Bay, 21, 281n179; Mississauga hunting grounds north of, 143, 145; Mississaugas of, 45-46; and Mohawks of, 67, 88, 174; salmon fishing in, 30; treaty at Carrying Place of, 146, 241(a); unsurrendered islands in, 43-44, 79, 143
Bear Tribe, 133
Beattie, John: witness to Treaty 76, 254(a)
Beausoleil First Nation, 3, 46; and civilization efforts, 41, 46; complaints from Chiefs and warriors, 53; lifting of nets by, 55; move from Coldwater, 33; move to Christian Island, 135; move to Matchedash Bay, 50; refusal to move to industrial schools, 41; resolutions hiring lawyers, 100; schools, 47; settlement near Penetanguishene, 46. *See also* Beausoleil Island; Christian Island Band; Coldwater
Beausoleil Island, 50, 135
beaver hunting grounds: north of Lake Ontario, 4; referred to in 1701 treaty, 258nn48-50
Bell, John: witness to Robinson-Huron Treaty, 251(a)
Belleville, 43
Bellomont, Governor, 7
Beman, Elisha: Commissioner for Province of Upper Canada in Treaty 16, and confirmatory surrender, 245(a)
Benidickson, Jamie, xi
Bennett, W.H., 102
Benson, Sam, 111
Bever, Isaac, 286n103
Bever, John, 286n103
Bick, C.F., 164
Big Canoe, Chief Charles (Chippewa), 66; delegations to Ottawa, 216; and education, 209; and fishing licences, 66; protesting charges against members, 88-89; and land claim, 100-1; signatory to Williams Treaty, 131, 216; testimony before Williams Treaties Commission, 131
Big Canoe, Chief John E. (Chippewa, Georgina Island), 131-32
Bigcanoe, Chief Charles. *See* Big Canoe, Chief Charles
Biggar, Oliver Mowat, 127, 284n18
Bigman, James, 286n87
Bigman, John (Mississauga): signatory to Treaty 78, 254(a)
Bigwin, Chief John (Chippewa): delegations to Ottawa, 216; evidence before Williams Treaties Commission, 133-34; and Rama land claim, 126-27; signatory to surrender of Coldwater Tract (Treaty 48), 250(a); signatory to Williams Treaty, 153, 216; understanding of treaty rights, 153, 160-62, 164-65
Bigwin, William: signatory to Williams Treaty, 76
Bigwin Island, 134
Bigwind, Chief James (Chippewa): signatory to sale of estate and interest in Orillia (Treaty 66), 252(a), 253(a); signatory to surrender of fishing islands (Treaty 76), 253(a)
Bigwind, Thomas: signatory to Williams Treaty, 76
Bigwing, Chief John. *See* Bigwin, Chief John
Bigwing, James (Chippewa): signatory to surrender of Coldwater Tract (Treaty 48), 250(a)
Black, Moses, 286n103
Black River, 5, 132, 133
Blackenbury, John. *See* Brackenbury, John
Bobcaygeon, 138
Bolen, Mrs. John, 210
Bond Head, Sir Francis, vii: civilization policy, 40; inducements to Indians during treaties, 63-64, 172; Lieutenant Governor of Upper Canada, 34; Manitoulin Island treaties, 34-37; treaty promises upheld by court, 173, 197; treaty with Ottawas and Chippewas (Treaty 45), 249(a); treaty with Saugeen peoples (Treaty 45½), 250(a)
Boudreau, J.F., 96
Boyle, David, 4
Brackenbury, John: witness to Treaties 13 and 13a, 243(a)
Brandão, José, x, 258n48
Brant, Captain Joseph, 16
Brant, Clare, 159
Bray, Samuel, 102, 140
British North America Act (1867), 80, 82, 236
Brock, Township of, 137, 142
Bronhead, Lieutenant John: witness to Treaty 8, 242(a)
Brooking, Lieutenant Arthur Holden: witness to Treaty 5, 243(a)
Bruce, Colonel R., 31; Superintendent General of Indian Affairs, 44
Bruce Peninsula, 2, 35, 87
Buck, Chief John: and wampum belts, 29-30

Buckhorn Lake, 174, 216
Buckquaquet, Chief (Chippewa, Eagle Tribe): Crown promises to, 24; signatory to Treaty 20, 246(a)
Buller, John: witness to Treaty 3¾, 242(a)
Bunevairear, Alexander Kaquta (Chippewa, Saugeen): signatory to Treaty 45½, 250(a)
Bureau pour la défense des indigènes, 150
Burlington Bay: provisional surrender by Mississaugas of lands extending from (Treaty 19), 246(a); surrender of, by Chippewas, 19; warfare at, 5
Burnham, J.H., 97, 117-18, 258n54, 282n192
Burns, Alexander: Commissioner for Province of Upper Canada, 243(a); signatory to Treaty 5, 243(a)
Burnt River, 138
Bushkong River, 138
Butler, Major John, 16; as colonel, 20; witness to Treaty 3, 241(a)
Butter, John. *See* Butler, Major John

Cabot, Reverend J., 97
Cadot, Louis: witness to Robinson-Huron Treaty, 251(a)
Cahgagewin (Chippewa, Snake Tribe): signatory to Treaty 20, 246(a)
Cahgahkishinse, Chief (Chippewa, Pike Tribe): signatory to Treaty 20, 246(a)
Cain, W.C., 98, 127, 147, 157, 169, 171
Caldwell v. Fraser, 276n2
Callieres, Chevalier de, 9
Camement D'ou Island, 54
Cameron, D.: Commissioner for Province of Upper Canada, signatory to Treaty 14, 244(a); witness to Treaty 22, 248(a)
Campbell, James J., 100, 107
Campbell, T.E., 42
Canada West, 37
Cape Croker, 50, 52-53, 65, 72, 87, 97
Cape Croker Band. *See* Cape Croker; Chippewas of Nawash; Saugeen Ojibway
Cape Vesey, 43
Cartier, Jacques: and St. Lawrence Iroquois, 2
Cat Fish Tribe (Chippewa): surrenders by chiefs of (Treaty 18), 245(a)
Cataracckui Lake, 4. *See also* Lake Ontario
Cataraqua. *See* Cataraqui
Cataraqui: Mississauga hunting grounds at, 74. *See also* Kingston
Catty, Lieutenant J.P.: witness to Treaty 22, 248(a)
Cayuga Nation, 3; Deskaheh, chief of, 149. *See also* Deskaheh; Iroquois; League of Nations; *Redman's Appeal for Justice;* Six Nations
census, federal, of Ontario, (1871): hunting and fishing by Mississaugas and Chippewas, 75, 137-38, 141, 206, 270n27, 286n87, 286n103
Chabondashea (Chippewa): signatory to Treaty 5, 243(a)
Chamberlain, A.F., describing: farming, 137; hunting and fishing, 12-13; Scugog, 209-10, 285n82; spearing, 84
Charles, Wellington, 114, 207
Chase, John, 145
Chase, John P., 286n103
Chechalk (Mississauga): signatory to 1806 treaty, 244(a); signatory to Treaty 13, 243(a); signatory to Treaty 13a, 243(a)
Chemong: defined, 45
Chemong Lake. *See* Mud Lake
Cheneebeesh: oral history of, 5
Chew, Manley, 102-3, 129
Chew, W. Johnson: employee of Indian Department, 242(a); witness to Treaty 3¾, 242(a); witness to Treaty 5, 243(a)
Chief (Chief's) Island, 159, 163
Chiefs of Ontario, 214-15
Chigenaus (Ojibway): signatory to Robinson-Superior Treaty, 251(a)
Chippawa Nation. *See* Chippewas; Ojibway
Chippewa (American), xiii, 219-21, 226-27, 297n104
Chippewas (Canadian), xii; and A.G. Chisholm, 149, 151; of Alnwick, 45; of Beausoleil, 53; compensation under Williams Treaties, 152; defined, 3; and 1818 treaty, 179; encroachments by white men into hunting grounds of, 76-77, 125; and fishing leases, 54; forced to leave seasonal villages, 44; of Georgina Island, 72; in Great Lakes and Upper Mississippi Valley, 1; and hunting and fishing, 10, 13, 80, 127; land claim of, 74, 126; land claim with Mississaugas, 75, 77-79, 99, 104, 128, 149; and Mississaugas at Balsam Lake, 137; of Nawash, 197; Rama Band of, 25, 102; report of Williams Treaties Commissioners concerning, 146; retainer of lawyers by, 100; of Saugeen, 197; and Saugeen Ojibway, 26, 34, 36; similarities to American Chippewa, 220-21; of Snake Island, 66; surrenders by, 18-19, 22, 243(a), 245(a), 249(a); *Statement of Case* filed on behalf of, by Canada, 74; and Williams Treaties Commission,

131-33; and Williams Treaty, 155-56, 231, 233. *See also* Ojibway
Chippewas of Alnwick. *See* Alnwick First Nation; Chippewas; Ojibway
Chippewas of Lake Huron, 53; surrenders by, 250(a), 252(a). *See also* Chippewas; Ojibway
Chippewas of Lake Simcoe, 53; surrenders by, 250(a), 252(a). *See also* Chippewas
Chippewas of Nawash, 52-53, 58, 65, 67; commercial fishing licence; 72, 91, 107, 120, 197; and enlistment in war, 120; and hunting on Saugeen Peninsula, 87; racism toward, 97. *See also* Cape Croker; Chippewas; *Imperial Proclamation*; Ojibway; Saugeen Ojibway
Chippewas of Rama, 151. *See also* Chippewas; Rama First Nation
Chippewas of Saugeen, 197. *See also* Chippewas; *Imperial Proclamation*; Saugeen Nation; Saugeen Ojibway
Chippewas of Snake Island. *See* Chippewas; Snake Island First Nation
Chippewawa Nation. *See* Chippewas; Ojibway
Chippeway Tribe. *See* Chippewas; Ojibway
Chisholm, A.G., 126, 149, 151
Chisholm, George: Commissioner for Province of Upper Canada, 242(a); signatory to Treaty 8, 242(a)
Chitewainganing, 42
Christian Island, 55; islands reserved, 253(a); lifting of nets at, 65, 136. *See also* Christian Island Band
Christian Island Band, 3; A.G. Chisholm, 149, 151; and Beausoleil Island, 50; and Chief Henry Jackson, 216; complaints from Chiefs and warriors of, 53; fishery lease to, 55; fishing licence to, 66-67; General Indian Council meeting at, 121; land claims by, 78, 125-26, 131; and lawyers, 100-1, 103-4, 126-27; protests over fishing, 53, 55, 65, 67; reliance on interpreters, 212; schools, 47; timber rights, 55; and Walter Simon, 147; Williams Treaties Commission hearings at, 131, 135-37, 212; Williams Treaties signed at, 149, 151, 154
Cigar Island, 52
civilization policy: and agriculture, 121, 207, 295n30; American, 221; Crown, xii; failure of, 47-48, 200, 236, 266n60; formalized, 38-40; and Indian harvesting activities, xii; as means of freeing up lands for whites, xiii; resisted by Mississaugas, 31, xiii
Claus, John: witness to Treaty 18, 245(a)
Claus, William: background, 22-23; Deputy Superintendent of Indian Affairs, 179; and 1818 treaty, 179; journal of negotiations with Chippewas, 24; and surrender of reserve lands, 248(a); treaties with Chippewas, 243(a), 245(a), 246(a); treaties with Mississaugas, 242(a), 243(a), 245(a), 246(a)
Clear Lake, 112
Cleland, Charles E.: testimony in *Mille Lacs* case, 212, 220, 227-28, 299n169
Cleland, Chuck. *See* Cleland, Charles E.
Clench, J.B.: Superintendent of Indian Affairs, 249(a); witness to Treaty 40½, 249(a)
close season: fishing, 63, 71, 73
Cobb, George: interviews with elders, 4, 257nn28-29, 271n64
Cochrane, Captain W.M.: witness to confirmatory surrender, 245(a); witness to Treaty 16, 245(a)
Cockburn, James, 58-59; legal opinion on Indian fisheries, 62, 64, 68, 83, 95, 113, 139
Coffin, N.: witness to Treaty 22, 248(a)
Colborne, Sir John, 28-29; and model villages, 32-33. *See also* Coldwater
Coldwater: hunting grounds at, 134; model village at, 32, 42, 250(a); surrender of (Treaty 48), 250(a). *See also* Aisance, Chief John; Yellowhead, Chief William
Colewater. *See* Coldwater
Collingwood, 64
Collins, John: Deputy Surveyor General, 16; and Toronto Carrying Place, 16; witness to Treaty 13 (Gunshot Treaty), 241(a)
Colpoys Bay, 46
Colwater River, 103
Comego, George, 286n103
Comego, John, 143
Comego, Peter, 120
Comego, Samson, 120
Comigo, William, 286n103
Comingo, George. *See* Comego, George
Commanda, Barney, 112
Commanda, Moses, 112
common law: and Aboriginal perspective, 200; and Aboriginal title, 57; American, 230; and Cockburn opinion on Indian rights, 59, 83; and pre-existing Aboriginal rights, 203; and public rights, 83; reception of, in Upper Canada, 57; and

riparian rights, 61, 93n5; rules of, in freshwater lakes, 60; treaty right to moderate living, under American, 297n99; use of gunshot to set water boundaries under, 17
Confederacy, Iroquois. *See* Five Nations
Confederation, 73
Conn, H.R., 177-78
Constitution Act (1982), 180
Cooks' Bay: surrender of lands bounded by (Treaty 18), 245(a)
Cooper, Astley P. *See* Cooper, Captain Arthur P.
Cooper, Captain Arthur P.: witness to Robinson-Huron Treaty, 251(a); witness to Robinson-Superior Treaty, 251(a)
Copegog, Frank, 126
Copegog, Frederick: signatory to Williams Treaty, 76
Coppewy, William, 286n87
Copway, Chief George, 36, 44; description of Iroquois warfare, 6
Copway, John, 29
Couchiching Lake. *See* Lake Couchiching
Cowie, Hank. *See* Cowie, Henry
Cowie, Henry, 119; referred to in *Howard,* 184; signatory to Williams Treaty, 119, 202
Cown, George: Lands Department, witness to Treaty 5, 243(a)
Coyle, Michael, xi
Crane, Chief Jacob (Mississauga), 22, 29, 45; signatory to Treaty 78, 254(a)
Crane, Jacob, Jr. (Mississauga): signatory to Treaty 78, 254(a)
Crane Tribe (Chippewa), 22; surrenders by chiefs of (Treaty 20), 246(a)
Crawford, William Redford: and purported purchase of waterways from Mississaugas, 16-17; of the Royal Regiment of New York, 16; and Treaty 3, 241(a). *See also* Crawford purchase
Crawford purchase, 260n14
Credit River, 2-3, 28, 35, 41; reservation of, for Mississaugas, 20; spearing at, 84; surrender by Mississaugas of, 246(a); white control of fisheries at, 56
Crosbie, John, 192
Crow, Captain John (Mississauga), 22, 29; signatory to Treaty 78, 254(a)
Crow, David, 145
Crow, Henry, 75
Crow, William, 286n103
Crowe, Chief Alfred, 116-17, 119; referred to in *Howard,* 184; signatory to Williams Treaty, 119, 184
Crowe, Jeremiah, 141
Crown: Law Advisors of the, 42; legal opinions of, 58
Crown civilization policy. *See* civilization policy
Crown lands, defined, 273n133
Crown Lands Department, federal, 53, 55, 268n107
Crown Lands Department, Ontario, 78
Crowther, Lieutenant William L.: witness to 1806 treaty, 244(a); witness to Treaty 14, 244(a)
Crowther, William M. *See* Crowther, Lieutenant William L.
Crozier, Arthur, 102
Cruikshank, E.A., 257n27
Curve Lake. *See* Mud Lake
Curve Lake First Nation. *See* Mud Lake First Nation
Cusick, David, 11

Davidson, James: hospital staff, 244(a); witness to 1806 treaty, 244(a); witness to Treaty 14, 244(a)
Davies, Sir Louis H., 105
Dawson, Simon, 54
deadfalls: used in hunting, 12. *See also* deer-hunting
Dean, William, 25
de la Potherie, Bacqueville, 6
de la Ronde, Joseph, 76
de la Ronde, Paul, 74-76
Decker, George Palmer, 149-50
Deer Tribe, 33. *See also* Reindeer Tribe
deer-hunting: and Aboriginal law-breakers, 106; and Algonquins of Golden Lake, 177; and American Chippewa, 220; evidence of in Williams Treaties Commission hearings, 131-32, 134-35, 138, 145; and hunting grounds, 143; Mississauga methods of, 12-13, 85; prohibitions against nets and snares in, 283n216; and Rama Band resolution concerning, 163; restricted by legislation, 86-87; state jurisdiction over, in Minnesota, 225-26
DeLaunay, David, 195
delegation of federal jurisdiction: challenged, 126, 283n14; evidence of, 276n25; legality of, 277n27, 279n97, 283n14; as operational matter, xiii; over Indian hunting and fishing, to Ontario, 92-93, 95-97, 195, 237
delegations: evidence of Ralph Loucks concerning, 202; and Johnson Paudash, 211; members of, 216; sent by Mississaugas and Chippewas to Ottawa, 78, 126-27

Delgamuukw v. British Columbia, 237, 294n2
Densmore, Frances, 220
Department of Justice, federal: opinion regarding fisheries jurisdiction, 68, 94; retainer of O.M. Biggar by, 127; and R.V. Sinclair, 207
Deskaheh, 149-50, 239. *See also* Cayuga Nation; Iroquois; League of Nations
Detroit, 7
Detroit, Treaty of, 298n120
Devil's Bird (Chippewa): signatory to Treaty 18, 245(a)
Dickson, Chief Justice Brian (Supreme Court of Canada), 238
dish with one spoon: and hunting by Iroquois, 29; and Joseph Brant, 16; 1701 treaty, oral history of, 7, 9, 16
Dodge, Governor, 223
Dokis (Ojibway): signatory to Robinson-Huron Treaty, 251(a)
Dorchester, Lord, 18
Douglas, Howard: witness to Treaty 8, 242(a)
Dowaganhaes, 7. *See also* Far Indians
Dowaganhaws. *See* Dowaganhaes
Draper, W.H., 42, 139
Duck Island, 43
Dupont, Charles, 65

Eagle Tribe (Mississaugas), 22; surrender by chiefs (Treaty 19), 246(a)
Edwards, Frank, 177
Edwards, W. Stuart, 126
Elliott, Adam: witness to Treaty 45½, 250(a)
Elliott, David: former Chief, 137; signatory to Williams Treaty, 137
Elliott, T.H., 87
Emily Creek, 90
Emily Lake, 90
encroachments: into Aboriginal lands and waters, xiv; and Bond Head Treaties, 34, 36; by commercial fishermen, 76; conflict between white and Aboriginal fishermen over, 64; as Crown policy, 38; and fishery leases, to prevent, 26; and George Ironside, 43; and Indian rents, 61; at Kingston, by Americans, 74; legalized, xiv; and Lieutenant-Governor Simcoe, 15; in muskrat trapping grounds, 140, 206; in northern hunting grounds, 77; relocation of Mississaugas and Chippewas because of, 44; at Rice Lake and Mud Lake, 29; at Saugeen fisheries, 36; by squatters, 39; steps taken by Mississaugas and Chippewas to prevent, 13; supported by law advisors of the Crown, 42; by white men into reserved Mississauga fisheries, 28-29; at Wikwemikong, 43
Eshevince, John, 286n103
Espaniole: signatory to Treaty 45, 249(a)
Esquabe, James, 132
Etobicoke, Township of: referred to in Treaty 19, 246(a)
Etobicoke River: reservation of fisheries by Mississaugas, 20
Euro-centrism, xiii
Evans, James: witness to Treaty 45½, 250(a)
Evans, Kelly, 109-10, 117
Evans and Evans (law firm), 98
Evany, James (schoolteacher): witness to Treaty No. 20, 22
Executive Council (Upper Canada), 40
extinguishment: in American cases, 218; arguments in *Howard,* 187, 231; burden of proving, 182; of Indian title, 74; intention of Williams Treaties Commissioners, 154; in *Mille Lacs* case, 231; of pre-existing treaty rights, x; by Williams Treaties, 152

Fairfield, Benjamin, Jr.: witness to Treaty 27, 247(a)
False Duck's Island, 43
Fanning, George, 121
Far Indians: warfare with Iroquois, 6. *See also* Dowaganhaes
Farrington, James, 174
Fawn, John (Mississauga), 286n87; signatory to Treaty 78, 254(a)
Fawn, Russell, 164
Fawn, Sampson, 208
Fawn, Solomon, 286n87
Férard, M., 266n54
Ferguson, Captain George R.: witness to 1806 treaty, 244(a); witness to Treaty 14, 244(a)
Ferguson, G.H., 169
Ferguson, John: Indian Department, 247(a); treaty with Mississaugas of the Bay of Quinte, 247(a); witness to Treaty 27¼, 248(a)
Ferguson, Lieutenant Alexander: witness to confirmatory surrender, 245(a); witness to Treaty 16, 245(a)
Ferguson, William Nassau, 283n14
Field, Talfourd W.: District Agent, 250(a); witness to Treaty 45½, 250(a)
fish fence: at Machickning, 5, 11-12; use of, by Ojibway, 11
fisheries (Great Lakes): commercial leases in, 52; fish production in, 222; and

hand-held nets, 2; size of, 50; as source of revenue, 51
Fisheries Act (federal), 48-49, 55, 57, 59, 61, 266n64; and Ontario, 53
Fisheries Act (Ontario), 80
Fisheries and Oceans, Department of, xi, 190-93, 195-96; and delegation of fisheries authority, 276n25. *See also* delegation of federal jurisdiction
Fisheries Branch, 55-56, 60
Fisheries Department, 83. *See also* Marine and Fisheries, Department of
Fisheries Reference: to the Judicial Committee of the Privy Council, 92-93, 96-97, 237; new legislation following, 105; to the Supreme Court of Canada, 80-82
fishery leases: under federal *Fisheries Act,* 49, 56; at Garden River, 54; issued to Chippewas and Mississaugas, 54-55; issued to white men, 52; and Saugeen Indians, 26; unfairness to Indians, 70. *See also Fisheries Act* (federal)
fishing, 10-12, 25, 28, 50; Aboriginal perspective on treaty rights to, 153, 165; by Anishnabe, 1; in Great Lakes, 222; interference with, 269n10; intra-government conflicts over, 62; protected in 1818 treaty, 24; by Rama Band, 55; restricted after *Howard,* 197; by Saugeen peoples, 2; with seine nets, 52; by white men, 88. *See also* fishing islands; fishing stations; pike; salmon trout; sturgeon; treaty rights; whitefish
fishing islands: as camping grounds, 262n63; at Chemong Lake, 97; in Georgian Bay, 253(a); importance of to Aboriginal peoples, 25-26, 35, 43; at Lake Simcoe, 48, 253(a); reservation by Alnwick, 79; in Robinson-Huron Treaty, 251(a); surrender of, at Rice Lake, 254(a). *See also* fishing; fishing stations
fishing stations: and First Nations in Lake Huron, 52
Five Nations, xii; killed while hunting, 7; peace agreement with Indian allies of French, 8-9; and protection of water rights in 1701 treaty, xii; and wampum belts, 6. *See also* Cayuga Nation; Iroquois; Mohawks; Oneida Nation; Onondaga Nation
Flat Mouth, Chief, 223
Fond du Lac Band (American Chippewa), 299n168, 300n197
Fox Island, 4
Franklin, Robert, 143-46
Fraser, Frederick C.M.: witness to signature of Peter Gadahgegwun, 253(a)
Frasure, Thomas (Mississauga, Grape Island): signatory to Treaty 77, 254(a)
French River, 113
fur trade: Iroquois warfare to control, 3, 6

Gadahgegwun, Peter (Chippewa): Chippewa, signatory to surrender of fishing islands (Treaty 76), 253(a); sale of estate and interest in Orillia (Treaty 66), 252(a), 253(a)
Gade-que-gun, Peter. *See* Gadahgegwun, Peter
Gainfort, Ensign William: witness to Treaty 3¾, 242(a)
Game and Fish Act (Ontario), 178
Game and Fisheries Act (Ontario), 105, 115
Game and Fisheries Amendment Act (Ontario), 279n 124
Game, Furbearing Animals and Fisheries Act (Ontario), 279n124
Game Protection Act (Ontario), 106, 174
Garden River, 54
Garden River Band, 63
Garfunkle, J., 114
Garrow, Wilson, 152
Gemoaghpenasse: oral history of, 5
General, Levi. *See* Deskaheh
George, Jonas, 134
George, Samson, 126, 135
George, Sampson. *See* George, Samson
Georgian Bay: and Bond Head Treaty, 173; Cape Croker Indians of, 67; Chippewa claim to Moose Deer Point, in, 138; close season in, 73, 88; and commercial fishing, 25; and Deer Tribe, 33; federal fishing licences in, 95; lands reserved by Lieutenant-Governor Simcoe along, 132; leases from First Nations to white men in, 27; nets lifted at, 55; trade, 2; and Trent Canal system, 21, 281n179; warfare at, 5; white control of fisheries in, 56; and Williams Treaties, 155, 157
Georgina, Township of, 137, 142
Georgina Island, 66, 114, 130-32, 207
Georgina Island First Nation, 3, 66, 75, 88; land claim by, 78, 100, 104, 126, 151-52
Gheghets Islands, 26
Gibb, Alexander, 75
Gibbard, William, 49-53, 55-57, 221, 268n119
Gibbons, Colonel. *See* Givins, Colonel James
Gibson, J.M., 86, 106, 119
Gilbert, Henry, 224
gill nets. *See* nets, fishing

Gitskan, 213
Givens, Saltern, 30
Givins, Colonel James: as agent of Indians in Treaty 5, 243(a); Chief Superintendent, Indian Affairs, 250(a); and 1818 treaty; 23; errors in 1818 treaty, 25, 36, 264n123; Superintendent of Indian Affairs in Treaty 16, 245(a); and surrender of Coldwater Tract, 250(a); witness to Treaty 19, 246(a); witness to Treaty 20, 246(a); witness to Treaty 22, 248(a)
Gladue, R. v., 216-17
Glenelg, Lord, 35
Golden Eagle. *See* Quinepenon, Chief
Gonthier, Charles (Supreme Court of Canada), 188-89
Good, Reg, x, xi
Goodman, A.K., 103
Goodman and Galbraith (law firm), 103
Goose, George, 106
Goudreau, F., 105
Graham, George P., 150
Grand River, 31, 272n75
Grant, George: and loss of Canadian identity, ix
Grape Island: surrender by Mississaugas of, 254(a). *See also* Alnwick First Nation
Grassy Point, 43, 85
Great Lakes: fisheries, 50
Green, James: and deficiencies in Mississauga surrenders, 18-19
Green's Island, 43
Gruet, William: interpreter, Indian Department, 245(a); and Treaty 16, 245(a); and Treaty 18, 246(a); and Treaty 20, 246(a); and Treaty 22, 248(a)
Guananoque, 43
Guillet, George, 79
Gull Lake, 137
Gunshot Treaty (Treaty No. 13), 17, 99, 141, 145-46, 148, 155, 261nn51-52

Hagen, Indian Agent, 103
Haglan, J.D., 97
Hah-wah-quash-kum, James (Mississauga, Alnwick): signatory to Treaty 49, 251(a)
half-breeds, 51, 284n18
Haliburton, 137
Hamilton, R.: witness to Treaty 3, 241(a)
Hamilton, W.B.: witness to Robinson-Huron Treaty, 252(a); witness to signature of Chief James Aissance, Treaty 66, 253(a)
Hammond, J. Hugh, 101, 103, 285n65
Hampton, Howard, 190-93, 195-96
Hands, William, Jr.: clerk, Indian Department, 246(a); witness to Treaty 19, 246(a); witness to Treaty 20, 246(a)
Hannipeaux, T.M., 266n54
harping-irons (harpoons), 10
Harring, Sidney L., 68, 115
Harris, Douglas, xi
Hatterick's Point, 5
Hawkins, Major J.P.: witness to Treaty 27¼, 248(a)
Hawkins, William, 33
Henderson, Bill, x, xi; and Supreme Court of Canada, ix, 186
Hennepin, Louis, 10
Henvey Inlet Band, 177
Hepburn, William: witness to surrender of Coldwater Tract, 250(a)
herring: amounts caught by Saugeen Ojibway, 50; fishing by Ojibway, 10; in Great Lakes, 52; quantity of, 27-28, 52
Hiawatha First Nation. *See* Rice Lake First Nation
Higginson, J.M., 36, 42
Hill, Chief John W. (Mohawk), 30
Hodgson, Chris: Ontario Minister of Natural Resources, 197
Holland River, 131; referred to in Treaty 18, 245(a)
Holmes, Joan, x
honour of the Crown, 235; failure to uphold, xiii
Howard, George Henry: charges against, ix, 181; exercise of rights by, 205; statement of facts concerning, 181; support of community for, x
Howard, Hanlon, 184, 186, 216; referred to in *Howard,* 184; signatory to Williams Treaty, 184, 186, 216
Howard, Henlon. *See* Howard, Hanlon
Howard, Henry, 75
Howard, James, 77
Howard, Madden, 77, 142; referred to in *Howard,* 184; signatory to Williams Treaty, 142, 184
Howard, R. v., 180, 196, 212-17; analysis of, xiv; Court of Appeal decision in, 186-87, 201; District Court appeal of, 185; erroneous assumptions by the courts in, xiv; evidence in, 114, 181-83, 201; injustice of decision in, xiv; submissions by Ontario during, 204, 239; Supreme Court of Canada decision in, xii, 187-89; trial decision in, 184-85
Howard # 2, R. v., 189
Howe, Joseph: Secretary of State, 75
Hudson's Bay Company, 52, 121
Hunter, A.F., 4, 257n27
Hunter, Pierre, 121

Hunter, W.H., 100-1, 103, 277n50
hunting and fishing, Aboriginal: by Anishnabe, 1; archaeological evidence of, 1; census information concerning, 75-76; and Crown civilization policy, 38-41; by Mississaugas and Chippewas, xiv, 10-13; at Rama, 67. *See also* deer-hunting; fishing; treaty rights
Hurlburt, Silvester: witness to Treaty 40½, 249(a); witness to Treaty 49, 250(a)
Huron Church Reserve: surrender of land and water in, 19
Huron Fishing Company: leases with Saugeen, 26-27, 262n66
Huron Nation, 2
Hurons: and fish-netting, 12

ice-fishing: by Ojibway, 11
Idowe-kesis (Ojibway): signatory to Robinson-Huron Treaty, 252(a)
Imperial Proclamation (1847), 37-38, 107. *See also* Saugeen Nation; Saugeen Ojibway
Indian, James (Mississauga, Grape Island): signatory to Treaty 77, 254(a)
Indian Act: amended, 103, 206; first, 62; and game laws, 109; and Indian Branch, 62; and Indians as non-persons, 207
Indian Affairs, Department of, 17; and Aboriginal rights, 104; and Cape Croker Band, 107; claims submitted by, on behalf of Indians, 78-79; and compulsory education for Indians, 210; dispute with Mohawks of Bay of Quinte, 174; and J.D. McLean, 97; jurisdiction over Indian fishing islands, 97-98; and Mississauga land claim, 99; non-interference in Indian hunting matters, 87, 89; position concerning white farmers, 117; proposal for free Indian fishing licences, 90; protests to, by Rama Band, 162; and provincial jurisdiction over Indians, 236; and Reginald Rimmer, 94; unwillingness to protect Indians, 111; and Williams Treaties, 151, 167; and Williams Treaties Commissioners, 183
Indian affairs, management of, in British North America, 14
Indian and Northern Affairs, Department of, 191. *See also* Indian and Northern Affairs Canada
Indian and Northern Affairs Canada, xi
Indian Branch, 62
Indian Citizenship Act, 227
Indian Commission of Ontario, 179
Indian Removal Act, 33, 222
Indian Self-Determination Act, 297n103
Indian Territory, 9, 14-15. *See also Royal Proclamation of 1763*
industrial school, at Alnwick, 46
Ingall, Lieutenant F.L.: witness to Treaty 45½, 250(a)
Ingersoll, Alex, 133
Ingersoll, Sampson, 134
Ingersoll, William, 133
Ininwayu, John (Ojibway): signatory to Robinson-Superior Treaty, 251(a)
Iron, Joseph, 106, 286n87
Irons, Herb, 85
Irons, Isaac (Mississauga), 75, 286n87; signatory to Treaty 78, 254(a)
Irons, Mrs. Herbert, 211
Irons, Mrs. Wellington, 211
Ironside, George: Superintendent, Indian Affairs, 43, 51, 266n54; witness to Robinson-Huron Treaty, 251(a); witness to Robinson-Superior Treaty, 251(a)
Iroquois: xii, 3; cornfields, 45; hunting, 4, 6; wars, 3-4, 256n19. *See also* Cayuga Nation; Five Nations; Grand River; Mohawks; Mohawks of the Bay of Quinte; Oneida Nation; Onondaga Nation; Six Nations; Tyendinaga
Irwin, Ron, 190, 194
Itawabonen (Mississauga of the Bay of Quinte): signatory to Treaty 27, 247(a)

Jack, William, 286n103
jack-lighting, 84
Jackson, Chief Henry, 127, 136, 216; signatory to Williams Treaty, 136, 216
Jackson, R. v., 189
Jacobs, David, 176
Jacobs, Peter, 47
Jacobs, Thomas, 75
James, Lawrence, 177
Jarvis, Colonel Samuel Peters: Chief Superintendent of Indian Affairs, 31; and civil action against Mohawks, 30-31; and extinguishment, 37, 164n123; position on title deeds, 32; and reserve at Manitoulin Island, 36-37; succeeded by William Claus, 25
Jarvis, William: Secretary, Indian Affairs, 241(a); and Simcoe grant to Six Nations at Tyendinaga, 241(a)
Jenkins, J.A. (District Court), 185-86
Jesuit missionaries, 2, 6
Jewett, Pauline, 175
Jirons, Isaac. *See* Irons, Isaac
Joan Holmes and Associates, xi
John, Captain: and complaints of encroachment, 29; and Treaty 20, 22
Johnson, Chief Isaac, 4, 117, 137, 209-10,

285n82, 286n87; signatory to Williams Treaty, 117, 137, 210
Johnson, Ian, 182-83, 185, 205
Johnson, Mary, 73, 271n64
Johnson, Miles, 286n87
Johnson, Mrs. Amos, 211
Johnson, Mrs. Isaac, 137
Johnson, Sir John: and Crawford purchase, 16-17; and Treaty 13 (Gunshot Treaty), 241(a)
Johnson, Thomas, 286n87
Johnston, Darlene, x, 257n34
Johnston, George: witness to Robinson-Huron Treaty, 251(a)
Johnston, Isaac. *See* Johnson, Chief Isaac
Jones, A.: witness to Treaty 3¾, 242(a)
Jones, Chief John (Chippewa): sale of estate and interest in Orillia (Treaty 66), 252(a), 253(a)
Jones, Henry (Chippewa): signatory to surrender of Coldwater Tract, 250(a)
Jones, Peter, 28-29, 31
Jones and Nadjiwon, R. v., 290n112
Joseph, Benjamin (Chippewa): signatory to surrender of Coldwater Tract, 250(a)
jurisdiction: delegation to Ontario by federal government, of fisheries, xiii; discussed in *Fisheries Reference,* 62, 93-94; disputes with Ontario over, 105, 190-92, 197; divided, 91; failure to protect, 236-37; federal-State, over Indians, 233; gaps due to divided, 97-98; over Indian hunting, 108-9, 118; over Indians, 14, 120; intra-governmental disputes over, 62, 82; over Property and Civil Rights, 80, 81; off-reserve, 122, 177; over Sea-Coasts and inland fisheries, 80. *See also* delegation of federal jurisdiction

Kabiatsiwaybegebe (Mississauga of the Bay of Quinte): signatory to Treaty 27, 247(a); signatory to Treaty 27¼, 248(a)
Kabratsiwaybiyebe. *See* Kabiatsiwaybegebe
Kadegegwon, Thomas (Spotted Feather), 135
Kagishewawetung (Ojibway): signatory to Robinson-Huron Treaty, 252(a)
Kakekijick (Mississauga of the Bay of Quinte): signatory to Treaty 27, 247(a)
Kaqueticum, Chief (Chippewa, Cat Fish Tribe): signatory to Treaty 18, 245(a); as Snake, signatory to Treaty 45, 249(a)
Katouche, (Mississauga of the Bay of Quinte): signatory to Treaty 27, 247(a)
Kautabus (Mississauga): signatory to Treaty 3, 241(a)
Ka-wa-gah-mong River, 136
Kawartha Lakes, 45, 138, 281n179
Kawwahkitahqubi (Mississauga, Otter Tribe): signatory to Treaty 19, 246(a)
Kay, W.J., 122
Keating, J.W., 30
Keating, T.W.: witness to Robinson-Huron Treaty, 251(a)
Kebonecence (Mississauga): signatory to Treaty 13, 243(a); signatory to Treaty 14, 244(a); witness to unnumbered treaty (1806), 245(a)
Kechegom (Mississauga of the Bay of Quinte): signatory to Treaty 27, 247(a)
Keeshick, Charles (Chippewa): signatory to Treaty 66, 253(a)
Kempenfelt Bay: referred to in Treaty 18, 245(a)
Keokonse (Ojibway): signatory to Robinson-Huron Treaty, 251(a)
Kerr, John, 99, 101
Kerr, R.: witness to Treaty 3, 241(a)
Kerr, William, 144
Kettle Point Indians, 54
Kimewen: signatory to Treaty 45, 249(a)
Kinaybicoinini (Chippewa): signatory to confirmatory surrender, 245(a); signatory to Treaty 16, 245(a)
King, Township of: referred to in Treaty 18, 245(a)
Kingston, 43; Mississauga hunting grounds at, 74. *See also* Cataraqui
Kitchemokomon: signatory to Treaty 45, 249(a)
Kitchipossegun (Ojibway): signatory to Robinson-Huron Treaty, 251(a)
Kiwaishe (Mississauga of the Bay of Quinte): signatory to Treaty 27, 247(a)
Knott, Alex, 119, 216
Knott, Keith, 215
Kohl, Johann Georg, 10, 219, 229
Komonjeveweny (Mississauga of the Bay of Quinte): signatory to Treaty 27, 247(a)
Koshee Lake, 134, 159
Koshog, 135
Kowgisawis (Saugeen): signatory to Treaty 45½, 250(a)

Lacasse, Jean-Pierre, xi
Lake, John, 145
Lake Couchiching: Chippewa request to use fisheries in, 66, 111; hunting and fishing grounds of Chippewa, 159, 162; Indians residing on shores of, 253(a); Iroquois warfare at, 4, 6
Lake Dalyrymple, 163
Lake Erie, 4, 8

Lake George, 54
Lake Huron: Chippewas of, 53; fisheries in, 51-52, 56, 84; fishery leases, 26, 54; hunting by Ojibway at, 80; and Huron Fishing Company, 27; Indians of, 83; Kettle Point Indians of, 54, 56
Lake Joseph, 131-32
Lake Muskoka, 33, 132-33
Lake Nipigon, 86
Lake Nipissing, 74; hunting at, 143-44; Indians of, 83, 113
Lake of Plains. *See* Rice Lake
Lake of the Burning Plains. *See* Rice Lake
Lake Ontario, 2, 3; as beaver hunting ground 4; unsurrendered islands in, 43. *See also* Cataracckui Lake
Lake Scugog, 45
Lake Simcoe, 2, 66, 72; Chippewas of, 53; close season in, 113; referred to in Treaty 20, 246(a), 281n179; warfare between Ojibway and Iroquois at, 5; white control of fisheries at, 56
Lake Simcoe, County of, 146
Lake Simcoe Indians, 72
Lake St. John, 164
Lake Superior, 52, 222; Indians of, 83, 224
lake trout, 25. *See also* fishing
Lake Winnibigoshish Band (Chippewa), 224
land claim, of Mississaugas and Chippewas, 74, 77; and Band lawyers, 98, 111, 149; and Chief Daniel Whetung, Jr., 216; confirmed by William Spragge, 75; explained by Johnson Paudash at Commission hearings, 182; international context of, 151; opinion of Reginald Rimmer concerning, 95, 99; rejected by Ontario, 80; tabled with Provincial Treasurers, 79; and William Plummer, 76-77; and Williams Treaties, 204. *See also* Williams Treaties
Latchford, Frank, 112
League of Nations, 149-51
Lefebvre, Marion, 195
Lindsay, 138
Lines, Nathaniel: interpreter, Treaty 13 (Gunshot Treaty), 241(a)
Little Lake George, 54
Little Mud Lake, 174
Loucks, Ralph: evidence in *Howard,* 114, 183-85, 187-88, 200, 205-6, 209-10, 230
Lougheed, Sir James, 207
Louis XIV (King of France), 7
Lund, Thomas, xi, 229-30, 299n169
Lytwyn, Victor, x, 258n48

Macdonald, Sir John A., 78
MacDonnell, Allan: witness to Robinson-Huron Treaty, 251(a)
MacDonnell, J.P., 80
Machickning, 11. *See also* fish fence
MacInnes, T.R.L., 175
Mackenzie, A.F., 163-65, 167, 174, 176
Mackenzie, Alexander, 68
Mackinac, 220
MacRae, J.A., 101, 142
Maghegabo, 223
Magna Carta, 58
Mahshkigance, 103
Mahzenahegaseebe River. *See* Credit River
Maisquaso (Ojibway): signatory to Robinson-Huron Treaty, 251(a)
Maitland, Sir Peregrine: Lieutenant-Governor, and new annuity scheme, 21
Male Devil (Chippewa, Pike Tribe): signatory to Treaty 18, 245(a)
Mangan, Joseph, 167
manidogizisons, 12
Manitobinince. *See* Devil's Bird
Manitonobe. *See* Male Devil
Manitonshanise (Ojibway): signatory to Robinson-Superior Treaty, 251(a)
Manitoulin Island, 2; First Nations of, 63, 110; jack-lighting at, 84; protests by Aboriginal fishermen at, 55; as reserve for Indian allies, 34-35, 42-43, 50, 92; sturgeon fishing at, 84
Manitowab, 103
Manitowaning, 43, 63, 71
manual labour schools, 41
Manypenny, George: as US treaty commissioner, 224-25, 228
map, of 1701 treaty with Iroquois, 8
Maracle, 67
Marine and Fisheries, Department of (federal): closed season for fishing, 73; criticism of Indian fishing, 89; delegation of authority to Ontario, 95-96, 276n25; and Department of Indian Affairs, 68, 104; and *Fisheries Reference,* 91; jurisdiction over Indian fishing, 62, 71; jurisdictional dispute with Ontario over fishing licences, 105; non-recognition of Indian rights, 65-68, 71, 83, 91-92, 113; refusal to issue licences to Indians, 72, 90, 92; and Snake Island First Nation, 66; and spearing, 84; support for provincial position on Indian rights, 113; and William Plummer, 66. *See also* Whitcher, William F.
Marsden, Norman, 145
Marsden, Sarah, 138
Marsden, Thomas, 138, 286n103; witness to Treaty 77, 254(a)

Marsden, William (Mississauga): signatory to Treaty 78, 254(a)
Martell, William, 163; signatory to Williams Treaty, 163
Martin, Michael, xi
Mashekyash (Ojibway): signatory to Robinson-Huron Treaty, 252(a)
Matchadash, Township of, 163
Matchedash Bay: blank surrender of, 16; invalidity of surrender of, 18; reference to in Williams Treaties, 155; settlement at, 50
Mattotow (Mississauga): signatory to Treaty 3, 241(a)
McCamus, R., 116
McCarthy, Leighton, 121
McClurg, G. Mills, 100, 111, 111n143
McClurken, James, xi, 226, 228, 299n169
McCuaig, John, 51, 56
McCue, Alfred: signatory to Williams Treaty, 128
McCue, James (Mississauga): signatory to Treaty 78, 254(a)
McCue, William, 286n87
McDonald, Alexander, 27
McDonald, D., 161
McDonald, John: Deputy Surveyor, 27
McDonnell, Alexander: Assistant Secretary, Indian Affairs, 245(a); witness to Treaty 18, 245(a); witness to Treaty 22, 248(a)
McFadden, Uriah, 128, 135, 147
McGill, John: Adjutant, 241(a); witness to Treaty 3, 241(a); witness to Treaty 5, 243(a)
McGregor, Alexander, 27, 27n74
McKenna, J.A.J., 98-100
McKenzie, Colonel, 72
McKirdy, William, 86
McLachlin, Chief Justice Beverley (Supreme Court of Canada), 201
McLean, Donald: Commissioner for Upper Canada, 244(a); witness to 1806 treaty, 244(a); witness to Treaty 14, 244(a)
McLean, J.D., 91, 122, 129; and Cape Croker Band, 107-9; and delegation of federal authority to Ontario, 92; and game laws, 111; and Hiawatha First Nation, 116-17; and jurisdiction over Lake Scugog; 98; and Justice Department, 94, and Mississauga land claim, 126; obstruction of Band lawyers by, 101-4; and provincial jurisdiction, 176; and Rama, 113-14; reference to during Williams Treaties Commission hearings, 134
McNachten, Colonel Neil, 116
McPhee, J.L., 89
Medegwaub. *See* Metigwob, Chief
Meighen, Arthur: Prime Minister, 119-20, 154
Mekis (Ojibway): signatory to Robinson-Huron Treaty, 251(a)
Menominee Tribe, 263n106
Meredith, William, 121
Messissaque Indian Nation: and Treaty 3, 241(a); and Treaty 3¾, 242(a). *See also* Mississaugas
Messissagues, 18. *See also* Mississaugas
Methodist: manual labour school at Alnwick, 47 missionaries, 45
Metiewabe. *See* Metigwob, Chief
Metigomin (Ojibway): signatory to Robinson-Huron Treaty, 252(a)
Metigwab, Chief. *See* Metigwob, Chief
Metigwob, Chief (Saugeen): and Manitoulin Island surrender, 34-35, 264n114; signatory to Treaty 45½, 250(a)
Mettawansh (Saugeen): signatory to Treaty 45½, 250(a)
Michigan, 219
Michilimackinac, 6
Mille Lacs, 225
Mille Lacs Band of Chippewa, 187, 219-20, 223. *See also Mille Lacs Band of Chippewa Indians and U.S. v. State of Minnesota*
Mille Lacs Band of Chippewa Indians and U.S. v. State of Minnesota, 298n112; consolidated with Fond du Lacs, 300n197; Court of Appeal decision, 232-33; evidence at, 227-31; trial decision, 231-32; US Supreme Court decision, 233-34. *See also* Mille Lacs Band of Chippewa
Mills, David, 68-70
Mimewawapenasse (Ojibway): signatory to Robinson-Huron Treaty, 252(a)
Minden (Ontario): and trapping, 134, 137
Ministry of Natural Resources (Ontario), xi; and *Howard,* 179-80, 189-90, 193-95, 197
Mishe-muckqua (Ojibway): signatory to Robinson-Superior Treaty, 251(a)
Mishequonga (Ojibway): signatory to Robinson-Huron Treaty, 252(a)
Mishoquetto (Ojibway): signatory to Robinson-Huron Treaty, 251(a)
Misquuckkey (Musquakie). *See* Yellowhead, Chief William
Mississauga tract: surrender of, 246(a)
Mississagua Tribe of Indians of Kingston: surrender of Wahboose Island, 250(a)

Mississaguas of the Bay of Quinte. *See* Mississaugas of the Bay of Quinte
Missisague Nation. *See* Mississaugas
Mississagi River, 2
Mississaqua Nation. *See* Mississaugas
Mississauga Point, 43
Mississaugas: xii, 2; arguments in *Howard,* 188; articles of Williams Treaty affecting, 155; and basket clause, 23, 233; and Canada-Ontario Agreement, 125, 128; and charges against Mud Lake Band, 178; commission reports concerning, 146, 157; Crown treaties with, 15-16, 19-22; defined, 3; dish with one spoon, 29; encroachments into lands of, 76-77; evidence concerning, in *Howard,* 182-84; fisheries at Credit River, 20-21, 28-29; fishery leases, 54; and game laws, 106; of Grape Island, 45; hunting and fishing rights, 127; hunting grounds, 74; and I.E. Weldon, 129; and influence of Six Nations, 151; Iroquois term for, 8; land claim of, 74-76, 78-79, 99-100, 118, 126; new treaty with, xiii; payment under Williams Treaty affecting, 152-53; peace agreement with Iroquois, 9; pressured to surrender fishing islands, 44; and *R. v. Taylor and Williams,* 179-80, 204-5; requests by Williams Treaties Commissioners for information concerning, 148; requests for information from Indian Affairs by, 126; and reserved fisheries, 30; response of Crown to land claim, 102, 104; resettlements by, 44-45; response to Crown civilization policy, 31; and salmon spearing, 84; settlements at Credit, Thames, Otonabee, and Moira Rivers, 3, 5; significance of hunting and fishing to, xiv, 10-13, 86; similarities to American Chippewa, 220, 223, 226; in south-central Ontario, 1; *Statement of Case* filed by Canada on behalf of, 74; surrenders by, 15-17, 21, 242(a), 243(a), 244(a), 248(a), 249(a); treaties with Crown, 102, 117; warfare with Iroquois, 5-6; and Williams Treaties Commission, 131, 137-44. *See also* Alnwick First Nation; Mississaugas of New Credit; Mississaugas of the Bay of Quinte; Mud Lake First Nation; Rice Lake First Nation; Scugog Island First Nation
Mississaugas of New Credit, 160; complaints of encroachment by, 28-29; and Johnson Paudash, 126, 160; legislation protecting, 29; reservation of fisheries, 20
Mississaugas of the Bay of Quinte, 45; surrenders by, 247(a), 249(a), 250(a). *See also* Mississaugas
Mississaugue Nation. *See* Mississaugas
Mississgua Tribe of the Bay of Quinte. *See* Mississaugas of the Bay of Quinte
Mississippi Band (Chippewa), 224
Mississippi River, 33
Mnjikaning First Nation, 3, 5. *See also* Rama First Nation
model villages: at Sarnia, Coldwater, and Credit River, 32; surrender of Coldwater Tract, 250(a); and Treaty 48, 250(a)
moderate living: treaty right to, under American law, 297n99
Mohawks: lands at Tyendinaga, 30, 44-45; peace agreement with Mississaugas, 9; war with Ojibways, 3-5. *See also* Brant, Captain Joseph; Five Nations; Mohawks of the Bay of Quinte; Six Nations; Tyendinaga
Mohawks of the Bay of Quinte, 30, 45, 67, 88, 173-74. *See also* Tyendinaga
Moira River, 56
Mokommunish: signatory to Treaty 45½, 249(a)
Monague, Enoch, 136
Monckton, Governor Robert, 14
Moodie, Kathleen, 130, 145, 152
Moon River, 102-3, 136, 163
Moose Deer Point, 132, 135, 138, 157, 159; and promises by Williams Treaties Commissioners, 162-63, 166
Morrice, J.L., 260n22
Morrison, Jim, x
Muckata Mishaquet (Ojibway): signatory to Robinson-Huron Treaty, 251(a)
Mud Creek, 88
Mud Lake, 3; blanket-fishing at, 84; encroachments at, 29; fishing islands, 97; flooding, 140; food-fishing licences at, 111; hunting grounds at, 80, 159; Indians of, 13, 45, 73, 174; Iroquois warfare at, 5-6; move from Balsam Lake to, 45-46; muskrat trapping at, 13. *See also* Mud Lake First Nation
Mud Lake, Indian agency, 80
Mud Lake Band. *See* Mud Lake First Nation
Mud Lake First Nation, 3, 22; annuities paid to under Chippewa treaties, 22; charges against members of, 167-68, 175-76, 178-79; claim for flooding, 140; claim to unsurrendered lands, 75-76; concerns over trapping, 140, 154; and Crown school proposal, 41; education at, 47, 210; exclusive rights to hunt and fish, 90; fishing islands, 97; fishing

licences, 111; guiding licences, 108; hunting camps, 85; and hunting grounds, 80; hunting, trapping, and fishing rights, 118; land claim, 78; land claims meeting, 78; move from Balsam Lake, 45-46, 204-5; no on-reserve waters, 175; oral history of peddling, 73; oral history of trap-lines, 119; oral history of winter camps, 85; perspective on Williams Treaty, 168; petition to sell fish, 175; political activism, 216; and *R. v. Taylor and Williams,* 204-5; racism toward, 216; resolution to retain lawyers, 100; sale of game by members of, 87; and special rights, 118, 175; terms of Williams Treaty affecting, 154; trapping by, 87; understanding of English, 211; and Williams Treaties Commission hearings, 131, 138; Williams Treaties Commissioners report concerning, 153; Williams Treaty signed by, 149. *See also* delegations; Mississaugas; Whetung, Chief Daniel, Jr.; Whetung, Chief Joseph
Mulligan, T. Murray, 176
Munceytown, chiefs of, 35
Murney, Henry: witness to Treaty 27, 247(a)
muskelonge, 11
Muskigonce, Chief (Chippewa, Otter Tribe): signatory to Treaty 18, 245(a)
Muskoka lakes, 111, 136
Muskoka River, 132
Muskosh River, 136
Muskrat, Joseph (Mississauga), 286n87; signatory to Treaty 78, 254(a)
muskrat trapping, 13; and Algonquins of Golden Lake, 117; ambiguities in Williams Treaties concerning, 201, 206; arguments before Supreme Court of Canada about, 187; close season, 106; evidence of during the Williams Treaties Commission hearings, 77, 132-33, 135, 138; and I.E. Weldon, 147; jurisdiction over, 97; limits on, 86-87; and report of Williams Treaties Commissioners concerning claim to, 154; requirement of licence for, 115; violence concerning, 88, 128
muskrats: described by Catherine Parr Trail, 45; and sales of, 85, 87; when can be caught, 284n30
Musquakie. *See* Yellowhead, Chief William
Musquosh River, 102, 163

Naganasaway (Mississauga): signatory to Treaty 27¼, 248(a)
Nagishking, J.B., 67
Nahwahquashkum, James (Mississauga of the Bay of Quinte): signatory to Treaty 40½, 249(a)
Nainawmutteebe: signatory to Treaty 45, 249(a)
Naineshunk, Thomas (Chippewa): signatory to surrender of Coldwater Tract, 250(a)
Naiquakan (Mississauga): signatory to Treaty 27¼, 248(a)
Nakawagan. *See* Naiquakan
Namassin (Ojibway): signatory to Robinson-Huron Treaty, 251(a)
Nanaghskung, James B., 270n27
Nandgisking, Chief Joseph B., 78; interpreter during Treaty 66, 253(a); interpreter during Treaty 76, 254(a)
Nanegeshking, Thomas (Chippewa): signatory to surrender of fishing islands in Treaty 76, 253(a)
Nanegeshkung, Joseph. *See* Nandgisking, Chief Joseph B.
Nanfan, Lieutenant Governor John: and Crown promises of protection for Iroquois hunting and fishing, 7-8, 258n49; and 1701 treaty, 7-8
Nanigishking (Chief). *See* Nandgisking, Chief Joseph B.
Nanigishkung family hunting grounds, 132
Naningeshkung, Joseph. *See* Nandgisking, Chief Joseph B.
Naningeshkung, Thomas (Chief): Chippewa, sale of estate and interest in Orillia (Treaty 66), 252(a), 253(a)
Naningishkung, Thomas. *See* Nanegeshking, Thomas
Naoquagabo (Ojibway): signatory to Robinson-Huron Treaty, 251(a)
Narrows, Lake Simcoe: model village at, 33; warfare at, 5
National Indian Brotherhood, 177
navigable waters: Aboriginal permission required to travel, 15; federal jurisdiction over, 96; Indian title in, 95. *See also Royal Proclamation of 1763*
Nawacamigo (Mississauga of the Bay of Quinte): signatory to Treaty 27, 247(a); signatory to Treaty 27¼, 248(a)
Nawakeshecom (Mississauga of the Bay of Quinte): signatory to Treaty 27, 247(a)
Nawaquarkecom (Mississauga): signatory to Treaty 27¼, 248(a)
Neace: signatory to Treaty 13 (Gunshot Treaty), 241(a)
Nebenaigoching (Ojibway): signatory to Robinson-Huron Treaty, 251(a)

Need, Thomas, 11; and Ojibway hunting territories, 13
Negigance, 103
Nelles, Robert: Commissioner for Province of Upper Canada, 242(a); witness to Treaty 8, 242(a)
nets, fishing: charges against Mohawks at Tyendinaga for using, 126, 173-74, 283n14, 291n114; destroyed as penalty under *Fisheries Act,* 73; gill, 2, 10, 81; seine, 52, 81, 87
Nevoiquequah (Mississauga): signatory to Treaty 22, 248(a)
Newcombe, E.L., 92, 104-5, 202-3
Nichols, John D., xi, 228-29, 230, 299n169
Ningawson (Chippewa): signatory to Treaty 5, 243(a)
Nipissing, 1
Nitinowinin (Mississauga of the Bay of Quinte): signatory to Treaty 27, 247(a)
Nogee, Peter (Mississauga), 286n87; signatory to Treaty 78, 254(a)
Nogeh, Peter. *See* Nogee, Peter
Nongonseway (Mississauga of the Bay of Quinte): signatory to Treaty 27, 247(a)
North American Indian Brotherhood, 216
North Caribou Lake, 25
North Gwillimbury, Township of, 75, 137, 142
North-west Angle Treaty, 54, 60
Nott, Captain, 22
Nottawasaga, 136

Oak Tribe, 133. *See also* White Oak Tribe
Ocheek (Ojibway): signatory to Robinson-Huron Treaty, 252(a)
Odawas. *See* Ottawas
Office of Native Affairs (Ontario), 191
ogemah: role in Ojibway culture, 13
O-ge-mah-be-nah-ke, 5
Ojebways. *See* Ojibway
Ojibway, 1-3, 7, 30, 33, 263n106; agriculture, 46, 80; and American Revolution, 15; and *Commanda* case, 112; and Crawford Purchase, 17; cultural differences with Europeans, 159-60; cultural values in negotiations, 159-60, 214; difficulty in interpreting language, 213, 220, 227-30; dish with one spoon, 9, 29; and 1818 treaty, 22; fishing methods, 10-11, 84; hunting and fishing, 12, 46; and manual labour schools, 40; men accused of horse-stealing, 210; muskrat trapping, 115; and the North-west Angle Treaty, 60; referred to in Robinson-Superior Treaty, 251(a); reservation of fishing islands by, 26; of southern Ontario, 206; specialized words for fishing, 10, 81; treaty negotiations with Crown, 32, 212; warfare with Iroquois, 3-5. *See also* Chippewas; Mississaugas
Okamapenes (Mississauga): signatory to Treaty 3¾, 242(a); signatory to Treaty 8, 242(a); signatory to Treaty 13, 243(a); signatory to Treaty 13a, 243(a); signatory to Treaty 14, 244(a); signatory to unnumbered treaty (1806), 244(a)
okeau: fish decoys, 10
Okemabenasse. *See* Okamapenes
Okemapenesse. *See* Okamapenes
Omassanahsqutawah (Chippewa): signatory to Treaty 5, 243(a)
O'Meara, Reverend D., 266n54
Ominayak, Bernard, 215
Oneida Nation, 3; and fishing feasts, 12
Oningegun (Ojibway): signatory to Robinson-Huron Treaty, 252(a)
Onondaga Nation, 3
Ontario Federation of Anglers and Hunters, 191-92, 194
Ontario Fishery Regulations, 190-91
Ontario government: and public rights, xiii. *See* Ministry of Natural Resources
oral history, 4, 5, 9, 85, 258n54, 282n192, 284n30
Orillia, Township of, 5, 41; referred to in Treaty 66, 252(a)
Osenego (Mississauga): signatory to 1806 treaty, 244(a); signatory to Treaty 13, 243(a); signatory to Treaty 14, 244(a)
Otonabee River, 2; and George Henry Howard, ix; muskrat trapping at, 116, 119; referred to in *Howard,* 181, 187-88, 201; warfare at, 5-6
Ottawa Valley, 4
Ottawas, 1, 2, 263n106; surrender of Manitoulin Island by (Treaty 45), 249(a)
Ottawawa, Great Lake of: claim to by Ottawas, 8. *See also* Lake Huron
Otter Tribe: surrender, by Chippewa chiefs of (Treaty 18), 245(a); surrender, by Mississauga chiefs of (Treaty 19), 246(a)
Outaouan. *See* Ottawas
Owen Sound, 35, 48, 50

Pagahmagabow, Francis, 120
Pagitaniquatoibe (Mississauga, Otter Tribe): signatory to Treaty 19, 246(a)
Pahbewun, Jacob (Mississauga of the Bay

of Quinte): signatory to Treaty 40½, 249(a); signatory to Treaty 49, 251(a)
Pahtaush, Captain George. *See* Pahtoshe, Chief
Pahtaush, George. *See* Pahtoshe, Chief
Pahtaush, M.G., 78
Pahtoshe, Captain. *See* Pahtoshe, Chief
Pahtoshe, Chief (Chippewa, Crane Tribe), 4, 22, 28 23, 29; signatory to Treaty 20, 247(a)
Paimauqumestcam: signatory to Treaty 45, 249(a)
Paimausegai: signatory to Treaty 45, 249(a)
Pamadusgodayong. *See* Rice Lake
Pamequonaishcung (Ojibway): signatory to Robinson-Huron Treaty, 251(a)
Panaissy (Ojibway): signatory to Robinson-Huron Treaty, 252(a)
Papasainse (Ojibway): signatory to Robinson-Huron Treaty, 252(a)
Papewan. *See* Papiwom
Papiwom (Mississauga of the Bay of Quinte): signatory to Treaty 27, 247(a); signatory to Treaty 27¼, 248(a)
Pakquan. *See* Pokquan, Chief
Paqwatchinini (Ojibway): signatory to Robinson-Huron Treaty, 252(a)
Patchey, Peter (Mississauga): signatory to Treaty 78, 254(a)
Patequan: signatory to 1806 treaty, 244 (a); signatory to Treaty 3¾, 242(a); signatory to Treaty 8, 242(a); signatory to Treaty 14, 244(a)
Paterson, Adam: Commissioner, Queen's Bench, 252(a); witness to Treaty 66, 252(a), witness to Treaty 76, 254(a)
Pathegezhick, Jacob (Mississauga of the Bay of Quinte): signatory to Treaty 40½, 249(a); signatory to Treaty 49, 250(a)
Patopkquan. *See* Patequan
Paudash, Captain. *See* Pahtoshe, Chief
Paudash, Chief Robert: census information concerning, 101, 282n192, 286n99; delegation to Ottawa, 127, 216; education level, 209; and error in 1818 treaty, 101; evidence before Williams Treaties Commission, 141-42, 212; knowledge of English, 212, 216; opposition to guiding licences, 106; oral history of, 5, 9, 258n54; signatory to Williams Treaty, 212, 216. *See also Howard, R. v.;* Rice Lake First Nation
Paudash, George (Mississauga), 209; referred to in *Howard,* 184; signatory to Treaty 78, 254(a); signatory to Williams Treaty, 184; testimony before Williams Treaties Commissioners, 77
Paudash, Johnson, 120, 286n85; education level, 211; and Gunshot Treaty, 17; and *Howard* case, 184-86; as member of delegations to Ottawa, 216; military service, 120; and Mississaugas of New Credit, 160; oral history of 5; referred to by I.E. Weldon, 147; referred to by Ralph Loucks, 184; requests for information from Indian Affairs, 97, 126, 167; signatory to Williams Treaty, 184, 216; testimony before Williams Treaties Commission, 5, 17, 77, 142, 211. *See also Howard, R. v.;* Rice Lake First Nation
Paudauh, M.G.: interpreter during Treaty 78, 254(a)
Paull, Andrew, 216
Paushetaunonquitohe (Mississauga): signatory to Treaty 22, 248(a)
Pautunseway: signatory to Treaty 45, 249(a)
Pawgawaznine, John (Chippewa): signatory to surrender of Coldwater Tract (Treaty 48), 250(a)
Pawiss (Ojibway): signatory to Robinson-Huron Treaty, 252(a)
Pazhhegezhick, Jacob. *See* Pathegezhick, Jacob
Peau de Chat, Joseph (Ojibway): signatory to Robinson-Superior Treaty, 251(a)
Pedley, Frank, 101, 119
peep-hole fishing: by Ojibway, 11, 84
Pejehejeck (Mississauga): signatory to Treaty 27¼, 248(a)
Pem-e-dash-cou tay-ang. *See* Rice Lake
Penetanguishene: hunting grounds at, 134; settlement near, 46
Penetanguishene Harbour: cession of land and water of, 19; referred to in Robinson-Huron Treaty, 251(a); surrender of by Chippewas, 18
Penetangushene Harbour. *See* Penetanguishene Harbour
Pennefather Report, 17, 43, 46, 209
Pesciatawick: signatory to Treaty 45, 249(a)
Peterborough, 5, 45, 87
Peters, Chief Gord, 196-97
Peters, John, 286n103
Petun, 2
Phipps, J.C., 63-64, 71
Pierce, Franklin, 223
Pigeon, John (Mississauga of Grape Island): signatory to Treaty 77, 254(a)
Pigeon Lake, 85
Pigeon River: referred to in Robinson-Superior Treaty, 251(a)

pike: caught by Chippewas at Beausoleil Island, 50; caught with decoys, 11; at Muskoka River, 131; netted by Mille Lacs Chippewa, 226; spearing of prohibited, 71. *See also* fishing; nets, fishing
Pike Tribe (Chippewa), 22; surrenders by chiefs of, 245(a), 246(a)
Pillager Band of Chippewa, 224
Pininse (Chippewa, White Oak Tribe): signatory to Treaty 20, 247(a)
Pishikinse, Chief (Chippewa, Rein Deer Tribe): signatory to Treaty 20, 247(a)
Plummer, William: and Indian fishing rights, 64-67, 69-71; and Mississauga land claim, 76-78; retired, 98
Pokquan, Chief, 16; signatory to Treaty 13 (Gunshot Treaty), 241(a)
Point au Pelee, 74
Point Pleasant, 43
Ponekeosh (Ojibway): signatory to Robinson-Huron Treaty, 251(a)
Port Carling, 132, 159, 163
Port Hope, 23
Portage Bay, 84
Potaquan. *See* Patequan
Potash, Chief Robert. *See* Paudash, Chief Robert
Potawatomie, 36, 263n106
Pottawatomi. *See* Potawatomie
Power, A., 94
Prescott, General Robert, 18
Price, David: interpreter during 1806 treaty, 244(a); interpreter during Treaty 14, 244(a)
Price, W.H., 160
Prince, John, 48-49
Procter, Henry: Commissioner for Province of Upper Canada, 245(a); witness to confirmatory surrender, 245(a); witness to Treaty 16, 245(a)
Protests, First Nation: against ban on spear fishing, 71; against encroachments into fisheries, 28, 177; against exclusion from muskrat trapping, 115; against exclusion from unceded fisheries, 107; against fishery leases, 52-53; against hunting charges, 89, 110, 160, 165; against restrictions on food-fishing, 177; against restrictions on guiding, 106; against squatters on unceded lands, 75; against Williams Treaties provisions, 183; by American Chippewa, 227; by destroying fishing stations, 56-57; by lifting nets, 55
Protle, Louis: witness to Treaty 13 (Gunshot Treaty), 241(a)

Quanibbenon. *See* Quinepenon, Chief
Quenepenon. *See* Quinepenon, Chief
Quennippenon. *See* Quinepenon, Chief
Quinepenon, Chief (Mississauga): principal chief at Twelve Mile Creek, 20; requests for Crown protection, 20-21; signatory to 1806 treaty, 244(a); signatory to Treaty 8, 242(a); signatory to Treaty 13, 243(a); signatory to Treaty 13a, 243(a); signatory to Treaty 14, 244(a)
Quinepono. *See* Quinepenon, Chief

Rae, Bob, 193
Rama Band. *See* Rama First Nation
Rama First Nation: Aboriginal perspective on Williams Treaty, 165-66, 204, 213; census information, 270n27; charges against members, 88-89, 160, 164-65; civilization efforts, 46; Coldwater settlement, 33; commercial fishing, 55, 67; compensation under Williams Treaties, 151, 153; delegations to Ottawa, 125-26; domestic fishing, 113; education, 47; encroachments into hunting grounds of, 74, 102, 125; evidence before Williams Treaties Commission, 130-38, 212; fishing by, 55, 111, 113; fishing lease, 53, 66; fishing licences, 67; as hunters and fishermen, 75; hunting grounds, 74, 162; industrial schools, 41; intention of Williams Treaties Commissioners concerning, 168; land claims, 78, 100, 104, 126, 151; land claims meetings, 78; lawyers, 100-1, 103-4; minutes of negotiation, 158-59; off-reserve fishing by, 111; post-treaty conduct, 160-63, 204; Sparrow Lake, 66, 133; trade and barter in fish, 25; understanding of English, 212; warfare with Iroquois, 6; and Williams Treaties, 154, 158-59, 213-14; Williams Treaties Commissioners' report about reserve of, 153; Williams Treaties signed by, 149. *See also* Rama reserve; Snache, Sam; Williams, Gilbert; Williams Treaties; Williams Treaties Commission; Yellowhead, Chief William
Rama reserve, 5; right to fish on, 165; Williams Treaties Commissioners' report about, 153. *See also* Rama First Nation
Reach township, 137, 142
Redman's Appeal for Justice, 150, 287n8. *See also* Deskaheh
Reed, Hayter, 71, 83, 88-92
Reigo, John, 286n87

Rein Deer Tribe. *See* Reindeer Tribe
Reindeer Tribe (Chippewa), 22, 133; and Treaty 18, 245(a); and Treaty 20, 246(a)
Rice, Henry, 225
Rice, John, 75; interpreter during Treaty 77, 254(a)
Rice Lake: blanket-fishing at, 84; deer-hunting at, 12-13; excluded from Williams Treaty, 155; fishing islands in, 79; flooding, 140; Indians of, 13; Iroquois warfare at, 4, 6; jurisdiction over, 97-98; Mississauga name for, 12, 44; muskrat hunting at, 116, 202; reserve at, 205; reserved for Mississaugas, 17; serpent mounds at, 4-5, 257n27; settlement at, 44; surrender of fishing islands in, 254(a); unceded islands in, 96
Rice Lake Band. *See* Rice Lake First Nation
Rice Lake First Nation, 3, 41, 46, 77, 97, 116, 119; appointment of lawyers, 100; ban on ice-fishing by members of, 175-76; charges against member of, 181; civilization efforts concerning, 46; compensation paid under Williams Treaties, 152; delegations from, 78; education, 47; and *Howard,* 181, 183, 187-88; land claims, 74-76, 78, 100-2; muskrat trapping by, 154, 201-2; perspective on treaties, 83; placarding of marshes, 116; protests against encroachments, 28-29, 116; request for title deeds, 31; and school proposal, 41; schooling for, 47; and signing of Williams Treaty affecting, 149; trapping rights, 128, 187; understanding of English, 211; understanding of Williams Treaty, 183, 201-2, 211-12; and Williams Treaties Commission, 131, 141-43. *See also* Howard, George Henry; *Howard, R. v.;* Paudash, Chief Robert; Paudash, Johnson; Williams Treaties; Williams Treaties Commission
Ricelake, John, 286n87
Rideau water system, 21
rights, Aboriginal: xii, xiii, 15; burden of proof in cases involving, 182; and Cockburn opinion, 60; at common-law, 57; denied by Crown, 83; evidentiary difficulties proving, 199; extinguishment of, 32; ignored by Crown, 71; as inherent rights, 215; and legal tests of, 199-200; on-reserve, 120; and Ontario game laws, 174; position of Indian Affairs concerning, 104; position of Ontario concerning, 113; pre-existing, 203; recognized in *Sparrow,* 192; unceded in northern Ontario, 169; unprotected by Crown, 97, 236; violation of, 236; and Williams Treaties, 233
Rimmer, Reginald: law clerk, and opinions, 94, 98-101
riparian lands, 60
riparian rights: 173, 175; legal concept of, 61; misapplication of, to Aboriginal title, 61
Ritchie, L., 173
Robertson, D., 174
Robinson, W.B.: and Robinson-Huron Treaty, 252(a); and Robinson-Superior Treaty, 251(a)
Robinson-Huron Treaty: referred to in Mississauga land claim, 63, 88, 102, 108, 112-13, 119, 134, 136-37, 148, 157, 178, 233; in surrender, 252(a)
Robinson-Superior Treaty, 119, 251(a)
Rogers, E.S., 86, 121
Rogers, Robert, 103
Rousseau, J.B.: and Collins agreement, 16; French-Canadian interpreter, 16; witness to 1806 treaty, 244(a); witness to Treaty 8, 242(a); witness to Treaty 13, 243(a); witness to Treaty 14, 244(a)
Royal Commission on Aboriginal Peoples, 121, 166, 172, 191, 201, 203, 214, 235-37
Royal Proclamation of 1763, 9, 14, 99, 102, 163, 259n3; and Aboriginal title to waters, 19; and English common law, 57; and law advisors of the Crown, 58-59; legal status of, 15; and Mississauga land claim, 104; and *Quebec Act,* 15; surrenders under, 14-15; transactions with individuals prohibited under, 26. *See also* Aboriginal title; Indian Territory
Rubin, Jeffrey Z., 213
Russeau, John. *See* Rousseau, J.B.
Russell, Peter: deficiencies in Mississauga treaties, 18; as member of Executive Council, Upper Canada; 18; witness to Treaty 3, 241(a)
Ryan, Joan, 215
Ryswick, Treaty of, 7

Sahgahnahquothoabe, James (Mississauga of the Bay of Quinte): signatory to Treaty 40½, 249(a); signatory to Treaty 49, 250(a)
Sahgahnaquottwabe, James. *See* Sahgahnahquothoabe, James
Sahiquage. *See* Lake Erie
salmon trout, 28; fished by Saugeen Ojibway, 50
Sander, Frank E.A., 213
Sandy Island Band, 46; education at, 47

Saniard, James, 286n87
Sanson, David Laing: witness to Treaty 76, 254(a)
Sarnia, model village at, 32
Saugeen, school at, 266n60
Saugeen culture, 1, 256n9
Saugeen Indians. *See* Saugeen Nation
Saugeen Nation, 26-27, 50, 52, 87; Bond Head treaty (Treaty 45½), 34-35, 173, 250a; fishing islands, 26; Imperial Proclamation of 1847, 37-38; villages, 46; violence on fishing grounds, 36. *See also* Chippewas of Saugeen; *Imperial Proclamation;* Saugeen Ojibway
Saugeen Ojibway (Chippewas), 26; court proceedings involving, 197-98, 214; fishing licences, 58, 72, 197; leases to Huron Fishery Company, 26; petition by chiefs, 53; villages, 50, 72. *See also* Chippewas of Nawash; Chippewas of Saugeen; *Jones and Nadjiwon, R. v.*
Saugeen Peninsula. *See* Bruce Peninsula
Saugeen River, 36
Saukings. *See* Saugeen Nation. *See also* Saugeen Ojibway
Sault River, 54
Sault Ste. Marie: fisheries in, 51; reservation of fishing island at, 26
Sawyer, Joseph, 28
Schofield, James: signatory to Treaty 78, 254(a)
Schoolcraft, Henry, 222
Scott, Duncan Campbell: and A.S. Williams, 140; Deputy Superintendent of Indian Affairs, 119; and Deskaheh, 150-51; and judge in *Sero v. Gault,* 173; and promise to protect Mississauga trapping in Rice Lake, 128; and unceded lands in Northern Ontario, 169-71; views of Indians, 208-9; and Williams Treaties Commissioners, 146, 156, 159, 163
Scott, Township of, 142
Scugog, Township of, 142
Scugog Island First Nation, 3; charges against members, 88, 117; civilization efforts concerning, 46; claim to unsurrendered lands, 75; and I.E. Weldon, 128-29, 208; and industrial school proposal, 41; land claims meeting, 78, 85; move from Balsam Lake, 45; oral history of warfare with Iroquois, 4; protests over trapping restrictions, 106; resolution to retain lawyers, 100; school at, 47; understanding of English, 209-10; and Williams Treaties Commission, 131, 137-38; Williams Treaties Commissioners' reports concerning, 153, 156; Williams Treaty affecting, 149, 154
Scugog Lake: jurisdiction over islands in, 98
Scugog Lake Band. *See* Scugog Island First Nation
Scugog reserve, 137; Williams Treaties Commissioners' report about, 153. *See also* Scugog Island First Nation
seine nets. *See* nets, fishing
Selby, P.: Assistant Secretary, Indian Affairs, 243(a); witness to 1806 treaty, 244(a); witness to Treaty 13, 243(a); witness to Treaty 13a, 243(a); witness to Treaty 14, 244(a)
Sequine River, 103
Sero, Elizabeth, 173. *See also Sero v. Gault*
Sero v. Gault, 126, 283n14, 291n114
serpent mounds, 4, 257n27
Shabokeshuk (Ojibway), 113; signatory to Robinson-Huron Treaty, 251(a)
Shabokishick. *See* Shabokeshuk
Shaule, Dan, x
Shawandais (Mississauga of the Bay of Quinte): signatory to Treaty 27, 247(a); signatory to Treaty 27¼, 248(a)
Shawenakeshick (Ojibway): signatory to Robinson-Huron Treaty, 251(a)
Shawenauseway: signatory to Treaty 45, 249(a)
Shawgashe (Chippewa): signatory to surrender of Coldwater Tract, 250(a)
Shawondaise. *See* Shawandais
Shawonebin (Ojibway): signatory to Robinson-Huron Treaty, 252(a)
Shawwenwabung (Chippewa): signatory to surrender of Coldwater Tract (Treaty 48), 250(a)
Sheaffe, Captain R.H.: witness to Treaty 3¾, 242(a)
Shebageshick, Michel (Ojibway): signatory to Robinson-Superior Treaty, 251(a)
Shebeshe (Mississauga of the Bay of Quinte): signatory to Treaty 27, 247(a); signatory to Treaty 27¼, 248(a)
Shebeshee. *See* Shebeshe
Shegwanaindand, 43
Shenaoqum (Ojibway): signatory to Robinson-Huron Treaty, 252(a)
Shewitigan (Mississauga): signatory to Treaty 27¼, 248(a)
Shilling: family hunting grounds, 133
Shilling, Enoch, 138
Shilling, James: signatory to Williams Treaty, 76

Shilling, John S., 286n103
Shilling, Joseph (Chippewa): signatory to surrender of Coldwater Tract (Treaty 48), 250(a)
Shilling, Joseph, Jr., 75, 137-38; signatory to Williams Treaty, 75
Shilling, Rebecca, 137-38
Shilling, Stanley, 164
Shilling, Thomas: witness to Treaty 76, 254(a)
Shinguakouce (Ojibway): signatory to Robinson-Huron Treaty, 251(a)
Shipegew, James, 286n103
Shiwitagon (Mississauga of the Bay of Quinte): signatory to Treaty 27, 247(a)
Short, John (Mississauga): signatory to Treaty 78, 254(a)
Shunyung, 5. *See also* Lake Simcoe
Sifton, Clifford, 91-92, 98, 101; replaced by Robert Rogers, 103
Simcoe, David, 135
Simcoe, John, 89
Simcoe, Lieutenant Governor John Graves: grant of lands to Six Nations at Tyendinaga (Treaty 3½), 241(a); lands reserved by, 102, 132, 137, 142
Simon, Walter, 135-36, 147, 212
Simpson, John: signatory to Treaty 66, 252(a); signatory to Treaty 77, 254(a)
Simpson, W.: witness to Robinson-Huron Treaty, 252(a)
Sinclair, R.V., 104, 116, 128, 145, 147, 149, 154, 203, 230
Sioux Lookout, 121
Six Nations, 16, 30-31, 120; grant of land to, at Tyendinaga (Treaty 3½), 241(a); and League of Nations, 149-51; surrender of lands by Mississaugas for, 16; and Tuscaroras, 15. *See also* Five Nations; Iroquois
Sixteen Mile Creek: referred to in Treaty 19, 246(a); reservation of fisheries at by Mississaugas, 20
Skene, Charles, 66-67, 69-70
Skene, Lieutenant D.J.: witness to Treaty 22, 248(a)
Skull Island, 5
Skunk, Joseph (Mississauga of Grape Island): signatory to Treaty 77, 254(a)
Skye, Luke T. (Mississauga): signatory to Treaty 78, 254(a)
Slonim, Marc, x
Smart, J., 106
Smith, David William: witness to Treaty 3, 241(a)
Smith, H.M.: witness to 1806 treaty, 244(a); witness to Treaty 14, 244(a)
Smith, Major Samuel: witness to Treaty 5, 243(a)
Smith, William, 91
Smock, Tara, x
Smoke, Jack, 145
Smoke, Moses, 145
Smoke-House Island, 52
Smyth, Lieutenant William: witness to Treaty 27¼, 248(a)
Snache, Sam, 134-35, 163, 216; signatory to Williams Treaty, 216
Snake (Chippewa): signatory to Treaty 45, 249(a). *See* Kaqueticum, Chief
Snake, Chief. *See* Kaqueticum, Chief
Snake, Chief Joseph (Chippewas), 32-33; sale of estate and interest in Orillia (Treaty 66), 252(a), 253(a); signatory to surrender of fishing islands (Treaty 76), 253(a)
Snake, James, 132
Snake, Sam. *See* Snache, Sam
Snake, William: signatory to Williams Treaty, 76
Snake Island, 66, 159
Snake Island First Nation, 41, 46, 66, 114; request for fishing island by chiefs, 66; resolution to retain lawyers, 100
Snake Tribe (Chippewa), 22; surrender by chief of (Treaty 20), 246(a)
Snowstorm, John, 286n103. *See also* Storm, John
Soper, Robert (Mississauga): signatory to Treaty 78, 254(a)
Sophiasburgh, 43
South Bay, 43
Sparrow, R. v., 186, 192, 194
Sparrow Lake, 66, 133-34, 159, 162
spearing (fish), 10, 12; banned, 71, 84; criticisms of, 48-49, 69, 71; and Lake Simcoe Indians, 72; Ojibway terms for, 10; and Robinson-Huron Treaty, 70
special rights, Aboriginal: Aboriginal perspective on, 172; advancement of "equal rights" over special rights, xiii; and Hayter Reed, 83-84, 92; and *Howard*, 185, 188-89, 239; Imperial policy, 236; and Indian Affairs, 119, 178; and James Cockburn, 58-59, 62, 113; and J.D. McLean, 116, 176; and Law Advisors of the Crown, 42, 58; and Marine and Fisheries, 91; Ontario's position concerning, x, 104, 188-89, 200, 239; and Ralph Loucks, 184, 200; recognized by legislation, 82; and Supreme Court of Canada, 239; in water, 170; and William Whitcher, 64, 113
Spielmann, Roger, 159

Spragge, William, 74-75
squatters: at Grand River, 311; and patents to, 73-74
Squaw Island, 65
St. Croix Valley, 220
St. Germain, Jacob, 164
St. Lawrence Iroquois, 2
St. Lawrence River: fishing islands in, 79
St. Peters, Treaty of, 219-23, 299n147
Stanour, Henry: Chippewa, signatory to surrender of Coldwater Tract (Treaty 48), 250(a)
Starna, William (Dr.), x
Stewart, Charles, 127, 149-51
Stinson, Chief J.B., 111, 132, 163; signatory to Williams Treaty, 163
Stinson, Joseph: General Superintendent of Wesleyan Missions, 250(a); witness to Treaty 45½, 250(a)
Stinson, Sandford, 164
Storm, John (Mississauga of Grape Island): signatory to Treaty 77, 254(a)
sturgeon: fishing, by Ojibway, 10; size of, 25
Sturgeon Lake, 90
Sunday, Jacob (Mississauga of the Bay of Quinte): signatory to Treaty 40½, 249(a); signatory to Treaty 49, 250(a); signatory to Treaty 77, 254(a)
Sunday, John (Mississauga of the Bay of Quinte), 265n34; signatory to Treaty 40½, 249(a); signatory to Treaty 49, 250(a); signatory to Treaty 77, 254(a)
surrenders: ambiguities in, 201-2; by Chippewas, 22, 24; Crown policy concerning, 14; early, 14; effect of, in *Mille Lacs* case, 230, 231-32; errors in Mississauga, 17-19, 25; excluding fisheries, 50, 53, 60, 63, 165; excluding fishing islands, 71; excluding game, 53, 63, 139, 153, 165; and extinguishment of Aboriginal title, 37; of hunting grounds, 39; of hunting rights in northern Ontario, 156; of Manitoulin Island, 34; in Manypenny treaties, 229; by Mississaugas, 9, 16-17, 20-21, 23; and preexisting treaty rights, 168, 182, 187, 205; presumption in American cases concerning effect of, 218; by Rama, 159, 161-62; and reservations from, 26; and *Royal Proclamation of 1763,* 15; by Saugeen people, 35, 37; in Treaty 9 adhesions, 171-72; and Williams Treaties, 98, 130, 134, 146-48, 152, 157
Surtees, Robert J., 17, 35
Sutton West, Indian agent, 122
Swamp. *See* Muskigonce, Chief
Swege, Lake of. *See* Lake Erie
Syrette, Vernon, 215

Tabandan. *See* Tabandon
Tabandon (Mississauga): signatory to Treaty 3¾, 242(a); signatory to Treaty 8, 242(a)
Tagawinini (Ojibway): signatory to Robinson-Huron Treaty, 251(a)
Talbot River: warfare at, 5
Tanner, Helen, xi, 299n169
Tauney, John, 75
Tawackkuck: signatory to Treaty 45, 249(a)
Taylor, David, 174, 177
Taylor, Dow: oral history, 284n30
Taylor, Ester: oral history, 295n26
Taylor, George, 286n87
Taylor, Hirum, 176
Taylor, James, 286n87
Taylor, President, 223
Taylor, Short Tom, 85, 210, 257n27. *See also* Cobb, George
Taylor, Tall Tom, 5, 85, 257n28. *See also* Cobb, George
Taylor, Thomas, 286n87
Taylor, Tom. *See* Cobb, George; Taylor, Tall Tom
Taylor, Wayne, 179
Taylor, William, 176
Taylor and Williams, R. v., 179-80, 184, 186, 204-5
Ten-Mile Creek, 28
Terminal Woodland period, 2
Thackeray, John: Indian Agent, Alnwick, 83, 98-99
Thames River, 2; white control of fisheries at, 56
Thomas, Chief Jake, 9, 258n53
Thompson, Alfred A.: witness to Robinson-Huron Treaty, 252(a)
Thompson, John S., 81
Tighe, J.L.: Assistant Surgeon, 248(a); witness to Treaty 22, 248(a)
Tilton, J., 72
Timber Island, 43
Tinsley, E.R., 108-9, 111
Titus, F.E., 170, 260n22
Tobin, Brian, 190, 192-96
Toronto: Carrying Place, 16
Totomenai, Jacob Wasseba (Ojibway): signatory to Robinson-Superior Treaty, 251(a)
Traill, Catharine Parr, 45
trapping, 77
Treaty, adhesions to No. 9, 171; negotiations, 208

Treaty of 1818, 22
Treaty of 1701: Iroquois, xii, 8; map of beaver hunting ground in, 8. *See also* Nanfan, Lieutenant Governor John
Treaty No. 13. *See* Gunshot Treaty
treaty rights: ix, x, xi, xiii; Aboriginal perspective of, Crown position on, 106-7, 119, 237; in adjacent waters, retained by Williams Treaties First Nations, 194; ambiguities concerning, in Williams Treaties, 202, 204-5, 215, 217; of American Chippewa, 227, 231; at American law, 219; charges against Indians exercising, 112; and *Constitution Act* (1982), 180; and decision in *Howard,* 185, 186, 189; decision not to inform Indians of, 178; denied by Crown, 56, 83, 88, 117; early Imperial policy concerning, 19; in 1818 treaty with Chippewas and Mississaugas, 22, 29, 88; extinguished in Williams Treaties, ix, x, 155, 162, 166, 168, 183; interpretation of, by courts, xiii; in Manypenny treaties, 225, 228; of Mille Lacs Band, 226, 233-34; in Minnesota, 225; negotiated with Iroquois, 8; promise of exclusive fishing rights, 32; provincial jurisdiction over, 82, 108, 119, 177, 179, 236; and public rights, 50, 68; referred to in Williams Treaties Commission hearings, 133-34, 140, 143; in Robinson-Huron Treaty, 70; of Saugeen Ojibway, 72, 173; and 1701 treaty, 6; under Treaty of Washington, 230; in US, xiii. *See also* Aboriginal title; common law; special rights, Aboriginal
Trent Canal, 97; flooding, 140; jurisdiction over, 281n179
Trent River, 21
Trent University, oral history project, 4
Trent Valley, 98
trout, 27
Tudhope, Melvin B.: Band lawyer, 135, 166
Twelve-Mile Creek: encroachments into reserved Mississauga fisheries, 28; referred to in Treaty 19, 246(a); reservation of fisheries by Mississaugas in, 20
Tyendinaga, 30, 45, 173-74, 207
Tyendinaga, Township of: grant to Six Nations at (Treaty 3½), 241(a)

Union of Ontario Indians, 179, 182
United Bands, 126
Uxbridge township, 137, 142

Van Antwerp, Ver Planck, 223
Vankoughnet, Lawrence, 69, 71; and Mississauga land claim, 76, 78
Vaughan, Township of: referred to in Treaty 19, 246(a)
vision quests, 46

Wabakanyne. *See* Wabukanyne
Wabakeek (Mississauga): signatory to Treaty 27¼, 248(a)
Wabakegego (Mississauga): signatory to 1806 treaty, 244(a); signatory to Treaty 14, 244(a)
Wabaninship (Mississauga): signatory to Treaty 3, 241(a)
Wabanip (Mississauga): signatory to Treaty 3, 241(a); signatory to Treaty 8, 242(a)
Wabanose (Mississauga): signatory to 1806 treaty, 244(a); signatory to Treaty 8, 242(a); signatory to Treaty 13, 243(a); signatory to Treaty 14, 244(a)
Wabanosh. *See* Wabanose
Wabanzik (Mississauga): signatory to Treaty 27¼, 248(a)
Wabeckeneme. *See* Wabukanyne
Wabenenguan (Chippewa): signatory to Treaty 5, 243(a)
Wabokekik (Ojibway): signatory to Robinson-Huron Treaty, 251(a)
Wabosek (Mississauga of the Bay of Quinte): signatory to Treaty 27, 247(a)
Wabukanyne (Mississauga): signatory to 1806 treaty, 244(a); signatory to Treaty 13 (confirmatory surrender) 243(a); signatory to Treaty 13 (Gunshot Treaty), 241(a); signatory to Treaty 27, 248(a); signatory to Treaty 27¼, 248(a)
Waganhaes. *See* Dowaganhaes; Far Indians
Wagemauquin: signatory to Treaty 45, 249(a)
wages: in Victorian era, 268n115, 288n18
Wahbone Young (Chippewa): signatory to surrender of Coldwater Tract, 250(a)
Wakanye (Mississauga): signatory to Treaty 14, 244(a)
Waquacomiek (Ojibway): signatory to Robinson-Huron Treaty, 252(a)
Walker Head, Sir Edmund: Governor General, 74
Wallis, Howard, 118
wampum belts, 6-7; and dish with one spoon, 16, 29
Wanapenant: signatory to Treaty 3¾, 242(a)
Waquimakong. *See* Wikwemikong
War of 1812, 21
Warren, Charles W.: witness to Treaty 40½, 249(a)

Wa-sha-gee-siks. *See* George, Jonas
Washburn, D.: witness to Treaty 27, 247(a)
Washington, Treaty of, 224
Waswanay, Asa (Ojibway): signatory to Robinson-Huron Treaty, 251(a)
Watachewana (Ojibway): signatory to Robinson-Huron Treaty, 252(a)
Watson, Adam, 58, 113, 139
Watson, Peter, 22, 29
wawasque. *See* deer-hunting
weirs, fishing: use of by Ojibway, 11
Weldon, I.E., 128-29, 146-47, 151, 208, 211
Weggishigomin (Mississauga, Eagle Tribe): signatory to Treaty 19, 246(a); signatory to Treaty 22, 248(a)
Weiguesquome. *See* Weggishigomin
Wequameking. *See* Wikwemikong
West Gwillimbury, Township of, 132
Wet'suwet'en, 213
Whetung, Arthur, 167-68
Whetung, Chief Daniel, Jr.: activism, 216, 297n84; concern over muskrat trapping issue at Williams Treaties Commission hearings, 139, 154, 206; education, 211; married to Muriel Whetung, 210; protests against guiding licences, 108; protests against restrictions on muskrat trapping, 106; signatory to Williams Treaty, 108, 216; and special rights, 175, 230; testimony concerning treaty rights at Williams Treaties Commission hearings, 139; trapper, 122; used as interpreter, 212. *See also* Mud Lake First Nation; Williams Treaties; Williams Treaties Commission
Whetung, Chief Joseph, 75, 117-18, 122, 127, 209, 216; signatory to Williams Treaty, 216
Whetung, Clifford, 87, 158
Whetung, Daniel, Sr.: evidence at Williams Treaties Commission, 138-39; farmer, 138; and Henry Wickham, 90; signatory to Williams Treaty, 90. *See also* Mud Lake First Nation; Williams Treaties; Williams Treaties Commission
Whetung, Muriel, 210
Whitcher, William F., 60, 62-64, 66-68, 71-72, 113, 269n138
White, Bruce, 299n169
White Oak Tribe (Chippewa), 22; surrender by chief of (Treaty 20), 246(a)
whitefish, 25, 27-28, 87; quantities sold by Saugeen Ojibway, 50
Wiarton, 97
Wickham, Henry, 90, 138-39
Wikwemikong, 43, 57, 63-64, 87
Wildlife Service (US), 218
Wilkins, Robert, 286n103
Willcocks, William: Commissioner for Province of Upper Canada, 243(a); witness to Treaty 5, 243(a)
Williams, A.E., 111n143
Williams, Angus Seymour, 3, 208; chair of Williams Treaties Commission, 128; completion of Williams Treaties, 166-68; as Indian Affairs departmental solicitor, 140, 203; misunderstanding of land claim, 144; questions about Gunshot Treaty, 145; questions concerning unsurrendered lands, 135-38, 141-42; report to Ontario Premier, 152. *See also* Williams Treaties; Williams Treaties Commission
Williams, A.S. *See* Williams, Angus Seymour
Williams, Captain J.W.: witness to Treaty 13, 243(a); witness to Treaty 13a, 243(a)
Williams, Doug, 179
Williams, Gilbert, 75, 157, 162, 216; signatory to Williams Treaty, 75, 132, 216
Williams, Paul, 179
Williams, Sam, 163; signatory to Williams Treaty, 163
Williams Treaties, xii, xiii; ambiguities in, 201-2; articles of, 154-56; compensation paid under, 152; copies not provided to First Nations, 153; expert evidence concerning, 182; failure to mention treaty rights within, x; interpreted, 285n70; rushed, xiii; signatories to, 126, 128, 131-32, 136-37, 141-42, 152, 163, 204-5, 211-12, 213, 215-16; signed, 149; terms of, 154
Williams Treaties Commission: agreement with Ontario to establish, 128; alleged promises by, 133-34, 164-66, 214; and Alnwick, 143; appointment of commissioners, 127-28; and basket clause, 155-56, 203-4; and Chief Daniel Whetung, Jr., 139, 141; and Chief Joseph Whetung, 127; and Chief Robert Paudash, 142; and Christian Island, 135; and common-law, 230; concerns about encroachment in hunting grounds raised with, 77; concerns about trapping raised with, 77, 154, 201-2, 206; and 1818 treaties, 138; expert evidence about, 182; failure to provide copies of treaties to First Nations, 153, 168; and Georgina Island, 130; and Gunshot Treaty, 17, 145; and *Howard*, 186-87; and I.E. Weldon, 146-47, 208;

and interpreters, 183, 212; and Johnson Paudash, 17, 77, 142; and Kathleen Moodie, 130; mandate of, 128-31, 133, 143, 155; and Minutes of Surrender, 157; and Mud Lake, 138; negotiations with First Nations, 152-53, 157-60; oral history of Iroquois warfare before, 4-5; *per diems* paid to, 152; powers of, 129; and pre-existing treaty rights, x, 202; preparation of treaties by, 147-48, 287n124; and Rama, 132-33, 158, 162-64; reports of, 146, 152-53, 157-59, 206, 210; response to requests by chiefs, 159, 201; and Rice Lake, 141; and Robinson-Huron Treaty, 136-37; and Scugog Island, 137; signing of treaties, 149, 151; and Sparrow Lake, 162, 164; and surrendered lands, 135, 137, 140, 145, 205; transcripts, 206, 208, 211; understanding of treaty rights, 139. *See also* basket clause; *Howard, R. v.;* McFadden, Uriah; Moodie, Kathleen; Sinclair, R.V.; Williams, Angus Seymour; Williams Treaties; Williams Treaties First Nations

Williams Treaties First Nations, 190-91, 195; extinguishment of rights by Supreme Court of Canada in *Howard,* xii; harvesting agreements with Ontario, 197; Ojibway-speaking, 1. *See also* Alderville First Nation; Beausoleil First Nation; Georgina Island First Nation; Mnjikaning First Nation; Mud Lake First Nation; Rice Lake First Nation; Scucog Island First Nation; Williams Treaties; Williams Treaties Commission

Wilson, Joseph: witness to Robinson-Huron Treaty, 251(a)

Windawtegowinini (Ojibway): signatory to Robinson-Huron Treaty, 251(a)

Windigo: fears of, 12

Winnibago Tribe, 263n106

Wisconsin, 219

Wright, John, 226

Wright, Roland, 266n64

Wobekenense (Mississauga of the Bay of Quinte): signatory to Treaty 27, 247(a)

Wobukeek (Mississauga of the Bay of Quinte): signatory to Treaty 27, 247(a)

Woo, Li Xiu, 150

Wright, James, 4

Xoshee Lake, 164

Yellow Head. *See* Yellowhead, Chief William

Yellow-head, William. *See* Yellowhead, Chief William

Yellowhead, Benjamin: signatory to Williams Treaty, 76

Yellowhead, Chief William (Chippewa, Reindeer Tribe): and model villages, 32-33, 36, 41; sale of estate and interest in Orillia (Treaty 66), 252(a), 253(a); signatory to confirmatory surrender of Treaty 16, 245(a); signatory to surrender of Coldwater Tract (Treaty 48), 250(a); signatory to Treaty 16, 245(a); signatory to Treaty 18, 245(a)

Yellowhead, Edward: signatory to Williams Treaty, 76

Yellowhead, Elijah, 133

Yellowhead, Joseph, 22

Yellowhead, Sampson, 134, 285n65

York, Chief Alder, 126, 132, 134-35, 162-63, 166, 216; signatory to Williams Treaty, 125, 216

York, County of, 146

Young, Chief George (Chippewa): Chippewa, signatory to surrender of fishing islands (Treaty 76), 253(a); sale of estate and interest in Orillia (Treaty 66), 252(a), 254(a)

Ziontz, Chestnut, Varnell, Berley & Slonim: law firm in *Mille Lacs* case, x